Java™ Cookbook

Other Java™ Titles from O'Reilly

Creating Effective JavaHelp™

Database Programming with JDBC™
and Java™

Developing Java Beans™

Enterprise JavaBeans™

Java™ 2D Graphics

Java™ and XML

Java™ Cryptography

Java™ Distributed Computing

Java™ Enterprise in a Nutshell

The Java™ Enterprise CD Bookshelf

Java™ Examples in a Nutshell

Java™ Foundation Classes in a Nutshell

Java™ I/O

Java™ in a Nutshell

Java™ Internationalization

Java™ Message Service

Java™ Network Programming

Java™ Performance Tuning

Java™ Professional Library

Java™ Security

JavaServer™ Pages

Java™ Servlet Programming

Java™ Swing

Java™ Threads

Jini™ in a Nutshell

Learning Java™

Java™ Cookbook

Ian F. Darwin

O'REILLY®

Beijing · Cambridge · Farnham · Köln · Paris · Sebastopol · Taipei · Tokyo

Java™ Cookbook
by Ian F. Darwin

Published by O'Reilly & Associates, Inc., 101 Morris Street, Sebastopol, CA 95472.

Editor: Mike Loukides

Production Editor: Emily Quill

Cover Designer: Hanna Dyer

Printing History:

> June 2001:   First Edition.

Nutshell Handbook, the Nutshell Handbook logo, and the O'Reilly logo are registered trademarks of O'Reilly & Associates, Inc. The association between the image of a domestic chicken and Java is a trademark of O'Reilly & Associates, Inc. Java and all Java-based trademarks and logos are trademarks or registered trademarks of Sun Microsystems, Inc., in the United States and other countries. O'Reilly & Associates, Inc. is independent of Sun Microsystems.

Many of the designations used by manufacturers and sellers to distinguish their products are claimed as trademarks. Where those designations appear in this book, and O'Reilly & Associates, Inc. was aware of a trademark claim, the designations have been printed in caps or initial caps.

Library of Congress Cataloging-in-Publication Data

Darwin, Ian F.
    Java cookbook/Ian Darwin.
        p. cm.
    ISBN 0-596-00170-3
    1. Java (Computer program language). I. Title.

QA76.73.J38 D348 2001
005.2'762–dc21   2001035421

Table of Contents

Preface

If you know a little Java™, great. If you know more Java, even better! This book is ideal for anyone who knows some Java and wants to learn more.

I started programming in C in 1980 while working at the University of Toronto, and C served me quite well through the 1980s and into the 1990s. In 1995, as the nascent language Oak was being renamed Java, I had the good fortune to be told about it by my colleague J. Greg Davidson. I sent an email to the address Greg provided, and got this mail back:

```
From scndprsn.Eng.Sun.COM!jag Wed Mar 29 19:43:54 1995
Date: Wed, 29 Mar 1995 16:47:51 +0800
From: jag@scndprsn.Eng.Sun.COM (James Gosling)
To: ian@scooter.Canada.Sun.COM, ian@darwinsys.com
Subject: Re: WebRunner
Cc: goltz@sunne.East.Sun.COM
Content-Length: 361
Status: RO
X-Lines: 9


> Hi. A friend told me about WebRunner(?), your extensible network
> browser. It and Oak(?) its extention language, sounded neat. Can
> you please tell me if it's available for play yet, and/or if any
> papers on it are available for FTP?

Check out http://java.sun.com
(oak got renamed to java and webrunner got renamed to
 hotjava to keep the lawyers happy)
```

I downloaded HotJava and began to play with it. At first I wasn't sure about this newfangled language, which looked like a mangled C/C++. I wrote test and demo programs, sticking them a few at a time into a directory that I called *javasrc* to keep it separate from my C source (as often the programs would have the same name). And as I learned more about Java, I began to see its advantages for many kinds of work, such as the automatic memory reclaim and the elimination of pointer calculations. The *javasrc* directory kept growing. I wrote a Java course for Learning Tree, and the directory kept growing faster, reaching the point where it needed subdirectories. Even then, it became increasingly difficult to find things, and it soon became evident that some kind of documentation was needed.

In a sense, this book is the result of a high-speed collision between my *javasrc* directory and a documentation framework established for another newcomer language. In O'Reilly's *Perl Cookbook,* Tom Christiansen and Nathan Torkington worked out a very successful design, presenting the material in small, focused articles called "recipes." The original model for such a book is, of course, the familiar kitchen cookbook. There is a long history of using the term "cookbook" to refer to an enumeration of how-to recipes relating to computers. On the software side, Donald Knuth applied the "cookbook" analogy to his book *The Art of Computer Programming* (Addison Wesley), first published in 1968. On the hardware side, Don Lancaster wrote *The TTL Cookbook* (Sams). (Transistor-transistor logic, or TTL, was the small-scale building block of electronic circuits at the time.) Tom and Nathan worked out a successful variation on this, and I recommend their book for anyone who wishes to, as they put it, "learn more Perl." Indeed, the work you are now reading intends to be a book for the person who wishes to "learn more Java."

The code in each recipe is intended to be self-contained; feel free to borrow bits and pieces of any of it for use in your own projects.

Who This Book Is For

I'm going to assume that you know the basics of Java. I won't tell you how to `println` a string and a number at the same time, or how to write a class that extends `Applet` and prints your name in the window. I'll presume you've taken a Java course or studied an introductory book such as O'Reilly's *Learning Java* or *Java in a Nutshell.* However, Chapter 1 covers some techniques that you might not know very well and that are necessary to understand some of the later material. Feel free to skip around! Both the printed version of the book and the (eventual) electronic copy are heavily cross-referenced.

What's in This Book?

Unlike my Perl colleagues Tom and Nathan, I don't have to spend as much time on the oddities and idioms of the language; Java is refreshingly free of strange quirks. But that doesn't mean it's trivial to learn well! If it were, there'd be no need for this book. My main approach, then, is to concentrate on the Java APIs: I'll teach you by example what the APIs are and what they are good for.

Like Perl, Java is a language that grows on you and with you. And, I confess, I use Java most of the time nowadays. Things I'd once done in C are now—except for device drivers and legacy systems—done in Java.

But Java is suited to a different range of tasks than Perl. Perl (and other scripting languages such as awk and Python) are particularly suited to the "one-liner" utility task. As Tom and Nathan show, Perl excels at things like printing the 42nd line from a file. While it can certainly do these things, Java, because it is a compiled, object-oriented language, seems more suited to "development in the large" or enterprise applications development. Indeed, much of the API material added in Java 2 was aimed at this type of development. However, I will necessarily illustrate many techniques with shorter examples and even code fragments. Be assured that every line of code you see here has been compiled and run.

Many of the longer examples in this book are tools that I originally wrote to automate some mundane task or another. For example, `MkIndex` (described in Chapter 17) reads the top-level directory of the place where I keep all my Java example source code and builds a browser-friendly *index.html* file for that directory. For another example, the body of the book itself was partly composed in XML, a recent simplification that builds upon a decade of experience in SGML (the parent standard that led to the tag-based syntax of HTML). It is not clear at this point if XML will primarily be useful as a publishing format or as a data manipulation format, or if its prevalence will further blur that distinction, though it seems that the blurring of distinctions is more likely. However, I used XML here to type in and mark up the original text of some of the chapters of this book. The text was then converted to FrameMaker input by the `XmlForm` program. This program also handles—by use of another program, `GetMark`—full and partial code insertions from the source directory. `XmlForm` is discussed in Chapter 21.

Let's go over the organization of this book. I start off *Chapter 1, Getting Started: Compiling, Running, and Debugging,* by describing some methods of compiling your program on different platforms, running them in different environments (browser, command line, windowed desktop), and debugging. Chapter 2, *Interacting with the Environment,* moves from compiling and running your program to getting it to adapt to the surrounding countryside—the other programs that live in your computer.

The next few chapters deal with basic APIs. Chapter 3, *Strings and Things,* concentrates on one of the most basic but powerful data types in Java, showing you how to assemble, dissect, compare, and rearrange what you might otherwise think of as ordinary text.

Chapter 4, *Pattern Matching with Regular Expressions*, teaches you how to use the powerful regular expressions technology from Unix in many string-matching and pattern-matching problem domains. This is the first chapter that covers a non-standard API—there is not yet a regular expression API in standard Java—so I talk about several regular expression packages.

Chapter 5, *Numbers*, deals both with built-in types such as `int` and `double`, as well as the corresponding API classes (`Integer`, `Double`, etc.) and the conversion and testing facilities they offer. There is also brief mention of the "big number" classes. Since Java programmers often need to deal in dates and times, both locally and internationally, Chapter 6, *Dates and Times*, covers this important topic.

The next two chapters cover data processing. As in most languages, *arrays* in Java are linear, indexed collections of similar-kind objects, as discussed in Chapter 7, *Structuring Data with Java*. This chapter goes on to deal with the many "Collections" classes: powerful ways of storing quantities of objects in the `java.util` package. Additional data structuring and programming tips appear in Chapter 8, *Object-Oriented Techniques*.

The next few chapters deal with aspects of traditional input and output. Chapter 9, *Input and Output*, details the rules for reading and writing files. (Don't skip this if you think files are boring, as you'll need some of this information in later chapters: you'll read and write on serial or parallel ports in Chapter 11, and on a socket-based network connection in Chapter 15!) Chapter 10, *Directory and Filesystem Operations*, shows you everything else about files—such as finding their size and last-modified time—and about reading and modifying directories, creating temporary files, and renaming files on disk. Chapter 11, *Programming Serial and Parallel Ports*, shows how you can use the `javax.comm` API to read/write on serial and parallel ports without resorting to coding in C.

Chapter 12, *Graphics and Sound*, leads us into the GUI development side of things. This chapter is a mix of the lower-level details, such as drawing graphics and setting fonts and colors, and very high-level activities, such as controlling a playing video clip or movie. Then, in Chapter 13, *Graphical User Interfaces*, I cover the higher-level aspects of a GUI, such as buttons, labels, menus, and the like—the GUI's predefined components. Once you have a GUI (really, before you actually write it), you'll want to read Chapter 14, *Internationalization and Localization*, so your programs can work as well in Akbar, Afghanistan, Algiers, Amsterdam, or Angleterre as they do in Alberta or Arkansas or Alabama . . .

Since Java was originally promulgated as "the programming language for the Internet," it's only fair that we spend some of our time on networking in Java. Chapter 15, *Network Clients*, covers the basics of network programming from the client side, focusing on sockets. We'll then move to the server side in Chapter 16,

Server-Side Java: Sockets. In Chapter 17, *Network Clients II: Applets and Web Clients,* you'll learn more client-side techniques. Some specialized server-side techniques for the Web are covered in Chapter 18, *Web Server Java: Servlets and JSP*. Finally, programs on the Net often need to generate electronic mail, so this section ends with Chapter 19, *Java and Electronic Mail.*

Chapter 20, *Database Access,* covers the Java Database Connectivity package (JDBC), showing how you can connect to local or remote relational databases, store and retrieve data, and find out information about query results or about the database.

Another form of storing and exchanging data is XML. Chapter 21, *XML,* discusses XML's formats and some operations you can apply using SAX and DOM, two standard Java APIs.

Chapter 22, *Distributed Java: RMI,* takes the distributed notion one step further and discusses Remote Methods Invocation, Java's standard remote procedure call mechanism. RMI lets you build clients, servers, and even "callback" scenarios, using a standard Java mechanism—the Interface—to describe the contract between client and server.

Chapter 23, *Packages and Packaging,* shows how to create packages of classes that work together. This chapter also talks about "deploying" or distributing and installing your software.

Chapter 24, *Threaded Java,* tells you how to write classes that appear to do more than one thing at a time and let you take advantage of powerful multiprocessor hardware.

Chapter 25, *Introspection, or "A Class Named Class",* lets you in on such big secrets as how to write API cross reference documents mechanically and how web browsers are able to load any old applet—never having seen that particular class before—and run it.

Sometimes you already have code written and working in another language that can do part of your work for you, or you want to use Java as part of a larger package. Chapter 26, *Dealing With Other Languages,* shows you how to run an external program (compiled or script) and also interact directly with "native code" in C/C++.

There isn't room in an 800-page book for everything I'd like to tell you about Java. The Afterword presents some closing thoughts and a link to my online summary of Java APIs that every Java developer should know about.

No two programmers or writers will agree on the best order for presenting all the Java topics. To help you find your way around, there are extensive cross-references, mostly by recipe number.

Platform Notes

In its short history, Java has gone through four major versions. The first official release is known as Java JDK 1.0, and its last bug-fixed version is 1.0.2. The second major release is Java JDK 1.1, and the latest bug-fixed version is 1.1.9, though it may be up from that by the time you read this book. The third major release, in December 1998, was to be known as Java JDK 1.2, but the Sun marketing gremlins abruptly renamed JDK 1.2 at the time of its release to Java 2, and the implementation is known as Java SDK 1.2. The current version as of this writing is Java 2 SDK 1.3 (JDK 1.3), which was released in 2000. Around the same time, two other packages, one low-end and one high-end, were announced. At the low end, Java Micro Edition (JME) is designed for tiny devices, such as Palm computers, telephones, and the like. At the high end, the Java 2 Enterprise Edition (J2EE) extends Java 2 by adding additional features for enterprise or large-scale distributed commercial applications. One of the key features of the Enterprise Edition is Enterprise Java-Beans™ (EJB). EJB has little in common with client-side JavaBeans except the name. Many Java pundits (including myself) believe that EJB will become a significant player in the development of large commercial applications, perhaps the most significant development of this era.

As we go to press, Java 2 Version 1.4 is about to appear. It entered beta (which Sun calls "early access") around the time of the book's completion, so I can only mention it briefly. You should cast your sights on *http://java.sun.com* to see what's new in 1.4 and how it affects the programs in the book.

This book is aimed at the Java 2 platform. By the time of publication, I expect that all Java implementations will be fairly close to conforming to the Java 2 specification. I have used four platforms to test this code for portability. The official "reference platform" is Sun's Java 2 Solaris Reference Implementation, which I used on a Sun SPARCStation running Solaris. To give a second Unix flavor, I've tested with Kaffe* and with Sun's Linux JDK running under the OpenBSD Unix-like system. For the mass market, I've used Sun's Java 2 Win32 (Windows 95/98/NT) implementation. And, "for the rest of us," I've run some of the programs on Apple's MacOS Runtime for Java (MRJ) running under MacOS 8 on a Power Macintosh and a few on MacOS X (which Apple wants you to pronounce "Oh Ess Ten," despite the way they've been writing it for the last three years). However, since Java is portable, I anticipate that the examples will work on MacOS X except where extra APIs are required. Not every example has been tested on every platform, but all have been tested on at least one, and most on more than one.

---

* Kaffe, the Swedish word for coffee, is an open source (GNU Public License) Java implementation that runs on just about any Unix or Unix-like system, and has been ported to other platforms such as Win32.

The Java API consists of two parts, core APIs and non-core APIs. The core is, by definition, what's included in the JDK that you download for free from *http://java. sun.com.* Non-core is everything else. But even this "core" is far from tiny: it weighs in at around 50 packages and well over a thousand public classes, each with up to 30 or more public methods. Programs that stick to this core API are reasonably assured of portability to any Java 2 platform.

The non-core APIs are further divided into standard extensions and non-standard extensions. All standard extensions have package names beginning with `javax.`,* and reference implementations are available from Sun. A Java licensee (like, say, Apple or Microsoft) is not required to implement every standard extension, but if they do, the interface of the standard extension should be adhered to. This book will call your attention to any code that depends on a standard extension. There is little code that depends on non-standard extensions other than code listed in the book itself (the major exception is the Regular Expressions API used in Chapter 4). My own package, `com.darwinsys.util`, contains some utility classes used here and there; you will see an import for this at the top of any file that uses classes from it.

Other Books

There is a lot of useful information packed into this book. However, due to the breadth of topics, it is not possible to give book-length treatment to any one topic. Because of this, the book also contains references to many web sites and other books. This is in keeping with my target audience: the person who wants to learn more about Java.

O'Reilly & Associates publishes one of the largest—and, I think, the best—selection of Java books on the market. As the API continues to expand, so does the coverage. You can find the latest versions and ordering information on O'Reilly's Java books in the back pages of this book or online at *http://java.oreilly.com*, and you can buy them at most bookstores, both physical and virtual. You can also read them online through a paid subscription service; see *http://safari.oreilly.com.* While many are mentioned at appropriate spots in the book, a few deserve special mention here.

First and foremost, David Flanagan's *Java in a Nutshell* offers a brief overview of the language and API, and a detailed reference to the most essential packages. This is handy to keep beside your computer.

Learning Java, by Patrick Niemeyer and Joshua Peck, contains a slightly more leisurely introduction to the language and the APIs.

---

* Note that not all packages named `javax.` are extensions: `javax.swing` and its sub-packages—the Swing GUI packages—used to be extensions, but are now core.

A definitive (and monumental) description of programming the Swing GUI is *Java Swing,* by Robert Eckstein, Marc Loy, and Dave Wood.

Java Servlets, by Jason Hunter, and *JavaServer Pages,* by Hans Bergsten, are both ideal for the server-side web developer.

Java Virtual Machine, by Jon Meyer and Troy Downing, will intrigue the person who wants to know more about what's under the hood.

Java Network Programming and *Java I/O,* by Elliotte Rusty Harold, and *Database Programming with JDBC and Java,* by George Reese, are also useful references.

There are many more; see the O'Reilly web site for an up-to-date list.

Other Java Books

Never consider releasing a GUI application unless you have read Sun's official *Java Look and Feel Design Guidelines* (Addison Wesley). This work presents the views of a large group of human factors and user-interface experts at Sun who have worked with the Swing GUI package since its inception; they tell you how to make it work well.

Finally, while authors at other publishing houses might be afraid to mention a book that their publisher might think of as competition to their own, I have found Patrick Chan's *Java Developer's Almanac* (Addison Wesley) a useful addition to my library and a natural complement to my book. While my book features much more detail and discussion than his short "examplets," the main part of Patrick's book is a large alphabetical (by class, not by package) reference to the core API. As the core part of his book was produced mechanically using Reflection, the book has a relatively low cover price. By the way, I show you how to generate books like Patrick's (see Recipe 25.7), but he doesn't show you how to write a book like mine.

General Programming Books

Donald E. Knuth's *The Art of Computer Programming* has been a source of inspiration to students of computing since its first publication by Addison Wesley in 1968. Volume 1 covers *Fundamental Algorithms,* Volume 2 is *Seminumerical Algorithms,* and Volume 3 is *Sorting and Searching.* The remaining four volumes in the projected series were never completed. Although his examples are far from Java (he invented a hypothetical assembly language for his examples), many of his discussions of algorithms—of how computers ought to be used to solve real problems—are as relevant today as 30 years ago.*

---

* With apologies for algorithm decisions that are less relevant today given the massive changes in computing power now available.

The Elements of Programming Style, by Kernighan and Plauger, set the style (literally) for a generation of programmers with examples from various structured programming languages. Brian Kernighan also wrote (with P. J. Plauger) a pair of books, *Software Tools* and *Software Tools in Pascal,* which demonstrated so much good advice on programming that I used to advise all programmers to read them. However, these three books are somewhat dated now; many times I wanted to write a follow-on book in a more modern language, but instead defer to *The Practice of Programming,* Brian's follow-on (co-written by Rob Pike) to the *Software Tools* series. This book continues the Bell Labs (now part of Lucent) tradition of excellence in software textbooks. I have even adapted one bit of code from their book, in Recipe 3.13.

Design Books

Peter Coad's *Java Design* (PTR-PH/Yourdon Press) discusses the issues of object-oriented analysis and design specifically for Java. Coad is somewhat critical of Java's implementation of the observable-observer paradigm and offers his own replacement for it.

One of the most famous books on object-oriented design in recent years is *Design Patterns,* by Gamma, Helm, Johnson, and Vlissides (Addison Wesley). These authors are often collectively called "the gang of four," resulting in their book sometimes being referred to as "the GOF book." One of my colleagues called it "the best book on object-oriented design ever," and I think he's probably not far off the mark.

Another group of important books on object-oriented design is the UML series by "the Three Amigos" (Booch, Jacobson, and Rumbaugh). Their major works are the *UML User Guide, UML Process,* and others. A smaller and more approachable book in the same series is Martin Fowler's *UML Distilled.*

Conventions Used in This Book

This book uses the following conventions.

Programming Conventions

I use the following terminology in this book. A *program* means either an applet, a servlet, or an application. An *applet* is for use in a browser. A *servlet* is similar to an applet but for use in a server. An *application* is any other type of program. A desktop application (a.k.a. *client*) interacts with the user. A server program deals with a client indirectly, usually via a network connection.

The examples shown are in two varieties. Those that begin with zero or more import statements, a Javadoc comment, and a public class statement are complete examples. Those that begin with a declaration or executable statement, of course, are excerpts. However, the full versions of these excerpts have been compiled and run, and the online source includes the full versions.

Recipes are numbered by chapter and number, so, for example, Recipe 7.5 refers to the fifth recipe in Chapter 7.

Typesetting Conventions

The following typographic conventions are used in this book:

Italic

> is used for commands, filenames, and URLs. It is also used to define new terms when they first appear in the text.

`Constant width`

> is used in code examples to show partial or complete Java source code program listings. It is also used for class names, method names, variable names, and other fragments of Java code.

Many programs are accompanied by an example showing them in action, run from the command line. These will usually show a prompt ending in either $ for Unix or > for Microsoft, depending on which computer I was using that day. Text before this prompt character can be ignored; it will be a pathname or a hostname, again depending on the system.

Comments and Questions

As mentioned earlier, I've tested all the code on at least one of the reference platforms, and most on several. Still, there may be platform dependencies, or even bugs, in my code or in some important Java implementation. Please report any errors you find, as well as your suggestions for future editions, by writing to:

> O'Reilly & Associates, Inc.
> 101 Morris Street
> Sebastopol, CA 95472
> (800) 998-9938 (in the United States or Canada)
> (707) 829-0515 (international or local)
> (707) 829-0104 (fax)

To ask technical questions or comment on the book, send email to:

> *bookquestions@oreilly.com*

There is an O'Reilly web site for the book, listing errata, examples, or any additional information. You can access this page at:

http://www.oreilly.com/catalog/javacook/

I also have a personal web site for the book:

http://javacook.darwinsys.com

Both sites will list errata and plans for future editions. You'll also find the source code for all the Java code examples to download; *please* don't waste your time typing them in again! For specific instructions, see the next section.

Getting the Source Code

From my web site *http://javacook.darwinsys.com*, just follow the Download link and you will be presented with three choices:

1. Download the entire source archive as a single large zip file

2. Download individual source files, indexed alphabetically as well as by chapter

3. Download the binary JAR file for the `com.darwinsys.util` package needed to compile many of the other programs

Most people will choose either #1 or #2, but anyone who wants to compile my code will need #3. See Recipe 1.4 for information on using these files.

Downloading the entire source archive (#1) gives a large zip file that contains all the files from the book (and more). This archive can be unpacked with *jar* (see Recipe 23.3), the free zip program from Info-ZIP, the commercial WinZip or PKZIP, or any compatible tool. The files are organized into subdirectories by topic; there is one for strings (Chapter 3), regular expressions (Chapter 4), numbers (Chapter 5) and so on. The archive also contains the index by name and index by chapter files from the download site, so you can easily find the files you need.

Downloading individual files is easy too: simply follow the links either by the file/subdirectory name or by chapter. Once you see the file you want in your browser, use File->Save or the equivalent, or just copy and paste it from the browser into an editor or IDE.

The files will be updated periodically, so if there are differences between what's printed in the book and what you get, be glad, for you'll have received the benefit of hindsight.

Acknowledgments

My life has been touched many times by the flow of the fates bringing me into contact with the right person to show me the right thing at the right time. Steve Munroe, with whom I've long since lost touch, introduced me to computers—in particular an IBM 360/30 at the Toronto Board of Education that was bigger than a living room, had 32 or 64K of memory, and had perhaps the power of a PC/XT—in 1970. (Are you out there somewhere, Steve?) Herb Kugel took me under his wing at the University of Toronto while I was learning about the larger IBM mainframes that came later. Terry Wood and Dennis Smith at the University of Toronto introduced me to mini- and micro-computers before there was an IBM PC. On evenings and weekends, the Toronto Business Club of Toastmasters International (*http://www.toastmasters.org*) and Al Lambert's Canada SCUBA School allowed me to develop my public speaking and instructional abilities. Several people at the University of Toronto, but especially Geoffrey Collyer, taught me the features and benefits of the Unix operating system at a time when I was ready to learn it.

Greg Davidson of UCSD taught the first Learning Tree course I attended, and welcomed me as a Learning Tree instructor. Years later, when the Oak language was about to be released on Sun's web site, Greg encouraged me to write to James Gosling and find out about it. James's reply of March 29th, 1995, that the lawyers had made them rename the language to Java and that it was "just now" available for download, is the prized first entry in my saved Java mailbox. Mike Rozek took me on as a Learning Tree course author for a Unix course and two Java courses. After Mike's departure from the company, Francesco Zamboni, Julane Marx, and Jennifer Urick in turn provided product management of these courses. Jennifer also arranged permission for me to "reuse some code" in this book that had previously been used in my Java course notes. Finally, thanks to the many Learning Tree instructors and students who showed me ways of improving my presentations. I still teach for "The Tree" and recommend their courses for the busy developer who wants to zero in on one topic in detail over four days. Their web site is *http://www.learningtree.com*.

Closer to this project, Tim O'Reilly believed in "the little Lint book" when it was just a sample chapter, enabling my early entry into the circle of O'Reilly authors. Years later, Mike Loukides encouraged me to keep trying to find a Java book idea that both he and I could work with. And he stuck by me when I kept falling behind the deadlines. Mike also read the entire manuscript and made many sensible comments, some of which brought flights of fancy down to earth. Jessamyn Read turned many faxed and emailed scratchings of dubious legibility into the quality illustrations you see in this book. And many, many other talented people at O'Reilly & Associates helped put this book into the form in which you now see it.

I also must thank my reviewers, first and foremost my dear wife Betty Cerar, who may still think Java is some kind of caffeinated beverage that I drink while programming, but whose passion for clear expression and correct grammar has benefited much of my writing. Jonathan Knudsen, Andy Oram, and David Flanagan commented on the outline when it was little more than a list of chapters and recipes, and yet were able to see the kind of book it could become, and to suggest ways to make it better. Learning Tree instructor Jim Burgess read most of the book with a very critical eye on locution, formulation, and code. Bil Lewis and Mike Slinn (*mslinn@mslinn.com*) made helpful comments on multiple drafts of the book. Ron Hitchens (*ron@ronsoft.com*) and Marc Loy carefully read the entire final draft. Editor Sue Miller helped shepherd the manuscript through the somewhat energetic final phases of production. Sarah Slocombe read the XML chapter in its entirety and made many lucid suggestions, though unfortunately time did not permit me to include all of them. Each of these people made this book better in many ways, particularly by suggesting additional recipes or revising existing ones. Any faults that remain are surely my own.

I've used a variety of tools and operating systems in preparing, compiling, and testing the book. The developers of OpenBSD (*http://www.openbsd.org*), "the proactively secure Unix-like system," deserve thanks for making a stable and secure Unix clone that is also closer to traditional Unix than other freeware systems. I used the *vi* editor (*vi* on OpenBSD and *vim* on MS-Windows) while inputting the original manuscript in XML, and Adobe FrameMaker to format the documents. Each of these is an excellent tool in its own way. If you're wondering how I got from XML to Frame, the answer will be given in Chapter 21.

No book on Java would be complete without a quadrium* of thanks to James Gosling for inventing the first Unix Emacs, the *sc* spreadsheet, the NeWS window system, and Java. Thanks also to his employer Sun Microsystems (NASDAQ SUNW) for creating not only the Java language but an incredible array of Java tools and API libraries freely available over the Internet.

Thanks to Tom and Nathan, for the *Perl Cookbook*. Without them I might never have come up with the format for this book.

Willi Powell of Apple Canada provided MacOS X access.

Thanks to the Tim Horton's Donuts in Bolton, Ontario for great coffee and for not enforcing the 20-minute table limit on the weird guy with the computer.

To each and every one of you, my sincere thanks.

---

* It's a good thing he only invented four major technologies, not five, or I'd have to rephrase that to avoid infringing on an Intel trademark.

1

Getting Started: Compiling, Running, and Debugging

1.0. Introduction

This chapter covers some entry-level tasks that you simply need to know how to do before you can go on—it is said you must crawl before you can walk, and walk before you can ride a bicycle. Before you can try out anything else in the book, you need to be able to compile and run your Java, so I start there, showing several ways: the JDK way, the Mac way, and the Integrated Development Environment (IDE) way. Then I'll discuss a few details about applets, in case you are working on them. Deprecation warnings come next, as you're likely to meet them in maintaining "old" Java code.*

If you're already happy with your IDE, you may wish to skip some or all of this material. It's here to ensure that everybody can compile and debug their programs before we move on.

1.1. Compiling and Running Java: JDK

Problem

You need to compile and run your Java program.

Solution

This is one of the few areas where your computer's operating system impinges into Java's portability, so let's get it out of the way first.

---

* There is humor in the phrase "old Java code," which should be apparent when you realize that Java has been in circulation for under five years at the time of this book's first printing.

JDK

Using the command-line Java Development Kit (JDK) may be the best way to keep up with the very latest improvements from Sun/JavaSoft. This is not the fastest compiler available by any means; the compiler is written in Java and interpreted at compile time, making it a sensible bootstrapping solution, but not necessarily optimal for speed of development. Nonetheless, using Sun's JDK (or Java SDK), the commands are *javac* to compile and *java* to run your program. For example:

```
C:\javasrc>javac HelloWorld.java


C:\javasrc>java HelloWorld
Hello, World


C:\javasrc>
```

As you can see from the compiler's (lack of) output, this compiler works on the Unix "no news is good news" philosophy: if a program was able to do what you asked it to, it shouldn't bother nattering at you to say that it did so. Many people use this compiler or one of its clones. The *javac* and *java* commands are available with the JDK on both Windows and Unix, and under MacOS X if you have installed the bundled Developer Tools package.

There is an optional setting called CLASSPATH, discussed in Recipe 2.5, that controls where Java looks for classes. CLASSPATH, if set, is used by both *javac* and *java*. In older versions of Java you had to set your CLASSPATH to include "." even to run a simple program from the current directory; this is no longer true on Sun's current Java implementations. It may be true on some of the clones.

Command-line alternatives

Sun's *javac* compiler is the official reference implementation. But it is itself written in Java, and hence must be interpreted at runtime. Recognizing the slowness of compilation as a significant hindrance to developers, Sun's Java folk went back and rewrote the compiler from scratch, discarding some old baggage and using new language features. This new compiler (still named *javac*) was unveiled for early access in May 1999 and released later that year. It is about twice as fast as the original Java compiler—a big improvement—but still slower than some other compilers. Symantec's Java compiler and Microsoft's J++ (a Java-like language) are written in C/C++, so they are quite a bit faster than an interpreted Java compiler.

In order to speed up my compilations, I have used Jikes, a freeware compiler written in C++. Jikes is fast, free, and available both for MS-Windows and for Unix. It's also easy to install. For MS-Windows (Win32), Linux, and other Unix systems, you can find binaries of the current version on IBM's Jikes web site. If you are using OpenBSD, NetBSD, or FreeBSD, you should only need to run:

```
cd /usr/ports/lang/jikes; sudo make install
```

or just download the package file and use pkg_add to get it installed. Visit *http:// oss.software.ibm.com/developerworks/opensource/jikes/* for Jikes information and downloads.

A key benefit of Jikes is that it gives much better error messages than the JDK compilers do. It will alert you to slightly misspelled names, for example. Its messages are often a bit verbose, but you can use the +E option to make it print them in a shorter format. Jikes has many other command-line options, many that are the same as the JDK compiler's, but some that go beyond them. See Jikes's online documentation for details.

An older C++-based Java compiler, Guavac, is not considered finished. Indeed, its author has stopped maintaining it. Nonetheless, I was able to use Guavac 1.2 to compile many of the examples in this book (note that the Guavac version number of 1.2 is unrelated to the Sun JDK version number 1.2). See *ftp://sunsite.org.uk/ packages/guavac/* for information on Guavac.

Another alternative technology is Kaffe, a product that Transvirtual (*http:// www.transvirtual.com*) licenses but also makes available in open source form under the standard GNU Public License. Kaffe aims to be a complete JDK replacement, though it has moved rather slowly past the JDK 1.1 level and is, as of this writing, still not quite a complete Java 2 clone. Again, on OpenBSD there is a port, and on Linux there are RPMs available. Visit Transvirtual's web site for the latest information on Kaffe.

One last freeware package is Japhar, a Java runtime clone, available from *http:// www.japhar.org.*

MacOS

The JDK is purely command-line-based. At the other end of the spectrum in terms of keyboard-versus-visual, we have the Apple Macintosh. Whole books have been written about how great the Mac is, and I won't step into that debate. I will, however, comment on how lamentable it is that Apple let its Java implementation lag behind current standards. Users of MacOS 8 and 8.5 have put up with Java 1.8 for several years. MacOS X (Release 10 of MacOS) is a new technology base built upon a BSD Unix base. As such, it has a regular command line as well as all the traditional Mac tools. And it features a full Java 2 implementation, including Swing.

For MacOS 8, if you've followed Apple's directions for installing the MacOS Runtime for Java (MRJ), you can compile by dragging a file to, or double-clicking on, the "javac" icon (I've made aliases for this icon and friends on my desktop). Once the dialog shown in Figure 1-1 appears, you can click on "Do Javac" (or just press Enter on the keyboard), first changing any options if you want.

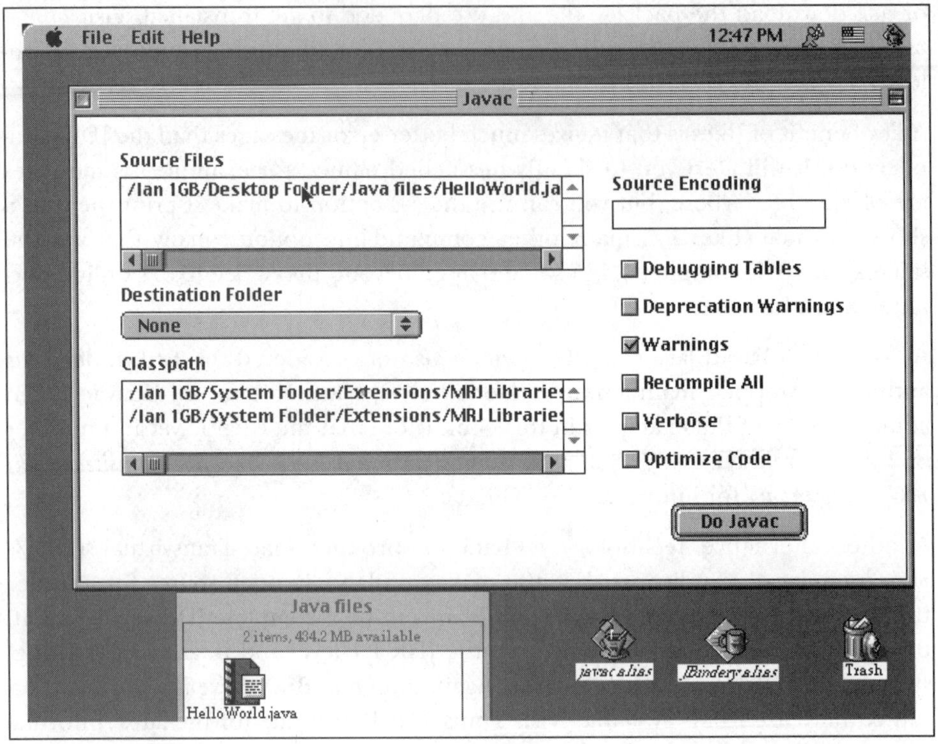

Figure 1-1. MacOS 8 Javac window

You will then see the Java console window stating that it ran *javac* (as shown in Figure 1-2). This *javac* is a Mac port of the JDK version, so it also runs on "no news is good news." As this is a Mac, you'll see the resulting class file appear in your destination folder as soon as it's been created (which happens only if there are no compilation errors).

You now have a class file, and you want to run it. That's where the JBindery program comes in. JBindery can do two things: run a Java class file directly or make it into a "clickable" runnable program. We'll start it by dragging the class file onto the Jbindery icon; the program starts as shown in Figure 1-3.

As we are running a simple command-line program rather than a windowed application, after we click on "Run," the JBindery screen is replaced by a Java Console showing the command output, as in Figure 1-4.

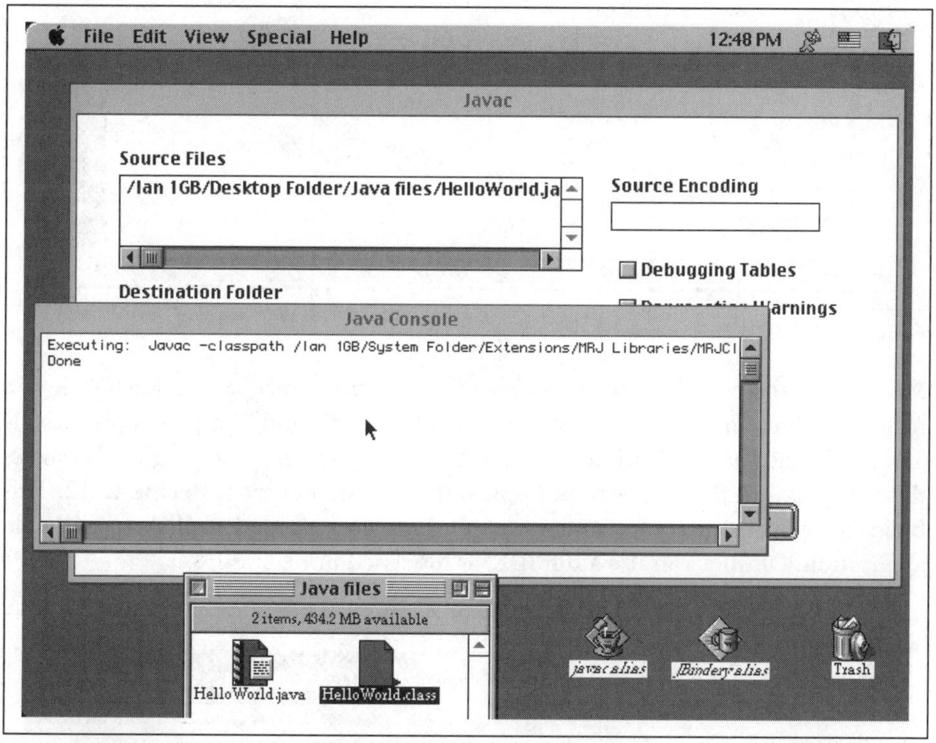

Figure 1-2. MacOS 8 compilation completed (MRJ)

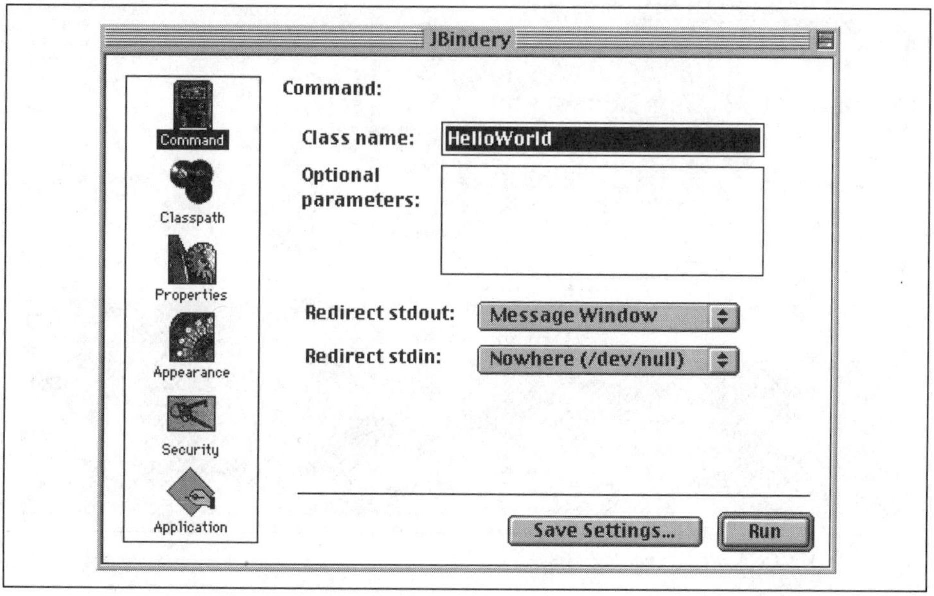

Figure 1-3. MacOS 8 JBindery window

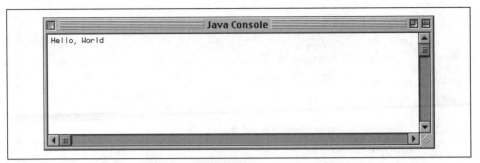

Figure 1-4. MacOS 8 Java Console showing program output

Macintosh users who can run MacOS X have more choice. Since MacOS X is a hybrid of Unix and MacOS X, they can use the command-line JDK tools directly and then build the application using the "Build Application" tool. Figure 1-5 shows this running with the Application Look and Feel Switcher from Recipe 13.12. This builds a folder or directory containing all the pieces needed to make a clickable application. Or, they can use a full IDE, as discussed in Recipe 1.3.

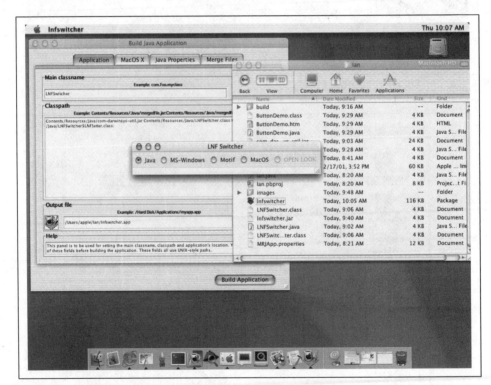

Figure 1-5. MacOS X application builder

1.2. Editing and Compiling with a Color-Highlighting Editor

Problem

You are tired of command-line tools but not ready for an IDE.

Solution

Use a color-highlighting editor.

Discussion

It's less than an IDE (see the next recipe), but more than a command line. What is it? It's an editor with Java support. Tools such as TextPad (*http://www.textpad.com*), Visual Slick Edit, and others are low-cost windowed editors (primarily for MS-Windows) that have some amount of Java recognition built in, and the ability to compile from within the editor. TextPad has quite a number of file types that it recognizes, including batch files and shell scripts, C, C++, Java, JSP (see Recipe 18.6), JavaScript (a client-side web technology), and many others. For each of these, it uses color highlighting to show which part of the file being edited comprises keywords, comments, quoted strings, and so on. This is very useful in spotting when part of your code has been swallowed up by an unterminated /* comment or a missing quote. While this isn't the same as the deep understanding of Java that a full IDE might possess, experience has shown that it definitely aids programmer productivity. TextPad also has a "compile Java" command and a "run external program" command. Both of these have the advantage of capturing the entire command output into a window, which may be easier to scroll than a command-line window on some platforms. On the other hand, you don't see the command results until the program terminates, which can be most uncomfortable if your GUI application throws an exception before it puts up its main window. Despite this minor drawback, TextPad is a very useful tool. Other editors that include color highlighting include *vim* (an enhanced version of the Unix tool *vi*, available for MS-Windows and Unix platforms; see *http://www.vim.org*), the ever-popular Emacs editor, and many others.

1.3. Compiling, Running, and Testing with an IDE

Problem

Several tools are too many.

Solution

Use an integrated development environment.

Discussion

Many programmers find that using a handful of separate tools—a text editor, a compiler, and a runner program, not to mention a debugger (see Recipe 1.12)—is too many. An *integrated development environment* (IDE*) integrates all of these into a single toolset with a (hopefully consistent) graphical user interface. There are many IDEs to choose from, ranging from text editors that allow you to compile and run a Java program, all the way up to fully integrated tools with their own compilers and virtual machines. Class browsers and other features of IDEs round out the purported ease-of-use feature-sets of these tools. It has been argued many times whether an IDE really makes you more productive or if you just have more fun doing the same thing. However, even the JDK maintainers at Sun admit (perhaps for the benefit of their advertisers) that an IDE is often more productive, although it hides many implementation details and tends to generate code that locks you into a particular IDE. Sun's Java Jumpstart CD (part of *Developer Essentials*) said, at one time:

> The JDK software comes with a minimal set of tools. Serious developers are advised to use a professional Integrated Development Environment with JDK 1.2 software. Click on one of the images below to visit external sites and learn more.

This is followed by some (presumably paid) advertising links to Inprise/Borland JBuilder, WebGain Visual Cafe, and Sybase PowerJ development suites.

I don't plan to debate the IDE versus the command-line process; I'm just going to show a few examples of using a couple of the Java-based IDEs. One that runs on both MS-Windows and Unix platforms is Forte, which is a free download from Sun. Originally created by NetBeans.com, this IDE was so good that Sun bought the company, and now distributes the IDE for free. Forte is also open sourced. You

---

* It takes too long to say, or type, Integrated Development Environment, so I'll use the term IDE from here on. I know you're good at remembering acronyms, especially TLAs.

can download the compiled version from *http://www.sun.com/forte/fff/** and the open source version from *http://www.netbeans.org.*

Forte comes with a variety of templates. In Figure 1-6, I almost selected the MDI (multiple-document interface) template, but instead opted for the Swing `JFrame` template.

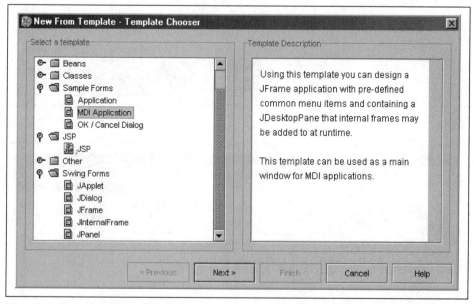

Figure 1-6. Forte: "New From Template" dialog

Then in Figure 1-7, Forte lets me specify a class name and package name for the new program I am building.

In Figure 1-8, I am building the GUI using Forte's GUI builder. Select a visual component in the upper right, and click on the form where you want it. While there are several things about Forte that most people (including myself) find quirky, I do like the fact that it defaults to using a `BorderLayout`; some other IDEs default to using no layout at all, and the resulting GUIs do not resize gracefully.

I also like the way Forte handles GUI action handlers (see Recipe 13.4). You simply double-click on the GUI control you want to handle actions for, and Forte creates an action handler for it and puts you into the editor to type the code for the action handler. In this case I made a deliberate typing error to show the effects; when I click the Build Project menu item, the offending line of code is highlighted in

---

* The *fff* stands for Forte For Java; there are also Forte IDEs for other languages.

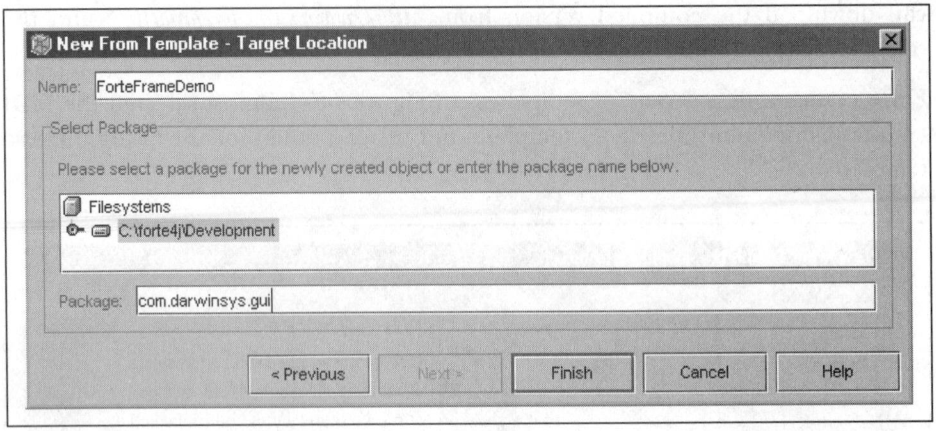

Figure 1-7. Forte: name that class

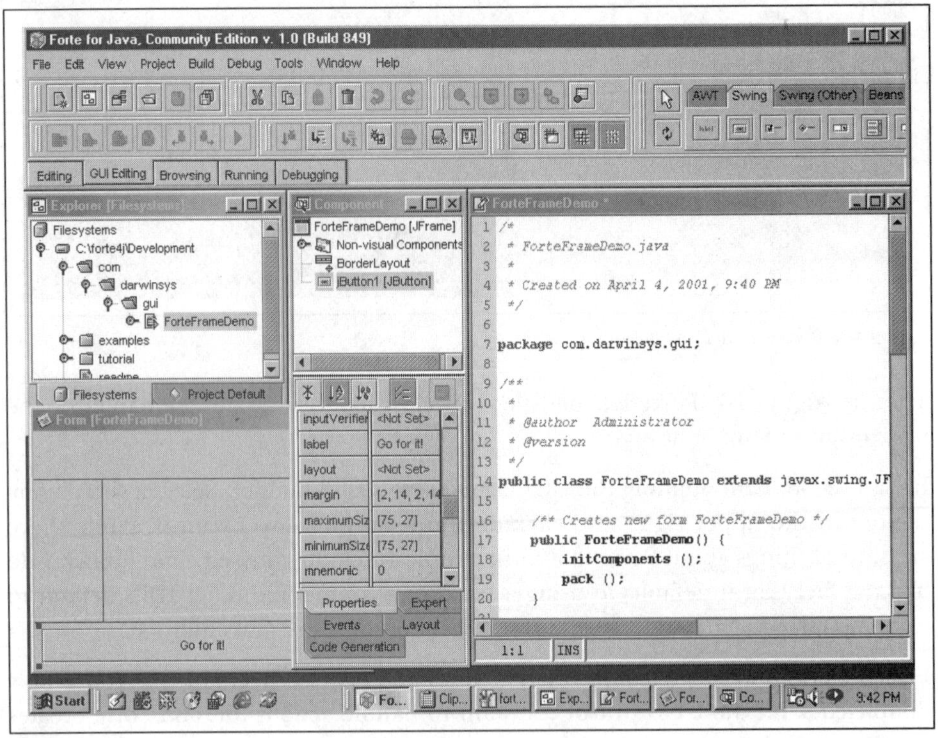

Figure 1-8. Forte: GUI building

bright red, both in the source code and in the error listing from the compiler (see Figure 1-9).

Some people don't like the user interface of Forte. There are many popular IDEs for Java, especially on the MS-Windows platform, and almost everybody who uses

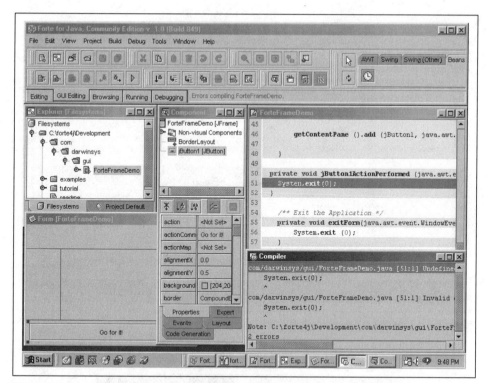

Figure 1-9. Forte: compilation error highlighted

one has a favorite, such as Borland JBuilder, WebGain Visual Cafe, or IBM Visual Age for Java. Most of them have a free version and a Pro version. For up-to-date comparisons, you may want to consult the glossy magazines, since IDEs are updated relatively often.

On MacOS X, the bundled Developer Tools includes a reasonably good IDE, shown in Figure 1-10. MetroWerks CodeWarrior and other IDEs are also available for MacOS X.

Figure 1-11 shows the MacOS X bundled IDE running a trivial application built using its default frame-based template.

What about the speed of IDEs? One way to categorize an IDE is by whether it was written to be as portable as Java or to run well on only one platform. Forte, JBuilder, and others are written in Java and can, in theory, be run on any platform that has Java 2 support. Visual Cafe, IBM Visual Age for Java, MetroWerks CodeWarrior, and others are built out of existing frameworks and provided as compiled binaries; these have major components that depend on one or another platform and cannot be "run anywhere." The native code IDEs tend to be a bit faster, although the difference is diminishing as Java runtimes get better and as

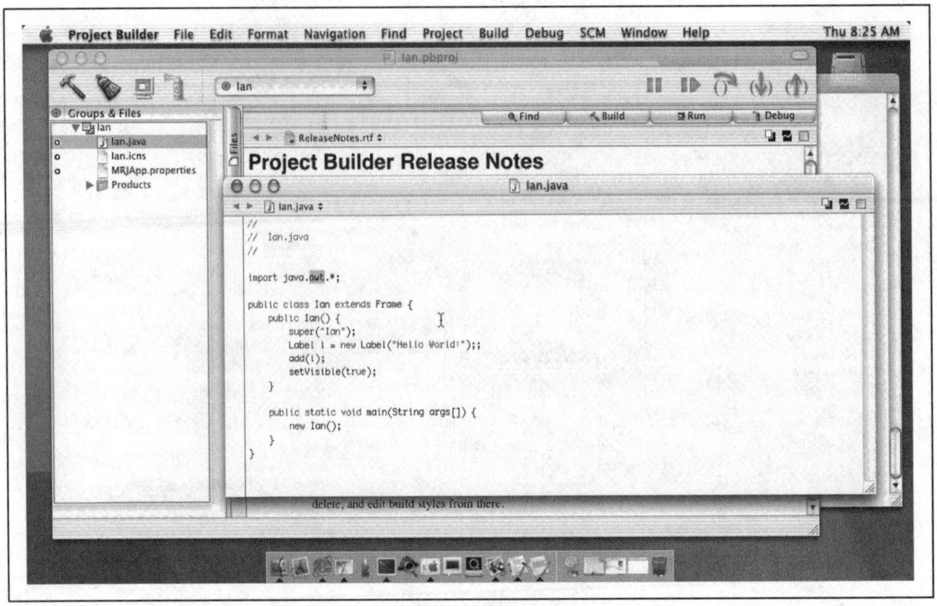

Figure 1-10. MacOS X Developer Tools IDE: main windows

Figure 1-11. MacOS X Developer Tools IDE: application built and running

computers get faster. When was the last time you bought a new computer system with a Pentium 133 processor?

1.4. Using Classes from This Book

Problem

You want to try out my examples and/or use my utility classes.

Solution

Download the latest zip file of the booksource files and unzip it. Install the class JAR file in your CLASSPATH. Or download just the files you need.

Discussion

You can download the latest version of the source code for all the examples in the book from the book web site, *http://javacook.darwinsys.com*. You will get two files. First is the source code, in a file called *javacooksrc.jar*, which you should unzip someplace convenient or wherever you like to keep source code. Second is a file called *com-darwinsys-util.jar*, which you need to set in your CLASSPATH (see Recipe 2.5) or *JDKHOME/jre/lib/ext* directory. The files are roughly organized in per-chapter directories, but there is a lot of overlap and cross-referencing. Because of this, I have prepared a cross-reference file named *index-bychapter.html*. There is also a mechanically generated file called *index-byname.html*, which you can use if you know the name of the file you want (and remember that Java source files almost always have the same name as the public class they contain). The canonical index file, *index.html*, links to both these files.

Once you've set your CLASSPATH, you can compile. In most directories you can simply say *javac *.java* or *jikes *.java*. Of course, not everybody likes typing those commands, so there is a makefile for the *make* utility. *make* is standard on Unix and readily available for MS-Windows from, for example, the GNUwin32 project (see *http://www.cygnus.com/gnuwin32/*). There is also a top-level makefile that visits the subdirectories and runs *make* in each of them. These makefiles have been tested with *gmake* (GNU *make* 3.79.1), BSD *make* (OpenBSD 2.8), and they should work with almost any reasonably modern *make* program or equivalent.

There may also be times when you don't want to download the entire archive—if you just need a bit of code in a hurry—so you can access those index files and the resulting directory, for "anyplace, anytime access" on the same web site.

1.5. Automating Compilation with jr

Problem

You get tired of typing *javac* and *java* commands.

Solution

Use my *jr* script.

Discussion

Although it may be tedious, there is some logic behind the fact that the compilation command (*javac*, *jikes*, etc.) requires you to include the filename extension, and the running command (*java*) requires you to omit the filename extension— you can't type *java HelloWorld.class* and have it run the `HelloWorld` program from the current directory. The compiler is actually reading a source file, while the *java* command is running a class, a class that might be located someplace in your CLASSPATH (see Recipe 2.5). It is common for JDK users to use a batch script or command file to automate this. Mine is called *jr*, for Java compile and Run. The Unix version is *jr*, a shell script:

```
javac $1.java && java $*
```

The `$*` gets expanded to include `$1` and any other arguments. The MS-Windows version is *jr.bat*:

```
javac %1.java

if errorlevel 1 goto norun

java %1    %2 %3 %4 %5 %6

:norun
```

For people using MS-Windows who have no experience using batch files for compilation, fear not. You could just copy this *jr.bat* file into the *JDKHOME/bin* directory. But the problem then is that when you deinstall that JDK version and install a new one, you'd lose *jr*. What I usually do on MS-Windows is this: just create a directory that won't conflict with anything else, such as *C:\bin* ("bin" being an old name for binary programs; by tradition all of one's own programs go there). Just add this to your PATH setting, either in your *autoexec.bat* file or in your Control Panel settings. Copy *jr.bat* into this directory, and you're done! From then on you can just give commands such as *jr HelloWorld*. The script will run *javac HelloWorld.java* for you and, if there are no errors, it will run *java HelloWorld*.

Feel free to improve upon this and to call it whatever you like.

1.6. *Automating Compilation with make*

Problem

You get tired of typing *javac* and *java* commands.

Solution

Use the *make* utility to direct your compilations.

Discussion

The Unix operating system has long had to deal with automating large or repetitive compilations. The most enduring tool for this purpose is *make*, invented by Stu Feldman at Bell Laboratories in the mid-1970s and still widely used. There have been literally dozens of *make*-like programs over the years. The X Window System has *imake*, which is really a front-end to *make*. Linux and GNU enthusiasts have *gmake*, and BSD systems feature BSD *make*; one or another will be installed under the name *make*. The cygwin32 project features its own *make*, a version of *gmake*. *make* consults a file called *Makefile* (or *makefile*) in the current directory to figure out what you want done and how to do it. A makefile to build one Java program could be as simple as this:

```
all:
      javac HelloWorld.java
```

Makefiles can be much more involved. One common feature is to parameterize a makefile so that if you need to port the code to a new platform or you distribute your source code to others to port, all the necessary makefile changes are in one place. For example, to use *make* variables to let the user compile with either *javac* or Jikes, and to add a rule to remove the **.class* files after a round of debugging, the makefile might grow somewhat, as shown here. Note that lines beginning with the pound sign (#) are comments for the reader and are ignored by *make*:

```
# Makefile for Acme FlutterBox program.
# Uncomment one of these compiler definitions:
#JAVAC= javac
JAVAC=    jikes +E

compile:
        $(JAVAC)  *.java

clean:
        @rm -f *.class
```

All modern Unix systems and most MS-Windows IDEs ship with some version of *make*. Java became popular after the current fragmentation of Unix into multiple systems maintained by different groups, so many current *make* programs do not come preconfigured with "convenience" rules for Java; they all come with rules for C and other older languages. Thus you may want to provide a "default" rule for compiling from *FILE.java* into *FILE.class*. The way you do this will vary from one version of *make* to another, so please see your system's documentation. For one such rule, see the file *jmake.rules* in the source distribution. For some slightly more involved, but still relatively simple, examples of using *make*, consult the files named *Makefile* in the source distribution.*

See Also

The sidebar "Make Versus Ant."

Also, you may want to refer to the book *Using Make and Imake* (O'Reilly).

1.7. Automating Compilation with Ant

Problem

You get tired of typing *javac* and *java* commands.

Solution

Use the Ant program to direct your compilations.

Discussion

The intricacies of makefiles and their importabilities have led to the development of a pure-Java solution for automating the build process. *Ant* is free software; it is available in source form or ready-to-run from the Apache Foundation's Jakarta project web site, at *http://jakarta.apache.org/ant/*. Like *make*, Ant uses a file or files—written in XML—listing what to do and, if necessary, how to do it. These rules are intended to be platform-independent, though you can of course write platform-specific recipes if necessary.

To use Ant you must create a 15–30 line file specifying various options. This file should be called *build.xml;* if you call it anything else, you'll have to give a special command-line arguments every time you run Ant. Example 1-1 shows the build script used to build the files in the *starting* directory. See Recipe 21.0 for discussion

---

* The one bit of *make* syntax that isn't explained is VARIABLE?=VALUE, which sets VARIABLE to VALUE only if it is not set. This is often used in *make* to pass a variable down and allow it to have a default value in the sub-makefile, but be overridden from the "main" makefile.

of the XML syntax. For now, note that the <!-- tag begins an XML comment, which extends to the --> tag.

Example 1-1. Ant example file (build.xml)

```
<project name="Java Cookbook Examples" default="compile" basedir=".">

  <!-- set global properties for this build -->
  <property name="src" value="."/>
  <property name="build" value="build"/>
  <!-- Specify the compiler to use.
    Using jikes is supported but requires rt.jar in classpath. -->
  <property name="build.compiler" value="modern"/>

  <target name="init">
    <!-- Create the time stamp -->
    <tstamp/>
    <!-- Create the build directory structure used by compile -->
    <mkdir dir="${build}"/>
  </target>

  <!-- specify what to compile. This builds everything -->
  <target name="compile" depends="init">

    <!-- Compile the java code from ${src} into ${build} -->
    <javac srcdir="${src}" destdir="${build}"
           classpath="../com-darwinsys-util.jar"/>
  </target>

</project>
```

When you run Ant, it produces a reasonable amount of notification as it goes, similar to *make*:

```
$ ant  compile
Buildfile: build.xml
Project base dir set to: /home/ian/javasrc/starting
Executing Target: init
Executing Target: compile
Compiling 19 source files to /home/ian/javasrc/starting/build
Performing a Modern Compile
Copying 22 support files to /home/ian/javasrc/starting/build
Completed in 8 seconds
$
```

See Also

The sidebar "Make Versus Ant."

Make Versus Ant

Both *make* and Ant have advantages and disadvantages, detractors and advocates. I'll try to stay neutral, though I admit I have been using *make* for 15 years longer than I've been using Ant.

make files are shorter. No contest. *make* has its own language instead of using XML, so it can be a lot more terse. *make* runs faster; it's written in C.

Ant files can do more. The *javac* task in Ant, for example, automatically finds all the **.java* files in subdirectories. With *make*, a sub-*make* is normally required. And the `include` directive for subdirectories differs between GNU *make* and BSD *make*.

Ant has special knowledge of CLASSPATH, making it easy to set a CLASSPATH in various ways for compile time. See the CLASSPATH setting in Example 1-1. You may have to duplicate this in other ways—shell scripts or batch files— for manually running or testing your application.

make is simpler to extend, but harder to do so portably. You can write a one-line *make* rule for getting a CVS archive from a remote site, but you may run into incompatibilities between GNU *make*, BSD *make*, etc. There is a built-in Ant task for getting an archive from CVS using Ant; it was written as a Java source file instead of just a series of command-line commands.

make has been around much longer. There are millions (literally) more *make* files than Ant files. Developers outside of Java have by and large not heard of Ant; they almost all use *make*. Most non-Java open source projects use *make*.

make is easier to start with. Ant's advantages make more sense on larger projects. Yet of the two, only *make* has been used on the really large projects. Telephone switch source code consists of hundreds of thousands of source files containing tens or hundreds of millions of lines of source code. *make* is used here. The use of Ant is growing steadily, particularly now that most of the widely used Java IDEs (JBuilder, Visual Age for Java, NetBeans Forte, and others), have interfaces to Ant. Most Java open source projects use Ant.

make is included with most Unix and Unix-like systems and shipped with many Windows IDEs. Ant is not included with any operating systems but is included with many open source Java packages.

make has remained mostly compatible over its 20-year history. The Ant developers are planning to break backward compatibility after only a couple of years (in Version 2.0, due out later in 2001), though there is another tool, Amber, that will provide compatibility with Ant in addition to adding new features.

To sum up, *make* and Ant are both good tools. Use whichever one you choose in your own projects, but be prepared to use both in code you receive.

1.8. Running Applets

Problem

You want to run an applet.

Solution

Write some HTML and point a browser at it.

Discussion

An *applet* is simply a Java class that extends `java.applet.Applet`, and in doing so inherits the functionality it needs to be viewable inside a web page in a Java-enabled web browser.* All that's necessary is an HTML page referring to the applet. This HTML page requires a minimum of three *attributes*, or modifiers: the applet itself, and the width and height it needs on-screen, in screen dots or pixels. This is not the place for me to teach you the syntax of HTML—there is some of that in Recipe 17.1—but I'll show my HTML applet template file. Many of the IDEs will write a page like this for you if you use their "build new applet" wizards.

```
<HTML>
<HEAD><TITLE>A Demonstration</TITLE></HEAD>
<BODY>
<H1>My TEMPLATE Applet</H1>
<APPLET CODE="CCC.class"  WIDTH="200" HEIGHT="200">
</APPLET>
</BODY>
</HTML>
```

You can probably intuit from this just about all you need to get started. For a little more detail, see Recipe 17.1. Once you've created this file (replacing the *CCC* with the actual name of your applet) and placed it in the same directory as the class file, you need only tell the browser to view the HTML page, and the applet should be included in it.

All right, so the applet appeared and it even almost worked. Make a change to the Java source and recompile. Click the browser's Reload button. Chances are you're still running the old version! Browsers aren't very good at debugging applets. You can sometimes get around this by holding down the Shift key while you click Reload. But to let you be sure, there is a program in the JDK known as `Appletviewer`, a kind of mini-browser. You need to give it the HTML file, just like a regular browser. Sun's AppletViewer (shown in Figure 1-12 under MS-Windows)

---

* Includes Netscape, MS Explorer, Sun's HotJava demonstration browser, and others.

has an explicit reload button that actually reloads the applet. And it has other features such as debugging hooks and other information displays. It also has a View-> Tag menu that lets you resize the window until the applet looks best, and then you can copy and paste the tag—including the adjusted WIDTH and HEIGHT tags— into a longer HTML document.

Figure 1-12. Sun JDK AppletViewer

The MacOS X runtime includes Apple's own implementation (shown in Figure 1-13), which is more colorful but slightly less featureful—I could not find the Reload item in its menu. It does, however, let you load a new HTML file by typing (or browsing), so you can get the same effect as Reload just by clicking on the Open button again.

Figure 1-13. Apple MacOS X applet launcher

Neither the Sun version nor the Apple version is a full applet runtime; features such as jumping to a new document do not work. But it is a good tool for debugging applets. Learn to use the AppletViewer that comes with your JDK or IDE.

See Also

The bad news about applets is that they either can't use features of newer Java versions or they run into the dreaded browser-incompatibility issue. In Recipe 23.5, I show using the Java Plug-in to get around this. In Recipe 23.11, I talk about Java Web Start, a relatively new technique for distributing applications over the Web in a way similar to how applets are downloaded.

1.9. Dealing with Deprecation Warnings

Problem

Your code used to compile cleanly, but now gives deprecation warnings.

Solution

You must have blinked :-). Either live with the warnings—live dangerously—or revise your code to eliminate the warnings.

Discussion

Each new release of Java includes a lot of powerful new functionality, but at a price: during the evolution of this new stuff, Java's maintainers find some old stuff that wasn't done right and shouldn't be used anymore because they can't really fix it. In building JDK 1.1, for example, they realized that the `java.util.Date` class had some serious limitations with regard to internationalization. Accordingly, many of the `Date` class methods and constructors are marked "deprecated." To *deprecate* something means, according to my *Concise Oxford Dictionary of Current English*, to "express wish against or disapproval of." Java's developers are therefore expressing a wish that you no longer do things the old way. Try compiling this code:

```
import java.util.Date;

/** Demonstrate deprecation warning */
public class Deprec {

    public static void main(String[] av) {

        // Create a Date object for May 5, 1986
        // EXPECT DEPRECATION WARNING
        Date d = new Date(86, 04, 05);// May 5, 1986
        System.out.println("Date is " + d);
    }
}
```

What happened? When I compile it on Java 2, I get this warning:

```
C:\javasrc>javac Deprec.java
Note: Deprec.java uses or overrides a deprecated API.  Recompile with
"-deprecation" for details.
1 warning
C:\javasrc>
```

So, we follow orders. Recompile with –deprecation for details:

```
C:\javasrc>javac -deprecation Deprec.java
Deprec.java:10: warning: constructor Date(int,int,int) in class java.util.Date has
been deprecated
            Date d = new Date(86, 04, 05);          // May 5, 1986
                     ^

1 warning

C:\javasrc>
```

The warning is simple: the Date constructor that takes three integer arguments has been deprecated. How do you fix it? The answer is, as in most questions of usage, to refer to the Javadoc documentation for the class. In Java 2, the introduction to the Date page says, in part:

> The class Date represents a specific instant in time, with millisecond precision.
>
> Prior to JDK 1.1, the class Date had two additional functions. It allowed the interpretation of dates as year, month, day, hour, minute, and second values. It also allowed the formatting and parsing of date strings. Unfortunately, the API for these functions was not amenable to internationalization. As of JDK 1.1, the Calendar class should be used to convert between dates and time fields and the DateFormat class should be used to format and parse date strings. The corresponding methods in Date are deprecated.

And more specifically, in the description of the three-integer constructor, it says:

> Date(int year, int month, int date)
>
> Deprecated. As of JDK version 1.1, replaced by Calendar.set(year + 1900, month, date) or GregorianCalendar(year + 1900, month, date).

As a general rule, when something has been deprecated, you should not use it in any new code and, when maintaining code, strive to eliminate the deprecation warnings. As we shall see in Recipe 2.1, there is already at least one example of a deprecation warning method that has altogether stopped working.

The main areas of deprecation warnings in the standard API are Date (as mentioned), the JDK 1.0 event handling, and some methods—a few of them important—in the Thread class.

You can also deprecate your own code. Just put a doc comment with the @deprecated tag immediately before the class or method you wish to deprecate. Using doc comments is described in Recipe 23.2.

1.10. *Conditional Debugging without #ifdef*

Problem

You want conditional compilation and Java doesn't seem to provide it.

Solution

Use constants or command-line arguments, depending upon the goal.

Discussion

Some older languages such as C, PL/I, and C++ provide a feature known as *conditional compilation*. Conditional compilation means that parts of the program can be included or excluded at compile time based upon some condition. One thing it's often used for is to include or exclude debugging print statements. When the program appears to be working, the developer is struck by a fit of hubris and removes all the error checking :-). A more common rationale is that the developer wants to make the finished program smaller—a worthy goal—or run faster by removing conditional statements.

Although Java lacks any explicit conditional compilation, there is a kind of conditional compilation implicit in the language. All Java compilers must do *flow analysis* to ensure that all paths to a local variable's usage pass through a statement that assigns it a value first, that all returns from a function pass out via someplace that provides a return value, and so on. Imagine what the compiler will do when it finds an `if` statement whose value is known to be false at compile time. Why should it even generate code for the condition? True, you say, but how can the results of an `if` statement be known at compile time? Simple: through `final boolean` variables. Further, if the value of the `if` condition is known to be false, then the body of the `if` statement should not be emitted by the compiler either. Presto—instant conditional compilation!

```
// IfDef.java
final boolean DEBUG = false;
System.out.println("Hello, World ");
if (DEBUG) {
        System.out.println("Life is a voyage, not a destination");
}
```

Compilation of this program and examination of the resulting class file reveals that the string "Hello" does appear, but the conditionally printed epigram does not. The entire `println` has been omitted from the class file. So Java does have its own conditional compilation mechanism.

```
darian$ jr IfDef
 jikes +E  IfDef.java
 java IfDef
Hello, World
darian$ strings IfDef.class | grep Life # not found!
darian$ javac IfDef.java # try another compiler
darian$ strings IfDef.class | grep Life # still not found!
darian$
```

What if we want to use debugging code similar to this, but have the condition applied at runtime? We can use `System.properties` (Recipe 2.2) to fetch a variable. Recipe 1.11 uses my `Debug` class as example of a class whose entire behavior is controlled this way.

But this is as good a place as any to interject about another feature, inline code generation. The C world has a language keyword `__inline`, which is a hint to the compiler that the function (method) is not needed outside the current source file. Therefore, when the C compiler is generating machine code, a call to the `__inline` function can be replaced by the actual method body, eliminating the overhead of pushing arguments onto a stack, passing control, retrieving parameters, and returning values. In Java, making a method final enables the compiler to know that it can be inlined, or emitted in line. This is an optional optimization that the compiler is not obliged to perform, but may for efficiency.

1.11. *Debugging Printouts*

Problem

You want to have debugging statements left in your code to be enabled at runtime.

Solution

Use my `Debug` class.

Discussion

Instead of using the conditional compilation mechanism of Recipe 1.10, you may want to leave your debugging statements in the code, but enable them only at runtime, when a problem surfaces. This is a good technique for all but the most compute-intensive applications because the overhead of a simple `if` statement is not all that great. Let's combine the flexibility of runtime checking with the simple `if` statement to debug a hypothetical `fetch()` method (part of `Fetch.java`):

```
String name = "poem";
if (System.getProperty("debug.fetch") != null) {
```

```
        System.err.println("Fetching " + name);
    }
    value = fetch(name);
```

Then, we can compile and run this normally and the debugging statement will be omitted. But if we run it with a –D argument to enable `debug.fetch`, the printout will occur:

```
> java Fetch              # See? No output
> java -Ddebug.fetch Fetch
Fetching poem
>
```

Of course this kind of `if` statement is tedious to write in large quantities, so I have encapsulated it into a `Debug` class, which is part of my `com.darwinsys.util` package. `Debug.java` appears in full at the end of this chapter, in Recipe 1.18. My `Debug` class also provides the string "debug". as part of the `System.getProperty()`, so we can simplify the previous `Fetch` example as follows (code in *FetchDebug.java*):

```
String name = "poem", value;
Fetch f = new Fetch();
Debug.println("fetch", "Fetching " + name);
value = f.fetch(name);
```

Running it behaves identically to the original `Fetch`:

```
> java FetchDebug        # again, no output
> java -Ddebug.fetch FetchDebug
Fetching poem
>
```

1.12. Using a Debugger

Problem

That debugging printout code is still not enough.

Solution

Use a debugger.

Discussion

The JDK includes a command-line-based debugger, *jdb*, and there are any number of IDEs that include their own debugging tools. If you've focused on one IDE, learn to use the debugger that it provides. If you're a command-line junkie like me, you may want to learn at least the basic operations of *jdb*.

Here is a buggy program. It has intentionally had bugs introduced so that you can see their effects in a debugger.

```
/** This program exhibits some bugs, so we can use a debugger */
public class Buggy {
    static String name;

    public static void main(String[] args) {
        int n = name.length();// bug # 1

        System.out.println(n);

        name += "; The end.";// bug #2
        System.out.println(name); // #3
    }
}
```

Here is a session using *jdb* to find these bugs:

```
ian> java Buggy
Exception in thread "main" java.lang.NullPointerException
        at Buggy.main(Compiled Code)
ian> jdb Buggy
Initializing jdb...
0xb2:class(Buggy)
> run
run Buggy
running ...
main[1]
Uncaught exception: java.lang.NullPointerException
        at Buggy.main(Buggy.java:6)
        at sun.tools.agent.MainThread.runMain(Native Method)
        at sun.tools.agent.MainThread.run(MainThread.java:49)

main[1] list
2          public class Buggy {
3                  static String name;
4
5                  public static void main(String[] args) {
6        =>                int n = name.length();  // bug # 1
7
8                          System.out.println(n);
9
10                         name += "; The end.";   // bug #2
main[1] print Buggy.name
Buggy.name = null
main[1] help
** command list **
threads [threadgroup]     -- list threads
thread <thread id>        -- set default thread
```

```
    suspend [thread id(s)]        -- suspend threads (default: all)
    resume [thread id(s)]         -- resume threads (default: all)
    where [thread id] | all    -- dump a thread's stack
    wherei [thread id] | all   -- dump a thread's stack, with pc info
    threadgroups                  -- list threadgroups
    threadgroup <name>            -- set current threadgroup

    print <id> [id(s)]            -- print object or field
    dump <id> [id(s)]             -- print all object information


    locals                        -- print all local variables in current stack frame


    classes                       -- list currently known classes
    methods <class id>            -- list a class's methods

    stop in <class id>.<method>[(argument_type,...)] -- set a breakpoint in a method
    stop at <class id>:<line>  -- set a breakpoint at a line
    up [n frames]                 -- move up a thread's stack
    down [n frames]               -- move down a thread's stack
    clear <class id>.<method>[(argument_type,...)]    -- clear a breakpoint in a method
    clear <class id>:<line>    -- clear a breakpoint at a line
    step                          -- execute current line
    step up                       -- execute until the current method returns to its
    caller
    stepi                         -- execute current instruction
    next                          -- step one line (step OVER calls)
    cont                          -- continue execution from breakpoint

    catch <class id>              -- break for the specified exception
    ignore <class id>             -- ignore when the specified exception

    list [line number|method]  -- print source code
    use [source file path]        -- display or change the source path

    memory                        -- report memory usage
    gc                            -- free unused objects

    load classname                -- load Java class to be debugged
    run <class> [args]            -- start execution of a loaded Java class
    !!                            -- repeat last command
    help (or ?)                   -- list commands
    exit (or quit)                -- exit debugger
    main[1] exit
    ian>
```

There are many other debuggers available; a look in the current Java magazines will inform you of them. Many of them will work remotely, since the Java debugging API (that which the debuggers use) is network-based.

1.13. Unit Testing: Avoid the Need for Debuggers

Problem

You don't want to have to debug your code.

Solution

Use unit testing to validate each class as you develop it.

Discussion

Stopping to use a debugger is time-consuming. Better to test beforehand. The methodology of *unit testing* has been around for a long time, but has been overshadowed by newer methodologies. Unit testing is a tried and true means of getting your code tested in small pieces. Typically, in an OO language like Java, unit testing is applied to individual classes, in contrast to "black box" testing where the entire application is tested.

I have long been an advocate of this very basic testing methodology. Indeed, developers of the software methodology known as Extreme Programming (XP for short; see *http://www.extremeprogramming.org*) advocate writing the unit tests *before* you write the code, and also advocate running your tests almost every time you compile. This group of extremists has some very well-known leaders, including Gamma and Beck of *Design Patterns* fame. While I am not yet ready to unconditionally endorse all aspects of Extreme Programming, I certainly go along with their advocacy of unit testing.

Indeed, many of my classes come with a "built-in" unit test. Classes that are not main programs in their own right often include a `main` method that just tests out the functionality of the class. Here is an example:

```
/** A simple class used to demonstrate unit testing. */
public class Person {
    protected String fullName;
    protected String firstName, lastName;

    /** Construct a Person using his/her first+last names. */
    public Person(String firstName, String lastName) {
        this.firstName = firstName;
        this.lastName = lastName;
    }

    /** Get the person's full name */
    public String getFullName() {
```

```
        if (fullName != null)
            return fullName;
        return firstName + " " + lastName;
    }

    /** Simple test program. */
    public static void main(String[] argv) {
        Person p = new Person("Ian", "Darwin");
        String f = p.getFullName();
        if (!f.equals("Ian Darwin"))
            throw new IllegalStateException("Name concatenation broken");
        System.out.println("Fullname " + f + " looks good");
    }

}
```

What surprised me is that, before encountering XP, I used to think I did this often, but an actual inspection of two projects indicated that only about a third of my classes had test cases, either inside or externally. Clearly what is needed is a uniform methodology. That is provided by JUnit.

JUnit is a Java-centric methodology for providing test cases. You can freely download JUnit from the obvious web site, *http://www.junit.org*. JUnit is a very simple but useful testing tool. It is easy to use; you just write a test class that has a series of methods whose names begin with `test`. JUnit uses introspection (see Chapter 25) to find all these methods, and runs them for you! There are extensions to JUnit for purposes as diverse as load testing and testing Enterprise JavaBeans (EJB); there are links to these on the JUnit web site.

How do you get started using JUnit? All that's necessary is to write a test. Here I have excerpted the test from my `Person` class and placed it into a class `PersonTest`. Note the obvious naming pattern.

```
    import junit.framework.*;

    /** A simple test case for Person */
    public class PersonTest extends TestCase {

        /** JUnit test classes require this constructor */
        public PersonTest(String name) {
            super(name);
        }

        public void testNameConcat() {
            Person p = new Person("Ian", "Darwin");
            String f = p.getFullName();
            assertEquals(f, "Ian Darwin");
        }

    }
```

To run it, I need only compile the test and invoke the test harness `junit`:

```
daroad.darwinsys.com$ jikes PersonTest.java
daroad.darwinsys.com$ java junit.textui.TestRunner PersonTest
.
Time: 0.188

OK (1 tests)

daroad.darwinsys.com$
```

The use of a full class name is a bit tedious, so I have a script named *jtest* that invokes this; I just say *jtest Person* and it runs the previous command for me.

```
#!/bin/sh

exec java junit.textui.TestRunner ${1}Test
```

See Also

If you prefer flashier GUI output, there are several JUnit variants (built using Swing and AWT; see Chapter 13) that will run the tests with a GUI.

JUnit offers classes for building comprehensive test suites and comes with considerable documentation of its own; download the program from the web site listed earlier.

Also, for testing graphical components, I have developed a simple component tester; it is described in Recipe 12.2.

Remember: Test early, test often!

1.14. Decompiling Java Class Files

Problem

You lost the source code.

Solution

If you still have the class files, decompile them.

Discussion

Have you ever looked at a class file by accident? Open it in a text editor, for example, and you might see this. You've never done this by accident, right? Sure, I believe you . . .

```
^H^@Z^C^@^@^@P^H^@[^H^@n^H^@o^H^@p^H^@q^H^@r^H^@s^H^@t^H^@v^H^@y^H
^@z^H^@{^H^@}^H^@Ç^H^@ä^H^@à^H^@á^H^@ª^H^@º^G^@ç^G^@Æ^G^@ô^G^@ö^G^@ò^G^@û^G^@ù^G
^@ÿ^G^@...^G^@Ü^G^@¢^G^@£^G^@¥
^@^V^@@
^@^\^@@
^@!^@A
^@^Y^@B
^@^[^@C
```

There's no resemblance to the Java source file that you wrote and spent so long fussing over the formatting of. What did it get you? Nothing here. The class file is a binary file that can't be inspected easily. However, it is in a well-documented format, and there's the rub. Once a format is known, files can be examined. One example of a Java program that examines other Java programs is *javap*, which gives you the external view of a class file. I'll show you in Recipe 25.2 just how this part of *javap* works and how you can write your own tools that process other Java classes. Meanwhile, this discussion is about decompilation. Let's suppose you have put some meat through a meat grinder. It's been converted to zillions of little bits. It might, in fact, look a bit like the class file seen here. Now suppose that unbeknownst to you, your paycheck fell into the meat and went through the grinder. Ugh! But the real question is, can you put the paycheck back together from the little pieces in the output? A related question is whether you can put a Java source file back together from the little pieces in the class file.

The task seems impossible. The file appears inscrutable. How can it be un-ground? But computer geeks like to work with files, and restoring structure to them is one part of that. When the infamous Internet Worm struck in 1988, it was only a matter of hours before security experts had taken the binary compiled program—most OSes' equivalent of a class file—and turned it back into source code without any tools other than debuggers, dumps, and manuals. So it is possible to take an object file and turn it back into some kind of source file. Now the ground-up paycheck, if you find the pieces and tape it back together, will still have bumps (not to mention the smell of salami or pastrami as appropriate). And a decompiled file will have one major bump: no comments! All the comments will be gone. But hopefully you can get back something that will take the place of your lost source file.

The first tool for reverse compilation of Java class files was called *Mocha*. Written by the late HanPeter van Vliet of the Netherlands, this tool showed a generation of early Java hackers that it was possible to decompile Java. Here is `HelloWorld` and its decompilation:

```
/**
 * Your basic, minimal, Hello World type program in Java.
 */

public class HelloWorld {
```

```
    public static void main(String[] argv) {
        System.out.println("Hello, World");

    }
}
```

The result of compiling it and then decompiling it is:

```
/* Decompiled by Mocha from HelloWorld.class */
/* Originally compiled from HelloWorld.java */

import java.io.PrintStream;

public class HelloWorld
{

    public static void main(String astring[])
    {
        System.out.println("Hello, World");
    }

    public HelloWorld()
    {
    }
}
```

Perhaps not as pretty, and with less of the abbreviation that is common practice in Java. The null constructor for HelloWorld actually does exist in the compiled class (as you can verify by running *javap* on it), so Mocha dutifully generates it.

Well, Mocha is OK, and the price is right—it's free. However, I did mention that it's no longer being maintained; it reportedly has problems with some of the class file constructs generated by current compilers. The O'Reilly web site for this book includes a link to Mocha.

A newer tool is *Jad,* written in C++. Jad is free but closed source (available in binary only); see *http://www.geocities.com/SiliconValley/Bridge/8617/jad.html.* There are also several commercial decompilers that keep abreast of the latest versions of Java; check one of the Java resource sites or magazines for the ones that are currently available.

1.15. Preventing Others from Decompiling Your Java Files

Problem

But I don't *want* people to be able to decompile my Java programs!

Solution

Obfuscate them.

Discussion

It has been said that for any weapon there is a defense, and for any defense there is a weapon. If the weapon is a decompiler, then the defense is something called an obfuscator. An obfuscator takes your program and tries to make it obscure, so that decompilation either will not work or will not be useful.

Because Mr. van Vliet, the late inventor of Mocha, did not release its source code, nobody else can take it over and maintain it, as we don't have the source. Or do we? Of course! That's it! We'll just run it through itself. Well, if you can download a copy, you can try it. But what you'll find is that it doesn't work. The entire program has been obfuscated. Yes, Mr. van Vliet also wrote the first Java obfuscator, partly in reaction to all the people who flamed him on the Net for releasing Mocha. Due to his untimely death, his obfuscator is no longer available.

There are, of course, commercial obfuscation programs that will do some degree of obfuscation. Some of them actually encrypt the file and use a custom class loader to decrypt it at runtime. I suppose if you wanted to keep people from learning how your program worked, which you well might for commercial or other reasons, you'd want to use one of these tools. Again, a Java resource web site or a current Java developer's magazine would be the place to go for the latest versions.

1.16. Getting Readable Tracebacks

Problem

You're getting an exception stack trace at runtime, but most of the important parts don't have line numbers.

Solution

Disable JIT and run it again. Or use the current HotSpot runtime.

Discussion

When a Java program throws an exception, the exception propagates up the call stack until there is a `catch` clause that matches it. If none is found, the Java interpreter program catches it and prints a stack traceback showing all the method calls that got from the top of the program to the place where the exception was thrown.

You can print this traceback yourself in any catch clause: the **Throwable** class has several methods called **printStackTrace()**.

The Just-In-Time (JIT) translation process consists of having the Java runtime convert part of your compiled class file into machine language, so that it can run at full execution speed. This is a necessary step for making Java programs run under interpretation and still be acceptably fast. However, until recently its one drawback was that it generally lost the line numbers. Hence, when your program died, you still got a stack traceback but it no longer showed the line numbers where the error occurred. So we have the tradeoff of making the program run faster, but harder to debug. The latest versions of Sun's Java runtime include the HotSpot Just-In-Time translator, which doesn't have this problem.

If you're still using an older (or non-Sun) JIT, there is a way around this. If the program is getting a stack traceback and you want to make it readable, you need only disable the JIT processing. How you do this depends upon what release of Java you are using. In the JDK 1.2 (Java 2), you need only set the environment variable JAVA_COMPILER to the value NONE, using the appropriate *set* command.

```
C:\> set JAVA_COMPILER=NONE # DOS, MS-Windows
setenv JAVA_COMPILER NONE     # UNIX Csh
export JAVA_COMPILER=NONE # UNIX Ksh, modern sh
```

To make this permanent, you would set it in the appropriate configuration file on your system; on Windows NT, you could also set this in the System Control Panel. You might well wish to make this setting the default, since using the JIT does take longer for startup, in return for faster execution. I ran JabaDex, my personal information manager application (see *http://www.darwinsys.com/jabadex/*) six times, thrice with JIT and thrice without; the results appear in Table 1-1.

Table 1-1. JIT and NOJIT timings

With JIT	**NOJIT**
46 seconds	34 seconds
37 seconds	28 seconds
34 seconds	29 seconds
Average: 39 seconds	Average: 30.3 seconds

As you can see, the average startup times are nearly 25% faster without JIT. Note that this includes reading a 500-line file and scanning it; that part of the code would definitely benefit from a JIT. Ideally we'd have selective control over JIT.

An easier way to disable JIT temporarily, and one that does not require changing the setting in your configuration files or Control Panel, is the −D command-line option, which updates the system properties. Just set `java.compiler` to NONE on the command line:

```
java -Djava.compiler=NONE  myapp
```

Note that the `-D` command-line option overrides the setting of the JAVA_COM-PILER environment variable.

On earlier releases, there was a command-line flag `-nojit`, but this was discontinued in favor of the more verbose `-D` option.

As mentioned, Sun's new HotSpot JIT—included in many JDK 1.2 and JDK 1.3 releases—generally provides tracebacks even with JIT mode enabled.

1.17. Finding More Java Source Code

Problem

You want even more Java code examples to look at.

Solution

Use The Source, Luke.

Discussion

Java source code is everywhere. As mentioned in the Preface, all the code examples from this book can be downloaded from the O'Reilly site (*http://java.oreilly.com*). What I didn't tell you, but what you might have realized by extension, is that the source examples from *all* the O'Reilly Java books are available there too: the *Java Examples in a Nutshell* book; the *Java Swing* book; all of them.

Another valuable resource is the source code for the Java API. You may not have realized it, but the source code for all the public parts of the Java API are included with each release of the Java Development Kit. Want to know how `java.util.ArrayList` actually works? You have the source code. Got a problem making a `JTable` behave? Sun's JDK includes the source for all the public classes! Look for a file called *src.zip* or *src.jar*; some versions unzip this and some do not.

If that's not enough, you can get the source for all of the JDK for free over the Internet just by committing to the Sun Java Community Source License and downloading a large file. This includes the source for the public and non-public parts of the API, as well as the compiler (written in Java) and a large body of code written in "native" code (C/C++): the runtime itself and the interfaces to the native library. For example, `java.io.Reader` has a method called `read()`, which reads bytes of data from a file or network connection. This is written in C because it actually calls the `read()` system call for Unix, MS-Windows, MacOS, Palm, BeOS, or whatever. The JDK source kit includes the source of all this stuff.

And ever since the early days of Java, there have been a number of web sites set up to distribute free-software or open source Java, just as with most other modern "evangelized" languages such as Perl, Python, Tk/Tcl, and others. (In fact, if you need native code to deal with some oddball filesystem mechanism in a portable way, beyond the material in Chapter 10 of this book, the source code for the above-mentioned languages' runtime systems might be a good place to look.)

I'd like to mention several web sites of lasting value:

- Gamelan has been around almost forever (in Java time). The URL *http://www.gamelan.com* still worked the last I checked, but the site has been (naturally) commercialized, and is now part of *http://www.developer.com*.

- The Giant Java Tree is more recent, and is limited to code that is covered by the GNU Public License. There is a great deal of source code stored there, all of which can be freely downloaded. See *http://www.gjt.org*.

- The CollabNet open source marketplace is not specific to Java, but offers a meeting place for people who want open source code written and those willing to fund its development. See *http://www.collab.net*.

- SourceForge, also not specific to Java, offers free public hosting of open-sourced projects. See *http://www.sourceforge.com*.

- Finally, the author of this book maintains a small Java site at *http://www.darwinsys.com/java/*, which may be of value. This is the prime spot to obtain the JabaDex program, a longer (6,000-line) application that demonstrates some of the principles and practices discussed in the book. There is also a listing of Java resources and material related to this book.

As with all free software, please be sure that you understand the ramifications of the various licensing schemes. Code covered by the GPL, for example, automatically transfers the GPL to any code that uses even a small part of it. And even once looking at Sun's Java implementation details (the licensed download mentioned previously) may prevent you from ever working on a "clean-room" reimplementation of Java, the free-software Kaffe, or any commercial implementation. Consult a lawyer. Your mileage may vary. Despite these caveats, the source code is an invaluable resource to the person who wants to learn more Java.

1.18. Program: Debug

Most of the chapters of this book will end with a "Program" recipe that illustrates some aspect of the material covered in the chapter. Example 1-2 is the source code for the Debug utility mentioned in Recipe 1.11.

Example 1-2. Debug.java

```java
package com.darwinsys.util;

/** Utilities for debugging
 */
public class Debug {
    /** Static method to see if a given category of debugging is enabled.
     * Enable by setting e.g., -Ddebug.fileio to debug file I/O operations.
     * Use like this:<BR>
     * if (Debug.isEnabled("fileio"))<BR>
     *   System.out.println("Starting to read file " + fileName);
     */
    public static boolean isEnabled(String category) {
        return System.getProperty("debug." + category) != null;
    }

    /** Static method to println a given message if the
     * given category is enabled for debugging.
     */
    public static void println(String category, String msg) {
        if (isEnabled(category))
            System.out.println(msg);
    }
    /** Same thing but for non-String objects (think of the other
     * form as an optimization of this).
     */
    public static void println(String category, Object stuff) {
        println(category, stuff.toString());
    }
}
```

2

Interacting with the Environment

2.0. Introduction

This chapter describes how your Java program can deal with its immediate surroundings, what we call the *runtime environment*. In one sense, everything you do in a Java program using almost any Java API involves the environment. Here we focus more narrowly on things that directly surround your program. Along the way we'll meet the System class, which knows a lot about our system.

Two other runtime classes deserve brief mention. The first, java.lang.Runtime, lies behind many of the methods in the System class. System.exit(), for example, just calls Runtime.exit(). This is technically part of "the environment," but the only time we use it directly is to run other programs, which is covered in Recipe 26.1. The java.awt.Toolkit object is also part of the environment and is discussed in Chapter 12.

2.1. Getting Environment Variables

Problem

You want to get at environment variables from within your Java program.

Solution

Don't.

Discussion

The seventh edition of Unix, released in 1979, had an exciting new feature known as *environment variables*. Environment variables are in all modern Unix systems and in most later command-line systems such as the DOS subsystem underlying MS-Windows, but are not in Macintosh computers, Palm Pilots, SmartCards, or other Java environments. Environment variables are commonly used for customizing an individual computer user's runtime environment, hence the name. To take one example that will be familiar to most readers, on Unix or DOS the environment variable PATH determines where the system will look for executable programs. So of course the issue comes up: "How do I get at environment variables from my Java program?"

The answer is that you can do this in some versions of Java, but you shouldn't. Java is designed to be a portable runtime environment. As such, you should not depend on operating system features that don't exist on every single Java platform. I just mentioned several Java platforms that don't have environment variables.

Oh, all right, if you insist. There is a `static` method called `getenv()` in class `java.lang.System`. Let's try it out. But remember, you made me do it. First, the code. All we need is this line in a main program:

```
System.out.println("System.getenv(\"PATH\") = " + System.getenv("PATH"));
```

Let's try compiling it:

```
C:\javasrc>javac GetEnv.java
Note: GetEnv.java uses or overrides a deprecated API. Recompile with -deprecation
for details.
```

That message is seldom welcome news. We'll do as it says:

```
C:\javasrc>javac -deprecation GetEnv.java
GetEnv.java:9: Note: The method java.lang.String getenv(java.lang.String) in class
java.lang.System has been deprecated.
System.out.println("System.getenv(\"PATH\") = " + System.getenv("PATH"));
                                                          ^
Note: GetEnv.java uses or overrides a deprecated API.  Please consult the
documentation for a better alternative.
1 warning
```

But it's only a warning, right? What the heck. Let's try running the program!

```
C:\javasrc>java  GetEnv
Exception in thread "main" java.lang.Error: getenv no longer supported, use
properties and -D instead: PATH
        at java.lang.System.getenv(System.java:602)
        at GetEnv.main(GetEnv.java:9)
```

Well, of all the non-backwards-compatible things! It used to work, in JDK 1.1, but it really and truly doesn't work anymore in Java 2. I guess we'll just have to do what the error message tells us, which is to learn about "properties and –D instead." In fact, that's our very next recipe.

2.2. System Properties

Problem

You need to get information from the system properties.

Solution

Use `System.getProperty()` or `System.getProperties()`.

Discussion

What is a property anyway? A property is just a name and value pair stored in a `java.util.Properties` object, which we'll discuss more fully in Recipe 7.7. So if I chose to, I could store the following properties in a `Properties` object called `ian`:

```
name=Ian Darwin
favorite_popsicle=cherry
favorite_rock group=Fleetwood Mac
favorite_programming_language=Java
pencil color=green
```

The `Properties` class has several forms of its retrieval method. You could, for example, say `ian.getProperty("pencil color")` and get back the string "green". You can also provide a default: say `ian.getProperty("pencil color", "black")`, and if the property has not been set you would get the default value "black".

For now, we're concerned with the `System` class and its role as keeper of the particular `Properties` object that controls and describes the Java runtime. The `System` class has a static `Properties` member whose content is the merger of operating system specifics (`os.name`, for example), system and user tailoring (`java.class.path`), and properties defined on the command line (as we'll see in a moment). Note that the use of periods in these names (like `os.arch`, `os.version` and `java.class.path`, `java.lang.version`) makes it look as though there is a hierarchical relationship similar to that for class names. The `Properties` class, however, imposes no such relationships: each key is just a string, and dots are not special.

To retrieve one system-provided property, use `System.getProperty()`. If you want them all, use `System.getProperties()`. Accordingly, if I wanted to find out if the `System Properties` had a property named "pencil color", I could say:

```
String color = System.getProperty("pencil color");
```

But what will that return? Surely Java isn't clever enough to know about everybody's favorite pencil color? Right you are! But we can easily tell Java about our pencil color (or anything else we want to tell it) using the –D argument.

The –D option argument is used to predefine a value in the system properties object. It must have a name, an equals sign, and a value, which are parsed the same way as in a properties file (see below). You can have more than one –D definition after your class name on the Java command. On Unix or MS-Windows command-line mode, use this:

```
java -D"pencil color=Deep Sea Green" SysPropDemo
```

Using MRJ or an IDE, put the variable's name and value in the appropriate dialog box when running the program. The `SysPropDemo` program is short; its essence is this one line:

```
System.getProperties().list(System.out);
```

When run this way, the program prints around 50 lines, looking something like:

```
java.library.path=/usr/local/linux-jdk1.2/jre/lib/i386/...
java.vm.specification.vendor=Sun Microsystems Inc.
sun.io.unicode.encoding=UnicodeLittle
pencil color=Deep Sea Green
file.encoding=ANSI_X3.4-1968
java.specification.vendor=Sun Microsystems Inc.
user.language=en
```

The program also has code to extract just one or a few properties, so you can say:

```
$ java SysPropDemo os.arch
os.arch = x86
```

See Also

The Javadoc page for `java.util.Properties` lists the exact rules used in the `load()` method, as well as other details.

Recipe 7.7 lists more details on using and naming your own `Properties` files.

2.3. Writing JDK Release–Dependent Code

Problem

You need to write code that depends on the JDK release.

Solution

Don't do this.

Discussion

Although Java is meant to be portable, there are some significant variations in Java runtimes. Sometimes you need to work around a feature that may be missing in older runtimes, but want to use it if it is present. So one of the first things you want to know is how to find out the JDK release corresponding to the Java runtime. This is easily obtained with System.getProperty():

```
System.out.println(System.getProperty("java.specification.version"));
```

Running this on Java 2 prints "1.2", as in JDK 1.2. Alas, not everyone is completely honest. Kaffe 1.5 certainly has some features of Java 2, but it is not yet a complete implementation of the Java 2 libraries. Yet it happily reports itself as "1.2" also. *Caveat hactor!*

Accordingly, you may want to test for the presence or absence of particular classes. One way to do this is with Class.forName("class"), which throws an exception if the class cannot be loaded—a good indication that it's not present in the runtime's library. Here is code for this, from an application wanting to find out whether the JDK 1.1 or later components are available:

```
/** Test for JDK >= 1.1 */
public class TestJDK11 {
    public static void main(String[] a) {
        // Check for JDK >= 1.1
        try {
            Class.forName("java.lang.reflect.Constructor");
        } catch (ClassNotFoundException e) {
            String failure =
                "Sorry, but this version of MyApp needs \n" +
                "a Java Runtime based on Java JDK 1.1 or later";
            System.err.println(failure);
            throw new IllegalArgumentException(failure);
        }
        System.out.println("Happy to report that this is JDK1.1");
        // rest of program would go here...
```

```
        return;
    }
}
```

To check if the runtime includes the Swing components with their final names,* you could use:

```
Class.forName("javax.swing.JButton");
```

It's important to distinguish between testing this at compile time and at runtime. In both cases, this code must be compiled on a system that includes the classes you are testing for—JDK 1.1 and Swing, respectively. These tests are only attempts to help the poor backwaters Java runtime user trying to run your up-to-date application. The goal is to provide this user with a message more meaningful than the simple "class not found" error that the runtime will give. It's also important to note that this test becomes unreachable if you write it inside any code that depends on the code you are testing for. The check for Swing won't ever see the light of day on a JDK 1.1 system if you write it in the constructor of a `JPanel` subclass (think about it). Put the test early in the main flow of your application, before any GUI objects are constructed. Otherwise the code will just sit there wasting space on Java 2 systems and never getting run on Java 1.1 systems.

As for what the class `Class` actually does, we'll defer that until Chapter 25.

2.4. Writing Operating System–Dependent Code

Problem

You need to write code that depends on the underlying operating system.

Solution

Again, don't do this. Or, if you must, use `System.properties`.

Discussion

While Java is designed to be portable, there are some things that aren't. These include such variables as the filename separator. Everybody on Unix knows that the filename separator is a slash character (/) and that a backwards slash or backslash (\) is an escape character. Back in the late 1970s, a group at Microsoft was actually

---

* Old-timers will remember that on the preliminary Swing releases, the name of this class was `com.sun.java.swing.JButton`.

working on Unix—their version was called Xenix, later taken over by SCO—and the people working on DOS saw and liked the Unix filesystem model. MS-DOS 2.0 didn't have directories, it just had "user numbers" like the system it was a clone of, Digital Research CP/M (itself a clone of various other systems). So the Microsoft folk set out to clone the Unix filesystem organization. Unfortunately, they had already committed the slash character for use as an option delimiter, for which Unix had used a dash (-). And the PATH separator (:) was also used as a "drive letter" delimiter, as in C: or A:. So we now have commands like this:

System	Directory list command	Meaning	Example PATH setting
Unix	*ls -R /*	Recursive listing of /, the top-level directory	*PATH=/bin:/usr/bin*
DOS	*dir/s *	Directory with subdirectories option (i.e., recursive) of \, the top-level directory (but only of the current drive)	*PATH=C:\windows; D:\mybins*

Where does this get us? If we are going to generate filenames in Java, we need to know whether to put a / or a \ or some other character; the Mac, for example, uses : between filenames and directories. Java has two solutions to this. First, when moving between Unix and Microsoft systems, at least, it is *permissive:* either / or \ can be used, and the code that deals with the operating system sorts it out. Second, and more generally, Java makes the platform-specific information available in a platform-independent way. First, for the file separator (and also the PATH separator), the `java.io.File` class (see Chapter 10) makes available some static variables containing this information. Since the `File` class is platform-dependent, it makes sense to anchor this information here. The variables are:

Name	Type	Meaning
separator	static String	The system-dependent filename separator character, e.g., / or \
separatorChar	static char	The system-dependent filename separator character, e.g., / or \
pathSeparator	static String	The system-dependent path separator character, represented as a string for convenience
pathSeparatorChar	static char	The system-dependent path separator character

Both filename and path separators are normally characters, but are also available in `String` form for convenience.

A second, more general, mechanism is the system `Properties` object mentioned in Recipe 2.2. You can use this to determine the operating system you are running on. Here is code that simply lists the system properties; it can be informative to run this on several different implementations:

```
import java.util.*;
/**
 * Demonstrate System Properties
 */
public class SysPropDemo {
    public static void main(String argv[]) {
        System.out.println("System Properties:");
        Properties p = System.getProperties();
        p.list(System.out);
    }
}
```

Some OSes, for example, provide a mechanism called "the null device" that can be used to discard output (typically used for timing purposes). Here is code that asks the system properties for the "os.name", and uses it to make up a name that can be used for discarding data. If no null device is known for the given platform, we return the name *junk*, which means that on such platforms, we'll occasionally create, well, junk files. I just remove these files when I stumble across them.

```
/** Some things that are System dependent.
 * All methods are static, like java.lang.Math.
 */
public class SysDep {
    /** Return the name of the Null device on platforms which support it,
     * or "jnk" otherwise.
     */
    public static String getDevNull() {
        String sys = System.getProperty("os.name");
        if (sys==null || sys.indexOf("Mac") >= 0)
            return "junk";
        if (sys.startsWith("Windows"))
            return "NUL:";
        return "/dev/null";
    }
}
```

2.5. *Using CLASSPATH Effectively*

Problem

You need to keep your class files in a common directory or you're wrestling with CLASSPATH.

Solution

Set CLASSPATH to the list of directories and/or JAR files that contain the classes you want.

Discussion

CLASSPATH is one of the more interesting aspects of using Java. You can store your class files in any of a number of directories, JAR files, or zip files. Just like the PATH your system uses for finding programs, the CLASSPATH is used by the Java runtime to find classes. Even when you type something as simple as *java Hello-World*, the Java interpreter looks in each of the places named in your CLASSPATH until it finds a match. Let's work through an example.

The CLASSPATH can be set as an environment variable on systems that support this (at least Unix and MS-Windows). You set it in the same syntax as your PATH environment variable. PATH is a list of directories to look in for programs; CLASS-PATH is a list of directories or JAR files to look in for classes.

Alternatively, you can set your CLASSPATH right on the command line:

```
java -classpath \c:\ian\classes MyProg
```

Suppose your CLASSPATH were set to *C:\classes;.* on MS-Windows, or *~/classes:.* on Unix (on the Mac, you can set the CLASSPATH with JBindery). Suppose you had just compiled a file named *HelloWorld.java* into *HelloWorld.class*, and went to run it. On Unix, if you run one of the kernel tracing tools (trace, strace, truss, ktrace) you would probably see the Java program open (or stat, or access) the following files:

- Some file(s) in the JDK directory;

- Then *~/classes/HelloWorld.class*, which it probably wouldn't find;

- And *./HelloWorld.class*, which it would find, open, and read into memory.

The "some file(s) in the JDK directory" is release-dependent. On JDK 1.2 it can be found in the system properties:

```
sun.boot.class.path = C:\JDK1.2\JRE\lib\rt.jar;C:\JDK1.2\JRE\lib\i18n.jar;C:\
JDK1.2\JRE\classes
```

The file *rt.jar* is the RunTime stuff; *i18n.jar* is the internationalization; and *classes* is an optional directory where you can install additional classes.

Suppose you had also installed the JAR file containing the supporting classes for programs from this book, *com-darwinsys-util.jar*. You might then set your CLASS-PATH to *C:\classes;C:\classes\com-darwinsys-util.jar;* on MS-Windows, or *~/classes:~/classes/com-darwinsys-util.jar:.* on Unix. Notice that you *do* need to list the JAR file explicitly. Unlike a single class file, placing a JAR file into a directory listed in your CLASSPATH does not suffice to make it available.

Note that certain specialized programs (such as a web server running servlets; see Chapter 18) may not use either bootpath or CLASSPATH as shown; they provide their own `ClassLoader` (see Recipe 25.4 for information on class loaders).

Another useful part of the JDK is *javap*, which by default prints the external face of a class file: its full name, its public methods and fields, and so on. If you ran a command like *javap HelloWorld* under kernel tracing, you would find that it opened, seeked around in, and read from a file *\jdk\lib\tools.jar*, and then got around to looking for your `HelloWorld` class, as previously. Yet there is no entry for this in your CLASSPATH setting. What's happening here is that the *javap* command sets its CLASSPATH internally to include the *tools.jar* file. If it can do this, why can't you? You can, but not as easily as you might expect. If you try the obvious first attempt at doing a `setProperty("java.class.path")` to itself plus the delimiter plus *jdk/lib/tools.jar*, you won't be able to find the JavaP class (`sun.tools.java.JavaP`); the CLASSPATH is set in the `java.class.path` at the beginning of execution, before your program starts. You can try it manually and see that it works if you set it beforehand:

```
C:\javasrc>java -classpath /jdk1.2/lib/tools.jar sun.tools.javap.JavaP
Usage: javap <options> <classes>...
```

If you need to do this in an application, you can either set it in a startup script, as we did here, or write C code to start Java, which is described in Recipe 26.5.

How can you easily store class files into a directory in your CLASSPATH? The *javac* command has a -d dir option, which specifies where the compiler output should go. For example, using -d to put the `HelloWorld` class file into my */classes* directory, I just say:

```
javac -d /classes HelloWorld.java
```

Then, as long as this directory remains in my CLASSPATH, I can access the class file regardless of my current directory. That's one of the key benefits of using CLASSPATH.

Managing CLASSPATH can be tricky, particularly when you alternate among several JVMs, as I do, or if you have multiple directories in which to look for JAR files. You may want to use some sort of batch file or shell script to control this. Here is part of the script that I use. It was written for the Korn shell on Unix, but similar scripts could be written in the C shell or as a DOS batch file.

```
# These guys must be present in my classpath...
export CLASSPATH=/home/ian/classes/com-darwinsys-util.jar:

# Now a for loop, testing for .jar/.zip or [ -d ... ]
```

```
OPT_JARS="$HOME/classes $HOME/classes/*.jar
    ${JAVAHOME}/jre/lib/ext/*.jar
    /usr/local/antlr-2.6.0"

for thing in $OPT_JARS
do
    if [ -f $thing ]; then        //must be either a file...
        CLASSPATH="$CLASSPATH:$thing"
    else if [ -d $thing ]; then          //or a directory
        CLASSPATH="$CLASSPATH:$thing"
    fi
done
CLASSPATH="$CLASSPATH:."
```

This builds a minimum CLASSPATH out of *com.darwinsys-util.jar*, then goes through a list of other files and directories to check that each is present on this system (I use this script on several machines on a network), and ends up adding a dot (.) to the end of the CLASSPATH.

2.6. *Using Extensions or Other Packaged APIs*

Problem

You have a JAR file of classes you want to use.

Solution

On JDK 1.2 or later, simply copy the JAR into *JDKHOME/jre/lib/ext/*.

Discussion

The Java API has grown by leaps and bounds since its first public release in 1995. It is now considered sufficiently functional for writing robust applications, but the areas to which it is being applied continue to grow. There are many specialized APIs that may require more resources than you have on a given Java platform. Many of the new APIs from Sun are in the form of *standard extensions* and have package names beginning in javax. to indicate that. Classes in packages named java. or javax. are treated as built-in classes by a web browser for purposes of applet security, for example. Each extension is distributed in the form of a JAR file (see Recipe 23.3).

If you have Java 1.1 or some clone, you will need to add each such JAR file to your CLASSPATH, as in Recipe 2.5.

In Java 2, as you accumulate these and other optional APIs contained in JAR files, you can simply drop these JAR files into the Java Extensions Mechanism directory, typically something like *\jdk1.2\jre\lib\ext.*, instead of listing each JAR file in your

CLASSPATH variable and watching CLASSPATH grow and grow and grow. Effective with Java 2, the runtime looks here for any and all JAR and zip files, so no special action is needed. In fact, unlike many other system changes, you do not even need to reboot your computer, since this directory is scanned each time the JVM starts up. You may, however, need to restart a long-running program such as an IDE for it to notice the change. Try it and see first.

2.7. Parsing Command-Line Arguments

Problem

You need to parse command-line options. Java doesn't provide an API for it.

Solution

Look in the `args` array passed as an argument to `main`. Or use my `GetOpt` class.

Discussion

The Unix folk have had to deal with this longer than anybody, and they came up with a C-library function called `getopt`.* `getopt` processes your command-line arguments and looks for single-character options set off with dashes and optional arguments. For example, the command:

```
sort -n -o outfile myfile1 yourfile2
```

runs the standard *sort* program. The -n tells it that the records are numeric rather than textual, and the -o outfile tells it to write its output into a file named *outfile*. The remaining words, *myfile1* and *yourfile2*, are treated as the input files to be sorted. On a Microsoft-based platform such as Windows 95, command arguments are set of with slashes (/). We will use the Unix form—a dash—in our API, but feel free to change the code to use slashes.

As in C, the `getopt()` method is used in a `while` loop. It returns once for each valid option found, returning the value of the character that was found or zero when all options (if any) have been processed.

Here is a program that uses my `GetOpt` class just to see if there is a -h (for help) argument on the command line:

```
import com.darwinsys.util.GetOpt;

/** Trivial demonstration of GetOpt. If -h present, print help.
 */
```

---

* There are several variations on `getopt` in the Unix world; my version emulates fairly closely the original AT&T standard one. The newer ones offer more frills such as long-name arguments, but the basic operation is pretty similar.

```java
public class GetOptSimple {
    public static void main(String[] args) {
        GetOpt go = new GetOpt("h");
        char c;
        while ((c = go.getopt(args)) != 0) {
            switch(c) {
            case 'h':
                helpAndExit(0);
                break;
            default:
                System.err.println("Unknown option in " +
                    args[go.getOptInd()-1]);
                helpAndExit(1);
            }
        }
        System.out.println();
    }

    /** Stub for providing help on usage
     * You can write a longer help than this, certainly.
     */
    static void helpAndExit(int returnValue) {
        System.err.println("This would tell you how to use this program");
        System.exit(returnValue);
    }
}
```

The following longer demo program has several options:

```java
import com.darwinsys.util.GetOpt;

/** Simple demonstration of GetOpt. Accept the '-n' and '-o outfile'
 * options as shown for sort, and also -h for help.
 */
public class GetOptDemo {
    public static void main(String[] args) {
        GetOpt go = new GetOpt("hno:");
        boolean numeric_option = false;
        String outFileName = "(standard output)";
        char c;
        while ((c = go.getopt(args)) != GetOpt.DONE) {
            switch(c) {
            case 'h':
                doHelp(0);
                break;
            case 'n':
                numeric_option = true;
                break;
            case 'o':
                outFileName = go.optarg();
```

```
                    break;
                default:
                    System.err.println("Unknown option character " + c);
                    doHelp(1);
                }
            }
            System.out.print("Options: ");
            System.out.print("Numeric: " + numeric_option + ' ');
            System.out.print("Output: " + outFileName + "; ");
            System.out.println("Inputs: ");
            if (go.getOptInd()-1 == args.length) {
                doFile("(standard input)");
            } else for (int i=go.getOptInd()-1; i<args.length; i++)
                doFile(args[i]);
        }

        /** Stub for providing help on usage
         * You can write a longer help than this, certainly.
         */
        static void doHelp(int returnValue) {
            System.err.println("Usage: GetOptDemo [-h][-n][-o outfile] file ...");
            System.exit(returnValue);
        }

        /** Stub to demonstrate processine one file. */
        static void doFile(String fileName) {
            System.out.println(fileName + ' ');
        }
    }
```

If we invoke it several times with different options, here's how it behaves:

```
C:\javasrc\environ>java GetOptDemo
Options: Numeric: false Output: (standard output) ; Input: (standard input)

C:\javasrc\environ>java GetOptDemo -h
Usage: GetOptDemo [-h][-n][-o outfile] file ...

C:\javasrc\environ>java GetOptDemo -n a b c
Options: Numeric: true Output: (standard output) ; Input: b c

C:\javasrc\environ>java GetOptDemo -n -o resultfile file1 file2
Options: Numeric: true Output: resultfile ; Input: file2
```

Here is a longer example using GetOpt:

```
public class GetOptTest {
    public static void main(String argv[]) {
        String goodArgChars = "o:h", goodArgs[]  = {
            "-h", "-o", "outfile", "infile"
        };
```

```
        String badArgChars = "f1o", badArgs[]  = {
            "-h", "-o", "outfile", "infile"
        };
        process(goodArgChars, goodArgs);
        process(badArgChars, goodArgs);
        process(badArgChars, badArgs);
    }


    /** Private function, for testing. */
    private static void process(String argChars, String[] args) {

        System.out.println("** START ** " + argChars + '(' + args.length + ')');

        GetOpt go = new GetOpt(argChars);

        char c;
        while ((c = go.getopt(args)) != 0) {
            System.out.print("Found " + c);
            if (go.optarg() != null)
                System.out.print("; Option " + go.optarg());
            System.out.println();
        }
        for (int i=go.optind(); i<args.length; i++)
            System.out.println("Filename-like arg " + args[i]);
    }
}
```

This program (which I used to test the GetOpt class while I was writing it) demonstrates several uses of getopt, some successful and some (by design) unsuccessful. It prints the successes and failures as it goes:

```
$ java GetOptTest
** START ** o:h(4)
Found h
Found o; Option outfile
** START ** f1o(4)
Bad option
Found o
Filename-like arg infile
At least one user error found
** START ** f1o(4)
Bad option
Found o
Filename-like arg infile
At least one user error found
$
```

GetOpt is an adequate tool for processing command-line options. You may come up with something better and contribute it to the Java world; this is left as an exercise for the reader.

3

Strings and Things

3.0. *Introduction*

Character strings are an inevitable part of just about any programming task. We use them for printing messages to the user, for referring to files on disk or other external media, and for people's names, addresses, and affiliations. The uses of strings are many, almost without number (actually, if you need numbers, we'll get to them in Chapter 5).

If you're coming from a programming language like C, you'll need to remember that `String` is a defined type (class) in Java. That is, a string is an object, and therefore has methods. It is not an array of characters and should not be thought of as an array. Operations like `fileName.endsWith(".gif")` and `extension.equals(".gif")` (and the equivalent `".gif".equals(extension)`) are commonplace.

Notice that a given `String` object, once constructed, is immutable. That is, once I have said `String s = "Hello" + yourName;` then the particular object that reference variable `s` refers to can never be changed. You can assign `s` to refer to a different string, even one derived from the original, as in `s = s.trim()`. And you can retrieve characters from the original string using `charAt()`, but it isn't called `getCharAt()` because there is not, and never will be, a `setCharAt()` method. Even methods like `toUpperCase()` don't change the `String`; they return a new `String` object containing the translated characters. If you need to change characters within a `String`, you should instead create a `StringBuffer` (possibly initialized to the starting value of the `String`), manipulate the `StringBuffer` to your heart's content, and then convert that to `String` at the end, using the ubiquitous `toString()` method.

How can I be so sure they won't add a `setCharAt()` method in the next release? Because the immutability of strings is one of the fundamentals of the Java Virtual Machine. Remember that Java is the one language that takes multiprocessing (threads) seriously. And takes security seriously. Got that in mind? Good. Now think about applets, which are prevented from accessing many local resources. Consider the following scenario: Thread A starts up another Thread B. Thread A creates a string called s containing a filename, saves a reference s2 to it, and passes s to some method that requires permission. This method will certainly call the Java Virtual Machine's `SecurityManager`[*] object, if one is installed (as it certainly will be in an applet environment). Then, in the nanoseconds between the time the `SecurityManager` passes its approval on the named file and the time the I/O system actually gets around to opening the file, Thread B changes the string referred to by s2, to refer to a system file. Poof! If you could do this, the entire notion of Java security would be a joke. But of course, they thought of that, so you can't. While you can, at any time, assign a new `String` reference to s, this never has any effect on the string that s used to refer to. Except, of course, if s were the only reference to that `String`, it is now eligible for garbage collection—it may go up the pipe!

Remember also that the `String` is a very fundamental type in Java. Unlike most of the other classes in the core API, the behavior of strings is not changeable; the class is marked `final` so it cannot be subclassed. So you can't declare your own `String` subclass. Think if you could—you could masquerade as a `String`, but provide a `setCharAt()` method! Again, they thought of that. If you don't believe me, try it out:

```
/**
 * If this class could be compiled, Java security would be a myth.
 */
public class WolfInStringsClothing extends java.lang.String {
    public void setCharAt(int index, char newChar) {
        // The implementation of this method
        // is left as an exercise for the reader.
        // Hint: compile this code exactly as-is before bothering!
    }
}
```

Got it? They thought of that!

Of course you do need to be able to modify strings. There are methods that extract part of a `String`; these are covered in the first few recipes in this chapter. And there is `StringBuffer`, an important class that deals in characters and strings

---

[*] `SecurityManager` is a class that is consulted on whether the current application is allowed to do certain things, such as open local disk files, open arbitrary network connections, etc. Applets run with a more restrictive security manager than do normal applications, for example.

and has many methods for changing the contents, including, of course, a
`toString()` method. Reformed C programmers should note that Java strings are
not arrays of chars as in C, so you must use methods for such operations as processing a string one character at a time; see Recipe 3.4. Figure 3-1 shows an overview of `String`, `StringBuffer`, and C-language strings.

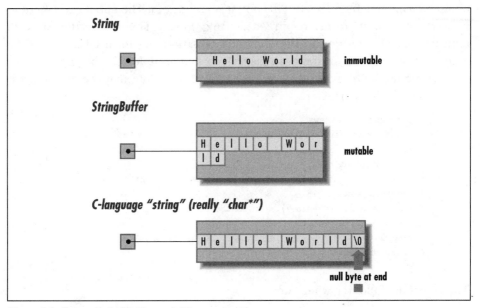

Figure 3-1. String, StringBuffer, and C-language strings

While we haven't discussed the details of the `java.io` package yet (we will, in
Chapter 9), you need to be able to read text files for some of these programs. Even
if you're not familiar with `java.io`, you can probably see from the examples that
read text files that a `BufferedReader` allows you to read "chunks" of data, and
that this class has a very convenient `readLine()` method.

We won't show you how to sort an array of strings here; the more general notion
of sorting a collection of objects is discussed in Recipe 7.8.

3.1. Taking Strings Apart with Substrings

Problem

You want to break a string apart into substrings by position.

Solution

Use the `String` object's `substring()` method.

Discussion

The substring() method constructs a new String object made up from a run of characters contained somewhere in the original string, the one whose substring() you called. The name of this method, substring(), violates the stylistic dictum that words should be capitalized; if Java were 100.0% consistent, this would be named subString. But it's not; it's substring. The substring method is overloaded: both forms require a starting index. The one-argument form returns from startIndex to the end. The two-argument form takes an ending index (not a length, as in some languages), so that an index can be generated by the String methods indexOf() or lastIndexOf(). Note that the end index is one beyond the last character!

```
// File SubStringDemo.java
public static void main(String[] av) {
    String a = "Java is great.";
    System.out.println(a);
    String b = a.substring(5);// b is the String "is great."
    System.out.println(b);
    String c = a.substring(5,7);// c is the String "is"
    System.out.println(c);
    String d = a.substring(5,a.length());// d is "is great."
    System.out.println(d);
}
```

This prints the following when run:

```
> java SubStringDemo
Java is great.
is great.
is
is great.
>
```

3.2. Taking Strings Apart with StringTokenizer

Problem

You need to take a string apart into words or tokens.

Solution

Construct a StringTokenizer around your string and call its methods hasMoreTokens() and nextToken(). These implement the Iterator design pattern (see Recipe 7.4). In addition, StringTokenizer implements the

Enumeration interface (also in Recipe 7.4), but if you use the methods thereof you will need to cast the results to String:

```
// StrTokDemo.java
StringTokenizer st = new StringTokenizer("Hello World of Java");

while (st.hasMoreTokens())
    System.out.println("Token: " + st.nextToken());
```

The StringTokenizer normally breaks the String into tokens at what we would think of as "word boundaries" in European languages. Sometimes you want to break at some other character. No problem. When you construct your StringTokenizer, in addition to passing in the string to be tokenized, pass in a second string that lists the "break characters." For example:

```
// StrTokDemo2.java
StringTokenizer st = new StringTokenizer("Hello, World|of|Java", ", |");

while (st.hasMoreElements())
    System.out.println("Token: " + st.nextElement());
```

But wait, there's more! What if you are reading lines like:

```
FirstName|Lastname|Company|PhoneNumber
```

and your dear old Aunt Begonia hasn't been employed for the last 38 years? Her "Company" field will in all probability be blank.* If you look very closely at the previous code example, you'll see that it has two delimiters together (the comma and the space), but if you run it there are no "extra" tokens. That is, the StringTokenizer normally discards adjacent consecutive delimiters. For cases like the phone list, where you need to preserve null fields, there is good news and bad news. The good news is you can do it; you simply add a second argument of true when constructing the StringTokenizer, meaning that you wish to see the delimiters as tokens. The bad news is that you now get to see the delimiters as tokens, so you have to do the arithmetic yourself. Want to see it? Run this program:

```
// StrTokDemo3.java
StringTokenizer st =
    new StringTokenizer("Hello, World|of|Java", ", |", true);

while (st.hasMoreElements())
    System.out.println("Token: " + st.nextElement());
```

and you get this output:

```
C:\javasrc>java  StrTokDemo3
Token: Hello
Token: ,
```

---

* Unless, perhaps, you're as slow at updating personal records as I am.

```
Token:
Token: World
Token: |
Token: of
Token: |
Token: Java
```

This isn't how you'd like `StringTokenizer` to behave, ideally, but it is serviceable enough most of the time. Example 3-1 processes and ignores consecutive tokens, returning the results as an array of strings.

Example 3-1. StrTokDemo4.java (StringTokenizer)

```java
import java.util.*;

/** Show using a StringTokenizer including getting the delimiters back */
public class StrTokDemo4 {
    public final static int MAXFIELDS = 5;
    public final static String DELIM = "|";

    /** Processes one String, returns it as an array of fields */
    public static String[] process(String line) {
        String[] results = new String[MAXFIELDS];

        // Unless you ask StringTokenizer to give you the tokens,
        // it silently discards multiple null tokens.
        StringTokenizer st = new StringTokenizer(line, DELIM  true);

        int i = 0;
        // stuff each token into the current user
        while (st.hasMoreTokens()) {
            String s = st.nextToken();
            if (s.equals(DELIM)) {
                if (i++>=MAXFIELDS)
                    // This is messy: See StrTokDemo4b which uses
                    // a Vector to allow any number of fields.
                    throw new IllegalArgumentException("Input line " +
                        line + " has too many fields");
                continue;
            }
            results[i] = s;
        }
        return results;
    }

    public static void printResults(String input, String[] outputs) {
        System.out.println("Input: " + input);
        for (int i=0; i<outputs.length; i++)
            System.out.println("Output " + i + " was: " + outputs[i]);
    }
```

Example 3-1. StrTokDemo4.java (StringTokenizer) (continued)

```
public static void main(String[] a) {
    printResults("A|B|C|D", process("A|B|C|D"));
    printResults("A||C|D", process("A||C|D"));
    printResults("A|||D|E", process("A|||D|E"));
}
}
```

When you run this, you will see that A is always in Field 1, B (if present) in Field 2, and so on. In other words, the null fields are being handled properly.

```
Input: A|B|C|D
Output 0 was: A
Output 1 was: B
Output 2 was: C
Output 3 was: D
Output 4 was: null
Input: A||C|D
Output 0 was: A
Output 1 was: null
Output 2 was: C
Output 3 was: D
Output 4 was: null
Input: A|||D|E
Output 0 was: A
Output 1 was: null
Output 2 was: null
Output 3 was: D
Output 4 was: E
```

3.3. *Putting Strings Together with + and StringBuffer*

Problem

You need to put some `String` pieces back together.

Solution

Use string concatenation: the + operator. The compiler will construct a `StringBuffer` for you and use its `append()` methods. Or better yet, construct it yourself. Conveniently, the `append()` method returns a reference to the `StringBuffer` itself, so that statements like the `.append(...).append(...)` are fairly common. You might even see this third way in a `toString()` method. Example 3-2 shows the three ways of concatenating strings.

Example 3-2. StringBufferDemo.java

```java
/**
 * StringBufferDemo: construct the same String three different ways.
 */
public class StringBufferDemo {
    public static void main(String[] argv) {
        String s1 = "Hello" + ", " + "World";
        System.out.println(s1);

        // Build a StringBuffer, and append some things to it.
        StringBuffer sb2 = new StringBuffer();
        sb2.append("Hello");
        sb2.append(',');
        sb2.append(' ');
        sb2.append("World");

        // Get the StringBuffer's value as a String, and print it.
        String s2 = sb2.toString();
        System.out.println(s2);

        // Now do the above all over again, but in a more
        // concise (and typical "real-world" Java) fashion.

        StringBuffer sb3 = new StringBuffer().append("Hello").
            append(',').append(' ').append("World");
        System.out.println(sb3.toString());

        // Exercise for the reader: do it all again but without
        // creating ANY temporary variables.
    }
}
```

In fact, all the methods that modify more than one character of a `StringBuffer`'s contents—(append(), delete(), deleteCharAt(), insert(), replace(), and reverse())— return a reference to the `StringBuffer` to facilitate this style of coding.

3.4. Processing a String One Character at a Time

Problem

You want to process the contents of a string one character at a time.

Solution

Use a for loop and the String's charAt() method.

Discussion

A string's charAt() method retrieves a given character by index number (starting at zero) from within the String object. To process all the characters in a String, one after another, use a for loop ranging from zero to String.length()-1. Here we process all the characters in a String:

```
// StrCharAt.java
String a = "A quick bronze fox leapt a lazy bovine";
for (int i=0; i < a.length(); i++)
    System.out.println("Char " + i + " is " + a.charAt(i));
```

A *checksum* is a numeric quantity representing and confirming the contents of a file. If you transmit the checksum of a file separately from the contents, a recipient can checksum the file—assuming the algorithm is known—and verify that the file was received intact. Example 3-3 shows the simplest possible checksum, computed just by adding the numeric value of each character together. It should produce the value "1248" if the input is "an apple a day". Note that on files, it will not include the values of the newline characters; to fix this, retrieve System.getProperty("line.separator"); and add its character value(s) into the sum at the end of each line. Or, give up on line mode and read the file a character at a time.

Example 3-3. CheckSum.java

```
/** CheckSum one file, given an open BufferedReader. */
public int process(BufferedReader is) {
    int sum = 0;
    try {
        String inputLine;

        while ((inputLine = is.readLine()) != null) {
            int i;
            for (i=0; i<inputLine.length(); i++) {
                sum += inputLine.charAt(i);
            }
        }
        is.close();
    } catch (IOException e) {
        System.out.println("IOException: " + e);
    } finally {
        return sum;
    }
}
```

3.5. Aligning Strings

Problem

You want to align strings left, right, or centered.

Solution

Do the math yourself, and use substring (Recipe 3.1) and a StringBuffer (Recipe 3.3). Or, just use my StringAlign class, which is based on the java.text.Format class.

Discussion

Centering, or left- or right-aligning text, comes up surprisingly often. Suppose you want to print a simple report with centered page numbers. There doesn't seem to be anything in the standard API that will do the job fully for you. But I have written a class called StringAlign that will. Here's how you might use it:

```
/* Align a page number on a 70-character line. */
public class StringAlignSimple {

    public static void main(String[] args) {
        // Construct a "formatter" to center strings.
        StringAlign formatter = new StringAlign(70, StringAlign.JUST_CENTER);
        // Try it out, for page "i"
        System.out.println(formatter.format("- i -"));
        // Try it out, for page 4. Since this formatter is
        // optimized for Strings, not specifically for page numbers,
        // we have to convert the number to a String
        System.out.println(formatter.format(Integer.toString(4)));
    }
}
```

If we compile and run this class, it prints the two demonstration line numbers centered, as shown:

```
> jikes +E -d . StringAlignSimple.java
> java StringAlignSimple
                                - i -
                                  4
>
```

Here is the code for the StringAlign class. Note that this class extends a class called Format. In the package java.text there is a series of Format classes; they all have at least one method called format(). It is thus in a family with numerous other formatters such as DateFormat, NumberFormat, and others that we'll meet in upcoming chapters.

```java
import java.text.*;

/** Bare-minimum String formatter (string aligner). */
public class StringAlign extends Format {
    /* Constant for left justification. */
    public static final int JUST_LEFT = 'l';
    /* Constant for centering. */
    public static final int JUST_CENTRE = 'c';
    /* Centering Constant, for those who spell "centre" the American way. */
    public static final int JUST_CENTER = JUST_CENTRE;
    /** Constant for right-justified Strings. */
    public static final int JUST_RIGHT = 'r';

    /** Current justification */
    private int just;
    /** Current max length */
    private int maxChars;

    public StringAlign(int maxChars, int just) {
        switch(just) {
        case JUST_LEFT:
        case JUST_CENTRE:
        case JUST_RIGHT:
            this.just = just;
            break;
        default:
            throw new IllegalArgumentException("invalid justification arg.");
        }
        if (maxChars < 0) {
            throw new IllegalArgumentException("maxChars must be positive.");
        }
        this.maxChars = maxChars;
    }

    /** Format a String */
    public StringBuffer format(
        Object obj, StringBuffer where, FieldPosition ignore)  {

        String s = (String)obj;
        String wanted = s.substring(0, Math.min(s.length(), maxChars));

        // If no space left for justification, return maxChars' worth */
        if (wanted.length() > maxChars) {
            where.append(wanted);
        }
        // Else get the spaces in the right place.
        else switch (just) {
            case JUST_RIGHT:
                pad(where, maxChars - wanted.length());
```

```
                   where.append(wanted);
                   break;
              case JUST_CENTRE:
                   int startPos = where.length();
                   pad(where, (maxChars - wanted.length())/2);
                   where.append(wanted);
                   pad(where, (maxChars - wanted.length())/2);
                   // Adjust for "rounding error"
                   pad(where, maxChars - (where.length() - startPos));
                   break;
              case JUST_LEFT:
                   where.append(wanted);
                   pad(where, maxChars - wanted.length());
                   break;
              }
         return where;
     }


     protected final void pad(StringBuffer to, int howMany) {
         for (int i=0; i<howMany; i++)
             to.append(' ');
     }


     /** Convenience Routine */
     String format(String s) {
         return format(s, new StringBuffer(), null).toString();
     }


     /** ParseObject is required, but not useful here. */
     public Object parseObject (String source, ParsePosition pos)  {
         return source;
     }


}
```

See Also

The alignment of numeric columns is considered in Chapter 5.

3.6. Converting Between Unicode Characters and Strings

Problem

You want to convert between Unicode characters and Strings.

Solution

Since both Java chars and Unicode characters are 16 bits in width, a char can hold any Unicode character. The charAt() method of String returns a Unicode character. The StringBuffer append() method has a form that accepts a char. Since char is an integer type, you can even do arithmetic on chars, though this is not necessary as frequently as in, say, C. Nor is it often recommended, since the Character class provides the methods for which these operations were normally used in languages such as C. Here is a program that uses arithmetic on chars to control a loop, and also appends the characters into a StringBuffer (see Recipe 3.3):

```
/**
 * Conversion between Unicode characters and bytes
 */
public class UnicodeChars {
    public static void main(String[] argv) {
        StringBuffer b = new StringBuffer();
        for (char c = 'a'; c<'d'; c++) {
            b.append(c);
        }
        b.append('\u00a5');// Japanese Yen symbol
        b.append('\u01FC');// Roman AE with acute accent
        b.append('\u0391');// GREEK Capital Alpha
        b.append('\u03A9');// GREEK Capital Omega

        for (int i=0; i<b.length(); i++) {
            System.out.println("Character #" + i + " is " + b.charAt(i));
        }
        System.out.println("Accumulated characters are " + b);
    }
}
```

When you run it, the expected results are printed for the ASCII characters. On my Unix system, the default fonts don't include all the additional characters, so they are either omitted or mapped to irregular characters. We will see in Recipe 12.3 how to draw text in other fonts.

```
C:\javasrc\strings>java  UnicodeChars
Character #0 is a
Character #1 is b
Character #2 is c
Character #3 is %
Character #4 is |
Character #5 is
Character #6 is )
Accumulated characters are abc%|)
```

My Windows system doesn't have most of those characters either, but it at least prints the ones it knows are lacking as question marks (Windows system fonts are more homogenous than those of the various Unix systems, so it is easier to know what won't work). On the other hand, it tries to print the Yen sign as a Spanish capital Enye (N with a ~ over it). Amusingly, if I capture the console log under MS-Windows into a file and display it under Unix, the Yen symbol now appears:

```
Character #0 is a
Character #1 is b
Character #2 is c
Character #3 is ¥
Character #4 is ?
Character #5 is ?
Character #6 is ?
Accumulated characters are abc¥???
```

See Also

The Unicode program in this book's online source displays any 256-character section of the Unicode character set. Documentation listing every character in the Unicode character set can be downloaded along with supporting documentation from the Unicode Consortium at *http://www.unicode.org*.

3.7. Reversing a String by Word or Character

Problem

You wish to reverse a string, a character or word at a time.

Solution

You can reverse a string by character easily, using a StringBuffer. There are several ways to reverse a string a word at a time. One natural way is to use a StringTokenizer and a *stack*. Stack is a class (defined in java.util; see Recipe 7.15) that implements an easy-to-use last-in, first-out (LIFO) stack of objects.

Discussion

To reverse the characters in a string, use the StringBuffer reverse() method.

```
// StringRevChar.java
String sh = "FCGDAEB";
System.out.println(sh + " -> " + new StringBuffer(sh).reverse());
```

The letters in this example list the order of the sharps in the key signatures of Western music; in reverse, it lists the order of flats. Alternately, of course, you could reverse the characters yourself, using character-at-a-time mode (see Recipe 3.4).

A popular *mnemonic* or memory aid for the order of sharps and flats consists of one word for each sharp instead of just one letter, so we need to reverse this one word at a time. Example 3-4 adds each one to a `Stack` (see Recipe 7.15), then process the whole lot in LIFO order, which reverses the order.

Example 3-4. StringReverse.java

```
String s = "Father Charles Goes Down And Ends Battle";

// Put it in the stack frontwards
Stack myStack = new Stack();
StringTokenizer st = new StringTokenizer(s);
while (st.hasMoreTokens()) myStack.push(st.nextElement());

// Print the stack backwards
System.out.print('"' + s + '"' + " backwards by word is:\n\t\"");
while (!myStack.empty()) {
    System.out.print(myStack.pop());
    System.out.print(' ');
}
System.out.println('"');
```

3.8. Expanding and Compressing Tabs

Problem

You need to convert space characters to tab characters in a file, or vice versa. You might want to replace spaces with tabs to save space on disk, or go the other way to deal with a device or program that can't handle tabs.

Solution

Use my `Tabs` class or its subclass `EnTab`.

Discussion

Example 3-5 is a listing of `EnTab`, complete with a sample main program. The program works a character at a time; if the character is a space, we see if we can coalesce it with previous spaces to output a single tab character. This program depends on the `Tabs` class, which we'll come to shortly. The `Tabs` class is used to

decide which column positions represent tab stops and which do not. The code
also has several Debug printouts. (Debug was introduced in Recipe 1.11.)

Example 3-5. Entab.java

```java
import com.darwinsys.util.Debug;
import java.io.*;

/** entab- replace blanks by tabs and blanks.
 * Transmuted from K&R Software Tools book into C.
 * Transmuted again, years later, into Java.
 */
public class EnTab {

    /** Main program: just create an EnTab program, and pass
     * the standard input or the named file(s) through it.
     */
    public static void main(String[] argv) throws IOException {
        EnTab et = new EnTab(8);
        if (argv.length == 0)// do standard input
            et.entab(new BufferedReader(
                new InputStreamReader(System.in)));
        else for (int i=0; i<argv.length; i++) {// do each file
            et.entab(new BufferedReader(new FileReader(argv[i])));
        }
    }


    /** The Tabs (tab logic handler) */
    protected Tabs tabHandler;
    /** A symbolic constant for end-of-file */
    public static int EOF = -1;

    /** Constructor: just save the tab values.
     * @arguments n The number of spaces each tab is to replace.
     */
    public EnTab(int n) {
        tabHandler = new Tabs(n);
    }


    /** putchar - convenience routine for printing one character */
    protected void putchar(int ch) {
        System.out.print((char)ch);
    }


    /** entab: process one entire file, replacing blanks with tabs.
     * @argument is A BufferedReader opened to the file to be read.
     */
    public void entab(BufferedReader is) throws IOException {
        String line;
```

Example 3-5. Entab.java (continued)

```
        int c, col = 0, newcol;

    // main loop: process entire file one char at a time.
    do {
        newcol = col;
        // If we get a space, increment column count; if this
        // takes us to a tab stop, output a tab character.
        while ((c = is.read()) == ' ') {
            Debug.println("space", "Got space at " + col);
            newcol++;
            if (tabHandler.tabpos(newcol)) {
                Debug.println("tab", "Got a Tab Stop " + newcol);
                putchar('\t');
                col = newcol;
            }
        }
        // If we're just past a tab stop, we need to put the
        // "leftover" spaces back out, since we just consumed
        // them in the "while c ... == ' ')" loop above.
        while (col < newcol) {
            Debug.println("pad", "Padding space at " + col);
            putchar(' ');
            col++;
        }
        Debug.println("out", "End of loop, c is " + c);

        // Now either we're at the end of the input file,
        // or we have a plain character to output.
        // If the "plain" char happens to be \r or \n, then
        // output it, but also set col back to 1.
        // This code for \r and \n should satisfy Unix, Mac and MS.
        if (c != EOF) {
            putchar(c);
            col = (c == '\n' || c == '\r' ? 1 : col + 1);
        }
    } while (c != EOF);
    System.out.flush();// output everything for this file.
    }
}
```

As the comments state, this code was patterned after a program in Kernighan and Plauger's classic work *Software Tools*. While their version was in a language called *RatFor* (Rational Fortran), my version has been through several translations since then, though I've tried to preserve the overall structure. This is not the most "natural" way of writing the code in Java, which would be the line-at-a-time mode. I've left this C-language relic to provide some hints on translating a working C program written in this character-at-a-time style into Java. This version tries to work correctly on Windows, Unix, or the Macintosh, since it resets the column count whenever it finds either a return (\r) or a newline (\n); see Recipe 2.4. Java is platform independent, but it's possible to write platform-dependent code—I would have done so were it not for the code that handles both. The code still may not work on some odd platforms that don't use either of the two line-ending characters.

The Detab program in Example 3-6 doesn't have this problem, as it reads a line at a time.

Example 3-6. Detab.java

```
public void detab(BufferedReader is) throws IOException {
    String line;
    char c;
    int col;
    while ((line = is.readLine()) != null) {
        col = 0;
        for (int i=0; i<line.length(); i++) {
            // Either ordinary character or tab.
            if ((c=line.charAt(i)) != '\t') {
                System.out.print(c); // Ordinary
                ++col;
                continue;
            }
            do { // Tab, expand it, must put >=1 space
                System.out.print(' ');
            } while (!tabpos(++col));
        }
        System.out.println();
    }
}
```

The Tabs class provides two methods, settabpos() and istabstop(). Example 3-7 is the source for the Tabs class.

Example 3-7. Tabs.java

```
import com.darwinsys.util.Debug;

/** Basic tab-character handling stuff.
 * <p>
 * N.B. Can only handle equally-spaced tab stops as written.
 */
public class Tabs {
    /** tabs every so often */
    public final static int DEFTABSPACE =    8;
    /** the current tab stop setting. */
    protected int tabSpace = DEFTABSPACE;
```

Example 3-7. Tabs.java (continued)

```
/** The longest line that we worry about tabs for. */
public final static int MAXLINE = 250;
/** the current tab stops */
protected boolean[] tabstops;

/** Construct a Tabs object with a given tab stop settings */
public Tabs(int n) {
    tabstops = new boolean[MAXLINE];
    tabSpace = n;
    settabs();
}

/** Construct a Tabs object with a default tab stop settings */
public Tabs() {
    tabstops = new boolean[MAXLINE];
    settabs();
}

/** settabs - set initial tab stops */
public void settabs() {
    int i;
    for (i = 0; i < tabstops.length; i++) {
        tabstops[i] = 0 == (i % tabSpace);
        Debug.println("settabs", "Tabs[" + i + "]=" + tabstops[i]);
    }
}

/** tabpos - returns true if given column is a tab stop.
 * If current input line is too long, we just put tabs whereever,
 * no exception is thrown.
 * @argument col - the current column number
 */
boolean tabpos(int col) {
    if (col > tabstops.length-1)
        return true;
    else
        return tabstops[col];
}
}
```

3.9. Controlling Case

Problem

You need to convert strings to uppercase or lowercase, or to compare strings without regard for case.

Solution

The `String` class has a number of methods for dealing with documents in a particular case. `toUpperCase()` and `toLowerCase()` each return a new string that is a copy of the current string, but converted as the name implies. Each can be called either with no arguments or with a `Locale` argument specifying the conversion rules; this is necessary because of internationalization. Java provides significantly more internationalization and localization features than ordinary languages, a feature that will be covered in Chapter 14. While the `equals()` method tells you if another string is exactly the same, there is also `equalsIgnoreCase()`, which tells you if all characters are the same regardless of case. Here, you can't specify an alternate locale; the system's default locale is used.

```
// Case.java
String name = "Java Cookbook";
System.out.println("Normal:\t" + name);
System.out.println("Upper:\t" + name.toUpperCase());
System.out.println("Lower:\t" + name.toLowerCase());
String javaName = "java cookBook"; // As if it were Java identifiers :-)
if (!name.equals(javaName))
    System.err.println("equals() correctly reports false");
else
    System.err.println("equals() incorrectly reports true");
if (name.equalsIgnoreCase(javaName))
    System.err.println("equalsIgnoreCase() correctly reports true");
else
    System.err.println("equalsIgnoreCase() incorrectly reports false");
```

If you run this, it prints the first name changed to uppercase and lowercase, then reports that both methods work as expected.

```
C:\javasrc\strings>java  Case
Normal: Java Cookbook
Upper:  JAVA COOKBOOK
Lower:  java cookbook
equals() correctly reports false
equalsIgnoreCase() correctly reports true
```

3.10. Indenting Text Documents

Problem

You need to indent (or "undent" or "dedent") a text document.

Solution

To indent, either generate a fixed-length string and prepend it to each output line, or use a for loop and print the right number of spaces.

```
// Indent.java
/** the default number of spaces. */
static int nSpaces = 10;

while ((inputLine = is.readLine()) != null) {
    for (int i=0; i<nSpaces; i++) System.out.print(' ');
    System.out.println(inputLine);
}
```

A more efficient approach to generating the spaces might be to construct a long string of spaces and use substring() to get the number of spaces you need.

To undent, use substring to generate a string that does not include the leading spaces. Be careful of inputs that are shorter than the amount you are removing! By popular demand, I'll give you this one too. First, though, here's a demonstration of an Undent object created with an undent value of 5, meaning remove up to five spaces (but don't lose other characters in the first five positions).

```
$ java Undent
Hello World
Hello World
 Hello
Hello
      Hello
Hello
        Hello
 Hello


^C
$
```

I test it by entering the usual test string "Hello World", which prints fine. Then "Hello" with one space, and the space is deleted. With five spaces, exactly the five spaces go. With six or more spaces, only five spaces go. And a blank line comes out as a blank line (i.e., without throwing an Exception or otherwise going berserk). I think it works!

```
import java.io.*;

/** Undent - remove up to 'n' leading spaces
 */
public class Undent {
    /** the maximum number of spaces to remove. */
    protected int nSpaces;
```

```
    Undent(int n) {
        nSpaces = n;
    }

public static void main(String[] av) {
    Undent c = new Undent(5);
    switch(av.length) {
        case 0: c.process(new BufferedReader(
                    new InputStreamReader(System.in))); break;
        default:
      for (int i=0; i<av.length; i++)
            try {
                c.process(new BufferedReader(new FileReader(av[i])));
            } catch (FileNotFoundException e) {
                System.err.println(e);
            }
        }
    }

    /** process one file, given an open BufferedReader */
    public void process(BufferedReader is) {
        try {
            String inputLine;

            while ((inputLine = is.readLine()) != null) {
                int toRemove = 0;
                for (int i=0; i<nSpaces && i < inputLine.length(); i++)
                    if (Character.isSpace(inputLine.charAt(i)))
                        ++toRemove;
                System.out.println(inputLine.substring(toRemove));
            }
            is.close();
        } catch (IOException e) {
            System.out.println("IOException: " + e);
        }
    }
}
```

3.11. Entering Non-Printable Characters

Problem

You need to put non-printable characters into strings.

Solution

Use the backslash character and one of the Java string escapes.

Discussion

The Java string escapes are listed in Table 3-1.

Table 3-1. String escapes

To get:	Use this:	Notes
Tab	\t	
Linefeed (Unix newline)	\n	See System.getProperty("line.separator"), which gives you the platform's line end.
Carriage return	\r	
Form feed	\f	
Backspace	\b	
Single quote	\'	
Double quote	\"	
Unicode character	\u*NNNN*	Four hexadecimal digits (no \x as in C/C++). See *http://www.unicode.org* for codes.
Octal(!) character	*NNN*	Who uses octal (base 8) these days?
Backslash	\\	

Here is a code example that shows most of these in action:

```
// StringEscapes.java
System.out.println("Java Strings in action:");
// System.out.println("An alarm or alert: \a");// not supported
System.out.println("An alarm entered in Octal: \007");
System.out.println("A tab key: \t(what comes after)");
System.out.println("A newline: \n(what comes after)");
System.out.println("A UniCode character: \u0207");
System.out.println("A backslash character: \\");
```

If you have a lot of non-ASCII characters to enter, you may wish to consider using Java's input methods, discussed briefly in the JDK online documentation.

3.12. Trimming Blanks from the End of a String

Problem

You need to work on a string without regard for extra leading or trailing spaces a user may have typed.

Solution

Use the String class trim() method.

Discussion

Example 3-8 uses `trim()` to strip an arbitrary number of leading spaces and/or tabs from lines of Java source code in order to look for the characters `//+` and `//-`. These are special (to me) Java comments I use to mark the parts of the programs in this book that I want to include in the printed copy.

Example 3-8. GetMark.java (trimming and comparing strings)

```
/** the default starting mark. */
public final String startMark = "//+";
/** the default ending mark. */
public final String endMark = "//-";
/** True if we are currently inside marks. */
protected boolean printing = false;


    try {
      String inputLine;

      while ((inputLine = is.readLine()) != null) {
             if (inputLine.trim().equals(startMark)) {
                 printing = true;
             } else if (inputLine.trim().equals(endMark)) {
                 printing = false;
             } else if (printing)
                 System.out.println(inputLine);
         }
         is.close();
    } catch (IOException e) {
      // not shown
    }
  }
```

3.13. Parsing Comma-Separated Data

Problem

You have a string or a file of lines containing comma-separated values (CSV) that you need to read in. Many MS-Windows-based spreadsheets and some databases use CSV to export data.

Solution

Use my CSV class or a regular expression (see Chapter 4).

Discussion

CSV is deceptive. It looks simple at first glance, but the values may be quoted or unquoted. If quoted, they may further contain escaped quotes. This far exceeds the capabilities of the `StringTokenizer` class (Recipe 3.2). Either considerable Java coding or the use of regular expressions is required. I'll show both ways.

First, a Java program. Assume for now that we have a class called CSV that has a no-argument constructor, and a method called `parse()` that takes a string representing one line of the input file. The `parse()` method returns a list of fields. For flexibility, this list is returned as an `Iterator` (see Recipe 7.4). I simply use the Iterator's `hasNext()` method to control the loop, and its `next()` method to get the next object.

```java
import java.util.*;

/* Simple demo of CSV parser class.
 */
public class CSVSimple {
    public static void main(String[] args) {
        CSV parser = new CSV();
        Iterator it = parser.parse(
            "\"LU\",86.25,\"11/4/1998\",\"2:19PM\",+4.0625");
        while (it.hasNext()) {
            System.out.println(it.next());
        }
    }
}
```

After the quotes are escaped, the string being parsed is actually the following:

```
"LU",86.25,"11/4/1998","2:19PM",+4.0625
```

Running `CSVSimple` yields the following output:

```
> java CSVSimple
LU
86.25
11/4/1998
2:19PM
+4.0625
>
```

But what about the CSV class itself? Oh yes, here it is. This is my translation of a CSV program written in C++ by Brian W. Kernighan and Rob Pike that appeared in their book *The Practice of Programming*. Their version commingled the input processing with the parsing; my CSV class does only the parsing, since the input could be coming from any of a variety of sources. The main work is done in `parse()`, which delegates handling of individual fields to advquoted() in cases where the field begins with a quote, and otherwise to advplain().

```java
import com.darwinsys.util.*;
import java.util.*;

/** Parse comma-separated values (CSV), a common Windows file format.
 * Sample input: "LU",86.25,"11/4/1998","2:19PM",+4.0625
 * <p>
 * Inner logic adapted from a C++ original that was
 * Copyright (C) 1999 Lucent Technologies
 * Excerpted from 'The Practice of Programming'
 * by Brian W. Kernighan and Rob Pike.
 * <p>
 * Included by permission of the http://tpop.awl.com/ web site,
 * which says:
 * "You may use this code for any purpose, as long as you leave
 * the copyright notice and book citation attached." I have done so.
 * @author Brian W. Kernighan and Rob Pike (C++ original)
 * @author Ian F. Darwin (translation into Java and removal of I/O)
 */
public class CSV {

    public static final String SEP = ",";

    /** Construct a CSV parser, with the default separator (`,'). */
    public CSV() {
        this(SEP);
    }

    /** Construct a CSV parser with a given separator. Must be
     * exactly the string that is the separator, not a list of
     * separator characters!
     */
    public CSV(String sep) {
        fieldsep = sep;
    }

    /** The fields in the current String */
    protected ArrayList list = new ArrayList();

    /** the separator string for this parser */
    protected String fieldsep;

    /** parse: break the input String into fields
     * @return java.util.Iterator containing each field
     * from the original as a String, in order.
     */
    public Iterator parse(String line)
```

```
    {
        StringBuffer sb = new StringBuffer();
        list.clear();// discard previous, if any
        int i = 0;

        if (line.length() == 0) {
            list.add(line);
            return list.iterator();
        }

        do {
            sb.setLength(0);
            if (i < line.length() && line.charAt(i) == '"')
                i = advquoted(line, sb, ++i);// skip quote
            else
                i = advplain(line, sb, i);
            list.add(sb.toString());
            i++;
        } while (i < line.length());

        return list.iterator();
    }

    /** advquoted: quoted field; return index of next separator */
    protected int advquoted(String s, StringBuffer sb, int i)
    {
        int j;

        // Loop through input s, handling escaped quotes
        // and looking for the ending " or , or end of line.

        for (j = i; j < s.length(); j++) {
            // found end of field if find unescaped quote.
            if (s.charAt(j) == '"' && s.charAt(j-1) != '\\') {
                int k = s.indexOf(fieldsep, j);
                Debug.println("csv", "j = " + j + ", k = " + k);
                if (k == -1) {// no separator found after this field
                    k += s.length();
                    for (k -= j; k-- > 0; ) {
                        sb.append(s.charAt(j++));
                    }
                } else {
                    --k;// omit quote from copy
                    for (k -= j; k-- > 0; ) {
                        sb.append(s.charAt(j++));
                    }
                    ++j;// skip over quote
                }
                break;
```

```
        }
            sb.append(s.charAt(j));// regular character.
        }
        return j;
    }

    /** advplain: unquoted field; return index of next separator */
    protected int advplain(String s, StringBuffer sb, int i)
    {
        int j;

        j = s.indexOf(fieldsep, i); // look for separator
        Debug.println("csv", "i = " + i + ", j = " + j);
        if (j == -1) {                  // none found
            sb.append(s.substring(i));
            return s.length();
        } else {
            sb.append(s.substring(i, j));
            return j;
        }
    }
}
```

In the online source directory you'll find *CSVFile.java*, which reads a file a line at a time and runs it through `parse()`. You'll also find Kernighan and Pike's original C++ program.

We haven't discussed regular expressions yet (we will in Chapter 4). However, many readers will be familiar with REs in a general way, so the following example will demonstrate the power of REs as well as provide code for you to reuse. Note that this program replaces *all* the code in both *CSV.java* and *CSVFile.java*. The key to understanding REs is that a little specification can match a lot of data.

```
import com.darwinsys.util.Debug;
import java.io.*;
import org.apache.regexp.*;

/* Simple demo of CSV matching using Regular Expressions.
 * Does NOT use the "CSV" class defined in the Java CookBook.
 * RE Pattern from Chapter 7, Mastering Regular Expressions (p. 205, first edn.)
 */
public class CSVRE {
    /** The rather involved pattern used to match CSV's consists of three
     * alternations: the first matches quoted fields, the second unquoted,
     * the third null fields
     */
    public static final String CSV_PATTERN =
        "\"([^\"\\\\]*(\\\\.[^\"\\\\]*)*)\",?|([^,]+),?|,";
```

```
public static void main(String[] argv) throws IOException, RESyntaxException
{
    String line;

    // Construct a new Regular Expression parser.
    Debug.println("regexp", "PATTERN = " + CSV_PATTERN); // debug
    RE csv = new RE(CSV_PATTERN);

    BufferedReader is = new BufferedReader(new InputStreamReader(System.in));

    // For each line...
    while ((line = is.readLine()) != null) {
        System.out.println("line = `" + line + "'");

        // For each field
        for (int fieldNum = 0, offset = 0; csv.match(line, offset);
            fieldNum++) {

            // Print the field (0=null, 1=quoted, 3=unquoted).
            int n = csv.getParenCount()-1;
            if (n==0)// null field
                System.out.println("field[" + fieldNum + "] = `'");
            else
                System.out.println("field[" + fieldNum + "] = `" +
                    csv.getParen(n) + "'");

            // Skip what already matched.
            offset += csv.getParen(0).length();
        }
    }
}
}
```

It is sometimes downright scary how much mundane code you can eliminate with a single, well-formulated regular expression.

3.14. Program: A Simple Text Formatter

This program is a very primitive text formatter, representative of what people used on most computing platforms before the rise of standalone graphics-based word processors, laser printers, and, eventually, desktop publishing, word processors, and desktop office suites. It simply reads words from a file—previously created with a text editor—and outputs them until it reaches the right margin, when it calls `println()` to append a line ending. For example, here is an input file:

```
It's a nice
day, isn't it, Mr. Mxyzzptllxy?
I think we should
go for a walk.
```

Given the above as its input, the Fmt program will print the lines formatted neatly:

```
It's a nice day, isn't it, Mr. Mxyzzptllxy? I think we should go for a
walk.
```

As you can see, it has fitted the text we gave it to the margin and discarded all the line breaks present in the original. Here's the code:

```java
import java.io.*;
import java.util.*;

/**
 * Fmt - format text (like Berkeley Unix fmt).
 */
public class Fmt {
    /** The maximum column width */
    public static final int COLWIDTH=72;
    /** The file that we read and format */
    BufferedReader in;

    /** If files present, format each, else format the standard input. */
    public static void main(String[] av) throws IOException {
        if (av.length == 0)
            new Fmt(System.in).format();
        else for (int i=0; i<av.length; i++)
            new Fmt(av[i]).format();
    }

    /** Construct a Formatter given a filename */
    public Fmt(String fname) throws IOException {
        in = new BufferedReader(new FileReader(fname));
    }

    /** Construct a Formatter given an open Stream */
    public Fmt(InputStream file) throws IOException {
        in = new BufferedReader(new InputStreamReader(file));
    }

    /** Format the File contained in a constructed Fmt object */
    public void format() throws IOException {
        String w, f;
        int col = 0;
        while ((w = in.readLine()) != null) {
            if (w.length() == 0) {// null line
                System.out.print("\n");// end current line
                if (col>0) {
                    System.out.print("\n");// output blank line
                    col = 0;
                }
                continue;
            }
```

```
                    // otherwise it's text, so format it.
                    StringTokenizer st = new StringTokenizer(w);
                    while (st.hasMoreTokens()) {
                        f = st.nextToken();

                        if (col + f.length() > COLWIDTH) {
                            System.out.print("\n");
                            col = 0;
                        }
                        System.out.print(f + " ");
                        col += f.length() + 1;
                    }
                }
                if (col>0) System.out.print("\n");
                in.close();
            }
        }
```

A slightly fancier version of this program, Fmt2, is in the online source for this book. It uses "dot commands"—lines beginning with periods—to give limited control over the formatting. A family of "dot command" formatters includes Unix's *roff, nroff, troff,* and *groff,* which are in the same family with programs called *runoff* on Digital Equipment systems. The original for this is J. Saltzer's runoff, which first appeared on Multics and from there made its way into various OSes. To save trees, I did not include Fmt2 here; it subclasses Fmt and overrides the format() method to include additional functionality.

3.15. *Program: Soundex Name Comparisons*

The difficulties in comparing (American-style) names inspired the development of the Soundex algorithm, in which each of a given set of consonants maps to a particular number. This was apparently devised for use by the Census Bureau to map similar-sounding names together on the grounds that in those days many people were illiterate and could not spell their parents' names correctly. But it is still useful today: for example, in a company-wide telephone book application. The names Darwin and Derwin, for example, map to D650, and Darwent maps to D653, which puts it adjacent to D650. All of these are historical variants of the same name. Suppose we needed to sort lines containing these names together: if we could output the Soundex numbers at the front of each line, this would be easy. Here is a simple demonstration of the Soundex class:

```
/** Simple demonstration of Soundex.  */
public class SoundexSimple {

    /** main */
    public static void main(String[] args) {
```

```
        String[] names = {
            "Darwin, Ian",
            "Davidson, Greg",
            "Darwent, William",
            "Derwin, Daemon"
        };
        for (int i = 0; i< names.length; i++)
            System.out.println(Soundex.soundex(names[i]) + ' ' + names[i]);
    }
}
```

Let's run it:

```
> jikes +E -d . SoundexSimple.java
> java SoundexSimple | sort
D132 Davidson, Greg
D650 Darwin, Ian
D650 Derwin, Daemon
D653 Darwent, William
>
```

As you can see, the Darwin-variant names (including Daemon Derwin*) all sort together and are distinct from the Davidson (and Davis, Davies, etc.) names that normally appear between Darwin and Derwin when using a simple alphabetic sort. The Soundex algorithm has done its work.

Here is the `Soundex` class itself; it uses `Strings` and `StringBuffers` to convert names into Soundex codes. There is a JUnit test (see Recipe 1.13) online, *SoundexTest.java*.

```
import com.darwinsys.util.Debug;
/**
 * Soundex - the Soundex Algorithm, as described by Knuth
 * <p>
 * This class implements the soundex algorithm as described by Donald
 * Knuth in Volume 3 of <I>The Art of Computer Programming</I>.  The
 * algorithm is intended to hash words (in particular surnames) into
 * a small space using a simple model which approximates the sound of
 * the word when spoken by an English speaker.  Each word is reduced
 * to a four character string, the first character being an upper case
 * letter and the remaining three being digits. Double letters are
 * collapsed to a single digit.
 *
 * <h2>EXAMPLES</h2>
 * Knuth's examples of various names and the soundex codes they map
 * to are:
```

---

* In Unix terminology, a *daemon* is a server. The word has nothing to do with demons, but refers to a helper or assistant. Derwin Daemon is actually a character in Susannah Coleman's "Source Wars" online comic strip; see *http://darby.daemonnews.org.*

```
 *  <b>Euler, Ellery -> E460
 *  <b>Gauss, Ghosh -> G200
 *  <b>Hilbert, Heilbronn -> H416
 *  <b>Knuth, Kant -> K530
 *  <b>Lloyd, Ladd -> L300
 *  <b>Lukasiewicz, Lissajous -> L222
 *
 *  <h2>LIMITATIONS</h2>
 *  As the soundex algorithm was originally used a <B>long</B> time ago
 *  in the United States of America, it uses only the English alphabet
 *  and pronunciation.
 *  <p>
 *  As it is mapping a large space (arbitrary length strings) onto a
 *  small space (single letter plus 3 digits) no inference can be made
 *  about the similarity of two strings which end up with the same
 *  soundex code.  For example, both "Hilbert" and "Heilbronn" end up
 *  with a soundex code of "H416".
 *  <p>
 *  The soundex() method is static, as it maintains no per-instance
 *  state; this means you never need to instantiate this class.
 *
 *  @author Perl implementation by Mike Stok (<stok@cybercom.net>) from
 *  the description given by Knuth.  Ian Phillips (<ian@pipex.net>) and
 *  Rich Pinder (<rpinder@hsc.usc.edu>) supplied ideas and spotted
 *  mistakes.
 */
public class Soundex {

    /* Implements the mapping
     * from: AEHIOUWYBFPVCGJKQSXZDTLMNR
     * to:   00000000111122222222334556
     */
    public static final char[] MAP = {
        //A  B   D   D   E   F   G   H   I   J   K   L   M
        '0','1','2','3','0','1','2','0','0','2','2','4','5',
        //N  O   P   W   R   S   T   U   V   W   X   Y   Z
        '5','0','1','2','6','2','3','0','1','0','2','0','2'
    };

    /** Convert the given String to its Soundex code.
     * @return null If the given string can't be mapped to Soundex.
     */
    public static String soundex(String s) {

        // Algorithm works on uppercase (mainframe era).
        String t = s.toUpperCase();

        StringBuffer res = new StringBuffer();
        char c, prev = '?';
```

```
    // Main loop: find up to 4 chars that map.
    for (int i=0; i<t.length() && res.length() < 4 &&
         (c = t.charAt(i)) != ','; i++) {

        // Check to see if the given character is alphabetic.
        // Text is already converted to uppercase. Algorithm
        // only handles ASCII letters, do NOT use Character.isLetter()!
        // Also, skip double letters.
        if (c>='A' && c<='Z' && c != prev) {
            prev = c;

            // First char is installed unchanged, for sorting.
            if (i==0)
                res.append(c);
            else {
                char m = MAP[c-'A'];
                Debug.println("inner", c + " --> " + m);
                if (m != '0')
                    res.append(m);
            }
        }
    }
    if (res.length() == 0)
        return null;
    for (int i=res.length(); i<4; i++)
        res.append('0');
    return res.toString();
    }
}
```

Pattern Matching with
Regular Expressions

4.0. Introduction

Suppose you have been on the Internet for a few years and have been very faithful about saving all your correspondence, just in case you (or your lawyers, or the prosecution) need a copy. The result is that you have a 50-megabyte disk partition dedicated to saved mail. And let's further suppose that you remember that there is one letter, somewhere in there, from someone named Angie or Anjie. Or was it Angy? But you don't remember what you called it or where you stored it. Obviously, you will have to go look for it.

But while some of you go and try to open up all 15,000,000 documents in a word processor, I'll just find it with one simple command. Any system that provides regular expression support will allow me to search for the pattern:

```
An[^ dn]
```

in all the files. The "A" and the "n" match themselves, in effect finding words that begin with "An", while the cryptic [^ dn] requires the "An" to be followed by a character other than a space (to eliminate the very common English word "an" at the start of a sentence) or "d" (to eliminate the common word "and") or "n" (to eliminate Anne, Announcing, etc.). Has your word processor gotten past its splash screen yet? Well, it doesn't matter, because I've already found the missing file. To find the answer, I just typed the command:*

```
grep 'An[^ dn]' *
```

---

* Non-Unix fans rejoice, for you can do this on Win32 using a package alternately called CygWin (after Cygnus Software) or GnuWin32 (*http://sources.redhat.com/cygwin/*). Or you can use my Grep program in Recipe 4.8 if you don't have grep on your system. Incidentally, the name grep comes from an ancient Unix line editor command g/RE/p, the command to globally find the RE (regular expression) in all lines in the edit buffer and print the lines that match: just what the grep program does to lines in files.

Regular expressions, or REs for short, provide a concise and precise specification of patterns to be matched in text. Java 2 did not include any facilities for describing regular expressions in text. This is mildly surprising given how powerful regular expressions are, how ubiquitous they are on the Unix operating system where Java was first brewed, and how powerful they are in modern scripting languages like sed, awk, Python, and Perl.

At any rate, there were no RE packages for Java when I first learned the language, and because of this, I wrote my own RE package. More recently, I had planned to submit a JSR* to Sun Microsystems, proposing to add to Java a regular expressions API similar to the one used in this chapter. However, the Apache Jakarta Regular Expressions project† has achieved sufficient momentum to become nearly a standard, but without the politics and meetings required of a JSR. Accordingly, my JSR has not been submitted yet. Conveniently, the Jakarta folk used a similar syntax to mine, so I was mostly able to migrate to theirs just by changing the imports. However, the Apache code is vastly more efficient than mine and should be used whenever possible. Mine was written for pedagogical display, and compiles the RE into an array of SubExpression objects. The Jakarta package, borrowing a trick from Java,‡ compiles to an array of integer commands, making it run much faster: around a factor of 3 or 4, even for simple cases like searching for the string "java" in a few dozen files. There are in fact a half dozen or so regular expression packages for Java; see Table 4-1.

Table 4-1. Java RE packages

Package	Notes	URL
Richard Emberson's	Unknown license; not being maintained.	None; posted to *advanced-java@berkeley.edu*
Ian Darwin's RE	Simple, but SLOW. Incomplete; didactic.	*http://www.darwinsys.com/java/*
Apache Jakarta RegExp (original by Jonathan Locke)	Apache (BSD-like) license.	*http://jakarta.apache.org/regexp/*

---

* A JSR is a Java Standards Request, the process by which new standards are submitted by the Java Community and discussed in public prior to adoption. See Sun's Java Community web site (*http://developer.java.sun.com/developer/community/*).

† Apache has, in fact, two regular expressions packages. The second, Oro, provides full Perl5-style regular expressions, AWK-like regular expressions, glob expressions, and utility classes for performing substitutions, splits, filtering filenames, etc. This library is the successor to the OROMatcher, AwkTools, PerlTools, and TextTools libraries from ORO, Inc. (*http://www.oroinc.com*).

‡ Java perhaps got the idea from the UCSD P-system, which used portable bytecodes in the early 1980s and ran on all the popular microcomputers of the day.

Table 4-1. Java RE packages (continued)

Package	Notes	URL
Apache Jakarta ORO	Apache license. More comprehensive?	*http://jakarta.apache.org/ oro/*
Daniel Savarese	Unknown.	*http://www.cs.umd.edu/ users/dfs/java/*
"GNU Java Regexp"	GPL; fairly fast.	*http://www.gjt.org* (Giant Java Tree)

The syntax of REs themselves is discussed in Recipe 4.1, hints on using them in Recipe 4.2, and the syntax of the Java API for using REs in Recipe 4.3.

See Also

O'Reilly's *Mastering Regular Expressions* by Jeffrey E. F. Friedl is the definitive guide to all the details of regular expressions. Most introductory Unix tomes include some discussion of REs; O'Reilly's *UNIX Power Tools* devotes a chapter to them.

4.1. Regular Expression Syntax

Problem

You need to learn the syntax of regular expressions.

Solution

Consult Table 4-2 for a list of the regular expression characters that the Apache Regular Expression API matches.

Table 4-2. Regular expression syntax

Subexpression	Will match:	Notes
General		
a	The letter a (and similarly for any other Unicode character not listed in this table)	
^	Start of line/string	
$	End of line/string	
.	Any one character	
[...]	"Character class"; any one character from those listed	
[^...]	Any one character not from those listed	

Table 4-2. Regular expression syntax (continued)

Subexpression	Will match:	Notes
Normal (greedy) multipliers ("greedy closures")		
{m,n}	Multiplier (closure) for from m to n repetitions	
{m,}	Multiplier for from m repetitions on up	
{,n}	Multiplier for 0 up to n repetitions	
*	Multiplier for 0 or more repetitions	Short for {0,}
+	Multiplier for 1 or more repetitions	Short for {1,}
?	Multiplier for 0 or 1 repetitions	Short for {0,1}
Reluctant (non-greedy) multipliers ("reluctant closures")		
*?	Reluctant multiplier: 0 or more	
+?	Reluctant multiplier: 1 or more	
??	Reluctant multiplier: 0 or 1 times	
Alternation and grouping		
( )	Grouping	
|	Alternation	
Escapes and shorthands		
\	Escape character: turns metacharacters off, and turns following alphabetics (t, w, d, and s) into metacharacters.	
\t	Tab character	
\w	Character in a word	Use \w+ for a word
\d	Numeric digit	Use \d+ for a number
\s	Whitespace	Space, tab, etc., as determined by java.lang.Character. isWhitespace()
\W, \D, \S	Inverse of above (\W is a non-word character, etc.)	
POSIX-style character classes		
[:alnum:]	Alphanumeric characters	
[:alpha:]	Alphabetic characters	
[:blank:]	Space and tab characters	
[:space:]	Space characters	
[:cntrl:]	Control characters	
[:digit:]	Numeric digit characters	
[:graph:]	Printable and visible characters (not spaces)	

Table 4-2. Regular expression syntax (continued)

Subexpression	Will match:	Notes
[:print:]	Printable characters	
[:punct:]	Punctuation characters	
[:lower:]	Lowercase characters	
[:upper:]	Uppercase characters	
[:xdigit:]	Hexadecimal digit characters	
[:javastart:]	Start of a Java language identifier	Not in POSIX
[:javapart:]	Part of a Java identifier	Not in POSIX

These pattern characters can be used in any combination that makes sense. For example, a+ means any number of occurrences of the letter a, from one up to a million or a gazillion. The pattern Mrs?\. matches Mr. or Mrs.. And, .* means "any character, any number of times," and is similar in meaning to most command-line interpreters' meaning of *.

It's important to remember that REs will match anyplace possible in the input, and that patterns ending in a greedy closure will consume as much as possible without compromising any other subexpressions.

Also, unlike some RE packages, the Apache package was designed to handle Unicode characters from the beginning. Actually, it came for free, as its basic units are the Java char and String variable, which are Unicode-based. In fact, the standard Java escape sequence \u*nnnn* is used to specify a Unicode character in the pattern. And we use methods of java.lang.Character to determine Unicode character properties, such as whether or not a given character is a space.

4.2. How REs Work in Practice

Problem

You want to know how these metacharacters work in practice.

Solution

Wherein I give a few more examples for the benefit of those who have not been exposed to REs.

In building patterns, you can use any combination of ordinary text and the *metacharacters* or special characters in Table 4-2. For example, the two-character RE ^T would match beginning of line (^) immediately followed by a capital T, i.e., any line beginning with a capital T. It doesn't matter whether the line begins with *Tiny trumpets,* or *Titanic tubas,* or *Triumphant trombones,* as long as the capital T is present in the first position.

But here we're not very far ahead. Have we really invested all this effort in RE technology just to be able to do what we could already do with the `java.lang.String` method `startsWith()`? Hmmm, I can hear some of you getting a bit restless. Stay in your seats! What if you wanted to match not only a letter T in the first position, but also a vowel (a, e, i, o, or u) immediately after it, followed by any number of letters in a word, followed by an exclamation point? Surely you could do this in Java by checking `startsWith("T")` and `charAt(1) == 'a' || charAt(1) == 'e'`, and so on? Yes, but by the time you did that, you'd have written a lot of very highly specialized code that you couldn't use in any other application. With regular expressions, you can just give the pattern `^T[aeiou]\w*`. That is, `^` and `T` as before, followed by a *character class* listing the vowels, followed by any number of word characters (`\w*`), followed by the exclamation point.

"But wait, there's more!" as my late great boss Yuri Rubinsky used to say. What if you want to be able to change the pattern you're looking for *at runtime?* Remember all that Java code you just wrote to match `T` in column 1 plus a vowel, some word-characters and an exclamation point? Well, it's time to throw it out. Because this morning we need instead to match Q, followed by a letter other than u, followed by a number of digits, followed by a period. While some of you start writing a new function to do that, the rest of us will just saunter over to the RegExp Bar & Grille, order a `^Q[^u]\d+\.` from the bartender, and be on our way.

Huh? Oh, the `[^u]` means "match any one character that is not the character u." The `\d+` means one or more numeric digits. Remember that + is a multiplier meaning one or more, and `\d` is any one numeric digit. (Remember that `\n`—which sounds as though it might mean numeric digit—actually means a newline.) Finally, the `\.`? Well, . by itself is a metacharacter. Single metacharacters are switched off by preceding them with an escape character. No, don't hit that ESC key on your keyboard. The RE "escape" character is a backslash. Preceding a metacharacter like . with escape turns off its special meaning. Preceding a few selected alphabetic characters (n, r, t, s, w) with escape turns them into metacharacters. In some other implementations, escape also precedes (,), <, and > to turn them into metacharacters.

One good way to think of regular expressions is as a "little language" for matching patterns of characters in text contained in strings. Give yourself extra points if you've already recognized this as the design pattern known as *Interpreter.* A regular expression API is an interpreter for matching regular expressions.

As for how REs work in theory—the logic behind it and the different types of RE engines—the reader is referred to the book *Mastering Regular Expressions.*

4.3. Using Regular Expressions in Java

Problem

You're ready to utilize regular expression processing to beef up your Java code.

Solution

Use the Apache Jakarta Regular Expressions Package, `org.apache.regexp`.

Discussion

As mentioned, the Apache project develops and maintains a regular expressions API. To ensure that you get the latest version, I don't include it in the source archive for this book; you should download it from *http://jakarta.apache.org/regexp/*. The good news is that it's actually easy to use. If all you need is to find out whether a given string matches an RE, just construct the RE and call its boolean `match()` method:

```
RE r = new RE(pattern); // Construct an RE object
boolean found = r.match(input); // Use it to match an input.
if (found) {
    // it matched... do something with it...
}
```

A complete program constructing an RE and using it to `match()` is shown here:

```
import org.apache.regexp.*;

/**
 * Simple example of using RE class.
 */
public class RESimple {
    public static void main(String[] argv) throws RESyntaxException {
        String pattern = "^Q[^u]\\d+\\.";
        String input = "QA777. is the next flight. It is on time.";

        RE r = new RE(pattern); // Construct an RE object

        boolean found = r.match(input); // Use it to match an input.

        System.out.println(pattern +
            (found ? " matches " : " doesn't match ") + input);
    }
}
```

The class RE provides the public API shown in Example 4-1. Unix users and Perl regulars may wish to skip this section, after glancing at the first few examples to

---

Remember This!

Remember that because an RE will be compiling strings that are also compiled by *javac*, you will probably need two levels of escaping for any special characters, including backslash, double quotes, and so on. For example, the RE:

```
"You said it\."
```

has to be typed like this to be a Java language `String`:

```
"\"You said it\\.\""
```

---

see the syntactic details of how we've adapted regular expressions into the form of a Java API.

Example 4-1. The Java Regular Expression API

```
/** The main public API of org.apache.regexp.RE.
 * Prepared in machine readable by javap and Ian Darwin.
 */
public class RE extends Object {
    // Constructors
    public RE();
    public RE(String patt) throws RESyntaxException;
    public RE(String patt, int flg) throws RESyntaxException;
    public RE(REProgram patt);
    public RE(REProgram patt, int flg);

    public boolean match(String in);
    public boolean match(String in, int index);
    public boolean match(CharacterIterator where, int index);
    public String[] split(String)[];
    public String[] grep(Object[] in);
    public String subst(String in, String repl);
    public String subst(String in, String repl, int how);

    public String getParen(int level);
    public int getParenCount();
    public final int getParenEnd(int level);
    public final int getParenLength(int level);
    public final int getParenStart(int level);

    public int getMatchFlags();
    public void setMatchFlags(int flg);
    public REProgram getProgram();
    public void setProgram(REProgram prog);
}
```

This API is large enough to require some explanation. As you can see, there are several forms of the method called `match()` that return `true` or `false`. The simplest usage is to construct an RE and call its `match()` method against an input string, as in Example 4-1. This compiles the pattern given as the constructor argument into a form that can be compared against the `match()` argument fairly efficiently, then goes through and matches it against the string. The overloaded form `match(String in, int index)` is the same, except that it allows you to skip characters from the beginning. The third form, which takes a `CharacterIterator` as its argument, will be covered in Recipe 4.7.

4.4. Testing REs Interactively

Problem

You want to try out REs interactively before committing them to Java code.

Solution

Use the provided `REDemo` program.

Discussion

`REDemo` is a program in the `org.apache.regexp` package that lets you see the code that a RE compiles into, and also lets you watch it match interactively. You can change the RE or the string being matched easily, as it is a GUI application. Just give the command:

```
> java org.apache.regexp.REDemo
```

Figure 4-1 shows the program in action.

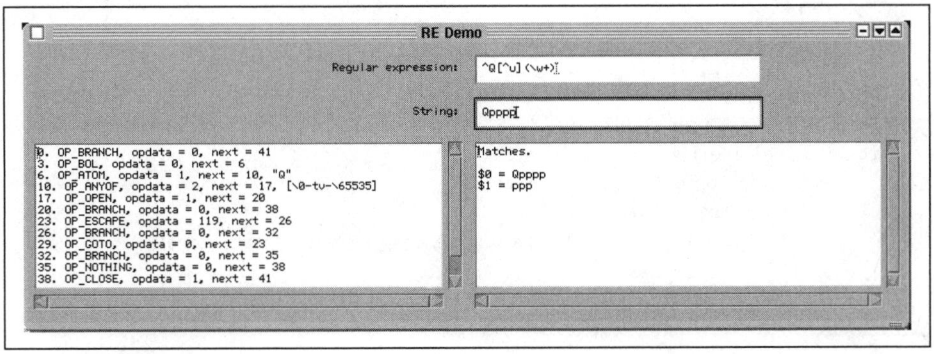

Figure 4-1. REDemo in action

In the upper-right box you type the RE you want to test, and below that a test string to match it against. In the lower-left window, you see the compiled expression, and in the lower-right, you see what matched. $0 is the entire match, and $1 and up are tagged subexpressions that matched. Experiment to your heart's content. When you have the RE the way you want it, you can paste it into your Java program. Remember to escape (backslash) any characters that are treated specially by Java and RE, such as the backslash itself, double quotes, \u, and others.

4.5. Finding the Matching Text

Problem

You need to find the text that matched the RE.

Solution

Sometimes you need to know more than just whether an RE matched an input string. In editors and many other tools, you will want to know exactly what characters were matched. Remember that with multipliers such as *, the length of the text that was matched may have no relationship to the length of the pattern that matched it. Do not underestimate the mighty .*, which will happily match thousands or millions of characters if allowed to. As you can see from looking at the API, you can find out whether a given match succeeds just by using match(), as we've done up to now. But it may be more useful to get a description of what it matched by using one of the getParen() methods.

The notion of parentheses is central to RE processing. REs may be nested to any level of complexity. The getParen() methods let you retrieve whatever matched at a given parenthesis level. If you haven't used any explicit parens, you can just treat whatever matched as "level zero." For example:

```
// Part of REmatch.java
String patt = "Q[^u]\\d+\\.";
RE r = new RE(patt);
String line = "Order QT300. Now!";
if (r.match(line)) {
    System.out.println(patt + " matches '" +
        r.getParen(0) +
        "' in '" + line + "'"); Match whence = RE.match(patt, line);
}
```

When run, this prints:

```
Q[^u]\d+\. matches "QT300." in "Order QT300. Now!"
```

It is also possible to get the starting and ending indexes and the length of the text that the pattern matched (remember that \d+ can match any number of digits in the input). You can use these in conjunction with the `String.substring()` methods as follows:

```
// Part of REsubstr.java -- Prints exactly the same as REmatch.java
if (r.match(line)) {
    System.out.println(patt + " matches '" +
        line.substring(r.getParenStart(0), r.getParenEnd(0)) +
        ' in '" + line + "'");
}
```

Suppose you need to extract several items from a string. If the input is:

```
Smith, John
Adams, John Quincy
```

and you want to get out:

```
John Smith
John Quincy Adams
```

just use:

```
// from REmatchTwoFields.java
// Construct an RE with parens to "grab" both field1 and field2
RE r = new RE("(.*), (.*)");
if (!r.match(inputLine))
    throw new IllegalArgumentException("Bad input: " + inputLine);
System.out.println(r.getParen(2) + ' ' + r.getParen(1));
```

4.6. *Replacing the Matching Text*

As we saw in the previous recipe, regular expression patterns involving multipliers can match a lot of input characters with a very few metacharacters. We need a way to replace the text that matched the RE without changing other text before or after it. We could do this manually using the `String` method `substring()`. However, because it's such a common requirement, the regular expression API provides it for us in methods named `subst()`. In all these methods, you pass in the string in which you want the substitution done, as well as the replacement text or "right-hand side" of the substitution. This term is historical; in a text editor's substitute command, the left-hand side is the pattern and the right-hand side is the replacement text.

```
// class SubDemo
// Quick demo of substitution: correct "demon" and other
// spelling variants to the correct, non-satanic "daemon".

// Make an RE pattern to match almost any form (deamon, demon, etc.).
```

```
String patt = "d[ae]{1,2}mon";

// A test input.
String input = "Some say Unix hath demons in it!";

// Run it from a RE instance and see that it works
RE r = new RE(patt);
System.out.println(input + " --> " + r.sub(input, "daemon"));
```

Sure enough, when you run it, it does what it should:

```
C:\javasrc\RE>java SubDemo
Some say Unix hath demons in it! --> Some say Unix hath deamons in it!
```

4.7. Printing All Occurrences of a Pattern

Problem

You need to find all the strings that match a given RE in one or more files or other sources.

Solution

This example reads through a file using a `ReaderCharacterIterator`, one of four `CharacterIterator` classes in the Jakarta RegExp package. Whenever a match is found, I extract it from the `CharacterIterator` and print it.

The other character iterators are `StreamCharacterIterator` (as we'll see in Chapter 9, streams are 8-bit bytes, while readers handle conversion among various representations of Unicode characters), `CharacterArrayIterator`, and `StringCharacterIterator`. All of these character iterators are interchangeable; apart from the construction process, this program would work on any of them. Use a `StringCharacterIterator`, for example, to find all occurrences of a pattern in the (possibly long) string you get from a `JTextArea`'s `getText()` method, described in Chapter 13.

This code takes the `getParen()` methods from Recipe 4.5, the `substring` method from the `CharacterIterator` interface, and the `match()` method from the RE, and simply puts them all together. I coded it to extract all the "names" from a given file; in running the program through itself, it prints the words "import", "org", "apache", "regexp", and so on.

```
> jikes +E -d . ReaderIter.java
> java ReaderIter ReaderIter.java
import
org
apache
```

```
regexp
import
java
io
import
com
darwinsys
util
Debug
Demonstrate
the
Character
Iterator
interface
print
```

I interrupted it here to save paper. The source code for this program is fairly short:

```java
import org.apache.regexp.*;
import java.io.*;
import com.darwinsys.util.Debug;

/** Demonstrate the CharacterIterator interface: print
 * all the strings that match a given pattern from a file.
 */
public class ReaderIter {
    public static void main(String[] args) throws Exception {
        // The RE pattern
        RE patt = new RE("[A-Za-z][a-z]+");
        // A FileReader (see the I/O chapter)
        Reader r = new FileReader(args[0]);
        // The RE package ReaderCharacterIterator, a "front end"
        // around the Reader object.
        CharacterIterator in = new ReaderCharacterIterator(r);
        int end = 0;

        // For each match in the input, extract and print it.
        while (patt.match(in, end)) {
            // Get the starting position of the text
            int start = patt.getParenStart(0);
            // Get ending position; also updates for NEXT match.
            end = patt.getParenEnd(0);
            // Print whatever matched.
            Debug.println("match", "start=" + start + "; end=" + end);
            // Use CharacterIterator.substring(offset, end);
            System.out.println(in.substring(start, end));
        }
    }
}
```

4.8. Printing Lines Containing a Pattern

Problem

You need to look for lines matching a given RE in one or more files.

Solution

As I've mentioned, once you have an RE package, you can write the *grep* program. I gave an example of the Unix *grep* program earlier. *grep* is called with some optional arguments, followed by one required regular expression pattern, followed by an arbitrary number of filenames. It prints any line that contains the pattern, differing from Recipe 4.7, which only prints the matching text itself. For example:

```
grep "[dD]arwin" *.txt
```

searches for lines containing either "darwin" or "Darwin" on any line in any file whose name ends in ".txt".* Example 4-1 is the source for the first version of a program to do this, called Grep1. It doesn't yet take any optional arguments, but it handles the full set of regular expressions that the RE class implements. We haven't covered the `java.io` package for input and output yet (see Chapter 9), but our use of it here is simple enough that you can probably intuit it. Later in this chapter, Recipe 4.13 presents a Grep2 program that uses my GetOpt (see Recipe 2.7) to parse command-line options.

```
import org.apache.regexp.*;
import java.io.*;

/** A command-line grep-like program. No options, but takes a pattern
 * and an arbitrary list of text files.
 */
public class Grep1 {
    /** The pattern we're looking for */
    protected RE pattern;
    /** The Reader for the current file */
    protected BufferedReader d;

    /** Construct a Grep object for each pattern, and run it
     * on all input files listed in argv.
     */
    public static void main(String[] argv) throws Exception {
```

---

* On Unix, the shell or command-line interpreter expands *.txt* to match all the filenames, but the normal Java interpreter does this for you on systems where the shell isn't energetic or bright enough to do it.

```
        if (argv.length < 1) {
            System.err.println("Usage: Grep pattern [filename]");
            System.exit(1);
        }

        Grep1 pg = new Grep1(argv[0]);

        if (argv.length == 1)
            pg.process(new InputStreamReader(System.in),
                "(standard input", false);
        else
            for (int i=1; i<argv.length; i++) {
                pg.process(new FileReader(argv[i]), argv[i], true);
            }
    }

    public Grep1(String arg) throws RESyntaxException {
        // compile the regular expression
        pattern = new RE(arg);
    }

    /** Do the work of scanning one file
     * @param patt RE Regular Expression object
     * @param ifile Reader Reader object already open
     * @param fileName String Name of the input file
     * @param printFileName Boolean - true to print filename
     * before lines that match.
     */
    public void process(
        Reader ifile, String fileName, boolean printFileName) {

        String line;

        try {
            d = new BufferedReader(ifile);

            while ((line = d.readLine()) != null) {
                if (pattern.match(line)) {
                    if (printFileName)
                        System.out.print(fileName + ": ");
                    System.out.println(line);
                }
            }
            d.close();
        } catch (IOException e) { System.err.println(e); }
    }
}
```

4.9. Controlling Case in match() and subst()

Problem

You want to find text regardless of case.

Solution

Use the `flags` static `int` variable RE.MATCH_CASEINDEPENDENT to indicate that matching should be case-independent ("fold" or ignore differences in case) or RE_MATCH_NORMAL to request normal, case-sensitive matching behavior. These flags can either be passed to the RE constructor method, as in:

```
// CaseMatch.java
RE r = new RE(pattern, RE.MATCH_CASEINDEPENDENT);
r.match(input);// will match case-insensitively
```

or passed to the RE's `setMatchFlags()` method before calling `match()`, as in:

```
r.setMatchFlags(RE.MATCH_NORMAL);
r.match(input);// will match case-sensitively
If we print the results of both match operations
+ jikes +E -d . CaseMatch.java
+ java CaseMatch
MATCH_CASEINDEPENDENT match true
MATCH_NORMAL match was false
```

The full source for this example is online as *CaseMatch.java*.

4.10. Precompiling the RE

Problem

You need to use the same RE many times over.

Solution

Precompile it using class `recompile` and include the resulting code fragment into your Java source code.

Discussion

Some REs never change. Those that don't can be precompiled to speed up your program's initialization. The class `recompile` (the only class in this API whose name doesn't fit the Java capitalization style rules) contains a main program that requires two arguments: a Java identifier prefix and an RE pattern. When running it, remember that you should quote the RE pattern, as many of the special characters are the same for the REs as they are for many command-line interpreters. You run it by giving the *java* command, the full class name, the identifier prefix, and the RE pattern as one command line. Once you've seen that the RE is correct, you can run the command again, redirecting the results into a new Java file. You can then edit this file into a complete program or copy it into an existing Java file.

```
> java org.apache.regexp.recompile Name "[A-Z][a-z]+"

    // Pre-compiled regular expression '[A-Z][a-z]+'
    private static char[] NamePatternInstructions =
    {
        0x007c, 0x0000, 0x0019, 0x005b, 0x0001, 0x0005, 0x0041,
        0x005a, 0x005b, 0x0001, 0x0005, 0x0061, 0x007a, 0x007c,
        0x0000, 0x0006, 0x0047, 0x0000, 0xfff8, 0x007c, 0x0000,
        0x0003, 0x004e, 0x0000, 0x0003, 0x0045, 0x0000, 0x0000,
    };

    private static RE NamePattern =
        new RE(new REProgram(NamePatternInstructions));
> java org.apache.regexp.recompile Name "[A-Z][a-z]+" > Name.java
>
```

The stuff that looks like a dump listing (the numbers with 0x at the front) are not a compiled Java program, but rather a compiled regular expression. It is there to speed up the runtime execution of your program.

The file (*Name.java* in this example) can be edited to start a new Java program or copied into an existing file. On some platforms, you can bypass that step and simply select the text with the mouse, copy it, and paste it into an editor or IDE editing window. In either case, the goal is to avoid manually retyping it; that would be error-prone and downright foolish.

4.11. Matching Newlines in Text

Problem

You need to match newlines in text.

Solution

Use \n or \r.

See also the `flags` constant RE.MATCH_MULTILINE, which makes newlines match as beginning-of-line and end-of-line (^ and $).

Discussion

While line-oriented tools from Unix such as *sed* and *grep* match regular expressions one line at a time, not all tools do. The *sam* text editor from Bell Laboratories was the first interactive tool I know of to allow multiline regular expressions; the Perl scripting language followed shortly. In our API, the newline character by default has no special significance. The `BufferedReader` method `readLine()` normally strips out whichever newline characters it finds. If you read in gobs of characters using some method other than `readLine()`, you may have \n in your text string. Since it's just an ordinary character, you can match it with `.*` or similar multipliers, and, if you want to know exactly where it is, \n or \r in the pattern will match it as well. In other words, to this API, a newline character is just another character with no special significance. You can recognize a newline either by the metacharacter \n, or you could also refer to it by its numerical value, \u000a.

```java
import org.apache.regexp.*;

/**
 * Show line ending matching using RE class.
 */
public class NLMatch {
    public static void main(String[] argv) throws RESyntaxException {

        String input = "I dream of engines\nmore engines, all day long";
        System.out.println("INPUT: " + input);
        System.out.println();

        String[] patt = {
            "engines\nmore engines",
            "engines$"
        };

        for (int i = 0; i < patt.length; i++) {
            System.out.println("PATTERN " + patt[i]);

            boolean found;
            RE r = new RE(patt[i]);

            found = r.match(input);
            System.out.println("DEFAULT match " + found);

            r.setMatchFlags(RE.MATCH_MULTILINE);
            found = r.match(input);
            System.out.println("MATCH_MULTILINE match was " + found);
            System.out.println();
        }
    }
}
```

If you run this code, the first pattern (with the embedded \n) always matches, while the second pattern (with $) matches only when MATCH_MULTILINE is set.

```
> java NLMatch
INPUT: I dream of engines
more engines, all day long

PATTERN engines
more engines
DEFAULT match true
MATCH_MULTILINE match was true

PATTERN engines$
DEFAULT match false
MATCH_MULTILINE match was true
```

4.12. Program: Data Mining

Suppose that I, as a published author, want to track how my book is selling in comparison to others. This information can be obtained for free just by clicking on the page for my book on any of the major bookseller sites, reading the sales rank number off the screen, and typing the number into a file, but that's tedious. As I somewhat haughtily wrote in the book that this example looks for, "computers get paid to extract relevant information from files; people should not have to do such mundane tasks." This program uses the regular expressions API and, in particular, newline matching to extract a value from an HTML page. It also reads from a URL (discussed later in Recipe 17.6.) The pattern to look for is something like this (bear in mind that the HTML may change at any time, so I want to keep the pattern fairly general):

```
<b>QuickBookShop.web Sales Rank: </b>
26,252
</font><br>
```

As the pattern may extend over more than one line, I read the entire web page from the URL into a single long string using my `FileIO.readerAsString()` method (see Recipe 9.5) instead of the more traditional line-at-a-time paradigm. I then plot a graph using an external program (see Recipe 26.1); this could (and should) be changed to use a Java graphics program. The complete program is shown in Example 4-2.

Example 4-2. BookRank.java

```
import java.io.*;
import com.darwinsys.util.FileIO;
import java.net.*;
import java.text.*;
```

Example 4-2. BookRank.java (continued)

```java
import java.util.*;
import org.apache.regexp.*;

/** Graph of a book's sales rank on a given bookshop site.
 */

public class BookRank {
    public final static String ISBN = "0937175307";
    public final static String DATA_FILE = "lint.sales";
    public final static String GRAPH_FILE = "lint.png";
    public final static String TITLE = "Checking C Prog w/ Lint";
    public final static String QUERY = "
            "http://www.quickbookshops.web/cgi-bin/search?isbn=";

    /** Grab the sales rank off the web page and log it. */
    public static void main(String[] args) throws Exception {

        // Looking for something like this in the input:
        //    <b>QuickBookShop.web Sales Rank: </b>
        //    26,252
        //    </font><br>

        // From Patrick Killelea <badraig@yahoo.com>: match number with
        // comma included, just print as is. Loses if you fall below 100,000.
        RE r = new RE("\..web Sales Rank: </b>\\s*(\\d*),*(\\d+)\\s");

        // Read the given search URL looking for the rank information.
        // Read as a single long string, so can match multi-line entries.
        // If found, append to sales data file.
        BufferedReader is = new BufferedReader(new InputStreamReader(
            new URL(QUERY + ISBN).openStream()));
        String input = FileIO.readerToString(is);
        if (r.match(input)) {
            PrintWriter FH = new PrintWriter(
                new FileWriter(DATA_FILE, true));
            String date = // `date +'%m %d %H %M %S %Y'`;
                new SimpleDateFormat("MM dd hh mm ss yyyy ").
                format(new Date());
            FH.println(date + r.getParen(1) + r.getParen(2));
            FH.close();
        }

        // Draw the graph, using gnuplot.

        String gnuplot_cmd =
            "set term png\n" +
            "set output \"" + GRAPH_FILE + "\"\n" +
            "set xdata time\n" +
```

Example 4-2. BookRank.java (continued)

```
            "set ylabel \"Amazon sales rank\"\n" +
            "set bmargin 3\n" +
            "set logscale y\n" +
            "set yrange [1:60000] reverse\n" +
            "set timefmt \"%m %d %H %M %S %Y\"\n" +
            "plot \"" + DATA_FILE +
                "\" using 1:7 title \"" + TITLE + "\" with lines\n"
        ;

        Process p = Runtime.getRuntime().exec("/usr/local/bin/gnuplot");
        PrintWriter gp = new PrintWriter(p.getOutputStream());
        gp.print(gnuplot_cmd);
        gp.close();
    }
}
```

4.13. Program: Full Grep

Now that we've seen how the regular expressions package works, it's time to write `Grep2`, a full-blown version of the line-matching program with option parsing. Table 4-3 lists some typical command-line options that a Unix implementation of *grep* might include.

Table 4-3. Grep command-line options

Option	Meaning
-c	Count only: don't print lines, just count them
-f pattern	Take pattern from file named after -f instead of from command line
-h	Suppress printing filename ahead of lines
-i	Ignore case
-l	List filenames only: don't print lines, just the names they're found in
-n	Print line numbers before matching lines
-s	Suppress printing certain error messages
-v	Invert: print only lines that do NOT match the pattern

We discussed the `GetOpt` class back in Recipe 2.7. Here we use it to control the operation of an application program. As usual, since `main()` runs in a static context but our application main line does not, we could wind up passing a lot of information into the constructor. Because we have so many options, and it would be inconvenient to keep expanding the options list as we add new functionality to the program, we use a kind of `Collection` called a `BitSet` to pass all the true/false arguments: true to print line numbers, false to print filenames, etc. (Collections are covered in Chapter 7.) A `BitSet` is much like a `Vector` (see Recipe 7.3) but is specialized to store only boolean values, and is ideal for handling command-line arguments.

The program basically just reads lines, matches the pattern in them, and if a match is found (or not found, with –v), prints the line (and optionally some other stuff too). Having said all that, the code is shown in Example 4-3.

Example 4-3. Grep2.java

```
import org.apache.regexp.*;
import com.darwinsys.util.*;
import java.io.*;
import java.util.*;

/** A command-line grep-like program. Some options, and takes a pattern
 * and an arbitrary list of text files.
 */
public class Grep2 {
    /** The pattern we're looking for */
    protected RE pattern;
    /** The Reader for the current file */
    protected BufferedReader d;
    /** Are we to only count lines, instead of printing? */
    protected boolean countOnly = false;
    /** Are we to ignore case? */
    protected boolean ignoreCase = false;
    /** Are we to suppress print of filenames? */
    protected boolean dontPrintFileName = false;
    /** Are we to only list names of files that match? */
    protected boolean listOnly = false;
    /** are we to print line numbers? */
    protected boolean numbered = false;
    /** Are we to be silent bout errors? */
    protected boolean silent = false;
    /** are we to print only lines that DONT match? */
    protected boolean inVert = false;

    /** Construct a Grep object for each pattern, and run it
     * on all input files listed in argv.
     */
    public static void main(String[] argv) throws RESyntaxException {

        if (argv.length < 1) {
            System.err.println("Usage: Grep pattern [filename...]");
            System.exit(1);
        }
        String pattern = null;

        GetOpt go = new GetOpt("cf:hilnsv");
        BitSet args = new BitSet();
```

Example 4-3. Grep2.java (continued)

```java
        char c;
        while ((c = go.getopt(argv)) != 0) {
            switch(c) {
                case 'c':
                    args.set('C');
                    break;
                case 'f':
                    try {
                        BufferedReader b = new BufferedReader
                                (new FileReader(go.optarg()));
                        pattern = b.readLine();
                        b.close();
                    } catch (IOException e) {
                        System.err.println("Can't read pattern file " +
                                go.optarg());
                        System.exit(1);
                    }
                    break;
                case 'h':
                    args.set('H');
                    break;
                case 'i':
                    args.set('I');
                    break;
                case 'l':
                    args.set('L');
                    break;
                case 'n':
                    args.set('N');
                    break;
                case 's':
                    args.set('S');
                    break;
                case 'v':
                    args.set('V');
                    break;
            }
        }

        int ix = go.getOptInd();

        if (pattern == null)
            pattern = argv[ix-1];

        Grep2 pg = new Grep2(pattern, args);

        if (argv.length == ix)
            pg.process(new InputStreamReader(System.in), "(standard input)");
```

Example 4-3. Grep2.java (continued)

```java
            else
                for (int i=ix; i<argv.length; i++) {
                    try {
                        pg.process(new FileReader(argv[i]), argv[i]);
                    } catch(Exception e) {
                        System.err.println(e);
                    }
                }
        }

    public Grep2(String arg, BitSet args) throws RESyntaxException {
        // compile the regular expression
        if (args.get('C'))
            countOnly = true;
        if (args.get('H'))
            dontPrintFileName = true;
        if (args.get('I'))
            ignoreCase = true;
        if (args.get('L'))
            listOnly = true;
        if (args.get('N'))
            numbered = true;
        if (args.get('S'))
            silent = true;
        if (args.get('V'))
            inVert = true;
        int caseMode = ignoreCase?RE.MATCH_CASEINDEPENDENT:RE.MATCH_NORMAL;
        pattern = new RE(arg, caseMode);
    }

    /** Do the work of scanning one file
     * @parampattRERegular Expression object
     * @paramifileReaderReader object already open
     * @paramfileName StringName of the input file
     */
    public void process(Reader ifile, String fileName) {

        String line;
        int matches = 0;

        try {
            d = new BufferedReader(ifile);

            while ((line = d.readLine()) != null) {
                if (pattern.match(line)) {
                    if (countOnly)
                        matches++;
                    else {
```

Example 4-3. Grep2.java (continued)

```
                    if (!dontPrintFileName)
                        System.out.print(fileName + ": ");
                    System.out.println(line);
                    }
            } else if (inVert) {
                System.out.println(line);
                }
        }
        if (countOnly)
            System.out.println(matches + " matches in " + fileName);
        d.close();
    } catch (IOException e) { System.err.println(e); }
    }
}
```

5

Numbers

5.0. Introduction

Numbers are basic to just about any computation. They're used for array indexes, temperatures, salaries, ratings, and an infinite variety of things. Yet they're not as simple as they seem. With floating-point numbers, how accurate is accurate? With random numbers, how random is random? With strings that should contain a number, what actually constitutes a number?

Java has several built-in types that can be used to represent numbers, summarized in Table 5-1. Note that unlike languages like C or Perl, which don't specify the size or precision of numeric types, Java—with its goal of portability—specifies these exactly, and states that they are the same on all platforms.

Table 5-1. Numeric types

Built-in type	**Object wrapper**	**Size (bits)**	**Contents**
byte	Byte	8	Signed integer
short	Short	16	Signed integer
int	Integer	32	Signed integer
long	Long	64	Signed integer
float	Float	32	IEEE-754 floating point
double	Double	64	IEEE-754 floating point
char	Character	16	Unsigned Unicode character

As you can see, Java provides a numeric type for just about any purpose. There are four sizes of signed integers for representing various sizes of whole numbers. There are two sizes of floating-point numbers to approximate real numbers. There is also a type specifically designed to represent and allow operations on Unicode characters.

When you read a string from user input or a text file, you need to convert it to the appropriate type. The object wrapper classes in the second column have several functions, but one of the most important is to provide this basic conversion functionality—replacing the C programmer's *atoi/atof* family of functions and the numeric arguments to *scanf.*

Going the other way, you can convert any number (indeed, anything at all in Java) to a string just by using string concatenation. If you want a little bit of control over numeric formatting, Recipe 5.7 shows you how to use some of the object wrappers' conversion routines. And if you want full control, it also shows the use of `NumberFormat` and its related classes to provide full control of formatting.

As the name *object wrapper* implies, these classes are also used to "wrap" a number in a Java object, as many parts of the standard API are defined in terms of objects. Later on, Recipe 9.16 shows using an `Integer` object to save an `int`'s value to a file using *object serialization,* and retrieving the value later.

But I haven't yet mentioned the issues of floating point. Real numbers, you may recall, are numbers with a fractional part. There is an infinity of possible real numbers. A floating-point number—what a computer uses to approximate a real number—is not the same as a real number. There are only a finite number of floating-point numbers: only 2^{32} different bit patterns for `floats`, and 2^{64} for `doubles`. Thus, most real values only have an approximate correspondence to floating point. The result of printing the real number 0.3, as in:

```
// RealValues.java
System.out.println("The real value 0.3 is " + 0.3);
```

results in this printout:

```
The real value 0.3 is 0.29999999999999999
```

Surprised? More surprising is this: you'll get the same output on any conforming Java implementation. I ran it on machines as disparate as a Pentium with Open-BSD and Kaffe, a Pentium with Windows 95 and JDK 1.2, and a PowerPC Macintosh with MRJ. Always the same answer.

One thing to be aware of is that the difference between a real value and its floating-point approximation can accumulate if the value is used in a computation; this is often called *rounding error.* Continuing the previous example, the real 0.3 multiplied by 3 yields:

```
The real 0.3 times 3 is 0.89999999999999991
```

And what about random numbers? How random are they? You have probably heard the expression "pseudo-random numbers." All conventional random number generators, whether written in Fortran, C, or Java, generate pseudo-random numbers. That is, they're not truly random! True randomness can only come from specially built hardware: an analog source of Brownian noise connected to an analog-to-digital converter, for example.* This is not your average PC! However, pseudo-random number generators (PRNG for short) are good enough for most purposes, so we use them. Java provides one random generator in the base library java.lang.Math, and several others; we'll examine these in Recipe 5.12.

Java comes with a math library class java.lang.Math plus several other areas of mathematical functionality. The class java.lang.Math contains an entire "math library" in one class, including trigonometry, conversions of all kinds (including degrees to radians and back), rounding, truncating, square root, minimum, and maximum. It's all there. Check the Javadoc for java.lang.Math.

The package java.Math contains support for "big numbers"—those larger than the normal built-in long integers, for example. See Recipe 5.18.

Java works hard to ensure that your programs are reliable. The usual ways you'd notice this are in the common requirement to catch potential exceptions—all through the Java API—and in the need to "cast" or convert when storing a value that might or might not fit into the variable you're trying to store it in. I'll show examples of these.

Overall, Java's handling of numeric data fits well with the ideals of portability, reliability, and ease of programming.

See Also

The *Java Language Specification*. The Javadoc page for java.lang.Math.

5.1. Checking Whether a String Is a Valid Number

Problem

You need to check if a given string contains a valid number, and if so, convert it to binary (internal) form.

---

* For a low-cost source of randomness, check out *http://lavarand.sgi.com*. These folks use digitized video of 1970s "lava lamps" to provide "hardware-based" randomness. Fun!

Solution

Use the appropriate wrapper class's conversion routine and catch the
NumberFormatException. This code converts a string to a double:

```
// StringToDouble.java
public static void main(String argv[]) {
    String aNumber = argv[0];// not argv[1]
    double result;
    try {
        result = Double.parseDouble(aNumber);
    } catch(NumberFormatException exc) {
        System.out.println("Invalid number " + aNumber);
        return;
    }
    System.out.println("Number is " + result);
}
```

Discussion

Of course, that lets you validate only numbers in the format that the designers of
the wrapper classes expected. If you need to accept a different definition of
numbers, you could use regular expressions (see Chapter 4) to make the determi-
nation.

There may also be times when you want to tell if a given number is an integer
number or a floating-point number. One way is to check for the characters ., d, or
e in the input; if it is present, convert the number as a double, otherwise, convert
it as an int:

```
// GetNumber.java
System.out.println("Input is " + s);
if (s.indexOf('.') >0 ||
    s.indexOf('d') >0 || s.indexOf('e') >0)
    try {
        dvalue = Double.parseDouble(s);
        System.out.println("It's a double: " + dvalue);
        return;
    } catch (NumberFormatException e) {
        System.out.println("Invalid a double: " + s);
        return;
    }
else // did not contain . or d or e, so try as int.
    try {
        ivalue = Integer.parseInt(s);
        System.out.println("It's an int: " + ivalue);
        return;
    } catch (NumberFormatException e2) {
        System.out.println("Not a number:" + s);
    }
}
```

A more involved form of parsing is offered by the `DecimalFormat` class, discussed in Recipe 5.7.

5.2. Storing a Larger Number in a Smaller

Problem

You have a number of a larger type and you want to store it in a variable of a smaller type.

Solution

Cast the number to the smaller type. (A *cast* is a type listed in parentheses before a value that causes the value to be treated as though it were of the listed type.)

For example, to cast a `long` to an `int`, you need a cast. To cast a `double` to a `float`, you also need a cast.

Discussion

This causes newcomers some grief, as the default type for a number with a decimal point is `double`, not `float`. So code like:

```
float f = 3.0;
```

won't even compile! It's as if you had written:

```
double tmp = 3.0;
float f = tmp;
```

You can fix it either by making `f` be a `double`, by making the 3.0 be a `float`, by putting in a cast, or by assigning an integer value of 3:

```
double f = 3.0;
float f = 3.0f;
float f = 3f;
float f = (float)3.0;
float f = 3;
```

The same applies when storing an `int` into a `short`, `char`, or `byte`:

```
// CastNeeded.java
public static void main(String argv[]) {
    int i, k;
    double j = 2.75;
    i = j;          // EXPECT COMPILE ERROR
    i = (int)j;// with cast; i gets 2
    System.out.println("i =" + i);
    byte b;
```

```
    b = i;        // EXPECT COMPILE ERROR
    b = (byte)i;// with cast, i gets 2
    System.out.println("b =" + b);
}
```

The lines marked EXPECT COMPILE ERROR will not compile unless either commented out or changed to be correct. The lines marked "with cast" show the correct forms.

5.3. Taking a Fraction of an Integer Without Using Floating Point

Problem

You want to multiply an integer by a fraction without converting the fraction to a floating-point number.

Solution

Multiply the integer by the numerator and divide by the denominator.

This technique should be used only when efficiency is more important than clarity, as it tends to detract from the readability—and therefore the maintainability—of your code.

Discussion

Since integers and floating-point numbers are stored differently, it may sometimes be desirable and feasible, for efficiency purposes, to multiply an integer by a fractional value without converting the values to floating point and back, and without requiring a "cast":

```
/** Compute the value of 2/3 of 5 */
public class FractMult {
    public static void main(String u[]) {

        double d1 = 0.666 * 5;// fast but obscure and inaccurate: convert
        System.out.println(d1); // 2/3 to 0.666 in programmer's head

        double d2 = 2/3 * 5;// wrong answer - 2/3 == 0, 0*5.0 = 0.0
        System.out.println(d2);

        double d3 = 2d/3d * 5;// "normal"
        System.out.println(d3);

        double d4 = (2*5)/3d;// one step done as integers, almost same answer
        System.out.println(d4);
```

```
        int i5 = 2*5/3;// fast, approximate integer answer
        System.out.println(i5);
    }
}
```

Running it looks like this:

```
$ java  FractMult
3.33
0.0
3.333333333333333
3.3333333333333335
3
$
```

5.4. Ensuring the Accuracy of Floating-Point Numbers

Problem

You want to know if a floating-point computation generated a sensible result.

Solution

Compare with the INFINITY constants, and use `isNaN()` to check for "not a number."

Fixed-point operations that can do things like divide by zero will result in Java notifying you abruptly by throwing an exception. This is because integer division by zero is considered a *logic error*.

Floating-point operations, however, do not throw an exception, because they are defined over an (almost) infinite range of values. Instead, they signal errors by producing the constant POSITIVE_INFINITY if you divide a positive floating-point number by zero, the constant NEGATIVE_INFINITY if you divide a negative floating-point value by zero, and `NaN`, (Not a Number) if you otherwise generate an invalid result. Values for these three public constants are defined in both the `Float` and the `Double` wrapper classes. The value `NaN` has the unusual property that it is not equal to itself, that is, `NaN != NaN`. Thus, it would hardly make sense to compare a (possibly suspect) number against `NaN`, because the expression:

```
x == NaN
```

can therefore never be true. Instead, the methods `Float.isNaN(float)` and `Double.isNaN(double)` must be used:

```
// InfNan.java
public static void main(String argv[]) {
```

```
    double d = 123;
    double e = 0;
    if (d/e == Double.POSITIVE_INFINITY)
        System.out.println("Check for POSITIVE_INFINITY works");
    double s = Math.sqrt(-1);
    if (s == Double.NaN)
        System.out.println("Comparison with NaN incorrectly returns true");
    if (Double.isNaN(s))
        System.out.println("Double.isNaN() correctly returns true");
}
```

Note that this, by itself, is not sufficient to ensure that floating-point calculations have been done with adequate accuracy. For example, the following program demonstrates a contrived calculation, Heron's formula for the area of a triangle, both in float and in double. The double values are correct, but the floating-point value comes out as zero due to rounding errors. This is because, in Java, operations involving only float values are performed as 32-bit calculations. Related languages such as C automatically promote these to double during the computation, which can eliminate some loss of accuracy.

```
/** Compute the area of a triangle using Heron's Formula.
 * Code and values from Prof W. Kahan and Joseph D. Darcy.
 * See http://www.cs.berkeley.edu/~wkahan/JAVAhurt.pdf.
 * Derived from listing in Rick Grehan's Java Pro article (October 1999).
 * Simplified and reformatted by Ian Darwin.
 */
public class Heron {
    public static void main(String[] args) {
        // Sides for triangle in float
        float af, bf, cf;
        float sf, areaf;

        // Ditto in double
        double ad, bd, cd;
        double sd, aread;

        // Area of triangle in float
        af = 12345679.0f;
        bf = 12345678.0f;
        cf = 1.01233995f;

        sf = (af+bf+cf)/2.0f;
        areaf = (float)Math.sqrt(sf * (sf - af) * (sf - bf) * (sf - cf));
        System.out.println("Single precision: " + areaf);

        // Area of triangle in double
        ad = 12345679.0;
        bd = 12345678.0;
        cd = 1.01233995;
```

```
        sd = (ad+bd+cd)/2.0d;
        aread =         Math.sqrt(sd * (sd - ad) * (sd - bd) * (sd - cd));
        System.out.println("Double precision: " + aread);
    }
}
```

Let's run it. To ensure that the rounding is not an implementation artifact, I'll try
it both with Sun's JDK and with Kaffe:

```
$ java Heron
Single precision: 0.0
Double precision: 972730.0557076167
$ kaffe Heron
Single precision: 0.0
Double precision: 972730.05570761673
```

If in doubt, use double!

5.5. Comparing Floating-Point Numbers

Problem

You want to compare two floating-point numbers for equality.

Solution

Based on what we've just discussed, you probably won't just go comparing two floats
or doubles for equality. You might expect the floating-point wrapper classes, Float
and Double, to override the equals() method, and they do. The equals()
method returns true if the two values are the same bit for bit, that is, if and only if
the numbers are the same, or are both NaN. It returns false otherwise, including if
the argument passed in is null, or if one object is +0.0 and the other is –0.0.

If this sounds weird, remember that the complexity comes partly from the nature
of doing real number computations in the less-precise floating-point hardware,
and partly from the details of the IEEE Standard 754, which specifies the floating-
point functionality that Java tries to adhere to, so that underlying floating-point
processor hardware can be used even when Java programs are being interpreted.

To actually compare floating-point numbers for equality, it is generally desirable
to compare them within some tiny range of allowable differences; this range is
often regarded as a tolerance or as *epsilon*. Example 5-1 shows an equals()
method you can use to do this comparison, as well as comparisons on values of
NaN. When run, it prints that the first two numbers are equal within epsilon.

```
$ java FloatCmp
True within epsilon 1.0E-7
$
```

Example 5-1. FloatCmp.java

```java
/**
 * Floating-point comparisons.
 */
public class FloatCmp {
    public static void main(String[] argv) {
        double da = 3 * .3333333333;
        double db = 0.99999992857;

        // Compare two numbers that are expected to be close.
        final double EPSILON = 0.0000001;
        if (da == db) {
            System.out.println("Java considers " + da + "==" + db);
        } else if (equals(da, db, 0.0000001)) {
            System.out.println("True within epsilon " + EPSILON);
        } else {
            System.out.println(da + " != " + db);
        }

        double d1 = Double.NaN;
        double d2 = Double.NaN;
        if (d1 == d2)
            System.err.println("Comparing two NaNs incorrectly returns true.");
        if (!new Double(d1).equals(new Double(d2)))
            System.err.println("Double(NaN).equal(NaN) incorrectly returns false.");
    }

    /** Compare two doubles within a given epsilon */
    public static boolean equals(double a, double b, double eps) {
        // If the difference is less than epsilon, treat as equal.
        return Math.abs(a - b) < eps;
    }
}
```

Note that neither of the `System.err` messages about "incorrect returns" prints. The point of this example with NaNs is that you should always make sure values are not NaN before entrusting them to `Double.equals()`.

5.6. *Rounding Floating-Point Numbers*

Problem

You need to round floating-point numbers to integer or to a particular precision.

Solution

If you simply cast a floating value to an integer value, Java will truncate the value. A value like 3.999999 casted to an `int` or `long` will give 3, not 4. To round these properly, use `Math.round()`. There are two forms; if you give it a `double`, you get a `long` result. If you give it a `float`, you get an `int`.

What if you don't like the rounding rules used by `round`? If you wanted to round numbers greater than 0.54 instead of the normal 0.5, you could write your own version of `round()`:

```
// Round.java
/** Round a number up if its fraction exceeds this threshold. */
public static final double THRESHOLD = 0.54;
/* Return the closest long to the argument.
 * ERROR CHECKING OMITTED.
 */
static long round(double d) {
    long di = (long)Math.floor(d);// integral value below (or ==) d
    if ((d - di) > THRESHOLD)
        return di + 1;
    else return di;
}
```

If you need to display a number with less precision than it normally gets, you will probably want to use a `DecimalFormat` object.

5.7. Formatting Numbers

Problem

You need to format numbers.

Solution

Use a `NumberFormat` subclass.

There are several reasons why Java doesn't provide the traditional *printf/scanf* functions from the C programming language. First, these depend on variable-length argument lists, which makes strict type checking impossible. Second and more importantly, they mix together formatting and input/output in a very inflexible way. Programs using *printf/scanf* can be very hard to internationalize, for example.

JDK 1.1 introduced a new package, `java.text`, which is full of formatting routines as general and flexible as anything you might imagine. As with *printf*, there is

an involved formatting language, described in the Javadoc page. Consider the presentation of long numbers. In North America, the number one thousand twenty-
four and a quarter is written 1,024.25, in most of Europe it is 1 024.25, and in
some other part of the world it might be written 1.024,25. Not to mention how
currencies and percentages get formatted! Trying to keep track of this yourself
would drive the average small software shop around the bend rather quickly.

Fortunately, the `java.text` package includes a `Locale` class, and, furthermore,
the Java runtime automatically sets a default `Locale` object based on the user's
environment; e.g., on the Macintosh and MS-Windows, the user's preferences; on
Unix, the user's environment variables. (To provide a non-default locale, see
Recipe 14.8.) To provide formatters customized for numbers, currencies, and percentages, the `NumberFormat` class has static *factory methods* that normally return a
`DecimalFormat` with the correct pattern already instantiated. A `DecimalFormat`
object appropriate to the user's locale can be obtained from the factory method
`NumberFormat.getInstance()` and manipulated using set methods. The
method `setMinimumIntegerDigits()`, a bit surprisingly, turns out to be the easy
way to generate a number format with leading zeros. Here is an example:

```
import java.text.*;
import java.util.*;

/*
 * Format a number our way and the default way.
 */
public class NumFormat2 {
    /** A number to format */
    public static final double data[] = {
        0, 1, 22d/7, 100.2345678
    };

    /** The main (and only) method in this class. */
    public static void main(String av[]) {
        // Get a format instance
        NumberFormat form = NumberFormat.getInstance();

        // Set it to look like 999.99[99]
        form.setMinimumIntegerDigits(3);
        form.setMinimumFractionDigits(2);
        form.setMaximumFractionDigits(4);

        // Now print using it.
        for (int i=0; i<data.length; i++)
            System.out.println(data[i] + "\tformats as " +
                form.format(data[i]));
    }
}
```

This prints the contents of the array using the `NumberFormat` instance form:

```
$ java NumFormat2
0.0      formats as 000.00
1.0      formats as 001.00
3.142857142857143        formats as 003.1429
100.2345678      formats as 100.2346
$
```

You can also construct a `DecimalFormat` with a particular pattern, or change the pattern dynamically using `applyPattern()`. The pattern characters are shown in Table 5-2.

Table 5-2. DecimalFormat pattern characters

Character	Meaning
#	Numeric digit (leading zeros suppressed)
0	Numeric digit (leading zeros provided)
.	Locale-specific decimal separator (decimal point)
,	Locale-specific grouping separator (comma in English)
–	Locale-specific negative indicator (minus sign)
%	Shows the value as a percentage
;	Separates two formats: the first for positive and the second for negative values
'	Escapes one of the above characters so it appears
Anything else	Appears as itself

The `NumFormatTest` program uses one `DecimalFormat` to print a number with only two decimal places, and a second to format the number according to the default locale:

```
// NumFormatTest.java
/** A number to format */
public static final double intlNumber = 1024.25;
/** Another number to format */
public static final double ourNumber = 100.2345678;
NumberFormat defForm = NumberFormat.getInstance();
NumberFormat ourForm = new DecimalFormat("##0.##");
// toPattern() shows the combination of #0., etc
// that this particular local uses to format with
System.out.println("defForm's pattern is " +
    ((DecimalFormat)defForm).toPattern());
System.out.println(intlNumber + " formats as " +
    defForm.format(intlNumber));
System.out.println(ourNumber + " formats as " +
    ourForm.format(ourNumber));
System.out.println(ourNumber + " formats as " +
    defForm.format(ourNumber) + " using the default format");
```

This program prints the given pattern and then formats the same number using several formats:

```
$ java NumFormatTest
defForm's pattern is #,##0.###
1024.25 formats as 1,024.25
100.2345678 formats as 100.23
100.2345678 formats as 100.235 using the default format
$
```

See Also

O'Reilly's *Java I/O*, Chapter 16.

5.8. Converting Between Binary, Octal, Decimal, and Hexadecimal

Problem

You want to display an integer as a series of bits, for example when interacting with certain hardware devices. You want to convert a binary number or a hexadecimal value into an integer.

Solution

The class `java.lang.Integer` provides the solutions. Use `toBinaryString()` to convert an integer to binary. Use `valueOf()` to convert a binary string to an integer:

```
// BinaryDigits.java
String bin = "101010";
System.out.println(bin + " as an integer is " + Integer.valueOf(bin, 2));
int i = 42;
System.out.println(i + " as binary digits (bits) is " +
    Integer.toBinaryString(i));
```

This program prints the binary as an integer, and an integer as binary:

```
$ java BinaryDigits
101010 as an integer is 42
42 as binary digits (bits) is 101010
$
```

Discussion

`Integer.valueOf()` is more general than binary formatting. It will also convert a string number from any radix to `int`, just by changing the second argument. Octal is base 8, decimal is 10, hexadecimal 16. Going the other way, the `Integer` class includes `toBinaryString()`, `toOctalString()`, and `toHexString()`.

The `String` class itself includes a series of static methods, `valueOf(int)`, `valueOf(double)`, and so on, that also provide default formatting. That is, they return the given numeric value formatted as a string.

5.9. Operating on a Series of Integers

Problem

You need to work on a range of integers.

Solution

For a contiguous set, use a `for` loop.

Discussion

To process a contiguous set of integers, Java provides a `for` loop. Loop control for the `for` loop is in three parts: initialize, test, and change. If the test part is initially false, the loop will never be executed, not even once.

For discontinuous ranges of numbers, use a `java.util.BitSet`.

The following program demonstrates all of these techniques:

```java
import java.util.BitSet;

/** Operations on series of numbers */
public class NumSeries {
    public static void main(String[] args) {

        // When you want an ordinal list of numbers, use a for loop
        // starting at 1.
        for (int i = 1; i <= 12; i++)
            System.out.println("Month # " + i);

        // When you want a set of array indexes, use a for loop
        // starting at 0.
        for (int i = 0; i < 12; i++)
            System.out.println("Month " + months[i]);

        // For a discontiguous set of integers, try a BitSet

        // Create a BitSet and turn on a couple of bits.
        BitSet b = new BitSet();
```

```
        b.set(0);// January
        b.set(3);// April

        // Presumably this would be somewhere else in the code.
        for (int i = 0; i<12; i++) {
            if (b.get(i))
                System.out.println("Month " + months[i] + " requested");
        }
    }
    /** The names of the months. See Dates/Times chapter for a better way */
    protected static String months[] = {
        "January", "February", "March", "April",
        "May", "June", "July", "August",
        "September", "October", "November", "December"
    };
}
```

5.10. Working with Roman Numerals

Problem

You need to format numbers as Roman numerals. Perhaps you've just written the next *Titanic* or *Star Wars* episode and you need to get the copyright date correct. Or, on a more mundane level, you need to format page numbers in the front matter of a book.

Solution

Use my `RomanNumberFormat` class:

```
// RomanNumberSimple.java
RomanNumberFormat nf = new RomanNumberFormat();
int year = Calendar.getInstance().get(Calendar.YEAR);
System.out.println(year + " -> " + nf.format(year));
```

The use of `Calendar` to get the current year is explained in Recipe 6.1. Running `RomanNumberSimple` looks like this:

```
+ jikes +E -d . RomanNumberSimple.java
+ java RomanNumberSimple
2000 -> MM
```

Discussion

There is nothing in the standard API to format Roman numerals. However, the `java.text.Format` class is designed to be subclassed for precisely such unanticipated purposes, so I have done just that and developed a class to format numbers as Roman numerals. Here is a better and complete example program of using it to format the current year. I can pass a number of arguments on the command line, including a "-" where I want the year to appear (note that these arguments are normally not quoted; the "-" must be an argument all by itself, just to keep the program simple). I use it as follows:

```
$ java RomanYear   Copyright (c) - Ian Darwin
Copyright (c) MMI Ian Darwin
$
```

The code for the RomanYear program is simple, yet it correctly gets spaces around the arguments.

```java
import java.util.*;

/** Print the current year in Roman Numerals */
public class RomanYear {

    public static void main(String[] argv) {

        RomanNumberFormat rf = new RomanNumberFormat();
        Calendar cal = Calendar.getInstance();
        int year = cal.get(Calendar.YEAR);

        // If no arguments, just print the year.
        if (argv.length == 0) {
            System.out.println(rf.format(year));
            return;
        }

        // Else a micro-formatter: replace "-" arg with year, else print.
        for (int i=0; i<argv.length; i++) {
            if (argv[i].equals("-"))
                System.out.print(rf.format(year));
            else
                System.out.print(argv[i]);// e.g., "Copyright"
            System.out.print(' ');
        }
        System.out.println();
    }
}
```

Now here's the code for the RomanNumberFormat class. I did sneak in one additional class, java.text.FieldPosition. A FieldPosition simply represents the position of one numeric field in a string that has been formatted using a variant of NumberFormat.format(). You construct it to represent either the integer part or the fraction part; though of course, Roman numerals don't have fractional parts. The FieldPosition methods getBeginIndex() and getEndIndex() indicate where in the resulting string the given field wound up.

Example 5-2 is the class that implements Roman number formatting. As the comments indicate, the one limitation is that the input number must be less than 4,000.

Example 5-2. RomanNumberFormat.java

```java
import java.text.*;
import java.util.*;

/**
 * Roman Number class. Not localized, since Latin's a Dead Dead Language
 * and we don't display Roman Numbers differently in different Locales.
 * Filled with quick-n-dirty algorithms.
 */
public class RomanNumberFormat extends Format {

    /** Characters used in "Arabic to Roman", that is, format() methods. */
    static char A2R[][] = {
            { 0, 'M' },
            { 0, 'C', 'D', 'M' },
            { 0, 'X', 'L', 'C' },
            { 0, 'I', 'V', 'X' },
    };

    /** Format a given double as a Roman Numeral; just truncate to a
     * long, and call format(long).
     */
    public String format(double n) {
        return format((long)n);
    }

    /** Format a given long as a Roman Numeral. Just call the
     * three-argument form.
     */
    public String format(long n) {
        if (n < 0 || n >= 4000)
            throw new IllegalArgumentException(n + " must be >= 0 && < 4000");
        StringBuffer sb = new StringBuffer();
        format(new Integer((int)n), sb, new FieldPosition(NumberFormat.INTEGER
                FIELD));
        return sb.toString();
    }

    /* Format the given Number as a Roman Numeral, returning the
     * Stringbuffer (updated), and updating the FieldPosition.
     * This method is the REAL FORMATTING ENGINE.
     * Method signature is overkill, but required as a subclass of Format.
     */
    public StringBuffer format(Object on, StringBuffer sb, FieldPosition fp) {
```

Example 5-2. RomanNumberFormat.java (continued)

```
    if (!(on instanceof Number))
        throw new IllegalArgumentException(on + " must be a Number object");
    if (fp.getField() != NumberFormat.INTEGER_FIELD)
        throw new IllegalArgumentException(fp +
                        " must be FieldPosition(NumberFormat.INTEGER_FIELD");
    int n = ((Number)on).intValue();

    // First, put the digits on a tiny stack. Must be 4 digits.
    for (int i=0; i<4; i++) {
        int d=n%10;
        push(d);
        // System.out.println("Pushed " + d);
        n=n/10;
    }

    // Now pop and convert.
    for (int i=0; i<4; i++) {
        int ch = pop();
        // System.out.println("Popped " + ch);
        if (ch==0)
            continue;
        else if (ch <= 3) {
            for(int k=1; k<=ch; k++)
                sb.append(A2R[i][1]); // I
        }
        else if (ch == 4) {
            sb.append(A2R[i][1]);// I
            sb.append(A2R[i][2]);// V
        }
        else if (ch == 5) {
            sb.append(A2R[i][2]);// V
        }
        else if (ch <= 8) {
            sb.append(A2R[i][2]);// V
            for (int k=6; k<=ch; k++)
                sb.append(A2R[i][1]);// I
        }
        else { // 9
            sb.append(A2R[i][1]);
            sb.append(A2R[i][3]);
        }
    }
    // fp.setBeginIndex(0);
    // fp.setEndIndex(3);
    return sb;
}
```

Example 5-2. RomanNumberFormat.java (continued)

```
/** Parse a generic object, returning an Object */
public Object parseObject(String what, ParsePosition where) {
    throw new IllegalArgumentException("Parsing not implemented");
    // TODO PARSING HERE
    // if (!(what instanceof String)
    //   throw new IllegalArgumentException(what + " must be String");
    // return new Long(0);
}

/* Implement a toy stack */
protected int stack[] = new int[10];
protected int depth = 0;

/* Implement a toy stack */
protected void push(int n) {
    stack[depth++] = n;
}
/* Implement a toy stack */
protected int pop() {
    return stack[--depth];
}
}
```

Several of the public methods are required because I wanted it to be a subclass of `Format`, which is abstract. This accounts for some of the complexity, like having three different format methods.

Note that the `parseObject()` method is also required, but we don't actually implement parsing in this version. This is left as the usual exercise for the reader.

See Also

The O'Reilly book *Java I/O* has an entire chapter on `NumberFormat`, and develops an `ExponentialNumberFormat` subclass.

The online source has `ScaledNumberFormat`, which prints numbers with a maximum of four digits and a computerish scale factor (B for bytes, K for kilo-, M for mega-, and so on).

5.11. Formatting with Correct Plurals

Problem

You're printing something like `"We used" + n + " items"`, but in English, "We used 1 items" is ungrammatical. You want "We used 1 item".

Solution

Use a `ChoiceFormat` or a conditional statement.

Use Java's ternary operator (cond ? `trueval` : `falseval`) in a string concatenation. Both zero and plurals get an "s" appended to the noun in English ("no books, one book, two books"), so we only need to test for n==1.

```
// FormatPlurals.java
public static void main(String argv[]) {
    report(0);
    report(1);
    report(2);
}
/** report -- using conditional operator */
public static void report(int n) {
    System.out.println("We used " + n + " item" + (n==1?"":"s"));
}
```

Does it work?

```
$ java FormatPlurals
We used 0 items
We used 1 item
We used 2 items
$
```

The final `println` statement is short for:

```
if (n==1)
    System.out.println("We used " + n + " item");
else
    System.out.println("We used " + n + " items");
```

This is a lot shorter, in fact, so the ternary conditional operator is worth learning.

In JDK 1.1 or later, the `ChoiceFormat` is ideal for this. It is actually capable of much more, but here I'll show only this simplest use. I specify the values 0, 1, and 2 (or more), and the string values to print corresponding to each number. The numbers are then formatted according to the range they fall into:

```
import java.text.*;
/**
 * Format a plural correctly, using a ChoiceFormat.
 */
public class FormatPluralsChoice extends FormatPlurals {
        static double[] limits = { 0, 1, 2 };
        static String[] formats = { "items", "item", "items"};
        static ChoiceFormat myFormat = new ChoiceFormat(limits, formats);
```

```
public static void main(String[] argv) {
    report(0);        // inherited method
    report(1);
    report(2);
}
}
```

This generates the same output as the basic version.

5.12. Generating Random Numbers

Problem

You need to generate random numbers in a hurry.

Solution

Use `java.lang.Math.random()` to generate random numbers. There is no claim that the random values it returns are very *good* random numbers, however. This code exercises the `random()` method:

```
// Random1.java
// java.lang.Math.random() is static, don't need to construct Math
System.out.println("A random from java.lang.Math is " + Math.random());
```

Note that this method only generates double values. If you need integers, you need to scale and round:

```
/** Generate random ints by scaling from Math.random().
 * Prints a series of 100 random integers from 1 to 10, inclusive.
 */
public class RandomInt {
    public static void main(String[] a) {
        for (int i=0; i<100; i++)
            System.out.println(1+(int)(Math.random() * 10));
    }
}
```

See Also

Recipe 5.13 is an easier way to get random integers. Also see the Javadoc documentation for `java.lang.Math`, and the warning in this chapter's Introduction about pseudo-randomness versus real randomness.

5.13. Generating Better Random Numbers

Problem

You need to generate better random numbers.

Solution

Construct a `java.util.Random` object (not just any old random object) and call its
next*() methods. These methods include `nextBoolean()`, `nextBytes()` (which
fills the given array of bytes with random values), `nextDouble()`, `nextFloat()`,
`nextInt()`, `nextLong()`. Don't be confused by the capitalization of Float,
Double, etc. They return the primitive types `boolean`, `float`, `double`, etc., not the
capitalized wrapper objects. Clear enough? Maybe an example will help:

```
// Random2.java
// java.util.Random methods are non-static, do need to construct Math
Random r = new Random();
for (int i=0; i<10; i++)
    System.out.println("A double from java.util.Random is " + r.nextDouble());
for (int i=0; i<10; i++)
    System.out.println("An integer from java.util.Random is " + r.nextInt());
```

You can also use the `java.util.Random` `nextGaussian()` method, as shown
next. The `nextDouble()` methods try to give a "flat" distribution between 0 and
1.0 in which each value has an equal chance of being selected. A Gaussian or normal distribution is a bell-curve of values from negative infinity to positive infinity,
with the majority of the values around zero (0.0).

```
// Random3.java
Random r = new Random();
for (int i=0; i<10; i++)
    System.out.println("A gaussian random double is " + r.nextGaussian());
```

To illustrate the different distributions, I generated 10,000 numbers first using
`nextRandom()` and then using `nextGaussian()`. The code for this is in
Random4.java (not shown here) and is a combination of the previous programs
with code to print the results into files. I then plotted histograms using the R statis-
tics package (see *http://www.r-project.org*). The results are shown in Figure 5-1.

See Also

The Javadoc documentation for `java.util.Random`, and the warning in the
Introduction about pseudo-randomness versus real randomness.

For cryptographic use, see class `java.security.SecureRandom`, which provides
cryptographically strong pseudo-random number generators (PRNG).

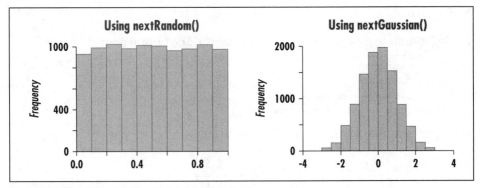

Figure 5-1. Flat (left) and Gaussian (right) distributions

5.14. Calculating Trigonometric Functions

Problem

You need to compute sine, cosine, and other trigonometric functions.

Solution

Use the trig functions in `java.lang.Math`. Like `java.lang.Math.random()`, all the methods of the `Math` class are static, so no `Math` instance is necessary. This makes sense, as none of these computations maintains any state. Here is a program that computes a few trigonometric values and displays the values of `E` and `PI` that are available in the math library:

```
// Trig.java
System.out.println("Java's PI is " + Math.PI);
System.out.println("Java's e is " + Math.E);
System.out.println("The cosine of 1.1418 is " + Math.cos(1.1418));
```

Java 1.3 (Java 2 JDK 1.3) includes a new class, `java.lang.StrictMath`, which is intended to perform most of the same operations with greater cross-platform repeatability.

5.15. Taking Logarithms

Problem

You need to take the logarithm of a number.

Solution

For logarithms to base e, use `java.lang.Math`'s `log()` function:

```
// Logarithm.java
double someValue;
// compute someValue...
double log_e = Math.log(someValue);
```

For logarithms to other bases, use the identity that:

$$\log_n(x) = \frac{\log_e(x)}{\log_e(n)}$$

where x is the number whose logarithm you want, n is any desired base, and e is the natural logarithm base. I have a simple `LogBase` class containing code that implements this functionality:

```
// LogBase.java
public static double log_base(double base, double value) {
    return Math.log(value) / Math.log(base);
}
```

Discussion

My `log_base` function allows you to compute logs to any positive base. If you have to perform a lot of logs to the same base, it is more efficient to rewrite the code to cache the `log(base)` once. Here is an example of using `log_base`:

```
// LogBaseUse.java
public static void main(String argv[]) {
    double d = LogBase.log_base(10, 10000);
    System.out.println("log10(10000) = " + d);
}
log10(10000) = 4.0
```

5.16. Multiplying Matrixes

Problem

You need to multiply a pair of two-dimensional arrays, as is common in mathematical and engineering applications.

Solution

Use the following code as a model.

Discussion

It is straightforward to multiply an array of a numeric type. The code in
Example 5-3 implements matrix multiplication.

Example 5-3. Matrix.java

```java
/**
 * Multiply two matrices.
 * Only defined for int: clone the code (or wait for Templates)
 * for long, float, and double.
 */
public class Matrix {

    /* Matrix-multiply two arrays together.
     * The arrays MUST be rectangular.
     * @author Tom Christiansen & Nathan Torkington, Perl Cookbook version.
     */
    public static int[][] multiply(int[][] m1, int[][] m2) {
        int m1rows = m1.length;
        int m1cols = m1[0].length;
        int m2rows = m2.length;
        int m2cols = m2[0].length;
        if (m1cols != m2rows)
            throw new IllegalArgumentException(
                "matrices don't match: " + m1cols + " != " + m2rows);
        int[][] result = new int[m1rows][m2cols];

        // multiply
        for (int i=0; i<m1rows; i++)
            for (int j=0; j<m2cols; j++)
                for (int k=0; k<m1cols; k++)
                result[i][j] += m1[i][k] * m2[k][j];

        return result;
    }

    public static void mprint(int[][] a) {
        int rows = a.length;
        int cols = a[0].length;
        System.out.println("array["+rows+"]["+cols+"] = {");
        for (int i=0; i<rows; i++) {
            System.out.print("{");
            for (int j=0; j<cols; j++)
                System.out.print(" " + a[i][j] + ",");
            System.out.println("},");
        }
        System.out.println(":;");
    }
}
```

Here is a program that uses the `Matrix` class to multiply two arrays of `int`s:

```
// MatrixUse.java
int x[][] = {
    { 3, 2, 3 },
    { 5, 9, 8 },
};
int y[][] = {
    { 4, 7 },
    { 9, 3 },
    { 8, 1 },
};
int z[][] = Matrix.multiply(x, y);
Matrix.mprint(x);
Matrix.mprint(y);
Matrix.mprint(z);
```

See Also

Consult a book on numerical methods for more things to do with matrixes. There are commercial libraries that will do this for you, such as the Visual Numerics *vni* library, which can be downloaded from *http://www.vni.com*.

5.17. Using Complex Numbers

Problem

You need to manipulate complex numbers, as is common in mathematical, scientific, or engineering applications.

Solution

Java does not provide any explicit support for dealing with complex numbers. You could keep track of the real and imaginary parts and do the computations yourself, but that is not a very well-structured solution.

A better solution, of course, is to use a class that implements complex numbers. I provide just such a class. First, an example of using it:

```
// ComplexDemo.java
Complex c = new Complex(3,  5);
Complex d = new Complex(2, -2);
System.out.println(c + ".getReal() = " + c.getReal());
System.out.println(c + " + " + d + " = " + c.add(d));
System.out.println(c + " + " + d + " = " + Complex.add(c, d));
System.out.println(c + " * " + d + " = " + c.multiply(d));
```

Example 5-4 is the complete source for the `Complex` class, and shouldn't require much explanation. To keep the API general, I provide—for each of add, subtract, and multiply—both a static method that works on two complex objects, and a non-static method that applies the operation to the given object and one other object.

Example 5-4. Complex.java

```java
/** A class to represent Complex Numbers. A Complex object is
 * immutable once created; the add, subtract and multiply routines
 * return newly-created Complex objects containing the results.
 *
 */
public class Complex {
    /** The real part */
    private double r;
    /** The imaginary part */
    private double i;
    /** Construct a Complex */
    Complex(double rr, double ii) {
        r = rr;
        i = ii;
    }
    /** Display the current Complex as a String, for use in
     * println() and elsewhere.
     */
    public String toString() {
        StringBuffer sb = new StringBuffer().append(r);
        if (i>0)
            sb.append('+');// else append(i) appends - sign
        return sb.append(i).append('i').toString();
    }
    /** Return just the Real part */
    public double getReal() {
        return r;
    }
    /** Return just the Real part */
    public double getImaginary() {
        return i;
    }
    /** Return the magnitude of a complex number */
    public double magnitude() {
        return Math.sqrt(r*r + i*i);
    }

    /** Add another Complex to this one */
    public Complex add(Complex other) {
        return add(this, other);
    }
    /** Add two Complexes */
    public static Complex add(Complex c1, Complex c2) {
```

Example 5-4. Complex.java (continued)

```
        return new Complex(c1.r+c2.r, c1.i+c2.i);
    }

    /** Subtract another Complex from this one */
    public Complex subtract(Complex other) {
        return subtract(this, other);
    }
    /** Subtract two Complexes */
    public static Complex subtract(Complex c1, Complex c2) {
        return new Complex(c1.r-c2.r, c1.i-c2.i);
    }


    /** Multiply this Complex times another one */
    public Complex multiply(Complex other) {
        return multiply(this, other);
    }
    /** Multiply two Complexes */
    public static Complex multiply(Complex c1, Complex c2) {
        return new Complex(c1.r*c2.r - c1.i*c2.i, c1.r*c2.i + c1.i*c2.r);
    }
}
```

5.18. Handling Very Large Numbers

Problem

You need to handle integer numbers larger than `Long.MAX_VALUE` or floating-point values larger than `Double.MAX_VALUE`.

Solution

Use the `BigInteger` or `BigDecimal` values in package `java.math`:

```
// BigNums.java
System.out.println("Here's Long.MAX_VALUE: " + Long.MAX_VALUE);
BigInteger bInt = new BigInteger("3419229223372036854775807");
System.out.println("Here's a bigger number: " + bInt);
System.out.println("Here it is as a double: " + bInt.doubleValue());
```

Note that the constructor takes the number as a string. Obviously you couldn't just type the numeric digits, since by definition these classes are designed to represent numbers larger than will fit in a Java `long`.

Discussion

Both `BigInteger` and `BigDecimal` objects are immutable; that is, once constructed, they always represent a given number. That said, there are a number of

methods that return new objects that are mutations of the original, such as
negate(), which returns the negative of the given BigInteger or BigDecimal.
There are also methods corresponding to most of the Java language built-in operators defined on the base types int/long and float/double. The division
method makes you specify the rounding method; consult a book on numerical
analysis for details. Here is a simple stack-based calculator using BigDecimal as its
numeric data type:

```java
import java.math.BigDecimal;
import java.util.Stack;

/** A trivial reverse-polish stack-based calculator for big numbers */
public class BigNumCalc {

    /** an array of Objects, simulating user input */
    public static Object[] input = {
        new BigDecimal("34192292233720368854775807.23343"),
        new BigDecimal("2.0"),
        "*",
        "=",
    };

    public static void main(String[] args) {
        Stack s = new Stack();
        for (int i = 0; i < input.length; i++) {
            Object o = input[i];
            if (o instanceof BigDecimal)
                s.push(o);
            else if (o instanceof String) {
                switch (((String)o).charAt(0)) {
                case '+':
                    s.push(((BigDecimal)s.pop()).add((BigDecimal)s.pop()));
                    break;
                case '-':
                    s.push(((BigDecimal)s.pop()).subtract((BigDecimal)s.pop()));
                    break;
                case '*':
                    s.push(((BigDecimal)s.pop()).multiply((BigDecimal)s.pop()));
                    break;
                case '/':
                    s.push(((BigDecimal)s.pop()).divide((BigDecimal)s.pop(),
                        BigDecimal.ROUND_UP));
                    break;
                case '=':
                    System.out.println(s.pop());
                    break;
                default:
                    throw new IllegalStateException("Unknown OPERATOR popped");
                }
            } else {
```

```
                    throw new IllegalStateException("Syntax error in input");
            }
        }
    }
}
```

Running this produces the expected (very large) value:

```
> jikes +E -d . BigNumCalc.java
> java BigNumCalc
6838458446744073709551614.466860
>
```

The current version has its inputs hardcoded, but in real life you can use regular expressions to extract words or operators from an input stream (as in Recipe 4.7) or use the StreamTokenizer approach of the simple calculator (Recipe 9.12). The stack of numbers is maintained using a java.util.Stack (Recipe 7.15).

BigInteger is mainly useful in cryptographic and security applications. Its method isProbablyPrime() can create prime pairs for public key cryptography. BigDecimal might also be useful in computing the size of the universe.

5.19. Program: TempConverter

The program shown in Example 5-5 prints a table of Fahrenheit temperatures (still used in daily life weather reporting in the United States) and the corresponding Celsius temperatures (used in science everywhere, and in daily life in most of the world).

Example 5-5. TempConverter.java

```
import java.text.*;

/* Print a table of fahrenheit and celsius temperatures
 */
public class TempConverter {

    public static void main(String[] args) {
        TempConverter t = new TempConverter();
        t.start();
        t.data();
        t.end();
    }

    protected void start() {
    }

    protected void data() {
        for (int i=-40; i<=120; i+=10) {
            float c = (i-32)*(5f/9);
            print(i, c);
```

Example 5-5. TempConverter.java (continued)

```
        }
    }

    protected void print(float f, float c) {
        System.out.println(f + " " + c);
    }

    protected void end() {
    }
}
```

This works, but these numbers print with about 15 digits of (useless) decimal fractions! The second version of this program subclasses the first and uses a `DecimalFormat` to control the formatting of the converted temperatures (Example 5-6).

Example 5-6. TempConverter2.java

```
import java.text.*;

/* Print a table of fahrenheit and celsius temperatures, a bit more neatly.
 */
public class TempConverter2 extends TempConverter {
    protected DecimalFormat df;

    public static void main(String[] args) {
        TempConverter t = new TempConverter2();
        t.start();
        t.data();
        t.end();
    }

    // Constructor
    public TempConverter2() {
        df = new DecimalFormat("##.###");
    }

    protected void print(float f, float c) {
        System.out.println(f + " " + df.format(c));
    }

    protected void start() {
        System.out.println("Fahr    Centigrade.");
    }

    protected void end() {
        System.out.println("-------------------");
    }
}
```

This works, and the results are better than the first version's, but still not right:

```
C:\javasrc\numbers>java  TempConverter2
Fahr    Centigrade.
-40.0 -40
-30.0 -34.444
-20.0 -28.889
-10.0 -23.333
0.0 -17.778
10.0 -12.222
20.0 -6.667
30.0 -1.111
40.0 4.444
50.0 10
```

It would look neater if we lined up the decimal points, but Java has nothing in its standard API for doing this. This is deliberate! They wanted to utterly break the ties with the ancient IBM 1403 line printers and similar monospaced devices such as typewriters, "dumb" terminals,* and DOS terminal windows. However, with a bit of simple arithmetic, the FieldPosition from Recipe 5.10 can be used to figure out how many spaces need to be prepended to line up the columns; the arithmetic is done in print(), and the spaces are put on in prependSpaces(). The result is much prettier:

```
C:\javasrc\numbers>java  TempConverter3
Fahr    Centigrade.
 -40    -40
 -30    -34.444
 -20    -28.889
 -10    -23.333
   0    -17.778
  10    -12.222
  20     -6.667
  30     -1.111
  40      4.444
  50    10
  60    15.556
  70    21.111
  80    26.667
  90    32.222
 100    37.778
 110    43.333
 120    48.889
-------------------
```

---

* My children are quick to remind me that "dumb" means "incapable of speech." Nobody who has used, say, a TTY33 or a DecWriter 100 dumb terminal will claim that they are incapable of speech. Intelligible speech yes, but they certainly did talk at you while they were printing . . .

And the code (Example 5-7) is only ten lines longer!

Example 5-7. TempConverter3.java

```java
import java.text.*;

/* Print a table of fahrenheit and celsius temperatures, with decimal
 * points lined up.
 */
public class TempConverter3 extends TempConverter2 {
    protected FieldPosition fp;
    protected DecimalFormat dff;

    public static void main(String[] args) {
        TempConverter t = new TempConverter3();
        t.start();
        t.data();
        t.end();
    }

    // Constructor
    public TempConverter3() {
        super();
        dff = new DecimalFormat("##.#");
        fp = new FieldPosition(NumberFormat.INTEGER_FIELD);
    }

    protected void print(float f, float c) {
        String fs = dff.format(f, new StringBuffer(), fp).toString();
        fs = prependSpaces(4 - fp.getEndIndex(), fs);

        String cs = df.format(c, new StringBuffer(), fp).toString();
        cs = prependSpaces(4 - fp.getEndIndex(), cs);

        System.out.println(fs + "   " + cs);
    }

    protected String prependSpaces(int n, String s) {
        String[] res = {
            "", " ", "  ", "   ", "    ", "     "
        };
        if (n<res.length)
            return res[n] + s;
        throw new IllegalStateException("Rebuild with bigger \"res\" array.");
    }
}
```

Remember, though, that the fields will line up only if you use a fixed-width font, such as Courier or LucidaSansTypewriter. If you want to line it up in a graphical display, you'll need to use Java's font capability (see Recipe 12.5) or use a JTable (see the Javadoc for javax.swing.JTable or the O'Reilly book *Java Swing*).

5.20. Program: Number Palindromes

My wife, Betty, recently reminded me of a theorem that I must have studied in high school but whose name I have long since forgotten: that any positive integer number can be used to generate a palindrome by adding to it the number comprised of its digits in reverse order. Palindromes are sequences that read the same in either direction, such as the name "Anna" or the phrase "Madam, I'm Adam" (being non-strict and ignoring spaces and punctuation). We normally think of palindromes as composed of text, but the concept can be applied to numbers: 13531 is a palindrome. Start with the number 72, for example, and add to it the number 27. The results of this addition is 99, which is a (short) palindrome. Starting with 142, add 241, and you get 383. Some numbers take more than one try to generate a palindrome. 1951 + 1591 yields 3542, which is not palindromic. The second round, however, 3542 + 2453, yields 5995, which is. The number 17,892, which my son Benjamin picked out of the air, requires 12 rounds to generate a palindrome, but it does terminate:

```
C:\javasrc\numbers>java  Palindrome 72 142 1951 17892
Trying 72
72->99
Trying 142
142->383
Trying 1951
Trying 3542
1951->5995
Trying 17892
Trying 47763
Trying 84537
Trying 158085
Trying 738936
Trying 1378773
Trying 5157504
Trying 9215019
Trying 18320148
Trying 102422529
Trying 1027646730
Trying 1404113931
17892->2797227972

C:\javasrc\numbers>
```

If this sounds to you like a natural candidate for recursion, you are correct. *Recursion* involves dividing a problem into simple and identical steps, which can be implemented by a function that calls itself and provides a way of termination. Our basic approach, as shown in method `findPalindrome`, is:

```
long findPalindrome(long num) {
    if (isPalindrome(num))
        return num;
    return findPalindrome(num + reverseNumber(num));
}
```

That is, if the starting number is already a palindromic number, return it; otherwise, add it to its reverse, and try again. The version of the code shown here handles simple cases directly (single digits are always palindromic, for example). We won't think about negative numbers, as these have a character at the front that loses its meaning if placed at the end, and hence are not strictly palindromic. Further, there are certain numbers whose palindromic forms are too long to fit in Java's 64-bit `long` integer. These will cause underflow, which is trapped and then an error message like "too big" is reported. Having said all that, Example 5-8 shows the code.

Example 5-8. Palindrome.java

```
/** Compute the Palindrome of a number by adding the number composed of
 * its digits in reverse order, until a Palindrome occurs.
 * e.g., 42->66 (42+24); 1951->5995 (1951+1591=3542; 3542+2453=5995).
 * <P>TODO: Do we need to handle negative numbers?
 */
public class Palindrome {
    public static void main(String[] argv) {
        for (int i=0; i<argv.length; i++)
            try {
                long l = Long.parseLong(argv[i]);
                if (l < 0) {
                    System.err.println(argv[i] + " -> TOO SMALL");
                    continue;
                }
                System.out.println(argv[i] + "->" + findPalindrome(l));
            } catch (NumberFormatException e) {
                System.err.println(argv[i] + "-> INVALID");
            } catch (IllegalStateException e) {
                System.err.println(argv[i] + "-> TOO BIG(went negative)");
            }
    }

    /** find a palindromic number given a starting point, by
     * calling ourself until we get a number that is palindromic.
     */
    static long findPalindrome(long num) {
        if (num < 0)
            throw new IllegalStateException("went negative");
        if (isPalindrome(num))
            return num;
```

Example 5-8. Palindrome.java (continued)

```java
        System.out.println("Trying " + num);
        return findPalindrome(num + reverseNumber(num));
    }

    /** The number of digits in Long.MAX_VALUE */
    protected static final int MAX_DIGITS = 19;

    // digits array is shared by isPalindrome and reverseNumber,
    // which cannot both be running at the same time.

    /* Statically allocated array to avoid new-ing each time. */
    static long[] digits = new long[MAX_DIGITS];

    /** Check if a number is palindromic. */
    static boolean isPalindrome(long num) {
        if (num >= 0 && num <= 9)
            return true;
        int nDigits = 0;
        while (num > 0) {
            digits[nDigits++] = num % 10;
            num /= 10;
        }
        for (int i=0; i<nDigits/2; i++)
            if (digits[i] != digits[nDigits - i - 1])
                return false;
        return true;
    }

    static long reverseNumber(long num) {
        int nDigits = 0;
        while (num > 0) {
            digits[nDigits++] = num % 10;
            num /= 10;
        }
        long ret = 0;
        for (int i=0; i<nDigits; i++) {
            ret *= 10;
            ret += digits[i];
        }
        return ret;
    }
}
```

See Also

People using Java in scientific or large-scale numeric computing should check out the Java Grande Forum (*http://www.javagrande.org*), a discussion group that aims to work with Sun to ensure Java's usability in these realms.

6

Dates and Times

6.0. Introduction

Yes, Java *is* Y2K safe. That was the first date-related question people asked before 2,000 AD rolled around, so I'll answer it up front. The difficulties of date handling in Java arise not from Y2K issues but from Y1970 issues.

When Java was devised in the early 1990s, there was already considerable awareness in the computing industry of the impending problems with some old code. In fairness to practitioners of the 1970s and 1980s, I must add that not all of us ignored the Y2K issue. I read a key early warning sounded around 1974 in Datamation or JACM, and many of my colleagues from that time forward (myself included) paid close attention to issues of date survivability, as did the developers of the Java API.

In the earliest releases of Java, there was a class called Date designed for representing and operating upon dates. Its problems were that it was Anglocentric—like much of Java 1.0—and that its dates began with the Unix time epoch: January 1, 1970. The year is an integer whose minimum value 70 is treated as 1970, so 99 is 1999, 100 is 2000, and so on. Consequently, there is no general Y2K problem with Java. The problem remains that those of us ancient enough to have been born before that venerable year of 1970 in the history of computing—the time when Unix was invented—found ourselves unable to represent our birth dates, and this made us grumpy and irritable.

The Anglocentricity and 1970-centricity could have been vanquished with Java 1.1. A new class, Calendar, was devised, with hooks for representing dates in any date scheme such as the western (Christian) calendar, the Hebrew calendar, the Islamic calendar, the Chinese calendar, and even Star Trek Star dates. Unfortunately, there wasn't enough time to implement any of these. In fact, only the

GregorianCalendar class appears in Java 1.1, and Java 2 does little to solve the problem (though it does fix the Date class to allow it to represent years before 1970.) You may have to go to other sources to get additional Calendar classes; one source is listed in Recipe 6.3.

The Calendar class can represent any date, BC or AD, in the western calendar. A separate Java int variable, with 32 bits of storage, is allocated for each item such as year, month, day, and so on. Years are signed, negative numbers meaning before the calendar epoch and positive numbers after it. The term *epoch* means the beginning of recorded time. In the western world, our calendar epoch is the imaginary year 0, representing the putative birth year of Jesus Christ. This is such an important event that the years before it are called Before Christ or BC, and dates since then are called . . . well, not After Christ, but the Latin *anno domini*, meaning "in the year of our Lord." Because that takes too long to say and write, we use the acronym AD, thus proving that computerists take no blame whatsoever for inventing the use of acronyms. In the modern spirit of political correctness, these terms have been renamed to BCE (Before Common Era) and CE (Common Era), but to most westerners born before about 1980 they will always be BC and AD. The GregorianCalendar class, intended to represent western or Christian dates, also uses BC and AD.

Where was I? Oh yes, Java. As ints in Java are 32 bits, that allows 2^{31}, or 2,147,483,648, years. Let's say roughly two billion years. I, for one, am not going to worry about this new Y2B menace—even if I'm still around, I'm sure they'll have gone to a 64-bit integer by then.

Fortunately, in Java 2 (JDK 1.2), the Date class was changed to use long values, and it can now represent a much wider range of dates. And what about this new DateFormat class? Well, it does provide a great deal of flexibility in the formatting of dates. Plus, it's bidirectional—it can parse dates too. We'll see it in action in Recipes 6.2 and 6.5.

Note also that some of these classes are in java.text while others are in java.util. Package java.text contains classes and interfaces for handling text, dates, numbers, and messages in a manner independent of natural languages, while java.util contains the collections framework, legacy collection classes, event model, date and time facilities, internationalization, and miscellaneous utility classes. You'll need to import both packages in most date-related programs.

6.1. Finding Today's Date

Problem

You want to find today's date.

Solution

Use a Date object's toString() method.

Discussion

The quick and simple way to get today's date and time is to construct a Date object with no arguments in the constructor call, and call its toString() method:

```
// Date0.java
System.out.println(new java.util.Date());
```

However, for reasons just outlined, we want to use a Calendar object. Just use Calendar.getInstance().getTime(), which returns a Date object (even though the name makes it seem like it should return a Time value*), and print the resulting Date object, either using its toString() method or a DateFormat object. You might be tempted to construct a GregorianCalendar object, using the no-argument constructor, but if you do this, your program will not give the correct answer when non-western locales get Calendar subclasses of their own (in some future release of Java). The static factory method Calendar.getInstance() returns a localized Calendar subclass for the locale you are in. In North America and Europe it will likely return a GregorianCalendar, but in other parts of the world it might (someday) return a different kind of Calendar.

Do *not* try to use a GregorianCalendar's toString() method; the results are truly impressive, but not very interesting. Sun's implementation prints all its internal state information; Kaffe's inherits Object's toString(), which just prints the class name and the hashcode. Neither is useful for our purposes.

```
// Date1,.javaj
ava.util.GregorianCalendar[time=932363506950,areFieldsSet=true,areAllFieldsSet=tru
e,lenient=true,zone=java.util.SimpleTimeZone[id=America/Los_Angeles,offset=-
28800000,dstSavings=3600000,useDaylight=true,startYear=0,startMode=3,startMonth=3,
startDay=1,startDayOfWeek=1,startTime=7200000,endMode=2,endMonth=9,endDay=-
1,endDayOfWeek=1,endTime=7200000],firstDayOfWeek=1,minimalDaysInFirstWeek=1,ERA=1,
YEAR=1999,MONTH=6,WEEK_OF_YEAR=30,WEEK_OF_MONTH=4,DAY_OF_MONTH=18,DAY_OF_
YEAR=199,DAY_OF_WEEK=1,DAY_OF_WEEK_IN_MONTH=3,AM_PM=1,HOUR=10,HOUR_OF_
DAY=22,MINUTE=51,SECOND=46,MILLISECOND=950,ZONE_OFFSET=-28800000,DST_
OFFSET=3600000]
```

Calendar's getTime() returns a Date object, which can be passed to println() to print today's date (and time) in the traditional (but non-localized) format:

```
// Date2.java
System.out.println(Calendar.getInstance().getTime());
```

---

* Just to be clear: Date's getTime() returns the time in seconds, while Calendar's getTime() returns a Date.

To print the date in any other format, use a `java.text.DateFormat`, which you'll meet in Recipe 6.2.

6.2. Printing Date/Time in a Specified Format

Problem

You want to print the date and/or time in a specified format.

Solution

Use a `java.text.DateFormat`.

Discussion

To print the date in the correct format for whatever locale your software lands in, simply use the default `DateFormat` formatter, which is obtained by calling `DateFormat.getInstance()`.

Suppose you want the date printed, but instead of the default format "Sun Jul 18 16:14:09 PDT 1999", you want it printed like "Sun 1999.07.18 at 04:14:09 PM PDT". A look at the Javadoc page for `SimpleDateFormat`—the only non-abstract subclass of `DateFormat`—reveals that it has a rich language for specifying date and time formatting. To use a default format, of course, we can just use the `Date` object's `toString()` method, and for a localized default format, we use `DateFormat.getInstance()`. But to have full control and get the "Sun 1999.07.18 at 04:14:09 PM PDT", we construct an instance explicitly, like so:

```
new SimpleDateFormat ("E yyyy.MM.dd 'at' hh:mm:ss a zzz");
```

E means the day of the week; `yyyy`, `MM`, and `dd` are obviously year, month, and day. The quoted string `'at'` means the string "at". `hh:mm:ss` is the time; a means A.M. or P.M., and `zzz` means the time zone. Some of these are more memorable than others; I find the `zzz` tends to put me to sleep. Here's the code:

```
// DateDemo.java
Date dNow = new Date();

/* Simple, Java 1.0 date printing */
System.out.println("It is now " + dNow.toString());

// Use a SimpleDateFormat to print the date our way.
SimpleDateFormat formatter
    = new SimpleDateFormat ("E yyyy.MM.dd 'at' hh:mm:ss a zzz");
System.out.println("It is " + formatter.format(dNow));
```

There are many format symbols; a list is shown in Table 6-1.

Table 6-1. SimpleDateFormat format codes

Symbol	Meaning	Presentation	Example
G	Era designator	Text	AD
y	Year	Number	2001
M	Month in year	Text and Number	July or 07
d	Day in month	Number	10
h	Hour in A.M./P.M. (1~12)	Number	12
H	Hour in day (0~23)	Number	0
m	Minute in hour	Number	30
s	Second in minute	Number	43
S	Millisecond	Number	234
E	Day in week	Text	Tuesday
D	Day in year	Number	360
F	Day of week in month	Number	2 (second Wed. in July)
w	Week in year	Number	40
W	Week in month	Number	1
a	A.M./P.M. marker	Text	PM
k	Hour in day (1~24)	Number	24
K	Hour in A.M./P.M. (0~11)	Number	0
z	Time zone	Text	Eastern Standard Time
'	Escape for text	Delimiter	
"	Single quote	Literal	'

You can use as many of the given symbols as needed. Where a format can be used either in text or numeric context, you can set it to longer form by repetitions of the character. For codes marked "Text", four or more pattern letters will cause the formatter to use the long form, whereas fewer will cause it to use the short or abbreviated form if one exists. Thus, E might yield Mon, whereas EEEE would yield Monday. For those marked "Number", the number of repetitions of the symbol gives the minimum number of digits. Shorter numbers are zero-padded to the given number of digits. The year is handled specially: yy yields a two-digit year (98, 88, 00, 01 . . .), whereas yyyy yields a valid year (2001). For those marked "Text and Number", three or more symbols causes it to use text, while one or two make it use a number: MM might yield 01, while MMM would yield January.

6.3. Representing Dates in Other Epochs

Problem

You need to deal with dates in a form other than the Gregorian Calendar used in the western world.

Solution

Visit the IBM alphaWorks web site.

Discussion

As of Java 2, the only non-abstract Calendar subclass is the GregorianCalendar, as mentioned previously. However, others do exist. Check out the IBM alphaWorks web site (*http://alphaworks.ibm.com*), which has a large collection of freely available Java software (mostly without source code, alas). Search for "calendar", and you'll find a set of calendars—Hebrew, Islamic, Buddhist, Japanese, and even an Astronomical Calendar class—that covers most of the rest of the world.

These work in a similar fashion to the standard GregorianCalendar class, but have constants for month names and other information relevant to each particular calendar.

6.4. Converting YMDHMS to a Calendar or Epoch Seconds

Problem

You have year, month, day, hour, minute, and maybe even seconds, and you need to convert it to a Calendar or a Date.

Solution

Use the Calendar class's set(y,m,d,h,m[,s]) method, which allows you to set the date/time fields to whatever you wish. Note that when using this form and providing your own numbers or when constructing either a Date or a GregorianCalendar object, the month value is zero-based while all the other values are true-origin. Presumably, this is to allow you to print the month name from an array without having to remember to subtract one, but it is confusing.

```
// GregCalDemo.java
GregorianCalendar d1 = new GregorianCalendar(1986, 04, 05); // May 5
```

```
GregorianCalendar d2 = new GregorianCalendar();// today
Calendar d3 = Calendar.getInstance();// today

System.out.println("It was then " + d1.getTime());
System.out.println("It is now " + d2.getTime());
System.out.println("It is now " + d3.getTime());
d3.set(Calendar.YEAR, 1915);
d3.set(Calendar.MONTH, Calendar.APRIL);
d3.set(Calendar.DAY_OF_MONTH, 12);
System.out.println("D3 set to " + d3.getTime());
```

This prints the dates as shown:

```
It was then Mon May 05 00:00:00 PDT 1986
It is now Sun Jul 18 22:51:47 PDT 1999
It is now Sun Jul 18 22:51:47 PDT 1999
D3 set to Mon Apr 12 22:51:47 PDT 1915
```

6.5. *Parsing Strings into Dates*

Problem

You need to convert user input into `Date` or `Calendar` objects.

Solution

Use a `DateFormat`.

Discussion

The `DateFormat` class introduced in Recipe 6.2 has some additional methods, notably `parse()`, which tries to parse a string according to the format stored in the given `DateFormat` object.

```
// DateParse1.java
SimpleDateFormat formatter
    = new SimpleDateFormat ("yyyy-MM-dd");
String input = args.length == 0 ? "1818-11-11" : args[0];
System.out.print(input + " parses as ");
Date t;
try {
    t = formatter.parse(input);
    System.out.println(t);
} catch (ParseException e) {
    System.out.println("unparseable using " + formatter);
}
```

This will parse any date back to Year Zero and well beyond Year 2000.

What if the date is embedded in an input string? You could, of course, use the string's substring() method to extract it, but there is an easier way. The ParsePosition object from java.text is designed to represent (and track) the position of an imaginary cursor in a string. Suppose we have genealogical data with input strings representing the times of a person's life:

```
BD: 1913-10-01 Vancouver, B.C.
DD: 1983-06-06 Toronto, ON
```

This lists one person's birth date (BD) and place, and death date (DD) and place. We can parse these using String.indexOf(' ') to find the space after the : character, DateFormat parse() to parse the date, and String.substring() to get the city and other geographic information. Here's how:

```java
// DateParse2.java
SimpleDateFormat formatter =
    new SimpleDateFormat ("yyyy-MM-dd");
String input[] = {
    "BD: 1913-10-01 Vancouver, B.C.",
    "MD: 1948-03-01 Ottawa, ON",
    "DD: 1983-06-06 Toronto, ON" };
for (int i=0; i<input.length; i++) {
    String aLine = input[i];
    String action;
    switch(aLine.charAt(0)) {
        case 'B': action = "Born"; break;
        case 'M': action = "Married"; break;
        case 'D': action = "Died"; break;
        // others...
        default: System.err.println("Invalid code in " + aLine);
        continue;
    }
    int p = aLine.indexOf(' ');
    ParsePosition pp = new ParsePosition(p);
    Date d = formatter.parse(aLine, pp);
    if (d == null) {
        System.err.println("Invalid date in " + aLine);
        continue;
    }
    String location = aLine.substring(pp.getIndex());
    System.out.println(
        action + " on " + d + " in " + location);
}
```

This works like I said it would:

```
Born on Wed Oct 01 00:00:00 PDT 1913 in  Vancouver, B.C.
Married on Mon Mar 01 00:00:00 PST 1948 in  Ottawa, ON
Died on Mon Jun 06 00:00:00 PDT 1983 in  Toronto, ON
```

Note that the polymorphic form of `parse()` that takes one argument throws a `ParseException` if the input cannot be parsed, while the form that takes a `ParsePosition` as its second argument returns `null` to indicate failure.

6.6. Converting Epoch Seconds to DMYHMS

Problem

You need to convert a number of seconds since 1970 into a `Date`.

Solution

Just use the `Date` constructor.

Discussion

"The Epoch" is the time at the beginning of time as far as modern operating systems go. Unix time, and some versions of MS-Windows time, count off inexorably the seconds since the epoch. On systems that store this in a 32-bit integer, time is indeed running out. Let's say we wanted to find out when the Unix operating system, whose 32-bit versions use a 32-bit date, will get into difficulty. We take a 32-bit integer of all ones, and construct a `Date` around it. The `Date` constructor needs the number of milliseconds since 1970, so we multiply by 1,000:

```
/** When does the UNIX date get into trouble? */

public class Y2038 {
    public static void main(String[] a) {

        // This should yield 2038AD, the hour of doom for the
        // last remaining 32-bit UNIX systems (there will be
        // millions of 64-bit UNIXes by then).

        long expiry = 0x7FFFFFFFL * 1000;

        System.out.println("32-bit UNIX expires on " +
            Long.toHexString(expiry) + " or " +
            new java.util.Date(expiry));
        // Why doesn't it?

        // Try going from msec of current time into a Date
        long now = System.currentTimeMillis();
        System.out.println(
            "Passing " + Long.toHexString(now) + " --> " +
            new java.util.Date(now));

    }
}
```

Sure enough, the program reports that 32-bit Unixes will expire in the year 2038 (you might think I knew that in advance if you were to judge by the name I gave the class; in fact, my web site has carried the Y2038 warning to Unix users for several years now). At least Unix system managers have more warning than most of the general public had for the original Y2K problem.

```
> java Y2038
32-bit UNIX expires on 1f3fffffc18 or Mon Jan 18 22:14:07 EST 2038
Passing e29cfe1432 --> Fri Nov 03 19:08:25 EST 2000
>
```

At any rate, if you need to convert seconds since 1970 to a date, you know how.

6.7. Adding to or Subtracting from a Date or Calendar

Problem

You need to add or subtract a fixed amount to or from a date.

Solution

As we've seen, Date has a getTime() method that returns the number of seconds since the epoch as a long. To add or subtract, you just do arithmetic on this value. Here's a code example:

```
// DateAdd.java
/** Today's date */
Date now = new Date();

long t = now.getTime();

t -= 700*24*60*60*1000;

Date then = new Date(t);

System.out.println("Seven hundred days ago was " + then);
```

Discussion

A cleaner variant is to use the Calendar's add() method:

```
import java.text.*;
import java.util.*;

/** DateCalAdd -- compute the difference between two dates.
 */
```

```
public class DateCalAdd {
    public static void main(String[] av) {
        /** Today's date */
        Calendar now = Calendar.getInstance();

        /* Do "DateFormat" using "simple" format. */
        SimpleDateFormat formatter
            = new SimpleDateFormat ("E yyyy.MM.dd 'at' hh:mm:ss a zzz");
        System.out.println("It is now " +
            formatter.format(now.getTime()));

        now.add(Calendar.DAY_OF_YEAR, - (365 * 2));
        System.out.println("Two years ago was " +
            formatter.format(now.getTime()));
    }
}
```

Running this reports the current date and time, and the date and time two years ago:

```
> java DateCalAdd
It is now Fri 2000.11.03 at 07:16:26 PM EST
Two years ago was Wed 1998.11.04 at 07:16:26 PM EST
```

6.8. Difference Between Two Dates

Problem

You need to compute the difference between two dates.

Solution

Convert to Date objects if necessary, call their getTime() methods, and subtract. Format the result yourself.

Discussion

There is no general mechanism in the API for computing the difference between two dates. This is surprising, given how often it comes up in some types of commercial data processing. However, it's fairly simple to implement this yourself:

```
import java.util.*;

/** DateDiff -- compute the difference between two dates.
 */
public class DateDiff {
    public static void main(String[] av) {
```

```
        /** The ending date. This value
         * doubles as a Y2K countdown time.
         */
        Date d1 = new GregorianCalendar(1999,11,31,23,59).getTime();

        /** Today's date */
        Date d2 = new Date();

        // Get msec from each, and subtract.
        long diff = d2.getTime() - d1.getTime();

        System.out.println("Difference between " + d2 + "\n" +
            "\tand Y2K is " +
            (diff / (1000*60*60*24)) +
            " days.");
    }
}
```

Of course, I'm doing the final editing on this chapter long after the Y2K turnover, so it should print a positive value, and it does:

```
> java DateDiff
Difference between Fri Nov 03 19:24:24 EST 2000
        and Y2K is -307 days.
>
```

You saw Calendar's add() method in Recipe 6.7, but that only adds to the day, month, or year (or any other field) in the Calendar object; it does not add two Calendar dates together.

6.9. Comparing Dates

Problem

You need to compare two dates.

Solution

If the dates are in Date objects, compare with equals() and one of before() or after(). If the dates are in longs, compare with both == and one of < or >.

Discussion

While Date implements equals() like any good class, it also provides before(Date) and after(Date), which compare one date with another to see which happened first. This can be used to determine the relationship among any two dates, as in Example 6-1.

Example 6-1. CompareDates.java

```java
import java.util.*;
import java.text.*;

public class CompareDates {
    public static void main(String[] args) throws ParseException {

        DateFormat df = new SimpleDateFormat ("yyyy-MM-dd");

        // Get Date 1
        Date d1 = df.parse(args[0]);

        // Get Date 2
        Date d2 = df.parse(args[1]);

        String relation;
        if (d1.equals(d2))
            relation = "the same date as";
        else if (d1.before(d2))
            relation = "before";
        else
            relation = "after";
        System.out.println(d1 + " is " + relation + ' ' + d2);
    }
}
```

Running `CompareDates` with two close-together dates and the same date reveals that it seems to work:

```
> java CompareDates 2000-01-01 1999-12-31
Sat Jan 01 00:00:00 EST 2000 is after Fri Dec 31 00:00:00 EST 1999
> java CompareDates 2000-01-01 2000-01-01
Sat Jan 01 00:00:00 EST 2000 is the same date as Sat Jan 01 00:00:00 EST 2000
```

It would be interesting to see if `DateFormat.parse()` really does field rolling, as the documentation says. Apparently so!

```
> javaCompareDates 2001-02-29 2001-03-01
Thu Mar 01 00:00:00 EST 2001 is the same date as Thu Mar 01 00:00:00 EST 2001
>
```

Sometimes the API gives you a date as a `long`. For example, the `File` class has methods (detailed in Recipe 10.1) to give information such as when the last time a file on disk was modified. Example 6-2 shows a program similar to Example 6-1, but using the `long` value returned by the `File`'s `lastModified()` method.

Example 6-2. CompareFileDates.java

```
import java.util.*;
import java.io.File;

public class CompareFileDates {
    public static void main(String[] args) {
        // Get the timestamp from file 1
        String f1 = args[0];
        long d1 = new File(f1).lastModified();

        // Get the timestamp from file 2
        String f2 = args[1];
        long d2 = new File(f2).lastModified();

        String relation;
        if (d1 == d2)
            relation = "the same age as";
        else if (d1 < d2)
            relation = "older than";
        else
            relation = "newer than";
        System.out.println(f1 + " is " + relation + ' ' + f2);
    }
}
```

Running `CompareFileDates` on its source and class reveals that the class file is newer (that is, more up to date). Comparing a directory with itself gives the result of "the same age", as you'd expect:

```
> java CompareFileDates CompareFileDate.java CompareFileDate.class
CompareFileDate.java is older thanCompareFileDate.class
> java CompareFileDates . .
. is the same age as .
```

6.10. Day of Week/Month/Year or Week Number

Problem

You have a date and need to find what day of the week, month, or year that date falls on.

Solution

Use the `Calendar` class's `get()` method, which has constants for retrieving most such values.

Discussion

The `Calendar` class can return most of these:

```
// CalendarDemo.java
Calendar c = Calendar.getInstance();// today
System.out.println("Year: " + c.get(Calendar.YEAR));
System.out.println("Month: " + c.get(Calendar.MONTH));
System.out.println("Day: " + c.get(Calendar.DAY_OF_MONTH));
System.out.println("Day of week = " + c.get(Calendar.DAY_OF_WEEK));
System.out.println("Day of year = " + c.get(Calendar.DAY_OF_YEAR));
System.out.println("Week in Year: " + c.get(Calendar.WEEK_OF_YEAR));
System.out.println("Week in Month: " + c.get(Calendar.WEEK_OF_MONTH));
System.out.println("Day of Week in Month: " +
            c.get(Calendar.DAY_OF_WEEK_IN_MONTH));
System.out.println("Hour: " + c.get(Calendar.HOUR));
System.out.println("AM or PM: " + c.get(Calendar.AM_PM));
System.out.println("Hour (24-hour clock): " +
            c.get(Calendar.HOUR_OF_DAY));
System.out.println("Minute: " + c.get(Calendar.MINUTE));
System.out.println("Second: " + c.get(Calendar.SECOND));
```

This chatty program shows most of the fields in the `Calendar` class:

```
Year: 1999
Month: 6
Day: 19
Day of week = 2
Day of year = 200
Week in Year: 30
Week in Month: 4
Day of Week in Month: 3
Hour: 3
AM or PM: 1
Hour (24-hour clock): 15
Minute: 18
Second: 42
```

6.11. Calendar Page

Problem

You want a calendar for a given month of a given year, or of the current month and year.

Solution

Use `Calendar.get()` to find what day of the week the first of the month falls on, and format accordingly.

Discussion

Like the output of the Unix *cal* command, it is often convenient to view a month in compact form. The basic idea is to find what day of week the first of the month is and print blank columns for the days of the week before the month begins. Then, print the numbers from 1 to the end of the month, starting a new column after you get to the last day of each week.

Here's my program, compared to the Unix *cal* command:

```
daroad.darwinsys.com$ java CalendarPage 6 2000
June 2000
Su Mo Tu We Th Fr Sa
             1  2  3
 4  5  6  7  8  9 10
11 12 13 14 15 16 17
18 19 20 21 22 23 24
25 26 27 28 29 30
daroad.darwinsys.com$ cal 6 2000
      June 2000
Su Mo Tu We Th Fr Sa
             1  2  3
 4  5  6  7  8  9 10
11 12 13 14 15 16 17
18 19 20 21 22 23 24
25 26 27 28 29 30
```

The source code is simple and straightforward (Example 6-3).

Example 6-3. CalendarPage.java

```java
import java.util.*;
import java.text.*;

/** Print a month page.
 * Only works for the Western calendar.
 */
public class CalendarPage {

    /** The names of the months */
    String[] months = {
        "January", "February", "March", "April",
        "May", "June", "July", "August",
        "September", "October", "November", "December"
    };

    /** The days in each month. */
    public final static int dom[] = {
            31, 28, 31, 30,/* jan feb mar apr */
            31, 30, 31, 31, /* may jun jul aug */
```

Example 6-3. CalendarPage.java (continued)

```
        30, 31, 30, 31/* sep oct nov dec */
};

/** Compute which days to put where, in the Cal panel */
public void print(int mm, int yy) {
    /** The number of days to leave blank at the start of this month */
    int leadGap = 0;

    System.out.print(months[mm]);// print month and year
    System.out.print(" ");
    System.out.print(yy);
    System.out.println();

    if (mm < 0 || mm > 11)
        throw new IllegalArgumentException("Month " + mm + " bad, must be 0-11");
    GregorianCalendar calendar = new GregorianCalendar(yy, mm, 1);

    System.out.println("Su Mo Tu We Th Fr Sa");

    // Compute how much to leave before the first.
    // getDay() returns 0 for Sunday, which is just right.
    leadGap = calendar.get(Calendar.DAY_OF_WEEK)-1;

    int daysInMonth = dom[mm];
    if (calendar.isLeapYear(calendar.get(Calendar.YEAR)) && mm == 1)
        ++daysInMonth;

    // Blank out the labels before 1st day of month
    for (int i = 0; i < leadGap; i++) {
        System.out.print("   ");
    }

    // Fill in numbers for the day of month.
    for (int i = 1; i <= daysInMonth; i++) {

        // This "if" statement is simpler than fiddling with NumberFormat
        if (i<=9)
            System.out.print(' ');
        System.out.print(i);

        if ((leadGap + i) % 7 == 0)// wrap if end of line.
            System.out.println();
        else
            System.out.print(' ');
    }
    System.out.println();
}
```

Example 6-3. CalendarPage.java (continued)

```
/** For testing, a main program */
public static void main(String[] av) {
    int month, year;

    CalendarPage cp = new CalendarPage();

    // print the current month.
    if (av.length == 2) {
        cp.print(Integer.parseInt(av[0])-1, Integer.parseInt(av[1]));
    } else {
        Calendar c = Calendar.getInstance();
        cp.print(c.get(Calendar.MONTH), c.get(Calendar.YEAR));
    }
}
}
```

6.12. High-Resolution Timers

Problem

You need to time how long something takes.

Solution

Call `System.getTimeMillis()` twice, and subtract the first result from the second result.

Discussion

Needing a timer is such a common thing that, instead of making you depend on some external library, the developers of Java have built it in. The `System` class contains a static method that returns the current time (since 1970) in milliseconds. Thus, to time some event, use this:

```
long start = System.getTimeMillis();
method_to_be_timed();
long end = System.getTimeMillis(); l
ong elapsed = end - start;// time in msec.
```

Here is a short example to measure how long it takes a user to press return. We divide the time in milliseconds by a thousand to get seconds, and print it nicely using a `NumberFormat`:

```
// Timer0.java
long t0, t1;
System.out.println("Press return when ready");
```

```
t0=System.currentTimeMillis();
int b;
do {
    b = System.in.read();
} while (b!='\r' && b != '\n');

t1=System.currentTimeMillis();
double deltaT = t1-t0;
System.out.println("You took " +
    DecimalFormat.getInstance().format(deltaT/1000.) + " seconds.");
```

This longer example uses the same technique, but computes a large number of square roots and writes each one to a discard file using the getDevNull() method from Recipe 2.4:

```
import java.io.*;
import java.text.*;

/**
 * Timer for processing sqrt and I/O operations.
 */
public class Timer {
    public static void main(String argv[]) {
        try {
            new Timer().run();
        } catch (IOException e) {
            System.err.println(e);
        }
    }
    public void run() throws IOException {

        DataOutputStream n = new DataOutputStream(
            new BufferedOutputStream(new FileOutputStream(SysDep.getDevNull())));
        long t0, t1;
        System.out.println("Java Starts at " + (t0=System.currentTimeMillis()));
        double k;
        for (int i=0; i<100000; i++) {
            k = 2.1 * Math.sqrt((double)i);
            n.writeDouble(k);
        }
        System.out.println("Java Ends at " + (t1=System.currentTimeMillis()));
        double deltaT = t1-t0;
        System.out.println("This run took " +
            DecimalFormat.getInstance().format(deltaT/1000.) + " seconds.");
    }
}
```

Finally, this code shows a simpler, but less portable, technique for formatting a "delta t" or time difference. It works only for the English locale (or any other where the number one-and-a-half is written "1.5"), but it's simple enough to write the code inline. I show it here as a method for completeness, and confess to having used it this way on occasion:

```
/** Convert a long ("time_t") to seconds and thousandths. */
public static String msToSecs(long t) {
    return t/1000 + "." + t%1000;
}
```

6.13. Sleeping for a While

Problem

You need to sleep for a while.

Solution

Use `Thread.sleep()`.

Discussion

You can sleep for any period of time from one millisecond up to the lifetime of your computer. As I write this, for example, I have a chicken on the barbecue. My wife has instructed me (I'm as helpless with anything in the kitchen beyond spaghetti as she is with anything computish made since the days of MS-DOS Word Perfect) to check it every five minutes. Since I'm busy writing, time tends to fly. So, I needed a reminder service, and came up with this in a jiffy:

```
// Reminder.java
while (true) {
    System.out.println(new Date() + "\007");
    Thread.sleep(5*60*1000);
}
```

The 007 is not a throwback to the Cold War espionage thriller genre, but the ASCII character for a bell code, or beep. Had I written it as a windowed application using a frame, I could have called `Toolkit.beep()` instead, and by toggling the state of `setVisible()`, a pop-up would appear every five minutes.

With a bit more work, you could have a series of events, and wait until their due times, making a sort of mini-scheduler entirely in Java. In fact, we'll do that in Recipe 6.14.

6.14. Program: Reminder Service

The `ReminderService` program provides a simple reminder service. The `load()` method reads a plain text file containing a list of appointments like the ones shown here, using a `SimpleDateFormat`:

```
1999 07 17 10 30 Get some sleep.
1999 07 18 01 27 Finish this program
1999 07 18 01 29 Document this program
```

Example 6-4 shows the full program.

Example 6-4. ReminderService.java

```java
import java.io.*;
import java.text.*;
import java.util.*;
import javax.swing.*;

/**
 * Read a file of reminders, sleep until each is due, beep.
 */
public class ReminderService {
    class Item {
        Date due;
        String message;
        Item(Date d, String m) {
            due = d;
            message = m;
        }
    }

    ArrayList l = new ArrayList();

    public static void main(String argv[]) throws IOException {
        ReminderService rs = new ReminderService();
        rs.load();
        rs.run();
    }

    protected void load() throws IOException {

        BufferedReader is = new BufferedReader(
            new FileReader("ReminderService.txt"));
        SimpleDateFormat formatter =
            new SimpleDateFormat ("yyyy MM dd hh mm");
        String aLine;
        while ((aLine = is.readLine()) != null) {
            ParsePosition pp = new ParsePosition(0);
            Date date = formatter.parse(aLine, pp);
            if (date == null) {
                message("Invalid date in " + aLine);
                continue;
            }
            String mesg = aLine.substring(pp.getIndex());
            l.add(new Item(date, mesg));
```

Example 6-4. ReminderService.java (continued)

```java
            }
        }

    public void run() {
        System.out.println("ReminderService: Starting at " + new Date());
        while (!l.isEmpty()) {
            Date d = new Date();
            Item i = (Item)l.get(0);
            long interval = i.due.getTime() - d.getTime();
            if (interval > 0) {
                System.out.println("Sleeping until " + i.due);
                try {
                    Thread.sleep(interval);
                } catch (InterruptedException e) {
                    System.exit(1);// unexpected intr
                }
                message(i.due + ": " + i.message);
            } else
                message("MISSED " + i.message + " at " + i.due);
            l.remove(0);
        }
        System.exit(0);
    }
    void message(String message) {
        System.out.println("007" + message);
        JOptionPane.showMessageDialog(null,
            message,
            "Timer Alert",    // titlebar
            JOptionPane.INFORMATION_MESSAGE);// icon
    }
}
```

I create a nested class `Item` to store one notification, storing its due date and time and the message to display when it's due. The `load()` method reads the file containing the data and converts it, using the date parsing from Recipe 6.5. The `run()` method does the necessary arithmetic to `sleep()` for the right length of time to wait until the next reminder is needed. The reminder is then displayed both on the standard output (for debugging) and in a dialog window using the Swing `JOptionPane` (see Recipe 13.7). The `message()` method consolidates both displays, allowing you to add a control to use only standard output or only the dialog.

See Also

In JDK 1.3, the new class `java.util.Timer` can be used to implement much of the functionality of this reminder program.

7

Structuring Data
with Java

7.0. Introduction

Almost every application beyond "Hello World" needs to keep track of a certain amount of data. A simple numeric problem might work with three or four numbers only, but in most applications there are groups of similar data items. A GUI-based application may need to keep track of a number of dialog windows. A personal information manager or PIM needs to keep track of a number of, well, persons. An operating system (a real one) needs to keep track of who is allowed to log in, who is currently logged in, and what those users are doing. A library needs to keep track of who has books checked out and when they're due. A network server may need to keep track of its active clients. There are several patterns here, and they all revolve around what has traditionally been called *data structuring*.

There are data structures in the memory of a running program; there is structure in the data in a file on disk; and there is structure in the information stored in a database. In this chapter we concentrate on the first aspect: in-memory data. We'll cover the second aspect in Chapter 9, and the third in Chapter 20.

If you had to think about in-memory data, you might want to compare it to a collection of index cards in a filing box, or to a treasure hunt where each clue leads to the next. Or you might think of it like my desk—apparently scattered, but actually a very powerful collection filled with meaningful information. Each of these is a good analogy for a type of data structuring that Java provides. An array is a fixed-length linear collection of data items, like the card filing box: it can only hold so much, then it overflows. The treasure hunt is like a data structure called a *linked list*. Before Java 2 there was no standard linked list class, but you could (and still can) write your own "traditional data structure" classes. Finally, the complex collection represents Java's `Collection` classes, which are substantially revised and expanded in Java 2. A document entitled *Collections Framework Overview,* distributed with the Java Development Kit documentation (and stored as file */jdk1.x/docs/guide/ collections/overview.html*), provides a detailed discussion of the Collections Framework. The framework aspects of Java collections are summarized in Recipe 7.17.

Beware of some typographic issues. The word `Arrays` (in constant-width font) is short for the class `java.util.Arrays`, but in the normal typeface, the word "arrays" is simply the plural of "array." (and will be found capitalized at the beginning of a sentence). Also, note that the Java 2 additions `HashMap` and `HashSet` follow the rule of having a "mid-capital" at each word boundary, while the older `Hashtable` does not (the "t" is not capitalized).

There are several classes in `java.util` that are not covered in this chapter. All the classes whose names begin with `Abstract` are, in fact, abstract, and we discuss their non-abstract subclasses. `BitSet` is used less frequently than some of the classes discussed here, and is simple enough to learn on your own; I have examples of it in Recipes 2.7 and 5.9. The `StringTokenizer` class is covered in Recipe 3.2.

We'll start our discussion of data structuring techniques with one of the oldest structures, the array. Then we'll go through a variety of fancier structuring techniques using classes from `java.util`. At the end, we'll discuss the overall structure of the Collections Framework that is part of `java.util`.

7.1. Data Structuring Using Arrays

Problem

You need to keep track of a fixed amount of information and retrieve it (usually) sequentially.

Solution

Use an array.

Discussion

Arrays can be used to hold any linear collection of data. The items in an array must all be of the same type. You can make an array of any built-in type or any object type. For arrays of built-ins such as `ints`, `booleans`, etc., the data is stored in the array. For arrays of objects, a reference is stored in the array, so the normal rules of reference variables and casting apply. Note in particular that if the array is declared as Object[], then object references of any type can be stored in it without casting, though a valid cast is required to take an Object reference out and use it as its original type. I'll say a bit more on two-dimensional arrays in Recipe 7.16; otherwise, you should treat this as a review example.

```java
import java.util.*;
public class Array1  {
    public static void main(String argv[]) {
        int monthLen1[];// declare a reference
        monthLen1 = new int[12];// construct it
        int monthlen2[] = new int[12];// short form
        // even shorter is this initializer form:
        int monthLen3[] = {
                31, 28, 31, 30,
                31, 30, 31, 31,
                30, 31, 30, 31,
        };

        final int MAX = 10;
        Calendar days[] = new Calendar[MAX];
        for (int i=0; i<MAX; i++) {
            // Note that this actually stores GregorianCalendar
            // etc. instances into a Calendar Array
            days[i] = Calendar.getInstance();
        }

        // Two-Dimensional Arrays
        // Want a 10-by-24 array
        int me[][] = new int[10][];
        for (int i=0; i<10; i++)
            me[i] = new int[24];

        // Remember that an array has a ".length" attribute
        System.out.println(me.length);
        System.out.println(me[0].length);

    }
}
```

Arrays in Java work nicely. The type checking provides reasonable integrity, and array bounds are always checked by the runtime system, further contributing to reliability.

The only problem with arrays is: what if the array fills up and you still have data coming in? Solution in Recipe 7.2.

7.2. *Resizing an Array*

Problem

The array filled up, and you got an `ArrayIndexOutOfBoundsException`.

Solution

Make the array bigger.

Discussion

One approach is to allocate the array at a reasonable size to begin with, but if you find yourself with more data than will fit, reallocate a new, bigger array and copy the elements into it.* Here is code that does so:

```java
import java.util.*;
/** Re-allocate an array, bigger... */
public class Array2 {
    public static void main(String argv[]) {
        int nDates = 0;
        final int MAX = 10;
        Calendar dates[] = new Calendar[MAX];
        Calendar c;
        while ((c=getDate()) != null) {

            // if (nDates >= dates.length) {
            //    System.err.println("Too Many Dates! Simplify your life!!");
            //    System.exit(1);  // wimp out
            // }

            // better: reallocate, making data structure dynamic
            if (nDates >= dates.length) {
                Calendar tmp[] = new Calendar[dates.length + 10];
                System.arraycopy(dates, 0, tmp, 0, dates.length);
                dates = tmp;    // copies the array reference
                // old array will be garbage collected soon...
            }
            dates[nDates++] = c;
        }
        System.out.println("Array size = " + dates.length);
    }

    static int n;
```

---

* You could copy it yourself using a `for` loop if you wish, but `System.arrayCopy()` is likely to be faster because it's implemented in native code.

```
          /* Dummy method to return a sequence of 21 Calendar references,
           * so the array should be sized >= 21.
           */
          public static Calendar getDate() {
              if (n++ > 21)
                  return null;
              return Calendar.getInstance();
          }
      }
```

This technique will work reasonably well for simple linear collections of data. For data with a more variable structure, you will probably want to use a more dynamic approach, as in Recipe 7.3.

7.3. Like an Array, but More Dynamic

Problem

You don't want to worry about storage reallocation; you want a standard class to handle it for you.

Solution

Use a Vector. Or, in Java 2, an ArrayList.

Discussion

A Vector is just a standard class that encapsulates the functionality of an array but allows it to expand automatically. You can just keep on adding things to it, and each addition will behave the same. If you watch *really* closely you might notice a brief extra pause once in a while when adding objects, as Vector reallocates and copies. But you don't have to think about it.

However, because Vector is a class and isn't part of the syntax of Java, you can't use Java's array syntax; you must use methods to access the Vector data. There are methods to add objects, retrieve objects, find objects, and tell you how big the Vector is and how big it can become without having to reallocate. Like those of all the collection classes in java.util, Vector's storing and retrieval methods are defined in terms of java.lang.Object. But since Object is the ancestor of every defined type, you can store objects of any type in a Vector (or any collection), and cast it when retrieving it. If you need to store a small number of built-ins (like int, float, etc.) into a collection containing other data, use the appropriate wrapper class (see the Introduction to Chapter 5). To store booleans, either use a java.util.BitSet (see the online documentation) or the Boolean wrapper class.

Table 7-1 shows some of the most important methods of `Vector`. Equally important, those listed are also methods of the `List` interface, which we'll discuss shortly. This means that the same methods can be used with the newer `ArrayList` class and several other classes.

Table 7-1. List access methods

Method signature	Usage
add(Object o)	Add the given element at the end
add(int i, Object o)	Insert the given element at the specified position
clear()	Remove all element references from the `Collection`
contains(Object o)	True if the `Vector` contains the given `Object`
get(int i)	Return the object reference at the specified position
indexOf(Object o)	Return the index where the given object is found, or –1
remove(Object o) remove(int i)	Remove an object by reference or by position
toArray()	Return an array containing the objects in the `Collection`

This program, `VectorDemo`, stores data in a `Vector` and retrieves it for processing:

```
Vector v = new Vector();
StructureDemo source = new StructureDemo(15);

// Add lots of elements to the Vector...
v.add(source.getDate());
v.add(source.getDate());
v.add(source.getDate());

// Process the data structure using a for loop.
System.out.println("Retrieving by index:");
for (int i = 0; i<v.size(); i++) {
    System.out.println("Element " + i + " = " + v.get(i));
}
```

Note that `Vector` and `Hashtable` pre-date the `Collections` framework, so they provide methods with different names: `Vector` provides `addElement()` and `elementAt()`. In new code you should generally use the `Collections` methods `add()` and `get()`. The equivalent program done using an `ArrayList` (`ArrayListDemo.java`) looks like this:

```
ArrayList al = new ArrayList();

// Create a source of Objects
StructureDemo source = new StructureDemo(15);

// Add lots of elements to the ArrayList...
al.add(source.getDate());
```

```
al.add(source.getDate());
al.add(source.getDate());

// First print them out using a for loop.
System.out.println("Retrieving by index:");
for (int i = 0; i<al.size(); i++) {
    System.out.println("Element " + i + " = " + al.get(i));
}
```

As you can see, the structure is very similar. You might wonder, then, why they added `ArrayList` and didn't just keep `Vector`. One major difference is that the methods of `Vector` are *synchronized,* meaning that they can be accessed from multiple threads (see Recipe 24.5). This does mean more overhead, though, so in a single-threaded application it may be faster to use an `ArrayList` (see timing results in Recipe 7.18).

7.4. *Data-Independent Access with Iterators*

Problem

You want to write your code so that users don't have to know whether you store it in an `Array`, a `Vector`, an `ArrayList`, or even a doubly linked list of your own choosing.

Solution

Use one of the `Iterator` interfaces.

Discussion

If you are making collections of data available to other classes, you may not want the other classes to depend upon how you have stored the data, so that you can revise your class easily at a later time. Yet you need to publish a method that gives these classes access to your data. It is for this very purpose that the `Enumeration` and later the `Iterator` interfaces were included in the `java.util` package. These provide a pair of methods that allow you to *iterate,* or step through all the elements of a data structure without knowing or caring how the data is stored. The newer `Iterator` interface also allows deletions, though classes that implement the interface are free either to implement the use of deletions or to throw an `UnsupportedOperationException`.

Here is `IterDemo`, the previous `Vector` demo rewritten to use an `Iterator` to access the elements of the data structure:

```
Vector v = new Vector();
Enumeration e;
```

```
StructureDemo source = new StructureDemo(15);

// Add lots of elements to the Vector...
v.addElement(source.getDate());
v.addElement(source.getDate());
v.addElement(source.getDate());

// Process the data structure using an iterator.
int i = 0;
Iterator it = v.iterator();

// Remaining part of the code does not know or care
// if the data is an an array, a Vector, or whatever.
while (it.hasNext()) {
    Object o = it.next();
    System.out.println("Element " + i++ + " = " + o);
}
```

To demystify the `Iterator` and show that it's actually easy to build, we'll create our own `Iterator` in Recipe 7.14.

7.5. Structuring Data in a Linked List

Problem

Your data isn't suitable for use in an array.

Solution

Write your own data structure(s).

Discussion

Anybody who's taken Computer Science 101 (or any computer science course) should be familiar with the concepts of data structuring, such as linked lists, binary trees, and the like. While this is not the place to discuss the details of such things, I'll give a brief illustration of one of the more common ones, the linked list. A linked list is commonly used when you have an unpredictably large number of data items, wish to allocate just the right amount of storage, and usually want to access them in the same order that you created them. Figure 7-1 is a diagram showing the normal arrangement.

Here is code that implements a simple linked list:

```
/**
 * Linked list class, written out in full using Java.
 */
```

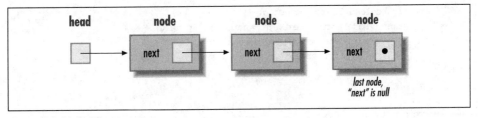

Figure 7-1. Linked list structure

```java
public class LinkList {
    public static void main(String argv[]) {
        System.out.println("Here is a demo of a Linked List in Java");
        LinkList l = new LinkList();
        l.add(new Object());
        l.add("Hello");
        System.out.println("Here is a list of all the elements");
        l.print();
        if (l.lookup("Hello"))
            System.err.println("Lookup works");
        else
            System.err.println("Lookup does not work");
    }

    /* A TNode stores one node or item in the linked list. */
    class TNode {
        TNode next;
        Object data;
        TNode(Object o) {
            data = o;
            next = null;
        }
    }
    protected TNode root;
    protected TNode last;

    /** Construct a LinkList: initialize the root and last nodes. */
    LinkList() {
        root = new TNode(this);
        last = root;
    }

    /** Add one object to the end of the list. Update the "next"
     * reference in the previous end, to refer to the new node.
     * Update "last" to refer to the new node.
     */
    void add(Object o) {
        last.next = new TNode(o);
        last = last.next;
    }
```

```
public boolean lookup(Object o) {
    for (TNode p=root.next; p != null; p = p.next)
        if (p.data==o || p.data.equals(o))
            return true;
    return false;
}


void print() {
    for (TNode p=root.next; p != null; p = p.next)
        System.out.println("TNode" + p + " = " + p.data);
}
}
```

This approach works reasonably well. But it turns out that many applications use linked lists. Why should each programmer have to provide his or her own linked list class, each with a slightly different set of bugs? You don't have to provide your own square root function or write your own Remote Method Invocation services. Accordingly, Java 2 does include a LinkedList class; here is a similar program that uses it:

```
import java.util.*;

/**
 * Demo 1.2 java.util.LinkedList; same example as my older LinkList class.
 */
public class LinkedListDemo {
    public static void main(String argv[]) {
        System.out.println("Here is a demo of Java 1.2's LinkedList class");
        LinkedList l = new LinkedList();
        l.add(new Object());
        l.add("Hello");

        System.out.println("Here is a list of all the elements");
        // ListIterator is discussed shortly.
        ListIterator li = l.listIterator(0);
        while (li.hasNext())
            System.out.println(li.next());

        if (l.indexOf("Hello") < 0)
            System.err.println("Lookup does not work");
        else
            System.err.println("Lookup works");
    }
}
```

As you can see, it does pretty much the same thing as my LinkList, but uses the existing class java.util.LinkedList instead of having you roll your own. The ListIterator class used here is an example of an Iterator, which was discussed in Recipe 7.4.

7.6. *Mapping with Hashtable and HashMap*

Problem

You need a one-way mapping from one data item to another.

Solution

Use a HashMap, or the older Hashtable.

Discussion

HashMap (added in Java 2) and Hashtable provide a one-way mapping from one set of object references to another. They are completely general purpose. I've used them to map AWT push buttons (see Recipe 13.4) to the URL to jump to when the button is pushed; to map names to addresses; and to implement a simple in-memory cache in a web server. You can map from anything to anything. Here we map from company names to addresses; the addresses here are String objects, but in real life they'd probably be Address objects.

```
// HashDemo.java
// Construct and load the HashMap. This simulates loading a database
// or reading from a file, or wherever the data is from.

// The hashtable maps from company name to company address.
// In a real application these would be an Address object.
HashMap h = new HashMap();

h.put("Adobe", "Mountain View, CA");
h.put("IBM", "White Plains, NY");
h.put("Learning Tree", "Los Angeles, CA");
h.put("O'Reilly & Associates", "Sebastopol, CA");
h.put("Netscape", "Mountain View, CA");
h.put("Sun", "Mountain View, CA");

    // Two versions of the "retrieval" phase.
    // Version 1: get one pair's value given its key
    // (presumably the key would really come from user input):
    String queryString = "O'Reilly & Associates";
    System.out.println("You asked about " + queryString + ".");
    String resultString = (String)h.get(queryString);
    System.out.println("They are located in: " + resultString);
    System.out.println();

    // Version 2: get ALL the keys and pairs
    // (maybe to print a report, or to save to disk)
    Iterator it = h.values().iterator();
```

```
    while (it.hasNext()) {
        String key = (String) it.next();
        System.out.println("Company " + key + "; " +
            "Address " + h.get(key));
        }
    }
}
```

7.7. Storing Strings in Properties and Preferences

Problem

You need to store keys and values that are both strings, possibly with persistence across runs of a program. For example: program customization.

Solution

Use a `java.util.Properties` object (or a `java.util.Prefs.Preferences` object in JDK 1.4).

Discussion

The `Properties` class is similar to a `HashMap` or `Hashtable` (it extends the latter), but with methods defined specifically for string storage and retrieval and for loading/saving. `Properties` objects are used throughout Java, for everything from setting the platform font names to customizing user applications into different `Locale` settings as part of internationalization and localization. When stored on disk, a `Properties` object looks just like a series of `name=value` assignments, with optional comments. Comments are added when you hand-edit a `Properties` file, ignored when the `Properties` object reads itself, and lost when you ask the `Properties` object to save itself to disk. Here is an example of a `Properties` file that could be used to internationalize the menus in a GUI-based program:

```
# Default properties for MenuIntl
program.title=Demonstrate I18N (MenuIntl)
program.message=Welcome to an English-localized Java Program
#
# The File Menu
#
file.label=File Menu
file.new.label=New File
file.new.key=N
file.open.label=Open...
file.open.key=O
```

```
file.save.label=Save
file.save.key=S
file.exit.label=Exit
file.exit.key=Q
```

Here is another example, showing some personalization properties:

```
name=Ian Darwin
favorite_popsicle=cherry
favorite_rock group=Fleetwood Mac
favorite_programming_language=Java
pencil color=green
```

A `Properties` object can be loaded from a file. The rules are flexible: either =, :, or spaces can be used after a key name and its values. Spaces after a non-space character are ignored in the key. Backslash can be used to continue lines or to escape other characters. Comment lines may begin with either # or !. Thus, a `Properties` file containing the previous items, if prepared by hand, could look like this:

```
# Here is a list of properties
! first, my name
name Ian Darwin
favorite_popsicle = cherry
favorite_rock\ group \
 Fleetwood Mac
favorite_programming_language=Java
pencil\ color green
```

Fortunately, when a `Properties` object writes itself to a file, it only uses the simple format:

```
key=value
```

Here is an example of a program that creates a `Properties` object adds into it the list of companies and their addresses from Recipe 7.6, and then loads additional properties from disk. To simplify the I/O processing, the program assumes that the `Properties` file to be loaded is contained in the standard input, as would be done using a command-line redirection on either Unix or DOS.

```
import java.util.*;

public class PropsCompanies {
    public static void main(String argv[]) throws java.io.IOException {
        Properties props = new Properties();

        // Get my data.
        props.setProperty("Adobe", "Mountain View, CA");
        props.setProperty("IBM", "White Plains, NY");
        props.setProperty("Learning Tree", "Los Angeles, CA");
```

```
        props.setProperty("O'Reilly & Associates", "Sebastopol, CA");
        props.setProperty("Netscape", "Mountain View, CA");
        props.setProperty("Sun", "Mountain View, CA");

        // Now load additional properties
        props.load(System.in);

        // Now list the merged Properties, using System.out
        props.list(System.out);
    }
}
```

Note that setProperty() was added in JDK 1.2; prior to that, the put() method of parent class HashTable was used.

Running it as:

```
    java PropsCompanies < PropsDemo.dat
```

produces the following output:

```
    -- listing properties --
    Sony=Japan
    Sun=Mountain View, CA
    IBM=White Plains, NY
    Netscape=Mountain View, CA
    Nippon_Kogaku=Japan
    Acorn=United Kingdom
    Adobe=Mountain View, CA
    Ericsson=Sweden
    O'Reilly & Associates=Sebastopol, CA
    Learning Tree=Los Angeles, CA
```

In case you didn't notice in either the HashMap or the Properties examples, the order that the outputs appear in these examples is neither sorted nor even the same order we put them in. The hashing classes and the Properties subclass make no claim about the order in which objects are retrieved. If you need them sorted, see Recipe 7.8.

As a convenient shortcut, my FileProperties class includes a constructor that takes a filename, and a no-argument load() method that takes a filename argument, as in:

```
    Properties p = new com.darwinsys.util.FileProperties("PropsDemo.dat");
```

Note that constructing a FileProperties causes it to be loaded, and therefore the constructor may throw a checked exception of class IOException.

The Preferences class java.util.Prefs.Preferences (new in Java 2 SDK 1.4) is intended to provide an easier-to-use mechanism for storing user customizations in a system-dependent way (which might mean dot files on Unix, a preferences file on the Mac, or the MS-Windows Registry on Microsoft systems). This new class provides a hierarchical set of nodes representing a user's preferences. Data is stored in the system-dependent storage format but can also be exported to or imported from an XML format.

Finally, though it is platform-specific, Cogent Logic produces a JNDI (Java Naming and Directory Interface) service provider for accessing the MS-Windows registry, which can also be used for preferences. JNDI is a general naming and directory lookup that, like `javax.preferences.prefs`, is better suited than `Properties` for dealing with hierarchical data. Cogent Logic's product gives you both local and (subject to security arrangements) remote access to preferences on an MS-Windows system. See *http://cogentlogic.com/jndi/*.

7.8. Sorting a Collection

Problem

You put your data into a collection in random order or used a `Properties` object that doesn't preserve the order, and now you want it sorted.

Solution

Use the static method `Arrays.sort()` or `Collections.sort()`, optionally providing a `Comparator`.

Discussion

If your data is in an array, you can sort it using the static `sort()` method of the `Arrays` utility class. If it is in a collection, you can use the static `sort()` method of the `Collections` class. Here is a set of strings being sorted, first in an `Array` and then in a `Vector`:

```
public class SortArray {
    public static void main(String[] unused) {
        String[] strings = {
            "painful",
            "mainly",
            "gaining",
            "raindrops"
        };
        Arrays.sort(strings);
        for (int i=0; i<strings.length; i++)
            System.out.println(strings[i]);
    }
}
```

```
public class SortCollection {
    public static void main(String[] unused) {
        Vector v = new Vector();
        v.add("painful");
        v.add("mainly");
        v.add("gaining");
        v.add("raindrops");

        Collections.sort(v);
        for (int i=0; i<v.size(); i++)
            System.out.println(v.elementAt(i));
    }
}
```

What if the default sort ordering isn't what you want? Well, there is a `Comparator` interface, and you can create an object that implements it and pass that as the second argument to sort. Fortunately, for the most common ordering next to the default, you don't have to; there is a public constant `String.CASE_INSENSITIVE_ORDER` that can be passed as this second argument. The `String` class defines it as "a `Comparator` that orders `String` objects as by `compareToIgnoreCase`." But if you need something fancier, you need to write a `Comparator`. Suppose that, for some strange reason, you need to sort strings the first character of each. One way to do this would be to write this `Comparator`:

```
public class SubstringComparator implements java.util.Comparator {
    public int compare(Object o1, Object o2) {
        String s1 = o1.toString().substring(1);
        String s2 = o2.toString().substring(1);
        return s1.compareTo(s2);
        // or, more concisely:
        // return o1.substring(1).equals(o2.substring(1));
    }
}
```

Using it is just a matter of passing it as the `Comparator` argument to the correct form of `sort()`, as shown here:

```
import java.util.*;

public class SubstrCompDemo {
    public static void main(String[] unused) {
        String[] strings = {
            "painful",
            "mainly",
            "gaining",
            "raindrops"
        };
        Arrays.sort(strings);
        dump(strings, "Using Default Sort");
```

```
        Arrays.sort(strings, new SubstringComparator());
        dump(strings, "Using SubstringComparator");

    }
    static void dump(String[] args, String title) {
        System.out.println(title);
        for (int i=0; i<args.length; i++)
            System.out.println(args[i]);
    }
}
```

Here is the output of running it:

```
$ java  SubstrCompDemo
Using Default Sort
gaining
mainly
painful
raindrops
Using SubstringComparator
raindrops
painful
gaining
mainly
```

And this is all as it should be.

On the other hand, you may be writing a class and want to build in the comparison functionality, so that you don't always have to remember to pass the Comparator with it. In this case, you can directly implement the java.lang.Comparable interface. The String class, the wrapper classes Byte, Character, Double, Float, Long, Short, and Integer, as well as BigInteger and BigDecimal from java.math, File from java.io, java.util.Date, and java.text.CollationKey all implement this interface, so arrays or Collections of these can be sorted without providing a Comparator. Classes that implement Comparable are said to have a "natural" ordering. The documentation strongly recommends that a class's natural ordering be consistent with its equals() method, and it is consistent with equals() if and only if e1.compareTo((Object)e2)==0 has the same boolean value as e1.equals((Object)e2) for every instance e1 and e2 of the given class. This means that if you implement Comparable, you should also implement equals(), and the logic of equals() should be consistent with the logic of the compareTo() method. Here, for example, is part of the appointment class Appt from a hypothetical scheduling program:

```
public class Appt implements Comparable {
    // much code and variables omitted - see online version
```

```
//------------------------------------------------------------------
//   METHODS - COMPARISON
//------------------------------------------------------------------
/** compareTo method, from Comparable interface.
 * Compare this Appointment against another, for purposes of sorting.
 * <P>Only date and time participate, not repetition!
 * Consistent with equals().
 * @return -1 if this<a2, +1 if this>a2, else 0.
 */
public int compareTo(Object o2) {
    Appt a2 = (Appt) o2;
    if (year < a2.year)
        return -1;
    if (year > a2.year)
        return +1;
    if (month < a2.month)
        return -1;
    if (month > a2.month)
        return +1;
    if (day < a2.day)
        return -1;
    if (day > a2.day)
        return +1;
    if (hour < a2.hour)
        return -1;
    if (hour > a2.hour)
        return +1;
    if (minute < a2.minute)
        return -1;
    if (minute > a2.minute)
        return +1;
    return target.compareTo(a2.target);
}


/** Compare this appointment against another, for equality.
 * Consistent with compareTo(). For this reason, only
 * date & time participate, not repetition.
 * @returns true if the objects are equal, false if not.
 */
public boolean equals(Object o2) {
    Appt a2 = (Appt) o2;
    if (year != a2.year ||
        month != a2.month ||
        day != a2.day ||
        hour != a2.hour ||
        minute != a2.minute)
        return false;
    return target.equals(a2.target);
}
```

If you're still confused between `Comparable` and `Comparator`, you're probably not alone. This table summarizes the two "comparison" interfaces:

Interface name	Description	Method(s)
java.lang.Comparable	Provides a natural order to objects. Used in the class whose objects are being sorted.	`int compareTo(Object o);` `boolean equals(Object c2)`
java.util.Comparator	Provides total control over sorting objects of another class. Standalone; pass to `sort()` method or `Collection` constructor.	`int compare(Object o1, Object o2);`

7.9. Sorting in Java 1.1

Problem

You need to sort, but you're still running on Java 1.1.

Solution

Provide your own sort routine, or use mine.

Discussion

If you're still running on a Java 1.1 platform, you won't have the `Arrays` or `Collections` classes and therefore must provide your own sorting. There are two ways of proceeding: using the system *sort* utility or providing your own sort algorithm. The former—running the *sort* program—can be accomplished by running an external program, which will be covered in Recipe 26.1. The code here re-casts the example from Recipe 7.8 into using our own `Sort`. The actual sorting code is not printed here; it is included in the online source files, since it is just a simple adaptation of the QuickSort example from the Sorting program in Sun's Java QuickSort Applet demonstration.

```
public class StrSort1_1 {
    /** The list of strings to be sorted */
    static public String a[] = {
        "Qwerty",
        "Ian",
        "Java",
        "Gosling",
        "Alpha",
        "Zulu"
    };
```

```
/** Simple main program to test the sorting */
public static void main(String argv[]) {
    System.out.println("StrSort Demo in Java");
    StringSort s = new StringSort();
    dump(a, "Before");
    s.QuickSort(a, 0, a.length-1);
    dump(a, "After");
}

static void dump(String a[], String title) {
    System.out.println("***** " + title + " *****");
    for (int i=0; i<a.length; i++)
        System.out.println("a["+i+"]="+a[i]);
}

}
```

7.10. Avoiding the Urge to Sort

Problem

Your data needs to be sorted, but you don't want to stop and sort it periodically.

Solution

Not everything that requires order requires an explicit *sort* operation. Just keep the data sorted at all times.

Discussion

You can avoid the overhead and elapsed time of an explicit sorting operation by ensuring that the data is in the correct order at all times. You can do this manually or, in Java 2, by using a TreeSet or a TreeMap. First, some code from a call tracking program that I first wrote on JDK 1.0 to keep track of people I had extended contact with. Far less functional than a Rolodex, my CallTrak program maintained a list of people sorted by last name and first name. For each person it also had the city, phone number, and email address. Here is a portion of the code that was the event handler for the New User push button:

```
/** The list of User objects. */
Vector usrList = new Vector();
/** The scrolling list */
java.awt.List visList = new List();
/** Add one (new) Candidate to the lists */
protected void add(Candidate c) {
    String n = c.lastname;
    int i;
```

```
    for (i=0; i<usrList.size(); i++)
        if (n.compareTo(((Candidate)(usrList.elementAt(i))).lastname) <= 0)
            break;
    visList.add(c.getName(), i);
    usrList.insertElementAt(c, i);
    visList.select(i);        // ensure current
}
```

This code uses the `String` class `compareTo(String)` routine. This has the same name and signature as the `compareTo(Object)` in `Comparable`, but was added to the `String` class in JDK 1.1, before the `Comparable` interface was defined.

If I were writing this code today, on Java 2, I would probably use a `TreeSet` (which keeps objects in order) or a `TreeMap` (which keeps the keys in order, and maps from keys to values; the keys would be the name and the values would be the `Candidate` objects). These both insert the objects into a tree in the correct order, so an `Iterator` that traverses the tree always returns the objects in sorted order. In addition, they have methods such as `headSet()` and `headMap()`, which give a new object of the same class containing objects lexically before a given value. The `tailSet()` and `tailMap()` methods return objects greater than a given value, and `subSet()` and `subMap()` return a range. The `first()` and `last()` methods retrieve the obvious components from the collection. The following program uses a `TreeSet` to sort some names:

```
// TreeSetDemo.java
/* A TreeSet keeps objects in sorted order. We use a
 * Comparator published by String for case-insensitive
 * sorting order.
 */
TreeSet tm = new TreeSet(String.CASE_INSENSITIVE_ORDER);
tm.add("Gosling");
tm.add("da Vinci");
tm.add("van Gogh");
tm.add("Java To Go");
tm.add("Vanguard");
tm.add("Darwin");
tm.add("Darwin");// TreeSet is Set, ignores duplicate. See Recipe 7.11.

// Since it is sorted we can ask for various subsets
System.out.println("Lowest (alphabetically) is " + tm.first());
// Print how many elements are greater than "k"
System.out.println(tm.tailSet("k").toArray().length +
    " elements higher than \"k\"");

// Print the whole list in sorted order
System.out.println("Sorted list:");
java.util.Iterator t = tm.iterator();
while (t.hasNext())
    System.out.println(t.next());
```

One last point to note is that if you have a `Hashtable` or `HashMap` (and Java 2), you can convert it to a `TreeMap`, and therefore get it sorted, just by passing it to the `TreeMap` constructor:

```
TreeMap sorted = new TreeMap(unsortedHashMap);
```

7.11. Sets

Problem

You want to ensure that only one copy of each unique value is stored in a collection.

Solution

Use a `Set`.

Discussion

The `Set` interface is a collection that maintains only one instance of each value. If you add into it an object that is equal (as defined by the `equals()` method) to another object, only one of the objects is maintained. By definition, it does not matter to you which of the two objects it keeps—the one in the collection or the one being added—since your objects' `equals()` method indicated they were both equal.

```
// SetDemo.java
HashSet h = new HashSet();
h.add("One");
h.add("Two");
h.add("One"); // DUPLICATE
h.add("Three");
Iterator it = h.iterator();
while (it.hasNext()) {
    System.out.println(it.next());
}
```

Not surprisingly, only the three distinct values are printed.

7.12. Finding an Object in a Collection

Problem

You need to see whether a given collection contains a particular value.

Solution

Ask the collection if it contains an object of the given value.

Discussion

If you have created the contents of a collection, you probably know what is in it and what is not. But if the collection is prepared by another part of a large application, or even if you've just been putting objects into it and now need to find out if a given value was found, this recipe's for you. There is quite a variety of methods, depending on which class of collection you have. The following methods can be used:

Method	Meaning	Implementing classes
binarySearch()	Fairly fast search	Arrays, Collections
contains()	Linear search	ArrayList, HashSet, Hashtable, LinkList, Properties, Vector
containsKey(), containsValue()	Checks if the collection contains the object as a Key or as a Value	HashMap, Hashtable, Properties, TreeMap
indexOf()	Returns location where object is found	ArrayList, LinkedList, List, Stack, Vector
search()	Linear search	Stack

This example plays a little game of "find the hidden number" (or "needle in a haystack"); the numbers to look through are stored in an array. As games go, it's fairly pathetic: the computer plays against itself, so you probably know who's going to win. I wrote it that way so I would know that the data array contains valid numbers. The interesting part is not the generation of the random numbers (discussed in Recipe 5.12). The array to be used with `Arrays.binarySearch()` must be in sorted order, but since we just filled it with random numbers, it isn't initially sorted. Hence we call `Arrays.sort()` on the array. Then we are in a position to call `Arrays.binarySearch()`, passing in the array and the value to look for. If you run the program with a number, it runs that many games and reports on how it fared overall. If you don't bother, it plays only one game.

```java
import java.util.*;

/** Array Hunt "game" (pathetic: computer plays itself).
 */
public class ArrayHunt {
    protected final static int MAX    = 4000; // how many random ints
    protected final static int NEEDLE = 1999; // value to look for
    int haystack[];
    Random r;
```

```java
public static void main(String argv[]) {
    ArrayHunt h = new ArrayHunt();
    if (argv.length == 0)
        h.play();
    else {
        int won = 0;
        int games = Integer.parseInt(argv[0]);
        for (int i=0; i<games; i++)
            if (h.play())
                ++won;
        System.out.println("Computer won " + won +
            " out of " + games + ".");
    }
}


/** Construct the hunting ground */
public ArrayHunt() {
    haystack = new int[MAX];
    r = new Random();
}


/** Play one game. */
public boolean play() {
    int i;
    // Fill the array with random data (hay?)
    for (i=0; i<MAX; i++) {
        haystack[i] = (int)(r.nextFloat() * MAX);
    }

    // Precondition for binarySearch() is that array be sorted!
    Arrays.sort(haystack);

    // Look for needle in haystack. :-)
    i = Arrays.binarySearch(haystack, NEEDLE);

    if (i >= 0) {// found it - hurray, we win!
        System.out.println("Value " + NEEDLE +
            " occurs at haystack[" + i + "]");
        return true;
    } else {     // not found, we lose.
        System.out.println("Value " + NEEDLE +
            " does not occur in haystack; nearest value is " +
            haystack[-(i+2)] + " (found at " + -(i+2) + ")");
        return false;
    }
}
}
```

Note that the `Collections.binarySearch()` works almost exactly the same way, except it looks in a `Collection`, which must be sorted (presumably using `Collections.sort`, as discussed in Recipe 7.8).

7.13. Converting a Collection to an Array

Problem

You have a `Collection` but you need a Java language array.

Solution

Use the `Collection` method `toArray()`.

Discussion

If you have an `ArrayList` or other `Collection` and you need a Java language array, you can get it just by calling the `Collection`'s `toArray()` method. With no arguments you get an array whose type is `Object[]`. You can optionally provide an array argument, which is used for two purposes:

1. The type of the array argument determines the type of array returned.

2. If the array is big enough (you can control this with the `Collection`'s `size()` method), then this array is filled and returned. If the array is not big enough, a new array is allocated instead. If you provide an array and there are objects in the `Collection` that cannot be casted to this type, then you get an `ArrayStoreException`.

Example 7-1 shows code for converting an `ArrayList` to an array of type `Object`.

Example 7-1. ToArray.java

```
import java.util.*;

/** ArrayList to array */
public class ToArray {
    public static void main(String[] args) {
        ArrayList al = new ArrayList();
        al.add("Blobbo");
        al.add("Cracked");
        al.add("Dumbo");
        // al.add(new Date());// Don't mix and match!

        // Convert a collection to Object[], which can store objects
        // of any type.
        Object[] ol = al.toArray();
```

Example 7-1. ToArray.java (continued)

```
        System.out.println("Array of Object has length " + ol.length);

        // This would throw an ArrayStoreException if the line
        // "al.add(new Date())" above were uncommented.
        String[] sl = (String[]) al.toArray(new String[0]);
        System.out.println("Array of String has length " + ol.length);
    }
}
```

7.14. Rolling Your Own Iterator

Problem

You have your own data structure, but you want to publish the data as an `Iterator` to provide generic access to it You need to write your own `Iterator`.

Solution

Just implement (or provide an inner class that implements) the `Iterator` (or `Enumeration`) interface.

Discussion

To make data from one part of your program available in a storage-independent way to other parts of the code, generate an `Iterator`. Here is a short program that constructs, upon request, an `Iterator` for some data that it is storing, in this case in an array. The `Iterator` interface has only three methods: `hasNext()`, `next()`, and `remove()`.

```
import java.util.*;

/** Demonstrate the Iterator interface (new in 1.2).
 */
public class IterDemo implements Iterator {
    protected String[] data = { "one", "two", "three" };

    protected int index = 0;

    /** Returns true if not at the end, i.e., if next() will return
     * an element. Returns false if next() will throw an exception.
     */
    public boolean hasNext() {
        return (index < data.length);
    }
```

```
/** Returns the next element from the data */
public Object next() {
    if (index >= data.length)
        throw new IndexOutOfBoundsException(
            "only " + data.length + " elements");
    return data[index++];
}


/** Remove the object that next() just returned.
 * An Iterator is not required to support this interface,
 * and we certainly don't. :-)
 */
public void remove() {
    throw new UnsupportedOperationException(
        "This demo does not implement the remove method");
}


/** Simple tryout */
public static void main(String unused[]) {
    IterDemo it = new IterDemo();
    while (it.hasNext())
        System.out.println(it.next());
}

}
```

The comments above the remove() method remind me of an interesting point. This interface introduces something new to Java, the *optional method*. Since there is no syntax for this and they didn't want to introduce any new syntax, the developers of the Collections Framework decided on an implementation using existing syntax. If they are not implemented, the optional methods are required to throw an UnsupportedOperationException if they ever get called. My remove() method does this. Note that UnsupportedOperationException is subclassed from RunTimeException, so it is not required to be declared or caught.

This code is unrealistic in several ways, but it does show the syntax and how the Iterator interface works. In real code, the Iterator and the data are usually separate objects (the Iterator might be an inner class from the data store class). Also, you don't even need to write this code for an array; you can just construct an ArrayList object, copy the array elements into it, and ask it to provide the Iterator. However, I believe it's worth showing this simple example of the internals of an Iterator so you can understand both how it works and how you could provide one for a more sophisticated data structure, should the need arise.

7.15. Stack

Problem

You need to process data in "last-in, first-out" (LIFO) or "most recently added" order.

Solution

Write your own code for creating a stack; it's easy. Or, use a `java.util.Stack`.

Discussion

You need to put things into a holding area quickly, and retrieve them in last-in, first-out order. This is a common data structuring operation and is often used to reverse the order of objects. The basic operations of any stack are `push()` (add to stack), `pop()` (remove from stack), and `peek()` (examine top element without removing). A simple stack for stacking only `int`s is in class `ToyStack`:

```
/** Toy Stack. */
public class ToyStack {

    /** The maximum stack depth */
    protected int MAX_DEPTH = 10;
    /** The current stack depth */
    protected int depth = 0;
    /* The actual stack */
    protected int stack[] = new int[MAX_DEPTH];

    /* Implement a toy stack version of push */
    protected void push(int n) {
        stack[depth++] = n;
    }
    /* Implement a toy stack version of pop */
    protected int pop() {
        return stack[--depth];
    }
    /* Implement a toy stack version of peek */
    protected int peek() {
        return stack[depth];
    }
}
```

If you are not familiar with the basic idea of a stack, you should work through the code here; if you are, skip ahead. While looking at it, of course, think about what happens if `pop()` is called when `push()` has never been called, or if `push()` is called to stack more data than will fit.

The `java.util.Stack` operation behaves in a similar fashion. However, instead of being built just for one type of primitive, such as Java `int`, the methods of `java.util.Stack` are defined in terms of `java.lang.Object` so that any kind of object can be put in and taken out. A cast will be needed when popping objects, if you wish to call any methods defined in a class below `Object`.

For an example of a `java.util.Stack` in operation, Recipe 5.18 provides a simple stack-based numeric calculator.

7.16. *Multidimensional Structures*

Problem

You need a two-, three-, or more dimensional array or `ArrayList`.

Solution

No problem. Java supports this.

Discussion

As mentioned back in Recipe 7.1, Java arrays can hold any reference type. Since an array is a reference type, it follows that you can have arrays of arrays or, in other terminology, *multidimensional* arrays. Further, since each array has its own length attribute, the columns of a two-dimensional array, for example, do not all have to be the same length (see Figure 7-2).

Here is code to allocate a couple of two-dimensional arrays, one using a loop and the other using an initializer. Both are selectively printed.

```
/** Show Two-Dimensional Array of Objects */
public class ArrayTwoDObjects {

    /** Return list of subscript names (unrealistic; just for demo). */
    public static String[][] getArrayInfo() {
        String info[][];
        info = new String[10][10];
        for (int i=0; i < info.length; i++) {
            for (int j = 0; j < info[i].length; j++) {
                info[i][j] = "String[" + i + "," + j + "]";
            }
        }
        return info;
    }
```

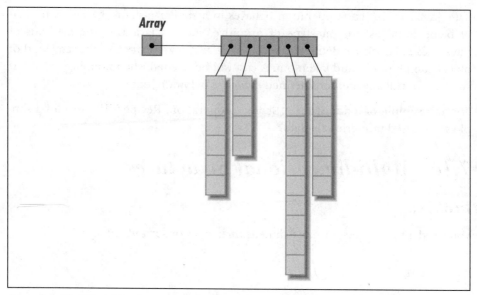

Figure 7-2. Multidimensional arrays

```java
/** Return list of allowable parameters (Applet method). */
public static String[][] getParameterInfo() {
    String param_info[][] = {
        {"fontsize",    "9-18",    "Size of font"},
        {"URL",    "-",    "Where to download"},
    };
    return param_info;
}


/** Run both initialization methods and print part of the results */
public static void main(String[] args) {
    print("from getArrayInfo", getArrayInfo());
    print("from getParameterInfo", getParameterInfo());
}


/** Print selected elements from the 2D array */
public static void print(String tag, String[][] array) {
    System.out.println("Array " + tag + " is " + array.length + " x " +
        array[0].length);
    System.out.println("Array[0][0] = " + array[0][0]);
    System.out.println("Array[0][1] = " + array[0][1]);
    System.out.println("Array[1][0] = " + array[1][0]);
    System.out.println("Array[0][0] = " + array[0][0]);
    System.out.println("Array[1][1] = " + array[1][1]);
}

}
```

Running it produces this output:

```
> java ArrayTwoDObjects
Array from getArrayInfo is 10 x 10
Array[0][0] = String[0,0]
Array[0][1] = String[0,1]
Array[1][0] = String[1,0]
Array[0][0] = String[0,0]
Array[1][1] = String[1,1]
Array from getParameterInfo is 2 x 3
Array[0][0] = fontsize
Array[0][1] = 9-18
Array[1][0] = URL
Array[0][0] = fontsize
Array[1][1] = -
>
```

The same kind of logic can be applied to any of the `Collections`. You could have an `ArrayList` of `ArrayLists`, or a `Vector` of linked lists, or whatever your little heart desires.

As Figure 7-2 shows, it is not necessary for the array to be "regular." That is, it's possible for each column of the 2D array to have a different height. That is why in the code example I used `array[0].length` for the length of the first column.

7.17. Finally, Collections

Problem

You're having trouble keeping track of all these lists, sets, and iterators.

Solution

There's a pattern to it. See Figure 7-3 and Table 7-2.

Discussion

Figure 7-3, in the fashion of the package-level class diagrams in the *Java in a Nutshell* books, shows the collection-based classes from package `java.util`.

See Also

The Javadoc documentation on `Collections`, `Arrays`, `List`, `Set`, and the classes that implement them provides more details than there's room for here. Table 7-2 may further help you to absorb the regularity of the Collections Framework.

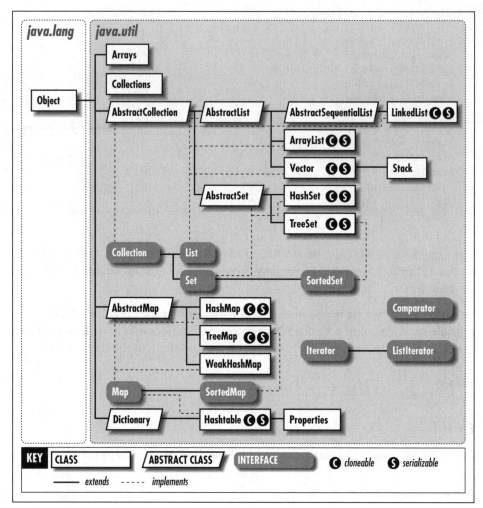

Figure 7-3. The Collections Framework

Table 7-2. Java Collections

Interfaces	Implementations			
	Resizable array	Hashed table	Linked list	Balanced tree
Set		HashSet		TreeSet
List	ArrayList, Vector		LinkList	
Map		HashMap, Hashtable		TreeMap

7.18. Program: Timing Comparisons

New developers sometimes worry about the overhead of these collections and think they should use arrays instead of data structures. To investigate, I wrote a

program that creates and accesses 250,000 objects, once through a Java array and
again through an ArrayList. This is a lot more objects than most programs use.
First the code for the Array version:

```
import com.darwinsys.util.MutableInteger;

/** Time a bunch of creates and gets through an Array */
public class Array {
    public static final int MAX = 250000;
    public static void main(String[] args) {
        System.out.println(new Array().run());
    }
    public int run() {
        MutableInteger list[] = new MutableInteger[MAX];
        for (int i=0; i<list.length; i++) {
            list[i] = new MutableInteger(i);
        }
        int sum = 0;
        for (int i=0; i<list.length; i++) {
            sum += list[i].getValue();
        }
        return sum;
    }
}
```

And the ArrayList version:

```
import java.util.ArrayList;

import com.darwinsys.util.MutableInteger;

/** Time a bunch of creates and gets through an Array */
public class ArrayLst {
    public static final int MAX = 250000;
    public static void main(String[] args) {
        System.out.println(new ArrayLst().run());
    }
    public int run() {
        ArrayList list = new ArrayList();
        for (int i=0; i<MAX; i++) {
            list.add(new MutableInteger(i));
        }
        int sum = 0;
        for (int i=0; i<MAX; i++) {
            sum += ((MutableInteger)list.get(i)).getValue();
        }
        return sum;
    }
}
```

The Vector-based version, ArrayVec, is sufficiently similar that I don't feel the need to kill a tree reprinting its code; it's online.

How can we time this? As covered in Recipe 25.5, you can either use the operating system's time command, if available, or just use a bit of Java that times a run of your main program. To be portable, I chose to use the latter, on an older, slower machine. Its exact speed doesn't matter, since the important thing is to compare only versions of this program running on the same machine.

Finally (drum roll, please) the results:

```
$ java Time Array
Starting class class Array
1185103928
runTime=4.310
$ java Time ArrayLst
Starting class class ArrayLst
1185103928
runTime=5.626
$ java Time ArrayVec
Starting class class ArrayVec
1185103928
runTime=6.699
$
```

Notice that I have ignored one oft-quoted bit of advice, that of giving a good initial estimate on the size of the ArrayList. I did time it that way as well; in this example, it made a difference of less than four percent in the total runtime.

The bottom line is that the efficiency of ArrayList is almost as good (75%) as that of arrays. The overhead of objects whose methods actually do some computation will almost certainly outweigh it. Unless you are dealing with millions of objects per minute, you probably don't need to worry about it. Vector is slightly slower, but still only about two-thirds the speed of the original array version.

8

Object-Oriented Techniques

8.0. Introduction

Java is an object-oriented (OO) language in the tradition of Simula-67, SmallTalk, and C++. It borrows syntax from the latter and ideas from SmallTalk. The Java API has been designed and built on the OO model. The *Design Patterns* (see the book of the same name) such as Factory and Delegate are used throughout; an understanding of these, though not required, will help you to better understand the use of the API.

Advice, or Mantras

There are any number of short bits of advice that I could give, and a few recurring themes that arise when learning the basics of Java, and then learning more Java.

Use the API

Can't say this often enough. A lot of the things you need to do have already been done by the good folks at JavaSoft. Learning the API well is a good grounds for avoiding that deadly "reinventing the flat tire" syndrome—coming up with a second-rate equivalent of a first-rate product that was available to you the whole time. This is, in fact, part of this book's mission—to prevent you from reinventing what's already there. One example of this is the Collections API in `java.util`, discussed in the previous chapter. It has a high degree of generality and regularity, so there is usually very little reason to invent your own data structuring code.

Generalize

There is a trade-off between generality (and the resulting reusability), which is emphasized here, and the convenience of application specificity. If you're writing one small part of a very large application designed according to OO design techniques, you'll have in mind a specific set of *use cases*. On the other hand, if you're writing "toolkit-style" code, you should write classes with few assumptions about how they'll be used. Making code easy to use from a variety of programs is the route to writing reusable code.

Read and write Javadoc

You've no doubt looked at the Java 2 online documentation in a browser, in part because I just told you to learn the API well. Do you think Sun hired millions of tech writers to produce all that documentation? No. That documentation exists because the developers of the API took the time to write Javadoc comments, those funny /** comments you've seen in code. So, one more bit of advice: use Javadoc. We finally have a good, standard mechanism for API documentation. And use it as you write the code—don't think you'll come back and write it in later. That kind of tomorrow never comes.

See Recipe 23.2 for details on using Javadoc.

Subclass early and often

I can't say this one enough either. Use subclassing. Use subclassing. Use subclassing. It is the best basis not only for avoiding duplication of code, but for developing software that works. See any number of good books on the topic of object- oriented design and programming for this. The topic of *Design Patterns* has recently evolved as a special case of "doing OO design while avoiding reinvention," hence a merger of these two bits of advice. That book is a good place to start.

Use design patterns

In the "Other Books" section of the Preface, I listed *Design Patterns* as one of the Very Important Books on object-oriented programming, as it provides a powerful catalog of things that programmers often reinvent. It is as important for giving a standard vocabulary of design as it is for its clear explanations of how the basic patterns work and how they can be implemented.

Here are some examples from the standard API:

Pattern name	Meaning	Examples in Java API
Factory	One class makes up instances for you, controlled by subclasses	getInstance (in Calendar, Format, Locale...); socket constructor; RMI InitialContext
Iterator	Loop over all elements in a collection, visiting each exactly once	Iterator; older Enumeration

Pattern name	Meaning	Examples in Java API
Singleton	Only one instance may exist	`java.awt.Toolkit`
Memento	Capture and externalize an object's state for later reconstruction	Object serialization
Command	Encapsulate requests, allowing queues of requests, undoable operations, etc.	`java.awt.Command`
Model-View-Controller	Model represents data; View is what the user sees; Controller responds to user request	Observer/Observable; see also Servlet Dispatcher (Recipe 18.8)

8.1. Printing Objects: Formatting with toString( )

Problem

You want your objects to have a useful default format.

Solution

Override the `toString()` method inherited from `java.lang.Object`.

Discussion

Whenever you pass an object to `System.out.println()` or any equivalent method, or involve it in string concatenation, Java will automatically call its `toString()` method. Java "knows" that every object has a `toString()` method, since `java.lang.Object` has one and all classes are ultimately subclasses of `Object`. The default implementation, in `java.lang.Object`, is neither pretty nor interesting: it just prints the class name, an @ sign, and the object's `hashCode()` value (see Recipe 8.3). For example, if you run this code:

```
/* Demonstrate toString() without an override */
public class ToStringWithout {
    int x, y;

    /** Simple constructor */
    public ToStringWithout(int anX, int aY) {
        x = anX; y = aY;
    }

    /** Main just creates and prints an object */
    public static void main(String[] args) {
        System.out.println(new ToStringWithout(42, 86));
    }
}
```

you might see this uninformative output:

```
ToStringWithout@990c747b
```

So, to make it print better, you should provide an implementation of `toString()`
that prints the class name and some of the important state in all but the most trivial classes. This gives you formatting control in `println()`, in debuggers, and anywhere your objects get referred to in a `String` context. Here is the previous
program done over with a `toString()` method:

```
/* Demonstrate toString() with an override */
public class ToStringWith {
    int x, y;

    /** Simple constructor */
    public ToStringWith(int anX, int aY) {
        x = anX; y = aY;
    }

    /** Override toString */
    public String toString() {
        return "ToStringWith[" + x + "," + y + "]";
    }
    /** Main just creates and prints an object */
    public static void main(String[] args) {
        System.out.println(new ToStringWith(42, 86));
    }
}
```

This version produces the more useful output:

```
ToStringWith[42,86]
```

8.2. Overriding the Equals Method

Problem

You want to be able to compare objects of your class.

Solution

Write an `equals()` method.

Discussion

How do you determine equality? For arithmetic or boolean operators, the answer is
simple: you test with the equals operator (==). For object references, though, Java
provides both == and the `equals()` method inherited from `java.lang.Object`.

The equals operator can be confusing, as it simply compares two object references to see if they refer to the same object. This is not what you want most of the time.

The inherited equals() method is also not as useful as you might imagine. Some people seem to start their life as Java developers thinking that the default equals() will magically do some kind of detailed, field-by-field or even binary comparison of objects. But it does *not* compare fields! It just does the simplest possible thing: it returns the value of an == comparison on the two objects involved! So, for anything useful, you will probably have to write an equals method. Note that both the equals and hashCode methods are used by hashes (Hashtable, HashMap; see Recipe 7.6). So if you think somebody using your class might want to create instances and put them into a hash, or even compare your objects, you owe it to them (and to yourself!) to implement equals() properly.

Here are the rules for an equals() method:

1. It is reflexive: x.equals(x) must be true.

2. It is symmetric: x.equals(y) must be true if and only if y.equals(x) is also true.

3. It is transitive: if x.equals(y) is true and y.equals(z) is true, then x.equals(z) must also be true.

4. It is consistent: multiple calls on x.equals(y) return the same value (unless state values used in the comparison are changed, as by calling a set method).

5. It is cautious: x.equals(null) must return false, rather than accidentally throwing a NullPointerException.

Here is a class that tries to implement these rules:

```
public class EqualsDemo {
    int int1;
    SomeClass obj1;

    /** Constructor */
    public EqualsDemo(int i, SomeClass o) {
        int1 = i;
        obj1 = o;
    }

    public EqualsDemo() {
        this(0, new SomeClass());
    }

    /** Typical run-of-the-mill Equals method */
    public boolean equals(Object o) {
        if (o == null)// caution
            return false;
```

```
        if (o == this)// optimization
            return true;


        // Castable to this class?
        if (!(o instanceof EqualsDemo))
            return false;

        EqualsDemo other = (EqualsDemo)o;// OK, cast to this class

        // compare field-by-field
        if (int1 != other.int1)// compare primitives directly
            return false;
        if (!obj1.equals(other.obj1))// compare objects using their equals
            return false;
        return true;
    }
}
```

And here is a `junit` test file (see Recipe 1.13) for the `EqualsDemo` class:

```
import junit.framework.*;
/** some junit test cases for EqualsDemo
 * writing a full set is left as "an exercise for the reader".
 * Run as: $ java junit.textui.TestRunner EqualsDemoTest
 */
public class EqualsDemoTest extends TestCase {

    /** an object being tested */
    EqualsDemo d1;
    /** another object being tested */
    EqualsDemo d2;

    /** init() method */
    public void setUp() {
        d1 = new EqualsDemo();
        d2 = new EqualsDemo();
    }

    /** constructor plumbing for junit */
    public EqualsDemoTest(String name) {
        super(name);
    }

    public void testSymmetry() {
        assert(d1.equals(d1));
    }

    public void testSymmetric() {
        assert(d1.equals(d2) && d2.equals(d1));
    }
```

```
        public void testCaution() {
            assert(!d1.equals(null));
        }
    }
```

With all that testing, what could go wrong? Well, some things still need care. What if the object is a *subclass* of EqualsDemo? We cast it and . . . compare only our fields! You probably should test explicitly with getClass() if subclassing is likely. And subclasses should call super.equals() to test all superclass fields.

What else could go wrong? Well, what if either obj1 or other.obj1 is null? You might have just earned a nice shiny new NullPointerException. So you also need to test for any possible null values. Good constructors can avoid these, as I've tried to do in EqualsDemo, or else test for them explicitly.

8.3. Overriding the Hashcode Method

Problem

You want to use your objects in a hash, and you need to write a hashCode().

Discussion

The hashCode() method is supposed to return an int that should uniquely identify different objects.

A properly written hashCode() method will follow these rules:

1. It is repeatable: hashCode(x) must return the same int when called again unless set methods have been called.

2. It is symmetric: if x.equals(y), then x.hashCode() must == y.hashCode(), i.e., either both return true, or both return false.

3. If !x.equals(y), it is not required that x.hashCode() != y.hashCode(), but doing so may improve performance of hash tables, i.e., hashes may call hashCode() before equals().

The default hashCode() on Sun's JDK returns a machine address, which conforms to Rule 1. Conformance to Rules 2 and 3 depends, in part, upon your equals() method. Here is a program that prints the hashcodes of a small handful of objects:

```
/** Display hashCodes from some objects */
public class PrintHashCodes {

    /** Some objects to hashCode() on */
```

```
protected static Object[] data = {
    new PrintHashCodes(),
    new java.awt.Color(0x44, 0x88, 0xcc),
    new SomeClass()
};

public static void main(String[] args) {
    System.out.println("About to hashCode " + data.length + " objects.");
    for (int i=0; i<data.length; i++) {
        System.out.println(data[i].toString() + " --> " +
            data[i].hashCode());
    }
    System.out.println("All done.");
}
}
```

What does it print?

```
> jikes +E -d . PrintHashCodes.java
> java PrintHashCodes
About to hashCode 3 objects.
PrintHashCodes@982741a0 --> -1742257760
java.awt.Color[r=68,g=136,b=204] --> -12285748
SomeClass@860b41ad --> -2046082643
All done.
>
```

The hashcode value for the Color object is interesting. It is actually computed as something like:

```
(r<<24 + g<<16 + b<<8 + alpha)
```

The "high bit" in this word having been set by shifting causes the value to appear negative when printed as a signed integer. Hashcode values are allowed to be negative.

8.4. The Clone Method

Problem

You want to clone yourself. Or at least your objects.

Solution

Override Object.clone().

Discussion

To *clone* something is to make a duplicate of it. The `clone()` method in Java makes an exact duplicate of an object. Why do we need cloning? Java's method calling semantics are call-by-reference, which allows the called method to modify the state of an object that is passed into it. Cloning the input object before calling the method would pass a copy of the object, keeping your original safe.

How can you clone? Cloning is not "enabled" by default in classes that you write.

```
Object o = new Object();
Object o2 = o.clone();
```

If you try calling `clone()` without any special preparation, as in this excerpt from *Clone0.java*, you will see a message like this (from the Jikes compiler; the *javac* message may not be as informative):

```
Clone0.java:4:29:4:37: Error: Method "java.lang.Object clone();" in class "java/
lang/Object" has protected or default access. Therefore, it is not accessible in
class "Clone0" which is in a different package.
```

You must take two steps to make your class cloneable:

1. Override `Object`'s `clone()` method.
2. Implement the empty Cloneable interface.

Using cloning

The class `java.lang.Object` declares its clone *protected* and *native*. Protected classes can be called by a subclass or those in the same package (i.e., `java.lang`), but not by unrelated classes. That is, you can call `Object.clone()`—the native method that does the magic of duplicating the object—only from within the object being cloned. Here is a simple example of a class with a clone method, and a tiny program that uses it:

```
public class Clone1 implements Cloneable {

    /** Clone this object. Just call super.clone() to do the work */
    public Object clone() throws CloneNotSupportedException {
        return super.clone();
    }

    int x;
    transient int y;// will be cloned, but not serialized

    public static void main(String[] args) {
        Clone1 c = new Clone1();
        c.x = 100;
        c.y = 200;
```

```
        try {
            Object d = c.clone();
            System.out.println("c=" + c);
            System.out.println("d=" + d);
        } catch (CloneNotSupportedException ex) {
            System.out.println("Now that's a surprise!!");
            System.out.println(ex);
        }
    }

    /** Display the current object as a string */
    public String toString() {
        return "Clone1[" + x + "," + y + "]";
    }
}
```

The clone() method in Object throws CloneNotSupportedException. This is to handle the case of inadvertently calling clone() on a class that isn't supposed to be cloned. Since most of the time you don't need to do anything with this exception, a clone method can simply declare this exception in its throws clause, and let the calling code deal with it.

Calling Object's clone() does a stateful, shallow copy down inside the JVM. That is, it creates a new object, and copies all the fields from the old object into the new. It then returns the new reference as an Object; you need to cast it to the appropriate object type. So if that's all there is, why do you even have to write this method? The reason is to give you a chance to do any preservation of state that is required in cloning your objects. For example, if your class has any references to other objects (and most real-world classes do), you may well want to clone them as well! The default clone method simply copies all the object's state, so that you now have two references to each object. Or you might have to close and reopen files, to avoid having two threads (see Chapter 24) reading from or writing into the same file. In effect, what you have to do here depends on what the rest of your class does.

Now suppose that you clone a class containing an array of objects. You now have two references to objects in the array, but further additions to the array will only be made in one array or the other. Imagine a Vector, Stack, or other collection class being used in your class, and your object gets cloned!

The bottom line is that most object references need to be cloned.

Even if you don't need clone(), your subclasses may! If you didn't provide clone() in a class subclassed from Object, your subclasses will probably get the Object version, which will cause problems if there are collections or other mutable objects referred to. As a general rule, you should provide clone() even if only your own subclasses would need it.

Difficulty in the standard API

The java.util.Observable class (designed to implement the Model-View-Controller pattern with AWT or Swing applications) contains a private Vector but no clone method to deep-clone it. Thus, Observable objects cannot safely be cloned, ever!

8.5. The Finalize Method

Problem

You want to have some action taken when your objects are removed from service.

Solution

Use finalize() but don't trust it; or, write your own end-of-life method.

Discussion

Developers coming from a C++ background tend to form a mental map that has a line of equivalency drawn from C++ destructors to Java finalizers. In C++, destructors are called automatically when you delete an object. Java, though, has no such operator as delete; objects are freed automatically by a part of the Java runtime called the *garbage collector*, or GC. GC runs as a background thread in Java processes and looks around every so often to see if there are any objects that are no longer referred to by any reference variable. When it runs, as it frees objects, it calls their finalize() methods.

For example, what if you (or some code you called) invoke System.exit()? In this case the entire JVM will cease to exists (assuming there isn't an applet-style security manager to deny it permission to do so) and the finalizer is never run. Similarly, a "memory leak" or mistakenly held reference to your object will also prevent finalizers from running.

Can't you just ensure that all finalizers get run simply by calling System.runFinalizersOnExit(true)? Not really! This method is deprecated (see Recipe 1.9); the documentation notes:

> This method is inherently unsafe. It may result in finalizers being called on live objects while other threads are concurrently manipulating those objects, resulting in erratic behavior or deadlock.

So what if you need some kind of cleanup? You must take responsibility for defining a method and invoking it before you let any object of that class go out of reference. You might call such a method cleanUp().

Java 2 SDK 1.3 introduced the runtime method addShutdownHook(), to which you pass a non-started Thread subclass object; if the virtual machine has a chance, it runs your shutdown hook code as part of termination. This will normally work, unless the VM was terminated abruptly as by a kill signal on Unix or a KillProcess on Win32, or the VM aborts due to detecting internal corruption of its data structures.

The bottom line? There's no guarantee, but finalizers and shutdown hooks both have pretty good odds of being run.

8.6. Using Inner Classes

Problem

You need to write a private class, or a class to be used in one other class at the most.

Solution

Use a non-public class or an inner class.

Discussion

A non-public class can be written as part of another class's source file, but is not included inside that class. An *inner class* is Java terminology for a class defined inside another class. Inner classes were first popularized with the advent of JDK 1.1 for use as event handlers for GUI applications (see Recipe 13.4), but they have a much wider application.

Inner classes can, in fact, be constructed in several contexts. An inner class defined as a member of a class can be instantiated anywhere in that class. An inner class defined inside a method can only be referred to later in the same method. Inner classes can also be named or anonymous. A named inner class has a full name that is compiler-dependent; the standard JVM uses a name like MainClass$InnerClass.class for the resulting file. An anonymous inner class, similarly, has a compiler-dependent name; the JVM uses MainClass$1.class, MainClass$2.class, and so on.

These classes cannot be instantiated in any other context; any explicit attempt to refer to, say, OtherMainClass$InnerClass, will be caught at compile time.

```java
import java.awt.event.*;
import javax.swing.*;

public class AllClasses {
    /** Inner class can be used anywhere in this file */
    public class Data {
        int x;
```

```
        int y;
    }
    public void getResults() {
        JButton b = new JButton("Press me");
        b.addActionListener(new ActionListener() {
            public void actionPerformed(ActionEvent evt) {
                System.out.println("Thanks for pressing me");
            }
        });
    }
}

/** Class contained in same file as AllClasses, but can be used
 * (with a warning) in other contexts.
 */
class AnotherClass {
    // methods and fields here...
}
```

8.7. *Providing Callbacks via Interfaces*

Problem

You want to provide *callbacks*; that is, have unrelated classes call back into your code.

Solution

One way is to use a Java interface.

Discussion

An *interface* is a class-like object that can contain only abstract methods and final fields. As we've seen, interfaces are used a lot in Java! In the standard API, the following are a few of the commonly used interfaces:

* `Runnable`, `Comparable`, and `Cloneable` (in `java.lang`)

* `List`, `Set`, `Map`, and `Enumeration/Iterator` (in the Collections API; see Chapter 7)

* `ActionListener`, `WindowListener`, and others (in the AWT GUI; see Recipe 13.4)

* `Driver`, `Connection`, `Statement`, and `ResultSet` (in JDBC; see Recipe 20.3)

* The "remote interface"—the contact between the client and the server—is specified as an `Interface` (in RMI, CORBA, and EJB)

Subclass, Abstract Class, or Interface?

There is usually more than one way to skin a cat. Some problems can be solved by subclassing, by use of abstract classes, or by interfaces. The following general guidelines may help:

- *Use an abstract class* when you want to provide a template for a series of subclasses, all of which may inherit some of their functionality from the parent class but are required to implement some of it themselves. (Any subclass of a geometric Shapes class might have to provide a computeArea() method; since the top-level Shapes class cannot do this, it would be abstract. This is implemented in Recipe 8.8.)

- *Subclass* whenever you want to extend a class and add some functionality to it, whether the parent class is abstract or not. See the standard Java APIs and the examples in Recipes 1.13, 5.10, 8.11, 9.7, and many others throughout this book.

- *Subclass* when you are required to extend a given class. Applets (see Recipe 17.2), servlets (Recipe 18.1), and others use subclassing to ensure "base" functionality in classes that are dynamically loaded (see Recipe 25.3).

- *Define an interface* when there is no common parent class with the desired functionality, and when you want only certain unrelated classes to have that functionality (see the PowerSwitchable interface in Recipe 8.7).

- *Use interfaces as "markers"* to indicate something about a class. The standard API uses Cloneable (Recipe 8.4) and Serializable (Recipe 9.16) as markers.

Suppose we are generating a futuristic building management system. To be energy-efficient, we want to be able to remotely turn off (at night and on weekends) such things as room lights and computer monitors, which use a lot of energy. Assume we have some kind of "remote control" technology: it could be a commercial version of BSR's house-light control technology "X10"; it could be BlueTooth or 802.11; it doesn't matter. What matters is that we have to be very careful what we turn off. It would cause great ire if we turned off computer processors automatically—people often leave things running overnight. It would be a matter of public safety if we ever turned off the building emergency lighting.* So we've come up with the design shown in Figure 8-1.

The code for these classes is not shown (it's pretty trivial) but it's in the online source. The top-level classes—those with names ending in Asset, and

---

* Of course these lights wouldn't have remote power-off. But the computers might, for maintenance purposes.

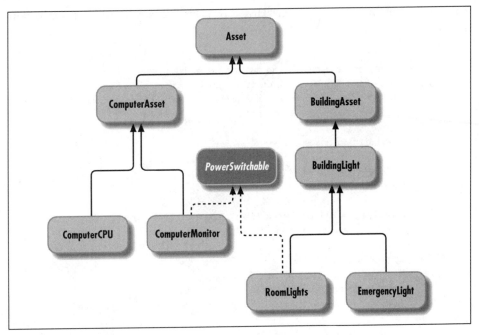

Figure 8-1. Classes for a building management system

BuildingLight—are abstract classes. You can't instantiate them, as they don't have any specific functionality. To ensure—both at compile time and at runtime—that we can never switch off the emergency lighting, we need only ensure that the class representing it, EmergencyLight, does not implement the PowerSwitchable interface.

Note that we can't very well use direct inheritance here. There is no common ancestor class that includes both ComputerMonitor and RoomLights that doesn't also include ComputerCPU and EmergencyLight. Use interfaces to define functionality in unrelated classes.

How we use these is demonstrated by the BuildingManagement class; this class is not part of the hierarchy shown in Figure 8-1, but instead uses a collection (actually an array, to make the code simpler for illustrative purposes) of Asset objects from that hierarchy.

Items that can't be switched must nonetheless be in the database, for various purposes (auditing, insurance, and so on). In the method that turns things off, the code is careful to check whether each object in the database is an instance of the PowerSwitchable interface. If so, the object is casted to PowerSwitchable so that its powerDown() method can be called. If not, the object is skipped, thus preventing any possibility of turning out the emergency lights or shutting off a machine that is busy running Seti@Home or a big Napster download. Or system backups.

```
/**
 * BuildingManagement - control an energy-saving building.
 * This class shows how we might control the objects in an office
 * that can safely be powered off at nighttime to save energy - lots of
 * it, when applied to a large office!
 */
public class BuildingManagement {

    Asset things[] = new Asset[24];
    int numItems = 0;

    /** goodNight is called from a timer Thread at 2200, or when we
     * get the "shutdown" command from the security guard.
     */
    public void goodNight() {
        for (int i=0; i<things.length; i++)
            if (things[i] instanceof PowerSwitchable)
                ((PowerSwitchable)things[i]).powerDown();
    }

    // goodMorning() would be the same, but call each one's powerUp().

    /** Add a Asset to this building */
    public void add(Asset thing) {
        System.out.println("Adding " + thing);
        things[numItems++] = thing;
    }

    /** The main program */
    public static void main(String[] av) {
        BuildingManagement b1 = new BuildingManagement();
        b1.add(new RoomLights(101));// control lights in room 101
        b1.add(new EmergencyLight(101));// and emerg. lights.
        // add the computer on desk#4 in room 101
        b1.add(new ComputerCPU(10104));
        // and its monitor
        b1.add(new ComputerMonitor(10104));

        // time passes, and the sun sets...
        b1.goodNight();
    }
}
```

When you run this program, it shows all the items being added, but only the PowerSwitchable ones being switched off:

```
> java BuildingManagement
Adding RoomLights@2dc77f32
```

```
Adding EmergencyLight@2e3b7f32
Adding ComputerCPU@2e637f32
Adding ComputerMonitor@2f1f7f32
Dousing lights in room 101
Dousing monitor at desk 10104
>
```

8.8. *Polymorphism/Abstract Methods*

Problem

You want each of a number of methods in subclasses to provide its own version of
a method.

Solution

Make the method abstract in the parent class; this makes the compiler ensure that
each subclass implements it.

Discussion

A hypothetical drawing program uses a Shape subclass for anything that is drawn.
Shape has an abstract method computeArea(), which computes the exact area of
the given shape:

```java
public abstract class Shape {
    protected int x, y;
    public abstract double computeArea();
}
```

A Rectangle subclass, for example, has a computeArea() that multiplies width
times height and returns the result:

```java
public class Rectangle extends Shape {
    double width, height;
    public double computeArea() {
        return width * height;
    }
}
```

A Circle subclass returns $\pi \times r$:

```java
public class Circle extends Shape {
    double radius;
    public double computeArea() {
        return Math.PI * radius * radius;
    }
}
```

This system has a very high degree of generality. In the main program we can pass over a collection of Shape objects and—here's the real beauty—call computeArea() on any Shape subclass object without having to worry about what kind of Shape it is. Java's polymorphic methods automatically call the correct computeArea() method in the class of which the object was originally constructed:

```
/** Part of a main program using Shape objects */
public class Main {

    Collection allShapes;// created in a Constructor, not shown

    /** Iterate over all the Shapes, getting their areas */
    public double totalAreas() {
        Iterator it = allShapes.iterator();
        double total = 0.0;
        while (it.hasNext()) {
            Shape s = (Shape)it.next();
            total += s.computeArea();
        }
        return total;
    }
}
```

This is a great boon for software maintenance: if a new subclass is added, the code in the main program does not change. Further, all the code that is specific to, say, polygon handling, is all in one place: in the source file for the Polygon class. This is a big improvement over older languages, where type fields in a structure or record were used with case or switch statements scattered all across the software. Java makes software more reliable and maintainable with the use of polymorphism.

8.9. Passing Values

Problem

You need to pass a number like an int into a routine, and get back the routine's updated version of that value in addition to the routine's return value.

This often comes up in working through strings; the routine may need to return a boolean, say, or the number of characters transferred, but also needs to increment an integer array or string index in the calling class.

It is also useful in constructors, which can't return a value but may need to indicate that they have "consumed" or processed a certain number of characters from within a string, such as when the string will be further processed in a subsequent call.

Solution

Use a specialized class such as the one presented here.

Discussion

The Integer class is one of Java's predefined Number subclasses, mentioned in the Introduction to Chapter 5. It serves as a wrapper for an int value, and also has static methods for parsing and formatting integers.

It's fine as it is, but you may want something simpler.

Here is a class I wrote, called MutableInteger, that is like an Integer but specialized by omitting the overhead of Number and providing only the set, get, and incr operations, the latter overloaded to provide a no-argument version that performs the increment (++) operator on its value, and also a one-integer version that adds that increment into the value (analogous to the += operator). Since Java doesn't support operator overloading, the calling class has to call these methods instead of invoking the operations syntactically, as you would on an int. For applications that need this functionality, the advantages outweigh this minor syntactic restriction. First let's look at an example of how it might be used. Assume you need to call a scanner function called, say, parse(), and get back both a boolean (indicating whether or not a value was found) and an integer value indicating where it was found:

```
import com.darwinsys.util.*;

/** Show use of MutableInteger to "pass back" a value in addition
 * to a function's return value.
 */
public class StringParse {
    /** This is the function that has a return value of true but
     * also "passes back" the offset into the String where a
     * value was found. Contrived example!
     */
    public static boolean parse(String in,
        char lookFor, MutableInteger whereFound) {
        int i = in.indexOf(lookFor);
        if (i == -1)
            return false;// not found
        whereFound.setValue(i);// say where found
        return true;// say that it was found
    }

    public static void main(String[] args) {
        MutableInteger mi = new MutableInteger();
        String text = "Hello, World";
```

```
        char c = 'W';
        if (parse(text, c, mi)) {
            System.out.println("Character " + c + " found at offset "
                + mi + " in " + text);
        } else {
            System.out.println("Not found");
        }
    }
}
```

Now many OO purists will argue—convincingly—that you shouldn't do this. That you can always rewrite it so there is only one return value. Either return and have the caller interpret a single value (in this case, return the offset in the return statement, and let the user know that –1 indicates not found), or define a trivial wrapper class containing both the integer and the boolean. However, there is precedent in the standard API: this code is remarkably similar to how the `ParsePosition` class (see Recipe 6.5) is used. Anyway, this functionality is requested often enough that I feel justified in showing how to do it, accompanied by this disclaimer: try to avoid doing it this way in new code!

Having said all that, here is the `MutableInteger` class:

```
package com.darwinsys.util;

/** A MutableInteger is like an Integer but mutable, to avoid the
 * excess object creation involved in
 * c = new Integer(c.getInt()+1)
 * which can get expensive if done a lot.
 * Not subclassed from Integer, since Integer is final (for performance :-))
 */
public class MutableInteger {
    private int value = 0;

    public MutableInteger() {
    }

    public MutableInteger(int i) {
        value = i;
    }

    public void incr() {
        value++;
    }

    public void decr() {
        value--;
    }
```

```
    public void setValue(int i) {
        value = i;
    }

    public int getValue() {
        return value;
    }

    public String toString() {
        return Integer.toString(value);
    }

    public static String toString(int val) {
        return Integer.toString(val);
    }

    public static int parseInt(String str) {
        return Integer.parseInt(str);
    }
}
```

See Also

As mentioned, this use of `MutableInteger` could be replaced with `ParsePosition`. However, `MutableInteger` has other uses; it makes a fine in-memory counter in a servlet (see Recipe 18.0).

8.10. Roll Your Own Exceptions

Problem

You'd like to use an application-specific exception class or two.

Solution

Go ahead and subclass `Exception` or `RuntimeException`.

Discussion

In theory you could subclass `Throwable` directly, but that's considered rude. You normally subclass `Exception` (if you want a checked exception) or `RuntimeException` (if you want an unchecked exception). Checked exceptions are those that an application developer is required to catch, or "throw away" by listing them in the `throws` clause of the invoking method.

When subclassing either of these, it is customary to provide at least a no-argument and a one-string argument constructor:

```
/** A ChessMoveException is thrown  when the user makes an illegal move. */
public class ChessMoveException extends RuntimeException {
        public ChessMoveException () {
                super();
        }
        public ChessMoveException (String msg) {
                super(msg);
        }
}
```

See Also

The Javadoc documentation for Exception lists a very large number of subclasses; you might look there first to see if there is one you can use.

8.11. Program: Plotter

Not because it is very sophisticated, but because it is simple, this program will serve as an example of some of the things we've covered in this chapter, and will also, in its subclasses, provide springboards for other discussions. This class describes a series of old-fashioned (i.e., common in the 1970s and 1980s) pen plotters. A pen plotter, in case you've never seen one, is a device that moves a pen around a piece of paper and draws things. It can lift the pen off the paper or lower it, and it can draw lines, letters, and so on. Before the rise of laser printers and ink-jet printers, pen plotters were the dominant means of preparing charts of all sorts, as well as presentation slides (this was, ah, well before the rise of programs like Harvard Presents and Microsoft PowerPoint). Today few companies still manufacture pen plotters, but I use them here because they are simple enough to be well understood from this brief description.

I'll present a high-level class that abstracts the key characteristics of a series of such plotters made by different vendors. It would be used, for example, in an analytical or data-exploration program to draw colorful charts showing the relationships found in data. But I don't want my main program to worry about the gory details of any particular brand of plotter, so I'll abstract into a Plotter class, whose source is as follows:

```
/**
 * Plotter abstract class. Must be subclassed
 * for X, DOS, Penman, HP plotter, etc.
 *
 * Coordinate space: X = 0 at left, increases to right.
 *        Y = 0 at top, increases downward (same as AWT).
 */
```

```java
public abstract class Plotter {
    public final int MAXX = 800;
    public final int MAXY = 600;
    /** Current X co-ordinate (same reference frame as AWT!) */
    protected int curx;
    /** Current Y co-ordinate (same reference frame as AWT!) */
    protected int cury;
    /** The current state: up or down */
    protected boolean penIsUp;
    /** The current color */
    protected int penColor;

    Plotter() {
        penIsUp = true;
        curx = 0; cury = 0;
    }
    abstract void rmoveTo(int incrx, int incry);
    abstract void moveTo(int absx, int absy);
    abstract void penUp();
    abstract void penDown();
    abstract void penColor(int c);

    abstract void setFont(String fName, int fSize);
    abstract void drawString(String s);

    /* Concrete classes */

    /** Draw a box of width w and height h */
    public void drawBox(int w, int h) {
        penDown();
        rmoveTo(w, 0);
        rmoveTo(0, h);
        rmoveTo(-w, 0);
        rmoveTo(0, -h);
        penUp();
    }

    /** Draw a box given an AWT Dimension for its size */
    public void drawBox(java.awt.Dimension d) {
        drawBox(d.width, d.height);
    }

    /** Draw a box given an AWT Rectangle for its location and size */
    public void drawBox(java.awt.Rectangle r) {
        moveTo(r.x, r.y);
        drawBox(r.width, r.height);
    }
}
```

Note the wide variety of abstract methods. Those related to motion, pen control, or drawing are left out, due to the number of different methods for dealing with them. However, the method for drawing a rectangle (drawBox) has a default implementation, which simply puts the currently selected pen onto the paper at the last-moved-to location, draws the four sides, and raises the pen. Subclasses for "smarter" plotters will likely override this method, but subclasses for less-evolved plotters will probably use the default version. There are also two overloaded convenience versions of this method, for the case where the client has an AWT Dimension for the size, or an AWT Rectangle for the location and size.

To demonstrate one of the subclasses of this program, consider the following simple "driver" program. The Class.forName() near the beginning of main will be discussed in Recipe 25.3; for now you can take my word that it simply creates an instance of the given subclass, which we store in a Plotter reference named "r" and use to draw the plot:

```
,/** Main program, driver for Plotter class.
 * This is to simulate a larger graphics application such as GnuPlot.
 */
public class PlotDriver {

    /** Construct a Plotter driver, and try it out. */
    public static void main(String[] argv)
    {
        Plotter r ;
        if (argv.length != 1) {
            System.err.println("Usage: PlotDriver driverclass");
            return;
        }
        try {
            Class c = Class.forName(argv[0]);
            Object o = c.newInstance();
            if (!(o instanceof Plotter))
                throw new ClassNotFoundException("Not instanceof Plotter");
            r = (Plotter)o;
        } catch (ClassNotFoundException e) {
            System.err.println("Sorry, "+argv[0]+" not a plotter class");
            return;
        } catch (Exception e) {
            e.printStackTrace();
            return;
        }
        r.penDown();
        r.penColor(1);
        r.moveTo(200, 200);
        r.penColor(2);
        r.drawBox(123, 200);
```

```
            r.rmoveTo(10, 20);
            r.penColor(3);
            r.drawBox(123, 200);
            r.penUp();
            r.moveTo(300, 100);
            r.penDown();
            r.setFont("Helvetica", 14);
            r.drawString("Hello World");
            r.penColor(4);
            r.drawBox(10, 10);
        }
    }
```

We'll see further examples of this Plotter class and its relatives in several upcoming chapters.

9

Input and Output

9.0 Introduction

Most programs need to interact with the outside world, and one common way of doing so is by reading and writing files. Files are normally on some persistent medium such as a disk drive, and, for the most part, we shall happily ignore the differences between a hard disk (and all the operating system–dependent filesystem types), a floppy or zip drive, a CD-ROM, and others. For now, they're just files.

Correcting Misconceptions

Java's approach to input/output is sufficiently different from that of older languages (C, Fortran, Pascal) that people coming from those languages are often critical of Java's I/O model. I can offer no better defense than that provided in the preface to Elliotte Rusty Harold's book *Java I/O*:

> Java is the first programming language with a modern, object-oriented approach to input and output. Java's I/O model is more powerful and more suited to real-world tasks than any other major language used today. Surprisingly, however, I/O in Java has a bad reputation. It is widely believed (falsely) that Java I/O can't handle basic tasks that are easily accomplished in other languages like C, C++, and Pascal. In particular, it is commonly said that:
>
> — I/O is too complicated for introductory students; or, more specifically, there's no good way to read a number from the console.
>
> — Java can't handle basic formatting tasks like printing PI with three decimal digits of precision.
>
> [Rusty's book shows] that not only can Java handle these two tasks with relative ease and grace; it can do anything C and C++ can do, and a whole lot more. Java's

I/O capabilities not only match those of classic languages like C and Pascal, they vastly surpass them.

The most common complaint about Java I/O among students, teachers, authors of textbooks, and posters to comp.lang.java is that there's no simple way to read a number from the console (System.in). Many otherwise excellent introductory Java books repeat this canard. Some textbooks go to great lengths to reproduce the behavior they're accustomed to from C or Pascal, apparently so teachers don't have to significantly rewrite the tired Pascal exercises they've been using for the last 20 years. However, new books that aren't committed to the old ways of doing things generally use command-line interfaces for basic exercises, then rapidly introduce the graphical user interfaces any real [desktop] program is going to use anyway. Apple wisely abandoned the command-line interface back in 1984, and the rest of the world is slowly catching up. Although System.in and System.out are certainly convenient for teaching and debugging, in 1999 no completed, cross-platform program should even assume the existence of a console for either input or output.

The second common complaint about Java I/O is that it can't handle formatted output; that is, that there's no equivalent of printf() in Java. In a very narrow sense, this is true, because Java does not support the variable length arguments lists a function like printf() requires. Nonetheless, a number of misguided souls (your author not least among them) [has] at one time or another embarked on futile efforts to reproduce printf() in Java. This may have been necessary in Java 1.0, but as of Java 1.1, it's no longer needed. The java.text package, described in Chapter 16 [of Rusty's book, and in Chapter 5 of the present work], provides complete support for formatting numbers. Furthermore, the java.text package goes way beyond the limited capabilities of printf(). It supports not only different precisions and widths, but also internationalization, currency formats, grouping symbols, and a lot more. It can easily be extended to handle Roman numerals, scientific or exponential notation, or any other number format you may require.

The underlying flaw in most people's analysis of Java I/O is that they've confused input and output with the formatting and interpreting of data. Java is the first major language to cleanly separate the classes that read and write bytes (primarily, various kinds of input streams and output streams) from the classes that interpret this data. You often need to format strings without necessarily writing them on the console. You may also need to write large chunks of data without worrying about what they represent. Traditional languages that connect formatting and interpretation of I/O and hard-wire a few specific formats are extremely difficult to extend to other formats. In essence, you have to give up and start from scratch every time you want to process a new format.

Furthermore, C's printf(), fprintf(), and sprintf() family only really works well on Unix (where, not coincidentally, C was invented). On other platforms the underlying assumption that every target may be treated as a file fails, and these standard library functions must be replaced by other functions from the host API.

Java's clean separation between formatting and I/O allows you to create new formatting classes without throwing away the I/O classes, and to write new I/O classes while still using the old formatting classes. Formatting and interpreting strings are fundamentally different operations from moving bytes from one device to another. Java is the first major language to recognize and take advantage of this.

To which I can only add, "Well said, Rusty." What Rusty doesn't mention is an obvious corollary of this flexibility: it can often take a bit more coding to do some of the command-line, standard-in/standard-out operations. You'll see most of these in this chapter, and you'll see throughout the book how flexible Java I/O really is.

This chapter covers all the normal input/output operations such as opening/closing and reading/writing files. Files are assumed to reside on some kind of file store or permanent storage. I don't discuss how such a filesystem or disk I/O system works—consult a book on operating system design for the general details, or a platform-specific book on system internals or filesystem design for such details. Network filesystems such as Sun's Network File System (NFS, common on Unix and available for Windows though products such as Hummingbird NFS), Macintosh Appletalk File System (available for Unix via NetATalk), and SMB (MS-Windows network filesystem, available for Unix with the freeware Samba program) are assumed to work "just like" disk filesystems, except where noted. And while you could even provide your own network filesystem layer using the material covered in Chapter 16, it is exceedingly difficult to design your own network virtual filesystem, and probably better to use one of the existing ones.

Streams and Readers/Writers

Java provides two sets of classes for reading and writing. The `Stream` section of package `java.io` (see Figure 9-1) is for reading or writing bytes of data. Older languages tended to assume that a byte (which is a machine-specific collection of bits, usually eight bits on modern computers) is exactly the same thing as a "character"—a letter, digit, or other linguistic element. However, Java is designed to be used interanationally, and eight bits is simply not enough to handle the many different character sets used around the world. Script-based languages like Arabic and Indian languages, and pictographic languages like Chinese, Japanese, and Korean each have many more than 256 characters, the maximum that can be represented in an eight-bit byte. The unification of these many character code sets is called, not surprisingly, Unicode. Actually, it's not the first such unification, but it's the most widely used standard at this time. Both Java and XML use Unicode as their character sets, allowing you to read and write text in any of these human languages. But you have to use `Readers` and `Writers`, not `Streams`, for textual data.

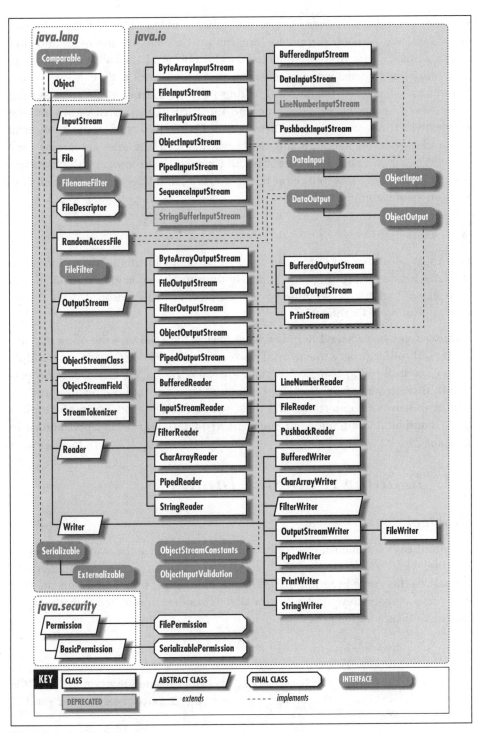

Figure 9-1. java.io classes

You see, Unicode itself doesn't solve the entire problem. Many of these human languages were used on computers long before Unicode was invented, and they didn't all pick the same representation as Unicode. And they all have zillions of files *encoded* in a particular representation that isn't Unicode. So conversion routines are needed when reading and writing to convert between Unicode `String` objects used inside the Java machine and the particular external representation that a user's files are written in. These converters are packaged inside a powerful set of classes called `Readers` and `Writers`. `Readers`/`Writers` are always used instead of `InputStreams`/`OutputStreams` when you want to deal with characters instead of bytes. We'll see more on this conversion, and how to specify which conversion, a little later in this chapter.

See Also

One topic *not* addressed here is the issue of hardcopy printing. Java includes two similar schemes for printing onto paper, both using the same graphics model as is used in AWT, the basic Window System package. For this reason, I defer discussion of printing to Chapter 12.

Another topic not covered here is that of having the read or write occur concurrently with other program activity. This requires the use of threads, or multiple flows of control within a single program. Threaded I/O is a necessity in many programs: those reading from slow devices such as tape drives, those reading from or writing to network connections, and those with a GUI. For this reason the topic is given considerable attention, in the context of multi-threaded applications, in Chapter 24.

9.1. Reading Standard Input

Problem

Despite Rusty's comments, you really do need to read from the standard input, or console. One reason is that simple test programs are often console-driven. Another is that some programs naturally require a lot of interaction with the user and you want something faster than a GUI (consider an interactive mathematics or statistical exploration program).

Solution

To read bytes, wrap a `BufferedInputStream()` around `System.in`. For the more common case of reading text, use an `InputStreamReader` and a `BufferedReader`.

Discussion

On most non-Macintosh desktop platforms, there is a notion of standard input—a keyboard, a file, or the output from another program—and standard output—a terminal window, a printer, a file on disk, or the input to yet another program. Most such systems also support a standard error output, so that error messages can be seen by the user even if the standard output is being redirected. When programs on these platforms start up, the three streams are preassigned to particular platform-dependent handles, or *file descriptors*. The net result is that ordinary programs on these operating systems can read the standard input or write to the standard output or standard error stream without having to open any files or make any other special arrangements.

Java continues this tradition, and enshrines it in the Java Standard Edition's System class. The static variables System.in, System.out, and System.err are connected to the three operating system streams before your program begins execution (an application is free to reassign these; see Recipe 9.6). So to read the standard input, you need only refer to the variable System.in and call its methods. For example, to read one byte from the standard input, you call the read method of System.in, which returns the byte in an int variable:

```
int b = System.in.read();
```

But is that enough? No, because the read() method can throw an IOException. So you must either declare that your program throws an IOException, as in:

```
public static void main(String ap[]) throws IOException {
```

Or, you can put a try/catch block around the read method:

```
int b = 0;
try {
    b = System.in.read();
} catch (Exception e) {
    System.out.println("Caught " + e);
}
System.out.println("Read this data: " + (char)b);
```

Note that I cavalierly convert the byte to a char for printing, assuming that you've typed a valid character in the terminal window.

Well, that certainly works, and gives you the ability to read a byte at a time from the standard input. But most applications are designed in terms of larger units, such as a line of text. For reading characters of text, using an input character converter so that your program will work with multiple input encodings around the world, you'll want to use a Reader class. The particular subclass that allows you to read lines of characters is a BufferedReader. But there's a hitch. Remember that I said there are two categories of input classes, Streams and Readers? But I also

said that System.in is a Stream, and you want a Reader. How to get from a
Stream to a Reader? There is a "crossover" class called an InputStream reader
that is tailor-made for this purpose. Just pass your Stream (like System.in) to the
InputStreamReader constructor, and you get back a Reader, which you in turn
pass to the BufferedReader constructor. The usual idiom for writing this in Java
is to nest the constructor calls:

```
BufferedReader is = new BufferedReader(new InputStreamReader(System.in);
```

Then you can read lines of text from the standard input using the readLine()
method. This method takes no argument, and returns a String that is made up
for you by readLine() containing the characters (converted to Unicode) from
the next line of text in the file. If there are no more lines of text, then the constant null is returned.

```
import java.io.*;

/**
 * Read and print, using BufferedReader from System.in, onto System.out
 */
public class CatStdin {

    public static void main(String av[]) {
        try {
            BufferedReader is = new BufferedReader(
                new InputStreamReader(System.in));
            String inputLine;

            while ((inputLine = is.readLine()) != null) {
                System.out.println(inputLine);
            }
            is.close();
        } catch (IOException e) {
            System.out.println("IOException: " + e);
        }
    }
}
```

And because it's something that people ask me over and over, I'll show how to
read an Integer from the standard input:

```
import java.io.*;
/**
 * Read an int from Standard Input
 */
public class ReadStdinInt {
    public static void main(String[] ap) {
        String line = null;
        int val = 0;
```

```
    try {
        BufferedReader is = new BufferedReader(
            new InputStreamReader(System.in));
        line = is.readLine();
        val = Integer.parseInt(line);
    } catch (NumberFormatException ex) {
        System.err.println("Not a valid number: " + line);
    } catch (IOException e) {
        System.err.println("Unexpected IO ERROR: " + e);
    }
    System.out.println("I read this number: " + val);
    }
}
```

There are many other things you might want to do with lines of text read from a
Reader. In the demo program shown in this recipe, I just printed them. In the
demo program in   Recipe 9.3, I convert them to integer values using
Integer.parseInt() (also see Recipe 5.1) or using a DecimalFormat
(Recipe 5.7). You can interpret them as dates (Recipe 6.5), or break them into
words with a StringTokenizer (Recipe 3.2). You can also process the lines as you
read them; several methods for doing so are listed in Recipe 9.12.

9.2. *Writing Standard Output*

Problem

You want your program to write to the standard output.

Solution

Use *System.out.*

Discussion

Again despite Rusty's quote, there are circumstances (such as a server program
with no connection back to the user's terminal) in which System.out can become
a very important debugging tool (assuming that you can find out what file the
server program has redirected standard output into; see Recipe 9.6).

System.out is a *PrintStream,* so in every introductory text you see a program containing this line, or one like it:*

```
System.out.println("Hello World of Java");
```

---

* All the examples in this recipe are found in one file, *PrintStandardOutput.java.*

The println method is polymorphic; there are forms of it for Object (which obviously calls the given object's toString() method), for String, and for each of the base types (int, float, boolean, etc.). Each takes only one argument, so it is common to use string concatenation:

```
System.out.println("The answer is " + myAnswer + " at this time.");
```

Remember that string concatenation is also polymorphic: you can "add" anything at all to a string, and the result is a string.

Up to here I have been using a Stream, System.out. What if you want to use a Writer? The PrintWriter class has all the same methods as PrintStream and a constructor that takes a Stream, so you can just say:

```
PrintWriter pw = new PrintWriter(System.out);
pw.println("The answer is " + myAnswer + " at this time.");
```

One caveat with this string concatenation is that if you are appending a bunch of things, and a number and a character come together at the front, they are added before concatenation due to the precedence rules. So don't do this:

```
System.out.println(i + '=' + " the answer.");
```

Assuming that i is an integer, then i + '=' (i added to the equals sign) is a valid *numeric* expression, which will result in a single value of type int. If the variable i has the value 42, and the character = in a Unicode (or ASCII) code chart has the value 61, then this will print:

```
103 the answer.
```

that is, the wrong value, and no equals sign. Safer methods include using parentheses, using double quotes around the equals sign, and using a StringBuffer (see Recipe 3.3) or a MessageFormat (see Recipe 14.10).

9.3. Opening a File by Name

Problem

The Java documentation doesn't have methods for opening files. How do I connect a filename on disk with a Reader, Writer, or Stream?

Solution

Construct a FileReader, a FileWriter, a FileInputStream, or a FileOutputStream.

Discussion

The action of constructing a `FileReader`, `FileWriter`, `FileInputStream`, or `FileOutputStream` corresponds to the "open" operation in most I/O packages. There is no explicit open operation, perhaps as a kind of rhetorical flourish of the Java API's object-oriented design. So to read a text file, you'd create, in order, a `FileReader` and a `BufferedReader`. To write a file a byte at a time, you'd create a `FileOutputStream`, and probably a `BufferedOutputStream` for efficiency:

```
// OpenFileByName.java
BufferedReader is = new BufferedReader(new FileReader("myFile.txt"));
BufferedOutputStream bytesOut = new BufferedOutputStream(
    new FileOutputStream("bytes.dat"));
...
bytesOut.close();
```

Remember that you will need to handle `IOException` around these calls.

9.4. Copying a File

Problem

You need to copy a file in its entirety.

Solution

Use a pair of `Streams` for binary data, or a `Reader` and a `Writer` for text, and a `while` loop to copy until end of file is reached on the input.

Discussion

This is a fairly common operation, so I've packaged it as a set of methods in a class I've called `FileIO` in my utilities package `com.darwinsys.util`. Here's a simple test program that uses it to copy a source file to a backup file:

```
import com.darwinsys.util.FileIO;

import java.io.*;

public class FileIOTest {
    public static void main(String[] av) {
        try {
            FileIO.copyFile("FileIO.java", "FileIO.bak");
            FileIO.copyFile("FileIO.class", "FileIO-class.bak");
        } catch (FileNotFoundException e) {
            System.err.println(e);
        } catch (IOException e) {
```

```
                    System.err.println(e);
            }
        }
    }
```

How does `FileIO` work? There are several forms of the `copyFile` method, depending on whether you have two filenames, a filename and a `PrintWriter`, and so on. See Example 9-1.

Example 9-1. FileIO.java

```java
package com.darwinsys.util;

import java.io.*;

/**
 * Some simple file I-O primitives reimplemented in Java.
 * All methods are static, since there is no state.
 */
public class FileIO {

    /** Copy a file from one filename to another */
    public static void copyFile(String inName, String outName)
    throws FileNotFoundException, IOException {
        BufferedInputStream is =
            new BufferedInputStream(new FileInputStream(inName));
        BufferedOutputStream os =
            new BufferedOutputStream(new FileOutputStream(outName));
        copyFile(is, os, true);
    }

    /** Copy a file from an opened InputStream to opened OutputStream */
    public static void copyFile(InputStream is, OutputStream os, boolean close)
    throws IOException {
        int b;              // the byte read from the file
        while ((b = is.read()) != -1) {
            os.write(b);
        }
        is.close();
        if (close)
            os.close();
    }

    /** Copy a file from an opened Reader to opened Writer */
    public static void copyFile(Reader is, Writer os, boolean close)
    throws IOException {
        int b;              // the byte read from the file
        while ((b = is.read()) != -1) {
            os.write(b);
        }
```

Example 9-1. FileIO.java (continued)

```
        is.close();
        if (close)
            os.close();
    }

    /** Copy a file from a filename to a PrintWriter. */
    public static void copyFile(String inName, PrintWriter pw, boolean close)
    throws FileNotFoundException, IOException {
        BufferedReader is = new BufferedReader(new FileReader(inName));
        copyFile(is, pw, close);
    }

    /** Open a file and read the first line from it. */
    public static String readLine(String inName)
    throws FileNotFoundException, IOException {
        BufferedReader is = new BufferedReader(new FileReader(inName));
        String line = null;
        line = is.readLine();
        is.close();
        return line;
    }

    /** The size of blocking to use */
    protected static final int BLKSIZ = 8192;

    /** Copy a data file from one filename to another, alternate method.
     * As the name suggests, use my own buffer instead of letting
     * the BufferedReader allocate and use the buffer.
     */
    public void copyFileBuffered(String inName, String outName) throws
            FileNotFoundException, IOException {
        InputStream is = new FileInputStream(inName);
        OutputStream os = new FileOutputStream(outName);
        int count = 0;// the byte count
        byte b[] = new byte[BLKSIZ];// the bytes read from the file
        while ((count = is.read(b)) != -1) {
            os.write(b, 0, count);
        }
        is.close();
        os.close();
    }

    /** Read the entire content of an Reader into a String */
    public static String readerToString(Reader is) throws IOException {
        StringBuffer sb = new StringBuffer();
        char[] b = new char[BLKSIZ];
        int n;
```

Example 9-1. FileIO.java (continued)

```
    // Read a block. If it gets any chars, append them.
    while ((n = is.read(b)) > 0) {
        sb.append(b, 0, n);
    }

    // Only construct the String object once, here.
    return sb.toString();
}

/** Read the content of a Stream into a String */
public static String inputStreamToString(InputStream is)
throws IOException {
    return readerToString(new InputStreamReader(is));
}
}
```

There is a test main program included in the online source, which copies the source and class files of this program. When I ran it for testing, I followed up by using *diff* (a text file compare program) on the text file and its backup, and *cmp* (a binary compare program) on the class files. Both of these programs operate on the Unix "no news is good news" principle: if they say nothing, it is because they found nothing of significance to report, i.e., no differences.

```
C:\javasrc\io>java IOUtil
C:\javasrc\io>diff IOUtil.java IOUtil-java.bak
C:\javasrc\io>cmp  IOUtil.class IOUtil-class.bak
C:\javasrc\io>
```

But wait! Did you look closely at the body of `copyTextFile()`? If you didn't, do it now. You'll notice that I cheated, and just reused `copyDataFile()`. Well, if I'm copying a file from one place on disk to another, why go through the overhead of converting it from external form to Unicode and back? Normally you won't have to. But if you have something like a network filesystem mounted from Windows to Unix or vice versa, better to do it a line at a time.

9.5. Reading a File into a String

Problem

You need to read the entire contents of a file into a string.

Solution

Use my `FileIO.readerToString()` method.

Discussion

This is not a common activity in Java, but there will be times when you really want
to do it. For example, you might want to load a file into a "text area" in a GUI. Or
process an entire file looking for multiline regular expressions (as in Recipe 4.12).
Even though there's nothing in the standard API to do this, it's still easy to accomplish with the `readerToString()` method in `com.darwinsys.util.FileIO`.
You just say something like the following:

```
Reader is = new FileReader(theFileName);
String input = FileIO.readerToString(is);
```

The `readerToString()` method is fairly simple, based on what you've already
seen:

```
// Part of com.darwinsys.util/FileIO.java

/** Read the entire content of an Reader into a String */
public static String readerToString(Reader is) throws IOException {
        StringBuffer sb = new StringBuffer();
        char[] b = new char[BLKSIZ];
        int n;

        // Read a block. If it gets any chars, append them.
        while ((n = is.read(b)) > 0) {
                sb.append(b, 0, n);
        }

        // Only construct the String object once, here.
        return sb.toString();
}

/** Read the content of a Stream into a String */
public static String inputStreamToString(InputStream is)
throws IOException {
        return readerToString(new InputStreamReader(is));
}
```

9.6. Reassigning the Standard Streams

Problem

You need to reassign one or more of the standard streams `System.in`,
`System.out`, or `System.err`.

Solution

Construct an InputStream or PrintStream as appropriate, and pass it to the appropriate set method in the System class.

Discussion

The ability to reassign these streams corresponds to what Unix (or DOS command line) users think of as *redirection,* or *piping.* This mechanism is commonly used to make a program read from or write to a file without having to explicitly open it and go through every line of code changing the read, write, print, etc., calls to refer to a different stream object. The *open* operation is performed by the command-line interpreter in Unix or DOS, or by the calling class in Java.

While you could just assign a new PrintStream to the variable System.out, you'd be considered antisocial, since there is a defined method to replace it carefully:

```
// Redirect.java
String LOGFILENAME = "error.log";
System.setErr(new PrintStream(new FileOutputStream(LOGFILENAME)));
System.out.println("Please look for errors in " + LOGFILENAME);
// Now to see somebody else's code writing to stderr...
int a[] = new int[5];
a[10] = 0;// here comes an ArrayIndexOutOfBoundsException
```

The stream you use can be one that you've opened, as here, or one you inherited:

```
System.setErr(System.out);// merge stderr and stdout to same output file.
```

It could also be a stream connected to or from another Process you've started (see Recipe 26.1), a network socket, or URL. Anything that can give you a stream can be used.

See Also

See Recipe 13.8, which shows how to reassign a file so that it gets "written" to a text window in a GUI application.

9.7. Duplicating a Stream as It Is Written

Problem

You want anything written to a stream, such as the standard output System.out or the standard error System.err, to appear there but *also* be logged into a file.

Solution

Subclass `PrintStream` and have its `write()` methods write to two streams. Then use `system.setErr()` or `setOut()` as in Recipe 9.6 to replace the existing standard stream with this "tee" `PrintStream` subclass.

Discussion

Classes are meant to be subclassed. Here we're just subclassing `PrintStream` and adding a bit of functionality: a second `PrintStream`! I wrote a class called `TeePrintStream`, named after the ancient Unix command *tee*. That command allowed you to duplicate, or "tee off," a copy of the data being written on a "pipeline" between two programs.

The original Unix *tee* command is used like this: the | character creates a pipeline in which the standard output of one program becomes the standard input to the next. This often-used example of pipes shows how many users are logged into a Unix server:

```
who | wc -l
```

This runs the *who* program (which lists who is logged into the system, one name per line along with the terminal port and login time) with its output, instead of going to the terminal, going into the standard input of the word count (*wc*) program. Here *wc* is being asked to count lines, not words; hence the -1 option. To *tee* a copy of the intermediate data into a file, you might say:

```
who | tee wholist | wc -l
```

which creates a file *wholist* containing the data. For the curious, the file *wholist* might look something like this:

```
ian        ttyC0     Mar 14 09:59
ben        ttyC3     Mar 14 10:23
ian        ttyp4     Mar 14 13:46   (daroad.darwinsys.com)
```

So the previous commands would both print 3 as their output.

`TeePrintStream` is an attempt to capture the spirit of the *tee* command. It can be used like this:

```
System.setErr(new TeePrintStream(System.err, "err.log"));
// ...lots of code that occasionally writes to System.err... Or might.
```

`System.setErr()` is a means of specifying the destination of text printed to `System.err` (there are also `System.setOut()` and `System.setIn()`). This code results in any messages that printed to `System.err` to print both to wherever `System.err` was previously directed (normally the terminal, but possibly a text window in an IDE) and into the file `err.log`.

This technique is not limited to the three standard streams. A TeePrintStream
can be passed to any method that wants a PrintStream. Or, for that matter, an
OutputStream. And you can adapt the technique for BufferedInputStreams,
PrintWriters, BufferedReaders, and so on.

Since TeePrintStream is fairly simple, I'll list the main parts of it here (see the
online source for the complete version):

```java
import java.io.*;

public class TeePrintStream extends PrintStream {
    protected PrintStream parent;
    protected String fileName;

    /* Construct a TeePrintStream given an existing Stream and a filename.
     */
    public TeePrintStream(PrintStream os, String fn) throws IOException {
        this(os, fn, false);
    }
    /* Construct a TeePrintStream given an existing Stream, a filename,
     * and a boolean to control the flush operation.
     */
    public TeePrintStream(PrintStream orig, String fn,
            boolean flush) throws IOException {
        super(new FileOutputStream(fn), flush);
        fileName = fn;
        parent = orig;
    }

    /** Return true if either stream has an error. */
    public boolean checkError() {
        return parent.checkError() || super.checkError();
    }

    /** override write(). This is the actual "tee" operation! */
    public void write(int x) {
        parent.write(x);// "write once; super.write(x); // write somewhere else"
    }
    /** override write() */
    public void write(byte[] x, int o, int l) {
        parent.write(x, o, l);
        super.write(x, o, l);
    }

    /** Close both streams. */
    public void close() {
        parent.close();
        super.close();
    }
}
```

It's worth mentioning that I do *not* need to override all the polymorphic forms of `print()` and `println()`. Since these all ultimately use one of the forms of `write()`, if you override the `print/println` methods to do the *tee*-ing as well, you can get several additional copies of the data written out.

9.8. Reading/Writing a Different Character Set

Problem

You need to read or write a text file using a particular encoding.

Solution

Convert the text to or from internal Unicode by specifying a converter when you construct an `InputStreamReader` or `PrintWriter`.

Discussion

Classes `InputStreamReader` and `OutputStreamWriter` are the bridge from byte-oriented `Streams` to character-based `Readers`. These classes read or write bytes and translate them to or from characters according to a specified character encoding. The Unicode character set used inside Java (`char` and `String` types) is a 16-bit character set. But most character sets, such as ASCII, Swedish, Spanish, Greek, Turkish, and many others, use only a small subset of that. In fact, many European language character sets fit nicely into 8-bit characters. Even the larger character sets (script-based and pictographic languages) don't all use the same bit values for each particular character. The *encoding*, then, is a mapping between Unicode characters and a particular external storage format for characters drawn from a particular national or linguistic character set.

To simplify matters, the `InputStreamReader` and `OutputStreamWriter` constructors are the only places where you can specify the name of an encoding to be used in this translation. If you do not, the platform's (or user's) default encoding will be used. `PrintWriters`, `BufferedReaders`, and the like all use whatever encoding the `InputStreamReader` or `OutputStreamWriter` class uses. Since these bridge classes only accept `Stream` arguments in their constructors, the implication is that if you want to specify a non-default converter to read/write a file on disk, you must start by constructing not a `FileReader/FileWriter`, but a `FileInputStream/FileOutputStream`!

```
// UseConverters.java
BufferedReader fromKanji = new BufferedReader(
```

```
    new InputStreamReader(new FileInputStream("kanji.txt"), "EUC_JP"));
PrintWriter toSwedish = new PrinterWriter(
    new OutputStreamWriter(new FileOutputStream("sverige.txt"), "Cp278"));
```

Not that it would necessarily make sense to read a single file from Kanji and output it in a Swedish encoding; for one thing, most fonts would not have all the characters of both character sets, and at any rate, the Swedish encoding certainly has far fewer characters in it than the Kanji encoding. Besides, if that were all you wanted, you could use a JDK tool with the ill-fitting name `native2ascii` (see its documentation for details). A list of the supported encodings is also in the JDK documentation, in the file *docs/guide/internat/encoding.doc.html*. A more detailed description is found in Appendix B of *Java I/O*.

9.9. Those Pesky End-of-Line Characters

Problem

You really want to know about end-of-line characters.

Solution

Use \r and \n in whatever combination makes sense.

Discussion

If you are reading text (or bytes containing ASCII characters) in line mode using the `readLine()` method, you'll never see the end-of-line characters, and so won't be cursed with having to figure out whether \n, \r, or \r\n appears at the end of each line. If you want that level of detail, you have to read the characters or bytes one at a time, using the readline methods. The only time I've found this necessary is in networking code, where some of the line-mode protocols assume that the line ending is \r\n. Even here, though, you can still work in line mode. When writing, send a \r\n. When reading, use `readLine()` and you won't have to deal with the characters.

```
outputSocket.print("HELO " + myName + "\r\n");
String response = inputSocket.readLine();
```

9.10. Beware Platform-Dependent File Code

Problem

Chastened by the previous recipe, you now wish to write only platform-independent code.

Solution

Use readLine() and println(). Never use \n by itself; use File.separator if you must.

Discussion

As mentioned in Recipe 9.9, if you just use readLine() and println(), you won't have to think about the line endings. But a particular problem, especially for recycled C programmers and their relatives, is using the \n character in text strings to mean a newline. What is particularly distressing about this code is that it will work—sometimes—usually on the developer's own platform. But it will surely someday fail, on some other system.

```
// BadNewline.java
String myName;
public static void main(String argv[]) {
    BadNewline jack = new BadNewline("Jack Adolphus Schmidt, III");
    System.out.println(jack);
}
/**
 * DON'T DO THIS. THIS IS BAD CODE.
 */
public String toString() {
    return "BadNewlineDemo@" + hashCode() + "\n" + myName;
}
```

```
// The obvious Constructor is not shown for brevity; it's in the code
```

The real problem is not that it will fail on some platforms, though. What's really wrong is that it mixes formatting and input/output, or tries to. Don't mix line-based display with toString(): avoid "multiline strings" output from toString() or any other string-returning method. If you need to write multiple strings, then say what you mean:

```
// GoodNewline.java
String myName;
public static void main(String argv[]) {
    GoodNewline jack = new GoodNewline("Jack Adolphus Schmidt, III");
    jack.print(System.out);
}

protected void print(PrintStream out) {
    out.println(toString());// classname and hashcode
    out.println(myName);// print name  on next line
}
```

9.11. Reading "Continued" Lines

Problem

You need to read lines that are continued with backslashes (\) or that are continued with leading spaces (such as email or news headers).

Solution

Use my `IndentContLineReader` or `EscContLineReader` classes.

Discussion

This functionality is likely to be reused, so it should be encapsulated in general-purpose classes. I offer the `IndentContLineReader` and `EscContLineReader` classes. `EscContLineReader` reads lines normally, but if a line ends with the escape character (by default, the backslash), then the escape character is deleted and the following line is joined to the preceding line. So if you have lines like this in the input:

```
Here is something I wanted to say:\
Try and Buy in every way.
Go Team!
```

and you read them using an `EscContLineReader`'s `readLine()` method, then you will get the following lines:

```
Here is something I wanted to say: Try and Buy in every way.
Go Team!
```

Note in particular that my reader *does* provide a space character between the abutted parts of the continued line. An `IOException` will be thrown if a file ends with the escape character.

`IndentContLineReader` reads lines, but if a line begins with a space or tab, that line is joined to the preceding line. This is designed for reading email or Usenet news ("message") header lines. Here is an example input file:

```
From: ian Tuesday, January 1, 2000 8:45 AM EST
To: Book-reviewers List
Received: by darwinsys.com (OpenBSD 2.6)
    from localhost
    at Tuesday, January 1, 2000 8:45 AM EST
Subject: Hey, it's 2000 and MY computer is still up
```

When read using an `IndentContLineReader`, this text will come out with the continued lines joined together into longer single lines:

```
From: ian Tuesday, January 1, 2000 8:45 AM EST
To: Book-reviewers List
Received: by darwinsys.com (OpenBSD 2.6) from localhost at Tuesday, January 1,
2000 8:45 AM EST
Subject: Hey, it's 2000 and MY computer is still up
```

This class has a `setContinueMode(boolean)` method, which lets you turn continuation mode off. This would normally be used to process the body of a message. Since the header and the body are separated by a null line in the text representation of messages, we can process the entire message correctly as follows:

```
IndentContLineReader is = new IndentContLineReader(
        new StringReader(sampleTxt));
    String aLine;
    // Print Mail/News Header
    System.out.println("----- Message Header -----");
    while ((aLine = is.readLine()) != null && aLine.length() > 0) {
        System.out.println(is.getLineNumber() + ": " + aLine);
    }
    // Make "is" behave like normal BufferedReader
    is.setContinuationMode(false);
    System.out.println();
    // Print Message Body
    System.out.println("----- Message Body -----");
    while ((aLine = is.readLine()) != null) {
        System.out.println(is.getLineNumber() + ": " + aLine);
```

Each of the three `Reader` classes is subclassed from `LineNumberReader` so that you can use `getLineNumber()`. This is a very useful feature when reporting errors back to the user who prepared an input file; it can save them considerable hunting around in the file if you tell them the line number on which the error occurred. The `Reader` classes are actually subclassed from an abstract `ContLineReader` subclass, which I'll present first (Example 9-2). This class encapsulates the basic functionality for keeping track of lines that need to be joined together, and for enabling/disabling the continuation processing.

Example 9-2. ContLineReader.java

```
import java.io.*;

/** Subclass of LineNumberReader to allow reading of continued lines
 * using the readLine() method. The other Reader methods (readInt()) etc.)
 * must not be used.  Must subclass to provide the actual implementation
 * of readLine().
 */
public abstract class ContLineReader extends LineNumberReader {
    /** Line number of first line in current (possibly continued) line */
    protected int firstLineNumber = 0;
    /** True if handling continuations, false if not; false == "PRE" mode */
```

Example 9-2. ContLineReader.java (continued)

```java
    protected boolean doContinue = true;

    /** Set the continuation mode */
    public void setContinuationMode(boolean b) {
        doContinue = b;
    }

    /** Get the continuation mode */
    public boolean isContinuation() {
        return doContinue;
    }

    /** Read one (possibly continued) line, stripping out the \ that
     * marks the end of each line but the last in a sequence.
     */
    public abstract String readLine() throws IOException;

    /** Read one real line. Provided as a convenience for the
     * subclasses, so they don't embarass themselves trying to
     * call "super.readLine()" which isn't very practical...
     */
    public String readPhysicalLine() throws IOException {
        return super.readLine();
    }

    // Can NOT override getLineNumber in this class to return the #
    // of the beginning of the continued line, since the subclasses
    // all call super.getLineNumber...

    /** Construct a ContLineReader with the default input-buffer size. */
    public ContLineReader(Reader in)  {
        super(in);
    }

    /** Construct a ContLineReader using the given input-buffer size. */
    public ContLineReader(Reader in, int sz)  {
        super(in, sz);
    }

    // Methods that do NOT work - redirect straight to parent

    /** Read a single character, returned as an int. */
    public int read() throws IOException {
        return super.read();
    }

    /** Read characters into a portion of an array. */
    public int read(char[] cbuf, int off, int len) throws IOException {
```

Example 9-2. ContLineReader.java (continued)

```
        return super.read(cbuf, off, len);
    }

    public boolean markSupported() {
        return false;
    }
}
```

The `ContLineReader` class ends with code for handling the `read()` calls so that the class will work correctly. The `IndentContLineReader` class extends this to allow merging of lines based on indentation. Example 9-3 shows the code for the `IndentContLineReader` class.

Example 9-3. IndentContLineReader.java

```
import java.io.*;

/** Subclass of ContLineReader for lines continued by indentation of
 * following line (like RFC822 mail, Usenet News, etc.).
 */
public class IndentContLineReader extends ContLineReader {
    /** Line number of first line in current (possibly continued) line */
    public int getLineNumber() {
        return firstLineNumber;
    }

    protected String prevLine;

    /** Read one (possibly continued) line, stripping out the '\'s that
     * mark the end of all but the last.
     */
    public String readLine() throws IOException {
        String s;

        // If we saved a previous line, start with it. Else,
        // read the first line of possible continuation.
        // If non-null, put it into the StringBuffer and its line
        // number in firstLineNumber.
        if (prevLine != null) {
            s = prevLine;
            prevLine = null;
        }
        else  {
            s = readPhysicalLine();
        }

        // save the line number of the first line.
        firstLineNumber = super.getLineNumber();
```

Example 9-3. IndentContLineReader.java (continued)

```java
        // Now we have one line. If we are not in continuation
        // mode, or if a previous readPhysicalLine() returned null,
        // we are finished, so return it.
        if (!doContinue || s == null)
            return s;

        // Otherwise, start building a stringbuffer
        StringBuffer sb = new StringBuffer(s);

        // Read as many continued lines as there are, if any.
        while (true) {
            String nextPart = readPhysicalLine();
            if (nextPart == null) {
                // Egad! EOF within continued line.
                // Return what we have so far.
                return sb.toString();
            }
            // If the next line begins with space, it's continuation
            if (nextPart.length() > 0 &&
                Character.isWhitespace(nextPart.charAt(0))) {
                sb.append(nextPart);// and add line.
            } else {
                // else we just read too far, so put in "pushback" holder
                prevLine = nextPart;
                break;
            }
        }

        return sb.toString();// return what's left
    }

    /* Constructors not shown */

    // Built-in test case
    protected static String sampleTxt =
        "From: ian today now\n" +
        "Received: by foo.bar.com\n" +
        "    at 12:34:56 January 1, 2000\n" +
        "X-Silly-Headers: Too Many\n" +
        "This line should be line 5.\n" +
        "Test more indented line continues from line 6:\n" +
        "    space indented.\n" +
        "    tab indented;\n" +
        "\n" +
        "This is line 10\n" +
        "the start of a hypothetical mail/news message, \n" +
        "that is, it follows a null line.\n" +
        "    Let us see how it fares if indented.\n" +
```

Example 9-3. IndentContLineReader.java (continued)

```
            " also space-indented.\n" +
            "\n" +
            "How about text ending without a newline?";

    // A simple main program for testing the class.
    public static void main(String argv[]) throws IOException {
        IndentContLineReader is = new IndentContLineReader(
            new StringReader(sampleTxt));
        String aLine;
        // Print Mail/News Header
        System.out.println("----- Message Header -----");
        while ((aLine = is.readLine()) != null && aLine.length() > 0) {
            System.out.println(is.getLineNumber() + ": " + aLine);
        }
        // Make "is" behave like normal BufferedReader
        is.setContinuationMode(false);
        System.out.println();
        // Print Message Body
        System.out.println("----- Message Body -----");
        while ((aLine = is.readLine()) != null) {
            System.out.println(is.getLineNumber() + ": " + aLine);
        }
        is.close();
    }
}
```

9.12. Scanning a File

Problem

You need to scan a file with more fine-grained resolution than the readLine() method of the BufferedReader class and its subclasses (discussed in Recipe 9.11).

Solution

Use a StreamTokenizer, readline() and a StringTokenizer, regular expressions (Chapter 4), or one of several scanning tools such as JavaCC.

Discussion

While you could, in theory, read the file a character at a time and analyze each character, that is a pretty low-level approach. The read() method in the Reader class is defined to return int, so that it can use the time-honored value −1

(defined as EOF in Unix *<stdio.h>* for years) to indicate that you have read to the
end of the file.

```
void doFile(Reader is) {
    int c;
    while ((c=is.read()) != -1) {
        System.out.print((char)c);
    }
}
```

The cast to char is interesting. The program will compile fine without it, but may
not print correctly (depending on the contents of the file).

We discussed the StringTokenizer class extensively in Recipe 3.2. The combination of readLine() and StringTokenizer provides a simple means of scanning
a file. Suppose you need to read a file in which each line consists of a name like
"user@host.domain", and you want to split the lines into the user part and the host
address part. You could use this:

```
// ScanStringTok.java
protected void process(LineNumberReader is) {
        String s = null;
        try {
            while ((s = is.readLine()) != null) {
                StringTokenizer st = new StringTokenizer(s, "@", true);
                String user = (String)st.nextElement();
                st.nextElement();
                String host = (String)st.nextElement();
                System.out.println("User name: " + user +
                    "; host part: " + host);

                // Presumably you would now do something
                // with the user and host parts...

            }

        } catch (NoSuchElementException ix) {
            System.err.println("Line " + is.getLineNumber() +
                ": Invalid input " + s);
        } catch (IOException e) {
            System.err.println(e);
        }
    }
```

The StreamTokenizer class in package java.util provides slightly more capabilities for scanning a file. It will read characters and assemble them into words, or
tokens. It will return these tokens to you along with a "type code" describing the
kind of token it found. This will either be one of four predefined types (String-
Tokenizer.TT_WORD, TT_NUMBER, TT_WORD, or TT_EOL for the end of

line), or the ASCII value of an ordinary character (such as 40 for the space character). Methods such as `ordinaryCharacter()` allow you to specify how to categorize characters, while others such as `slashSlashComment()` allow you to enable or disable features.

The example shows a `StreamTokenizer` used to implement a simple immediate-mode stack-based calculator:

```
2 2 + =
4
22 7 / =
3.141592857
```

I read tokens as they arrive from the `StreamTokenizer`. Numbers get put on the stack. The four operators (+, -, *, and /) are immediately performed on the two elements at the top of the stack, and the result is put back on the top of the stack. The = operator causes the top element to be printed, but is left on the stack so that you can say:

```
4 5 * = 2 / =
20.0
10.0
```

Here is the relevant code from `SimpleCalc`:

```java
public class SimpleCalc {
    /** The StreamTokenizer */
    protected  StreamTokenizer tf;

    /** The variable name (not used in this version) */
    protected String variable;
    /** The operand stack */
    protected Stack s;

    /** Construct a SimpleCalc from an existing Reader */
    public SimpleCalc(Reader rdr) throws IOException {
        tf = new StreamTokenizer(rdr);
        // Control the input character set:
        tf.slashSlashComments(true);// treat "//" as comments
        tf.ordinaryChar('-');// used for subtraction
        tf.ordinaryChar('/');// used for division

        s = new Stack();
    }

    protected void doCalc() throws IOException {
        int iType;
        double tmp;

        while ((iType = tf.nextToken()) != tf.TT_EOF) {
```

```
switch(iType) {
case StringTokenizer.TT_NUMBER:
    // Found a number, push value to stack
    push(tf.nval);
    break;
case StringTokenizer.TT_WORD:
    // Found a variable, save its name. Not used here. */
    variable = tf.sval;
    break;
case '+':
    // Found + operator, perform it immediately.
    push(pop() + pop());
    break;
case '-':
    // Found + operator, perform it (order matters).
    tmp = pop();
    push(pop() - tmp);
    break;
case '*':
    // Multiply works OK
    push(pop() * pop());
    break;
case '/':
    // Handle division carefully: order matters!
    tmp = pop();
    push(pop() / tmp);
    break;
case '=':
    System.out.println(peek());
    break;
default:
    System.out.println("What's this? iType = " + iType);
}
    }
  }
}
```

While `StreamTokenizer` is useful, it is limited in the number of different tokens that it knows and has no way of specifying that the tokens must appear in a particular order. To do more advanced scanning, you need to use some special-purpose scanning tools. Such tools have been known and used for a long time in the Unix realm. The best-known examples are yacc and lex, (discussed in the O'Reilly text *lex & yacc*). These tools let you specify the lexical structure of your input using regular expressions (see Chapter 4). For example, you might say that an email address consists of a series of alphanumerics, followed by an at sign (@), followed by a series of alphanumerics with periods embedded, as:

```
name:[A-Za-z0-9]+@[A-Za-z0-0.]
```

The tool will then write code that recognizes the characters you have described. There is also the grammatical specification, which says, for example, that the keyword ADDRESS must appear, followed by a colon, followed by a "name" token as previously defined.

One widely used scanning tool is *JavaCC*. Though still owned by Sun, it is being distributed and supported by WebGain (*http://www.webgain.com/products/metamata/java_doc.html*). JavaCC can be used to write grammars for a wide variety of programs, from simple calculators such as the one earlier in this recipe, through HTML and CORBA/IDL, up to full Java and C/C++ compilers. Examples of these are included with the JavaCC distribution. Unfortunately, the learning curve for parsers in general precludes providing a simple and comprehensive example here. Please refer to the documentation and the numerous examples provided with the JavaCC distribution.

That's all I have to say on scanning: simple line-at-a-time scanners using StringTokenizer, fancier token-based scanners using StreamTokenizer, and grammar-based scanners based on JavaCC and similar tools. Scan well and prosper!

9.13. Binary Data

Problem

You need to read or write binary data, as opposed to text.

Solution

Use a DataInputStream or DataOutputStream.

Discussion

The Stream classes have been in Java since the JDK 1.0 release and are optimal for reading/writing bytes, rather than characters. The "data" layer over them, comprising DataInputStream and DataOutputStream, are configured for reading and writing binary values, including all of Java's built-in types. Suppose that you want to write a binary integer plus a binary floating-point value into a file and read it back later. This code shows the writing part:

```
import java.io.*;
/** Write some data in binary. */
public class WriteBinary {
    public static void main(String argv[]) throws IOException {
        int i = 42;
        double d = Math.PI;
        String FILENAME = "binary.dat";
```

```
        DataOutputStream os = new DataOutputStream(
            new FileOutputStream(FILENAME));
        os.writeInt(i);
        os.writeDouble(d);
        os.close();
        System.out.println("Wrote " + i + ", " + d + " to file " + FILENAME);
    }
}
```

The reading part is left as an exercise for the reader. Should you need to write all the fields from an object, you should probably use an `ObjectDataStream`; see Recipe 9.16.

9.14. Seeking

Problem

You need to read from or write to a particular location in a file, such as an indexed file.

Solution

Use a `RandomAccessFile`.

Discussion

The class `java.io.RandomAccessFile` allows you to move the read/write position to any location within a file, or past the end when writing. This allows you to create or access "files with holes" on some platforms and lets you read/write indexed or other database-like files in Java. The primary methods of interest are `void(long where)`, which moves the position for the next read/write to `where`; `int skipBytes(int howmany)`, which moves the position forward by `howmany` bytes; and `long getFilePointer()`, which returns the position.

`RandomAccessFile` class also implements the `DataInput` and `DataOutput` interfaces, so everything I said about `DataStreams` in Recipe 9.13 also applies here. This example reads a binary integer from the beginning of the file, treats that as the position to read from, finds that position, and reads a string from that location within the file.

```
import java.io.*;

/**
 * Read a file containing an offset, and a String at that offset.
 */
public class ReadRandom {
```

```
        final static String FILENAME = "random.dat";
        protected String fileName;
        protected RandomAccessFile seeker;

        public static void main(String argv[]) throws IOException {
            ReadRandom r = new ReadRandom(FILENAME);

            System.out.println("Offset is " + r.readOffset());
            System.out.println("Message is \"" + r.readMessage() + "\".");
        }

        /** Constructor: save filename, construct RandomAccessFile */
        public ReadRandom(String fname) throws IOException {
            fileName = fname;
            seeker = new RandomAccessFile(fname, "r");
        }

        /** Read the Offset field, defined to be at location 0 in the file. */
        public int readOffset() throws IOException {
            seeker.seek(0);
            return seeker.readInt();
        }

        /** read the message at the given offset */
        public String readMessage() throws IOException {
            seeker.seek(readOffset());// move to where
            return seeker.readLine();// and read the String
        }
    }
```

9.15. Writing Data Streams from C

Problem

You need to exchange binary data between C and Java.

Solution

Use the network byte-ordering macros.

Discussion

The program that created the file *random.dat* read by the program in the previous recipe was not written in Java, but in C. Since the earliest days of the TCP/IP proto-col in the 1980s, and particularly on the 4.2 BSD version of Unix, there was an awareness that not all brands of computers store the bytes within a word in the same order, and there was a means for dealing with it. For this early heterogeneous network to function at all, it was necessary that a 32-bit word be interpreted correctly as a computer's network address, regardless of whether it originated on a PDP-11, a VAX, a Sun workstation, or any other kind of machine then prevalent (there were no "IBM PC" machines powerful enough to run TCP/IP at that time). So *network byte order* was established, a standard for which bytes go in which order on the network. And the network byte order macros were written: ntohl for network-to-host order for a long (32 bits), htons for host-to-network order for a short (16 bits), and so on. In most Unix implementations, these C macros live in one of the Internet header files, although in some newer systems they have been segregated out into a file like *<machine/endian.h>*, as on our OpenBSD system.

The designers of Java, working at Sun, were well aware of these issues, and chose to use network byte order in the Java Virtual Machine. Thus a Java program can read an IP address from a socket using a DataInputStream, or write an integer to disk that will be read from C using read() and the network byte order macros.

This C program writes the file *random.dat* read in Recipe 9.14. It uses the network byte order macros to make sure that the long integer (32 bits on most C compilers on the IBM PC) is in the correct order to be read as an int in Java.

```
/* Create the random-access file for the RandomAccessFile example
 */

#include <stdio.h>
#include <fcntl.h>
#include <stdlib.h>
#include <unistd.h>
#include <sys/types.h>
#include <machine/endian.h>

const off_t OFFSET = 1234;
const char* FILENAME = "random.dat";
const int MODE = 0644;
const char* MESSAGE = "Ye have sought, and ye have found!\r\n";

int
main(int argc, char **argv) {
    int fd;
    int java_offset;

    if ((fd = creat(FILENAME, MODE)) < 0) {
        perror(FILENAME);
        return 1;
    }

    /* Java's DataStreams etc. are defined to be in network byte order,
     * so convert OFFSET to network byte order.
     */
```

```
    java_offset = htonl(OFFSET);

    if (write(fd, &java_offset, sizeof java_offset) < 0) {
        perror("write");
        return 1;
    }

    if (lseek(fd, OFFSET, SEEK_SET) < 0) {
        perror("seek");
        return 1;
    }

    if (write(fd, MESSAGE, strlen(MESSAGE)) != strlen(MESSAGE)) {
        perror("write2");
        return 1;
    }

    if (close(fd) < 0) {
        perror("close!?");
        return 1;
    }

    return 0;
}
```

The same technique can be used in the other direction, of course, and when
exchanging data over a network socket, and anyplace else you need to exchange
binary data between Java and C.

9.16. Saving and Restoring Serialized Objects

Problem

You need to write and (later) read objects.

Solution

Use the object stream classes, `ObjectInputStream` and `ObjectOutputStream`.

Discussion

Object serialization is the ability to convert in-memory objects to an external form
that can be sent serially (a byte at a time) and back again. The "and back again"
may happen at a later time, or in another JVM on another computer (even one
that has a different byte order); Java handles differences between machines.
`ObjectInputStream` and `ObjectOutputStream` are specialized stream classes

designed to read and write objects. They can be used to save objects to disk, as I'll
show here, and are also useful in passing objects across a network connection, as
I'll show in Recipe 15.6. This fact was not lost on the designers of the remote
methods invocation, or RMI (see Chapter 22), which uses them for transporting
the data involved in remote method calls.

As you might imagine, if we pass an object such as MyData to the writeObject
method, and writeObject notices that one of the fields is itself an object such as
a String, that data will get serialized properly. In other words, writeObject
works *recursively*. So, we will give it an ArrayList of data objects. The first is a
java.util.Date, for versioning purposes. All remaining objects are of type
MyData.

To be serializable, the data must implement the empty Serializable interface.
Also, the keyword transient can be used for any data that should *not* be serialized. You might need to do this for security, or to prevent attempts to serialize a
reference to an object from a non-serializable class. Here we use it to prevent the
unencrypted passwords from being saved where they might be readable:

```
import java.io.*;
import java.util.*;

class MyData implements Serializable {
    String userName;
    String passwordCypher;
    transient String passwordClear;
    public MyData(String name, String clear) {
        userName = name;
        // Save the clear text p/w in the object, it won't get serialized
        passwordClear = clear;
        // So we must save the encryption! Encryption not shown here.
        passwordCypher = DES.encrypt(passwordClear);
    }
}


public class Serialize {
    protected static final String FILENAME = "serial.dat";

    public static void main(String s[]) throws IOException {
        ArrayList v = new ArrayList();
        // Gather the data
        MyData u1 = new MyData("Ian Darwin", "secret_java_cook");
        v.add(new Date());
        v.add(u1);
        v.add(new MyData("Abby Brant", "dujordian"));
        // Save the data to disk.
        ObjectOutputStream os = new ObjectOutputStream(
            new FileOutputStream(FILENAME));
```

```
            os.writeObject(v);
            os.close();
        }
    }
```

See Also

There are many other ways to serialize objects, depending upon your interchange goals. One way would be to write the individual data members into an XML file (see Chapter 21).

9.17. Preventing ClassCastExceptions with SerialVersionUID

Problem

Your class got recompiled, and you're getting ClassCastExceptions that you shouldn't.

Solution

Run serialver and paste its output into your classes before you start.

Discussion

When a class is undergoing a period of evolution, particularly a class being used in a networking context such as RMI or servlets, it may be useful to provide a serialVersionUID value in this class. This is a long integer that is basically a hash of the methods and fields in the class. Both the object serialization API (see Recipe 9.16) and the JVM, when asked to cast one object to another (common when using collections, as in Chapter 7), either look up or, if not found, compute this value. If the value on the source and destination do not match, a ClassCastException is thrown. Most of the time, this is the correct thing for Java to do.

However, there may be times when you want to allow a class to evolve in a compatible way, but you can't immediately replace all instances in circulation. You must be willing to write code to account for the additional fields being discarded if restoring from the longer format to the shorter, and having the default value (null for objects, 0 for numbers and false for boolean) if restoring from the shorter format to the longer. If you are only adding fields and methods in a reasonably compatible way, you can control the compatibility by providing a long int named serialVersionUID. The initial value should be obtained from a JDK tool called

serialver, which takes just the class name. Consider a simple class called
SerializableUser:

```
/** Demo of a data class that will be used as a JavaBean or as a data
 * class in a Servlet container; making it Serializable allows
 * it to be saved ("serialized") to disk or over a network connection.
 */
public class SerializableUser implements java.io.Serializable {
    public String name;
    public String address;
    public String country;

    // other fields, and methods, here...
}
```

I first compiled it with two different compilers to ensure that the value is a product of the class structure, not of some minor differences in class file format that
different compilers might emit:

```
$ jikes +E SerializableUser..java
$ serialver SerializableUser
SerializableUser:    static final long serialVersionUID = -7978489268769667877L;
$ javac SerializableUser.java
$ serialver SerializableUser
SerializableUser:    static final long serialVersionUID = -7978489268769667877L;
```

Sure enough, the class file from both compilers has the same hash. Now let's
change the file. I go in with a line editor and add a new field phoneNum right after
country:

```
$ ed SerializableUser.java
383
8
        public String country;
a
        public String phoneNum;

.
w
408
q
ian:145$ jikes +E SerializableUser.java
ian:146$ serialver SerializableUser
SerializableUser:    static final long serialVersionUID = -8339341455288589756L;
```

Notice how the addition of the field changed the serialVersionUID! Now, if I
had wanted this class to evolve in a compatible fashion, here's what I should have
done before I started expanding it. I copy and paste the original serialver output into the source file (again using a line editor to insert a line before the last
line):

```
$ ed SerializableUser.java
408
$i
    static final long serialVersionUID = -7978489268769667877L;
.
w
472
q
$ jikes +E SerializableUser.java
$ serialver SerializableUser
SerializableUser:    static final long serialVersionUID = -7978489268769667877L;
$
```

Now all is well: I can interchange serialized versions of this file.

Note that `serialver` is part of the "object serialization" mechanism, and there-fore only works on classes that implement the `Serializable` interface described in Recipe 9.16.

9.18. Reading and Writing JAR or Zip Archives

Problem

You need to create and/or extract from a JAR archive or a file in the PkZip or WinZip format.

Solution

You could use the *jar* program in the Java Development Kit, since its file format is identical with the zip format with the addition of the META-INF directory to con-tain additional structural information. But since this is a book about program-ming, you are probably more interested in the `ZipFile` and `ZipEntry` classes and the stream classes that they provide access to.

Discussion

The class `java.util.zip.ZipFile` is not an I/O class per se, but a utility class that allows you to read or write the contents of a JAR or zip-format file.* When con-structed, it creates a series of `ZipEntry` objects, one to represent each entry in the archive. In other words, the `ZipFile` represents the entire archive, and the `ZipEntry` represents one entry, or one file that has been stored (and compressed)

---

* There is no support for adding files to an existing archive, so make sure you put all the files in at once, or be prepared to re-create the file from scratch.

in the archive. The `ZipEntry` has methods like `getName()`, which returns the name that the file had before it was put into the archive, and `getInputStream()`, which gives you an `InputStream` that will transparently uncompress the archive entry by filtering it as you read it. To create a `ZipFile` object, you need either the name of the archive file or a `File` object representing it:

```
ZipFile zippy = new ZipFile(fileName);
```

If you want to see whether a given file is present in the archive, you can call the `getEntry()` method with a filename. More commonly, you'll want to process all the entries; for this, use the `ZipFile` object to get a list of the entries in the archive, in the form of an `Enumeration` (see Recipe 7.4):

```
Enumeration all = zippy.entries();
while (all.hasMoreElements()) {
    ZipEntry entry = (ZipEntry)all.nextElement();
```

We can then process each entry as we wish. A simple listing program could be:

```
if (entry.isDirectory())
    println("Directory: " + e.getName());
else
    println("File: " + e.getName());
```

A fancier version would extract the files. The program in Example 9-4 does both: it lists by default, but with the -x (extract) switch, it actually extracts the files from the archive.

Example 9-4. UnZip.java

```
import java.io.*;
import java.util.*;
import java.util.zip.*;

/**
 * UnZip -- print or unzip a JAR or PKZIP file using JDK1.1 java.util.zip.
 * Final command-line version: extracts files.
 */
public class UnZip {
    /** Constants for mode listing or mode extracting. */
    public static final int LIST = 0, EXTRACT = 1;
    /** Whether we are extracting or just printing TOC */
    protected int mode = LIST;

    /** The ZipFile that is used to read an archive */
    protected ZipFile zippy;

    /** The buffer for reading/writing the ZipFile data */
    protected byte[] b;
```

Example 9-4. UnZip.java (continued)

```java
/** Simple main program, construct an UnZipper, process each
 * .ZIP file from argv[] through that object.
 */
public static void main(String[] argv) {
    UnZip u = new UnZip();

    for (int i=0; i<argv.length; i++) {
        if ("-x".equals(argv[i])) {
            u.setMode(EXTRACT);
            continue;
        }
        String candidate = argv[i];
        // System.err.println("Trying path " + candidate);
        if (candidate.endsWith(".zip") ||
            candidate.endsWith(".jar"))
                u.unZip(candidate);
        else System.err.println("Not a zip file? " + candidate);
    }
    System.err.println("All done!");
}


/** Construct an UnZip object. Just allocate the buffer */
UnZip() {
    b = new byte[8092];
}


/** Set the Mode (list, extract). */
protected void setMode(int m) {
    if (m == LIST ||
        m == EXTRACT)
        mode = m;
}


/** For a given Zip file, process each entry. */
public void unZip(String fileName) {
    try {
        zippy = new ZipFile(fileName);
        Enumeration all = zippy.entries();
        while (all.hasMoreElements()) {
            getFile(((ZipEntry)(all.nextElement())));
        }
    } catch (IOException err) {
        System.err.println("IO Error: " + err);
        return;
    }
}
```

Example 9-4. UnZip.java (continued)

```
    /** Process one file from the zip, given its name.
     * Either print the name, or create the file on disk.
     */
    protected void getFile(ZipEntry e) throws IOException {
        String zipName = e.getName();
        if (mode == EXTRACT) {
            // double-check that the file is in the zip
            // if a directory, mkdir it (remember to
            // create intervening subdirectories if needed!)
            if (zipName.endsWith("/")) {
                new File(zipName).mkdirs();
                return;
            }
            // Else must be a file; open the file for output
            System.err.println("Creating " + zipName);
            FileOutputStream os = new FileOutputStream(zipName);
            InputStream  is = zippy.getInputStream(e);
            int n = 0;
            while ((n = is.read(b)) >0)
                os.write(b, 0, n);
            is.close();
            os.close();
        } else
            // Not extracting, just list
            if (e.isDirectory()) {
                System.out.println("Directory " + zipName);
            } else {
                System.out.println("File " + zipName);
            }
    }
}
```

9.19. Reading and Writing Compressed Files

Problem

You need to read or write files that have been compressed using GNU zip, or *gzip*. These files are usually saved with the extension *.gz*.

Solution

Use a GZipInputStream or GZipOutputStream as appropriate.

Discussion

The GNU *gzip/gunzip* utilities originated on Unix and are commonly used to compress files. Unlike the PkZip format discussed in Recipe 9.18, these programs do not combine the functionality of archiving and compressing, and are therefore easier to work with. However, because they are not archives, people often use them in conjunction with an archiver. On Unix, *tar* and *cpio* are common, with *tar* and *gzip* being the de facto standard combination. Many web sites and FTP sites make files available with the extension *.tar.gz*; such files originally had to be first decompressed with *gunzip* and then extracted with *tar*. As this became a common operation, modern versions of *tar* have been extended to support a -z option, which means to *gunzip* before extracting, or to *gzip* before writing, as appropriate.

You may find archived files in *gzip* format on any platform. If you do, they're quite easy to read, again using classes from the `java.util.zip` package. This program assumes that the gzipped file originally contained text (Unicode characters). If not, you would treat it as a stream of bytes, that is, use a `BufferedInputStream` instead of a `BufferedReader`.

```java
import java.io.*;
import java.util.zip.*;

public class ReadGZIP {
    public static void main(String argv[]) throws IOException {
        String FILENAME = "file.txt.gz";

        // Since there are 4 constructors here, I wrote them all out in full.
        // In real life you would probably nest these constructor calls.
        FileInputStream fin = new FileInputStream(FILENAME);
        GZIPInputStream gzis = new GZIPInputStream(fin);
        InputStreamReader xover = new InputStreamReader(gzis);
        BufferedReader is = new BufferedReader(xover);

        String line;
        // Now read lines of text: the BufferedReader puts them in lines,
        // the InputStreamReader does Unicode conversion, and the
        // GZipInputStream "gunzip"s the data from the FileInputStream.
        while ((line = is.readLine()) != null)
            System.out.println("Read: " + line);
    }
}
```

If you need to write files in this format, everything works as you'd expect: you create a `GZipOutputStream` and write on it, usually using it through a `DataOutputStream` or `BufferedReader`.

See Also

The `Inflater`/`Deflater` classes provide access to general-purpose compression and decompression. The `InflaterStream`/`DeflaterStream` stream classes provide an I/O-based implementation of `Inflater`/`Deflater`.

9.20. Program: Text to PostScript

There are several approaches to printing in Java. In a GUI application, or if you want to use the graphical facilities that Java offers (fonts, colors, drawing primitives, and the like), you should refer to Recipes 12.10 and 12.11. However, sometimes you simply want to convert text into a form that will display nicely on a printer that isn't capable of handling raw text on its own (such as most of the many PostScript devices on the market). The program in Example 9-5 shows code for reading one or more text files, and outputting each of them in a plain font with PostScript around it. Because of the nature of PostScript, certain characters must be "escaped"; this is handled in toPsString(), which in turn is called from doLine(). There is also code for keeping track of the current position on the page. The output of this program can be sent directly to a PostScript printer.

Example 9-5. PSFormatter.java

```
import java.io.*;

/** Text to PS */
public class PSFormatter {
    /** The current input source */
    protected BufferedReader br;
    /** The current page number */
    protected int pageNum;
    /** The current X and Y on the page */
    protected int curX, curY;
    /** The current line number on page */
    protected int lineNum;
    /** The current tab setting */
    protected int tabPos = 0;
    public static final int INCH = 72;// PS constant: 72 pts/inch

    // Page parameters
    /** The left margin indent */
    protected int leftMargin = 50;
    /** The top of page indent */
    protected int topMargin = 750;
    /** The bottom of page indent */
    protected int botMargin = 50;

    // FORMATTING PARAMETERS
    protected int points = 12;
    protected int leading = 14;

    public static void main(String[] av) throws IOException {
        if (av.length == 0)
            new PSFormatter(
                new InputStreamReader(System.in)).process();
```

Example 9-5. PSFormatter.java (continued)

```
        else for (int i = 0; i < av.length; i++) {
            new PSFormatter(av[i]).process();
        }
    }

    public PSFormatter(String fileName) throws IOException {
        br = new BufferedReader(new FileReader(fileName));
    }

    public PSFormatter(Reader in) throws IOException {
        if (in instanceof BufferedReader)
            br = (BufferedReader)in;
        else
            br = new BufferedReader(in);
    }

    /** Main processing of the current input source. */
    protected void process() throws IOException {

        String line;

        prologue();  // emit PostScript prologue, once.

        startPage();// emit top-of-page (ending previous)

        while ((line = br.readLine()) != null) {
            if (line.startsWith("\f") || line.trim().equals(".bp")) {
                startPage();
                continue;
            }
            doLine(line);
        }

        // finish last page, if not already done.
        if (lineNum != 0)
            println("showpage");
    }

    /** Handle start of page details. */
    protected void startPage() {
        if (pageNum++ > 0)
            println("showpage");
        lineNum = 0;
        moveTo(leftMargin, topMargin);
    }

    /** Process one line from the current input */
    protected void doLine(String line) {
```

Example 9-5. PSFormatter.java (continued)

```java
        tabPos = 0;
        // count leading (not imbedded) tabs.
        for (int i=0; i<line.length(); i++) {
            if (line.charAt(i)=='\t')
                tabPos++;
            else
                break;
        }
        String l = line.trim(); // removes spaces AND tabs
        if (l.length() == 0) {
            ++lineNum;
            return;
        }
        moveTo(leftMargin + (tabPos * INCH),
            topMargin-(lineNum++ * leading));
        println('(' + toPSString(l)+ ") show");

        // If we just hit the bottom, start a new page
        if (curY <= botMargin)
            startPage();
    }

    protected String toPSString(String o) {
        StringBuffer sb = new StringBuffer();
        for (int i=0; i<o.length(); i++) {
            char c = o.charAt(i);
            switch(c) {
                case '(':sb.append("\\("); break;
                case ')':sb.append("\\)"); break;
                default:sb.append(c); break;
            }
        }
        return sb.toString();
    }

    protected void println(String s) {
        System.out.println(s);
    }

    protected void moveTo(int x, int y) {
        curX = x;
        curY = y;
        println(x + " " + y + " " + "moveto");
    }

    void prologue() {
```

Example 9-5. PSFormatter.java (continued)

```
        println("%!PS-Adobe");
        println("/Courier findfont " + points + " scalefont setfont ");
    }
}
```

The program could certainly be generalized more, and certain features (such as wrapping long lines) could be handled. I could also wade into the debate among PostScript experts as to how much of the formatting should be done on the main computer and how much should be done by the PostScript program interpreter running in the printer. But perhaps I won't get into that discussion. At least, not today.

See Also

As mentioned, Recipes 12.10 and 12.11 contain "better" recipes for printing under Java.

9.21. Program: TarList (File Converter)

This program provides easy access to *tar*-format files using an interface similar to that used for zip archives in Recipe 9.18. Unix users will be familiar with the *tar* program, an archiver first written back in the mid-1970s. And JDK users might find the *tar* program syntax somewhat familiar, as it was the basis for the command-line Java Archiver (*jar*) program in the JDK, written 20 years later. If you're not a Unix user, don't dismay: just think of this as an example of a whole category of programs, those that need to repetitively read and write files in a special-purpose, predefined format. MS-Windows is full of special-purpose file formats, as are many other operating systems. Unlike *jar, tar* is just an archiver, not a combined archiver and compressor, so its format is somewhat simpler. In this section we'll develop a program that reads a *tar* archive and lists the contents. The `TarList` program combines several reading methods with several formatting methods. So the commands:

```
tar -xvf demo.tar
java TarList demo.tar
```

should produce the same output. And indeed they do, at least for some files and some versions of *tar*, when run on a small *tar* archive:

```
$ java TarList demo.tar
-rwxr-xr-x ian/wheel        734 1999-10-05 19:10 TarDemo.class
-rwxr-xr-x ian/wheel        431 1999-10-05 19:10 TarList.java
-rw-r--r-- ian/wheel          0 1999-10-05 19:10 a
-rw-r--r-- ian/wheel          0 1999-10-05 19:10 b link to a
lrwxr-xr-x ian/wheel          0 1999-10-05 19:10 c -> a
```

```
$ tar -tvf demo.tar
-rwxr-xr-x ian/wheel       734 1999-10-05 19:10 TarDemo.class
-rwxr-xr-x ian/wheel       431 1999-10-05 19:10 TarList.java
-rw-r--r-- ian/wheel         0 1999-10-05 19:10 a
-rw-r--r-- ian/wheel         0 1999-10-05 19:10 b link to a
lrwxr-xr-x ian/wheel         0 1999-10-05 19:10 c -> a
$
```

This example archive contains five files. The last two items, b and c, represent two
kinds of links, regular and symbolic. A *regular link* is simply an additional name for
a filesystem entry. In Win-32 terms, a *symbolic link* closely approximates a *LNK* file,
except it is maintained by the operating system kernel instead of by a user-level
programming library.

First let's look at the main program class, TarList (Example 9-6), which is fairly
simple. Its main method simply looks for a filename in the command-line arguments, passes it to the TarList constructor, and calls the list() method. The
list() method delegates the presentation formatting to a method called
toListFormat(), which demonstrates several techniques. The Unix permissions,
which consist of three octal digits (user, group, and other) representing three permissions (read, write, and execute) is formatted using a simple for loop and an
array of strings (see Recipe 7.1). A DecimalFormat (see Recipe 5.7) is used to format the "size" column to a fixed width. But since DecimalFormat apparently lacks
the capability to do fixed-width numeric fields with leading spaces instead of leading zeros, we convert the leading zeros to spaces. A DateFormat (see Recipe 6.2)
is used to format the date-and-time field. All of this formatting is done into a
StringBuffer (see Recipe 3.3), which at the very end is converted into a String
and returned as the value of the toListFormat() method.

Example 9-6. TarList.java

```java
import java.io.*;
import java.text.*;// only for formatting
import java.util.*;

/**
 * Demonstrate the Tar archive lister.
 */
public class TarList {
    public static void main(String[] argv) throws IOException, TarException {
        if (argv.length == 0) {
            System.err.println("Usage: TarList archive");
            System.exit(1);
        }
        new TarList(argv[0]).list();
    }
    /** The TarFile we are reading */
```

Example 9-6. TarList.java (continued)

```java
    TarFile tf;

    /** Constructor */
    public TarList(String fileName) {
        tf = new TarFile(fileName);
    }


    /** Generate and print the listing */
    public void list() throws IOException, TarException {
        Enumeration list = tf.entries();
        while (list.hasMoreElements()) {
            TarEntry e = (TarEntry)list.nextElement();
            System.out.println(toListFormat(e));
        }
    }


    protected StringBuffer sb;
    /** Shift used in formatting permissions */
    protected static int shft[] = { 6, 3, 0 };
    /** Format strings used in permissions */
    protected static String rwx[] = {
        "---", "--x", "-w-", "-wx",
        "r--", "r-x", "rw-", "rwx"
    };
    /** NumberFormat used in formatting List form string */
    NumberFormat sizeForm = new DecimalFormat("00000000");
    /** Date used in printing mtime */
    Date date = new Date();
    SimpleDateFormat dateForm =
        new SimpleDateFormat ("yyyy-MM-dd HH:mm");

    /** Format a TarEntry the same way that UNIX tar does */
    public String toListFormat(TarEntry e) {
        sb = new StringBuffer();
        switch(e.type) {
            case TarEntry.LF_OLDNORMAL:
            case TarEntry.LF_NORMAL:
            case TarEntry.LF_CONTIG:
            case TarEntry.LF_LINK:// hard link: same as file
                sb.append('-');// 'f' would be sensible
                break;
            case TarEntry.LF_DIR:
                sb.append('d');
                break;
            case TarEntry.LF_SYMLINK:
                sb.append('l');
                break;
            case TarEntry.LF_CHR:// UNIX device file
```

Example 9-6. TarList.java (continued)

```java
            sb.append('c');
            break;
        case TarEntry.LF_BLK:// UNIX device file
            sb.append('b');
            break;
        case TarEntry.LF_FIFO:// UNIX named pipe
            sb.append('p');
            break;
        default:      // Can't happen?
            sb.append('?');
            break;
    }

    // Convert e.g., 754 to rwxrw-r--
    int mode = e.getMode();
    for (int i=0; i<3; i++) {
        sb.append(rwx[mode >> shft[i] & 007]);
    }
    sb.append(' ');

    // owner and group
    sb.append(e.getUname()).append('/').append(e.getGname()).append(' ');

    // size
    // DecimalFormat can't do "%-9d", so we do part of it ourselves
    sb.append(' ');
    String t = sizeForm.format(e.getSize());
    boolean digit = false;
    char c;
    for (int i=0; i<8; i++) {
        c = t.charAt(i);
        if (!digit && i<(8-1) && c == '0')
            sb.append(' ');// leading space
        else {
            digit = true;
            sb.append(c);
        }
    }
    sb.append(' ');

    // mtime
    // copy file's mtime into Data object (after scaling
    // from "sec since 1970" to "msec since 1970"), and format it.
    date.setTime(1000*e.getTime());
    sb.append(dateForm.format(date)).append(' ');

    sb.append(e.getName());
    if (e.isLink())
```

Example 9-6. TarList.java (continued)

```
            sb.append(" link to " ).append(e.getLinkName());
        if (e.isSymLink())
            sb.append(" -> " ).append(e.getLinkName());

        return sb.toString();
    }
}
```

"But wait," you may be saying. "There's no I/O here!" Well, patient reader, your waiting is rewarded. For here is class `TarFile` (Example 9-7). As its opening comment remarks, *tar* files, unlike zip files, have no central directory, so you have to read the entire archive file to be sure of having a particular file's entry, or to know how many entries there are in the archive. I centralize this in a method called `readFile()`, but for efficiency I don't call this method until I need to; this technique is known as lazy evaluation (there are comments in the ToDo file on how to make it even lazier, at the cost of one more boolean variable). In this method I construct a `RandomAccessFile` (see Recipe 9.14) to read the data. Since I need to read the file sequentially but then may need to seek back to a particular location, I use a file that can be accessed randomly as well as sequentially. Most of the rest of the code has to do with keeping track of the files stored within the archive.

Example 9-7. TarFile.java

```
import java.io.*;
import java.util.*;

/**
 * Tape Archive Lister, patterned loosely after java.util.ZipFile.
 * Since, unlike Zip files, there is no central directory, you have to
 * read the entire file either to be sure of having a particular file's
 * entry, or to know how many entries there are in the archive.
 */

public class TarFile {
    /** True after we've done the expensive read. */
    protected boolean read = false;
    /** The list of entries found in the archive */
    protected Vector list;

    /** Size of header block on tape. */
    public static final intRECORDSIZE = 512;

    /* Size of each block, in records */
    protected intblocking;
    /* Size of each block, in bytes */
    protected intblocksize;
```

Example 9-7. TarFile.java (continued)

```java
/** File containing archive */
protected StringfileName;

/** Construct (open) a Tar file by name */
public TarFile(String name) {
    fileName = name;
    list = new Vector();
    read = false;
}

/** Construct (open) a Tar file by File */
public TarFile(java.io.File name) throws IOException {
    this(name.getCanonicalPath());
}

/** The main datastream. */
protected RandomAccessFile is;

/** Read the Tar archive in its entirety.
 * This is semi-lazy evaluation, in that we don't read the file
 * until we need to.
 * A future revision may use even lazier evaluation: in getEntry,
 * scan the list and, if not found, continue reading!
 * For now, just read the whole file.
 */
protected void readFile() throws IOException, TarException {
    is = new RandomAccessFile(fileName, "r");
    TarEntry hdr;
    try {
        do {
            hdr = new TarEntry(is);
            if (hdr.getSize() < 0) {
                System.out.println("Size < 0");
                break;
            }
            // System.out.println(hdr.toString());
            list.addElement(hdr);
            // Get the size of the entry
            int nbytes = hdr.getSize(), diff;
            // Round it up to blocksize.
            if ((diff = (nbytes % RECORDSIZE)) != 0) {
                nbytes -= diff; nbytes += RECORDSIZE;
            }
            // And skip over the data portion.
            // System.out.println("Skipping " + nbytes + " bytes");
            is.skipBytes(nbytes);
        } while (true);
    } catch (EOFException e) {
```

Example 9-7. TarFile.java (continued)

```java
            // OK, just stop reading.
        }
        // All done, say we've read the contents.
        read = true;
    }

    /* Close the Tar file. */
    public void close() {
        try {
            is.close();
        } catch (IOException e) {
            // nothing to do
        }
    }

    /* Returns an enumeration of the Tar file entries. */
    public Enumeration entries() throws IOException, TarException {
        if (!read) {
            readFile();
        }
        return list.elements();
    }

    /** Returns the Tar entry for the specified name, or null if not found. */
    public TarEntry getEntry(String name) {
        for (int i=0; i<list.size(); i++) {
            TarEntry e = (TarEntry)list.elementAt(i);
            if (name.equals(e.getName()))
                return e;
        }
        return null;
    }

    /** Returns an InputStream for reading the contents of the
     * specified entry from the archive.
     * May cause the entire file to be read.
     */
    public InputStream getInputStream(TarEntry entry) {
        return null;
    }

    /** Returns the path name of the Tar file. */
    public String getName() {
        return null;
    }

    /** Returns the number of entries in the Tar archive.
     * May cause the entire file to be read.
     */
```

Example 9-7. TarFile.java (continued)

```
    public int size() {
        return 0;
    }
}
```

"But my patience is nearly at an end! Where's the actual reading?" Indeed, you may well ask. But it's not there. The actual reading code is further delegated to `TarEntry`'s constructor, which we'll see in a minute. Since `TarFile` is patterned after `ZipFile` (see Recipe 9.18), it doesn't extend any of the I/O classes. Like `ZipFile`, a `TarFile` is an object that lets you get at the individual elements within a *tar*-format archive, each represented by a `TarEntry` object. If you want to find whether a particular file exists in the archive, you can call the `TarFile`'s `getEntry()` method. Or you can ask for all the entries, as we did previously in `TarList`. Having obtained one entry, you can ask for all the information about it, again as we did in `TarList`. Or you could ask for an `InputStream`, as we did for zip files. However, that part of the `TarEntry` class has been left as an exercise for the reader. Here, at last, is `TarEntry` (Example 9-8), whose constructor reads the archive header and stores the file's beginning location for you, for when you get around to writing the `getInputStream` method.

As mentioned, I use lazy evaluation, simply reading the bytes into some byte arrays, and don't convert them to strings or numbers until asked to. Notice also that the filenames and user/group names are treated as byte strings and converted as ASCII characters when needed as `Strings`. This makes sense, because the *tar* file format only uses ASCII characters at present. Some Unix implementations of *tar* explicitly look for null characters to end some of these strings; this will need work from the Unix standards people.

Example 9-8. TarEntry.java

```
import java.io.*;

/** One entry in an archive file.
 * @note
 * Tar format info taken from John Gilmore's public domain tar program,
 * @(#)tar.h 1.21 87/05/01Public Domain, which said:
 * "Created 25 August 1985 by John Gilmore, ihnp4!hoptoad!gnu."
 * John is now gnu@toad.com, and by another path tar.h is GPL'd in GNU Tar.
 */
public class TarEntry {
    /** Where in the tar archive this entry's HEADER is found. */
    public long fileOffset = 0;

    /** The maximum size of a name */
    public static final intNAMSIZ= 100;
```

Example 9-8. TarEntry.java (continued)

```java
    public static final intTUNMLEN= 32;
    public static final intTGNMLEN= 32;

    // Next fourteen fields constitute one physical record.
    // Padded to TarFile.RECORDSIZE bytes on tape/disk.
    // Lazy Evaluation: just read fields in raw form, only format when asked.

    /** File name */
    byte[]name = new byte[NAMSIZ];
    /** permissions, e.g., rwxr-xr-x? */
    byte[]mode = new byte[8];
    /* user */
    byte[]uid = new byte[8];
    /* group */
    byte[]gid = new byte[8];
    /* size */
    byte[]size = new byte[12];
    /* UNIX modification time */
    byte[]mtime = new byte[12];
    /* checksum field */
    byte[]chksum = new byte[8];
    byte type;
    byte[]linkName = new byte[NAMSIZ];
    byte[]magic = new byte[8];
    byte[]uname = new byte[TUNMLEN];
    byte[]gname = new byte[TGNMLEN];
    byte[]devmajor = new byte[8];
    byte[]devminor = new byte[8];

    // End of the physical data fields.

    /* The magic field is filled with this if uname and gname are valid. */
    public static final byte TMAGIC[] = {
        // 'u', 's', 't', 'a', 'r', ' ', ' ', '\0'
        0, 0, 0, 0, 0, 0, 0x20, 0x20, 0
    }; /* 7 chars and a null */

    /* Type value for Normal file, Unix compatibility */
    public static final intLF_OLDNORMAL ='\0';
    /* Type value for Normal file */
    public static final intLF_NORMAL = '0';
    /* Type value for Link to previously dumped file */
    public static final int LF_LINK = '1';
    /* Type value for Symbolic link */
    public static final int LF_SYMLINK = '2';
    /* Type value for Character special file */
    public static final int LF_CHR = '3';
    /* Type value for Block special file */
```

Example 9-8. TarEntry.java (continued)

```java
    public static final int LF_BLK = '4';
    /* Type value for Directory */
    public static final int LF_DIR = '5';
    /* Type value for FIFO special file */
    public static final int LF_FIFO = '6';
    /* Type value for Contiguous file */
    public static final int LF_CONTIG = '7';

    /* Constructor that reads the entry's header. */
    public TarEntry(RandomAccessFile is) throws IOException, TarException {

        fileOffset = is.getFilePointer();

        // read() returns -1 at EOF
        if (is.read(name) < 0)
            throw new EOFException();
        // Tar pads to block boundary with nulls.
        if (name[0] == '\0')
            throw new EOFException();
        // OK, read remaining fields.
        is.read(mode);
        is.read(uid);
        is.read(gid);
        is.read(size);
        is.read(mtime);
        is.read(chksum);
        type = is.readByte();
        is.read(linkName);
        is.read(magic);
        is.read(uname);
        is.read(gname);
        is.read(devmajor);
        is.read(devminor);

        // Since the tar header is < 512, we need to skip it.
        is.skipBytes((int)(TarFile.RECORDSIZE -
            (is.getFilePointer() % TarFile.RECORDSIZE)));

        // TODO if checksum() fails,
        //   throw new TarException("Failed to find next header");

    }

    /** Returns the name of the file this entry represents. */
    public String getName() {
        return new String(name).trim();
    }
```

Example 9-8. TarEntry.java (continued)

```java
public String getTypeName() {
    switch(type) {
    case LF_OLDNORMAL:
    case LF_NORMAL:
        return "file";
    case LF_LINK:
        return "link w/in archive";
    case LF_SYMLINK:
        return "symlink";
    case LF_CHR:
    case LF_BLK:
    case LF_FIFO:
        return "special file";
    case LF_DIR:
        return "directory";
    case LF_CONTIG:
        return "contig";
    default:
        throw new IllegalStateException("TarEntry.getTypeName: type "
            + type + " invalid");
    }
}

/** Returns the UNIX-specific "mode" (type+permissions) of the entry */
public int getMode() {
    try {
        return Integer.parseInt(new String(mode).trim(), 8) & 0777;
    } catch (IllegalArgumentException e) {
        return 0;
    }
}

/** Returns the size of the entry */
public int getSize() {
    try {
        return Integer.parseInt(new String(size).trim(), 8);
    } catch (IllegalArgumentException e) {
        return 0;
    }
}

/** Returns the name of the file this entry is a link to,
 * or null if this entry is not a link.
 */
public String getLinkName() {
    // if (isLink())
    //    return null;
    return new String(linkName).trim();
}
```

Example 9-8. TarEntry.java (continued)

```java
/** Returns the modification time of the entry */
public long getTime() {
    try {
        return Long.parseLong(new String(mtime).trim(),8);
    } catch (IllegalArgumentException e) {
        return 0;
    }
}

/** Returns the string name of the userid */
public String getUname() {
    return new String(uname).trim();
}

/** Returns the string name of the group id */
public String getGname() {
    return new String(gname).trim();
}

/** Returns the numeric userid of the entry */
public int getuid() {
    try {
        return Integer.parseInt(new String(uid).trim());
    } catch (IllegalArgumentException e) {
        return -1;
    }
}
/** Returns the numeric gid of the entry */
public int getgid() {
    try {
        return Integer.parseInt(new String(gid).trim());
    } catch (IllegalArgumentException e) {
        return -1;
    }
}

/** Returns true if this entry represents a file */
boolean isFile() {
    return type == LF_NORMAL || type == LF_OLDNORMAL;
}

/** Returns true if this entry represents a directory */
boolean isDirectory() {
    return type == LF_DIR;
}

/** Returns true if this a hard link (to a file in the archive) */
boolean isLink() {
```

Example 9-8. TarEntry.java (continued)

```
        return type == LF_LINK;
    }

    /** Returns true if this a symbolic link */
    boolean isSymLink() {
        return type == LF_SYMLINK;
    }

    /** Returns true if this entry represents some type of UNIX special file */
    boolean isSpecial() {
        return type == LF_CHR || type == LF_BLK || type == LF_FIFO;
    }

    public String toString() {
        return "TarEntry[" + getName() + ']';
    }
}
```

See Also

The `TarFile` example is one of the longest in the book. One could equally well use filter subclassing to provide encryption. One could even, in theory, write a Java interface to an encrypted filesystem layer, such as CFS (see *ftp://research.att.com/ dist/mab/cfs.ps*) or to a version-archiving system such as CVS (the Concurrent Versions System; see *http://www.cvs.org*). CVS is a good tool for maintaining source code; most large open source projects now use it (see *http://www.openbsd.org/why-cvs.html*). In fact, there is already a Java-based implementation of CVS* (see *http:// www.ice.com/java/jcvs/*). Either of these would be substantially more clever than my little tarry friend, but, I suspect, contain rather more code.

For all topics in this chapter, Rusty's book *Java I/O* should be considered the antepenultimate documentation. The penultimate reference is the Javadoc documentation, while the ultimate reference is, if you really need it, the source code for the Java API, to which I have not needed to make a single reference in writing this chapter.

---

* There are also CVS interfaces in many tools, including Ant (Recipe 1.7), and several IDEs (Recipe 1.3), including Forte, JBuilder, and probably others.

10

Directory and Filesystem Operations

10.0. Introduction

This chapter is largely devoted to one class: `java.io.File`. The `File` class gives you the ability to list directories, obtain file status, rename and delete files on disk, create directories, and perform other filesystem operations. Many of these would be considered "system programming" functions on some operating systems. Java makes them all as portable as possible.

Note that many of the methods of this class attempt to modify the permanent file store, or disk filesystem, of the computer you run them on. Naturally, you might not have permission to change certain files in certain ways. This can be detected by the Java Virtual Machine's (or the browser's, in an applet) `SecurityManager`, which will throw an instance of the unchecked exception `SecurityException`. But failure can also be detected by the underlying operating system: if the security manager approves it but the user running your program lacks permissions on the directory, for example, then you will either get back an indication (such as false), or an instance of the checked exception `IOException`. This must be caught (or declared in the `throws` clause) in any code that calls any method that tries to change the filesystem.

10.1. Getting File Information

Problem

You need to know all you can about a given file on disk.

Solution

Use a `java.io.File` object.

Discussion

The `File` class has a number of "informational" methods. To use any of these, you must construct a `File` object containing the name of the file it is to operate upon. It should be noted up front that creating a `File` object has no effect on the permanent filesystem; it is only an object in Java's memory. You must call methods on the `File` object in order to change the filesystem; as we'll see, there are numerous "change" methods, such as one for creating a new (but empty) file, one for renaming a file, etc., as well as many informational methods. Table 10-1 lists some of the informational methods.

Table 10-1. java.io.File methods

Return type	Method name	Meaning
boolean	exists()	True if something of that name exists
String	getCanonicalPath()	Full name
String	getName()	Relative filename
String	getParent()	Parent directory
boolean	canRead()	True if file is readable
boolean	canWrite()	True if file is writable
long	lastModified()	File modification time
long	length()	File size
boolean	isFile()	True if it's a file
boolean	isDirectory()	True if it's a directory (Note: it might be neither)

You can't change the name stored in a `File` object; you simply create a new `File` object each time you need to refer to a different file.

```java
import java.io.*;
import java.util.*;

/**
 * Report on a file's status in Java
 */
public class FileStatus {
    public static void main(String[] argv) throws IOException {

        // Ensure that a filename (or something) was given in argv[0]
        if (argv.length == 0) {
            System.err.println("Usage: Status filename");
```

```
            System.exit(1);
        }
        for (int i = 0; i< argv.length; i++) {
            status(argv[i]);
        }
    }

public static void status(String fileName) throws IOException {
    System.out.println("---" + fileName + "---");

    // Construct a File object for the given file.
    File f = new File(fileName);

    // See if it actually exists
    if (!f.exists()) {
        System.out.println("file not found");
        System.out.println();// Blank line
        return;
    }
    // Print full name
    System.out.println("Canonical name " + f.getCanonicalPath());
    // Print parent directory if possible
    String p = f.getParent();
    if (p != null) {
        System.out.println("Parent directory: " + p);
    }
    // Check if the file is readable
    if (f.canRead()) {
        System.out.println("File is readable.");
    }
    // Check if the file is writable
    if (f.canWrite()) {
        System.out.println("File is writable.");
    }
    // Report on the modification time.
    Date d = new Date();
    d.setTime(f.lastModified());
    System.out.println("Last modified " + d);

    // See if file, directory, or other. If file, print size.
    if (f.isFile()) {
        // Report on the file's size
        System.out.println("File size is " + f.length() + " bytes.");
    } else if (f.isDirectory()) {
        System.out.println("It's a directory");
    } else {
        System.out.println("I dunno! Neither a file nor a directory!");
    }
```

```
                System.out.println();// blank line between entries
        }
    }
```

When run with the three arguments shown, it produces this output:

```
C:\javasrc\dir_file>java  FileStatus    / /tmp/id /autoexec.bat
---/---
Canonical name C:\
File is readable.
File is writable.
Last modified Thu Jan 01 00:00:00 GMT 1970
It's a directory

---/tmp/id---
file not found

---/autoexec.bat---
Canonical name C:\AUTOEXEC.BAT
Parent directory: \
File is readable.
File is writable.
Last modified Fri Sep 10 15:40:32 GMT 1999
File size is 308 bytes.
```

As you can see, the so-called "canonical name" not only includes a leading directory root of C:\, but also has had the name converted to uppercase. You can tell I ran that on MS-Windows. On Unix, it behaves differently:

```
$ java FileStatus / /tmp/id /autoexec.bat
---/---
Canonical name /
File is readable.
Last modified October 4, 1999 6:29:14 AM PDT
It's a directory

---/tmp/id---
Canonical name /tmp/id
Parent directory: /tmp
File is readable.
File is writable.
Last modified October 8, 1999 1:01:54 PM PDT
File size is 0 bytes.

---/autoexec.bat---
file not found

$
```

On a typical Unix system there is no *autoexec.bat* file. And Unix filenames (like those on a Mac) can consists of upper- and lowercase characters: what you type is what you get.

10.2. Creating a File

Problem

You need to create a new file on disk, but you don't want to write into it.

Solution

Use a `java.io.File` object's `createNewFile()` method.

Discussion

You could easily create a new file by constructing a `FileOutputStream` or `FileWriter` (see Recipe 9.3). But then you'd have to remember to close it as well. Sometimes you want a file to exist, but you don't want to bother putting anything into it. This might be used, for example, as a simple form of interprogram communication: one program could test for the presence of a file, and interpret that to mean that the other program has reached a certain state. Here is code that simply creates an empty file for each name you give:

```java
import java.io.*;

/**
 * Create one or more files by name.
 * The final "e" is omitted in homage to the underlying UNIX system call.
 */
public class Creat {
    public static void main(String[] argv) throws IOException {

        // Ensure that a filename (or something) was given in argv[0]
        if (argv.length == 0) {
            System.err.println("Usage: Creat filename");
            System.exit(1);
        }

        for (int i = 0; i< argv.length; i++) {
            // Constructing a File object doesn't affect the disk, but
            // the createNewFile() method does.
            new File(argv[i]).createNewFile();
        }
    }
}
```

10.3. Renaming a File

Problem

You need to change a file's name on disk.

Solution

Use a `java.io.File` object's `renameTo()` method.

Discussion

For reasons best left to the gods of Java, the `renameTo()` method requires not the name you want the file renamed to, but another `File` object referring to the new name. So to rename a file you must create two `File` objects, one for the existing name and another for the new name. Then call the `renameTo` method of the existing-name's `File` object, passing in the second `File` object. This is easier to see than to explain, so here goes:

```
import java.io.*;

/**
 * Rename a file in Java
 */
public class Rename {
    public static void main(String[] argv) throws IOException {

        // Construct the file object. Does NOT create a file on disk!
        File f = new File("Rename.java~"); // backup of this source file.

        // Rename the backup file to "junk.dat"
        // Renaming requires a File object for the target.
        f.renameTo(new File("junk.dat"));
    }
}
```

10.4. Deleting a File

Problem

You need to delete one or more files from disk.

Solution

Use a `java.io.File` object's `delete()` method; it will delete files (subject to permissions) and directories (subject to permissions and to the directory being empty).

Discussion

This is not very complicated. Simply construct a `File` object for the file you wish
to delete, and call its `delete()` method:

```java
import java.io.*;

/**
 * Delete a file from within Java
 */
public class Delete {
    public static void main(String[] argv) throws IOException {

        // Construct a File object for the backup created by editing
        // this source file. The file probably already exists.
        // My editor creates backups by putting ~ at the end of the name.
        File bkup = new File("Delete.java~");
        // Quick, now, delete it immediately:
        bkup.delete();
    }
}
```

Just recall the caveat about permissions in the Introduction to this chapter: if you
don't have permission, you can get a return value of false or, possibly, a
`SecurityException`. Note also that there are some differences between platforms. Windows 95 allows Java to remove a file that has the read-only bit, but Unix
does not allow you to remove a file that you don't have permission on or to
remove a directory that isn't empty. Here is a version of `Delete` with error checking (and reporting of success, too):

```java
import java.io.*;

/**
 * Delete a file from within Java, with error handling.
 */
public class Delete2 {

    public static void main(String argv[]) {
        for (int i=0; i<argv.length; i++)
            delete(argv[i]);
    }

    public static void delete(String fileName) {
        try {
            // Construct a File object for the file to be deleted.
            File bkup = new File(fileName);
            // Quick, now, delete it immediately:
            if (!bkup.delete())
                System.out.println("** Deleted " + fileName);
```

```
            else
                System.err.println("Failed to delete " + fileName);
                } catch (SecurityException e) {
            System.err.println("Unable to delete " + fileName +
                "(" + e.getMessage() + ")");
            }
        }
    }
```

Running it we get this:

```
$ ls -ld ?
-rw-r--r--  1 ian  ian    0 Oct  8 16:50 a
drwxr-xr-x  2 ian  ian  512 Oct  8 16:50 b
drwxr-xr-x  3 ian  ian  512 Oct  8 16:50 c
$ java Delete2 ?
**Deleted** a
**Deleted** b
Failed to delete c
$ ls -l  c
total 2
drwxr-xr-x  2 ian  ian  512 Oct  8 16:50 d
$ java Delete2 c/d c
**Deleted** c/d
**Deleted** c
$
```

10.5. Creating a Transient File

Problem

You need to create a file with a unique temporary filename or arrange for a file to be deleted when your program is finished.

Solution

Use a `java.io.File` object's `createTempFile()` or `deleteOnExit()` method.

Discussion

The `File` object has a `createTempFile` method and a `deleteOnExit` method. The former creates a file with a unique name—in case several users run the same program at the same time on a server—and the latter arranges for any file (no matter how it was created) to be deleted when the program exits. Here we arrange for a backup copy of a program to be deleted on exit, and we also create a temporary file and arrange for it to be removed on exit. Sure enough, both files are gone after the program runs.

```java
import java.io.*;

/**
 * Work with temporary files in Java.
 */
public class TempFiles {
    public static void main(String[] argv) throws IOException {

        // 1. Make an existing file temporary

        // Construct a File object for the backup created by editing
        // this source file. The file probably already exists.
        // My editor creates backups by putting ~ at the end of the name.
        File bkup = new File("Rename.java~");
        // Arrange to have it deleted when the program ends.
        bkup.deleteOnExit();

        // 2. Create a new temporary file.

        // Make a file object for foo.tmp, in the default temp directory
        File tmp = File.createTempFile("foo", "tmp");
        // Report on the filename that it made up for us.
        System.out.println("Your temp file is " + tmp.getCanonicalPath());
        // Arrange for it to be deleted at exit.
        tmp.deleteOnExit();
        // Now do something with the temporary file, without having to
        // worry about deleting it later.
        writeDataInTemp(tmp.getCanonicalPath());
    }

    public static void writeDataInTemp(String tempnam) {
        // This version is dummy. Use your imagination.
    }
}
```

Notice that the `createTempFile` method is like `createNewFile` (see Recipe 10.2) in that it does create the file. Also be aware that, should the Java Virtual Machine terminate abnormally, the deletion will probably not occur. Finally, there is no way to undo the setting of `deleteOnExit()` short of something drastic like powering off the computer before the program exits.

10.6. Changing File Attributes

Problem

You want to change attributes of a file other than its name.

Solution

Use setReadOnly() or setLastModified().

Discussion

As we saw in Recipe 10.1, there are many methods that report on a file. By contrast, there are only a few that change the file.

setReadOnly() turns on read-only for a given file or directory. It returns true if it succeeds, otherwise false. There is no setReadWrite() (at least as of JDK 1.3; I don't know why this method was overlooked). Since you can't undo a setReadOnly(), use this method with care!

setLastModified() allows you to play games with the modification time of a file. This is normally not a good game to play, but is useful in some types of backup/ restore programs. This method takes an argument that is the number of milliseconds (not seconds) since the beginning of time (January 1, 1970). You can get the original value for the file by calling getLastModified() (see Recipe 10.1) or you can get the value for a given date by calling the Date class's getTime() method (see Recipe 6.1). setLastModified() returns true if it succeeded, and false otherwise.

The interesting thing is that the documentation claims that "File objects are immutable," meaning that their state doesn't change. But does calling setReadOnly() affect the return value of canRead()? Let's find out:

```
import java.io.*;

public class ReadOnly {
    public static void main(String[] a) throws IOException {

        File f = new File("f");

        if (!f.createNewFile()) {
            System.out.println("Can't create new file.");
            return;
        }

        if (!f.canWrite()) {
            System.out.println("Can't write new file!");
            return;
        }

        if (!f.setReadOnly()) {
            System.out.println("Grrr! Can't set file read-only.");
            return;
        }
```

```
        if (f.canWrite()) {
            System.out.println("Most immutable, captain!");
            System.out.println("But it still says canWrite() after setReadOnly");
            return;
        } else {
            System.out.println("Logical, captain!");
            System.out.println
                ("canWrite() correctly returns false after setReadOnly");
        }
    }
}
```

When I run it, this program reports what I (and I hope you) would expect:

```
$ jr ReadOnly
+ jikes +E -d . ReadOnly.java
+ java ReadOnly
Logical, captain!
canWrite() correctly returns false after setReadOnly
$
```

So, the immutability of a `File` object refers only to the pathname it contains, not
to its read-only-ness.

10.7. Listing a Directory

Problem

You need to list the filesystem entries named in a directory.

Solution

Use a `java.io.File` object's `list()` method.

Discussion

The `java.io.File` class contains several methods for working with directories.
For example, to list the filesystem entities named in the current directory, just
write:

```
String names = new File(".").list()
```

This can become a complete program with as little as the following:

```
/** Simple directory lister.
 */
public class Ls {
    public static void main(String argh_my_aching_fingers[]) {
        String[] dir = new java.io.File(".").list(); // Get list of names
```

```
            java.util.Arrays.sort(dir);// Sort it (Data Structuring chapter))
            for (int i=0; i<dir.length; i++)
                System.out.println(dir[i]);// Print the list
        }
    }
```

Of course, there's lots of room for elaboration. You could print the names in multiple columns across the page. Or even down the page, since you know the number of items in the list before you print. You could omit filenames with leading periods, as does the Unix *ls* program. Or print the directory names first; I once used a directory lister called *lc* that did this, and I found it quite useful. By constructing a new `File` object for each name, you could print the size of each, as per the DOS *dir* command or the Unix *ls –l* command (see Recipe 10.1). Or you could figure out whether each is a file, a directory, or neither. Having done that, you could pass each directory to your top-level function, and you'd have directory recursion (the Unix *find* command, or *ls –R*, or the DOS *DIR/S* command).

A more flexible way to list filesystem entries is with `list(FilenameFilter ff)`. `FilenameFilter` is a tiny little interface, with only one method: `boolean accept(File inDir, String fileName)`. Suppose you want a listing of only Java-related files (**.java*, **.class*, **.jar*, etc.). Just write the `accept()` method so that it returns true for these files and false for any others. Here is the `Ls` class warmed over to use a `FilenameFilter` instance (my `OnlyJava` class implements this interface) to restrict the listing:

```
import java.io.*;

/**
 * FNFilter - Ls directory lister modified to use FilenameFilter
 */
public class FNFilter {
    public static void main(String argh_my_aching_fingers[]) {
        // Generate the selective list, with a one-use File object.
        String[] dir = new java.io.File(".").list(new OnlyJava());
        java.util.Arrays.sort(dir);// Sort it (Data Structuring chapter))
        for (int i=0; i<dir.length; i++)
            System.out.println(dir[i]);// Print the list
    }
}

/** This class implements the FilenameFilter interface.
 * The Accept method only returns true for .java and .class files.
 */
class OnlyJava implements FilenameFilter {
    public boolean accept(File dir, String s) {
        if (s.endsWith(".java") || s.endsWith(".class") || s.endsWith(".jar"))
            return true;
```

```
        // others: projects, ... ?
        return false;
    }
}
```

The `FilenameFilter` need not be a separate class; the online code example `FNFilter2` implements the interface directly in the main class, resulting in a slightly shorter file. In a full-scale application, the list of files returned by the `FilenameFilter` would be chosen dynamically, possibly automatically based on what you were working on. As we'll see in Recipe 13.9, the file chooser dialogs implement a superset of this functionality, allowing the user to select interactively from one of several sets of files to be listed. This is a great convenience in finding files, just as it is here in reducing the number of files that must be examined.

10.8. Getting the Directory Roots

Problem

You want to know about all the top-level directories, such as C:\ and D:\ on MS-Windows.

Solution

Use the static method `File.listRoots()`.

Discussion

Speaking of directory listings, you surely know that all modern desktop computing systems arrange files into hierarchies of directories. But you might not know that on Unix all filenames are somehow "under" the single root directory named /, while on Microsoft platforms there is a root directory named \ in each disk drive (A:\ for the first floppy, C:\ for the first hard drive, and other letters for CD-ROM and network drivers). If you need to know about all the files on all the disks, then, you should find out what "directory root" names exist on the particular platform. The static method `listRoots()` returns (in an array of `File` objects) the available filesystem roots on whatever platform you are running on. Here is a short program to list these, along with its output:

```
C:> type DirRoots.java
import java.io.*;

public class DirRoots {
    public static void main(String argh_my_aching_fingers[]) {
        File[] drives = File.listRoots(); // Get list of names
        for (int i=0; i<drives.length; i++)
```

```
                System.out.println(drives[i]);// Print the list
        }
    }
C:> java DirRoots
A:\
C:\
D:\
C:>
```

As you can see, the program listed my floppy drive (even though the floppy drive was not only empty, but left at home while I wrote this recipe on my notebook computer in a parking lot), the hard disk drive, and the CD-ROM drive.

On Unix there is only one:

```
$ java DirRoots
/
$
```

One thing that is "left out" of the list of roots is the so-called UNC filename. UNC filenames are used on Microsoft platforms to refer to a network-available resource that hasn't been mounted locally on a particular drive letter. For example, my server (running Unix with the Samba SMB fileserver software) is named darian (made from my surname and first name), and my home directory on that machine is exported or shared with the name ian, so I could refer to a directory named *book* in my home directory under the UNC name *\\darian\ian\book*. Such a filename would be valid in any Java filename context (assuming you're running on MS-Windows), but you would not learn about it from the File.listRoots() method.

10.9. Making New Directories

Problem

You need to create a directory.

Solution

Use java.io.File's mkdir() or mkdirs() method.

Discussion

Of the two methods used for creating directories, mkdir() creates just one directory while mkdirs() creates any parent directories that are needed. For example, if */home/ian* exists and is a directory, then the calls:

```
new File("/home/ian/bin").mkdir();
new File("/home/ian/src").mkdir();
```

will succeed, whereas:

```
new File("/home/ian/once/twice/again").mkdir();
```

will fail, assuming that the directory *once* does not exist. If you wish to create a whole path of directories, you would tell `File` to make all the directories at once by using `mkdirs()`:

```
new File("/home/ian/once/twice/again").mkdirs();
```

Both variants of this command return `true` if they succeed and `false` if they fail. Notice that it is possible (but not likely) for `mkdirs()` to create some of the directories and then fail; in this case, the newly created directories will be left in the filesystem.

Notice the spelling: `mkdir()` is all lowercase. While this might be said to violate the normal Java naming conventions (which would suggest `mkDir()` as the name), it is the name of the underlying operating system call and command on both Unix and DOS (though DOS allows *md* as an alias at the command-line level).

10.10. Program: Find

This program implements a small subset of the MS-Windows Find Files dialog or the Unix *find* command. However, it has much of the structure needed to build a more complete version of either of these. It uses a custom filename filter controlled by the `-n` command-line option, which is parsed using my `GetOpt` (see Recipe 2.7).

```
import com.darwinsys.util.*;
import java.io.*;
import java.io.*;

/**
 * Find - find files by name, size, or other criteria. Non-GUI version.
 */
public class Find {
    /** Main program */
    public static void main(String[] args) {
        Find finder = new Find();
        GetOpt argHandler = new GetOpt("n:s:");
        int c;
        while ((c = argHandler.getopt(args)) != GetOpt.DONE) {
            switch(c) {
            case 'n': finder.filter.setNameFilter(argHandler.optarg()); break;
            case 's': finder.filter.setSizeFilter(argHandler.optarg()); break;
            default:
                System.out.println("Got: " + c);
                usage();
```

```
        }
    }
    if (args.length == 0 || argHandler.getOptInd()-1 == args.length) {
        finder.doName(".");
    } else {
        for (int i = argHandler.getOptInd()-1; i<args.length; i++)
            finder.doName(args[i]);
    }
}

protected FindFilter filter = new FindFilter();

public static void usage() {
    System.err.println(
        "Usage: Find [-n namefilter][-s sizefilter][dir...]");
    System.exit(1);
}

/** doName - handle one filesystem object by name */
private void doName(String s) {
    Debug.println("flow", "doName(" + s + ")");
    File f = new File(s);
    if (!f.exists()) {
        System.out.println(s + " does not exist");
        return;
    }
    if (f.isFile())
        doFile(f);
    else if (f.isDirectory()) {
        // System.out.println("d " + f.getPath());
        String objects[] = f.list(filter);

        for (int i=0; i<objects.length; i++)
            doName(s + f.separator + objects[i]);
    } else
        System.err.println("Unknown type: " + s);
}

/** doFile - process one regular file. */
private static void doFile(File f) {
    System.out.println("f " + f.getPath());
}
}
```

The program uses a class called **FindFilter** to implement matching:

```
import java.io.*;
import org.apache.regexp.*;
import com.darwinsys.util.Debug;
```

```java
/** Class to encapsulate the filtration for Find.
 * For now just setTTTFilter() methods. Really needs to be a real
 * data structure to allow complex things like
 *      -n "*.html" -a \( -size < 0 -o mtime < 5 \).
 */
public class FindFilter implements FilenameFilter {
    boolean sizeSet;
    int size;
    String name;
    RE nameRE;

    public FindFilter() {
    }

    void setSizeFilter(String sizeFilter) {
        size = Integer.parseInt(sizeFilter);
        sizeSet = true;
    }

    /** Convert the given shell wildcard pattern into internal form (an RE) */
    void setNameFilter(String nameFilter) {
        name = nameFilter;
        StringBuffer sb = new StringBuffer('^');
        for (int i = 0; i < nameFilter.length(); i++) {
            char c = nameFilter.charAt(i);
            switch(c) {
                case '.':sb.append("\\."); break;
                case '*':sb.append(".*"); break;
                case '?':sb.append('.'); break;
                default:sb.append(c); break;
            }
        }
        sb.append('$');
        Debug.println("name", "RE=\"" + sb + "\".");
        try {
            nameRE = new RE(sb.toString());
        } catch (RESyntaxException ex) {
            System.err.println("For shame! " + ex);
        }
    }

    /** Do the filtering. For now, only filter on name */
    public boolean accept(File dir, String fileName) {
        File f = new File(dir, fileName);
        if (f.isDirectory()) {
            return true;// allow recursion
        }
```

```
            if (name != null) {
                return nameRE.match(fileName);
            }

            // TODO size handling.

            // Catchall
            return false;
        }
    }
```

Exercise for the reader: in the source directory, you'll find a class called `FindNumFilter`, which is meant to (someday) allow relational comparison of sizes, modification times, and the like, as most `find` services already offer. Make this work from the command line, and write a GUI front-end to this program.

11

Programming Serial and Parallel Ports

11.0. Introduction

Peripheral devices are usually external to the computer.* Printers, mice, video cameras, scanners, data/fax modems, plotters, robots, telephones, light switches, weather gauges, Palm Computing Platform devices, and many others exist "out there," beyond the confines of your desktop or server machine. We need a way to reach out to them.

The Java Communications API not only gives us that, but cleverly unifies the programming model for dealing with a range of external devices. It supports both serial (RS232/434, COM, or tty) and parallel (printer, LPT) ports. We'll cover this in more detail later, but briefly, serial ports are used for modems and occasionally printers, and parallel ports are used for printers and sometimes (in the PC world) for Zip drives and other peripherals. Before USB (Universal Serial Bus) came along, it seemed that parallel ports would dominate for such peripherals, as manufacturers were starting to make video cameras, scanners, and the like. Now, however, USB has become the main attachment mode for such devices. One can imagine that future releases of Java Communications might expand the structure to include USB support (Sun has admitted that this is a possibility) and maybe other bus-like devices.

This chapter† aims to teach you the principles of controlling these many kinds of devices in a machine-independent way using the Java Communications API, which is in package `javax.comm`.

---

* Conveniently ignoring things like "internal modem cards" on desktop machines!

† This chapter was originally going to be a book. Ironic, since my first book for O'Reilly was originally going to be a chapter. So it goes.

I'll start this chapter by showing you how to get a list of available ports and how to control simple serial devices like modems. Such details as baud rate, parity, and word size are attended to before we can write commands to the modem, read the results, and establish communications. We'll move on to parallel (printer) ports, and then look at how to transfer data synchronously (using read/write calls directly) and asynchronously (using Java listeners). Then we build a simple phone dialer that can call a friend's voice phone for you—a simple phone controller, if you will. The discussion ends with a serial-port printer/plotter driver.

The Communications API

The Communications API is centered around the abstract class `CommPort` and its two subclasses, `SerialPort` and `ParallelPort`, which describe the two main types of ports found on desktop computers. `CommPort` represents a general model of communications, and has general methods like `getInputStream()` and `getOutputStream()` that allow you to use the information from Chapter 9 to communicate with the device on that port.

However, the constructors for these classes are intentionally non-public. Rather than constructing them, you instead use the static factory method `CommPortIdentifier.getPortIdentifiers()` to get a list of ports, let the user choose a port from this list, and call this `CommPortIdentifier`'s `open()` method to receive a `CommPort` object. You cast the `CommPort` object to a non-abstract subclass representing a particular communications device. At present, the subclass must be either `SerialPort` or `ParallelPort`.

Each of these subclasses has some methods that apply only to that type. For example, the `SerialPort` class has a method to set baud rate, parity, and the like, while the `ParallelPort` class has methods for setting the "port mode" to original PC mode, bidirectional mode, etc.

Both subclasses also have methods that allow you to use the standard Java event model to receive notification of events such as data available for reading, output buffer empty, and type-specific events such as ring indicator for a serial port and out-of-paper for a parallel port—as we'll see, the parallel ports were originally for printers, and still use their terminology in a few places.

About the Code Examples in This Chapter

Java Communication is a standard extension. This means that it is not a required part of the Java API, which in turn means that your vendor probably didn't ship it. You may need to download the Java Communications API from Sun's Java web site, *http://java.sun.com*, or from your system vendor's web site, and install it. If your platform or vendor doesn't ship it, you may need to find, modify, compile, and install some C code. Try my personal web site, too. And, naturally enough, to run some of the examples you will need additional peripheral devices beyond those normally provided with a desktop computer. Batteries—and peripheral devices— are not included in the purchase of this book.

See Also

Elliotte Rusty Harold's book *Java I/O* contains a chapter that discusses the Communications API in considerable detail, as well as some background issues such as baud rate that we take for granted here. Rusty also discusses some details that I have glossed over, such as the ability to set receive timeouts and buffer sizes.

This book is about portable Java. If you want the gory low-level details of setting device registers on a 16451 UART on an ISA or PCI PC, you'll have to look elsewhere; there are several books on these topics. If you really need the hardware details for I/O ports on other platforms such as Sun Workstations and Palm Computing Platform, consult either the vendor's documentation and/or the available open source operating systems that run on that platform.

11.1. Choosing a Port

Problem

You need to know what ports are available on a given computer.

Solution

Use `CommPortIdentifier.getPortIdentifiers()` to return the list of ports.

Discussion

There are many kinds of computers out there. It's unlikely that you'd find yourself running on a desktop computer with no serial ports, but you might find that there is only one and it's already in use by another program. Or you might want a parallel port and find that the computer has only serial ports. This program shows you how to use the static `CommPortIdentifier` method `getPortIdentifiers()`. This gives you an `Enumeration` (Recipe 7.4) of the serial and parallel ports available on your system. My routine `populate()` processes this list and loads it into a pair of `JComboBoxes` (graphical choosers; see Recipe 13.1), one for serial ports and one for parallel (there is also a third, unknown, to cover future expansion of the API). The routine `makeGUI` creates the `JComboBoxes` and arranges to notify us when the user picks one from either of the lists. The name of the selected port is displayed at the bottom of the window. So that you won't have to know much about it to use it, there are public methods getSelectedName( ), which returns the name of the last port chosen by either JComboBox and getSelectedIdentifier(), which returns an object called a CommPortIdentifier corresponding to the selected port name. Figure 11-1 shows the port chooser in action.

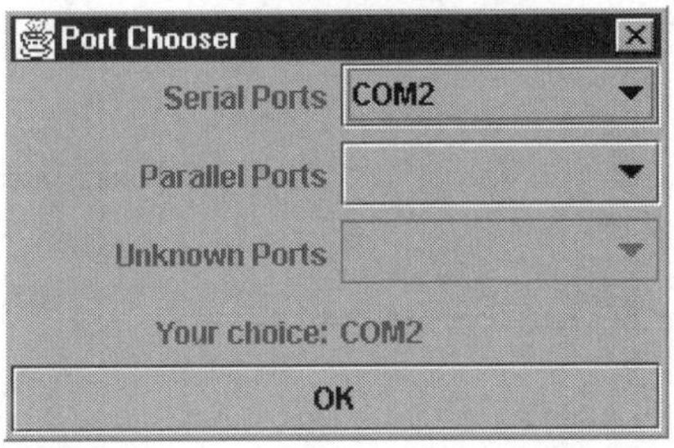

Figure 11-1. The Communications Port Chooser in action

Example 11-1 shows the code.

Example 11-1. PortChooser.java

```java
import java.io.*;
import javax.comm.*;
import java.awt.*;
import java.awt.event.*;
import javax.swing.*;
import java.util.*;

/**
 * Choose a port, any port!
 *
 * Java Communications is a "standard extension" and must be downloaded
 * and installed separately from the JDK before you can even compile this
 * program.
 *
 */
public class PortChooser extends JDialog implements ItemListener {
    /** A mapping from names to CommPortIdentifiers. */
    protected HashMap map = new HashMap();
    /** The name of the choice the user made. */
    protected String selectedPortName;
    /** The CommPortIdentifier the user chose. */
    protected CommPortIdentifier selectedPortIdentifier;
    /** The JComboBox for serial ports */
    protected JComboBox serialPortsChoice;
    /** The JComboBox for parallel ports */
    protected JComboBox parallelPortsChoice;
    /** The JComboBox for anything else */
```

Example 11-1. PortChooser.java (continued)

```java
    protected JComboBox other;
    /** The SerialPort object */
    protected SerialPort ttya;
    /** To display the chosen */
    protected JLabel choice;
    /** Padding in the GUI */
    protected final int PAD = 5;

    /** This will be called from either of the JComboBoxes when the
     * user selects any given item.
     */
    public void itemStateChanged(ItemEvent e) {
        // Get the name
        selectedPortName = (String)((JComboBox)e.getSource()).getSelectedItem();
        // Get the given CommPortIdentifier
        selectedPortIdentifier = (CommPortIdentifier)map.get(selectedPortName);
        // Display the name.
        choice.setText(selectedPortName);
    }

    /* The public "getter" to retrieve the chosen port by name. */
    public String getSelectedName() {
        return selectedPortName;
    }

    /* The public "getter" to retrieve the selection by CommPortIdentifier. */
    public CommPortIdentifier getSelectedIdentifier() {
        return selectedPortIdentifier;
    }

    /** A test program to show up this chooser. */
    public static void main(String[] ap) {
        PortChooser c = new PortChooser(null);
        c.setVisible(true);// blocking wait
        System.out.println("You chose " + c.getSelectedName() +
            " (known by " + c.getSelectedIdentifier() + ").");
        System.exit(0);
    }

    /** Construct a PortChooser --make the GUI and populate the ComboBoxes.
     */
    public PortChooser(JFrame parent) {
        super(parent, "Port Chooser", true);

        makeGUI();
        populate();
        finishGUI();
    }
```

Example 11-1. PortChooser.java (continued)

```
/** Build the GUI. You can ignore this for now if you have not
 * yet worked through the GUI chapter. Your mileage may vary.
 */
protected void makeGUI() {
    Container cp = getContentPane();

    JPanel centerPanel = new JPanel();
    cp.add(BorderLayout.CENTER, centerPanel);

    centerPanel.setLayout(new GridLayout(0,2, PAD, PAD));

    centerPanel.add(new JLabel("Serial Ports", JLabel.RIGHT));
    serialPortsChoice = new JComboBox();
    centerPanel.add(serialPortsChoice);
    serialPortsChoice.setEnabled(false);

    centerPanel.add(new JLabel("Parallel Ports", JLabel.RIGHT));
    parallelPortsChoice = new JComboBox();
    centerPanel.add(parallelPortsChoice);
    parallelPortsChoice.setEnabled(false);

    centerPanel.add(new JLabel("Unknown Ports", JLabel.RIGHT));
    other = new JComboBox();
    centerPanel.add(other);
    other.setEnabled(false);

    centerPanel.add(new JLabel("Your choice:", JLabel.RIGHT));
    centerPanel.add(choice = new JLabel());

    JButton okButton;
    cp.add(BorderLayout.SOUTH, okButton = new JButton("OK"));
    okButton.addActionListener(new ActionListener() {
        public void actionPerformed(ActionEvent e) {
            PortChooser.this.dispose();
        }
    });

}

/** Populate the ComboBoxes by asking the Java Communications API
 * what ports it has.  Since the initial information comes from
 * a Properties file, it may not exactly reflect your hardware.
 */
protected void populate() {
    // get list of ports available on this particular computer,
    // by calling static method in CommPortIdentifier.
    Enumeration pList = CommPortIdentifier.getPortIdentifiers();
```

Example 11-1. PortChooser.java (continued)

```
        // Process the list, putting serial and parallel into ComboBoxes
        while (pList.hasMoreElements()) {
            CommPortIdentifier cpi = (CommPortIdentifier)pList.nextElement();
            // System.out.println("Port " + cpi.getName());
            map.put(cpi.getName(), cpi);
            if (cpi.getPortType() == CommPortIdentifier.PORT_SERIAL) {
                serialPortsChoice.setEnabled(true);
                serialPortsChoice.addItem(cpi.getName());
            } else if (cpi.getPortType() == CommPortIdentifier.PORT_PARALLEL) {
                parallelPortsChoice.setEnabled(true);
                parallelPortsChoice.addItem(cpi.getName());
            } else {
                other.setEnabled(true);
                other.addItem(cpi.getName());
            }
        }
        serialPortsChoice.setSelectedIndex(-1);
        parallelPortsChoice.setSelectedIndex(-1);
    }

    protected void finishGUI() {
        serialPortsChoice.addItemListener(this);
        parallelPortsChoice.addItemListener(this);
        other.addItemListener(this);
        pack();
        addWindowListener(new WindowCloser(this, true));
    }
}
```

11.2. Opening a Serial Port

Problem

You want to set up a serial port and open it for input/output.

Solution

Use a CommPortIdentifier's open() method to get a SerialPort object.

Discussion

Now you've picked your serial port, but it's not ready to go yet. Baud rate. Parity. Stop bits. These things have been the bane of many a programmer's life. Having needed to work out the details of setting them on many platforms over the years, including CP/M systems, IBM PCs, and IBM System/370 mainframes, I can report that it's no fun. Finally, Java has provided a portable interface for setting all these parameters.

The steps in setting up and opening a serial port are as follows:

1. Get the name and `CommPortIdentifier` (which you can do using my `PortChooser` class).

2. Call the `CommPortIdentifier`'s `open()` method; cast the resulting `CommPort` object to a `SerialPort` object (this cast will fail if the user chose a parallel port!).

3. Set the serial communications parameters, such as baud rate, parity, stop bits, and the like, either individually or all at once using the convenience routing `setSerialPortParams()`.

4. Call the `getInputStream` and `getOutputStream` methods of the `SerialPort` object, and construct any additional `Stream` or `Writer` objects (see Chapter 9).

You are then ready to read and write on the serial port. Example 11-2 is code that implements all these steps for a serial port. Some of this code is for parallel ports, which we'll discuss in Recipe 11.3.

Example 11-2. CommPortOpen.java

```java
import java.awt.*;
import java.io.*;
import javax.comm.*;
import java.util.*;

/**
 * Open a serial port using Java Communications.
 *
 */
public class CommPortOpen {
    /** How long to wait for the open to finish up. */
    public static final int TIMEOUTSECONDS = 30;
    /** The baud rate to use. */
    public static final int BAUD = 9600;
    /** The parent Frame, for the chooser. */
    protected Frame parent;
    /** The input stream */
    protected DataInputStream is;
    /** The output stream */
    protected PrintStream os;
    /** The last line read from the serial port. */
    protected String response;
    /** A flag to control debugging output. */
    protected boolean debug = true;
```

Example 11-2. CommPortOpen.java (continued)

```java
/** The chosen Port Identifier */
CommPortIdentifier thePortID;
/** The chosen Port itself */
CommPort thePort;

public static void main(String[] argv)
    throws IOException, NoSuchPortException, PortInUseException,
        UnsupportedCommOperationException {

    new CommPortOpen(null).converse();

    System.exit(0);
}


/* Constructor */
public CommPortOpen(Frame f)
    throws IOException, NoSuchPortException, PortInUseException,
        UnsupportedCommOperationException {

    // Use the PortChooser from before. Pop up the JDialog.
    PortChooser chooser = new PortChooser(null);

    String portName = null;
    do {
        chooser.setVisible(true);

        // Dialog done. Get the port name.
        portName = chooser.getSelectedName();

        if (portName == null)
            System.out.println("No port selected. Try again.\n");
    } while (portName == null);

    // Get the CommPortIdentifier.
    thePortID = chooser.getSelectedIdentifier();

    // Now actually open the port.
    // This form of openPort takes an Application Name and a timeout.
    //
    System.out.println("Trying to open " + thePortID.getName() + "...");

    switch (thePortID.getPortType()) {
    case CommPortIdentifier.PORT_SERIAL:
        thePort = thePortID.open("DarwinSys DataComm",
            TIMEOUTSECONDS * 1000);
        SerialPort myPort = (SerialPort) thePort;
```

Example 11-2. CommPortOpen.java (continued)

```
        // set up the serial port
        myPort.setSerialPortParams(BAUD, SerialPort.DATABITS_8,
            SerialPort.STOPBITS_1, SerialPort.PARITY_NONE);
        break;

    case CommPortIdentifier.PORT_PARALLEL:
        thePort = thePortID.open("DarwinSys Printing",
            TIMEOUTSECONDS * 1000);
        ParallelPort pPort = (ParallelPort)thePort;

        // Tell API to pick "best available mode" - can fail!
        // myPort.setMode(ParallelPort.LPT_MODE_ANY);

        // Print what the mode is
        int mode = pPort.getMode();
        switch (mode) {
            case ParallelPort.LPT_MODE_ECP:
                System.out.println("Mode is: ECP");
                break;
            case ParallelPort.LPT_MODE_EPP:
                System.out.println("Mode is: EPP");
                break;
            case ParallelPort.LPT_MODE_NIBBLE:
                System.out.println("Mode is: Nibble Mode.");
                break;
            case ParallelPort.LPT_MODE_PS2:
                System.out.println("Mode is: Byte mode.");
                break;
            case ParallelPort.LPT_MODE_SPP:
                System.out.println("Mode is: Compatibility mode.");
                break;
            // ParallelPort.LPT_MODE_ANY is a "set only" mode;
            // tells the API to pick "best mode"; will report the
            // actual mode it selected.
            default:
                throw new IllegalStateException
                    ("Parallel mode " + mode + " invalid.");
        }
        break;
    default:// Neither parallel nor serial??
        throw new IllegalStateException("Unknown port type " + thePortID);
    }

    // Get the input and output streams
    // Printers can be write-only
    try {
        is = new DataInputStream(thePort.getInputStream());
```

Example 11-2. CommPortOpen.java (continued)

```
    } catch (IOException e) {
        System.err.println("Can't open input stream: write-only");
        is = null;
    }
    os = new PrintStream(thePort.getOutputStream(), true);
}


/** This method will be overridden by non-trivial subclasses
 * to hold a conversation.
 */
protected void converse() throws IOException {

    System.out.println("Ready to read and write port.");

    // Input/Output code not written -- must subclass.

    // Finally, clean up.
    if (is != null)
        is.close();
    os.close();
}
}
```

As noted in the comments, this class contains a dummy version of the **converse** method. In following sections we'll expand on the input/output processing by subclassing and overriding this method.

11.3. Opening a Parallel Port

Problem

You want to open a parallel port.

Solution

Use a CommPortIdentifier's open() method to get a ParallelPort object.

Discussion

Enough of serial ports! Parallel ports as we know 'em are an outgrowth of the "dot matrix" printer industry. Before the IBM PC, Tandy and other "pre-PC" PC makers needed a way to hook printers to their computers. Centronics, a company that made a variety of dot matrix printers, had a standard connector mechanism that caught on, changing only when IBM got into the act. Along the way, PC makers found they needed more speed, so they built faster printer ports. And peripheral makers took advantage of this by using the faster (and by now bidirectional) printer ports to hook up all manner of weird devices like scanners, SCSI and Ethernet controllers, and others via parallel ports. You can, in theory, open any of these devices and control them; the logic of controlling such devices is left as an exercise for the reader. For now we'll just open a parallel port.

Just as the `SerialPortOpen` program set the port's parameters, the `ParallelPortOpen` program sets the parallel port access type or "mode." Like baud rate and parity, this requires some knowledge of the particular desktop computer's hardware. There are several common modes, or types of printer interface and interaction. The oldest is "simple parallel port," which the API calls MODE_SPP. This is an output-only parallel port. Other common modes include EPP (extended parallel port, MODE_ECP) and ECP (extended communciation port, MODE_ECP). The API defines a few rare ones, as well as MODE_ANY, the default, and allows the API to pick the best mode. In my experience, the API doesn't always do a very good job of picking, either with MODE_ANY or with explicit settings. And indeed, there may be interactions with the BIOS (at least on a PC) and on device drivers (MS-Windows, Unix). What follows is a simple example that opens a parallel port (though it works on a serial port also), opens a file, and sends it; in other words, a very trivial printer driver. Now this is obviously *not* the way to drive printers. Most operating systems provide support for various types of printers (the MacOS and MS-Windows both do, at least; Unix tends to assume a PostScript or HP printer). This example, just to make life simple by allowing us to work with ASCII files, copies a short file of PostScript. The intent of the PostScript job is just to print the little logo in Figure 11-2.

Figure 11-2. PostScript printer output

The PostScript code used in this particular example is fairly short:

```
%!PS-Adobe

% Draw a circle of "Java Cookbook"
% simplified from Chapter 9 of the Adobe Systems "Blue Book",
% PostScript Language Tutorial and Cookbook
```

```
% center the origin
250 350 translate

/Helvetica-BoldOblique findfont
    30 scalefont
    setfont

% print circle of Java
0.4 setlinewidth% make outlines not too heavy
20 20 340 {
    gsave
    rotate 0 0 moveto
    (Java) true charpath stroke
    grestore
} for

% print "Java Cookbook" in darker outline
% fill w/ light gray to contrast w/ spiral
1.5 setlinewidth
0 0 moveto
(Java Cookbook) true charpath
gsave 1 setgray fill grestore
stroke

% now send it all to the printed page
showpage
```

It doesn't matter if you know PostScript; it's just the printer control language that
some printers accept. What matters to us is that we can open the parallel port,
and, if an appropriate printer is connected (I used an HP6MP, which supports
PostScript), the logo will print, appearing near the middle of the page.
Example 11-3 is a short program that again subclasses CommPortOpen, opens a file
that is named on the command line, and copies it to the given port. Using it looks
like this:

```
C:\javasrc\io\javacomm>java ParallelPrint javacook.ps
Mode is: Compatibility mode.
Can't open input stream: write-only

C:\javasrc\io\javacomm>
```

The message "Can't open input stream" appears because my notebook's printer
port is (according to the Java Comm API) unable to do bidirectional I/O. This is
in fact incorrect, as I have used various printer-port devices that require bidirectional I/O, such as the Logitech (formerly Connectix) QuickCam, on this same
hardware platform (but under Unix and MS-Windows, not using Java). This message is just a warning; the program works correctly despite it.

Example 11-3. ParallelPrint.com

```
import java.awt.*;
import java.io.*;
import javax.comm.*;

/**
 * Print to a serial port using Java Communications.
 *
 */
public class ParallelPrint extends CommPortOpen {

    protected static String inputFileName;

    public static void main(String[] argv)
        throws IOException, NoSuchPortException, PortInUseException,
            UnsupportedCommOperationException {

        if (argv.length != 1) {
            System.err.println("Usage: ParallelPrint filename");
            System.exit(1);
        }
        inputFileName = argv[0];

        new ParallelPrint(null).converse();

        System.exit(0);
    }

    /* Constructor */
    public ParallelPrint(Frame f)
        throws IOException, NoSuchPortException, PortInUseException,
            UnsupportedCommOperationException {

        super(f);
    }

    /**
     * Hold the (one-way) conversation.
     */
    protected void converse() throws IOException {

        // Make a reader for the input file.
        BufferedReader file = new BufferedReader(
            new FileReader(inputFileName));

        String line;
        while ((line = file.readLine()) != null)
            os.println(line);
```

Example 11-3. ParallePrint.com (continued)

```
            // Finally, clean up.
            file.close();
            os.close();
    }
}
```

11.4. *Resolving Port Conflicts*

Problem

Somebody else is using the port you want, and they won't let go!

Solution

Use a `PortOwnershipListener`.

Discussion

If you run the `CommPortOpen` program and select a port that is opened by a native program such as HyperTerminal on MS-Windows, you will get a `PortInUseException` after the timeout period is up:

```
C:\javasrc\commport>java CommPortOpen
Exception in thread "main" javax.comm.PortInUseException: Port currently owned by
Unknown Windows Application
        at javax.comm.CommPortIdentifier.open(CommPortIdentifier.java:337)
        at CommPortOpen.main(CommPortOpen.java:41)
```

If, on the other hand, you run two copies of `CommPortOpen` at the same time for the same port, you will see something like the following:

```
C:\javasrc\commport>java CommPortOpen
Exception in thread "main" javax.comm.PortInUseException: Port currently owned by
DarwinSys DataComm
        at javax.comm.CommPortIdentifier.open(CommPortIdentifier.java:337)
        at CommPortOpen.main(CommPortOpen.java:41)


C:\javasrc\commport>
```

To resolve conflicts over port ownership, you can register a `PortOwnershipListener` so that you will be told if another application wants to use the port. Then you can either close the port and the other application will get it, or ignore the request and the other program will get a `PortInUseException`, as we did here.

What is this "listener"? The Event Listener model is used in many places in Java. It may be best known for its uses in GUIs (see Recipe 13.4). The basic form is that you have to *register* an object as a *listener* with an *event source*. The event source will then call a well-known method to notify you that a particular event has occurred. In the GUI, for example, an event occurs when the user presses a button with the mouse; if you wish to monitor these events, you need to call the button object's `addActionListener()` method, passing an instance of the `ActionListener` interface (which can be your main class, an inner class, or some other class).

How does a listener work in practice? To simplify matters, we've again subclassed from our command-line program `CommPortOpen` to pop up a dialog if one copy of the program tries to open a port that another copy already has open. If you run two copies of the new program `PortOwner` at the same time, and select the same port in each, you'll see the dialog shown in Figure 11-3.

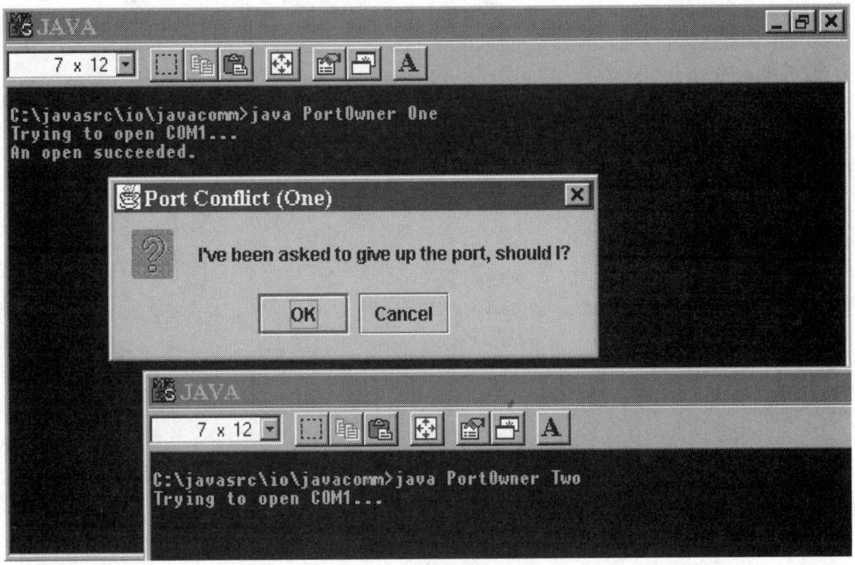

Figure 11-3. Port conflict resolution

The trick to make this happen is simply to add a `CommPortOwnershipListener` to the `CommPortIdentifier` object. You will then be called when any program gets ownership, gives up ownership, or if there is a conflict. Example 11-4 shows the program with this addition.

Example 11-4. PortOwner.java

```java
import javax.comm.*;
import java.io.*;
import javax.swing.*;

/** Demonstrate the port conflict resolution mechanism.
 * Run two copies of this program and choose the same port in each.
 */
public class PortOwner extends CommPortOpen {
    /** A name for showing which of several instances of this program */
    String myName;

    public PortOwner(String name)
        throws IOException, NoSuchPortException, PortInUseException,
            UnsupportedCommOperationException {

        super(null);
        myName = name;
        thePortID.addPortOwnershipListener(new MyResolver());
    }

    public void converse() {
        // lah de dah...
        // To simulate a long conversation on the port...

        try {
            Thread.sleep(1000 * 1000);
        } catch (InterruptedException cantHappen) {
            //
        }
    }

    /** An inner class that handles the ports conflict resolution. */
    class MyResolver implements CommPortOwnershipListener {
        protected boolean owned = false;
        public void ownershipChange(int whaHoppen) {
            switch (whaHoppen) {
            case PORT_OWNED:
                System.out.println("An open succeeded.");
                owned = true;
                break;
            case PORT_UNOWNED:
                System.out.println("A close succeeded.");
                owned = false;
                break;
            case PORT_OWNERSHIP_REQUESTED:
                if (owned) {
                    if (JOptionPane.showConfirmDialog(null,
                        "I've been asked to give up the port, should I?",
```

Example 11-4. PortOwner.java (continued)

```
                            "Port Conflict (" + myName + ")",
                            JOptionPane.OK_CANCEL_OPTION) == 0)
                        thePort.close();
                } else {
                    System.out.println("Somebody else has the port");
                }
            }
        }
    }

    public static void main(String[] argv)
        throws IOException, NoSuchPortException, PortInUseException,
            UnsupportedCommOperationException {

        if (argv.length != 1) {
            System.err.println("Usage: PortOwner aname");
            System.exit(1);
        }

        new PortOwner(argv[0]).converse();

        System.exit(0);
    }
}
```

Note the single argument to ownershipChange(). Do not assume that only your listener will be told when an event occurs; it will be called whether you are the affected program or simply a bystander. To see if you are the program being requested to give up ownership, you have to check to see if you already have the port that is being requested (for example, by opening it successfully!).

11.5. Reading and Writing: Lock Step

Problem

You want to read and write on a port, and your communications needs are simple.

Solution

Just use read and write calls.

Discussion

Suppose you need to send a command to a device and get a response back, and then send another, and get another. This has been called a "lock-step" protocol, since both ends of the communication are locked into step with one another, like soldiers on parade. There is no requirement that both ends be able to write at the same time (see Recipes 10.7 and 10.8 for this), since you know what the response to your command should be and don't proceed until you have received that response. A well-known example is using a standard Hayes-command-set modem to just dial a phone number. In its simplest form, you send the command string ATZ and expect the response OK, then send ATD with the number, and expect CONNECT. To implement this, we first subclass from `CommPortOpen` to add two functions, `send` and `expect`, which perform reasonably obvious functions for dealing with such devices. See Example 11-5.

Example 11-5. CommPortModem.java

```java
import java.awt.*;
import java.io.*;
import javax.comm.*;
import java.util.*;

/**
 * Subclasses CommPortOpen and adds send/expect handling for dealing
 * with Hayes-type modems.
 *
 */
public class CommPortModem extends CommPortOpen {
    /** The last line read from the serial port. */
    protected String response;
    /** A flag to control debugging output. */
    protected boolean debug = true;

    public CommPortModem(Frame f)
        throws IOException, NoSuchPortException, PortInUseException,
            UnsupportedCommOperationException {
        super(f);
    }

    /** Send a line to a PC-style modem. Send \r\n, regardless of
     * what platform we're on, instead of using println().
     */
    protected void send(String s) throws IOException {
        if (debug) {
            System.out.print(">>> ");
            System.out.print(s);
            System.out.println();
        }
        os.print(s);
        os.print("\r\n");

        // Expect the modem to echo the command.
```

Example 11-5. CommPortModem.java (continued)

```
            if (!expect(s)) {
                System.err.println("WARNING: Modem did not echo command.");
            }

            // The modem sends an extra blank line by way of a prompt.
            // Here we read and discard it.
            String junk = os.readLine();
            if (junk.length() != 0) {
                System.err.print("Warning unexpected response: ");
                System.err.println(junk);
            }
        }

    /** Read a line, saving it in "response".
     * @return true if the expected String is contained in the response, false if not.
     */
    protected boolean expect(String exp) throws IOException {
        response = is.readLine();
        if (debug) {
            System.out.print("<<< ");
            System.out.print(response);
            System.out.println();
        }
        return response.indexOf(exp) >= 0;
    }
}
```

Finally, Example 11-6 extends our `CommPortModem` program to initialize the modem and dial a telephone number.

Example 11-6. CommPortDial.java

```
import java.io.*;
import javax.comm.*;
import java.util.*;

/**
 * Dial a phone using the Java Communications Package.
 *
 */
public class CommPortDial extends CommPortModem {

    protected static String number = "000-0000";

    public static void main(String[] ap)
        throws IOException, NoSuchPortException,PortInUseException,
            UnsupportedCommOperationException {
        if (ap.length == 1)
```

Example 11-6. CommPortDial.java (continued)

```
        number = ap[0];
    new CommPortDial().converse();
    System.exit(0);
}


public CommPortDial()
    throws IOException, NoSuchPortException, PortInUseException,
        UnsupportedCommOperationException {
    super(null);
}


protected void converse() throws IOException {

    String resp;// the modem response.

    // Send the reset command
    send("ATZ");

    expect("OK");

    send("ATDT" + number);

    expect("OK");

    try {
        Thread.sleep(5000);
    } catch (InterruptedException e) {
        // nothing to do
    }
    is.close();
    os.close();
    }
}
```

11.6. Reading and Writing: Event-Driven

Problem

After the connection is made, you don't know what order to read or write in.

Solution

Use Java Communication Events to notify you when data becomes available.

Discussion

While lock-step mode is acceptable for dialing a modem, it breaks down when you have two independent agents communicating over a port. Either end may be a person, as in a remote login session, or a program, either a server or a client program. A client program, in turn, may be driven by a person (as is a web browser) or may be self-driven (such as an FTP client transferring many files at one request). You cannot predict, then, who will need to read and who will need to write. Consider the simplest case: the programs at both end try to read at the same time! Using the lock-step model, each end will wait forever for the other end to write something. This error condition is known as a *deadlock*, since both ends are locked up, dead, until a person intervenes, or the communication line drops, or the world ends, or the universe ends, or somebody making tea blows a fuse and causes one of the machines to halt.

There are two general approaches to this problem: event-driven activity, wherein the Communications API notifies you when the port is ready to be read or written, and threads-based activity, wherein each "direction" (from the user to the remote, and from the remote to the user) has its own little flow of control, causing only the reads in that direction to wait. We'll discuss each of these.

First, Example 11-7 reads from a serial port using the event-driven approach.

Example 11-7. SerialReadByEvents.java

```java
import java.awt.*;
import java.io.*;
import javax.comm.*;
import java.util.*;

/**
 * Read from a Serial port, notifying when data arrives.
 * Simulation of part of an event-logging service.
 */
public class SerialReadByEvents extends CommPortOpen
    implements SerialPortEventListener {

    public static void main(String[] argv)
        throws IOException, NoSuchPortException, PortInUseException,
            UnsupportedCommOperationException {

        new SerialReadByEvents(null).converse();
    }

    /* Constructor */
    public SerialReadByEvents(Frame f)
        throws IOException, NoSuchPortException, PortInUseException,
            UnsupportedCommOperationException {
```

Example 11-7. SerialReadByEvents.java (continued)

```
        super(f);
    }


    protected BufferedReader ifile;

    /**
     * Hold the conversation.
     */
    protected void converse() throws IOException {

        if (!(thePort instanceof SerialPort)) {
            System.err.println("But I wanted a SERIAL port!");
            System.exit(1);
        }
        // Tell the Comm API that we want serial events.
        ((SerialPort)thePort).notifyOnDataAvailable(true);
        try {
            ((SerialPort)thePort).addEventListener(this);
        } catch (TooManyListenersException ev) {
            // "CantHappen" error
            System.err.println("Too many listeners(!) " + ev);
            System.exit(0);
        }

        // Make a reader for the input file.
        ifile = new BufferedReader(new InputStreamReader(is));

        //
    }
    public void serialEvent(SerialPortEvent ev) {
        String line;
        try {
            line = ifile.readLine();
            if (line == null) {
                System.out.println("EOF on serial port.");
                System.exit(0);
            }
            os.println(line);
        } catch (IOException ex) {
            System.err.println("IO Error " + ex);
        }
    }
}
```

As you can see, the `serialEvent()` method does the `readLine()` calls. "But wait!" I hear you say. "This program is not a very meaningful example. It could just as easily be implemented using the lock-step method of Recipe 11.5." True enough, gentle reader. Have patience with your humble and obedient servant. Here is a program that will read from each and any of the serial ports, whenever data arrives. The program is representative of a class of programs called "data loggers," which receive data from a number (possibly a large number) of remote locations, and log them centrally. One example is a burglar alarm monitoring station, which needs to log activities such as the alarm being turned off at the close of the day, entry by the cleaners later, what time they left, and so on. And then, of course, it needs to notify the operator of the monitoring station when an unexpected event occurs. This last step is left as an exercise for the reader.

Example 11-8 makes use of the `EventListener` model and uses a unique instance of the inner class `Logger` for each serial port it's able to open.

Example 11-8. SerialLogger.java

```java
import java.io.*;
import javax.comm.*;
import java.util.*;

/**
 * Read from multiple Serial ports, notifying when data arrives on any.
 */
public class SerialLogger {

    public static void main(String[] argv)
        throws IOException, NoSuchPortException, PortInUseException,
            UnsupportedCommOperationException {

        new SerialLogger();
    }

    /* Constructor */
    public SerialLogger()
        throws IOException, NoSuchPortException, PortInUseException,
            UnsupportedCommOperationException {

        // get list of ports available on this particular computer,
        // by calling static method in CommPortIdentifier.
        Enumeration pList = CommPortIdentifier.getPortIdentifiers();

        // Process the list, putting serial and parallel into ComboBoxes
        while (pList.hasMoreElements()) {
            CommPortIdentifier cpi = (CommPortIdentifier)pList.nextElement();
            String name = cpi.getName();
            System.out.print("Port " + name + " ");
            if (cpi.getPortType() == CommPortIdentifier.PORT_SERIAL) {
                System.out.println("is a Serial Port: " + cpi);
```

Example 11-8. SerialLogger.java (continued)

```java
            SerialPort thePort;
            try {
                thePort = (SerialPort)cpi.open("Logger", 1000);
            } catch (PortInUseException ev) {
                System.err.println("Port in use: " + name);
                continue;
            }

            // Tell the Comm API that we want serial events.
            thePort.notifyOnDataAvailable(true);
            try {
                thePort.addEventListener(new Logger(cpi.getName(), thePort));
            } catch (TooManyListenersException ev) {
                // "CantHappen" error
                System.err.println("Too many listeners(!) " + ev);
                System.exit(0);
            }
        }
    }
}

/** Handle one port. */
public class Logger implements SerialPortEventListener {
    String portName;
    SerialPort thePort;
    BufferedReader ifile;
    public Logger(String name, SerialPort port) throws IOException {
        portName = name;
        thePort = port;
        // Make a reader for the input file.
        ifile = new BufferedReader(
            new InputStreamReader(thePort.getInputStream()));
    }
    public void serialEvent(SerialPortEvent ev) {
        String line;
        try {
            line = ifile.readLine();
            if (line == null) {
                System.out.println("EOF on serial port.");
                System.exit(0);
            }
            System.out.println(portName + ": " + line);
        } catch (IOException ex) {
            System.err.println("IO Error " + ex);
        }
    }
}
```

11.7. Reading and Writing: Threads

Problem

After the connection is made, you don't know what order to read or write in.

Solution

Use a *thread* to handle each direction.

Discussion

When you have two things that must happen at the same time or unpredictably, the normal Java paradigm is to use a thread for each. We will discuss threads in detail in Chapter 24, but for now, just think of a thread as a small, semi-independent flow of control within a program, just as a program is a small, self-contained flow of control within an operating system. The Thread API requires you to construct a method whose signature is `public void run()` to do the body of work for the thread, and call the `start()` method of the thread to "ignite" it and start it running independently. This example creates a `Thread` subclass called `DataThread`, which reads from one file and writes to another. `DataThread` works a byte at a time so that it will work correctly with interactive prompts, which don't end at a line ending. My now-familiar `converse()` method creates two of these `DataThreads`, one to handle data "traffic" from the keyboard to the remote, and one to handle bytes arriving from the remote and copy them to the standard output. For each of these the `start()` method is called. Example 11-9 shows the entire program.

Example 11-9. CommPortThreaded.java

```
import java.io.*;
import javax.comm.*;
import java.util.*;

/**
 * This program tries to do I/O in each direction using a separate Thread.
 */
public class CommPortThreaded extends CommPortOpen {

    public static void main(String[] ap)
        throws IOException, NoSuchPortException,PortInUseException,
            UnsupportedCommOperationException {
        CommPortThreaded cp;
        try {
            cp = new CommPortThreaded();
```

Example 11-9. CommPortThreaded.java (continued)

```
                    cp.converse();
            } catch(Exception e) {
                System.err.println("You lose!");
                System.err.println(e);
            }
        }
    }


    public CommPortThreaded()
        throws IOException, NoSuchPortException, PortInUseException,
            UnsupportedCommOperationException {
        super(null);
    }

    /** This version of converse() just starts a Thread in each direction.
     */
    protected void converse() throws IOException {

        String resp;// the modem response.

        new DataThread(is, System.out).start();
        new DataThread(new DataInputStream(System.in), os).start();


    }

    /** This inner class handles one side of a conversation. */
    class DataThread extends Thread {
        DataInputStream inStream;
        PrintStream pStream;

        /** Construct this object */
        DataThread(DataInputStream is, PrintStream os) {
            inStream = is;
            pStream = os;
        }


        /** A Thread's run method does the work. */
        public void run() {
            byte ch = 0;
            try {
                while ((ch = (byte)inStream.read()) != -1)
                    pStream.print((char)ch);
            } catch (IOException e) {
                System.err.println("Input or output error: " + e);
                return;
            }
        }

    }
}
```

11.8. Program: Penman Plotter

This program in Example 11-10 is an outgrowth of the `Plotter` class from Recipe 8.11. It connects to a *Penman* plotter. These serial-port plotters were made in the United Kingdom in the 1980s, so it is unlikely that you will meet one. However, there are several companies that still make pen plotters. See Figure 11-4 for a photograph of the plotter in action.

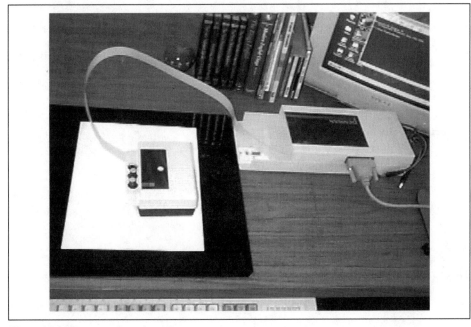

Figure 11-4. Penman plotter in action

Example 11-10. Penman.java

```java
import java.io.*;
import javax.comm.*;
import java.util.*;

/**
 * A Plotter subclass for drawing on a Penman plotter.
 * These were made in the UK and sold into North American markets.
 * It is a little "turtle" style robot plotter that communicates
 * over a serial port. For this, we use the "Java Communications" API.
 * Java Communications is a "standard extension" and must be downloaded
 * and installed separately from the JDK before you can even compile this
 * program.
 *
 */
```

Example 11-10. Penman.java (continued)

```java
public class Penman extends Plotter {
    private final String OK_PROMPT = "\r\n!";
    private final int MAX_REPLY_BYTES = 50;// paranoid upper bound
    private byte b, reply[] = new byte[22];
    private SerialPort tty;
    private DataInputStream is;
    private DataOutputStream os;

    /** Construct a Penman plotter object */
    public Penman() throws NoSuchPortException,PortInUseException,
            IOException,UnsupportedCommOperationException {
        super();
        init_comm("COM2");// setup serial commx
        init_plotter();// set plotter to good state
    }

    private void init_plotter() {
        send("I"); expect('!');// eat VERSION etc., up to !
        send("I"); expect('!');// wait for it!
        send("H");// find home position
        expect('!');// wait for it!
        send("A");// Set to use absolute coordinates
        expect('!');
        curx = cury = 0;
        penUp();
    }

    //
    // PUBLIC DRAWING ROUTINES
    //

    public void setFont(String fName, int fSize) {
        // Font name is ignored for now...

        // Penman's size is in mm, fsize in points (inch/72).
        int size = (int)(fSize*25.4f/72);
        send("S"+size + ","); expect(OK_PROMPT);
        System.err.println("Font set request: " + fName + "/" + fSize);
    }

    public void drawString(String mesg) {
        send("L" + mesg + "\r"); expect(OK_PROMPT);
    }

    /** Move to a relative location */
    public void rmoveTo(int incrx, int incry){
        moveTo(curx + incrx, cury + incry);
    }
```

Example 11-10. Penman.java (continued)

```java
/** move to absolute location */
public void moveTo(int absx, int absy) {
    System.err.println("moveTo ["+absx+","+absy+"]");
    curx = absx;
    cury = absy;
    send("M" + curx + "," + cury + ","); expect(OK_PROMPT);
}

private void setPenState(boolean up) {
    penIsUp = up;
    System.err.println("Pen Up is ["+penIsUp+"]");
}

public void penUp() {
    setPenState(true);
    send("U"); expect(OK_PROMPT);
}
public void penDown() {
    setPenState(false);
    send("D"); expect(OK_PROMPT);
}
public void penColor(int c) {
    penColor = (c%3)+1;// only has 3 pens, 4->1
    System.err.println("PenColor is ["+penColor+"]");
    send("P" + c + ","); expect(OK_PROMPT);
}

//
// PRIVATE COMMUNICATION ROUTINES
//

private void init_comm(String portName) throws
        NoSuchPortException, PortInUseException,
        IOException, UnsupportedCommOperationException {

    // get list of ports available on this particular computer.
    // Enumeration pList = CommPortIdentifier.getPortIdentifiers();

    // Print the list. A GUI program would put these in a chooser!
    // while (pList.hasMoreElements()) {
    //     CommPortIdentifier cpi = (CommPortIdentifier)pList.nextElement();
    //     System.err.println("Port " + cpi.getName());
    // }

    // Open a port.
    CommPortIdentifier port =
        CommPortIdentifier.getPortIdentifier(portName);
```

Example 11-10. Penman.java (continued)

```java
        // This form of openPort takes an Application Name and a timeout.
        tty = (SerialPort) port.openPort("Penman Driver", 1000);

        // set up the serial port
        tty.setSerialPortParams(9600, SerialPort.DATABITS_8,
            SerialPort.STOPBITS_1, SerialPort.PARITY_NONE);
        tty.setFlowcontrolMode(SerialPort.FLOWCTRL_RTSCTS_OUT|
            SerialPort.FLOWCTRL_RTSCTS_OUT);

        // Get the input and output streams
        is = new DataInputStream(tty.getInputStream());
        os = new DataOutputStream(tty.getOutputStream());
    }

    /** Send a command to the plotter. Although the argument is a String,
     * we send each char as a *byte*, so avoid 16-bit characters!
     * Not that it matters: the Penman only knows about 8-bit chars.
     */
    privatevoid send(String s) {
        System.err.println("sending " + s + "...");
        try {
            for (int i=0; i<s.length(); i++)
                os.writeByte(s.charAt(i));
        } catch(IOException e) {
            e.printStackTrace();
        }
    }

    /** Expect a given CHAR for a result */
    privatevoid expect(char s) {
        byte b;
        try {
            for (int i=0; i<MAX_REPLY_BYTES; i++){
                if ((b = is.readByte()) == s) {
                    return;
                }
                System.err.print((char)b);
            }
        } catch (IOException e) {
            System.err.println("Penman:expect(char "+s+"): Read failed");
            System.exit(1);
        }
        System.err.println("ARGHH!");
    }

    /** Expect a given String for a result */
    privatevoid expect(String s) {
        byte ans[] = new byte[s.length()];
```

Example 11-10. Penman.java (continued)

```
        System.err.println("expect " + s + " ...");
        try {
            is.read(ans);
        } catch (IOException e) {
            System.err.println("Penman:expect(String "+s+"): Read failed");
            System.exit(1);
        };
        for (int i=0; i<s.length() && i<ans.length; i++)
            if (ans[i] != s.charAt(i)) {
                System.err.println("MISMATCH");
                break;
            }
        System.err.println("GOT: " + new String(ans));


    }
}
```

See Also

In the online source there is a program called JModem, which implements remote connections (like *tip* or *cu* on Unix, or HyperTerminal on MS-Windows). It is usable, but too long to include in this book.

There are other specialized APIs for dealing with particular devices. For communicating with Palm Computing Platform devices, you can either use the Palm SDK for Java from Palm Computing, or the third-party API jSyncManager by Brad Barclay, which can be obtained from *http://web.idirect.com/~warp/*.

12

Graphics and Sound

12.0. Introduction

The Graphics class and the Component method paint() have survived virtually unchanged since the early days of Java. Together they provide a basic but quite functional graphics capability. The first printing API was put forward in 1.1, and it was promptly replaced in Java 2 (things change quickly in the online world). Both printing APIs, fortunately, are based on use of Graphics objects, so your drawing code does not have to change: only the details of getting the right kind of Graphics object change in moving from 1.1 to Java 2. The 2D (two-dimensional graphics) package is also based on Graphics: Graphics2D is a subclass of Graphics. To put the 2D graphics in perspective, think about the tremendous boost that the Adobe PostScript language gave to desktop publishing and printing. PostScript is both a scripting language and a *marking engine*: it has the ability to make a terrific variety of marks on paper. Since Java is already a comprehensive programming language, the 2D API needed only to add the marking engine. This it did very well, using several ideas imported from PostScript via Adobe's participation in the early design.

Also present from the beginning was the AudioClip class, which represents a playable sound file. In Java 2 this was extended to support additional formats (including MIDI) and to be usable from within an application as well. Meanwhile, the Java Media Framework—standard extension javax.media—provides for playing (and eventually recording) of audio, video, and possibly other media with much greater control over the presentation. You'll see examples in this chapter.

But first let's look at the Graphics class. Many of the code examples in this chapter can be used either in applications (which we'll see in Recipe 12.2) or in applets (discussed more in Chapter 17).

12.1. Painting with a Graphics Object

Problem

You want to draw something on the screen.

Solution

In your `paint()` method, use the provided `Graphics` object's drawing methods:

```
// graphics/PaintDemo.java
import java.awt.*;

public class PaintDemo extends Component {
    int rectX = 20, rectY = 30;
    int rectWidth = 50, rectHeight = 50;

    public void paint(Graphics g) {
        g.setColor(Color.red);
        g.fillRect(rectX, rectY, rectWidth, rectHeight);
    }
    public Dimension getPreferredSize() {
        return new Dimension(100, 100);
    }
}
```

Discussion

The `Graphics` class has a large set of drawing primitives. For each of Rect(angle), Arc, Ellipse, and Polygon, there is a draw method (draws just the outline) and a fill method (fills inside the outline). You don't need both, unless you want the outline and the interior (fill) of a shape to be different colors. The method `drawString()` and related methods let you print text on the screen (see Recipe 12.3). There are also `drawLine()`, which draws straight line segments, `setColor/getColor`, `setFont/getFont`, and many other methods. Too many to list here, in fact; see Sun's online documentation for `java.awt.Graphics`.

When to draw?

A common beginner's mistake used to be to call `getGraphics()` and call the `Graphics` object's drawing methods from within a main program or the constructor of a `Component` subclass. Fortunately we now have any number of books to tell us that the correct way to draw anything is with your component's paint method. Why? Because you can't draw in a window until it's actually been created and (on most window systems) mapped to the screen, and that takes much more time than your main program or constructor has. The drawing code needs to wait patiently until the window system notifies the Java runtime that it's time to paint the window.

Where do you put your drawing code? This is one situation where you need to think about AWT versus Swing. AWT, the basic windowing system (and the only one in JDK 1.1) uses a method called paint(). This method is still available in Swing, but due to interaction with borders and the like, it is recommended that you override paintComponent() instead. Both are called with a single argument of type Graphics. Your paintComponent() should start by calling super.paintComponent() with the same argument to ensure that components are painted in proper back-to-front order, while paint() should not call its parent. Some examples in this chapter use paint() and others use paintComponent(); the latter also usually extend JPanel. This allows better interaction with Swing, and also allows you to place these as the main component in a JFrame by calling setContentPane(), which eliminates an extra layer of container. (JFrame's ContentPane is discussed in Recipe 13.1.)

12.2. Testing Graphical Components

Problem

You don't want to have to write a little main program with a frame each time you write a subclass of Component.

Solution

Use my CompTest class, which has a main method that builds a frame and installs your component into it.

Discussion

CompTest is a small main program that takes a class name from the command line, instantiates it (see Recipe 25.3), and puts it in a JFrame, alone with an Exit button and its action handler. It also worries a bit over making sure the window comes out the right size. Many of these issues relate to the GUI rather than graphics, and are deferred to Chapter 13.

The class to be tested must be a subclass of Component, or an error message will be printed. This is very convenient for running small component classes, and I show a lot of these in this chapter and the next. Using it is simplicity itself; for example, to instantiate the DrawStringDemo2 class from Recipe 12.3, you just say:

```
java CompTest DrawStringDemo2
```

This is shown on the left side of Figure 12-1. It's interesting to try running it on some of the predefined classes. A JTree (Java's tree view widget, used in Recipe 19.9) no-argument constructor creates a JTree that comes up with a demonstration set of data, as in Figure 12-1, right.

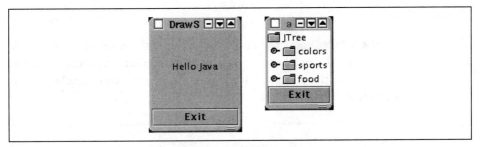

Figure 12-1. CompTest showing DrawStringDemo2 (left) and javax.swing.JTree (right)

Since little of this relates to the material in this chapter, I don't show the source for `CompTest`; however, it's included in the online code examples for the book.

12.3. Drawing Text

Problem

You need to draw text in a component.

Solution

Simply call the `drawString()` method in the `Graphics` class:

```
// graphics/DrawStringDemo.java
import java.awt.*;

public class DrawStringDemo extends Component {
    int textX = 10, textY = 20;
    public void paint(Graphics g) {
        g.drawString("Hello Java", textX, textY);
    }
    public Dimension getPreferredSize() {
        return new Dimension(100, 100);
    }
}
```

12.4. Drawing Centered Text in a Component

Problem

You want to draw text neatly centered in a component.

Solution

Measure the width and height of the string in the given font, and subtract it from the width and height of the component. Divide by two, and use this as your drawing location.

Discussion

The program `DrawStringDemo2` measures the width and height of a string (see Figure 12-2 for some attributes of the text). The program then subtracts the size of the text from the size of the component, divides this by two, and thereby centers the text in the given component.

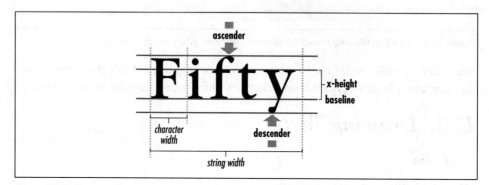

Figure 12-2. Font metrics

```
// file graphics/DrawStringDemo2.java
import java.awt.*;

public class DrawStringDemo2 extends Component {
    String message = "Hello Java";

    /** Paint is called (by AWT) when it's time to draw the text. */
    public void paint(Graphics g) {
        // Get the current Font, and ask it for its FontMetrics.
        FontMetrics fm = getFontMetrics(getFont());

        // Use the FontMetrics to get the width of the String.
        // Subtract this from width, divide by 2, that's our starting point.
        int textX = (getSize().width - fm.stringWidth(message))/2;
        if (textX<0)// If string too long, start at 0
            textX = 0;

        // Same as above but for the height
        int textY = (getSize().height - fm.getLeading())/2;
        if (textY<0)
            textY = 0;

        // Now draw the text at the computed spot.
        g.drawString(message, textX, textY);
    }

    public Dimension getPreferredSize() {
```

```
          return new Dimension(100, 100);
      }
  }
```

This is so common that you'd expect Java to have encapsulated the whole thing as a service, and in fact, Java does do this. What we have here is what most GUI component architectures call a *label*. As we'll see in Chapter 13, Java provides a `Label` component that allows for centered (or left- or right-aligned) text and supports the setting of fonts and colors; and `JLabel`, which provides image icons in addition to or instead of text.

12.5. *Drawing a Drop Shadow*

Problem

You want to draw text or graphical objects with a "drop shadow" effect, as in Figure 12-3.

Figure 12-3. Drop shadow text

Solution

Draw the component twice, with the darker shadow behind and the "real" color, slightly offset, in front.

Discussion

Program `DropShadow` does just this. It also uses a `Font` object from `java.awt` to exercise some control over the typeface.

The program in Example 12-1 is unabashedly an Applet; to run it, you should invoke it as `appletviewer DropShadow.htm`* (the details of such HTML files are in Recipe 17.1).

---

* In all my applet examples I use a filename ending in *htm* instead of the more traditional *html*, because the Javadoc program (see Recipe 23.2) will overwrite the *html* file without notice. `AppletViewer` doesn't care either way.

Example 12-1. DropShadow.java

```java
import java.applet.*;
import java.awt.*;

/**
 * DropShadow -- show overlapped painting.
 */
public class DropShadow extends Applet {
    /** The label that is to appear in the window */
    protected String theLabel = null;
    /** The width and height */
    protected int width, height;
    /** The name of the font */
    protected String fontName;
    /** The font */
    protected Font theFont;
    /** The size of the font */
    protected int fontSize = 18;
    /** The offset for the drop shadow */
    protected int theOffset = 3;
    /** True if we got all required parameters */
    protected boolean inittedOK = false;

    /** Called from the browser to set up. We want to throw various
     * kinds of exceptions but the API predefines that we don't, so we
     * limit ourselves to the ubiquitous IllegalArgumentException.
     */
    public void init() {
        // System.out.println("In DropShadow init()");

        theLabel = getParameter("label");
        if (theLabel == null)
                throw new IllegalArgumentException("LABEL is REQUIRED");
        // Now handle font stuff.
        fontName = getParameter("fontname");
        if (fontName == null)
                throw new IllegalArgumentException("FONTNAME is REQUIRED");
        String s;
        if ((s = getParameter("fontsize")) != null)
            fontSize = Integer.parseInt(s);
        if (fontName != null || fontSize != 0) {
            theFont = new Font(fontName, Font.BOLD + Font.ITALIC, fontSize);
            System.out.println("Name " + fontName + ", font " + theFont);
        }
        if ((s = getParameter("offset")) != null)
            theOffset = Integer.parseInt(s);
        setBackground(Color.green);
        inittedOK = true;
    }
```

Example 12-1. DropShadow.java (continued)

```
/** Paint method showing drop shadow effect */
public void paint(Graphics g) {
    if (!inittedOK)
        return;
    g.setFont(theFont);
    g.setColor(Color.black);
    g.drawString(theLabel, theOffset+30, theOffset+50);
    g.setColor(Color.white);
    g.drawString(theLabel, 30, 50);
}


/** Give Parameter info to the AppletViewer, just for those
 * writing HTML without hardcopy documentation :-)
 */
public String[][] getParameterInfo() {
    String info[][] = {
        { "label","string","Text to display" },
        { "fontname","name","Font to display it in" },
        { "fontsize","10-30?","Size to display it at" },
    };
    return info;
}
}
```

Standard AWT uses a very simple paint model for drawing. I guess that's why the method you have to write is called `paint()`. Let's go back to the paper age for a moment. If you paint something on a piece of paper and then paint over it with a different color, what happens? If you're old enough to remember paper, you'll know that the second color covers up the first color. Well, AWT works in pretty much the same way. No fair asking about water-based paints that run together; Java's painting is more like fast-drying oil paints. The fact that AWT retains all the bits (pixels, or picture elements) that you don't draw, plus the fact that methods like `drawString()` have extremely good aim, make it very easy to create a drop shadow and to combine graphics drawings in interesting ways.

Remember to draw from the back to the front, though. To see why, try interchanging the two calls to `drawString()` in the previous code.

A word of warning: don't mix drawing with added GUI components (see Chapter 13). For example, say you had a paint method in an applet or other container and had `add()`ed a button to it. This works on some implementations of Java, but not on others: only the painting or the button will appear, not both. It's not portable, so don't do it—you've been warned! Instead, you should probably use multiple components; see the `JFrame`'s `getContentPane()` and `getGlassPane()`, discussed in Chapter 8 of *Java Swing*, for details.

An alternative method of obtaining a drop shadow effect is covered Recipe 12.9.

12.6. Drawing an Image

Problem

You want to display an image, a preformatted bitmap, or raster file.

Solution

Use the `Graphics drawImage()` method in your paint routine. Image objects represent bitmaps. They are normally loaded from a file via `getImage()`, but can also be synthesized using `createImage()`. You can't construct them yourself, however: the `Image` class is abstract. Once you have an image, displaying it is trivial:

```
// File graphics/DrawImageDemo.java
public void paint(Graphics g) {
    g.drawImage(0, 0, myImage, this);
}
```

Discussion

You can get an image by using a routine named, naturally, `getImage()`. If your code will be used only in an applet, you can use the `Applet` method `getImage()`, but if you want it to run in an application as well, you need to use the Toolkit version. This form takes either a filename or a URL. The filename, of course, when it turns up in an applet, will fail with a security exception unless the user installs a policy file. Program `GetImage` shows the code for doing this both ways:

```
/*
 * For Applet, invoke as:
<APPLET CODE="GetImage" WIDTH="100" HEIGHT="100">
</APPLET>
 * For Application, just run it (has own main).
 */

import java.awt.*;
import java.net.*;// for URL class

/** This program, which can be an Applet or an Application,
 * shows a form of Toolkit.getImage() which works the same
 * in either Applet or Application!
 */
public class GetImage extends java.applet.Applet {

    Image image;

    public void init() {
        loadImage();
    }
```

```
      public void loadImage() {
          // Applet-only version:
          // Image = getImage(getCodeBase(), "Duke.gif");

          // Portable version: getClass().getResource() works in either
          // applet or application, 1.1 or 1.3, returns URL for file name.
          URL url = getClass().getResource("Duke.gif");
          image = getToolkit().getImage(url);
          // Shorter portable version: same but avoids temporary variables
          // image = getToolkit().getImage(getClass().getResource("Duke.gif"));
      }

      public void paint(Graphics g) {
          g.drawImage(image, 20, 20, this);
      }

      public static void main(String args[]) {
          Frame f = new Frame("GetImage");
          f.addWindowListener(new WindowCloser(f, true));
          GetImage myApplet = new GetImage();
          f.add(myApplet);
          myApplet.init();
          f.setSize(100, 100);
          f.setVisible(true);
          myApplet.start();
      }
  }
```

You may sometimes want to display an image more than once in the same panel. Example 12-2 is a program that paints its background with the same image over and over. We use the image's getWidth() and getHeight() methods to find the image's size, and the more regular getSize() method on the component itself. As usual, we don't hardcode the window size in the paint() method, since the user has the option of resizing with the mouse.

Example 12-2. TiledImageComponent.java

```
import com.darwinsys.util.WindowCloser;

import java.awt.*;
import java.awt.event.*;
import java.net.*;

/**
 * Demo of Tiled Image
 */
public class TiledImageComponent extends Container {
    TextField nameTF, passTF, domainTF;
    Image im;
```

Example 12-2. TiledImageComponent.java (continued)

```java
    String IMAGE_NAME = "background.gif";

    /** Set things up nicely. */
    public TiledImageComponent() {
        Label l;

        setLayout(new FlowLayout());
        add(l = new Label("Name:", Label.CENTER));
        add(nameTF=new TextField(10));

        add(l = new Label("Password:", Label.CENTER));
        add(passTF=new TextField(10));
        passTF.setEchoChar('*');

        add(l = new Label("Domain:", Label.CENTER));
        add(domainTF=new TextField(10));

        im = getToolkit().getImage(IMAGE_NAME);
    }

    /** paint() - just tile the background.  */
    public void paint(Graphics g) {
        // System.out.println("In paint()");
        if (im == null)
            return;
        int iw = im.getWidth(this), ih=im.getHeight(this);
        if (iw < 0 || ih < 0)// image not ready
            return;                // live to try again later.
        int w = getSize().width, h = getSize().height;
        // System.out.println(iw + "," + ih + "; " + w + ", " + h);
        for (int i = 0; i<w+iw; i+=iw) {
            for (int j = 0; j<h+ih; j+=ih) {
                // System.out.println("drawImage(im,"+i+","+j+")");
                g.drawImage(im, i, j, this);
            }
        }
    }


    public static void main(String[] av) {
        Frame f = new Frame("TiledImageComponent Demo");
        f.add(new TiledImageComponent());
        f.setSize(200, 200);
        f.setVisible(true);
        f.addWindowListener(new WindowCloser(f, true));
    }
}
```

In the paint() method, we must check that the image not only is not null, but
has a non-negative width and height—we are more careful than we were in the
previous, somewhat cavalier example. The image will be null only if something
went very wrong in the constructor, but it can have a negative size. How? In certain creation myths, time ran backward before the beginning of time; therefore,
before an image is fully created, its size is backwards, that is, it has a width and
height of –1. The getImage() method doesn't actually get the image, you see. It
creates the Image object, true, but it doesn't necessarily load all the bits: it starts a
background thread to do the reading, and returns. This dates from the days when
the Web was slower and took a long time to fully load an image. In particular,
there might be some image file formats (some kinds of TIFF files, perhaps) where
you don't know the actual image size until you've read the entire file. Thus, when
getImage() returns, the Image object is created, but its size is set to –1, –1. Since
there are now two threads running (see Chapter 24), there are two possible out-
comes. Either the image-reading thread reads enough to know the width and
height before you need them, or you need them before the thread reads enough
to know them. The curious-looking code in paint() is defensive about this. You
should be too.

But what if you really need the size of the image, for example to lay out a larger
panel? If you read a bit of the Image documentation, you might think you can use
the prepareImage() method to ensure that the object has been loaded. Unfortunately, this method can get you stuck in a loop if the image file is missing, because
prepareImage will never return true! If you need to be sure, you must construct a
MediaTracker object to ensure that the image has been loaded successfully. That
looks something like this:

```
/**
 * This CODE FRAGMENT shows using a MediaTracker to ensure
 * that an Image has been loaded successfully, then obtaining
 * its Width and Height. The MediaTracker can track an arbitrary
 * number of Images; the "0" is an arbitrary number used to track
 * this particular image.
 */
Image im;
int imWidth, imHeight;
public void setImage(Image i) {
    im = i;
    MediaTracker mt = new MediaTracker(this);
    // use of "this" assumes we're in a Component subclass.
    mt.addImage(im, 0);
    try {
        mt.waitForID(0);
    } catch(InterruptedException e) {
        throw new IllegalArgumentException(
            "InterruptedException while loading Image");
    }
```

```
    if (mt.isErrorID(0)) {
        throw new IllegalArgumentException(
                           "Couldn't load image");
    }
    imWidth  = im.getWidth(this);
    imHeight = im.getHeight(this);
}
```

You can ask the MediaTracker for its status at any time using the method status(int ID, boolean load), which returns an integer made by or-ing together the values shown in Table 12-1. The boolean load flag, if true, tells the MediaTracker to start loading any images that haven't yet been started. A related method, statusAll(), returns the inclusive or of any flags applying to images that have started loading.

Table 12-1. MediaTracker status values

Flag	Meaning
ABORTED	Downloading of at least one item was aborted.
COMPLETE	Downloading of all items completed without error.
ERRORED	Something went wrong while downloading at least one item.
LOADING	Downloading is ongoing.

You can shorten the previous code by using the Swing ImageIcon class, which includes this functionality. The ImageIcon class has several constructor forms, one of which takes just a filename argument. ImageIcon uses a MediaTracker internally; you can ask for its status using the ImageIcon's getImageLoadStatus() method, which returns the same values as MediaTracker's statusAll()/statusID().

12.7. *Playing a Sound File*

Problem

You want a quick and easy way to "make noise" or play an existing sound file.

Solution

Get an AudioClip object and use its play() method.

Discussion

This might seem out of place in the midst of all this Graphics code, but there's a pattern. We're moving from the simpler graphical forms to more dynamic multimedia. You can play a sound file using an AudioClip to represent it. Back in the

days of 1.0 and 1.1, you could do this only in an applet (or using unsupported
sun.java classes). But with Java 2, this capability was extended to applications.
Here is a program that plays either two demonstration files from a precompiled
list, or the list of files you give. Due to the applet legacy, each file must be given as
a URL.

```java
import java.applet.*;
import java.net.*;

/** Simple program to try out the "new Sound" stuff in JDK1.2 --
 * allows Applications, not just Applets, to play Sound.
 */
public class SoundPlay {
    static String defSounds[] = {
        "file:///javasrc/graphics/test.wav",
        "file:///music/midi/Beet5th.mid",
    };
    public static void main(String[] av) {
        if (av.length == 0)
            main(defSounds);
        else for (int i=0;i<av.length; i++) {
            System.out.println("Starting " + av[i]);
            try {
                URL snd = new URL(av[i]);
                // open to see if works or throws exception, close to free fd's
                // snd.openConnection().getInputStream().close();
                Applet.newAudioClip(snd).play();
            } catch (Exception e) {
                System.err.println(e);
            }
        }
        // With this call, program exits before/during play.
        // Without it, on some versions, program hangs forever after play.
        // System.exit(0);
    }
}
```

As the code comment reports, you can open the URL to see if it succeeds; if this
throws an IOException, there is not much point in trying the newAudioClip()
call, and catching it this way might allow you to print a better error message.

See Also

There are several limitations on the applet sound API. The JMFPlayer interface
discussed in Recipe 12.8 plays sound files with a volume control panel.

12.8. Displaying a Moving Image with Video

Problem

You want to display a video file within a Java program.

Solution

Use the Java Media Framework (JMF), a standard extension.

Discussion

Example 12-3 shows a program that displays a movie or other media file named on the command line. JMF is very flexible; this program will display (that is, play) an audio file with a volume control if the media object that you name contains a sound clip instead of a movie. Figure 12-4 shows JMFPlayer displaying a sound file and a movie.

Figure 12-4. JMFPlayer in action: audio (left), video (right)

Example 12-3. JMFPlayer.java

```
import com.darwinsys.util.WindowCloser;

import java.applet.*;
import java.awt.*;
import javax.swing.*;
import java.net.*;
import java.io.*;
import java.util.*;
import javax.media.*;

/**
 * Demonstrate simple code to play a movie with Java Media Framework.
 */
```

Example 12-3. JMFPlayer.java (continued)

```java
public class JMFPlayer extends JPanel implements ControllerListener {

    /** The player object */
    Player thePlayer = null;
    /** The parent Frame we are in. */
    JFrame parentFrame = null;
    /** Our contentpane */
    Container cp;
    /** The visual component (if any) */
    Component visualComponent = null;
    /** The default control component (if any) */
    Component controlComponent = null;
    /** The name of this instance's media file. */
    String mediaName;
    /** The URL representing this media file. */
    URL theURL;

    /** Construct the player object and the GUI. */
    public JMFPlayer(JFrame pf, String media) {
        parentFrame = pf;
        mediaName = media;
        // cp = getContentPane();
        cp = this;
        cp.setLayout(new BorderLayout());
        try {
            theURL = new URL(getClass().getResource("."), mediaName);
            thePlayer = Manager.createPlayer(theURL);
            thePlayer.addControllerListener(this);
        } catch (MalformedURLException e) {
            System.err.println("JMF URL creation error: " + e);
        } catch (Exception e) {
            System.err.println("JMF Player creation error: " + e);
            return;
        }
        System.out.println("theURL = " + theURL);

        // Start the player: this will notify our ControllerListener.
        thePlayer.start();// start playing
    }

    /** Called to stop the audio, as from a Stop button or menuitem */
    public void stop() {
        if (thePlayer == null)
            return;
        thePlayer.stop();// stop playing!
        thePlayer.deallocate();// free system resources
    }
```

Example 12-3. JMFPlayer.java (continued)

```java
    /** Called when we are really finished (as from an Exit button). */
    public void destroy() {
        if (thePlayer == null)
            return;
        thePlayer.close();
    }


    /** Called by JMF when the Player has something to tell us about. */
    public synchronized void controllerUpdate(ControllerEvent event) {
        // System.out.println("controllerUpdate(" + event + ")");
        if (event instanceof RealizeCompleteEvent) {
            if ((visualComponent = thePlayer.getVisualComponent()) != null)
                    cp.add(BorderLayout.CENTER, visualComponent);
            if ((controlComponent =
                thePlayer.getControlPanelComponent()) != null)
                    cp.add(BorderLayout.SOUTH, controlComponent);
            // re-size the main window
            if (parentFrame != null) {
                parentFrame.pack();
                parentFrame.setTitle(mediaName);
            }
        }
    }


    public static void main(String[] argv) {
        JFrame f = new JFrame("JMF Player Demo");
        Container frameCP = f.getContentPane();
        JMFPlayer p = new JMFPlayer(f, argv.length == 0 ?
            "file:///C:/music/midi/beet5th.mid" : argv[0]);
        frameCP.add(BorderLayout.CENTER, p);
        f.setSize(200, 200);
        f.setVisible(true);
        f.addWindowListener(new WindowCloser(f, true));
    }
}
```

The optional Java Media Framework includes much more functionality than this
example shows. However, the ability to display a QuickTime or MPEG movie with
only a few lines of code is one of JMF's most endearing young charms. We load the
media file from a URL and create a `Player` object to manage it. If it makes sense
for the given player to have a controller, it will have one, and we add it to the bottom of the applet. Controllers may include volume controls, forward/backward
buttons, position sliders, etc. However, we don't have to care: we get a component
that contains all the appropriate controls for the kind of media clip we've created

the player for. If the given player represents a medium with a visual component (like a movie or a bitmap image), we add this to the center of the applet.

See Also

Of course, there is much more to the JMF API than this. You can, for example, coordinate playing of audio and video with each other or with other events.

12.9. Drawing Text with 2D

Problem

You want fancier drawing abilities.

Solution

Use a `Graphics2D` object.

Discussion

The subject of the 2D graphics added in Java 2 could be the subject of an entire book, and in fact, it is. *Java 2D Graphics* by Jonathan Knudsen (O'Reilly) covers every imaginable aspect of this comprehensive new graphics package. Here I'll just show one example, that of drawing text with a textured background.

The `Graphics2D` class is a direct subclass of the original Java `Graphics` object. In fact, in Java 2, your `paint()` method is always called with an instance of `Graphics2D`. So, it suffices to begin your paint method by casting appropriately:

```
public void paint(Graphics g) {
    Graphics2D g2 = (Graphics2D) g;
```

You can then use any `Graphics2D` methods or any regular `Graphics` methods, getting to them with the object reference g2. One of the additional methods in `Graphics2D` is `setPaint()`, which can take the place of `setColor()` to draw with a solid color. However, it can also be called with several other types, and in this case we pass in an object called a `TexturePaint`, which refers to a pattern. Our pattern is a simple set of diagonal lines, but any pattern or even a bitmap from a file (see Recipe 12.6) can be used. Figure 12-5 shows the resulting screen (it looks even better in color).

The program that produced this is shown in Example 12-4.

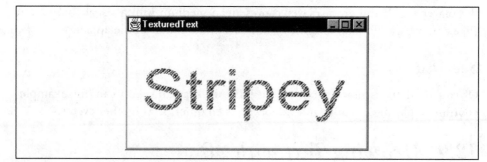

Figure 12-5. TexturedText: a tiny sample of the 2D API

Example 12-4. TexturedText.java

```java
import java.awt.*;
import java.awt.event.*;
import java.awt.image.*;

/** Text with a Texture
 */
public class TexturedText extends Component {
    /** The image we draw in the texture */
    protected BufferedImage bim;
    /** The texture for painting. */
    TexturePaint tp;
    /** The string to draw. */
    String mesg = "Stripey";
    /** The font */
    Font myFont = new Font("Lucida Regular", Font.BOLD, 72);

    /** "main program" method - construct and show */
    public static void main(String av[]) {
        // create a TexturedText object, tell it to show up
        final Frame f = new Frame("TexturedText");
        TexturedText comp = new TexturedText();
        f.add(comp);
        f.addWindowListener(new WindowAdapter() {
            public void windowClosing(WindowEvent e) {
                f.setVisible(false);
                f.dispose();
                System.exit(0);
            }
        });
        f.pack();
        f.setLocation(200, 200);
        f.setVisible(true);
    }
```

Example 12-4. TexturedText.java (continued)

```
protected static Color[] colors = {
    Color.green, Color.red, Color.blue, Color.yellow,
};

/** Construct the object */
public TexturedText() {
    super();
    setBackground(Color.white);
    int width = 8, height = 8;
    bim = new BufferedImage(width, height, BufferedImage.TYPE_INT_ARGB);
    Graphics2D g2 = bim.createGraphics();
    for (int i=0; i<width; i++) {
        g2.setPaint(colors[(i/2)%colors.length]);
        g2.drawLine(0, i, i, 0);
        g2.drawLine(width-i, height, width, height-i);
    }
    Rectangle r = new Rectangle(0, 0, bim.getWidth(), bim.getHeight());
    tp = new TexturePaint(bim, r);
}

public void paint(Graphics g) {
    Graphics2D g2 = (Graphics2D)g;
    g2.setRenderingHint(RenderingHints.KEY_ANTIALIASING,
        RenderingHints.VALUE_ANTIALIAS_ON);
    g2.setPaint(tp);
    g2.setFont(myFont);
    g2.drawString(mesg, 20, 100);
}

public Dimension getMinimumSize() {
    return new Dimension(250, 100);
}

public Dimension getPreferredSize() {
    return new Dimension(320, 150);
}
}
```

See Also

I have not discussed how to scale, rotate, or otherwise transmogrify an image using the `AffineTransform` class in Java 2D graphics, as this is beyond the scope of this book. Consult the previously mentioned *Java 2D Graphics*.

12.10. Printing: JDK 1.1

Problem

You need to generate hardcopy, and you're using JDK 1.1.

Solution

Use `java.awt.PrintJob`. Or, upgrade to JDK 1.2.

Discussion

The JDK 1.1 API puts your program in the driver's seat: you decide what to print and when to print it. But first, you have to let the user pick a printer, which you can do by calling the Toolkit method `getPrinterJob()`. This pops up a platform-specific print chooser dialog, and if the user picks a printer, you get back a `PrintJob` object (otherwise you get back null). Your program is in charge of pagination (breaking the data into pages) and drawing each page onto a print buffer. How? For each page you want to print, call the `PrintJob`'s `getGraphics()` method to retrieve a `Graphics` object. Use it as you will; any of its draw or fill methods will draw, not to the screen, but onto paper. Your best bet is to pass it to your `paint()` method, if you have one. This is one of the few places where you do call `paint()` directly. When the page is done, call the `Graphics` object's `dispose()` method. When the whole print job is done, call the `PrintJob`'s `end()` method, and you're finished—the data is on its way to the printer.

Here's a little program that displays a simple graphical component called a `DemoGFXCanvas`. When you click the Print button at the bottom, the program prints the contents of the `DemoGFXCanvas` (this is shown graphically in Figure 12-6). When you click on the Print button in the main window, the printer dialog shown at the bottom of the figure appears. Example 12-5 is the code that makes it all happen. (The push button and the `addActionListener` code will be explained in Chapter 13; suffice it to say that this causes an action to be performed when the button is pressed.)

Example 12-5. PrintDemoGfx (JDK 1.1 version)

```
import java.awt.*;
import java.awt.event.*;
import javax.swing.*;

/** PrintDemoGfx -- Construct and print a GfxDemoCanvas.  JDK1.1 VERSION. */
public class PrintDemoGfx1_1 {
```

Example 12-5. PrintDemoGfx (JDK 1.1 version) (continued)

```java
/** Simple demo main program. */
public static void main(String[] av) {
    final JFrame f = new JFrame("Printing Test Dummy Frame");

    // Construct the object we want to print. Contrived:
    // this object would already exist in a real program.
    final GfxDemoCanvas thing = new GfxDemoCanvas(500, 300);

    f.getContentPane().add(thing, BorderLayout.CENTER);

    JButton printButton = new JButton("Print");
    f.getContentPane().add(printButton, BorderLayout.SOUTH);

    printButton.addActionListener(new ActionListener() {
        public void actionPerformed(ActionEvent e) {

            PrintJob pjob = Toolkit.getDefaultToolkit().getPrintJob(f,
                "Printing Test", null);

            if (pjob == null)
                return;               // user cancelled

            // Fetch the Print Graphics object
            Graphics pg = pjob.getGraphics();

            // Now (drum roll please), ask "thing" to paint itself
            // on the printer, by calling its paint() method with
            // a Printjob Graphics instead of a Window Graphics.
            thing.paint(pg);
            pg.dispose(); // end of this page
            pjob.end();// end of print job.
        }
    });

    f.pack();
    f.setVisible(true);
}
}
```

One limitation of the 1.1 API is that it offers no way to print without a screen connection for the GUI-based printer dialog, so you can't use the 1.1 API in a background job or cron job on Unix, or in a service on other platforms. For that, use the Java 2 API.

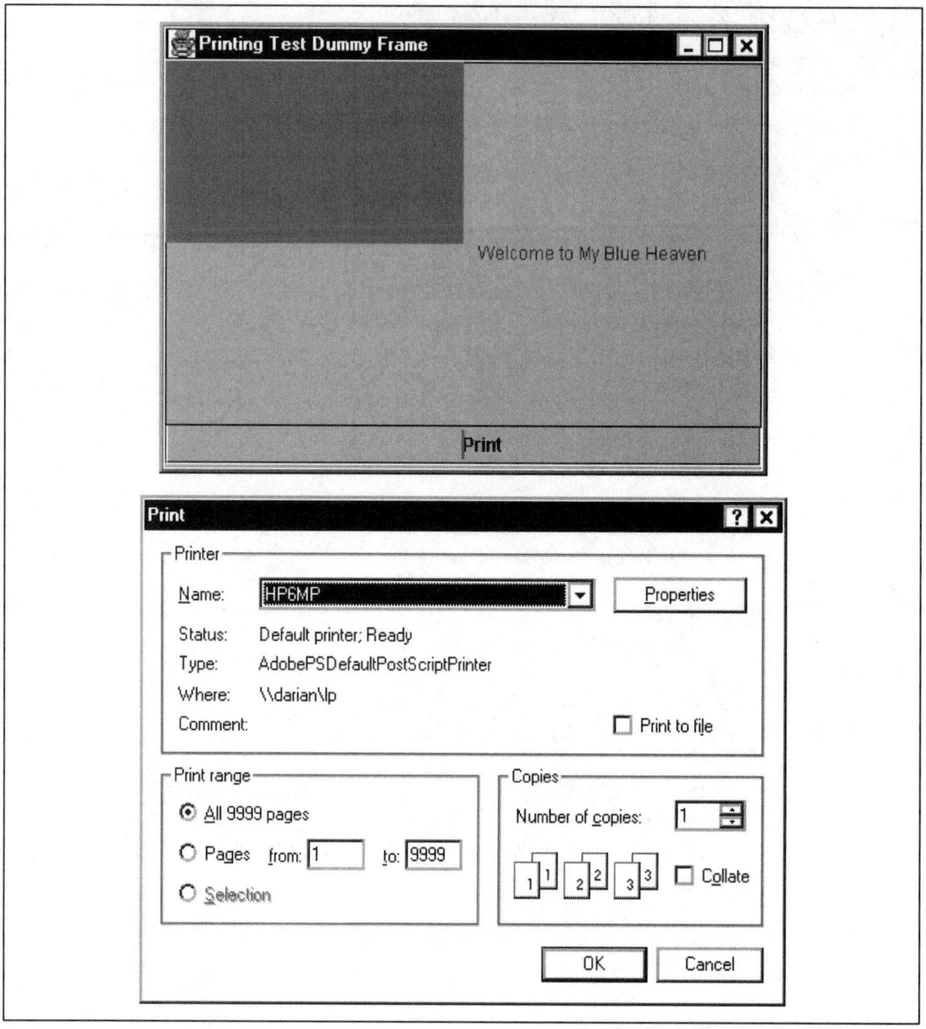

Figure 12-6. PrintDemoGfx program in action (main screen and MS-Windows print dialog)

12.11. Printing: Java 2

Problem

You need to generate hardcopy, and you're using Java 2.

Solution

Use `java.awt.print.PrinterJob`.

Discussion

Like its predecessor, the Java 2 printing API makes you divide the data into pages. Again, you start by getting a `PrinterJob` object to control your printing. You'll usually want to let the user pick a printer, which you do by calling the `PrinterJob`'s method `printerDialog()`. This pops up a platform-specific print chooser dialog, and if the user picks a printer, you get back a `PrinterJob` object (otherwise, again, you get back null). If you don't call `printerDialog()` and there is a default printer, your job will be sent to that printer (if there isn't a default printer, I don't know what happens). Unlike the 1.1 API, however, Java is in charge of what to print and in what order, though your program is still responsible for pagination and drawing each page onto a print buffer. You need to provide an object that implements the `Printable` interface (see Recipe 8.7). In this example, we pass an anonymous inner class (see Recipe 8.6); this is not required but as usual makes the code more succinct by eliminating having to write another class in another file and by keeping the action and the result together. Java calls this object's `print()` method once for each page the user has requested. This is more efficient than the 1.1 method, since if the user wants to print only page 57, you only get called once to print that page (in 1.1, you'd have to generate the intervening 56 pages and have the print system discard them). Note that the official documentation calls the third argument a `pageIndex`, but it's really a page number. Trust me. Presumably it's called a `pageIndex` to remind you that in some printing jobs (such as this book), there are unnumbered pages and pages with those funny little roman numerals at the front (see Recipe 5.10).

The screen shots in Figure 12-6 apply equally to this version of the program. And the source code is similar; see Example 12-6.

Example 12-6. PrintDemoGfx (Java 2 version)

```
import java.awt.*;
import java.awt.event.*;
import java.awt.print.*;
import javax.swing.*;

/** PrintDemoGfx -- Construct and print a GfxDemoCanvas. Java 2 VERSION. */
public class PrintDemoGfx {

    /** Simple demo main program. */
    public static void main(String[] av) throws PrinterException {
        final JFrame f = new JFrame("Printing Test Dummy Frame");

        // Construct the object we want to print. Contrived:
        // this object would already exist in a real program.
        final GfxDemoCanvas thing = new GfxDemoCanvas(400, 300);
```

Example 12-6. PrintDemoGfx (Java 2 version) (continued)

```java
        f.getContentPane().add(thing, BorderLayout.CENTER);

        JButton printButton = new JButton("Print");
        f.getContentPane().add(printButton, BorderLayout.SOUTH);

        printButton.addActionListener(new ActionListener() {
            public void actionPerformed(ActionEvent e) {
                try {
                    PrinterJob pjob = PrinterJob.getPrinterJob();
                    pjob.setJobName("DemoGfx - Graphics Demo Printout");
                    pjob.setCopies(1);
                    // Tell the print system how to print our pages.
                    pjob.setPrintable(new Printable() {
                        /** called from the printer system to print each page */
                        public int print(Graphics pg, PageFormat pf, int pageNum) {
                            if (pageNum>0)// we only print one page
                                return Printable.NO_SUCH_PAGE;// ie., end of job

                            // Now (drum roll please), ask "thing" to paint itself
                            // on the printer, by calling its paint() method with
                            // a Printjob Graphics instead of a Window Graphics.
                            thing.paint(pg);

                            // Tell print system that the page is ready to print
                            return Printable.PAGE_EXISTS;
                        }
                    });

                    if (pjob.printDialog() == false)// choose printer
                        return;        // user cancelled

                    pjob.print(); // Finally, do the printing.
                } catch (PrinterException pe) {
                    JOptionPane.showMessageDialog(f,
                        "Printer error" + pe, "Printing error",
                        JOptionPane.ERROR_MESSAGE);
                }
            }
        });

        f.pack();
        f.setVisible(true);
    }
}
```

See Also

The Java 2 API has other useful methods in the `PrinterJob` class; see the documentation. There are also `Paper`, `PageFormat`, and `Book` classes that describe a physical page, a page by size and orientation, and a collection of pages, respectively.

Both Java printing APIs require you to think in "page mode." That is, you must know where the page breaks are and request the start of each new page. This is optimal for graphically oriented programs, and less optimal for "report writing" applications; handling pagination for yourself can become quite a tedium. See the `HardCopyWriter` class in O'Reilly's *Java Examples in a Nutshell* for code that neatly paginates and prints plain text.

Another means of printing is to directly generate PostScript files or Acrobat PDF files. See Recipes 9.20 and 18.5 for these alternate paths to printing.

12.12. Program: PlotterAWT

In Recipe 8.11, we discussed a series of `Plotter` classes. The `PlotterAWT` class shown in Example 12-7 extends that to provide a "plot preview" service: before being plotted on a (probably slow) plotter, the plot is displayed in an AWT window using the `Graphics` drawing primitives.

Example 12-7. PlotterAWT.java

```
import java.awt.*;
import java.awt.event.*;

/**
 * A Plotter subclass for drawing into an AWT Window. Reflecting back
 * to AWT gives us a "known working" plotter to test on.
 * You can also steal this as a basis for your own plotter driver!
 */
public class PlotterAWT extends Plotter {
    Frame f;
    Image os;
    PCanvas p;
    Graphics g;
    Font font;
    FontMetrics fontMetrics;
    PlotterAWT() {
        super();
        f = new Frame("Plotter");
        p = new PCanvas(os, MAXX, MAXY);
        f.add(p);
        f.pack();
        f.setVisible(true);
        f.addWindowListener(new WindowAdapter() {
```

Example 12-7. PlotterAWT.java (continued)

```java
            public void windowClosing(WindowEvent e) {
                // If we do setVisible and dispose, then the Close completes
                PlotterAWT.this.f.setVisible(false);
                PlotterAWT.this.f.dispose();
                System.exit(0);
            }
        });
        g = p.getOsGraphics();
    }
    public void drawBox(int w, int h) {
        g.drawRect(curx, cury, w, h);
        p.repaint();
    }
    public void rmoveTo(int incrx, int incry){
        moveTo(curx += incrx, cury += incry);
    }
    public void moveTo(int absx, int absy){
        if (!penIsUp)
            g.drawLine(curx, cury, absx, absy);
        curx = absx;
        cury = absy;
    }
    public void setdir(float deg){}
    void penUp(){ penIsUp = true; }
    void penDown(){ penIsUp = false; }
    void penColor(int c){
        switch(c) {
        case 0: g.setColor(Color.white); break;
        case 1: g.setColor(Color.black); break;
        case 2: g.setColor(Color.red); break;
        case 3: g.setColor(Color.green); break;
        case 4: g.setColor(Color.blue); break;
        default: g.setColor(new Color(c)); break;
        }
    }
    void setFont(String fName, int fSize) {
        font = new Font(fName, Font.BOLD, fSize);
        fontMetrics = p.getFontMetrics(font);
    }
    void drawString(String s) {
        g.drawString(s, curx, cury);
        curx += fontMetrics.stringWidth(s);
    }

    /** A Member Class that contains an off-screen Image that is
     * drawn into; this component's paint() copies from there to
     * the screen. This avoids having to keep a list of all the
     * things that have been drawn.
     */
```

Example 12-7. PlotterAWT.java (continued)

```java
class PCanvas extends Canvas {
    int width;
    int height;

    PCanvas(Image im, int x, int y) {
        width = x;
        height = y;
        setBackground(Color.white);
        setForeground(Color.red);
    }

    public Graphics getOsGraphics() {
        checkOS();
        return g;
    }
    private void checkOS() {
        // This createImage fails mysteriously if done in a constructor!
        os = createImage(width, height);
        // System.out.println("PCanvas.checkOS(): image= " + os);
        if (os == null)
            throw new IllegalArgumentException("createImage failed");
        g = os.getGraphics();
    }

    public void paint(Graphics pg) {
        pg.drawImage(os, 0, 0, null);
    }
    public Dimension getPreferredSize() {
        return new Dimension(width, height);
    }
}
}
```

12.13. *Program: Grapher*

Grapher is a simple program to read a table of numbers and graph them. The input format is two or more lines that each contain an X and a Y value. The output is an on-screen display that can also be printed. Figure 12-7 shows the results of running it with the following simple data; the first column is the X coordinate and the second is the Y coordinate of each point. The program scales the data to fit the window.

```
1.5   5
1.7   6
1.8   8
2.2   7
```

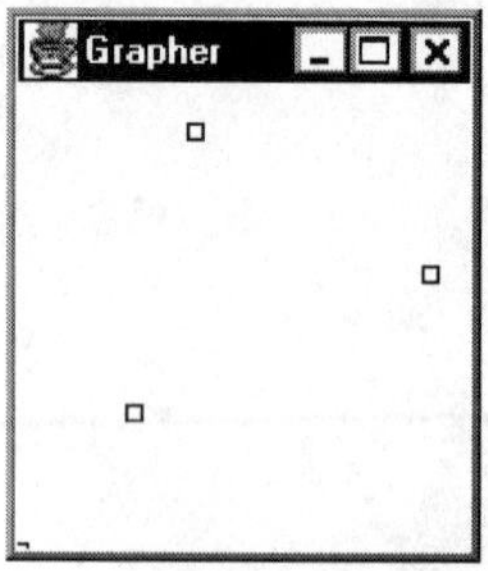

Figure 12-7. Grapher in action

Example 12-8 shows the code.

Example 12-8. Grapher.java

```java
import com.darwinsys.util.Debug;
import java.awt.*;
import java.awt.event.*;
import javax.swing.*;
import java.io.*;
import java.util.*;

/** Simple Graphing program.
 */
public class Grapher extends JPanel {
    /** Multiplier for range to allow room for a border */
    public final static float BORDERFACTOR = 1.1f;

    /* Small inner class to hold x, y. Called Apoint to differentiate
     * from java.awt.Point.
     */
    class Apoint {
        float x;
        float y;
        public String toString() {
            return "Apoint("+x+","+y+")";
        }
    }

    /** The list of Apoint points. */
    protected Vector data;

    /** The minimum and maximum X values */
    protected float minx = Integer.MAX_VALUE, maxx = Integer.MIN_VALUE;
    /** The minimum and maximum Y values */
    protected float miny = Integer.MAX_VALUE, maxy = Integer.MIN_VALUE;
    /** The number of data points */
```

Example 12-8. Grapher.java (continued)

```java
    protected int n;
    /** The range of X and Y values */
    protected float xrange, yrange;

    public Grapher() {
        data = new Vector();
    }

    /** Read the data file named. Each line has an x and a y coordinate. */
    public void read(String fname) {
        LineNumberReader is = null;
        try {
            is = new LineNumberReader(new FileReader(fname));

            String txt;
            // Read the file a line at a time, parse it, save the data.
            while ((txt = is.readLine()) != null) {
                StringTokenizer st = new StringTokenizer(txt);
                try {
                    Apoint d = new Apoint();
                    d.x = Float.parseFloat(st.nextToken());
                    d.y = Float.parseFloat(st.nextToken());
                    data.add(d);
                } catch(NumberFormatException nfe) {
                    System.err.println("Invalid number on line " +
                        is.getLineNumber());
                } // XXX catch out of range exception
            }
        } catch (FileNotFoundException e) {
            System.err.println("File " + fname + " unreadable: " + e);
        } catch (IOException e) {
            System.err.println("I/O error on line " + is.getLineNumber());
        }
        n = data.size();
        if (n < 2) {
            System.err.println("Not enough data points!");
            return;
        }

        // find min & max
        for (int i=0 ; i < n; i++) {
            Apoint d = (Apoint)data.elementAt(i);
            if (d.x < minx) minx = d.x;
            if (d.x > maxx) maxx = d.x;
            if (d.y < miny) miny = d.y;
            if (d.y > maxy) maxy = d.y;
        }
```

Example 12-8. Grapher.java (continued)

```java
        // Compute ranges
        xrange = (maxx - minx) * BORDERFACTOR;
        yrange = (maxy - miny) * BORDERFACTOR;
        Debug.println("range", "minx,x,r = " + minx +' '+ maxx +' '+ xrange);
        Debug.println("range", "miny,y,r = " + miny +' '+ maxy +' '+ yrange);
    }


    /** Called when the window needs painting.
     * Computes X and Y range, scales.
     */
    public void paintComponent(Graphics g) {
        super.paintComponent(g);
        Dimension s = getSize();
        if (n < 2) {
            g.drawString("Insufficient data", 10, 40);
            return;
        }

        // Compute scale factors
        float xfact = s.width  / xrange;
        float yfact = s.height / yrange;

        // Scale and plot the data
        for (int i=0 ; i < n; i++) {
            Apoint d = (Apoint)data.elementAt(i);
            float x = (d.x-minx) * xfact;
            float y = (d.y-miny) * yfact;
            Debug.println("point", "AT " + i + " " + d + "; " +
                "x = " + x + "; y = " + y);
            // Draw a 5-pixel rectangle centered, so -2 both x and y.
            // AWT numbers Y from 0 down, so invert:
            g.drawRect(((int)x)-2, s.height-2-(int)y, 5, 5);
        }
    }


    public Dimension getPreferredSize() {
        return new Dimension(150, 150);
    }

    public static void main(String[] rgs) {
        final JFrame f = new JFrame("Grapher");
        f.addWindowListener(new WindowAdapter() {
            public void windowClosing(WindowEvent e) {
                f.setVisible(false);
                f.dispose();
                System.exit(0);
            }
        });
```

Example 12-8. Grapher.java (continued)

```
      Grapher g = new Grapher();
      f.setContentPane(g);
      f.setLocation(100, 100);
      f.pack();
      if (rgs.length == 0)
          g.read("Grapher.dat");
      else
          g.read(rgs[0]);
      f.setVisible(true);
   }
}
```

Most of the complexity of `Grapher` lies in determining the range and scaling. You could obviously extend this to draw fancier drawings such as bar charts and the like. If pie charts interest you, see `ChartBean` in the online source.

13

Graphical User Interfaces

13.0. Introduction

Java has had windowing capabilities since its earliest days. The first version made public was the Abstract Windowing Toolkit, or AWT. AWT used the native toolkit components, so it was relatively small and simple. AWT suffered somewhat from being a "least common denominator"; a feature could not be added unless it could be implemented on all major platforms that Java supported. The second major implementation was the Swing classes, released in 1998 as part of the Java Foundation Classes. Swing is a full-function, professional-quality GUI toolkit designed to enable almost any kind of client-side GUI-based interaction. AWT lives on inside, or rather underneath, Swing, and for this reason many programs begin by importing both `java.awt` and `javax.swing`.

This chapter presents a few elements of Java windowing for the developer whose main exposure to Java has been on the server side. The examples are shown using Swing, rather than the obsolescent AWT components. For a slightly more detailed presentation, the reader is referred to *Learning Java*. For a very thorough presentation on all aspects of Swing, I recommend the O'Reilly book *Java Swing*, by Robert Eckstein, Marc Loy, and Dave Wood. At 1252 pages it's not an overnight read. But it *is* comprehensive.

Java's event model has evolved over time, too. In JDK 1.0, the writer of a windowed application had to write a single large event-handling method to deal with button presses from all the GUI controls in the window. This was simple for small programs, but did not scale well. My JabaDex application had one large event handler method that tried to figure out which of 50 or 60 GUI controls had caused an event, which was tedious and error prone. In JDK 1.1, the new delegation event model was introduced. In this model, events are given only to classes that request them, which is done by *registering* a *listener*. This is discussed in Recipe 13.4 and shown in Example 13-1. At the same time, the language was extended ever so slightly to include the notion of *inner classes*. An inner class is simply a class whose definition is contained inside the body of another class. We use examples of two types of inner classes here; for details on the half-dozen different categories of inner classes, the reader is referred to *Java in a Nutshell*.

For this chapter, I make the assumption that you have at least a basic understanding of what GUI components are, which ones should be used where, and so on. I will refer to JButton, JList, and JFrame, to name a few, without saying much more about their basics or functionality. If this stuff is mysterious to you, consult a good book on GUI design, such as the *Java Look and Feel Design Guidelines*.

Most of the GUI construction techniques in this chapter can be done for you, in some cases more quickly, by an integrated development environment (IDE). I have always believed, however, that understanding what goes on inside the code should be a prerequisite for being allowed to use an IDE. Those who disagree may be inclined to skip this chapter, go press a few buttons, and have the computer do the work for them. But you should at least skim this chapter to see what's going on, so you'll know where to look when you need it later.

13.1. Displaying GUI Components

Problem

You want to create some GUI components and have them appear in a window.

Solution

Create a JFrame and add the components to its ContentPane.

Discussion

The older Abstract Windowing Toolkit (AWT) had a simple frame component that allowed you to add components directly to it. "Good" programs always created a panel to fit inside the frame, and populated that. But some less-educated heathens often added components directly to the frame. The Swing JFrame is more complex; it comes with not one but two containers already constructed inside it. The ContentPane is the main container; you should normally use it as your JFrame's main container. The GlassPane has a clear background and sits over the top of the ContentPane; its primary use is in temporarily painting something over top of the main ContentPane. Because of this, you need to use the JFrame's getContentPane() method:

```
import java.awt.*;
import javax.swing.*;

public class ContentPane extends JFrame {
    public ContentPane() {
        Container cp = getContentPane();
        // now add Components to "cp"...
    }
}
```

Then you can add any number of components (including containers) into this existing container, using the Container's add() method:

```
import java.awt.*;
import java.awt.event.*;
import javax.swing.*;

/** Just a Frame
 */
public class JFrameDemo extends JFrame {
    boolean unsavedChanges = false;
    JButton quitButton;

    /** Construct the object including its GUI */
    public JFrameDemo() {
        super("JFrameDemo");
        getContentPane().add(quitButton = new JButton("Exit"));

        // These "action handlers" will be explained later in the chapter.
        quitButton.addActionListener(new ActionListener() {
            public void actionPerformed(ActionEvent e) {
                setVisible(false);
                dispose();
                System.exit(0);
            }
        });
        addWindowListener(new WindowAdapter() {
            public void windowClosing(WindowEvent e) {
                setVisible(false);
                dispose();
                System.exit(0);
            }
        });

        pack();
    }
}
```

This code compiles fine. But when we try to run it, of course, there is no main method. We need to create one:

```
public class JFrameDemoMain {
    // We need a main program to instantiate and show.
    public static void main(String[] args) {
        new JFrameDemo().setVisible(true);
    }
}
```

Now we can run it and have it display. But there are two problems: it starts off tiny (on MS-Windows) or huge (on X Windows). And, when we do resize it, only the buttons show, and it always takes up the full size of the window. To solve these problems, we need to discuss layout management, a topic to which we now turn our attention.

13.2. Designing a Window Layout

Problem

The default layout isn't good enough.

Solution

Learn to deal with a layout manager.

Discussion

The container classes such as Panel have the ability to contain a series of components. But there are many ways of arranging the components within a window. Rather than clutter up each container with a variety of different layout computations, the designers of the Java API used a sensible design pattern to divide the labor. A *layout manager* is an object that performs the layout computations for a container.* There are five common layout manager classes in the AWT package (see Table 13-1), plus a few more specialized ones in javax.swing. Plus, as we'll see in Recipe 13.14, it's not that big a deal to write your own!

---

* The LayoutManager specification is actually a Java interface, rather than a class, for historical reasons. In fact, it's two interfaces: quoting the code, interface LayoutManager2 extends LayoutManager. The extra features of the second interface don't concern us here; we want to concentrate on using the layout managers.

Table 13-1. Layout managers

Name	Notes	Default on
FlowLayout	Flows across the container	(J)Panel, (J)Applet
BorderLayout	Five "geographic" regions	(J)Frame, (J)Window
GridLayout	Regular grid (all items same size)	None
CardLayout	Display one of many components at a time; useful for wizard-style layouts	None
GridBagLayout	Very flexible but maximally complex	None

Since we've broached the subject of layout management, I should mention that each component has a method called getPreferredSize(), which the layout managers use in deciding how and where to place components. A well-behaved component overrides this method to return something meaningful. A button or label, for example, will indicate that it wishes to be large enough to contain its text and/or icon plus a bit of space for padding. And, if your JFrame is full of well-behaved components, you can set its size to be "just the size of all included components, plus a bit for padding," just by calling the pack() method, which takes no arguments. The pack() method goes around and asks each embedded component for its preferred size (and any nested container's getPreferredSize() will ask each of its components, and so on). The JFrame is then set to the best size to give the components their preferred sizes as much as is possible. If not using pack(), you need to call the setSize() method, which requires either a width and a height, or a Dimension object containing this information.

A FlowLayout is the default in JPanel and Applet/JApplet. It simply lays the components out along the "normal" axis (left to right in European and English-speaking locales, right to left in Hebrew or Arabic locales, and so on, as set by the user's Locale settings). The overall collection of them is centered within the window.

The default for JFrame and JWindow is BorderLayout. This explains the problem of the single button appearing in the JFrameDemo class at the end of the previous recipe. BorderLayout divides the screen into the five areas shown in Figure 13-1. If you don't specify where to place a component, it goes into the Center. And if you place multiple components in the same region (perhaps by adding several components without specifying where to place them!), only the last one appears.

So we can fix the previous version of the JFrameDemo in one of two ways. Either we can use a FlowLayout, or specify BorderLayout regions for the label and the button. The former being simpler, we'll try it out:

```
import java.awt.*;
import javax.swing.*;
```

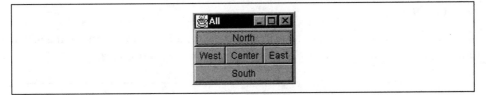

Figure 13-1. BorderLayout's five regions

```java
public class JFrameFlowLayout extends JFrame {
    public JFrameFlowLayout() {
        Container cp = getContentPane();

        // Make sure it has a FlowLayout layoutmanager.
        cp.setLayout(new FlowLayout());

        // now add Components to "cp"...
        cp.add(new JLabel("Wonderful?"));
        cp.add(new JButton("Yes!"));
        pack();
    }

    // We need a main program to instantiate and show.
    public static void main(String[] args) {
        new JFrameFlowLayout().setVisible(true);
    }
}
```

See Also

I have not discussed the details of the advanced layouts. For an example of a dialog layout using nested panels, see the font chooser in Recipe 13.13. For an example of a GridBagLayout, see the GUI network client in Recipe 17.3. For more details, see the AWT and Swing books.

13.3. A Tabbed View of Life

Problem

These layouts don't include a tab layout, and you need one.

Solution

Use a JTabbedPane.

Discussion

The JTabbedPane class acts as a combined container and layout manager. It implements a conventional tab layout, which looks like Figure 13-2.

Figure 13-2. JTabbedPane: two views in Java Look and one in MS-Windows Look

To add a tab to the layout, you do not use setLayout(). You simply create the JTabbedPane and call its addTab() method, passing in a String and a Component. Example 13-1 is the code for our simple program.

Example 13-1. TabPaneDemo.java

```java
import javax.swing.*;

public class TabPaneDemo {
    protected JTabbedPane tabPane;
    public TabPaneDemo() {
        tabPane = new JTabbedPane();
        tabPane.add(new JLabel("One", JLabel.CENTER), "First");
        tabPane.add(new JLabel("Two", JLabel.CENTER), "Second");
    }

    public static void main(String[] a) {
        JFrame f = new JFrame("Tab Demo");
        f.getContentPane().add(new TabPaneDemo().tabPane);
        f.setSize(120, 100);
        f.setVisible(true);
    }
}
```

See Also

The third screen shot in Figure 13-2 shows the program with a MS-Windows look and feel, instead of the default Java look and feel. See Recipe 13.12 for how to change the look and feel of a Swing-based GUI application.

13.4. Action Handling: Making Buttons Work

Problem

Your button doesn't do anything when the user presses it.

Solution

Add an `ActionListener` to do the work.

Discussion

There are about half-dozen different types of *event listeners*. The most common is the `ActionListener`, used by push buttons, text fields, and certain other components to indicate that the user has performed a high-level action such as activating a push button or pressing Return in a text field. The paradigm (shown in Figure 13-3) is that you create a `Listener` object, register it with the event source (such as the push button) and wait. Later, when and if the user pushes the button, the button will call your `Listener`.

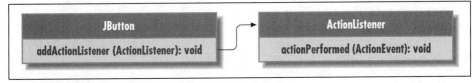

Figure 13-3. AWT listener relationships

Here's some simple code in which pushing a button causes the program to print a friendly message. This program is an applet (see Recipe 17.2), so it can use the `showStatus()` method to print its text:

```java
import java.applet.*;
import java.awt.*;
import java.awt.event.*;

/** Demonstrate use of Button */
public class ButtonDemo extends Applet implements ActionListener {
    Button b1;

    public ButtonDemo() {
        add(b1 = new Button("A button"));
        b1.addActionListener(this);
    }
```

```
    public void actionPerformed(ActionEvent event) {
        showStatus("Thanks for pushing my button!");
    }
}
```

This version does not use an inner class to handle the events, but does so itself by directly implementing the `ActionListener` interface. This works for small programs, but as an application grows, quickly becomes unserviceable; how do you sort out which button was pressed? To solve this problem, we normally use an inner class as the action handler, and have a different class for each button. First, let's write the previous code with two buttons, so you'll see what I mean:

```
import java.applet.*;
import java.awt.*;
import java.awt.event.*;

/** Demonstrate use of two buttons, using a single ActionListener,
 * being the class itself.
 */
public class ButtonDemo2a extends Applet implements ActionListener {
    Button b1, b2;

    public void init() {
        add(b1 = new Button("A button"));
        b1.addActionListener(this);

        add(b2 = new Button("Another button"));
        b2.addActionListener(this);
    }

    public void actionPerformed(ActionEvent e) {
        if (e.getSource() == b1)
            showStatus("Thanks for pushing my first button!");
        else
            showStatus("Thanks for pushing my second button!");
    }
}
```

Now here it is using a *member inner class,* that is, a class that is a named part of another class:

```
import java.applet.*;
import java.awt.*;
import java.awt.event.*;

/** Demonstrate use of two buttons, using a single ActionListener
 * made of a named inner class
 */
```

```
public class ButtonDemo2b extends Applet {
    Button b1, b2;
    ActionListener handler = new ButtonHandler();

    public void init() {
        add(b1 = new Button("A button"));
        b1.addActionListener(handler);

        add(b2 = new Button("Another button"));
        b2.addActionListener(handler);
    }

    class ButtonHandler implements ActionListener {
        public void actionPerformed(ActionEvent e) {
            if (e.getSource() == b1)
                showStatus("Thanks for pushing my first button!");
            else
                showStatus("Thanks for pushing my second button!");
        }
    }
}
```

Note that merely breaking the action handling code into its own class doesn't really contribute much to readability. But there is a way to use inner classes that does promote readability and maintainability. We create an inner class (see Recipe 8.6) for each event source: each button, each menu item, and so on. Sounds like a lot of work. And it would be, if you used the previous method. But there is a shorter way, using anonymous inner classes, described next.

13.5. Action Handling Using Anonymous Inner Classes

Problem

You want action handling with less creation of special classes.

Solution

Use anonymous inner classes.

Discussion

Anonymous inner classes are declared and instantiated at the same time, using the new operator with the name of an existing class or interface. If you name a class, it

will be subclassed; if you name an interface, the anonymous class will extend
`java.lang.Object` and implement the named interface. The paradigm is:

```
b.addActionListener(new ActionListener() {
    public void actionPerformed(ActionEvent e) {
        showStatus("Thanks for pushing my second button!");
        }
});
```

Did you notice the `});` by itself on the last line? Good, because it's important.
The `}` terminates the definition of the inner class, while the `)` ends the argument
list to the `addActionListener` method; the single argument inside the brackets is
an argument of type `ActionListener` that refers to the one and only instance
created of your anonymous class. Example 13-2 contains a complete example.

Example 13-2. ButtonDemo2c.java

```
import java.applet.*;
import java.awt.*;
import java.awt.event.*;

/** Demonstrate use of Button */
public class ButtonDemo2c extends Applet {
    Button b;

    public void init() {
        add(b = new Button("A button"));
        b.addActionListener(new ActionListener() {
            public void actionPerformed(ActionEvent e) {
                showStatus("Thanks for pushing my first button!");
            }
        });
        add(b = new Button("Another button"));
        b.addActionListener(new ActionListener() {
            public void actionPerformed(ActionEvent e) {
                showStatus("Thanks for pushing my second button!");
            }
        });
    }
}
```

The real benefit of these anonymous inner classes, by the way, is that they keep the
action handling code in the same place that the GUI control is being instantiated.
This saves a lot of looking back and forth to see what a GUI control really does.

Those `ActionListener` objects have no instance name and appear to have no
class name: is that possible? The former yes, but not the latter. In fact, class names
are assigned to anonymous inner classes by the compiler. After compiling and testing `ButtonDemo2c` with JDK 1.2, I list the directory in which I ran the program:

```
C:\javasrc\gui>ls -1 ButtonDemo2c*
ButtonDemo2c$1.class
ButtonDemo2c$2.class
ButtonDemo2c.class
ButtonDemo2c.htm
ButtonDemo2c.java
C:\javasrc\gui>
```

Those first two are the anonymous inner classes. Note that a different compiler might assign different names to them; it doesn't matter to us. A word for the wise: don't depend on those names!

See Also

Most IDEs (see Recipe 1.1) have drag-and-drop GUI builder tools that will make this task easier, at least for simpler projects.

13.6. Terminating a Program with "Window Close"

Problem

Nothing happens when you click on the close button on the title bar of an AWT Frame. When you do this on a Swing JFrame, the window disappears but the application does not exit.

Solution

Add a WindowListener; have it exit the application.

Discussion

Main windows—subclasses of java.awt.Window, such as (J)Frames and (J)Dialogs—are treated specially. Unlike all other Component subclasses, Window and its subclasses are not initially visible. This is sensible, as they have to be packed or resized, and you don't want the user to watch the components getting rearranged. Once you call a Window's setVisible(true) method, all components inside it become visible. And you can listen for WindowEvents on a Window.

The WindowListener interface contains a plenitude of methods to notify a listener when anything happens to the window. You can be told when the window is activated (gets keyboard and mouse events) or deactivated. Or you can find out when the window is iconified or de-iconified: these are good times to suspend and resume processing, respectively. You can be notified the first time the window is opened. And, most importantly for us, you can be notified when the user requests that the window be closed. (Some sample close buttons are show in Figure 13-4.) The windowClosing method of your WindowListener is called when the user clicks on the close button (this depends on the window system and, on X Windows, on the window manager) or sends the close message from the keyboard (normally Alt-F4).

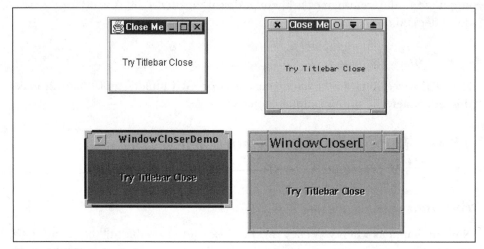

Figure 13-4. Some close buttons

The method signature is:

```
public void windowClosing(WindowEvent);
```

But this method comes from the interface WindowListener, which has half a dozen other methods. If you define a WindowListener and implement only this one method, the compiler will declare your class abstract and refuse to instantiate it. You might start by writing stub or dummy versions (methods whose body is just the two characters {}), but you'd then be doing more work than necessary, since there's already an "adapter" class that does this for all methods in the Listener interface. So you really need only to subclass from WindowAdapter, and override the one method, windowClosing, that you care about. Figure 13-5 shows this model.

Let's put this all together in some code examples. Class WindowDemo puts up a frame and, when you ask it to close, it does so. The online source includes class WindowDemo2, which is the same, but implemented as a Swing JFrame.

```
import java.awt.*;
import java.awt.event.*;
```

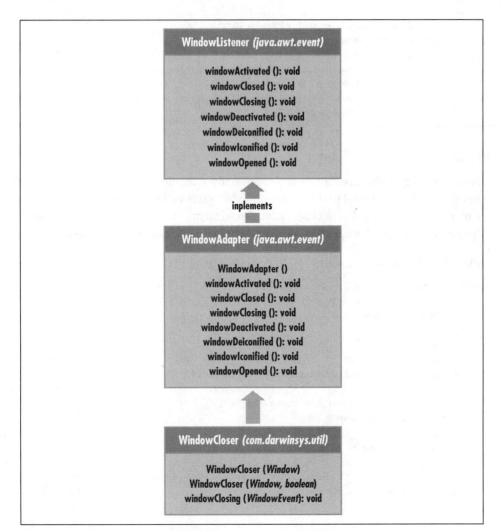

Figure 13-5. WindowListener, WindowAdapter, and my WindowCloser

```
/* Show an example of closing a Window.
 */
public class WindowDemo extends Frame {

    public static void main(String[] argv) {
        Frame f = new WindowDemo();
        f.setVisible(true);
    }
    public WindowDemo() {
        setSize(200, 100);
        addWindowListener(new WindowDemoAdapter());
    }
```

```
    /** Named Inner class that closes a Window. */
    class WindowDemoAdapter extends WindowAdapter {
        public void windowClosing(WindowEvent e) {
                System.out.println("Goodbye!");
                WindowDemo.this.setVisible(false);// window will close
                WindowDemo.this.dispose();// and be freed up.
                System.exit(0);
        }
    }
}
```

Since making a Window close—and optionally exit the program—is a common operation, I've encapsulated this into a small class called WindowCloser, which I've put into my public package com.darwinsys.util. Most AWT and Swing books have similar classes. Example 13-3 contains my WindowCloser class.

Example 13-3. WindowCloser.java

```
package com.darwinsys.util;

import java.awt.Window;
import java.awt.event.*;

/** A WindowCloser - watch for Window Closing events, and
 * follow them up with setVisible(false) and dispose().
 */
public class WindowCloser extends WindowAdapter {
    /** The window we close */
    Window win;
    /** True if we are to exit as well. */
    boolean doExit = false;

    public WindowCloser(Window w) {
        this(w, false);
    }
    public WindowCloser(Window w, boolean exit) {
        win = w;
        doExit = exit;
    }
    public void windowClosing(WindowEvent e) {
        win.setVisible(false);
        win.dispose();
        if (doExit)
            System.exit(0);
    }
}
```

Using it is straightforward:

```
import java.awt.*;
import java.awt.event.*;

/* Show an example of closing a Window.
 */
public class WindowCloserDemo {

    /* Main method */
    public static void main(String[] argv) {
        Frame f = new Frame("Close Me");
        f.add(new Label("Try Titlebar Close", Label.CENTER));
        f.setSize(100, 100);
        f.setVisible(true);
        f.addWindowListener(new WindowCloser(f, true));
    }
}
```

See Also

I've mentioned dispose() several times without saying much about it. The dispose() method (inherited from Window) causes the underlying (operating system–specific) window system resources to be released without totally destroying the Window. If you later call pack() or setVisible(true) on the Window, the native resources will be re-created. It's a good idea to dispose() a window if you won't be using it for a while, but not if there's a good chance you'll need it again soon.

There may be cases in which you don't even need a window closer. The Swing JFrame has a setDefaultCloseOperation() method, which controls the default behavior. You can pass it one of the values defined in the WindowConstants class:

WindowConstants.DO_NOTHING_ON_CLOSE
> Ignore the request.

WindowConstants.HIDE_ON_CLOSE
> Hide the window (default).

WindowConstants.DISPOSE_ON_CLOSE
> Hide and dispose the window.

WindowConstants.EXIT_ON_CLOSE
> JDK 1.3 (and later!). Exit the application on close, obviating the need for a WindowListener!

The action set by setDefaultCloseOperation() will be performed after your actionPerformed() method (the last, if more than one) returns.

There are several other multi-method interfaces, including MouseListener and ComponentListener, and an Adapter class for each of these.

13.7. Dialogs: When Later Just Won't Do

Problem

You need a bit of feedback from the user *right now*.

Solution

Use a JOptionPane method to show a prebuilt dialog.

Discussion

It's fairly common to want to confirm an action with the user or to bring some problem to their attention right away, rather than waiting for them to read a log-file that they might or might not get around to. These pop-up windows are called *Dialogs*. The JOptionPane class has a number of show...Dialog() methods that let you display most prebuilt dialogs, including those shown in Figure 13-6.

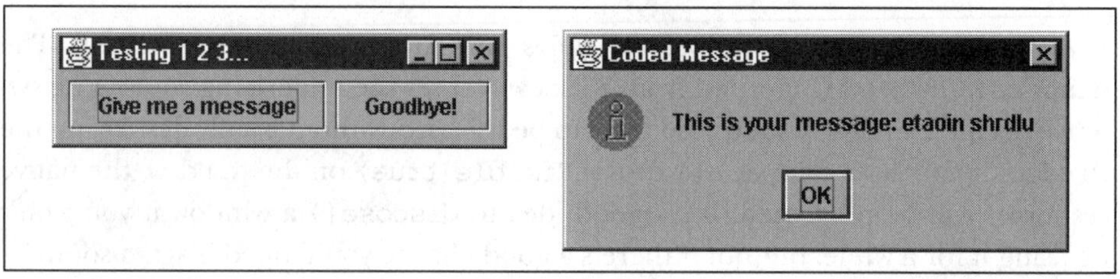

Figure 13-6. JOptionPane in action

The simplest form is showMessageDialog(), and its first argument is the owning Frame or JFrame. If you don't know it, pass null, but Java doesn't guarantee to give input focus back to your main window when the dialog is dismissed. The second argument is the message text, and the third is the title bar title. Last but not least is code telling which of several prebuilt bitmaps should be displayed. This program produces the "Coded Message" dialog in the figure:

```
import java.awt.*;
import java.awt.event.*;
import javax.swing.*;

/**
 * Demonstrate JOptionPane
 */
public class JOptionDemo extends JFrame {

    // Constructor
    JOptionDemo(String s) {
        super(s);
```

```
        Container cp = getContentPane();
        cp.setLayout(new FlowLayout());

        JButton b = new JButton("Give me a message");
        b.addActionListener(new ActionListener() {
            public void actionPerformed(ActionEvent e) {
                JOptionPane.showMessageDialog(
                    JOptionDemo.this,
                    "This is your message: etaoin shrdlu", "Coded Message",
                    JOptionPane.INFORMATION_MESSAGE);
            }
        });
        cp.add(b);

        b = new JButton("Goodbye!");
        b.addActionListener(new ActionListener() {
            public void actionPerformed(ActionEvent e) {
                System.exit(0);
            }
        });
        cp.add(b);

        // the main window
        setSize(200, 150);
        pack();
    }

    public static void main(String[] arg) {
        JOptionDemo x = new JOptionDemo("Testing 1 2 3...");
        x.setVisible(true);
    }
}
```

There are several other ways of using the JOptionPane class. For example, you can call its showDialog() method with a list of strings; each will be displayed on a push button in the dialog. This method blocks until the user selects one of the buttons; the return value of the method is an int telling which button the user clicked on (it returns the array index of the string whose button was pressed). There is also showInputDialog(), which lets you prompt the user for a data value. Very, very convenient!

See Also

JDialog lets you write arbitrary complicated dialogs. You subclass them in a manner similar to JFrame, specifying whether you want an application-modal or nonmodal dialog (a modal dialog locks out the rest of the application, which is less convenient for the user but much easier for the programmer). See the *Java Swing* book for information on JDialog.

13.8. Getting Program Output into a Window

Problem

You want to capture an input/output stream and display it in a text field.

Solution

Use an interconnected pair of piped streams and a Thread to read from the input half, and write it to the text area. You may also want to redirect System.out and System.err to the stream; see Recipe 9.6.

Discussion

The PipedInputStream and PipedOutputStream provide two streams (see the section "Streams and Readers/Writers" in Chapter 9) that are connected together by a buffer and are designed to provide communication between multiple threads (see Recipe 24.0).

As you'll see in Chapter 19, I am fairly aggressive in the pursuit of SPAM perpetrators. I have a program called TestOpenMailRelay, derived from the mail sender in Recipe 19.2, that I use to test whether remote servers are willing to accept mail from unknown third parties and forward it as their own. This gives these bastard messages a parent, just as many birds will glibly nest on a cuckoo's egg that has been snuck into their nest. This is the GUI for that program; both this and the main program are online in the email directory.

In the constructor, I arrange for the main class to write to the PipedOutputStream; the call to TestOpenMailRelay.process() passing the *ps* argument arranges this. That method will write its own output to the stream in addition to assigning standard output and standard error, so we should see anything it tries to print. To avoid long (possibly infinitely long!) delays, I start an additional thread to read from the pipe buffer. Figure 13-7 shows three windows: the program output window (the goal of this whole exercise), a terminal window from which I copied the IP address (some parts of the text in this window have been deliberately obfuscated), and another command window in which I started the GUI program running.

The code is shown in Example 13-4. Note that there's a problem that causes an IOException at the end of the first file; hopefully this will be corrected by the time you download the source code.

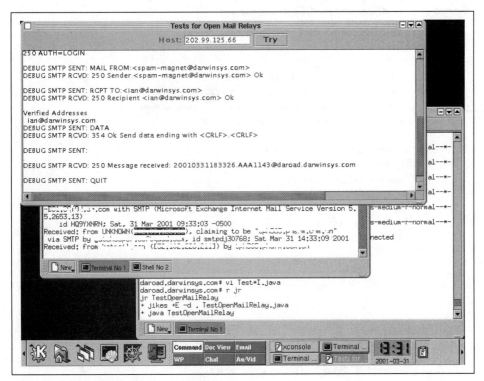

Figure 13-7. TestOpenMailRelayGUI in action

Example 13-4. TestOpenMailRelayGUI.java

```java
import java.awt.*;
import java.awt.event.*;
import javax.swing.*;
import java.io.*;


/** GUI for TestOpenMailRelay, lets you run it multiple times in one JVM
 * to avoid startup delay.
 *
 * Starts each in its own Thread for faster return to ready state.
 *
 * Uses PipedI/OStreams to capture system.out/err into a window.
 */
public class TestOpenMailRelayGUI extends JFrame {

    /** The one-line textfield for the user to type Host name/IP */
    JTextField hostTextField;
    /** Multi-line text area for results. */
    JTextArea results;
    /** The piped stream for the main class to write into "results" */
    PrintStream ps;
```

Example 13-4. TestOpenMailRelayGUI.java (continued)

```java
    /** The piped stream to read from "ps" into "results" */
    DataInputStream iis;

    /** This inner class is the action handler both for pressing
     * the "Try" button and also for pressing <ENTER> in the text
     * field. It gets the IP name/address from the text field
     * and passes it to process() in the main class.
     */
    ActionListener runner = new ActionListener() {
        public void actionPerformed(ActionEvent evt) {
            new Thread(new Runnable() {
                public void run() {
                    String host = hostTextField.getText().trim();
                    ps.println("Trying " + host);
                    TestOpenMailRelay.process(host, ps);
                }
            }).start();
        }
    };

    /** Construct a GUI and some I/O plumbing to get the output
     * of "TestOpenMailRelay" into the "results" textfield.
     */
    public TestOpenMailRelayGUI() throws IOException {
        super("Tests for Open Mail Relays");
        PipedInputStream is;
        PipedOutputStream os;
        JPanel p;
        Container cp = getContentPane();
        cp.add(BorderLayout.NORTH, p = new JPanel());

        // The entry label and text field.
        p.add(new JLabel("Host:"));
        p.add(hostTextField = new JTextField(10));
        hostTextField.addActionListener(runner);

        JButton b;
        p.add(b = new JButton("Try"));
        b.addActionListener(runner);

        results = new JTextArea(20, 60);
        // Add the text area to the main part of the window (CENTER).
        // Wrap it in a JScrollPane to make it scroll automatically.
        cp.add(BorderLayout.CENTER, new JScrollPane(results));

        pack();        // end of GUI portion
```

Example 13-4. TestOpenMailRelayGUI.java (continued)

```
        // Create a pair of Piped Streams.
        is = new PipedInputStream();
        os = new PipedOutputStream(is);

        iis = new DataInputStream(is);
        ps = new PrintStream(os);

        // Construct and start a Thread to copy data from "is" to "os".
        new Thread() {
            public void run() {
                try {
                    String line;
                    while ((line = iis.readLine()) != null) {
                        results.append(line);
                        results.append("\n");
                    }
                } catch(IOException ex) {
                        results.append("\n");
                        results.append("*** Input or Output error ***\n");
                        results.append(ex.toString());
                        return;
                }
            }
        }.start();
    }
}
```

13.9. Choosing a File with JFileChooser

Problem

You want to allow the user to select a file by name using a traditional windowed file dialog.

Solution

Use a JFileChooser.

Discussion

The JFileChooser dialog provides a fairly standard file chooser. It has elements of both an MS-Windows chooser and a Mac chooser, with more resemblance to the former than the latter. If you want to have control over what files appear, you need to provide one or more FileFilter subclasses. Each FileFilter subclass instance passed into the JFileChooser's addChoosableFileFilter() method becomes a selection in the chooser's "Files of Type:" choice. The default is "All Files (*.*)". Figure 13-8 shows my demo program in action.

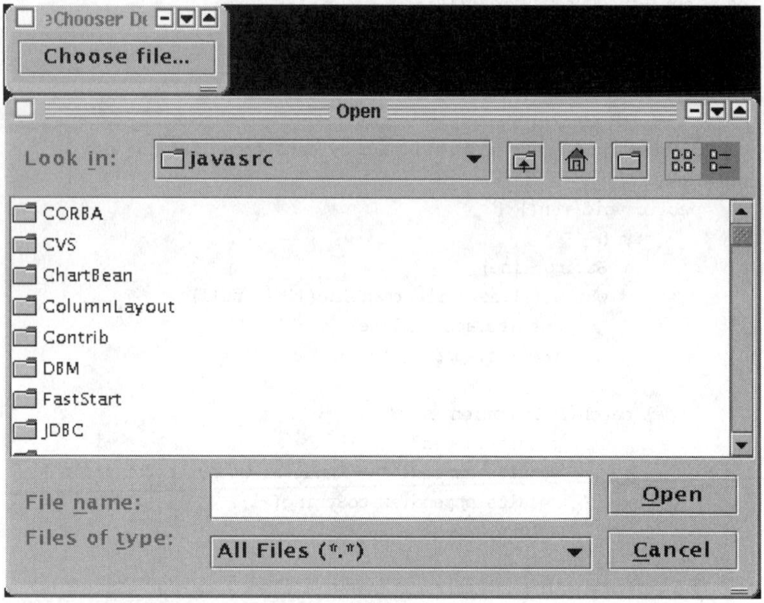

Figure 13-8. JFileChooserDemo in action

Let's look at the code for using the `JFileChooser`:

```java
import com.darwinsys.util.*;

import javax.swing.*;
import java.awt.event.*;
import java.io.*;
import java.util.*;

/** A simple demo of a JFileChooser in action. */
public class JFileChooserDemo extends JPanel {

    /** Constructor */
    public JFileChooserDemo(JFrame f) {
        final JFrame frame = f;
        final JFileChooser chooser = new JFileChooser();
        JFileFilter filter = new JFileFilter();
        filter.addType("java");
        filter.addType("class");
        filter.addType("jar");
        filter.setDescription("Java-related files");
        chooser.addChoosableFileFilter(filter);
```

```
        JButton b = new JButton("Choose file...");
        add(b);
        b.addActionListener(new ActionListener() {
            public void actionPerformed(ActionEvent e) {
            int returnVal = chooser.showOpenDialog(frame);
            if (returnVal == JFileChooser.APPROVE_OPTION) {
                System.out.println("You chose a file named: " +
                    chooser.getSelectedFile().getPath());
            } else {
                System.out.println("You did not choose a file.");
            }
            }
        });
    }


    public static void main(String[] args) {
        JFrame f = new JFrame("JFileChooser Demo");
        f.getContentPane().add(new JFileChooserDemo(f));
        f.pack();
        f.setVisible(true);
        f.addWindowListener(new WindowCloser(f, true));
    }
}
```

In this example, I set up a `FileFilter` for Java files. Note that `FileFilter` exists both in `javax.swing.filechooser` and `java.io` (an older version, not for use here; see Recipe 10.7). The `javax.swing.filechooser.FileFilter` interface has only two methods: `boolean accept(File)` and `String getDescription()`. This is enough for a totally fixed-function file filter: you could hardcode the list of extensions that should be accepted, for example. The following class is similar in spirit to the `ExtensionFileFilter` included in the JDK demo directory; Sun claims that its version will be moved into `javax.swing.filechooser` in a subsequent release of Swing.

```
import java.io.File;
import java.util.*;

/** A simple FileFilter class that works by filename extension,
 * like the one in the JDK demo called ExtentionFilter, which
 * has been announced to be supported in a future Swing release.
 */
class JFileFilter extends javax.swing.filechooser.FileFilter {
    protected String description;
    protected ArrayList exts = new ArrayList();

    public void addType(String s) {
        exts.add(s);
    }
```

```
/** Return true if the given file is accepted by this filter. */
public boolean accept(File f) {
    // Little trick: if you don't do this, only directory names
    // ending in one of the extensions appear in the window.
    if (f.isDirectory()) {
        return true;

    } else if (f.isFile()) {
        Iterator it = exts.iterator();
        while (it.hasNext()) {
            if (f.getName().endsWith((String)it.next()))
                return true;
        }
    }

    // A file that didn't match, or a weirdo (e.g. UNIX device file?).
    return false;
}

/** Set the printable description of this filter. */
public void setDescription(String s) {
    description = s;
}
/** Return the printable description of this filter. */
public String getDescription() {
    return description;
}
}
```

13.10. Choosing a Color

Problem

You want to allow the user to select a color from all the colors available on your computer.

Solution

Use Swing's JColorChooser.

Discussion

OK, so it may be just glitz or a passing fad, but with today's displays, the 13 original AWT colors are too limiting. Swing's JColorChooser lets you choose from zillions of colors. From a program's view, it can be used in three ways:

- Construct it and place it in a panel

- Call its `ConstructDialog()` and get a `JDialog` back

- Call its `showDialog()` and get back the chosen color

We'll use the last method, since it's the simplest and the most likely to be used in a real application. The user has several methods of operating the chooser, too:

Swatches mode
> The user can pick from one of a few hundred color variants.

HSB mode
> This one's my favorite. The user picks one of Hue, Saturation, or Brightness to be nailed down; by adjusting another by slider, there is a huge range of different pixel values to choose from, by clicking (or, more fun, *dragging*) in the central area. See Figure 13-9.

RGB mode
> The user picks Red, Green, and Blue components by sliders.

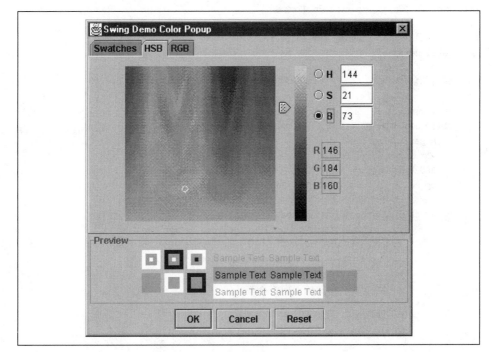

Figure 13-9. JColorChooser: HSB view in action

Example 13-5 contains a short program that makes it happen.

Example 13-5. JColorDemo.java

```java
import com.darwinsys.util.*;

import javax.swing.*;
import java.awt.*;
import java.awt.event.*;

/*
 * Colors - demo of Swing JColorChooser.
 * Swing's JColorChooser can be used in three ways:
 * <UL><LI>Construct it and place it in a panel;
 * <LI>Call its ConstructDialog() and get a JDialog back
 * <LI>Call its showDialog() and get back the chosen color
 * </UL>
 * <P>We use the last method, as it's the simplest, and is how
 * you'd most likely use it in a real application.
 *
 * Originally appeared in the Linux Journal, 1999.
 */
public class JColorDemo extends JFrame
{
    /** A canvas to display the color in. */
    JLabel demo;
    /** The latest chosen Color */
    Color lastChosen;

    /** Constructor - set up the entire GUI for this program */
    public JColorDemo() {
        super("Swing Color Demo");
        Container cp = getContentPane();
        JButton jButton;
        cp.add(BorderLayout.NORTH, jButton = new JButton("Change Color..."));
        jButton.setToolTipText("Click here to see the Color Chooser");
        jButton.addActionListener(new ActionListener() {
            public void actionPerformed(ActionEvent actionEvent)
            {
                Color ch = JColorChooser.showDialog(
                    JColorDemo.this,  // parent
                    "Swing Demo Color Popup",// title
                    getBackground());// default
                if (ch != null)
                    demo.setBackground(ch);
            }
        });
        cp.add(BorderLayout.CENTER, demo =
            new MyLabel("Your One True Color", 200, 100));
        demo.setToolTipText("This is the last color you chose");
        pack();
        addWindowListener(new WindowCloser(this, true));
```

Example 13-5. JColorDemo.java (continued)

```
    }

    /** good old main */
    public static void main(String[] argv)
    {
        new JColorDemo().setVisible(true);
    }
}
```

See Also

This program introduces `setToolTipText()`, a method to set the text for pop-up "tooltips" that appear when you position the mouse pointer over a component and don't do anything for a given time (initially half a second). Tooltips originated with Macintosh Balloon Help, and were refined into ToolTips under Microsoft Windows.* Tooltips are easy to use; the simplest form is shown here. For more documentation, see Chapter 3 of the *Java Swing* book.

13.11. Centering a Main Window

Problem

You want your main window to be centered on the screen.

Solution

First, be aware that some users on some platforms would rather that you didn't do this, as they have existing "placement" schemes. However, at least on MS-Windows, this technique is useful.

Subtract the width and height of the window from the width and height of the screen, divide by two, and go there.

Discussion

The code for this is pretty simple. The part that might take a while to figure out is the `Dimension` of the screen. There is a method `getScreenSize()` in the Toolkit class, and a static method `getDefaultToolkit()`. (The Toolkit class relates to the underlying windowing toolkit; there are several subclasses of it, one for X Windows on Unix, another for Macintosh, etc.) Put these together and you have the `Dimension` you need.

---

* See? I even said something nice about Microsoft. I do believe in credit where credit's due.

Centering a Window is such a common need that I have packaged it in its own little class UtilGUI, just as I did for the WindowCloser class in Recipe 13.6. Here is
the complete source for UtilGUI, which I'll use without comment from now on:

```
package com.darwinsys.util;

import java.awt.*;

/** Utilities for GUI work.
 */
public class UtilGUI {
    /** Centre a Window, Frame, JFrame, Dialog, etc. */
    public static void centre(Window w) {
        // After packing a Frame or Dialog, centre it on the screen.
        Dimension us = w.getSize(),
            them = Toolkit.getDefaultToolkit().getScreenSize();
        int newX = (them.width - us.width) / 2;
        int newY = (them.height- us.height)/ 2;
        w.setLocation(newX, newY);
    }
    /** Center a Window, Frame, JFrame, Dialog, etc.,
     * but do it the American Spelling Way :-)
     */
    public static void center(Window w) {
        UtilGUI.centre(w);
    }
}
```

To use it after the relevant import, you can simply say, for example:

```
myFrame.pack();
UtilGUI.centre(myFrame);
myFrame.setVisible(true);
```

13.12. Changing a Swing Program's Look and Feel

Problem

You want to change the look and feel of an application.

Solution

Use the static UIManager.setLookAndFeel() method. Maybe.

Discussion

If you wish to specify the entire look and feel for a program, set it with the static
UIManager.setLookAndFeel() method; the name you pass in must be the full

name (as a string) of a class that implements a Java look and feel. The details of writing a look and feel class are beyond this book; refer to the book *Java Swing* or the Sun documentation. But using these classes is easy. For example:

```
UIManager.setLookAndFeel("javax.swing.plaf.metal.MetalLookAndFeel");
```

This must appear before you create the GUI of the program, and can throw an exception if the class name is invalid.

People sometimes like to show off the fact that you can change the look and feel on the fly. You call `setLookAndFeel()` as previously, and then call the static `SwingUtilities.updateComponentTree()` for your `JFrame` and all detached trees, such as dialog classes. But before you rush out to do it, please be advised that the official Sun position is that you shouldn't! The official *Java Look and Feel Design Guideline* book says, on page 23 (first edition):

> Because there is far more to the design of an application than the look and feel of components, it is unwise to give end users the ability to swap look and feel while [running] your application. Switching look and feel designs in this way only swaps the look and feel designs from one platform to another. The layout and vocabulary used are platform-specific and do not change. For instance, swapping look and feel designs does not change the titles of the menus.

The book does recommend that you let users specify an alternate look and feel, presumably in your properties file, at program startup time. Even so, the capability to switch while an application is running is too tempting to ignore; even Sun's own Swing Demonstration (included with the Java SDK) offers a menu item to change its look and feel. Figure 13-10 is my nice little program in the Java style; see Example 13-6 for the source code.

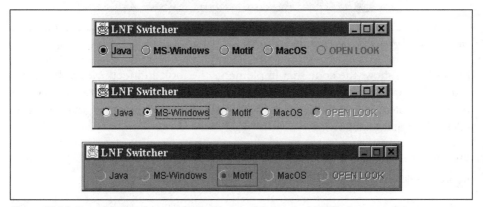

Figure 13-10. Java, MS-Windows, and Motif look and feel under MS-Windows

Figure 13-11 shows what happens when you request a look and feel that is unavailable on the current platform.

UI Failure ☒

ⓘ setLookAndFeel didn't work: java.lang.ClassNotFoundException: com.sun.java.swing.plaf.mac.MacLookAndFeel

OK

Figure 13-11. Look and feel request refused on MS-Windows

There's a bit of a cheat here: I had to resize it to get the disabled OPEN LOOK radio button to appear, due to what I think is a bug in JDK 1.2. If I try the MacOS look and feel under MS-Windows, I get the error dialog shown in Figure 13-11.

The OPEN LOOK design alluded to in the code is, well, not written yet. Vaporware. That's why it's grayed out.

Under MacOS X, the default look and feel is, of course, the MacOS X look and feel. You can also select the Java or Motif look, but not the MS-Windows look. See Figure 13-12.

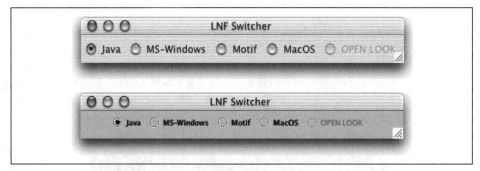

Figure 13-12. Look and feel switcher under MacOS X

Example 13-6 shows the code that implements the look and feel *switcher*. It's pretty straightforward based on what we've seen already. The only neat trick is that I've set the selected button back to what it was if the look and feel that the user selected is not available.

Example 13-6. LNFSwitcher.java

```
import com.darwinsys.util.*;

import java.awt.*;
import java.awt.event.*;
import java.io.*;
import javax.swing.*;
```

Example 13-6. LNFSwitcher.java (continued)

```java
import javax.swing.plaf.*;
import javax.swing.plaf.metal.*;

/**
 * A Look-and-feel switcher.
 */
public class LNFSwitcher {
    /** The frame. */
    protected JFrame theFrame;
    /** Its content pane */
    protected Container cp;

    /** Start with the Java look-and-feel, if possible */
    final static String PREFERREDLOOKANDFEELNAME =
        "javax.swing.plaf.metal.MetalLookAndFeel";
    protected String curLF = PREFERREDLOOKANDFEELNAME;
    protected JRadioButton previousButton;

    /** Construct a program... */
    public LNFSwitcher() {
        super();
        theFrame = new JFrame("LNF Switcher");
        theFrame.addWindowListener(new WindowCloser(theFrame, true));
        cp = theFrame.getContentPane();
        cp.setLayout(new FlowLayout());

        ButtonGroup bg = new ButtonGroup();

        JRadioButton bJava = new JRadioButton("Java");
        bJava.addActionListener(new LNFSetter(
            "javax.swing.plaf.metal.MetalLookAndFeel", bJava));
        bg.add(bJava);
        cp.add(bJava);

        JRadioButton bMSW  = new JRadioButton("MS-Windows");
        bMSW.addActionListener(new LNFSetter(
            "com.sun.java.swing.plaf.windows.WindowsLookAndFeel", bMSW));
        bg.add(bMSW);
        cp.add(bMSW);

        JRadioButton bMotif = new JRadioButton("Motif");
        bMotif.addActionListener(new LNFSetter(
            "com.sun.java.swing.plaf.motif.MotifLookAndFeel", bMotif));
        bg.add(bMotif);
        cp.add(bMotif);

        JRadioButton bMac = new JRadioButton("MacOS");
        bMac.addActionListener(new LNFSetter(
```

Example 13-6. LNFSwitcher.java (continued)

```
            "com.sun.java.swing.plaf.mac.MacLookAndFeel", bMac));
    bg.add(bMac);
    cp.add(bMac);

    // Following is a **hypothetical** addition!
    JRadioButton bOL = new JRadioButton("OPEN LOOK");
    bOL.addActionListener(new LNFSetter(
        "com.darwinsys.openlook.OpenLookAndFeel", bOL));
    bOL.setEnabled(false);// since it IS hypothetical
    bg.add(bOL);
    cp.add(bOL);

    // We "know" that the Java Look-and-feel is the default.
    previousButton = bJava;
    bJava.setSelected(true);

    theFrame.pack();
    theFrame.setVisible(true);
}

/* Class to set the Look and Feel on a frame */
class LNFSetter implements ActionListener {
    String theLNFName;
    JRadioButton thisButton;

    /** Called to setup for button handling */
    LNFSetter(String lnfName, JRadioButton me) {
        theLNFName = lnfName;
        thisButton = me;
    }

    /** Called when the button actually gets pressed. */
    public void actionPerformed(ActionEvent e) {
        try {
            UIManager.setLookAndFeel(theLNFName);
            SwingUtilities.updateComponentTreeUI(theFrame);
        } catch (Exception evt) {
            JOptionPane.showMessageDialog(null,
                "setLookAndFeel didn't work: " + evt,
                "UI Failure", JOptionPane.INFORMATION_MESSAGE);
            previousButton.setSelected(true);// reset the GUI to agree
        }
        previousButton = thisButton;
    }
}
```

Example 13-6. LNFSwitcher.java (continued)

```
public static void main(String[] argv) {
    new LNFSwitcher();
}
}
```

13.13. Program: Custom Font Chooser

Problem

You want to allow the user to select a font, but standard Java doesn't yet include a Font Chooser dialog.

Solution

Use my FontChooser dialog class.

Discussion

As we saw in Recipe 12.3, you can manually select a font by calling the `java.awt.Font` class constructor, passing in the name of the font, the type you want (plain, bold, italic, or bold+italic), and the point size:

```
Font f = new Font("Helvetica", Font.BOLD, 14);
setfont(f);
```

But this is not very flexible for interactive applications. You normally want the user to be able to choose fonts with the same ease as using a File Chooser dialog. Until the Java API catches up with this, you are more than welcome to use the Font Chooser that I wrote when faced with a similar need.

The source code is shown in Example 13-7; it ends, as many of my classes do, with a short main method that is both a test case and an example of using the class in action. The display is shown in Figure 13-13.

Example 13-7. FontChooser.java

```
import com.darwinsys.util.*;

import java.awt.*;
import java.awt.event.*;
import javax.swing.*;

/** A font selection dialog. AWT version.
 * <p>Note: can take a LONG time to start up on systems
 * with (literally) hundreds of fonts.
 */
```

Example 13-7. FontChooser.java (continued)

```
public class FontChooser extends Dialog {
    /** The font the user has chosen */
    protected Font resultFont;
    /** The resulting font name */
    protected String resultName;
    /** The resulting font size */
    protected int resultSize;
    /** The resulting boldness */
    protected boolean isBold;
    /** The resulting italicness */
    protected boolean isItalic;

    /** The list of Fonts */
    protected String fontList[];
    /** The file name chooser */
    protected List fNameChoice;
    /** The file size chooser */
    protected List fSizeChoice;
    /** The bold and italic choosers */
    Checkbox bold, italic;
    /** The list of font sizes */
    protected String fontSizes[] = {
        "8", "10", "11", "12", "14", "16", "18", "20", "24",
        "30", "36", "40", "48", "60", "72"
        };
    /** The display area. Use a JLabel as the AWT label doesn't always
     * honor setFont() in a timely fashion :-)
     */
    protected JLabel previewArea;

    /** Construct a FontChooser -- Sets title and gets
     * array of fonts on the system. Builds a GUI to let
     * the user choose one font at one size.
     */
    public FontChooser(Frame f) {
        super(f, "Font Chooser", true);

        Container cp = this;// or getContentPane() in Swing

        Panel top = new Panel();
        top.setLayout(new FlowLayout());

        fNameChoice = new List(8);
        top.add(fNameChoice);

        Toolkit toolkit = Toolkit.getDefaultToolkit();
        // For JDK 1.1: returns about 10 names (Serif, SansSerif, etc.)
```

Example 13-7. FontChooser.java (continued)

```
// fontList = toolkit.getFontList();
// For JDK 1.2: a much longer list; most of the names that come
// with your OS (e.g., Arial), plus the Sun/Java ones (Lucida,
// Lucida Bright, Lucida Sans...)
fontList = GraphicsEnvironment.getLocalGraphicsEnvironment().
    getAvailableFontFamilyNames();

for (int i=0; i<fontList.length; i++)
    fNameChoice.add(fontList[i]);
fNameChoice.select(0);

fSizeChoice = new List(8);
top.add(fSizeChoice);

for (int i=0; i<fontSizes.length; i++)
    fSizeChoice.add(fontSizes[i]);
fSizeChoice.select(5);

cp.add(BorderLayout.NORTH, top);

Panel attrs = new Panel();
top.add(attrs);
attrs.setLayout(new GridLayout(0,1));
attrs.add(bold  =new Checkbox("Bold", false));
attrs.add(italic=new Checkbox("Italic", false));

previewArea = new JLabel("Qwerty Yuiop", JLabel.CENTER);
previewArea.setSize(200, 50);
cp.add(BorderLayout.CENTER, previewArea);

Panel bot = new Panel();

Button okButton = new Button("Apply");
bot.add(okButton);
okButton.addActionListener(new ActionListener() {
    public void actionPerformed(ActionEvent e) {
        previewFont();
        dispose();
        setVisible(false);
    }
});

Button pvButton = new Button("Preview");
bot.add(pvButton);
pvButton.addActionListener(new ActionListener() {
    public void actionPerformed(ActionEvent e) {
```

Example 13-7. FontChooser.java (continued)

```java
                previewFont();
            }
        });

        Button canButton = new Button("Cancel");
        bot.add(canButton);
        canButton.addActionListener(new ActionListener() {
            public void actionPerformed(ActionEvent e) {
                // Set all values to null. Better: restore previous.
                resultFont = null;
                resultName = null;
                resultSize = 0;
                isBold = false;
                isItalic = false;

                dispose();
                setVisible(false);
            }
        });

        cp.add(BorderLayout.SOUTH, bot);

        previewFont();    // ensure view is up to date!

        pack();
        setLocation(100, 100);
    }

    /** Called from the action handlers to get the font info,
     * build a font, and set it.
     */
    protected void previewFont() {
        resultName = fNameChoice.getSelectedItem();
        String resultSizeName = fSizeChoice.getSelectedItem();
        int resultSize = Integer.parseInt(resultSizeName);
        isBold = bold.getState();
        isItalic = italic.getState();
        int attrs = Font.PLAIN;
        if (isBold) attrs = Font.BOLD;
        if (isItalic) attrs |= Font.ITALIC;
        resultFont = new Font(resultName, attrs, resultSize);
        // System.out.println("resultName = " + resultName + "; " +
        //         "resultFont = " + resultFont);
        previewArea.setFont(resultFont);
        pack();            // ensure Dialog is big enough.
    }
```

Example 13-7. FontChooser.java (continued)

```java
    /** Retrieve the selected font name. */
    public String getSelectedName() {
        return resultName;
    }
    /** Retrieve the selected size */
    public int getSelectedSize() {
        return resultSize;
    }

    /** Retrieve the selected font, or null */
    public Font getSelectedFont() {
        return resultFont;
    }

    /** Simple main program to start it running */
    public static void main(String[] args) {
        final JFrame f = new JFrame("Dummy");
        final FontChooser fc = new FontChooser(f);
        final Container cp = f.getContentPane();
        cp.setLayout(new GridLayout(0, 1));// one vertical column

        JButton theButton = new JButton("Change font");
        cp.add(theButton);

        final JLabel theLabel = new JLabel("Java is great!");
        cp.add(theLabel);

        // Now that theButton and theLabel are ready, make the action listener
        theButton.addActionListener(new ActionListener() {
            public void actionPerformed(ActionEvent e) {
                fc.setVisible(true);
                Font myNewFont = fc.getSelectedFont();
                System.out.println("You chose " + myNewFont);
                theLabel.setFont(myNewFont);
                f.pack();// again
                fc.dispose();
            }
        });

        f.pack();
        f.setVisible(true);
        f.addWindowListener(new WindowCloser(f, true));
    }
}
```

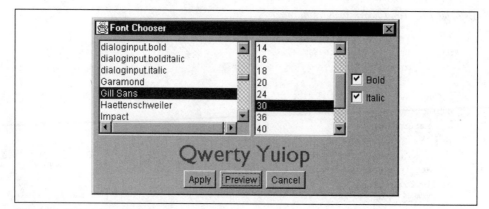

Figure 13-13. Font Chooser in action

13.14. Program: Custom Layout Manager

Problem

None of the standard layout managers does quite what you need.

Solution

Roll your own. All you need to do is implement the methods of the `java.awt.LayoutManager` interface.

Discussion

While many people are intimidated by the thought of writing their own layout manager, it beats the alternative of using only "the big five" layouts (`BorderLayout`, `CondLayout`, `FlowLayout`, `GridBagLayout`, and `GridLayout`). `BorderLayout` isn't quite flexible enough, and `GridBaglayout` is too complex for many applications. Suppose, for instance, that you wanted to lay out an arbitrary number of components in a circle. In a typical X Windows or MS-Windows application, you would write the geometry calculations within the code for creating the components to be drawn. This would work, but the code for the geometry calculations would be unavailable to anybody who needed it later. The `LayoutManager` interface is another great example of how the Java API's design promotes code reuse: if you write the geometry calculations as a layout manager, then anybody needing this type of layout could simply instantiate your `CircleLayout` class to get circular layouts.

As another example, consider the layout shown in Figure 13-14, where the labels column and the textfield column have different widths. Using the big five layouts, there's no good way to get this and still ensure that the columns line up and that you have control over the relative widths. Suppose you wanted the label field to take up 40% of the panel and the entry field to take up 60%. I'll implement a simple layout manager here, both to show you how easy it is and to give you a useful class for making panels like the one shown.

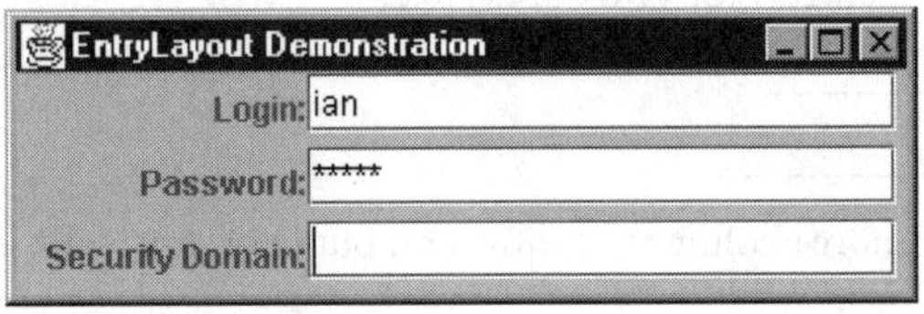

Figure 13-14. EntryLayout in action

Here are the methods for the `LayoutManager` interface:

Method name	Description
`preferredLayoutSize()`	Like `getPreferredSize()` for a component: the "best" size for the container
`minimumLayoutSize()`	Same, but for the minimum workable size
`layoutContainer()`	Perform the layout calculations, and resize and reposition all the components at the current size of the container
`addLayoutComponent()`	Associate a constraint with a given component (you normally store these mappings in a `java.util.HashMap()`)
`removeLayoutComponent()`	Remove a component from the `HashMap`

If you don't need `Constraint` objects (like `BorderLayout.NORTH` or a `GridBagConstraint` object), you can ignore the last two methods. Well, you can't ignore them completely. Since this is an interface, you must implement them. But they can be as simple as `{}`, that is, a null-bodied method.

That leaves only three serious methods. The first, `preferredLayoutSize()`, will normally loop through all the components—either in the `HashMap` if using constraints, or in array returned by the container's `getComponents()` method—asking each for its preferred size and adding them up, while partly doing the layout calculations. And `minimumLayoutSize()` is the same, for the smallest possible layout that will work. It may be possible for these methods to delegate either to a common submethod or to invoke `layoutContainer()`, depending upon how the given layout policy works.

Finally, the most important method is `layoutContainer()`. This method needs to examine all the components and decide where to put them and how big to make each one. Having made the decision, it can use setBounds() to set each one's position and size.

Other than a bit of error checking, that's all that's involved. Here's an example, EntryLayout, that implements the multi-column layout shown in Figure 13-14. Quoting its Javadoc documentation:

> A simple layout manager, for Entry areas like:
>
> Login: _____
>
> Password: _____
>
> Basically two (or more) columns of different, but constant, widths.
>
> Construct instances by passing an array of the column width percentages (as doubles, fractions from 0.1 to 0.9, so 40%, 60% would be {0.4, 0.6}). The length of this array uniquely determines the number of columns. Columns are forced to be the relevant widths. As with GridLayout, the number of items added must be an even multiple of the number of columns. If not, exceptions may be thrown!

First, let's look at the program that uses this layout to produce Figure 13-14. This program simply creates a JFrame, gets the contentPane container, and sets its layout to an instance of EntryLayout, passing an array of two doubles representing the relative widths (decimal fractions, not percentages) into the EntryLayout constructor. Then we add an even number of components, and call pack()—which will in turn call our preferredLayoutSize()—and setVisible(true).

```
import java.awt.*;
import java.awt.event.*;
import javax.swing.*;

/** Testbed for EntryLayout layout manager.
 */
public class EntryLayoutTest {

    /** "main program" method - construct and show */
    public static void main(String[] av) {
        final JFrame f = new JFrame("EntryLayout Demonstration");
        Container cp = f.getContentPane();
        double widths[] = { .33, .66 };
        cp.setLayout(new EntryLayout(widths));
        cp.add(new JLabel("Login:", SwingConstants.RIGHT));
        cp.add(new JTextField(10));
        cp.add(new JLabel("Password:", SwingConstants.RIGHT));
        cp.add(new JPasswordField(20));
        cp.add(new JLabel("Security Domain:", SwingConstants.RIGHT));
        cp.add(new JTextField(20));
        // cp.add(new JLabel("Monkey wrench in works"));
        f.pack();
```

```
        f.addWindowListener(new WindowCloser(f, true));
        f.setLocation(200, 200);
        f.setVisible(true);
    }
}
```

Nothing complicated about it. The last JLabel ("Monkey wrench in works") is commented out since, as noted, the LayoutManager throws an exception if the number of components is not evenly divisible by the number of columns. It was put in during testing and then commented out, but was left in place for further consideration.

Finally, let's look at the code for the layout manager itself, shown in Example 13-8. After some constants and fields and two constructors, the methods are listed in about the same order as the discussion earlier in this recipe; the dummy add/ remove component methods, then the preferredSize() and minimumLayoutSize() methods (which delegate to computeLayoutSize), and, finally, layoutContainer, which does the actual laying out of the components within the container. As you can see, the entire EntryLayout layout manager class is only about 140 lines, including a lot of comments.

Example 13-8. EntryLayout.java

```java
// package com.darwinsys.entrylayout;

import java.awt.*;
import java.util.*;

/** A simple layout manager, for Entry areas like:
 * <PRE>
 *    Login: _____
 * Password: _____
 * </PRE>
 * ...
 */
public class EntryLayout implements LayoutManager {
    /** The array of widths, as decimal fractions (0.4 == 40%, etc.). */
    protected final double[] widthPercentages;

    /** The number of columns. */
    protected final int COLUMNS;

    /** The default padding */
    protected final static int HPAD = 5, VPAD = 5;
    /** The actual padding */
    protected final int hpad, vpad;
```

Example 13-8. EntryLayout.java (continued)

```java
/** True if the list of widths was valid. */
protected boolean validWidths = false;

/** Construct an EntryLayout with widths and padding specified.
 * @param widthsArray of doubles specifying column widths.
 * @param h  Horizontal padding between items
 * @param v  Vertical padding between items
 */
public EntryLayout(double[] widths, int h, int v) {
    COLUMNS = widths.length;
    widthPercentages = new double[COLUMNS];
    for (int i=0; i<widths.length; i++) {
        if (widths[i] >= 1.0)
            throw new IllegalArgumentException(
                "EntryLayout: widths must be fractions < 1");
        widthPercentages[i] = widths[i];
    }
    validWidths = true;
    hpad = h;
    vpad = v;
}
/** Construct an EntryLayout with widths and with default padding amounts.
 * @param widthsArray of doubles specifying column widths.
 */
public EntryLayout(double[] widths) {
    this(widths, HPAD, VPAD);
}


/** Adds the specified component with the specified constraint
 * to the layout; required by LayoutManager but not used.
 */
public void addLayoutComponent(String name, Component comp) {
    // nothing to do
}


/** Removes the specified component from the layout;
 * required by LayoutManager, but does nothing.
 */
public void removeLayoutComponent(Component comp)  {
    // nothing to do
}


/** Calculates the preferred size dimensions for the specified panel
 * given the components in the specified parent container. */
public Dimension preferredLayoutSize(Container parent)  {
    // System.out.println("preferredLayoutSize");
    return computelayoutSize(parent, hpad, vpad);
}
```

Example 13-8. EntryLayout.java (continued)

```java
/** Find the minimum Dimension for the
 * specified container given the components therein.
 */
public Dimension minimumLayoutSize(Container parent)   {
    // System.out.println("minimumLayoutSize");
    return computelayoutSize(parent, 0, 0);
}

/** The width of each column, as found by computLayoutSize(). */
int[] widths;
/** The height of each row, as found by computLayoutSize(). */
int[] heights;

/** Compute the size of the whole mess. Serves as the guts of
 * preferredLayoutSize() and minimumLayoutSize().
 */
protected Dimension computelayoutSize(Container parent, int hpad, int vpad) {
    if (!validWidths)
        return null;
    Component[] components = parent.getComponents();
    Dimension contSize = parent.getSize();
    int preferredWidth = 0, preferredHeight = 0;
    widths = new int[COLUMNS];
    heights = new int[components.length / COLUMNS];
    // System.out.println("Grid: " + widths.length + ", " + heights.length);

    int i;
    // Pass One: Compute largest widths and heights.
    for (i=0; i<components.length; i++) {
        int row = i / widthPercentages.length;
        int col = i % widthPercentages.length;
        Component c = components[i];
        Dimension d = c.getPreferredSize();
        widths[col] = Math.max(widths[col], d.width);
        heights[row] = Math.max(heights[row], d.height);
    }

    // Pass two: aggregate them.
    for (i=0; i<widths.length; i++)
        preferredWidth += widths[i] + hpad;
    for (i=0; i<heights.length; i++)
        preferredHeight += heights[i] + vpad;

    // Finally, pass the sums back as the actual size.
    return new Dimension(preferredWidth, preferredHeight);
}
```

Example 13-8. EntryLayout.java (continued)

```java
/** Lays out the container in the specified panel. */
public void layoutContainer(Container parent) {
    // System.out.println("layoutContainer:");
    if (!validWidths)
        return;
    Component[] components = parent.getComponents();
    Dimension contSize = parent.getSize();
    for (int i=0; i<components.length; i++) {
        int row = i / COLUMNS;
        int col = i % COLUMNS;
        Component c = components[i];
        Dimension d = c.getPreferredSize();
        int colWidth = (int)(contSize.width * widthPercentages[col]);
        Rectangle r = new Rectangle(
            col == 0 ? 0 :
            hpad * (col-1) + (int)(contSize.width * widthPercentages[col-1]),
            vpad * (row) + (row * heights[row]) + (heights[row]-d.height),
            colWidth, d.height);
        // System.out.println(c.getClass() + "-->" + r);
        c.setBounds(r);
    }
}

}
```

See Also

As mentioned in the Introduction, there are a number of good books on window programming with Java. These discuss the many Swing components not covered here, such as JTable, JScrollPane, JList, and JTree, and many more. My JabaDex application contains examples of many of these, and some are used in later recipes in this book; for example, JTree is discussed in Recipe 19.9.

14

Internationalization and Localization

14.0. Introduction

"All the world's a stage," wrote William Shakespeare. But not all the players upon it speak the great Bard's native tongue. To be usable on a global scale, your software needs to communicate in many different languages. The menu labels, button strings, dialog messages, title bar titles, and even command-line error messages must be settable to the user's choice of language. This is the topic of *internationalization* and *localization*. Because these words take a long time to say and write, they are often abbreviated by their first and last letters and the count of omitted letters, that is, I18N and L10N.*

Java provides a `Locale` class to discover/control the internationalization settings. A default `Locale` is inherited from operating system runtime settings when Java starts up, and can be used most of the time!

See also the relatively new book *Java Internationalization*, by Andy Deitsch and David Czarnecki (O'Reilly).

14.1. Creating a Button with I18N Resources

Problem

You want your program to take "sensitivity lessons" so it can communicate well internationally.

---

* Sometimes written L9N by those who can't count, or who think that L10N that looks too much like "lion."

Ian's Basic Steps: Internationalization

Internationalization and localization consist of:

- Sensitivity training (Internationalization or I18N): making your software sensitive to these issues

- Language lessons (Localization or L10N): writing configuration files for each language

- Culture lessons (optional): customizing the presentation of numbers, fractions, dates, and message-formatting

---

Solution

Your program must obtain all control and message strings via the internationalization software. Here's how:

1. Get a `ResourceBundle`.

```
ResourceBundle b = ResourceBundle.getBundle("Menus");
```

I'll talk about `ResourceBundle` in Recipe 14.6, but briefly, a `ResourceBundle` represents a collection of name-value pairs (resources). The names are names you assign to each GUI control or other user interface text, and the values are the text to assign to each control in a given language.

2. Use this `ResourceBundle` to fetch the localized version of each control name.

Old way:

```
somePanel.add(new JButton("Exit"));
```

New way:

```
rb = ResourceBundle.getBundle("Widgets");
try { label = rb.getString("exit.label"); }
catch (MissingResourceException e) { label="Exit"; } // fallback
somePanel.add(new JButton(label));
```

This is quite a bit of code for one button, but distributed over all the widgets (buttons, menus, etc.) in a program, it can be as little as one line with the use of *convenience routines*, which I'll show in Recipe 14.3.

What happens at runtime?

The default locale is used, since we didn't specify one. The default locale is platform-dependent:

- Unix/POSIX: LANG environment variable (per user)
- Windows 95: Start->Control Panel->Regional Settings
- Others: see platform documentation

ResourceBundle.getBundle() locates a file with the named resource bundle name (Menus in the previous example), plus an underscore and the locale name (if any locale is set), plus another underscore and the locale variation (if any variation is set), plus the extension *.properties*. If a variation is set but the file can't be found, it falls back to just the country code. If that can't be found, it falls back to the original default. Table 14-1 shows some examples for various locales.

Table 14-1. Property filenames for different locales

Locale	Filename
Default locale	Menus.Properties
Swedish	Menus_sv.properties
Spanish	Menus_es.properties
French	Menus_fr.properties
French-Canadian	Menus_fr_CA.properties

Locale names are two-letter ISO language codes (lowercase); locale variations are two-letter ISO country codes (uppercase)

Setting the locale

On Windows, go into the Control Panel. Changing this setting entails a reboot, so exit any editor windows.

On Unix, set your LANG environment variable. For example, a Korn shell user in Mexico might have this line in his or her *.profile*:

```
export LANG=es_MX
```

On either system, for testing a different locale, you need only define the locale in the System Properties at runtime using the command-line option –D, as in:

```
java -Duser.language=es Browser
```

to run the program named Browser in the Spanish locale.

14.2. Listing Available Locales

Problem

You want to see what locales are available.

Solution

Call Locale.getAvailableLocales().

Discussion

A typical runtime may have dozens of locales available. The program ListLocales uses the method getAvailableLocales() and prints the list:

```
// File ListLocales.java
Locale[] list = Locale.getAvailableLocales();
        for (int i=0; i<list.length; i++)
            System.out.println(list[i]);
    }
}
```

The list is far too long to show here, as you can judge by the first few entries:

```
> java ListLocales
en
en_US
ar
ar_AE
ar_BH
ar_DZ
ar_EG
ar_IQ
ar_JO
ar_KW
ar_LB
ar_LY
ar_MA
ar_OM
ar_QA
ar_SA
ar_SD
ar_SY
ar_TN
ar_YE
be
be_BY
```

On my system the complete list has an even dozen dozen (144) locales, as listed by the command *java ListLocales | wc –l*.

14.3. Creating a Menu with I18N Resources

Problem

You want to internationalize an entire Menu.

Solution

Get the `Menu`'s label, and each `MenuItem`'s label, from a `ResourceBundle`.

Discussion

Fetching a single menu item is the same as fetching a button:

```
rb = getResourceBundle("Widgets");
try { label = rb.getString("exitMenu.label"); }
catch (MissingResourceException e) { label="Exit"; } // fallback
someMenu.add(new JMenuItem(label));
```

This is a lot of code, so we typically consolidate it in *convenience routines* (see Recipe 14.4). Here is sample code, using our convenience routines:

```
JMenu fm = mkMenu(rb, "file");
fm.add(mkMenuItem(rb, "file", "open"));
fm.add(mkMenuItem(rb, "file", "new"));
fm.add(mkMenuItem(rb, "file", "save"));
fm.add(mkMenuItem(rb, "file", "exit"));
mb.add(fm);
Menu um = mkMenu(rb, "edit");
um.add(mkMenuItem(rb, "edit", "copy"));
um.add(mkMenuItem(rb, "edit", "paste"));
mb.add(um);
```

14.4. Writing Internationalization Convenience Routines

Problem

You want convenience.

Solution

I've got it.

Discussion

Convenience routines are mini-implementations that can be more convenient and effective than the general-purpose routines. Here I present the convenience routines to create buttons, menus, etc. First, a simple one, `mkMenu()`:

```
/** Convenience routine to make up a Menu with its name L10N'd */
Menu mkMenu(ResourceBundle b, String menuName) {
    String label;
```

```
try { label = b.getString(menuName+".label"); }
catch (MissingResourceException e) { label=menuName; }
return new Menu(label);
}
```

There are many such routines that you might need; I have consolidated several of them into my class *I18N.java*, which is part of the com.darwinsys.util package. All methods are static, and can be used without having to instantiate an I18N object because they do not maintain any state across calls. The method mkButton() creates and returns a localized Button, and so on. The method mkDialog is slightly misnamed, since the JOptionPane method showMessageDialog() doesn't create and return a Dialog object, but it seemed more consistent to write it as shown here:

```java
package com.darwinsys.util;

import java.util.*;
import javax.swing.*;

/** Set of convenience routines for internationalized code.
 * All convenience methods are static, for ease of use.
 */
public class I18N {

    /** Convenience routine to make a JButton */
    public static JButton mkButton(ResourceBundle b, String name) {
        String label;
        try { label = b.getString(name+".label"); }
        catch (MissingResourceException e) { label=name; }
        return new JButton(label);
    }

    /** Convenience routine to make a JMenu */
    public static JMenu mkMenu(ResourceBundle b, String name) {
        String menuLabel;
        try { menuLabel = b.getString(name+".label"); }
        catch (MissingResourceException e) { menuLabel=name; }
        return new JMenu(menuLabel);
    }

    /** Convenience routine to make a JMenuItem */
    public static JMenuItem mkMenuItem(ResourceBundle b,
            String menu, String name) {

        String miLabel;
        try { miLabel = b.getString(menu + "." + name + ".label"); }
        catch (MissingResourceException e) { miLabel=name; }
        String key = null;
        try { key = b.getString(menu + "." + name + ".key"); }
        catch (MissingResourceException e) { key=null; }
```

```
        if (key == null)
            return new JMenuItem(miLabel);
        else
            return new JMenuItem(miLabel, key.charAt(0));
}

/** Show a JOptionPane message dialog */
public static void mkDialog(ResourceBundle b,JFrame parent,
    String dialogTag, String titleTag, int messageType) {
        JOptionPane.showMessageDialog(
            parent,
            getString(b, dialogTag, "DIALOG TEXT MISSING " + dialogTag),
            getString(b, titleTag, "DIALOG TITLE MISSING" + titleTag),
            messageType);
}

/** Just get a String (for dialogs, labels, etc.) */
public static String getString(ResourceBundle b, String name, String dflt) {
    String result;
    try {
        result = b.getString(name);
    } catch (MissingResourceException e) {
        result = dflt;
    }
    return result;
}
}
}
```

14.5. Creating a Dialog with I18N Resources

Problem

You want to internationalize a dialog.

Solution

Use a ResourceBundle.

Discussion

This is similar to the use of ResourceBundle in the previous recipes, and shows
the code for an internationalized version of the JOptionDemo program from
Recipe 13.7.

```
package com.darwinsys.util;

import java.awt.*;
import java.awt.event.*;
```

```java
import javax.swing.*;
import java.util.*;

/**
 * I18N'd JOptionPane
 */
public class JOptionDemo extends JFrame {

    ResourceBundle rb;

    // Constructor
    JOptionDemo(String s) {
        super(s);

        Container cp = getContentPane();
        cp.setLayout(new FlowLayout());

        rb = ResourceBundle.getBundle("Widgets");

        JButton b = I18N.mkButton(rb, "getButton");
        b.addActionListener(new ActionListener() {
            public void actionPerformed(ActionEvent e) {
                JOptionPane.showMessageDialog(
                    JOptionDemo.this,
                    rb.getString("dialog1.text"),
                    rb.getString("dialog1.title"),
                    JOptionPane.INFORMATION_MESSAGE);
            }
        });
        cp.add(b);

        b = I18N.mkButton(rb, "goodbye");
        b.addActionListener(new ActionListener() {
            public void actionPerformed(ActionEvent e) {
                System.exit(0);
            }
        });
        cp.add(b);

        // the main window
        setSize(200, 150);
        pack();
    }

    public static void main(String[] arg) {
        JOptionDemo x = new JOptionDemo("Testing 1 2 3...");
        x.setVisible(true);
    }
}
```

14.6. Creating a Resource Bundle

Problem

You need to create a resource bundle for use by I18N.

Solution

A resource bundle is just a collection of names and values. You can write a `java.util.ResourceBundle` subclass, but it is easier to create them as textual `Properties` files (see Recipe 7.7), which you then load with `ResourceBundle.getBundle()`. The files can be created using any text editor. Leaving it in a text file format also allows user customization; a user whose language is not provided for, or who wishes to change the wording somewhat due to local variations in dialect, will have no trouble editing the file.

Note that the resource bundle text file should not have the same name as any of your Java classes. The reason is that the `ResourceBundle` constructs a class dynamically, with the same name as the resource files. You can confirm this by running *java –verbose* on any of the programs that use the I18N class from this chapter.

Discussion

Here is a sample for a simple browser (see the `MenuIntl` program in Recipe 14.11):

```
# Default Menu properties
# The File Menu
file.label=File Menu
file.new.label=New File
file.new.key=N
```

Creating the default properties file will usually not be a problem, but creating properties files for other languages might. Unless you are a large multinational corporation, you will probably not have the resources (pardon the pun) to create resource files in-house. If you are shipping commercial software, you need to identify your target markets and understand which of these are most sensitive to wanting menus and the like in their own languages. Then, hire a professional translation service that has expertise in the required languages to prepare the files. Test them well before you ship, as you would any other part of your software.

If you need special characters, multiline text, or other complex entry, remember that a `ResourceBundle` is also a `Properties` file.

As an alternate approach, the next recipe describes a program that automates some of the work of isolating strings, creating resource files, and translating them to other languages.

14.7. JILTing Your Code

Nothing to do with jilting your lover, JILT is Sun's Java Internationalization and Localization Toolkit, Version 2.0. JILTing your code means processing it with JILT, which facilitates I18N and L10N'ing the Java classes. JILT has four GUI-based tools, which can be used independently, started from a GUI front-end called JILKIT. Figure 14-1 shows JILT in action.

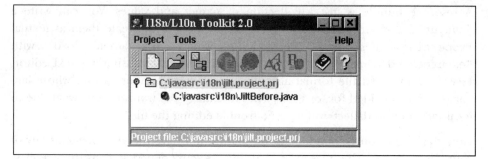

Figure 14-1. JILT in action

The tools are listed in Table 14-2.

Table 14-2. JILT programs

Tool	Function
I18N Verifier	Tests program for international use and suggests improvements.
Message Tool	Finds and allows you to edit hardcoded or inconsistent messages.
Translator	Translates messages in a resource bundle file into a given locale/language.
Resource Tool	Merges multiple resource files into a new resource bundle. Can also find differences between resource files.

It's worth noting that the time to learn these tools may overshadow their benefits on small projects, but on large projects will likely prove worthwhile.

Version 2 of the Translator ships with a Chinese dictionary, but you can provide your own dictionaries as well.

The Java Internationalization and Localization Toolkit can be downloaded for free from Sun's Java page, *http://java.sun.com/products/*.

14.8. Using a Particular Locale

Problem

You want to use a locale other than the default in a particular operation.

Solution

Use `Locale.getInstance(Locale)`.

Discussion

Classes that provide formatting services, such as `DateFormat` and `NumberFormat`, provide an overloaded `getInstance()` method that can be called either with no arguments or with a `Locale` argument.

To use these, you can use one of the predefined locale variables provided by the `Locale` class, or you can construct your own `Locale` object giving a language code and a country code:

```
Locale locale1 = Locale.FRANCE;// predefined
Locale locale2 = new Locale("en", "UK");// English, UK version
```

Either of these can be used to format a date or a number, as shown in class `UseLocales`:

```
import java.text.*;
import java.util.*;

/** Use some locales
 * choices or -Duser.lang= or -Duser.region=.
 */
public class UseLocales {
    public static void main(String[] args) {

        Locale frLocale = Locale.FRANCE;// predefined
        Locale ukLocale = new Locale("en", "UK");// English, UK version

        DateFormat defaultDateFormatter = DateFormat.getDateInstance(
            DateFormat.MEDIUM);
        DateFormat frDateFormatter = DateFormat.getDateInstance(
            DateFormat.MEDIUM, frLocale);
        DateFormat ukDateFormatter = DateFormat.getDateInstance(
            DateFormat.MEDIUM, ukLocale);

        Date now = new Date();
        System.out.println("Default: " + ' ' +
            defaultDateFormatter.format(now));
        System.out.println(frLocale.getDisplayName() + ' ' +
            frDateFormatter.format(now));
        System.out.println(ukLocale.getDisplayName() + ' ' +
            ukDateFormatter.format(now));
    }
}
```

The program prints the locale name and formats the date in each of the locales:

```
$ java UseLocales
Default:  Nov 30, 2000
French (France) 30 nov. 00
English (UK) Nov 30, 2000
$
```

14.9. Setting the Default Locale

Problem

You want to change the default Locale for all operations within a given Java runtime.

Solution

Set the system property user.language, or call Locale.setDefault().

Discussion

Here is a program called SetLocale, which takes the language and country codes from the command line, constructs a Locale object, and passes it to Locale.setDefault(). When run with different arguments, it prints the date and a number in the appropriate locale:

```
C:\javasrc\i18n>java SetLocale en US
6/30/00 1:45 AM
123.457

C:\javasrc\i18n>java SetLocale fr FR
30/06/00 01:45
123,457
```

The code is similar to the previous recipe in how it constructs the locale.

```java
import java.text.*;
import java.util.*;

/** Change the default locale */
public class SetLocale {
    public static void main(String[] args) {

        switch (args.length) {
        case 0:
            Locale.setDefault(Locale.FRANCE);
            break;
        case 1:
            throw new IllegalArgumentException();
```

```
            case 2:
                Locale.setDefault(new Locale(args[0], args[1]));
                break;
            default:
                System.out.println("Usage: SetLocale [language [country]]");
                // FALLTHROUGH
            }

            DateFormat df = DateFormat.getInstance();
            NumberFormat nf = NumberFormat.getInstance();

            System.out.println(df.format(new Date()));
            System.out.println(nf.format(123.4567));
        }
    }
```

14.10. Formatting Messages

Problem

Messages may need to be formatted differently in different languages.

Solution

Use a MessageFormat object.

Discussion

In English, for example, we say "file not found." But in other languages the word order is different: the word for "not found" might need to precede the word for "file." Java provides for this using the MessageFormat class. Suppose we want to format a message as follows:

```
$ java MessageFormatDemoIntl
At 3:33:02 PM on 01-Jul-00, myfile.txt could not be opened.
$ java -Duser.language=es MessageFormatDemoIntl
A 3:34:49 PM sobre 01-Jul-00, no se puede abrir la fila myfile.txt.
$
```

The MessageFormat in its simplest form takes a format string with a series of numeric indexes, and an array of objects to be formatted. The objects are inserted into the resulting string, where the given array index appears. Here is a simple example of a MessageFormat in action:

```
import java.text.*;

public class MessageFormatDemo {

    static Object[] data = {
```

```
            new java.util.Date(),
            "myfile.txt",
            "could not be opened"
    };

    public static void main(String[] args) {
        String result = MessageFormat.format(
            "At {0,time} on {0,date}, {1} {2}.", data);
        System.out.println(result);
    }
}
```

But we still need to internationalize this, so we'll add some lines to our widget's properties files. In the default (English) version:

```
# These are for MessageFormatDemo
#
filedialogs.cantopen.string=could not be opened
filedialogs.cantopen.format=At {0,time} on {0,date}, {1} {2}.
```

In the Spanish version, we'll add these lines:

```
# These are for MessageFormatDemo
#
filedialogs.cantopen.string=no se puede abrir la fila
filedialogs.cantopen.format=A {0,time} sobre {0,date}, {2} {1}.
```

Then MessageFormatDemo needs to have a ResourceBundle, and get both the format string and the message from the bundle. Here is MessageFormatDemoIntl:

```
import java.text.*;
import java.util.*;

public class MessageFormatDemoIntl {

    static Object[] data = {
            new Date(),
            "myfile.txt",
            null
    };

    public static void main(String[] args) {
        ResourceBundle rb = ResourceBundle.getBundle("Widgets");
        data[2] = rb.getString("filedialogs.cantopen.string");
        String result = MessageFormat.format(
            rb.getString("filedialogs.cantopen.format"), data);
        System.out.println(result);
    }
}
```

There is more to the MessageFormat than this; see the Javadoc page for more details and examples.

14.11. Program: MenuIntl

MenuIntl (shown in Example 14-1) is a complete version of the menu code presented in Recipe 14.3.

Example 14-1. MenuIntl.java

```java
import java.awt.*;
import java.awt.event.*;
import javax.swing.*;
import java.util.*;

/** This is a partly-internationalized version of MenuDemo.
 * To try it out, use
 *      java MenuIntl
 *      java -Duser.language=es MenuIntl
 */
public class MenuIntl extends JFrame {

    /** "main program" method - construct and show */
    public static void main(String[] av) {
        // create an MenuIntl object, tell it to show up
        new MenuIntl().setVisible(true);
    }

    /** Construct the object including its GUI */
    public MenuIntl() {
        super("MenuIntlTest");
        JMenuItem mi;// used in various spots

        Container cp = getContentPane();
        cp.setLayout(new FlowLayout());
        JLabel lab;
        cp.add(lab = new JLabel());

        addWindowListener(new WindowAdapter() {
            public void windowClosing(WindowEvent e) {
                setVisible(false);
                dispose();
                System.exit(0);
            }
        });
        JMenuBar mb = new JMenuBar();
        setJMenuBar(mb);

        ResourceBundle b = ResourceBundle.getBundle("Menus");

        String titlebar;
        try { titlebar = b.getString("program"+".title"); }
```

Example 14-1. MenuIntl.java (continued)

```java
        catch (MissingResourceException e) { titlebar="MenuIntl Demo"; }
        setTitle(titlebar);

        String message;
        try { message = b.getString("program"+".message"); }
        catch (MissingResourceException e) {
            message="Welcome to the world of Java";
        }
        lab.setText(message);

        JMenu fm = mkMenu(b, "file");
        fm.add(mi = mkMenuItem(b, "file", "open"));
        // In finished code there would be a call to
        // mi.addActionListener(...) after *each* of
        // these mkMenuItem calls!
        fm.add(mi = mkMenuItem(b, "file", "new"));
        fm.add(mi = mkMenuItem(b, "file", "save"));
        fm.add(mi = mkMenuItem(b, "file", "exit"));
        mi.addActionListener(new ActionListener() {
            public void actionPerformed(ActionEvent e) {
                MenuIntl.this.setVisible(false);
                MenuIntl.this.dispose();
                System.exit(0);
            }
        });
        mb.add(fm);

        JMenu vm = mkMenu(b,  "view");
        vm.add(mi = mkMenuItem(b, "view", "tree"));
        vm.add(mi = mkMenuItem(b, "view", "list"));
        vm.add(mi = mkMenuItem(b, "view", "longlist"));
        mb.add(vm);

        JMenu hm = mkMenu(b,  "help");
        hm.add(mi = mkMenuItem(b, "help", "about"));
        // mb.setHelpMenu(hm);// needed for portability (Motif, etc.).

        // the main window
        JLabel jl = new JLabel("Menu Demo Window");
        jl.setSize(200, 150);
        cp.add(jl);
        pack();
    }

    /** Convenience routine to make a JMenu */
    public JMenu mkMenu(ResourceBundle b, String name) {
        String menuLabel;
        try { menuLabel = b.getString(name+".label"); }
```

Example 14-1. MenuIntl.java (continued)

```
        catch (MissingResourceException e) { menuLabel=name; }
        return new JMenu(menuLabel);
    }

    /** Convenience routine to make a JMenuItem */
    public JMenuItem mkMenuItem(ResourceBundle b, String menu, String name) {
        String miLabel;
        try { miLabel = b.getString(menu + "." + name + ".label"); }
        catch (MissingResourceException e) { miLabel=name; }
        String key = null;
        try { key = b.getString(menu + "." + name + ".key"); }
        catch (MissingResourceException e) { key=null; }

        if (key == null)
            return new JMenuItem(miLabel);
        else
            return new JMenuItem(miLabel, key.charAt(0));
    }
}
```

14.12. Program: BusCard

This program may seem a bit silly, but it's a good example of configuring a variety
of user interface controls from a resource bundle. The BusCard program allows
you to create a digital business card ("interactive business card") on-screen (see
Figure 14-2). The labels for all the GUI controls, event the pull-down menu, are
loaded from a ResourceBundle.

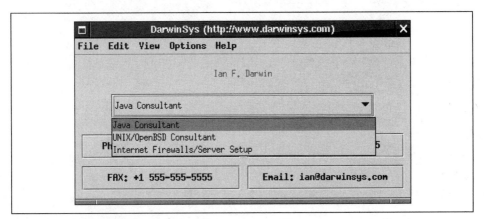

Figure 14-2. BusCard program in action

Example 14-2 shows the code for the BusCard program.

Example 14-2. BusCard.java

```java
import java.awt.*;
import java.awt.event.*;
import java.util.*;
import javax.swing.*;

/** Display your business-card information in a Java window.
 *
 * This is a first attempt. The next version should use a GridBagLayout.
 */
public class BusCard extends JFrame {

    JLabel nameTF;
    JComboBox jobChoice;
    JButton B1, B2, B3, B4;

    /** "main program" method - construct and show */
    public static void main(String[] av) {

        // create a BusCard object, tell it to show up
        new BusCard().setVisible(true);
    }

    /** Construct the object including its GUI */
    public BusCard() {
        super();

        Container cp = getContentPane();

        cp.setLayout(new GridLayout(0, 1));

        addWindowListener(new WindowAdapter() {
            public void windowClosing(WindowEvent e) {
                setVisible(false);
                dispose();
                System.exit(0);
            }
        });

        JMenuBar mb = new JMenuBar();
        setJMenuBar(mb);

        ResourceBundle b = ResourceBundle.getBundle("BusCard");

        JMenu aMenu;
        aMenu = I18N.mkMenu(b, "filemenu");
        mb.add(aMenu);
        JMenuItem mi = I18N.mkMenuItem(b, "filemenu", "exit");
```

Example 14-2. BusCard.java (continued)

```
        aMenu.add(mi);
    mi.addActionListener(new ActionListener() {
        public void actionPerformed(ActionEvent e) {
            System.exit(0);
        }
    });
    aMenu = I18N.mkMenu(b, "editmenu");
    mb.add(aMenu);
    aMenu = I18N.mkMenu(b, "viewmenu");
    mb.add(aMenu);
    aMenu = I18N.mkMenu(b, "optionsmenu");
    mb.add(aMenu);
    aMenu = I18N.mkMenu(b, "helpmenu");
    mb.add(aMenu);
    //mb.setHelpMenu(aMenu);// needed for portability (Motif, etc.).

    setTitle(I18N.getString(b, "card"+".company", "TITLE"));

    JPanel p1 = new JPanel();
    p1.setLayout(new GridLayout(0, 1, 50, 10));

    nameTF = new JLabel("My Name", JLabel.CENTER);
    nameTF.setFont(new Font("helvetica", Font.BOLD, 18));
    nameTF.setText(I18N.getString(b, "card"+".myname", "MYNAME"));
    p1.add(nameTF);

    jobChoice = new JComboBox();
    jobChoice.setFont(new Font("helvetica", Font.BOLD, 14));

    // Get Job Titles ofrom the Properties file loaded into "b"!
    String next;
    int i=1;
    do {
        next = I18N.getString(b, "job_title" + i++, null);
        if (next != null)
            jobChoice.addItem(next);
    } while (next != null);
    p1.add(jobChoice);

    cp.add(p1);

    JPanel p2 = new JPanel();
    p2.setLayout(new GridLayout(2, 2, 10, 10));

    B1 = new JButton();
    B1.setLabel(I18N.getString(b, "button1.label", "BUTTON LABEL"));
    p2.add(B1);
```

Example 14-2. BusCard.java (continued)

```
        B2 = new JButton();
        B2.setLabel(I18N.getString(b, "button2.label", "BUTTON LABEL"));
        p2.add(B2);

        B3 = new JButton();
        B3.setLabel(I18N.getString(b, "button3.label", "BUTTON LABEL"));
        p2.add(B3);

        B4 = new JButton();
        B4.setLabel(I18N.getString(b, "button4.label", "BUTTON LABEL"));
        p2.add(B4);
        cp.add(p2);

        pack();
    }
}
```

See Also

Other things may need to be internationalized as well:

Character comparisons
>   These are set separately on Unix/POSIX; on other operating systems, they depend on the default `Locale`.

Date and Time Formats
>   See `GregorianCalendar` and `DateFormat` in Recipe 6.0.

Number Formats
>   See `java.util.NumberFormat` in Recipe 5.7.

Message insertions
>   These appear in different orders in different languages (something the C-language `printf()` could never handle). See `java.util.MessageFormat` in Recipe 14.10.

Internationalization Caveats

Internationalizing your menus and push buttons is only one step. You also need to internationalize message text in dialogs as well as help files (see the JavaHelp API at *http://java.sun.com/products/javahelp/*).

Some items such as AWT `FileDialog` use native components; their appearance depends on the native operating system (your application can change its own default locale, but not the system's; therefore, if your customer has a differently internationalized copy of the same OS, the file dialogs will appear differently).

Documentation

A short, readable, non-Java-specific introduction to the overall topic of internationalization is *The Guide to Translation and Localization,* written by the staff of Lingo Systems and published by the IEEE Computer Society. For more on Java I18N, see the online documentation that ships with the JDK; start at *jdk1.x/docs/ guide/intl/index.html.* See also the O'Reilly book *Java Internationalization.*

The Last Word

Good luck. Bonne chance. Buena suerte . . .

15

Network Clients

15.0. Introduction

Java can be used to write several types of networked programs. In traditional socket-based code, the programmer is responsible for the entire interaction between the client and server. In higher-level types, such as RMI, CORBA, and EJB, the software takes over increasing degrees of control. Sockets are often used for connecting to "legacy" servers; if you were writing a new application from scratch, you'd be better off using a higher-level service.

It may be helpful to compare sockets with the telephone system. Telephones were originally used for analog voice traffic, which is pretty unstructured. Then it began to be used for some "layered" applications; the first widely popular one was facsimile transmission, or FAX. Where would FAX be without the widespread availability of voice telephony? The second wildly popular layered application is dialup TCP/IP. This coexisted with the World Wide Web to become popular as a mass-market service. Where would dialup IP be without widely deployed voice lines? And where would the Internet be without dialup IP?

Sockets are like that too. The Web, RMI, JDBC, CORBA, and EJB are all layered on top of sockets.

Ever since the alpha release of Java (originally as a sideline to the HotJava browser) in May of 1995, Java has been popular as a programming language for building network applications. It's easy to see why, particularly if you've ever built a networked application in C. First, C programmers have to worry about the platform they are on. Unix uses synchronous sockets, which work rather like normal disk files vis-a-vis reading and writing, while Microsoft OSes use asynchronous sockets, which use callbacks to notify when a read or write has completed. Java glosses over this distinction for you. Further, the amount of code needed to set up a socket in C is intimidating. Just for fun, Example 15-1 shows the "typical" C code for setting up a client socket. And remember, this is only the Unix part. And only the part that makes the connection. To be portable to MS-Windows, there would need to be additional conditional code (using C's #ifdef mechanism). And C's #include mechanism requires that exactly the right files be included and in exactly the right order; Java's import mechanism lets you use * to import a whole section of the API, and the imports can be listed in any order you like.

Example 15-1. C client setup

```c
/*
 * Simple demonstration of code to setup a client connection in C.
 */

#include <sys/types.h>
#include <sys/socket.h>
#include <netinet/in.h>
#include <netdb.h>
#include <stdio.h>
#include <string.h>
#include <fcntl.h>

int
main(int argc, char *argv[])
{
    char* server_name = "localhost";
    struct hostent *host_info;
    int sock;
    struct sockaddr_in server;

    /* Look up the remote host's IP address */
    host_info = gethostbyname(server_name);
    if (host_info == NULL) {
        fprintf(stderr, "%s: unknown host: %s\n", argv[0], server_name);
        exit(1);
    }

    /* Create the socket */
    if ((sock = socket(AF_INET, SOCK_STREAM, 0)) < 0) {
        perror("creating client socket");
        exit(2);
    }

    /* Set up the server's socket address */
    server.sin_family = AF_INET;
    memcpy((char *)&server.sin_addr, host_info->h_addr,
                    host_info->h_length);
```

Example 15-1. C client setup (continued)

```
    server.sin_port = htons(80);

    /* Connect to the server */
    if (connect(sock,(struct sockaddr *)&server,sizeof server) < 0) {
        perror("connecting to server");
        exit(4);
    }

    /* Finally, we can read and write on the socket. */
    /* ... */

    (void) close(sock);
}
```

In the first recipe, we'll see how to do the connect in essentially one line of Java (plus a bit of error handling). Then we'll cover error handling and transferring data over a socket. Next, we'll take a quick look at a datagram or UDP client that implements most of the TFTP (trivial file transfer protocol) that has been used for two decades to boot diskless workstations. We'll end with a program that connects interactively to a text-based server such as Telnet or email.

A common theme through most of these client examples is to use existing servers, so we don't have to generate both the client and the server at the same time. With one exception, all of these are services that exist on any standard Unix platform. If you can't find a Unix server near you to try them on, let me suggest that you take an old PC, maybe one that's underpowered for running the latest Microsoft software, and put up a free, open source Unix system on it. My personal favorite is OpenBSD, and the market's overall favorite is Linux. Both are readily available on CD-ROM, can be installed for free over the Internet, and offer all the standard services used in the client examples, including the time servers and TFTP. Both have free Java implementations available.

15.1. Contacting a Server

Problem

You need to contact a server using TCP/IP.

Solution

Just create a Socket, passing the hostname and port number into the constructor.

Discussion

There isn't much to this in Java, in fact. When creating a socket, you pass in the hostname and the port number. The `java.net.Socket` constructor does the `gethostbyname()` and the `socket()` system call, sets up the server's `sockaddr_in` structure, and executes the `connect()` call. All you have to do is catch the errors, which are subclassed from the familiar `IOException`. Example 15.2 sets up a Java network client, using `IOException` to catch errors.

Example 15-2. Connect.java (simple client connection)

```java
import java.net.*;

/*
 * A simple demonstration of setting up a Java network client.
 */
public class Connect {
    public static void main(String[] argv) {
        String server_name = "localhost";

        try {
            Socket sock = new Socket(server_name, 80);

            /* Finally, we can read and write on the socket. */
            System.out.println(" *** Connected to " + server_name  + " ***");

            /* . do the I/O here .. */

            sock.close();

        } catch (java.io.IOException e) {
            System.err.println("error connecting to " +
                server_name + ": " + e);
            return;
        }


    }
}
```

See Also

Java supports other ways of using network applications. You can also open a URL and read from it (see Recipe 17.6). You can write code so that it will run from a URL, when opened in a web browser, or from an application (see Recipe 17.9).

15.2. Finding and Reporting Network Addresses

Problem

You want to look up a host's address name or number, or get the address at the other end of a network connection.

Solution

Get an `InetAddress` object.

Discussion

The `InetAddress` object represents the Internet address of a given computer or host. There are no public constructors; you obtain an `InetAddress` by calling the static `byName()` method, passing in either a hostname like *www.darwinsys.com* or a network address as a string, like "1.23.45.67". All the "lookup" methods in this class can throw the checked exception `UnknownHostException`, which must be caught or declared on the calling method's header. None of these methods actually contacts the remote host, so they do not throw the other exceptions related to network connections.

The method `getHostAddress()` gives you the numeric IP address (as a string) corresponding to the `InetAddress`. The inverse is `getHostName()`, which reports the name of the `InetAddress`. This can be used to print the address of a host given its name, or vice versa:

```
// From InetAddrDemo.java
String ipNumber = "123.45.67.89";
String hostName = "www.darwinsys.com";
System.out.println(hostName + "'s address is " +
    InetAddress.byName(hostName).getHostAddress());
 System.out.println(ipNumber + "'s name is " +
    InetAddress.byName(ipNumber).getHostName());
```

You can also get an `InetAddress` from a `Socket` by calling its `getInetAddress()` method. You can construct a `Socket` using an `InetAddress` instead of a hostname string. So, to connect to port number "myPortNumber" on the same host as an existing socket, you'd use:

```
InetAddress remote = theSocket.getInetAddress();
Socket anotherSocket = new Socket(remote, myPortNumber);
```

Finally, to look up all the addresses associated with a host—a server may be on more than one network—use the static method `getAllByName(host)`, which returns an array of InetAddress objects, one for each IP address associated with the given name.

There is a static method getLocalHost(), which returns an InetAddress equivalent to "localhost" or 127.0.0.1. This can be used to connect to a server on the same machine as the client.

See Also

There is not yet a way to look up services, i.e., to find out that the HTTP service is on port 80. Full implementations of TCP/IP have always included an additional set of resolvers; in C, the call getservbyname("http", "tcp"); would look up the given service* and return a servent (service entry) structure whose s_port member would contain the value 80. The numbers of established services do not change, but when services are new or installed in non-routine ways, it is convenient to be able to change the service number for all programs on a machine or network (regardless of programming language) just by changing the services definitions. Java should provide this capability in a future release.

15.3. Handling Network Errors

Problem

You want more detailed reporting than just IOException if something goes wrong.

Solution

Catch a greater variety of exception classes. There are several subclasses of SocketException; the most notable of these are ConnectException and NoRouteToHostException. The names are self-explanatory: the first means that the connection was refused by the machine at the other end (the server machine), and the second completely explains the failure. Example 15-3 is an excerpt from the Connect program, enhanced to handle these conditions.

Example 15-3. ConnectFriendly.java

```
/* Client with error handling */
public class ConnectFriendly {
    public static void main(String[] argv) {
        String server_name = argv.length == 1 ? argv[0] : "localhost";
```

---

* The location where it is looked up varies. It might be in a file named /etc/services on Unix, or the services file under \windows or \winnt under MS-Windows; in a centralized registry such as Sun's Network Information Services (NIS, formerly YP); or in some other platform- or network-dependent location.

Example 15-3. ConnectFriendly.java (continued)

```
    int tcp_port = 80;
    try {
        Socket sock = new Socket(server_name, tcp_port);

        /* Finally, we can read and write on the socket. */
        System.out.println(" *** Connected to " + server_name  + " ***");
        /* ... */

        sock.close();

    } catch (UnknownHostException e) {
        System.err.println(server_name + " Unknown host");
        return;
    } catch (NoRouteToHostException e) {
        System.err.println(server_name + " Unreachable" );
        return;
    } catch (ConnectException e) {
        System.err.println(server_name + " connect refused");
        return;
    } catch (java.io.IOException e) {
        System.err.println(server_name + ' ' + e.getMessage());
        return;
    }
  }
}
```

15.4. Reading and Writing Textual Data

Problem

Having connected, you wish to transfer textual data.

Solution

Construct a `BufferedReader` or `PrintWriter` from the socket's `getInputStream()` or `getOutputStream()`.

Discussion

The `Socket` class has methods that allow you to get an `InputStream` or `OutputStream` to read from or write to the socket. There is no method to fetch a `Reader` or `Writer`, partly because some network services are limited to ASCII, but mainly because the `Socket` class was decided on before there were `Reader` and `Writer` classes. You can always create a `Reader` from an `InputStream` or a

`Writer` from an `OutputStream` using the conversion classes. The paradigm for the two most common forms is:

```
BufferedReader is = new BufferedReader(
    new InputStreamReader(sock.getInputStream()));
PrintWriter os = new PrintWriter(sock.getOutputStream(), true);
```

Here is code that reads a line of text from the "daytime" service, a service offered by full-fledged TCP/IP suites (such as those included with most Unixes). You don't have to send anything to the `Daytime` server; you simply connect and read one line. The server writes one line containing the date and time, and then closes the connection.

Running it looks like this. I started by getting the current date and time on the local host, then ran the `DaytimeText` program to see the date and time on the server (machine "darian" is my local server):

```
C:\javasrc\network>date
Current date is Sun 01-23-2000
Enter new date (mm-dd-yy):
C:\javasrc\network>time
Current time is  1:13:18.70p
Enter new time:
C:\javasrc\network>java DaytimeText darian
Time on darian is Sun Jan 23 13:14:34 2000
```

The code is in class `DaytimeText`, shown in Example 15-4.

Example 15-4. DaytimeText.java

```
/**
 * DaytimeText - connect to the Daytime (ascii) service.
 */
public class DaytimeText {
    public static final short TIME_PORT = 13;

    public static void main(String[] argv) {
        String hostName;
        if (argv.length == 0)
            hostName = "localhost";
        else
            hostName = argv[0];

        try {
            Socket sock = new Socket(hostName, TIME_PORT);
            BufferedReader is = new BufferedReader(new
                InputStreamReader(sock.getInputStream()));
            String remoteTime = is.readLine();
            System.out.println("Time on " + hostName + " is " + remoteTime);
        } catch (IOException e) {
```

Example 15-4. DaytimeText.java (continued)

```
            System.err.println(e);
        }
    }
}
```

The second example, shown in Example 15-5, shows both reading and writing on the same socket. The Echo server simply echoes back whatever lines of text you send it. It's not a very clever server, but it is a useful one: it helps in network testing, and also in testing clients of this type!

The converse() method holds a short conversation with the Echo server on the named host; if no host is named, it tries to contact localhost, a universal alias* for "the machine the program is running on."

Example 15-5. EchoClientOneLine.java

```
/**
 * EchoClientOneLine - create client socket, send one line,
 * read it back. See also EchoClient.java, slightly fancier.
 */
public class EchoClientOneLine {
    /** What we send across the net */
    String mesg = "Hello across the net";

    public static void main(String[] argv) {
        if (argv.length == 0)
            new EchoClientOneLine().converse("localhost");
        else
            new EchoClientOneLine().converse(argv[0]);
    }

    /** Hold one conversation across the net */
    protected void converse(String hostName) {
        try {
            Socket sock = new Socket(hostName, 7); // echo server.
            BufferedReader is = new BufferedReader(new
                InputStreamReader(sock.getInputStream()));
            PrintWriter os = new PrintWriter(sock.getOutputStream(), true);
            // Do the CRLF ourself since println appends only a \r on
            // platforms where that is the native line ending.
            os.print(mesg + "\r\n"); os.flush();
            String reply = is.readLine();
            System.out.println("Sent \"" + mesg  + "\"");
```

---

* It used to be universal, when most networked systems were administered by fulltime systems people who had been trained or served an apprenticeship. Today there are so many machines on the Internet that don't have localhost configured properly that there is a web site, *http://localhost.com*, which tells you about this problem if you type "localhost" into a web browser on a misconfigured machine.

Example 15-5. EchoClientOneLine.java (continued)

```
            System.out.println("Got  \"" + reply + "\"");
        } catch (IOException e) {
            System.err.println(e);
        }
    }
}
```

It might be a good exercise to isolate the reading and writing code from this method into a `NetWriter` class, possibly subclassing `PrintWriter` and adding the `\r\n` and the flushing.

15.5. Reading and Writing Binary Data

Problem

Having connected, you wish to transfer binary data.

Solution

Construct a `DataInputStream` or `DataOutputStream` from the socket's `getInputStream()` or `getOutputStream()`.

Discussion

The simplest paradigm is:

```
DataInputStream is = new DataInputStream(sock.getInputStream());
DataOutputStream is = new DataOutputStream(sock.getOutputStream());
```

If the volume of data might be large, insert a buffered stream for efficiency. The paradigm is:

```
DataInputStream is = new DataInputStream(
    new BufferedInputStream(sock.getInputStream()));
DataOutputStream is = new DataOutputStream(
    new BufferedOutputStream(sock.getOutputStream()));
```

This program uses another standard service that gives out the time, this time as a binary integer representing the number of seconds since 1900. Since the Java `Date` class base is 1970, we convert the time base by subtracting the difference between 1970 and 1900. When I used this exercise in a course, most of the students wanted to *add* this time difference, reasoning that 1970 is later. But if you think clearly, you'll see that there are fewer seconds between 1999 and 1970 than there are between 1999 and 1900, so subtraction gives the correct number of seconds. And since the `Date` constructor needs milliseconds, we multiply the number of seconds by 1,000.

The time base difference is the number of years multiplied by 365.25, multiplied by the number of seconds in a day. The earth's mean orbital period is approximately 365.23 days, but when you factor in the leap years correctly, you can use exactly 365 1/4 days per year in such calculations.

The integer that we read from the server is a C-language `unsigned int`. But Java doesn't provide an unsigned integer type; normally when you need an unsigned number, you use the next-larger integer type, which would be `long`. But Java 2 also doesn't give us a method to read an unsigned integer from a data stream. The `DataInputStream` method `readInt()` reads Java-style signed integers. There are `readUnsignedByte()` methods and `readUnsignedShort()` methods, but no `readUnsignedInt()` method. Accordingly, we synthesize the ability to read an unsigned `int` (which must be stored in a `long`, or else you'd lose the signed bit and be back where you started from) by reading unsigned bytes and reassembling them using Java's bit-shifting operators.

```
$ date
Fri Mar 30 10:02:28 EST 2001
$ java DaytimeBinary darian
Remote time is 3194953367
BASE_DIFF is 2208988800
Time diff == 985964567
Time on darian is Fri Mar 30 10:02:47 EST 2001
$
```

Looking at the output, you can see that the server agrees within a few seconds. So the date calculation code in Example 15-6 is probably correct.

Example 15-6. DaytimeBinary.java

```java
/**
 * DaytimeBinary - connect to the Daytime (ascii) service.
 */
public class DaytimeBinary {
    /** The TCP port for the binary time service. */
    public static final short TIME_PORT = 37;
    /** Seconds between 1970, the time base for Date(long) and Time.
     * Factors in leap years (up to 2100), hours, minutes, and seconds.
     * Subtract 1 day for 1900, add in 1/2 day for 1969/1970.
     */
    protected static final long BASE_DAYS =
        (long)(((1970 - 1900) * 365.25) - 1 + .5);
    /* Seconds since 1970 */
    public static final long BASE_DIFF = (BASE_DAYS * 24 * 60 * 60);
    /** Convert from seconds to milliseconds */
    public static final int MSEC = 1000;

    public static void main(String[] argv) {
```

Example 15-6. DaytimeBinary.java (continued)

```
    String hostName;
    if (argv.length == 0)
        hostName = "localhost";
    else
        hostName = argv[0];

    try {
        Socket sock = new Socket(hostName, TIME_PORT);
        DataInputStream is = new DataInputStream(new
            BufferedInputStream(sock.getInputStream()));
        // Need to read 4 bytes from the network, unsigned.
        // Do it yourself; there is no readUnsignedInt().
        // Long is 8 bytes on Java, but we are using the
        // existing daytime protocol, which uses 4-byte ints.
        long remoteTime = (
            ((long)(is.readUnsignedByte() & 0xff) << 24) |
            ((long)(is.readUnsignedByte() & 0xff) << 16) |
            ((long)(is.readUnsignedByte() & 0xff) <<  8) |
            ((long)(is.readUnsignedByte() & 0xff) <<  0));
        System.out.println("Remote time is " + remoteTime);
        System.out.println("BASE_DIFF is " + BASE_DIFF);
        System.out.println("Time diff == " + (remoteTime - BASE_DIFF));
        Date d = new Date((remoteTime - BASE_DIFF) * MSEC);
        System.out.println("Time on " + hostName + " is " + d.toString());
    } catch (IOException e) {
        System.err.println(e);
    }
  }
}
```

15.6. *Reading and Writing Serialized Data*

Problem

Having connected, you wish to transfer serialized object data.

Solution

Construct an `ObjectInputStream` or `ObjectOutputStream` from the socket's `getInputStream()` or `getOutputStream()`.

Discussion

Object serialization is the ability to convert in-memory objects to an external form that can be sent *serially* (a byte at a time). This is discussed in Recipe 9.16.

This program (and its server) operate one service that isn't normally provided by TCP/IP, as it is Java-specific. It looks rather like the `DaytimeBinary` program in the previous recipe, but the server sends us a `Date` object already constructed. You can find the server for this program in Recipe 16.3; Example 15-7 shows the client code.

Example 15-7. DaytimeObject.java

```java
/**
 * DaytimeObject - connect to the Daytime (ascii) service.
 */
public class DaytimeObject {
    /** The TCP port for the object time service. */
    public static final short TIME_PORT = 1951;

    public static void main(String[] argv) {
        String hostName;
        if (argv.length == 0)
            hostName = "localhost";
        else
            hostName = argv[0];

        try {
            Socket sock = new Socket(hostName, TIME_PORT);
            ObjectInputStream is = new ObjectInputStream(new
                BufferedInputStream(sock.getInputStream()));

            // Read and validate the Object
            Object o = is.readObject();
            if (!(o instanceof Date))
                throw new IllegalArgumentException("Wanted Date, got " + o);

            // Valid, so cast to Date, and print
            Date d = (Date) o;
            System.out.println("Time on " + hostName + " is " + d.toString());
        } catch (ClassNotFoundException e) {
            System.err.println("Wanted date, got INVALID CLASS (" + e + ")");
        } catch (IOException e) {
            System.err.println(e);
        }
    }
}
```

I ask the operating system for the date and time, and then run the program, which prints the date and time. The server and my desktop are within about ten seconds of agreement:

```
C:\javasrc\network>date
Current date is Sun 01-23-2000
```

```
Enter new date (mm-dd-yy):
C:\javasrc\network>time
Current time is  2:52:35.43p
Enter new time:
C:\javasrc\network>java DaytimeObject
Time on localhost is Sun Jan 23 14:52:25 GMT 2000
C:\javasrc\network>
```

15.7. UDP Datagrams

Problem

You need to use a datagram connection (UDP) instead of a stream connection (TCP).

Solution

Use `DatagramSocket` and `DatagramPacket`.

Discussion

Datagram network traffic is a kindred spirit to the underlying packet-based Ethernet and IP (Internet protocol) layers. Unlike a stream-based connection such as TCP, datagram transports such as UDP transmit each "packet" or chunk of data as a single entity with no necessary relation to any other. A common analogy is that TCP is like talking on the telephone, while UDP is like sending postcards, or maybe FAX messages.

The differences show up most in error handling. Packets can, like postcards, go astray. When was the last time the postman rang your bell to tell you that the post office had lost one of several postcards it was supposed to deliver to you? It doesn't happen, right? Because they don't keep track of them. On the other hand, when you're talking on the phone and there's a noise burst—like somebody yelling in the room, or even a bad connection—you can ask the person at the other end to repeat what they just said.

With a stream-based connection like a TCP socket, the network transport layer handles errors for you: it asks the other end to retransmit. With a datagram transport such as UDP, you have to handle retransmission yourself. Kind of like numbering the postcards you send, so that you can go back and resend any that don't arrive—a good excuse to return to your vacation spot, perhaps.

Another difference is that datagram transmission preserves message boundaries. That is, if you write 20 bytes and then write 10 bytes when using TCP, the program reading from the other end will not know if you wrote one chunk of 30 bytes, two

Ian's Basic Steps: UDP Client

UDP is a bit more involved, so I'll list the basic steps for generating a UDP client:

1. Create a `DatagramSocket` with no arguments (the form that takes two arguments is used on the server).

2. Optionally `connect()` the socket to an `InetAddress` (see Recipe 15.2) and port number.

3. Create one or more `DatagramPacket` objects; these are wrappers around a byte array that contains data you want to send and is filled in with data you receive.

4. If you did not `connect()` the socket, provide the `InetAddress` and port when constructing the `DatagramPacket`.

5. Set the packet's length, and use `sock.send(packet)` to send data to the server.

6. Use `sock.receive()` to retrieve data.

chunks of 15, or even 30 individual characters. With a `DatagramSocket`, you construct a `DatagramPacket` object for each buffer, and its contents are sent as a *single* entity over the network; its contents will not be mixed together with the contents of any other buffer. The `DatagramPacket` object has methods like `getLength()`, `setPort()`, and so on.

Example 15-8 is a short program that connects via UDP to the `Daytime` date and time server used in Recipe 15.4. Since there is no real notion of "connection" with UDP, even services that only send you data must be contacted by sending an empty packet, which the UDP server uses to return its response.

Example 15-8. DaytimeUDP.java

```java
public class DaytimeUDP {
    /** The UDP port number */
    public final static int DAYTIME_PORT = 13;

    /** A buffer plenty big enough for the date string */
    protected final static int PACKET_SIZE = 100;

    // main program
    public static void main(String[] argv) throws IOException {
        if (argv.length < 1) {
            System.err.println("usage: java DayTime host");
            System.exit(1);
        }
        String host = argv[0];
```

Example 15-8. DaytimeUDP.java (continued)

```
        InetAddress servAddr = InetAddress.getByName(host);
        DatagramSocket sock = new DatagramSocket();

        // Allocate the data buffer
        byte[] buffer = new byte[PACKET_SIZE];

        // The udp packet we will send and receive
        DatagramPacket packet = new DatagramPacket(
            buffer, PACKET_SIZE, servAddr, DAYTIME_PORT);

        /* Send empty max-length (-1 for null byte) packet to server */
        packet.setLength(PACKET_SIZE-1);
        sock.send(packet);
        Debug.println("net", "Sent request");

        // Receive a packet and print it.
        sock.receive(packet);
        Debug.println("net", "Got packet of size " + packet.getLength());
        System.out.print("Date on " + host + " is " +
            new String(buffer, 0, packet.getLength()));
    }
}
```

I'll run it to my server just to be sure that it works:

```
$ jikes +E -d . DaytimeUDP.java
$ java DaytimeUDP darian
Date on darian is Sat Jan 27 12:42:41 2001
$
```

15.8. Program: TFTP UDP Client

This program implements the client half of the TFTP application protocol, a well-known service that has been used in the Unix world for network booting of workstations since before Windows 3.1. I chose this protocol because it's widely implemented on the server side, so it's easy to find a test server for it.

The TFTP protocol is a bit odd. The client contacts the server on the well-known UDP port number 69, from a generated port number,[*] and the server responds to the client from a generated port number. Further communication is on the two generated port numbers.

---

[*] When the application doesn't care, these are usually made up by the operating system. For example, when you call a company from a pay phone or cell phone, the company doesn't usually care what number you are calling from, and if it does, there are ways to find out. Generated port numbers generally range from 1024 (the first non-privileged port; see Chapter 16) to 65535 (the largest value that can be held in a 16-bit port number).

Getting into more detail, as shown in Figure 15-1, the client initially sends a read request with the filename, and reads the first chunk of data. The read request consists of two bytes (a short) with the read request code (short integer with a value of 1, defined as OP_RRQ), two bytes for the sequence number, then the ASCII filename, null terminated, and the string octet, also null terminated. The server verifies that it can open the file and, if so, sends the first data packet (OP_DATA), and then reads again. This read-acknowledge cycle is repeated until all the data is read. Note that each packet is 516 bytes (512 bytes of data, plus 2 bytes for the packet type and 2 more for the packet number) except the last, which can be any length from 4 (zero bytes of data) to 515 (511 bytes of data). If there is a network I/O error, the packet is re-sent. If a given packet goes astray, both client and server are supposed to perform a timeout cycle. This client does not, but the server does. You could add timeouts using a thread; see Recipe 24.4. The client code is shown in Example 15-9.

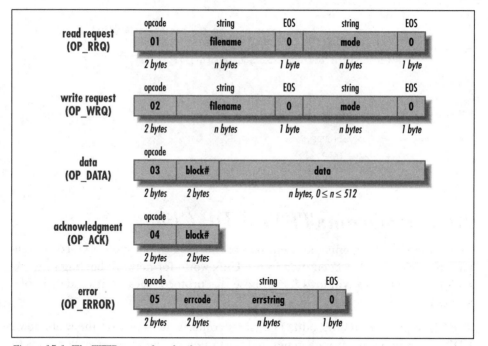

Figure 15-1. The TFTP protocol packet formats

Example 15-9. RemCat.java

```java
import java.io.*;
import java.net.*;

/**
 * RemCat - remotely cat (DOS type) a file, using the TFTP protocol.
```

Example 15-9. RemCat.java (continued)

```
 * Inspired by the "rcat" exercise in Learning Tree Course 363,
 * <I>UNIX Network Programming</I>, by Dr. Chris Brown.
 *
 * Note that the TFTP server is NOT "internationalized"; the name and
 * mode in the protocol are defined in terms of ASCII, not UniCode.
 */
public class RemCat {
    /** The UDP port number */
    public final static int TFTP_PORT = 69;
    /** The mode we will use - octet for everything. */
    protected final String MODE = "octet";

    /** The offset for the code/response as a byte */
    protected final int OFFSET_REQUEST = 1;
    /** The offset for the packet number as a byte */
    protected final int OFFSET_PACKETNUM = 3;

    /** Debugging flag */
    protected static boolean debug = false;

    /** TFTP op-code for a read request */
    public final int OP_RRQ = 1,
        /** TFTP op-code for a read request */
        OP_WRQ = 2,
        /** TFTP op-code for a read request */
        OP_DATA = 3,
        /** TFTP op-code for a read request */
        OP_ACK = 4,
        /** TFTP op-code for a read request */
        OP_ERROR = 5;
    protected final static int PACKET = 516;// == 2 + 2 + 512
    protected String host;
    protected InetAddress servAddr;
    protected DatagramSocket sock;
    protected byte buffer[];
    protected DatagramPacket inp, outp;

    /** The main program that drives this network client.
     * @param argv[0] hostname, running TFTP server
     * @param argv[1..n] filename(s), must be at least one
     */
    public static void main(String[] argv) throws IOException {
        if (argv.length < 2) {
            System.err.println("usage: java RemCat host filename[...]");
            System.exit(1);
        }
        if (debug)
            System.err.println("Java RemCat starting");
```

Example 15-9. RemCat.java (continued)

```
        RemCat rc = new RemCat(argv[0]);
        for (int i = 1; i<argv.length; i++) {
            if (debug)
                System.err.println("-- Starting file " +
                        argv[0] + ":" + argv[i] + "---");
            rc.readFile(argv[i]);
        }
    }


    RemCat(String host) throws IOException {
        super();
        this.host = host;
        servAddr = InetAddress.getByName(host);
        sock = new DatagramSocket();
        buffer = new byte[PACKET];
        inp = new DatagramPacket(buffer, PACKET);
        outp = new DatagramPacket(buffer, PACKET, servAddr, TFTP_PORT);
    }


    void readFile(String path) throws IOException {
        /* Build a tftp Read Request packet. This is messy because the
         * fields have variable length. Numbers must be in
         * network order, too; fortunately Java just seems
         * naturally smart enough :-) to use network byte order.
         */
        buffer[0] = 0;
        buffer[OFFSET_REQUEST] = OP_RRQ;// read request
        int p = 2;    // number of chars into buffer

        // Convert filename String to bytes in buffer , using "p" as an
        // offset indicator to get all the bits of this request
        // in exactly the right spot.
        path.getBytes(0, path.length(), buffer, p); // file name
        p += path.length();
        buffer[p++] = 0;// null byte terminates string

        // Similarly, convert MODE ("octet") to bytes in buffer
        MODE.getBytes(0, MODE.length(), buffer, p);
        p += MODE.length();
        buffer[p++] = 0;// null terminate

        /* Send Read Request to tftp server */
        outp.setLength(p);
        sock.send(outp);


        /* Loop reading data packets from the server until a short
         * packet arrives; this indicates the end of the file.
         */
```

Example 15-9. RemCat.java (continued)

```
        int len = 0;
        do {
            sock.receive(inp);
            if (debug)
                System.err.println(
                    "Packet # " + Byte.toString(buffer[OFFSET_PACKETNUM])+
                    "RESPONSE CODE " + Byte.toString(buffer[OFFSET_REQUEST]));
            if (buffer[OFFSET_REQUEST] == OP_ERROR) {
                System.err.println("remcat ERROR: " +
                    new String(buffer, 4, inp.getLength()-4));
                return;
            }
            if (debug)
                System.err.println("Got packet of size " +
                    inp.getLength());

            /* Print the data from the packet */
            System.out.write(buffer, 4, inp.getLength()-4);

            /* Ack the packet. The block number we
             * want to ack is already in buffer so
             * we just change the opcode. The ACK is
             * sent to the port number which the server
             * just sent the data from, NOT to port
             * TFTP_PORT.
             */
            buffer[OFFSET_REQUEST] = OP_ACK;
            outp.setLength(4);
            outp.setPort(inp.getPort());
            sock.send(outp);
        } while (inp.getLength() == PACKET);

        if (debug)
            System.err.println("** ALL DONE** Leaving loop, last size " +
                inp.getLength());
    }
}
```

To test this client, you would need a TFTP server. If you are on a Unix system that you administer, you can enable the TFTP server to test this client just by editing the file */etc/inetd.conf* and restarting (or just reloading, with *kill –HUP*) the `inetd` server. `inetd` is a program that listens for a wide range of connections and starts the servers only when a connection from a client comes along (a kind of lazy evaluation). Beware of security holes; don't turn a TFTP server loose on the Internet without first reading a good security book, such as O'Reilly's *Building Internet Firewalls*. I set up the traditional */tftpboot* directory, put this line in my *inetd.conf*, and reloaded inetd:

```
tftp  dgram udp wait root /usr/libexec/tftpd tftpd -s /tftpboot
```

(On MS Windows/NT, you could probably enable this from the Services Control Panel.) Then I put a few test files, one of them named *foo*, into the */tftpboot* directory. Running:

```
$ java RemCat localhost foo
```

produced what looked like the file. But just to be safe, I tested the output of RemCat against the original file, using the Unix *diff* comparison program. No news is good news:

```
$ java RemCat localhost foo | diff - /tftpboot/foo
```

So far so good. Let's not slip this program on an unsuspecting network without exercising the error handling at least briefly:

```
$ java RemCat localhost nosuchfile
remcat ERROR: File not found
$
```

15.9. *Program: Telnet Client*

This program is a simple Telnet client. Telnet, as you probably know, is the oldest surviving remote login program in use on the Internet. It began on the original ARPAnet and was later translated for the Internet. A Unix command-line client lives on, and there are several windowed clients in circulation. For security reasons, the use of Telnet as a means of logging in remotely over the Internet has largely been superseded by SSH (see *http://www.openssh.com*). However, a Telnet client remains a necessity for such purposes as connecting locally, as well as debugging textual socket servers and understanding their protocols. For example, it is common to connect from a Telnet client to an SMTP (email) server; you can often intuit quite a bit about the SMTP server even if you wouldn't normally type an entire mail session interactively.

When you need to have data copied in both directions at more or less the same time—from the keyboard to the remote program, and from the remote program to the screen—there are two approaches. Some I/O libraries in C have a function called poll() or select() that allows you examine a number of files to see which ones are ready for reading or writing. Java does not support this model. The other model, which works on most platforms and is the norm in Java, is to use two threads,* one to handle the data transfer in each direction. That is our plan here;

---

* A thread is one of (possibly) many separate flows of control within a single process; see Recipe 24.1.

the class `Pipe` encapsulates one thread and the code for copying data in one direction; two instances are used, one to drive each direction of transfer independently of the other.

This program allows you to connect to any text-based network service. For example, you can talk to your system's SMTP (simple mail transport protocol) server, or the `Daytime` server (port 13) used in several earlier recipes in this chapter.

```
$ java Telnet darian 13
Host darian; port 13
Connected OK
Sat Apr 28 14:07:41 2001
^C
$
```

The source code is shown in Example 15-10.

Example 15-10. Telnet.java

```java
import java.net.*;
import java.io.*;

/**
 * Telnet - very minimal (no options); connect to given host and service
 */
public class Telnet {
    String host;
    int portNum;
    public static void main(String[] argv) {
        new Telnet().talkTo(argv);
    }
    private void talkTo(String av[]) {
        if (av.length >= 1)
            host = av[0];
        else
            host = "localhost";
        if (av.length >= 2)
            portNum = Integer.parseInt(av[1]);
        else portNum = 23;
        System.out.println("Host " + host + "; port " + portNum);
        try {
            Socket s = new Socket(host, portNum);

            // Connect the remote to our stdout
            new Pipe(s.getInputStream(), System.out).start();

            // Connect our stdin to the remote
            new Pipe(System.in, s.getOutputStream()).start();

        } catch(IOException e) {
```

Example 15-10. Telnet.java (continued)

```
            System.out.println(e);
            return;
        }
        System.out.println("Connected OK");
    }
}


/** This class handles one side of the connection. */
/* This class handles one half of a full-duplex connection.
 * Line-at-a-time mode. Streams, not writers, are used.
 */
class Pipe extends Thread {
    DataInputStream is;
    PrintStream os;

    // Constructor
    Pipe(InputStream is, OutputStream os) {
        this.is = new DataInputStream(is);
        this.os = new PrintStream(os);
    }

    // Do something method
    public void run() {
        String line;
        try {
            while ((line = is.readLine()) != null) {
                os.print(line);
                os.print("\r\n");
                os.flush();
            }
        } catch(IOException e) {
            throw new RuntimeException(e.getMessage());
        }
    }
}
```

15.10. *Program: Chat Client*

This program is a simple Chat program. You can't break in on ICQ or AIM with it, because they each use their own protocol;* this one simply writes to and reads from a server, locating the server with the applet method `getCodeBase()`. The server for this will be presented in Chapter 16. How does it look when you run it? Figure 15-2 shows me chatting all by myself one day.

---

* For an open source program that "AIMs" to let you talk to both from the same program, check out *Jabber*, at *http://www.jabber.org*.

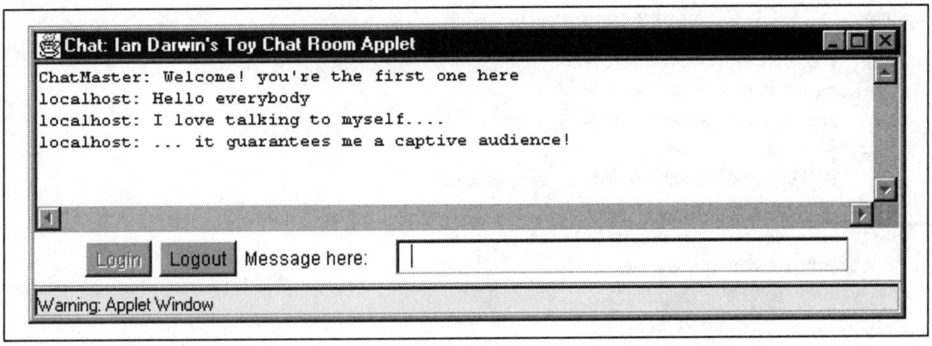

Figure 15-2. Chat client in action

The code is reasonably self-explanatory. We read from the remote server in a thread to make the input and the output run without blocking each other; this is discussed in Chapter 24. The reading and writing are discussed in this chapter. The program is an applet (see Recipe 17.2) and is shown in Example 15-11.

Example 15-11. ChatClient.java

```java
import java.applet.*;
import java.awt.*;
import java.awt.event.*;
import java.io.*;
import java.net.*;

/** Simple Chat Room Applet.
 * Writing a Chat Room seems to be one of many obligatory rites (or wrongs)
 * of passage for Java experts these days.
 * <P>
 * This one is a toy because it doesn't implement much of a command protocol, which
 * means we can't query the server as to * who's logged in,
 *  or anything fancy like that. However, it works OK for small groups.
 * <P>
 * Uses client socket w/ two Threads (main and one constructed),
 * one for reading and one for writing.
 * <P>
 * Server multiplexes messages back to all clients.
 * <P>
 * TODO in V2: use Java's MultiCastSocket, if it works OK on '95.
 */
public class ChatRoom extends Applet {
    /** The state */
    protected boolean loggedIn;
    /* The Frame, for a pop-up, durable Chat Room. */
    protected Frame cp;
    /** The default port number */
    protected static int PORTNUM = 7777;
```

Example 15-11. ChatClient.java (continued)

```java
    /** The actual port number */
    protected int port;
    /** The network socket */
    protected Socket sock;
    /** BufferedReader for reading from socket */
    protected BufferedReader is;
    /** PrintWriter for sending lines on socket */
    protected PrintWriter pw;
    /** TextField for input */
    protected TextField tf;
    /** TextArea to display conversations */
    protected TextArea ta;
    /** The Login button */
    protected Button lib;
    /** The LogOUT button */
    protected Button lob;
    /** The TitleBar title */
    final static String TITLE = "Chat: Ian Darwin's Toy Chat Room Applet";
    /** The message that we paint */
    protected String paintMessage;

    /** Init, inherited from Applet */
    public void init() {
        paintMessage = "Creating Window for Chat";
        repaint();
        cp = new Frame(TITLE);
        cp.setLayout(new BorderLayout());
        String portNum = getParameter("port");
        port = PORTNUM;
        if (portNum == null)
            port = Integer.parseInt(portNum);

        // The GUI
        ta = new TextArea(14, 80);
        ta.setEditable(false);// readonly
        ta.setFont(new Font("Monospaced", Font.PLAIN, 11));
        cp.add(BorderLayout.NORTH, ta);

        Panel p = new Panel();
        Button b;

        // The login button
        p.add(lib = new Button("Login"));
        lib.setEnabled(true);
        lib.requestFocus();
        lib.addActionListener(new ActionListener() {
            public void actionPerformed(ActionEvent e) {
                login();
```

Example 15-11. ChatClient.java (continued)

```java
                lib.setEnabled(false);
                lob.setEnabled(true);
                tf.requestFocus();// set keyboard focus in right place!
        }
    });

    // The logout button
    p.add(lob = new Button("Logout"));
    lob.setEnabled(false);
    lob.addActionListener(new ActionListener() {
        public void actionPerformed(ActionEvent e) {
                logout();
                lib.setEnabled(true);
                lob.setEnabled(false);
                lib.requestFocus();
        }
    });

    p.add(new Label("Message here:"));
    tf = new TextField(40);
    tf.addActionListener(new ActionListener() {
        public void actionPerformed(ActionEvent e) {
                if (loggedIn) {
                    pw.println(Chat.CMD_BCAST+tf.getText());
                    tf.setText("");
                }
        }
    });
    p.add(tf);

    cp.add(BorderLayout.SOUTH, p);

    cp.addWindowListener(new WindowAdapter() {
        public void windowClosing(WindowEvent e) {
                // If we do setVisible and dispose, then the Close completes
                ChatRoom.this.cp.setVisible(false);
                ChatRoom.this.cp.dispose();
                logout();
        }
    });
    cp.pack();
    // After packing the Frame, centre it on the screen.
    Dimension us = cp.getSize(),
        them = Toolkit.getDefaultToolkit().getScreenSize();
    int newX = (them.width - us.width) / 2;
    int newY = (them.height- us.height)/ 2;
    cp.setLocation(newX, newY);
    cp.setVisible(true);
```

Example 15-11. ChatClient.java (continued)

```java
        paintMessage = "Window should now be visible";
        repaint();
    }

    /** LOG ME IN TO THE CHAT */
    public void login() {
        if (loggedIn)
            return;
        try {
            sock = new Socket(getCodeBase().getHost(), port);
            is = new BufferedReader(new InputStreamReader(sock.getInputStream()));
            pw = new PrintWriter(sock.getOutputStream(), true);
        } catch(IOException e) {
            showStatus("Can't get socket: " + e);
            cp.add(new Label("Can't get socket: " + e));
            return;
        }

        // construct and start the reader: from server to textarea
        // make a Thread to avoid lockups.
        new Thread(new Runnable() {
            public void run() {
                String line;
                try {
                    while (loggedIn && ((line = is.readLine()) != null))
                        ta.append(line + "\n");
                } catch(IOException e) {
                    showStatus("GAA! LOST THE LINK!!");
                    return;
                }
            }
        }).start();

        // FAKE LOGIN FOR NOW
        pw.println(Chat.CMD_LOGIN + "AppletUser");
        loggedIn = true;
    }

    /** Log me out, Scotty, there's no intelligent life here! */
    public void logout() {
        if (!loggedIn)
            return;
        loggedIn = false;
        try {
            if (sock != null)
                sock.close();
        } catch (IOException ign) {
            // so what?
```

Example 15-11. ChatClient.java (continued)

```
        }
    }

    // It is deliberate that there is no STOP method - we want to keep
    // going even if the user moves the browser to another page.
    // Anti-social? Maybe, but you can use the CLOSE button to kill
    // the Frame, or you can exit the Browser.

    /** Paint paints the small window that appears in the HTML,
     * telling the user to look elsewhere!
     */
    public void paint(Graphics g) {
        Dimension d = getSize();
        int h = d.height;
        int w = d.width;
        g.fillRect(0, 0, w, 0);
        g.setColor(Color.black);
        g.drawString(paintMessage, 10, (h/2)-5);
    }
}
```

See Also

This chat applet might not work on all browser flavors; you might need the Java Plug-in. See Recipe 23.5.

There are many better-structured ways to write a chat client, including RMI, Java's Remote Methods Interface (see Recipe 22.0) and the Java Messaging Services, part of the Java 2 Enterprise Edition.

If you need to encrypt your socket connection, check out Sun's JSSE (Java Secure Socket Extension).

For a good overview of network programming from the C programmer's point of view, see the book *Unix Network Programming* by the late W. Richard Stevens. Despite the book's name, it's really about socket and TCP/IP/UDP programming, and covers all parts of the (Unix version) networking API and protocols such as TFTP in amazing detail.

16

Server-Side Java: Sockets

16.0. Introduction

Sockets form the underpinnings of all networking protocols. JDBC, RMI, CORBA, EJB, and the non-Java RPC (Remote Procedure Call), the foundation of the Network File System, or NFS: all of these are implemented by connecting various types of sockets together. Socket connections can be implemented in many languages, not just Java: C, C++, Perl, and Python are also popular, and many others are possible. A client or server written in any one of these languages can communicate with its opposite written in any of the other languages. Therefore, it's worth taking a quick look at how the ServerSocket behaves, even if you wind up utilizing the higher-level services such as RMI, JDBC, CORBA, or EJB.

The discussion looks first at the ServerSocket itself, then at writing data over a socket in various ways. Finally, there is a complete implementation of a usable network server written in Java: the chat server from the client in the previous chapter.

16.1. Opening a Server for Business

Problem

You need to write a socket-based server.

Solution

Create a ServerSocket for the given port number.

Discussion

The ServerSocket represents the "other end" of a connection, the server that waits patiently for clients to come along and connect to it. You construct a ServerSocket with just the port number;* since it doesn't need to connect to another host, it doesn't need a particular host's address as the client socket constructor does.

Assuming the ServerSocket constructor doesn't throw an exception, you're in business. Your next step is to await client activity, which you do by calling accept(). This call blocks until a client connects to your server; at that point, the accept() returns to you a Socket object (not a ServerSocket) that is connected in both directions to the Socket object on the client (or its equivalent, if written in another language). Example 16-1 shows the code for a socket-based server.

Example 16-1. Listen.java

```java
/**
 * Listen -- make a ServerSocket and wait for connections.
 */
public class Listen {
    /** The TCP port for the service. */
    public static final short PORT = 9999;

    public static void main(String[] argv) throws IOException {
        ServerSocket sock;
        Socket   clientSock;
        try {
            sock = new ServerSocket(PORT);
            while ((clientSock = sock.accept()) != null) {

                // Process it.
                process(clientSock);
            }

        } catch (IOException e) {
            System.err.println(e);
        }
    }

    /** This would do something with one client. */
```

---

* You can't just pick any port number for your own service, of course. There are certain well-known ports listed in your *services* file, such as 22 for Secure Shell, 25 for SMTP, and hundreds more. Also, on server-based operating systems, ports below 1024 are considered "privileged" ports, and require root or administrator privilege to create. This was an early form of security mechanism; today, with zillions of single-user desktops connected to the Internet, it provides little, but the restriction remains.

Example 16-1. Listen.java (continued)

```
    static void process(Socket s) throws IOException {
        System.out.println("Accept from client " + s.getInetAddress());
        // The conversation would be here.
        s.close();
    }
}
```

You would normally use the socket for reading and writing, as shown in the next few recipes.

You may want to listen only on a particular *network interface.* While we tend to think of network addresses as computer addresses, the two are not the same. A network address is actually the address of a particular network card, or network interface connection, on a given computing device. A desktop computer, laptop, Palm handheld, or cellular phone might have only a single interface, hence a single network address. But a large server machine might have two or more interfaces, usually when it is connected to several networks. A network *router* is a box (either special-purpose, e.g., Cisco, or general-purpose, e.g., a Unix host) that has interfaces on multiple networks *and* has both the capability and the administrative permission to forward packets from one network to another. A program running on such a server machine might want to provide services only to its inside network or its outside network. One way to accomplish this is by specifying the network interface to be listened on. Suppose you wanted to provide a different view of web pages for your intranet than you provided to outside customers. For security reasons, you probably wouldn't run both these services on the same machine. But if you wanted to, you could do this by providing the network interface addresses as arguments to the `ServerSocket` constructor.

However, to use this form of the constructor, you don't have the option of using a string for the network address's name, as you did with the client socket; you must convert it to an `InetAddress` object. You also have to provide a *backlog* argument, which is the number of connections that can queue up to be accepted before clients are told that your server is too busy. The complete setup is shown in Example 16-2.

Example 16-2. ListenInside.java

```
/**
 * ListenInside -- make a server socket that listens only on
 * a particular interface, in this case, one called "inside".
 */
public class ListenInside {
    /** The TCP port for the service. */
    public static final short PORT = 9999;
    /** The name of the network interface. */
```

Example 16-2. ListenInside.java (continued)

```
    public static final String INSIDE_HOST = "acmewidgets-inside";
    /** The number of clients allowed to queue */
    public static final int BACKLOG = 10;

    public static void main(String[] argv) throws IOException {
        ServerSocket sock;
        Socket   clientSock;
        try {
            sock = new ServerSocket(PORT, BACKLOG,
                InetAddress.getByName(INSIDE_HOST));
            while ((clientSock = sock.accept()) != null) {

                // Process it.
                process(clientSock);
            }

        } catch (IOException e) {
            System.err.println(e);
        }
    }

    /** This would do something with one client. */
    static void process(Socket s) throws IOException {
        System.out.println("Accept from inside " + s.getInetAddress());
        // The conversation would be here.
        s.close();
    }
}
```

The `InetAddress.getByName()` looks up the given hostname in a system-depen-dent way, referring to a configuration file in the */etc* or *\windows* directory, or to some kind of resolver such as the Domain Name Service. Consult a good book on networking and system administration if you need to modify this data.

16.2. *Returning a Response (String or Binary)*

Problem

You need to write a string or binary data to the client.

Solution

The socket gives you an `InputStream` and an `OutputStream`. Use them.

Discussion

The client socket examples in the previous chapter called the getInputStream()
and getOutputStream() methods. These examples do the same. The main difference is that they get the socket from a ServerSocket's accept() method, and
that normally the server creates or modifies the data and writes it to the client.
Example 16-3 is a simple Echo server, which the Echo client of Recipe 15.4 can
connect to. This server handles one complete connection with a client, then goes
back and does the accept() to wait for the next client.

Example 16-3. EchoServer.java

```
/**
 * EchoServer - create server socket, do I-O on it.
 */
public class EchoServer {
    /** Our server-side rendezvous socket */
    protected ServerSocket sock;
    /** The port number to use by default */
    public final static int ECHOPORT = 7;
    /** Flag to control debugging */
    protected boolean debug = true;

    /** main: construct and run */
    public static void main(String[] argv) {
        new EchoServer(ECHOPORT).handle();
    }

    /** Construct an EchoServer on the given port number */
    public EchoServer(int port) {
        try {
            sock = new ServerSocket(port);
        } catch (IOException e) {
            System.err.println("I/O error in setup");
            System.err.println(e);
            System.exit(1);
        }
    }

    /** This handles the connections */
    protected void handle() {
        Socket ios = null;
        BufferedReader is = null;
        PrintWriter os = null;
        while (true) {
            try {
                ios = sock.accept();
                System.err.println("Accepted from " +
```

Example 16-3. EchoServer.java (continued)

```
                        ios.getInetAddress().getHostName());
                is = new BufferedReader(
                    new InputStreamReader(ios.getInputStream(), "8859_1"));
                os = new PrintWriter(
                        new OutputStreamWriter(
                            ios.getOutputStream(), "8859_1"), true);
                String echoLine;
                while ((echoLine = is.readLine()) != null) {
                    System.err.println("Read " + echoLine);
                    os.print(echoLine + "\r\n");
                    System.err.println("Wrote " + echoLine);
                }
                System.err.println("All done!");
            } catch (IOException e) {
                System.err.println(e);
            } finally {
                try {
                    if (is != null)
                        is.close();
                    if (os != null)
                        os.close();
                    if (ios != null)
                        ios.close();
                } catch (IOException e) {
                    // These are unlikely, but might indicate that
                    // the other end shut down early, a disk filled up
                    // but wasn't detected until close, etc.
                    System.err.println("IO Error in close");
                }
            }
        }
        /*NOTREACHED*/
    }
}
```

To send a string across an arbitrary network connection, some authorities recommend sending both the carriage return and the newline character. This explains the `\r\n` in the code. The reason is that if the other end is a DOS program or a Telnet-like program, it may be expecting both characters. On the other hand, if you are writing both ends, you can simply use `println()`, followed always by an explicit `flush()` before you read, to prevent the deadlock of having both ends trying to read with one end's data still in the `PrintWriter`'s buffer!

If you need to process binary data, use the data streams from `java.io` instead of the readers/writers. I need a server for the `DaytimeBinary` program of Recipe 15.5. In operation, it should look like the following.

```
C:\javasrc\network>java DaytimeBinary
Reme time is 3161316799
BASE_DIFF is 2209032000
Time diff == 952284799
Time on localhost is Sun Mar 05 19:33:19 GMT 2000

C:\javasrc\network>time
Current time is  7:33:23.84p
Enter new time:

C:\javasrc\network>date
Current date is Sun 03-05-2000
Enter new date (mm-dd-yy):

C:\javasrc\network>
```

Well, it happens that I have such a program in my arsenal, so I present it in
Example 16-4. Note that it directly uses certain public constants defined in the cli-
ent class. Normally these are defined in the server class and used by the client, but
I wanted to present the client code first.

Example 16-4. DaytimeServer.java (binary server protocol)

```
/**
 * DaytimeServer - send the binary time.
 */
public class DaytimeServer {
    /** Our server-side rendezvous socket */
    ServerSocket sock;
    /** The port number to use by default */
    public final static int PORT = 37;

    /** main: construct and run */
    public static void main(String[] argv) {
        new DaytimeServer(PORT).runService();
    }

    /** Construct an EchoServer on the given port number */
    public DaytimeServer(int port) {
        try {
            sock = new ServerSocket(port);
        } catch (IOException e) {
            System.err.println("I/O error in setup\n" + e);
            System.exit(1);
        }
    }

    /** This handles the connections */
    protected void runService() {
        Socket ios = null;
```

Example 16-4. DaytimeServer.java (binary server protocol) (continued)

```
DataOutputStream os = null;
while (true) {
    try {
        System.out.println("Waiting for connection on port " + PORT);
        ios = sock.accept();
        System.err.println("Accepted from " +
            ios.getInetAddress().getHostName());
        os = new DataOutputStream(ios.getOutputStream());
        long time = System.currentTimeMillis();

        time /= DaytimeBinary.MSEC;// Daytime Protocol is in seconds

        // Convert to Java time base.
        time += DaytimeBinary.BASE_DIFF;

        // Write it, truncating cast to int since it is using
        // the Internet Daytime protocol which uses 4 bytes.
        // This will fail in the year 2038, along with all
        // 32-bit timekeeping systems based from 1970.
        // Remember, you read about the Y2038 crisis here first!
        os.writeInt((int)time);
        os.close();
    } catch (IOException e) {
        System.err.println(e);
    }
}
}
}
```

16.3. Returning Object Information

Problem

You need to return an object.

Solution

Create the object you need, and write it using an ObjectOutputStream created on top of the socket's output stream.

Discussion

In the previous chapter, you saw a program that read a Date object over an ObjectInputStream. This code is the other end of that process, the DaytimeObjectServer. Example 16-5 is a server that constructs a Date object each time it's connected to, and returns it.

Example 16-5. DaytimeObjectServer.java

```java
/*
 * DaytimeObject - connect to the Daytime (ascii) service.
 */
public class DaytimeObjectServer {
    /** The TCP port for the object time service. */
    public static final short TIME_PORT = 1951;

    public static void main(String[] argv) {
        ServerSocket sock;
        Socket  clientSock;
        try {
            sock = new ServerSocket(TIME_PORT);
            while ((clientSock = sock.accept()) != null) {
                System.out.println("Accept from " +
                    clientSock.getInetAddress());
                ObjectOutputStream os = new ObjectOutputStream(
                    clientSock.getOutputStream());

                // Construct and write the Object
                os.writeObject(new Date());

                os.close();
            }

        } catch (IOException e) {
            System.err.println(e);
        }
    }
}
```

16.4. Handling Multiple Clients

Problem

Your server needs to handle multiple clients.

Solution

Use a thread for each.

Discussion

In the C world, there are several mechanisms that allow a server to handle multiple clients. One is to use a special system call `select()` or `poll()`, which notifies the server when any of a set of file/socket descriptors is ready to read, ready to

write, or has an error. By including its *rendezvous socket* (equivalent to our
ServerSocket) in this list, the C-based server can read from any of a number of
clients in any order. Java does not provide this call, as it is not readily implement-
able on some Java platforms. Instead, Java uses the general-purpose Thread
mechanism, as described in Recipe 24.8. Threads are, in fact, one of the other
mechanisms available to the C programmer on most platforms. Each time the
code accepts a new connection from the ServerSocket, it immediately constructs and starts a new thread object to process that client.*

The code to implement accepting on a socket is pretty simple, apart from having
to catch IOExceptions:

```
/** Run the main loop of the Server. */
void runServer() {
    while (true) {
        try {
            Socket clntSock = sock.accept();
            new Handler(clntSock).start();
        } catch(IOException e) {
            System.err.println(e);
        }
    }
}
```

To use a thread, you must either subclass Thread or implement Runnable. The
Handler class must be a subclass of Thread for this code to work as written; if
Handler instead implemented the Runnable interface, the code would pass an
instance of the Runnable into the constructor for Thread, as in:

```
Thread t = new Thread(new Handler(clntSock));
t.start();
```

But as written, Handler is constructed using the normal socket returned by the
accept() call, and normally calls the socket's getInputStream() and
getOutputStream() methods and holds its conversation in the usual way. I'll
present a full implementation, a threaded echo client. First, a session showing it in
use:

```
$ java  EchoServerThreaded
EchoServerThreaded ready for connections.
Socket starting: Socket[addr=localhost/127.0.0.1,port=2117,localport=7]
Socket starting: Socket[addr=darian/192.168.1.50,port=13386,localport=7]
Socket starting: Socket[addr=darian/192.168.1.50,port=22162,localport=7]
```

---

* There are some limits to how many threads you can have, which affect only very large, enterprise-scale
  servers. You can't expect to have thousands of threads running in the standard Java runtime. For large,
  high-performance servers, you may wish to resort to native code (see Recipe 26.4) using select() or
  poll().

```
Socket ENDED: Socket[addr=darian/192.168.1.50,port=22162,localport=7]
Socket ENDED: Socket[addr=darian/192.168.1.50,port=13386,localport=7]
Socket ENDED: Socket[addr=localhost/127.0.0.1,port=2117,localport=7]
```

Here, I connected to the server once with my EchoClient program and, while still connected, called it up again (and again) with an operating system–provided Telnet client. The server communicated with all the clients concurrently, sending the answers from the first client back to the first client, and the data from the second client back to the second client. In short, it works. I ended the sessions with the end-of-file character in the program, and used the normal disconnect mechanism from the Telnet client. Example 16-6 is the code for the server.

Example 16-6. EchoServerThreaded.java

```java
/**
 * Threaded Echo Server, sequential allocation scheme.
 */
public class EchoServerThreaded {

    public static final int ECHOPORT = 7;

    public static void main(String[] av)
    {
        new EchoServerThreaded().runServer();
    }

    public void runServer()
    {
        ServerSocket sock;
        Socket clientSocket;

        try {
            sock = new ServerSocket(ECHOPORT);

            System.out.println("EchoServerThreaded ready for connections.");

            /* Wait for a connection */
            while(true){
                clientSocket = sock.accept();
                /* Create a thread to do the communication, and start it */
                new Handler(clientSocket).start();
            }
        } catch(IOException e) {
            /* Crash the server if IO fails. Something bad has happened */
            System.err.println("Could not accept " + e);
            System.exit(1);
        }
    }
```

Example 16-6. EchoServerThreaded.java (continued)

```
/** A Thread subclass to handle one client conversation. */
class Handler extends Thread {
    Socket sock;

    Handler(Socket s) {
        sock = s;
    }

    public void run()
    {
        System.out.println("Socket starting: " + sock);
        try {
            DataInputStream is = new DataInputStream(
                sock.getInputStream());
            PrintStream os = new PrintStream(
                sock.getOutputStream(), true);
            String line;
            while ((line = is.readLine()) != null) {
                os.print(line + "\r\n");
                os.flush();
            }
            sock.close();
        } catch (IOException e) {
            System.out.println("IO Error on socket " + e);
            return;
        }
        System.out.println("Socket ENDED: " + sock);
    }
}
```

There can be a performance issue if there are a lot of short transactions, since each client causes the creation of a new threaded object. If you know or can reliably predict the degree of concurrency that will be needed, an alternative paradigm involves the pre-creation of a fixed number of threads. But then how do you control their access to the ServerSocket? A look at the ServerSocket class documentation reveals that the accept() method is not synchronized, meaning that any number of threads can call the method concurrently. This could cause bad things to happen. So I use the synchronized keyword around this call to ensure that only one client runs in it at a time, because it updates global data. When there are no clients connected, you will have one (randomly selected) thread running in the ServerSocket object's accept() method, waiting for a connection, plus *n–1* threads waiting for the first thread to return from the method. As soon as the first thread manages to accept a connection, it goes off and holds its conversation, releasing its lock in the process so that another randomly chosen thread is allowed into the accept() method. Each thread's run() method has an indefinite loop beginning with an accept() and then holding the conversation. The result is that client connections can get started more quickly, at a cost of slightly greater server startup time. Doing it this way also avoids the overhead of constructing a new Handler or Thread object each time a request comes along. This general approach is similar to what the popular Apache web server does, though it normally creates a number of identical processes (instead of threads) to handle client connections. Accordingly, I have modified the EchoServerThreaded class shown in Example 16-7 to work this way.

Example 16-7. EchoServerThreaded2.java

```java
/**
 * Threaded Echo Server, pre-allocation scheme.
 */
public class EchoServerThreaded2 {

    public static final int ECHOPORT = 7;

    public static final int NUM_THREADS = 4;

    /** Main method, to start the servers. */
    public static void main(String[] av)
    {
        new EchoServerThreaded2(ECHOPORT, NUM_THREADS);
    }

    /** Constructor */
    public EchoServerThreaded2(int port, int numThreads)
    {
        ServerSocket servSock;
        Socket clientSocket;

        try {
            servSock = new ServerSocket(ECHOPORT);

        } catch(IOException e) {
            /* Crash the server if IO fails. Something bad has happened */
            System.err.println("Could not create ServerSocket " + e);
            System.exit(1);
            return;/*NOTREACHED*/
        }

        // Create a series of threads and start them.
        for (int i=0; i<numThreads; i++) {
            new Thread(new Handler(servSock, i)).start();
        }
    }
```

Example 16-7. EchoServerThreaded2.java (continued)

```java
    /** A Thread subclass to handle one client conversation. */
    class Handler extends Thread {
        ServerSocket servSock;
        int threadNumber;

        /** Construct a Handler. */
        Handler(ServerSocket s, int i) {
            super();
            servSock = s;
            threadNumber = i;
            setName("Thread " + threadNumber);
        }

        public void run()
        {
            /* Wait for a connection */
            while (true){
                try {
                    System.out.println( getName() + " waiting");

                    // Wait here for the next connection.
                    synchronized(servSock) {
                        Socket clientSocket = servSock.accept();
                    }
                    System.out.println(getName() + " starting, IP=" +
                        clientSocket.getInetAddress());
                    DataInputStream is = new DataInputStream(
                        clientSocket.getInputStream());
                    PrintStream os = new PrintStream(
                        clientSocket.getOutputStream(), true);
                    String line;
                    while ((line = is.readLine()) != null) {
                        os.print(line + "\r\n");
                        os.flush();
                    }
                    System.out.println(getName() + " ENDED ");
                    clientSocket.close();
                } catch (IOException ex) {
                    System.out.println(getName() + ": IO Error on socket " + ex);
                    return;
                }
            }
        }
    }
}
```

16.5. Network Logging

Problem

Your class is running inside a server container, and its debugging output is hard to obtain.

Solution

Use a network-based logger like the one shown here.

Discussion

Getting the debug output from a desktop client is fairly easy on most operating systems. But if the program you want to debug is running in a "container" like a servlet engine or EJB server, it can be difficult to obtain debugging output, particularly if the container is running on a remote computer. It would be convenient if you could have your program send messages back to a program on your desktop machine for immediate display. Needless to say, it's not that hard to do this with Java's socket mechanism. I have written a small, simple API to handle this type of logging function. The program being debugged is the "client" from a socket point of view—even though it may be running in a server-side container such as a web server or application server—since the "network client" is the program that initiates the connection. The program that runs on your desktop machine is the "server" program for sockets, since it waits for a connection to come along.

Example 16-8 is a simple client program called `NetLogSimple`.

Example 16-8. NetLogSimple.java

```java
/* A simple example of using the NetLog program.
 * Unrealistic in that it's standalone; this API is
 * intended for use inside another program, possibly
 * a servlet or EJB.
 */
public class NetLogSimple {

    public static void main(String[] args) throws java.io.IOException {

        System.out.println("NetLogSimple: Starting...");

        // Get the connection to the NetLog
        NetLog nl = new NetLog();

        // Show sending a String
        nl.log("Hello Java");
```

Example 16-8. NetLogSimple.java (continued)

```
        // Show sending Objects
        nl.log(new java.util.Date());
        nl.log(nl);

        // Show sending null and "" (normally an accident...)
        nl.log(null);
        nl.log("");

        // All done, close the log
        nl.close();

        System.out.println("NetLogSimple: Done...");
    }
}
```

In Figure 16-1, I show both the server and client running side by side.

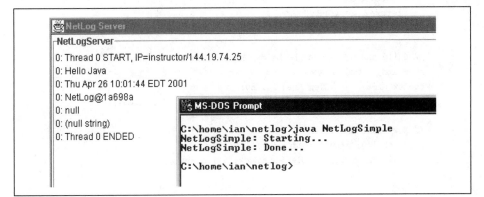

Figure 16-1. NetLog server and client

The client-side API and the server code are both online. Example 16-9 shows the code for the key parts of the server.

Example 16-9. NetLogServer.java

```
public class NetLogServer {

    public static final int PORT = 65432;

    public static final int NUM_THREADS = 8;

    JFrame theFrame;
    JTextArea theTextArea;

    /** Main method, to start the servers. */
```

Example 16-9. NetLogServer.java (continued)

```java
    public static void main(String[] av)
    {
        new NetLogServer(PORT, NUM_THREADS);
    }


    /** Constructor */
    public NetLogServer(int port, int numThreads)
    {
        ServerSocket servSock;
        Socket clientSocket;

        try {
            servSock = new ServerSocket(PORT);

        } catch(IOException e) {
            /* Crash the server if IO fails. Something bad has happened */
            System.err.println("Could not create ServerSocket " + e);
            System.exit(1);
            return;   /*NOTREACHED*/
        }

        // Build the GUI - must be before Handler constructors!
        theFrame  = new JFrame("NetLog Server");
        theTextArea = new JTextArea(24, 80);
        theFrame.getContentPane().add(new JScrollPane(theTextArea));

        // Now start the Threads
        for (int i=0; i<numThreads; i++) {
            new Thread(new Handler(servSock, i)).start();
        }

        theFrame.pack();
        theFrame.setVisible(true);
        theFrame.addWindowListener(new WindowAdapter() {
            public void windowClosing(WindowEvent we) {
                System.exit(0);
            }
        });

    }

    public synchronized void log(int tid, String s) {
        StringBuffer sb = new StringBuffer();
        sb.append(tid);
        sb.append(": ");

        if (s == null) {
            sb.append("(null)");
```

Example 16-9. NetLogServer.java (continued)

```
        }
        else if (s.length() == 0) {
            sb.append("(null string)");
        }
        else
            sb.append(s);

        sb.append('\n');
        theTextArea.append(sb.toString());
        theTextArea.setCaretPosition(theTextArea.getText().length());
        theFrame.toFront();
}

/** A Thread subclass to handle one client conversation. */
class Handler extends Thread {
    ServerSocket servSock;
    int tid;

    /** Construct a Handler. */
    Handler(ServerSocket s, int i) {
        super();
        servSock = s;
        tid = i;
        setName("Thread " + tid);
    }

    public void run()
    {
        /* Wait for a connection */
        while (true){
            try {
                // log(tid, getName() + " waiting");
                Socket clientSocket = servSock.accept();
                log(tid,getName() + " START, IP=" +
                    clientSocket.getInetAddress());
                BufferedReader is = new BufferedReader(
                    new InputStreamReader(clientSocket.getInputStream()));
                String line;
                while ((line = is.readLine()) != null) {
                    // System.out.println(">> " + line);
                    log(tid,line);
                }
                log(tid,getName() + " ENDED ");
                clientSocket.close();
            } catch (IOException ex) {
                log(tid, getName() + ": IO Error on socket " + ex);
                return;
            }
```

Example 16-9. NetLogServer.java (continued)

```
            }
        }
    }
}
```

See Also

If you want to run this on a network, you need to be very aware of security issues. One very common form of attack is a simple denial-of-service, during which the attacker makes a lot of connections to your server in order to slow it down. If you had extended this program by writing the log to disk, the attacker could fill up your disk by sending lots of garbage. However, because this example displays the log on the screen, you would see this happening. Don't leave the server running while you're not around to watch it!

The Apache Foundation Jakarta Project (*http://jakarta.apache.org*) offers log4j, which provides a similar service but is more fully fleshed out; it can write to a file, an OutputStream or Writer, or a remote log4j, Unix Syslog or NT Event Logger server. Java 2 SDK (JDK 1.4) includes a new Event Logger mechanism.

16.6. Program: A Java Chat Server

This program implements a simple chat server (Example 16-10) that works with the chat applet from Recipe 15.10. It accepts connections from an arbitrary number of clients; any message sent from one client is broadcast to all clients. In addition to ServerSockets, it demonstrates the use of threads (see Chapter 24). And since there are interactions among clients, this server needs to keep track of all the clients it has at any one time. I use an ArrayList (see Recipe 7.3) to serve as an expandable list, and am careful to use the synchronized keyword around all accesses to this list to prevent one thread from accessing it while another is modifying it (this is discussed in Chapter 24).

Example 16-10. ChatServer.java

```
/** Simple Chat Server to go with our Trivial Chat Client.
 *
 * Does not implement any form of "anonymous nicknames" - probably
 * a good thing, given how a few people have abused anonymous
 * chat rooms in the past.
 */
public class ChatServer {
    /** What I call myself in system messages */
    protected final static String CHATMASTER_ID = "ChatMaster";
    /** What goes between any handle and the message */
    protected final static String SEP = ": ";
```

Example 16-10. ChatServer.java (continued)

```java
/** The Server Socket */
protected ServerSocket servSock;
/** The list of my current clients */
protected ArrayList clients;
/** Debugging state */
private boolean DEBUG = false;

/** Main just constructs a ChatServer, which should never return */
public static void main(String[] argv) {
    System.out.println("DarwinSys Chat Server 0.1 starting...");
    ChatServer w = new ChatServer();
    w.runServer();// should never return.
    System.out.println("**ERROR* Chat Server 0.1 quitting");
}

/** Construct (and run!) a Chat Service */
ChatServer() {
    clients = new ArrayList();
    try {
        servSock = new ServerSocket(Chat.PORTNUM);
        System.out.println("DarwinSys Chat Server Listening on port " +
            Chat.PORTNUM);
    } catch(IOException e) {
        log("IO Exception in ChatServer.<init>");
        System.exit(0);
    }
}

public void runServer() {
    try {
        while (true) {
            Socket us = servSock.accept();
            String hostName = us.getInetAddress().getHostName();
            System.out.println("Accepted from " + hostName);
            ChatHandler cl = new ChatHandler(us, hostName);
            synchronized (clients) {
                clients.add(cl);
                cl.start();
                if (clients.size() == 1)
                    cl.send(CHATMASTER_ID,
                            "Welcome! you're the first one here");
                else {
                    cl.send(CHATMASTER_ID, "Welcome! you're the latest of " +
                            clients.size() + " users.");
                }
            }
        }
    } catch(IOException e) {
```

Example 16-10. ChatServer.java (continued)

```
            log("IO Exception in runServer: " + e);
            System.exit(0);
        }
    }

    protected void log(String s) {
        System.out.println(s);
    }

    /** Inner class to handle one conversation */
    protected class ChatHandler extends Thread {
        /** The client socket */
        protected Socket clientSock;
        /** BufferedReader for reading from socket */
        protected BufferedReader is;
        /** PrintWriter for sending lines on socket */
        protected PrintWriter pw;
        /** The client's host */
        protected String clientIP;
        /** String handle */
        protected String login;

        /* Construct a Chat Handler */
        public ChatHandler(Socket sock, String clnt) throws IOException {
            clientSock = sock;
            clientIP = clnt;
            is = new BufferedReader(
                new InputStreamReader(sock.getInputStream()));
            pw = new PrintWriter(sock.getOutputStream(), true);
        }

        /** Each ChatHandler is a Thread, so here's the run() method,
         * which handles this conversation.
         */
        public void run() {
            String line;
            try {
                while ((line = is.readLine()) != null) {
                    char c = line.charAt(0);
                    line = line.substring(1);
                    switch (c) {
                    case Chat.CMD_LOGIN:
                        if (!Chat.isValidLoginName(line)) {
                            send(CHATMASTER_ID, "LOGIN " + line + " invalid");
                            log("LOGIN INVALID from " + clientIP);
                            continue;
                        }
                        login = line;
```

Example 16-10. ChatServer.java (continued)

```
                    broadcast(CHATMASTER_ID, login +
                        " joins us, for a total of " +
                        clients.size() + " users");
                    break;
                case Chat.CMD_MESG:
                    if (login == null) {
                        send(CHATMASTER_ID, "please login first");
                        continue;
                    }
                    int where = line.indexOf(Chat.SEPARATOR);
                    String recip = line.substring(0, where);
                    String mesg = line.substring(where+1);
                    log("MESG: " + login + "-->" + recip + ": "+ mesg);
                    ChatHandler cl = lookup(recip);
                    if (cl == null)
                        psend(CHATMASTER_ID, recip + " not logged in.");
                    else
                        cl.psend(login, mesg);
                    break;
                case Chat.CMD_QUIT:
                    broadcast(CHATMASTER_ID, "Goodbye to "
                            + login + "@" + clientIP);
                    close();
                    return;  // END OF THIS CHATHANDLER

                case Chat.CMD_BCAST:
                    if (login != null)
                        broadcast(login, line);
                    else
                        log("B<L FROM " + clientIP);
                    break;
                default:
                    log("Unknown cmd " + c + " from " + login + "@" + clientIP);
                }
            }
        } catch (IOException e) {
            log("IO Exception: " + e);
        } finally {
            // the sock ended, so we're done, bye now
            // Can NOT send a good-bye message, until we have
            // a simple command-based protocol in place.
            System.out.println(login + SEP + "All Done");
            synchronized(clients) {
                clients.remove(this);
                if (clients.size() == 0) {
                    System.out.println(CHATMASTER_ID + SEP +
                        "Im so lonely I could cry...");
                } else if (clients.size() == 1) {
```

Example 16-10. ChatServer.java (continued)

```java
                        ChatHandler last = (ChatHandler)clients.get(0);
                        last.send(CHATMASTER_ID,
                            "Hey, you're talking to yourself again");
                    } else {
                        broadcast(CHATMASTER_ID,
                            "There are now " + clients.size() + " users");
                    }
                }
            }
        }

    protected void close() {
        if (clientSock == null) {
            log("close when not open");
            return;
        }
        try {
            clientSock.close();
            clientSock = null;
        } catch (IOException e) {
            log("Failure during close to " + clientIP);
        }
    }

    /** Send one message to this user */
    public void send(String sender, String mesg) {
        pw.println(sender + SEP + mesg);
    }

    /** Send a private message */
    protected void psend(String sender, String msg) {
        send("<*" + sender + "*>", msg);
    }

    /** Send one message to all users */
    public void broadcast(String sender, String mesg) {
        System.out.println("Broadcasting " + sender + SEP + mesg);
        for (int i=0; i<clients.size(); i++) {
            ChatHandler sib = (ChatHandler)clients.get(i);
            if (DEBUG)
                System.out.println("Sending to " + sib);
            sib.send(sender, mesg);
        }
        if (DEBUG) System.out.println("Done broadcast");
    }

    protected ChatHandler lookup(String nick) {
        synchronized(clients) {
```

Example 16-10. ChatServer.java (continued)

```
                  for (int i=0; i<clients.size(); i++) {
                      ChatHandler cl = (ChatHandler)clients.get(i);
                      if (cl.login.equals(nick))
                          return cl;
                  }
              }
              return null;
          }


          /** Present this ChatHandler as a String */
          public String toString() {
              return "ChatHandler[" + login + "]";
          }
      }
  }
}
```

I've used this code with a number of clients connected concurrently, and no difficulties were found.

See Also

The server side of any network mechanism is extremely sensitive to security issues. It is easy for one misconfigured or poorly written server program to compromise the security of an entire network! There are many books on network security, but two books stand out as worthy of mention: Cheswick and Bellovin's *Firewalls and Internet Security* and the more recent *Hacking Exposed,* by McCLure et al.

This completes my discussion of server-side Java using sockets. I'll next return to the client side to discuss applets and some useful client-side recipes. Later, in Chapter 22, I show an alternate technology that can be used to implement both sides of the chat program in a more object-oriented manner. Finally, a chat server could also be implemented using JMS (Java Message Service), a newer API that handles store-and-forward message processing. This is beyond the scope of this book, but there's an example of such a chat server in O'Reilly's book *Java Message Service.*

17

Network Clients II: Applets and Web Clients

17.0. Introduction

In Chapter 15, I discussed straightforward client applications that communicate over a socket. Now we'll turn our attention to a variety of other client topics. First let's look at Java-based web applet client programs. Applets are, as you probably know, small programs that run inside and under the control of a web browser. There's a discussion of `Applet` versus `JApplet` and the `Applet` methods. Deploying an applet is no different from deploying a web page—you simply copy it into the web server directory—but you need an HTML page to invoke it (discussed in Recipe 17.1). We'll then discuss some additional client-side topics, such as loading a URL, that apply both to applets and to applications. In Chapter 18, we'll talk about servlets, which are similar to applets but run inside the process of a web server. There are some issues on the applet deployment side; see Recipe 23.5 for a means of ensuring that a user's browser has a Java runtime compatible with your applet. Recipe 23.11 contains information on Java Web Start, which combines applet-like downloading with full application capabilities.

17.1. Embedding Java in a Web Page

Problem

You need to deploy a Java applet.

Solution

Use an APPLET tag in an HTML page.

Discussion

While this is not the place for a dissertation on the details of HTML, you should at least know that HTML is a tag-based textual language for writing web pages. The tags (officially called *elements*) have short names, such as P for paragraph and A for anchor (hyperlink). Tag names can be written in uppercase (as I do in this book) or lowercase, but be consistent. Tags are surrounded by angle brackets, < and >. Modifiers, called *attributes*, go between the tag name and the close angle brackets. For example, the body of a web page might be introduced by <BODY BGCOLOR=WHITE>, which gives that page the specified background color. Most tags, including BODY and P, have a corresponding end tag, consisting of a forward slash character (/) and the name of the tag. A paragraph, for example, should begin with <P> and end with </P>. In days of yore, it was common to simply use <P> between paragraphs, but this mistake stems from not understanding the nature of HTML tags as containers. You still see old pages done this way and, occasionally, very old books or web pages recommending this.

The most common method of embedding a Java applet is to use an APPLET tag. Other tags include OBJECT and EMBED, which I'll discuss briefly in Recipe 23.5. The APPLET tag has three required parameters (CODE/OBJECT, WIDTH, and HEIGHT) and several optional ones. Table 17-1 lists these parameters.

Table 17-1. Applet parameters

Parameter	Description
CODE	Name of applet class to run
OBJECT	Name of serialized applet to run
WIDTH	Width in pixels for applet display
HEIGHT	Height in pixels for applet display
CODEBASE	Directory (URL) from which to load class file
ARCHIVE	List of JAR archives in which to hunt for applet and resources
ALT	Alternate text to display if applet can't be loaded
NAME	Name of this applet instance
ALIGN	Horizontal alignment
VSPACE	Vertical space around applet, in pixels
HSPACE	Horizontal space around applet, in pixels

You may also wish to pass some parameters in to the applet. Since an applet has no main method, there is no command-line communication with the applet. Hence, the applet parameters are included in the HTML page: the PARAM tags go between the <APPLET> and </APPLET> tags. The following applet, for example, is an HTML file that demonstrates many of these parameters.

```
<APPLET>
    CODE="DemoApplet.class" WIDTH=400 HEIGHT=75
    CODEBASE="http://www.darwinsys.com/applets/"
    >
    <PARAM NAME="text" VALUE="Java is fun!">
    <HR>
    If you were using a Java-enabled browser,
    you would see the graphical results instead of this paragraph.
    <HR>
</APPLET>
```

17.2. Applet Techniques

Problem

You need to write an applet.

Solution

Write a class that extends `java.applet.Applet` or `javax.swing.JApplet`, and use some or all of the applet methods. Start with `Applet` if you want to use plain AWT and be portable to all browsers; use `JApplet` if you want Swing capabilities in your applet (but see the note at the end of this recipe under "See Also").

Discussion

The four `Applet` "life cycle" methods that an applet writer can implement are `init()`, `start()`, `stop()`, and `destroy()` (see Table 17-2). The applet's life cycle is more complex than that of a regular application, since the user can make the browser move to a new page, return to a previous page, reload the current page, etc. What's a poor applet to do?

Table 17-2. Applet methods

Method name	Function
init()	Initialize the applet (takes the place of a constructor).
start()	The page is loaded, and we're ready to display.
stop()	The user is leaving this page.
destroy()	The applet is being unloaded.

Applets normally use their `init()` method to initialize their state, the same functionality as a constructor in a non-applet class. This may seem a bit odd for those used to constructors in an OO language. However, it is mandatory for any methods that will call applet-specific methods, such as the all-important `getParameter()`.

Why? In brief, because the browser will first construct the applet—always with the no-argument constructor form, which is much easier for the browser (see Recipe 25.3)—and then call its setStub() method.* The AppletStub is an object provided by the browser, which provides a method getAppletContext(), which of course returns an AppletContext object. These are both *delegates* (in the design patterns sense). The AppletStub object contains the actual implementation of getParameter(), getCodeBase(), and getDocumentBase(). The AppletContext object contains the real implementations of most other applet-specific routines, including showStatus(), getImage(), and showDocument().

So, an applet constructor can't call getParameter(), getImage(), or showStatus() because the AppletStub isn't set until the applet's constructor returns. About the most a constructor can do is add GUI elements. Therefore, it is generally preferable to do all the applet's initialization in one place, so it might as well be the init() method, which a sane browser will call only once for each applet instance. This is why, in practice, most applets don't have any constructors: the default (no-argument) constructor is the only one ever called.

The start() method is called when the browser has fully loaded the applet and it's ready to go. This is the normal time for your applet to start threads (Chapter 24), audio or video (see Chapter 12), or anything else that takes time. The stop() method is called when the user gets bored and leaves the page.

The least commonly used applet method is destroy(); it is called when the browser removes your applet instance from memory and allows you to close files, network connections, etc. After that, it's all over.

All four methods are public, all return void, and all take no arguments. They are shown together in Example 17-1.

Example 17-1. AppletMethods.java

```
import java.applet.*;
import java.awt.*;
import java.net.*;

/** AppletMethods -- show stop/start and AudioClip methods */

public class AppletMethods extends Applet {
    /** AudioClip object, used to load and play a sound file. */
    AudioClip snd = null;

    /** Yes, applets can have constructors! */
```

---

* It didn't have to be this way. At the beginning of Java-browserdom, they could have said, "Let's just pass in the applet stub as an argument when constructing the applet." But they didn't, "and now it's too late," as Dr. Seuss once said.

Example 17-1. AppletMethods.java (continued)

```java
    public AppletMethods() {
        System.out.println("In Appletmethods::<init> No Arg form");
    }

    /** Initialize the sound file object and the GUI. */
    public void init() {
        System.out.println("In AppletMethods.init()");
        try {
            snd = getAudioClip(new URL(getCodeBase(), "laugh.au"));
        } catch (MalformedURLException e) {
            showStatus(e.toString());
        }
        setSize(200,100);// take the place of a GUI
    }

    /** Called from the Browser when the page is ready to go. */
    public void start() {
        System.out.println("In AppletMethods.start()");
        if (snd != null)
            snd.play();// loop() to be obnoxious...
    }

    /** Called from the Browser when the page is being vacated. */
    public void stop() {
        System.out.println("In AppletMethods.stop()");
        if (snd != null)
            snd.stop();// stop play() or loop()
    }

    /** Called from the Browser (when the applet is being un-cached?).
     * Not actually used here, but the println will show when it's called.
     */
    public void destroy() {
        System.out.println("In AppletMethods.destroy()");
    }

    public void paint(Graphics g) {
        g.drawString("Welcome to Java", 50, 50);
    }

    /** An alternate form of getParameter that lets
     * you provide a default value, since this is so common.
     */
    public String getParameter(String p, String def) {
        return getParameter(p)==null?def:getParameter(p);
    }
}
```

See Also

Applets based on `Applet` and using AWT will work on most browsers. Applets based on `JApplet` and/or using Swing components will need the Java Plug-in (see Recipe 23.5) to ensure that a compatible runtime is available.

17.3. Contacting a Server on the Applet Host

Problem

You want an applet to contact a socket-based server on the host from which it was loaded.

Solution

Use the method `getCodeBase()` to retrieve a URL for the applet host, and call the URL's `getHost()`. Use this to construct a client socket.

Discussion

For very good security reasons, applets are not permitted network access to servers on hosts other than the one from which the applet was loaded.

To reach a server on the download host, call the applet method `getCodeBase()`, which yields a URL for the applet host. Call this URL's `getHost()` method to get the hostname. Finally, use the hostname to open a client socket (see Recipe 15.1). For example:

```
URL u = getCodeBase();
String host = u.getHost();
Socket s = new Socket(host , MY_SERVER_PORT);
```

Of course, in real code you wouldn't create all those temporary variables:

```
Socket s = new Socket(getCodeBase().getHost(), MY_SERVER_PORT);
```

And, of course, you will need error handling. Example 17-2 shows an applet that constructs a sort of login dialog and passes the results to a socket-based server on the applet host, using exactly this technique. Figure 17-1 shows the screen display.

Example 17-2. SocketApplet.java

```
/** Initialize the GUI nicely. */
public void init() {
    Label aLabel;

    setLayout(new GridBagLayout());
    int LOGO_COL = 1;
```

Example 17-2. SocketApplet.java (continued)

```
int LABEL_COL = 2;
int TEXT_COL = 3;
int BUTTON_COL = 1;
GridBagConstraints gbc = new GridBagConstraints();
gbc.weightx = 100.0; gbc.weighty = 100.0;

gbc.gridx = LABEL_COL; gbc.gridy = 0;
gbc.anchor = GridBagConstraints.EAST;
add(aLabel = new Label("Name:", Label.CENTER), gbc);
gbc.anchor = GridBagConstraints.CENTER;
gbc.gridx = TEXT_COL; gbc.gridy = 0;
add(nameTF=new TextField(10), gbc);

gbc.gridx = LABEL_COL; gbc.gridy = 1;
gbc.anchor = GridBagConstraints.EAST;
add(aLabel = new Label("Password:", Label.CENTER), gbc);
gbc.anchor = GridBagConstraints.CENTER;
gbc.gridx = TEXT_COL; gbc.gridy = 1;
add(passTF=new TextField(10), gbc);
passTF.setEchoChar(*);

gbc.gridx = LABEL_COL; gbc.gridy = 2;
gbc.anchor = GridBagConstraints.EAST;
add(aLabel = new Label("Domain:", Label.CENTER), gbc);
gbc.anchor = GridBagConstraints.CENTER;
gbc.gridx = TEXT_COL; gbc.gridy = 2;
add(domainTF=new TextField(10), gbc);
sendButton = new Button("Send data");
gbc.gridx = BUTTON_COL; gbc.gridy = 3;
gbc.gridwidth = 3;
add(sendButton, gbc);

whence = getCodeBase();

// Now the action begins...
sendButton.addActionListener(new ActionListener() {
    public void actionPerformed(ActionEvent evt) {
        String name = nameTF.getText();
        if (name.length() == 0) {
            showStatus("Name required");
            return;
        }
        String domain = domainTF.getText();
        if (domain.length() == 0) {
            showStatus("Domain required");
            return;
        }
```

Example 17-2. SocketApplet.java (continued)

```
            showStatus("Connecting to host " + whence.getHost() +
                " as " + nameTF.getText());

            try {
                Socket s = new Socket(getCodeBase().getHost(),
                    SocketServer.PORT);
                PrintWriter pf = new PrintWriter(s.getOutputStream(), true);
                // send login name
                pf.println(nameTF.getText());
                // passwd
                pf.println(passTF.getText());
                // and domain
                pf.println(domainTF.getText());

                BufferedReader is = new BufferedReader(
                    new InputStreamReader(s.getInputStream()));
                String response = is.readLine();
                showStatus(response);
            } catch (IOException e) {
                showStatus("ERROR: " + e.getMessage());
            }
        }
    });
}
```

Figure 17-1. SocketApplet in action

17.4. Making an Applet Show a Document

Problem

You want an applet to transfer control to another web page.

Solution

Use the `AppletContext` method `showDocument()`.

Discussion

Any applet can request the browser that contains it to show a new web page by passing the new URL into the `showDocument()` method. Usually, the browser replaces the current page with the target page. This, of course, triggers a call to the applet's `stop()` method.

Note that the applet shown in Example 17-3 only works correctly in a full browser; the `AppletViewer` does not display HTML pages, so it ignores this method!

Example 17-3. ShowDocApplet.java

```
/** ShowDocApplet: Demonstrate showDocument().
 */
public class ShowDocApplet extends Applet {
    // String targetString = "http://www.darwinsys.com/javacook/secret.html";
    String targetString = "file:///c:/javasrc/network/ShowDocApplet.java";
    /** The URL to go to */
    URL targetURL;

    /** Initialize the Applet */
    public void init() {
        setBackground(Color.gray);
        try {
            targetURL = new URL(targetString);
        } catch (MalformedURLException mfu) {
            throw new IllegalArgumentException(
                "ShowDocApplet got bad URL " + targetString);
        }
        Button b = new Button("View Secret");
        add(b);
        b.addActionListener(new ActionListener() {
            public void actionPerformed(ActionEvent e) {
                getAppletContext().showDocument(targetURL);
            }
        });
    }

    public void stop() {
        System.out.println("Ack! Its been fun being an Applet. Goodbye!");
    }
}
```

Figure 17-2 shows the program in operation.

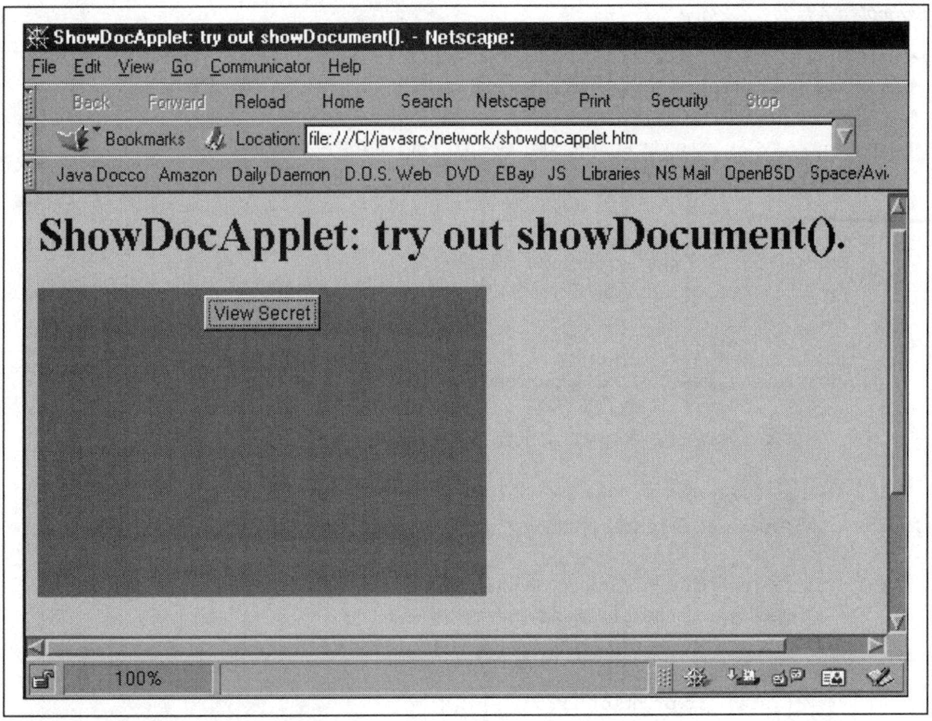

Figure 17-2. ShowDocApplet program

If the URL is unreachable, the browser will notify the user with a dialog, and the current page (including the applet) will be left in view.

17.5. *Making an Applet Run a CGI Script*

Problem

You want an applet to run a CGI script.

Solution

Just use showDocument( ) with the correct URL.

Discussion

It doesn't matter what type of target your URL refers to. It can be an HTML page, a plain text file, a compressed tar file to be downloaded, a CGI script, servlet, or JavaServer Page (Chapter 18). In all cases, you simply provide the URL. The Java applet for this appears in Example 17-4.

Example 17-4. TryCGI.java

```java
/**
 * Try running a CGI-BIN script from within Java.
 */
public class TryCGI extends Applet implements ActionListener {
    protected Button goButton;

    public void init() {
        add(goButton = new Button("Go for it!"));
        goButton.addActionListener(this);
    }

    public void actionPerformed(ActionEvent evt) {
        try {
            URL myNewURL = new URL("http://server/cgi-bin/credit");

            // debug...
            System.out.println("URL = " + myNewURL);

            // "And then a miracle occurs..."
            getAppletContext().showDocument(myNewURL);

        } catch (Exception err) {
            System.err.println("Error!

            showStatus("Error, look in Java Console for details!");
        }
    }
}
```

Since this is an applet, it requires an HTML page to invoke it. I used the HTML shown here:

```html
<HTML><HEAD>
<TITLE>Java Applets Can Run CGI's (at least on Netscape Navigator)</TITLE>
<BODY BGCOLOR="White">
<H1>Java Applets Can run CGI's (at least on Netscape Navigator)</H1>
<P>Click on the button on this little Applet for p(r)oof!
<APPLET CODE="TryCGI" WIDTH=100 HEIGHT=30>
<P>If you can see this, you need to get a Java-powered(tm) Web Browser
before you can watch for real.
</APPLET>
<HR>
<P>Use <A HREF="MakeHTML.java">The Source</A>, Luke.
```

17.6. *Reading the Contents of a URL*

Problem

You want to read the contents of a URL (which can include a CGI, servlet, etc.).

Solution

Use the URL's openConnection() or getContent() method. This is not dependent upon being in an applet.

Discussion

The URL class has several methods that allow you to read. The first and simplest, openStream(), returns an InputStream that can read the contents directly. The simple TextBrowser program shown here calls openStream() and uses this to construct a BufferedReader to read text lines from what is presumed to be a web server. I also demonstrate it reading a local file to show that almost any valid URL can be used:

```
$ java TextBrowser http://localhost/
*** Loading http://localhost/... ***
<HTML>
<HEAD>
    <TITLE>Ian Darwin's Webserver On The Road</TITLE>
    <LINK REL="stylesheet" TYPE="text/css" HREF="/stylesheet.css" TITLE="Style"> </
HEAD>
<BODY BGCOLOR="#c0d0e0">
<H1>Ian Darwin's Webserver On The Road</H1>
... (rest of body omitted) ...

$ java TextBrowser file:///etc/group
*** Loading file:///etc/group... ***
wheel:*:0:root
daemon:*:1:daemon
```

The next method, openConnection(), returns a URLConnection object. This allows you more flexibility, providing methods such as getHeaderField(), getLastModified(), and other detailed methods. The third URL method, getContent(), is more general. It returns an object that might be an InputStream, or an object containing the data. Use instanceof to determine which of several types was returned.

See Also

O'Reilly's *Java Network Programming* discusses this topic in considerable detail.

17.7. Extracting HTML from a URL

Problem

You need to extract all the HTML tags from a URL.

Solution

Use this simple HTML tag extractor.

Discussion

A simple HTML extractor can be made by reading a character at a time and look-ing for < and > tags. This is reasonably efficient if a `BufferedReader` is used.

The `ReadTag` program shown in Example 17-5 implements this; given a URL, it opens the file (similar to `TextBrowser` in Recipe 17.6) and extracts the HTML tags. Each tag is printed to the standard output.

Example 17-5. ReadTag.java

```
/** A simple but reusable HTML tag extractor.
 */
public class ReadTag {
    /** The URL that this ReadTag object is reading */
    protected URL myURL = null;
    /** The Reader for this object */
    protected BufferedReader inrdr = null;

    /* Simple main showing one way of using the ReadTag class. */
    public static void main(String[] args) throws MalformedURLException, IOException {
        if (args.length == 0) {
            System.err.println("Usage: ReadTag URL [...]");
            return;
        }

        for (int i=0; i<args.length; i++) {
            ReadTag rt = new ReadTag(args[0]);
            String tag;
            while ((tag = rt.nextTag()) != null) {
                System.out.println(tag);
            }
            rt.close();
        }
    }
```

Example 17-5. ReadTag.java (continued)

```java
/** Construct a ReadTag given a URL String */
public ReadTag(String theURLString) throws
        IOException, MalformedURLException {

    this(new URL(theURLString));
}


/** Construct a ReadTag given a URL */
public ReadTag(URL theURL) throws IOException {
    myURL = theURL;
    // Open the URL for reading
    inrdr = new BufferedReader(new InputStreamReader(myURL.openStream()));
}


/** Read the next tag.   */
public String nextTag() throws IOException {
    int i;
    while ((i = inrdr.read()) != -1) {
        char thisChar = (char)i;
        if (thisChar == '<') {
            String tag = readTag();
            return tag;
        }
    }
    return null;
}


public void close() throws IOException {
    inrdr.close();
}


/** Read one tag. Adapted from code by Elliotte Rusty Harold */
protected String readTag() throws IOException {
    StringBuffer theTag = new StringBuffer("<");
    int i = '<';

    while (i != '>' && (i = inrdr.read()) != -1) {
            theTag.append((char)i);
    }
    return theTag.toString();
}


/* Return a String representation of this object */
public String toString() {
    return "ReadTag[" + myURL.toString() + "]";
}
}
```

When I ran it on one system, I got the following output:

```
darian$ java ReadTag http://localhost/
<HTML>
<HEAD>
<TITLE>
</TITLE>
</HEAD>
<FRAMESET BORDER="0" ROWS="110, *" FRAMESPACING="0">
<FRAME NAME="header" SRC="header.html" SCROLLING="NO" MARGINHEIGHT="0"
FRAMEBORDER="0">
<FRAMESET COLS="130, *" FRAMESPACING="0">
<FRAME NAME="menu" SRC="menu.html" SCROLLING="NO" MARGINHEIGHT="0"
FRAMEBORDER="0">
<FRAME NAME="main" SRC="main.html" MARGINHEIGHT="15" MARGINWIDTH="15"
FRAMEBORDER="0">
</FRAMESET>
</FRAMESET>
</HTML>
darian$
```

17.8. Extracting URLs from a File

Problem

You need to extract just the URLs from a file.

Solution

Use ReadTag from Recipe 17.7, and just look for tags that might contain URLs.

Discussion

The program in Example 17-6 uses ReadTag from the previous recipe and checks each tag to see if it is a "wanted tag" defined in the array wantedTags. These include A (anchor), IMG (image), and APPLET tags. If it is determined to be a wanted tag, the URL is extracted from the tag and printed.

Example 17-6. GetURLs.java

```
public class GetURLs {
    /** The tag reader */
    ReadTag reader;

    public GetURLs(URL theURL) throws IOException {
        reader = new ReadTag(theURL);
    }
```

Example 17-6. GetURLs.java (continued)

```
    public GetURLs(String theURL) throws MalformedURLException, IOException {
        reader = new ReadTag(theURL);
    }

    /* The tags we want to look at */
    public final static String[] wantTags = {
        "<a ", "<A ",
        "<applet ", "<APPLET ",
        "<img ", "<IMG ",
        "<frame ", "<FRAME ",
    };

    public ArrayList getURLs() throws IOException {
        ArrayList al = new ArrayList();
        String tag;
        while ((tag = reader.nextTag()) != null) {
            for (int i=0; i<wantTags.length; i++) {
                if (tag.startsWith(wantTags[i])) {
                    al.add(tag);
                    continue;// optimization
                }
            }
        }
        return al;
    }

    public void close() throws IOException {
        if (reader != null)
            reader.close();
    }
    public static void main(String[] argv) throws
            MalformedURLException, IOException {
        String theURL = argv.length == 0 ?
            "http://localhost/" : argv[0];
        GetURLs gu = new GetURLs(theURL);
        ArrayList urls = gu.getURLs();
        Iterator urlIterator = urls.iterator();
        while (urlIterator.hasNext()) {
            System.out.println(urlIterator.next());
        }
    }
}
```

The GetURLs program prints the URLs contained in a given web page:

```
darian$ java GetURLs http://daroad
<IMG SRC="ian.gif">
<A ID="LinkLocal" HREF="webserver/index.html">
```

```
<A HREF="quizzes/">
<A HREF="servlets/IsItWorking">
<A HREF="demo.jsp">
<A ID=LinkRemote HREF="http://java.sun.com">
<A ID=LinkRemote HREF="http://www.openbsd.org">
<A ID=LinkRemote HREF="http://www.cpg.com">
<A ID=LinkRemote HREF="http://www.ssc.com">
<A ID=LinkRemote HREF="http://www.learningtree.com">
<A ID=LinkLocal HREF="javacook.html">
<A ID=LinkRemote HREF="http://java.oreilly.com">
<A ID=LinkLocal HREF="lookup/index.htm">
<A ID=LinkLocal HREF="readings/index.html">
<A ID=LinkLocal HREF="download.html">
<IMG SRC="miniduke.gif" BORDER=0>
darian$
```

The `LinkChecker` program in Recipe 17.11 will extract the HREF or SRC attributes, and validate them.

17.9. Converting a Filename to a URL

Problem

You require a URL, but you have a local file.

Solution

Use `getResource()` or `File.toURL()`.

Discussion

There are many operations that require a URL, but for which it would be convenient to refer to a file on the local filesystem or disk. For these, the convenience method `getResource()` in the class `java.lang.Class` can be used. This takes a filename and returns a URL for it:

```
public class GetResource {
    public static void main(String[] argv) {
        Class c = GetResource.class;
        java.net.URL u = c.getResource("GetResource.java");
        System.out.println(u);
    }
}
```

When I ran this code on Java 2 on my MS-Windows system, it printed:

```
file:/C:/javasrc/netweb/GetResource.java
```

Java 2 also introduced a toURL() method into the File class (Recipe 10.1). Unlike getResource(), this method can throw a MalformedURLException. This makes sense, since a File class can be constructed with arbitrary nonsense in the filename. So the previous code can be rewritten as:

```
public class FileToURL
{
    public static void main(String[] argv) throws MalformedURLException {
        java.net.URL u = new File("GetResource.java").toURL();
        System.out.println(u);
    }
}
```

Both programs print the same result:

```
> java FileToURL
file:/usr/home/ian/javasrc/netweb/GetResource.java
> java GetResource
file:/usr/home/ian/javasrc/netweb/GetResource.java
```

17.10. Program: MkIndex

This little program has saved me a great deal of time over the years. It reads a directory containing a large number of files, harking back from a time when I kept all my demonstration Java programs in a fairly flat directory structure. MkIndex, shown in Example 17-7, produces a better-formatted listing than the default directory that web servers generate. For one thing, it includes an alphabet navigator, which lets you jump directly to the section of files whose names begin with a certain letter, saving a lot of scrolling time or iterations with the browser's find menu. This program uses a File object (see Recipe 10.1) to list the files, and another to decide which are files and which are directories. It also uses Collections.sort (see Recipe 7.8) to sort the names alphabetically before generating the output. It writes its output to the file *index.html* in the current directory, even if an alternate directory argument is given. This is the default filename for most standard web servers; if your web server uses something different, of course, you can rename the file.

Example 17-7. MkIndex.java

```
/** MkIndex -- make a static index.html for a Java Source directory
 */
public class MkIndex {
    /** The output file that we create */
    public static final String OUTPUTFILE = "index-byname.html";
    /** The string for TITLE and H1 */
    public static final String TITLE =
        "Ian Darwin's Java Cookbook: Source Code: By Name";
    /** The main output stream */
    PrintWriter out;
```

Example 17-7. MkIndex.java (continued)

```java
    /** The background color for the page */
    public static final String BGCOLOR="#33ee33";
    /** The File object, for directory listing. */
    File dirFile;

    /** Make an index */
    public static void main(String[] args) throws IOException {
        MkIndex mi = new MkIndex();
        String inDir = args.length > 0 ? args[0] : ".";
        mi.open(inDir, OUTPUTFILE);// open files
        mi.BEGIN();// print HTML header
        mi.process();// do bulk of work
        mi.END();// print trailer.
        mi.close();// close files
    }

    void open(String dir, String outFile) {
        dirFile = new File(dir);
        try {
            out = new PrintWriter(new FileWriter(outFile));
        } catch (IOException e) {
            System.err.println(e);
        }
    }

    /** Write the HTML headers */
    void BEGIN() throws IOException {
        println("<HTML>");
        println("<HEAD>");
        println("    <META HTTP-EQUIV=\"Content-Type\"
            CONTENT=\"text/html; charset=iso-8859-1\">");
        println("    <META NAME=\"GENERATOR\" CONTENT=\"Java MkIndex\">");
        println("    <title>" + TITLE + "</title>");
        println("</HEAD>");
        println("<body bgcolor=\"" + BGCOLOR + "\">");
        println("<h1>" + TITLE + "</h1>");
        if (new File("about.html").exists()) {
            FileIO.copyFile("about.html", out, false);
        } else {
            println("<P>The following files are online.");
            println("Some of these files are still experimental!</P>");
            println("<P>Most of these files are Java source code.");
            println("If you load an HTML file from here, the applets will not run!");
            println("HTML files must be saved to disk and the applets compiled,");
            println("before you can run them!");
        }
        println("<P>All files are Copyright &copy;: All rights reserved.");
        println("See the accompanying <A HREF=\"legal-notice.txt\
            \">Legal Notice</A> for conditions of use.");
```

Example 17-7. MkIndex.java (continued)

```
        println("May be used by readers of my Java Cookbook for educational
            purposes,");
        println("and for commercial use if certain conditions are met.");
        println("</P>");
        println("<HR>");
    }


    /** Array of letters that exist. Should
     * fold case here so don't get f and F as distinct entries!
     * This only works for ASCII characters (8-bit chars).
     */
    boolean[] exists = new boolean[255];

    /** Vector for temporary storage, and sorting */
    ArrayList vec = new ArrayList();

    /** Do the bulk of the work */
    void process() throws IOException {

        System.out.println("Start PASS ONE -- from directory to Vector...");
        String[] fl = dirFile.list();
        for (int i=0; i<fl.length; i++) {
            String fn = fl[i];
            if (fn.startsWith("index")) { // we'll have no self-reference here!
                System.err.println("Ignoring " + fn);
                continue;
            } else if (fn.endsWith(".bak")) {// delete .bak files
                System.err.println("DELETING " + fn);
                new File(fn).delete();
                continue;
            } else if (fn.equals("CVS")) {// Ignore CVS subdirectories
                continue;              // don't mention it
            } else if (fn.charAt(0) == '.') {// UNIX dot-file
                continue;
            } else if (fn.endsWith(".class")) {// nag about .class files
                System.err.println("Ignoring " + fn);
                continue;
            } else if (new File(fn).isDirectory()) {
                vec.add(fn + "/");
            } else
                vec.add(fn);
            exists[fn.charAt(0)] = true;// only after chances to continue
        }

        System.out.println("Writing the Alphabet Navigator...");
        for (char c = 'A'; c<='Z'; c++)
            if (exists[c])
                print("<A HREF=\"#" + c + "\">" + c + "</A> ");
```

Example 17-7. MkIndex.java (continued)

```
        // ... (and the beginning of the HTML Unordered List...)
        println("<UL>");

        System.out.println("Sorting the Vector...");
        Collections.sort(vec, String.CASE_INSENSITIVE_ORDER);

        System.out.println("Start PASS TWO -- from Vector to " +
            OUTPUTFILE + "...");
        String fn;
        Iterator it = vec.iterator();
        while (it.hasNext()) {
            fn = (String)it.next();
            // Need to make a link into this directory.
            // IF there is a descr.txt file, use it for the text
            // of the link, otherwise, use the directory name.
            // But, if there is an index.html or index.html file,
            // make the link to that file, else to the directory itself.
            if (fn.endsWith("/")) {// directory
                String descr = null;
                if (new File(fn + "descr.txt").exists()) {
                    descr = com.darwinsys.util.FileIO.readLine(fn +
                        "descr.txt");
                };
                if (new File(fn + "index.html").exists())
                    mkDirLink(fn+"index.html", descr!=null?descr:fn);
                else if (new File(fn + "index.htm").exists())
                        mkDirLink(fn+"index.htm", descr!=null?descr:fn);
                else
                    mkLink(fn, descr!=null?descr:fn + " -- Directory");
            } else // file
                mkLink(fn, fn);
        }
        System.out.println("*** process - ALL DONE***");
    }

    /** Keep track of each letter for #links */
    boolean done[] = new boolean[255];

    void mkLink(String href, String descrip) {
        print("<LI>");
        char c = href.charAt(0);
        if (!done[c]) {
            print("<A NAME=\"" + c + "\">");
            done[c] = true;
        }
        println("<A HREF=\"" + href + "\">" + descrip + "</A>");
    }
```

Example 17-7. MkIndex.java (continued)

```
    void mkDirLink(String index, String dir) {
        // XXX Open the index and look for TITLE lines!
        mkLink(index, dir + " -- Directory");
    }

    /** Write the trailers and a signature */
    void END() {
        System.out.println("Finishing the HTML");
        println("</UL>");
        flush();
        println("<P>This file generated by ");
        print("<A HREF=\"MkIndex.java\">MkIndex</A>, a Java program, at ");
        println(new Date().toString());
        println("</P>");
        println("</BODY>");
        println("</HTML>");
    }

    /** Close open files */
    void close() {
        System.out.println("Closing output files...");
        if (out != null)
            out.close();
    }

    /** Convenience routine for out.print */
    void print(String s) {
        out.print(s);
    }

    /** Convenience routine for out.println */
    void println(String s) {
        out.println(s);
    }

    /** Convenience for out.flush(); */
    void flush() {
        out.flush();
    }
}
```

17.11. *Program: LinkChecker*

One of the hard parts of maintaining a large web site is ensuring that all the hypertext links, images, applets, and so forth remain valid as the site grows and changes. It's easy to make a change somewhere that breaks a link somewhere else, exposing your users to those "Doh!"-producing 404 errors. What's needed is a program to automate checking the links. This turns out to be surprisingly complex due to the variety of link types. But we can certainly make a start.

Since we already created a program that reads a web page and extracts the URL-containing tags (Recipe 17.8), we can use that here. The basic approach of our new LinkChecker program is this: given a starting URL, create a GetURLs object for it. If that succeeds, read the list of URLs and go from there. This program has the additional functionality of displaying the structure of the site using simple indentation in a graphical window, as shown in Figure 17-3.

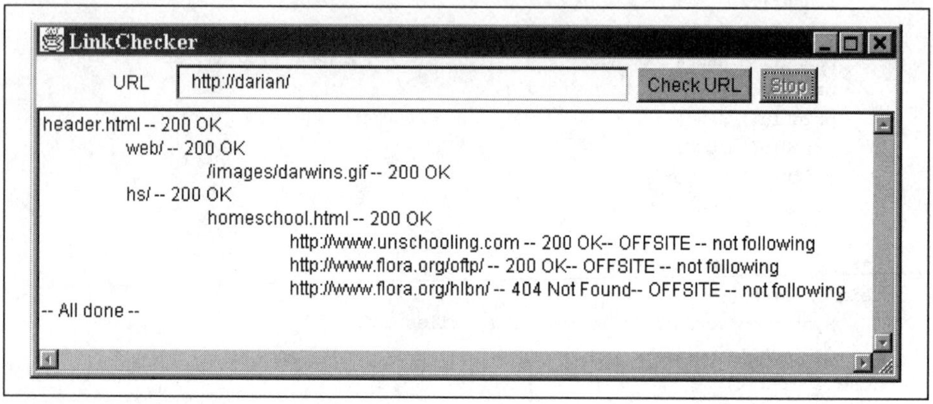

Figure 17-3. LinkChecker in action

So using the GetURLS class from Recipe 17.8, the rest is largely a matter of elaboration. A lot of this code has to do with the GUI (see Chapter 13). The code uses recursion: the routine checkOut() calls itself each time a new page or directory is started.

Example 17-8 shows the code for the LinkChecker program.

Example 17-8. LinkChecker.java

```
/** A simple HTML Link Checker.
 * Need a Properties file to set depth, URLs to check. etc.
 * Responses not adequate; need to check at least for 404-type errors!
 * When all that is (said and) done, display in a Tree instead of a TextArea.
 * Then use Color coding to indicate errors.
 */
public class LinkChecker extends Frame implements Runnable {
    protected Thread t = null;
    /** The "global" activation flag: set false to halt. */
    boolean done = false;
    protected Panel p;
    /** The textfield for the starting URL.
     * Should have a Properties file and a JComboBox instead.
     */
```

Example 17-8. LinkChecker.java (continued)

```
    protected TextField textFldURL;
    protected Button checkButton;
    protected Button killButton;
    protected TextArea textWindow;
    protected int indent = 0;

    public static void main(String[] args) {
        LinkChecker lc = new LinkChecker();
        lc.setSize(500, 400);
        lc.setLocation(150, 150);
        lc.setVisible(true);
        if (args.length == 0)
            return;
        lc.textFldURL.setText(args[0]);
    }

    public void startChecking() {
        done = false;
        checkButton.setEnabled(false);
        killButton.setEnabled(true);
        textWindow.setText("");
        doCheck();
    }

    public void stopChecking() {
        done = true;
        checkButton.setEnabled(true);
        killButton.setEnabled(false);
    }

    /** Construct a LinkChecker */
    public LinkChecker() {
        super("LinkChecker");
        addWindowListener(new WindowAdapter() {
            public void windowClosing(WindowEvent e) {
            setVisible(false);
            dispose();
            System.exit(0);
            }
        });
        setLayout(new BorderLayout());
        p = new Panel();
        p.setLayout(new FlowLayout());
        p.add(new Label("URL"));
        p.add(textFldURL = new TextField(40));
        p.add(checkButton = new Button("Check URL"));
        // Make a single action listener for both the text field (when
        // you hit return) and the explicit "Check URL" button.
```

Example 17-8. LinkChecker.java (continued)

```
        ActionListener starter = new ActionListener() {
            public void actionPerformed(ActionEvent e) {
                startChecking();
            }
        };
        textFldURL.addActionListener(starter);
        checkButton.addActionListener(starter);
        p.add(killButton = new Button("Stop"));
        killButton.setEnabled(false);// until startChecking is called.
        killButton.addActionListener(new ActionListener() {
            public void actionPerformed(ActionEvent e) {
                if (t == null || !t.isAlive())
                    return;
                stopChecking();
            }
        });
        // Now lay out the main GUI - URL & buttons on top, text larger
        add("North", p);
        textWindow = new TextArea(80, 40);
        add("Center", textWindow);
    }

    public void doCheck() {
        if (t!=null && t.isAlive())
            return;
        t = new Thread(this);
        t.start();
    }

    public synchronized void run() {
        textWindow.setText("");
        checkOut(textFldURL.getText());
        textWindow.append("-- All done --");
    }

    /** Start checking, given a URL by name.
     * Calls checkLink to check each link.
     */
    public void checkOut(String rootURLString) {
        URL rootURL = null;
        GetURLs urlGetter = null;

        if (done)
            return;
        if (rootURLString == null) {
            textWindow.append("checkOut(null) isn't very useful");
            return;
        }
```

Example 17-8. LinkChecker.java (continued)

```java
// Open the root URL for reading
try {
    rootURL = new URL(rootURLString);
    urlGetter = new GetURLs(rootURL);
} catch (MalformedURLException e) {
    textWindow.append("Can't parse " + rootURLString + "\n");
    return;
} catch (FileNotFoundException e) {
    textWindow.append("Can't open file " + rootURLString + "\n");
    return;
} catch (IOException e) {
    textWindow.append("openStream " + rootURLString + " " + e + "\n");
    return;
}

// If we're still here, the root URL given is OK.
// Next we make up a "directory" URL from it.
String rootURLdirString;
if (rootURLString.endsWith("/") ||
    rootURLString.endsWith("\\"))
        rootURLdirString = rootURLString;
else {
    rootURLdirString = rootURLString.substring(0,
        rootURLString.lastIndexOf('/'));// XXX or \
}

try {
    ArrayList urlTags = urlGetter.getURLs();
    Iterator urlIterator = urlTags.iterator();
    while (urlIterator.hasNext()) {
        if (done)
            return;
        String tag = (String)urlIterator.next();
        System.out.println(tag);

        String href = extractHREF(tag);

        for (int j=0; j<indent; j++)
            textWindow.append("\t");
        textWindow.append(href + " -- ");

        // Can't really validate these!
        if (href.startsWith("mailto:")) {
            textWindow.append(href + " -- not checking");
            continue;
        }

        if (href.startsWith("..") || href.startsWith("#")) {
```

Example 17-8. LinkChecker.java (continued)

```
                    textWindow.append(href + " -- not checking");
                    // nothing doing!
                    continue;
                }

                URL hrefURL = new URL(rootURL, href);

                // TRY THE URL.
                // (don't combine previous textWindow.append with this one,
                // since this one can throw an exception)
                textWindow.append(checkLink(hrefURL));

                // There should be an option to control whether to
                // "try the url" first and then see if off-site, or
                // vice versa, for the case when checking a site you're
                // working on on your notebook on a train in the Rockies
                // with no web access available.

                // Now see if the URL is off-site.
                if (!hrefURL.getHost().equals(rootURL.getHost())) {
                    textWindow.append("-- OFFSITE -- not following");
                    textWindow.append("\n");
                    continue;
                }
                textWindow.append("\n");

                // If HTML, check it recursively. No point checking
                // PHP, CGI, JSP, etc., since these usually need forms input.
                // If a directory, assume HTML or something under it will work.
                if (href.endsWith(".htm") ||
                    href.endsWith(".html") ||
                    href.endsWith("/")) {
                        ++indent;
                        if (href.indexOf(':') != -1)
                            checkOut(href);// RECURSE
                        else {
                            String newRef =
                                rootURLdirString + '/' + href;
                            checkOut(newRef);// RECURSE
                        }
                        --indent;
                }
            }
            urlGetter.close();
        } catch (IOException e) {
            System.err.println("Error " + ":(" + e +")");
        }
    }
```

Example 17-8. LinkChecker.java (continued)

```java
/** Check one link, given its DocumentBase and the tag */
public String checkLink(URL linkURL) {

    try {
        // Open it; if the open fails we'll likely throw an exception
        URLConnection luf = linkURL.openConnection();
        if (linkURL.getProtocol().equals("http")) {
            HttpURLConnection huf = (HttpURLConnection)luf;
            String s = huf.getResponseCode() + " " + huf.getResponseMessage();
            if (huf.getResponseCode() == -1)
                return "Server error: bad HTTP response";
            return s;
        } else if (linkURL.getProtocol().equals("file")) {
            InputStream is = luf.getInputStream();
            is.close();
            // If that didn't throw an exception, the file is probably OK
            return "(File)";
        } else
            return "(non-HTTP)";
    }
    catch (SocketException e) {
        return "DEAD: " + e.toString();
    }
    catch (IOException e) {
        return "DEAD";
    }
}

/** Read one tag. Adapted from code by Elliotte Rusty Harold */
public String readTag(BufferedReader is) {
    StringBuffer theTag = new StringBuffer("<");
    int i = '<';

    try {
        while (i != '>' && (i = is.read()) != -1)
            theTag.append((char)i);
    }
    catch (IOException e) {
        System.err.println("IO Error: " + e);
    }
    catch (Exception e) {
        System.err.println(e);
    }

    return theTag.toString();
}
```

Example 17-8. LinkChecker.java (continued)

```java
    /** Extract the URL from <sometag attrs HREF="http://foo/bar" attrs ...>
     * We presume that the HREF is correctly quoted!!!!!
     * TODO: Handle Applets.
     */
    public String extractHREF(String tag) throws MalformedURLException {
        String caseTag = tag.toLowerCase(), attrib;
        int p1, p2, p3, p4;

        if (caseTag.startsWith("<a "))
            attrib = "href";// A
        else
            attrib = "src";// image, frame
        p1 = caseTag.indexOf(attrib);
        if (p1 < 0) {
            throw new MalformedURLException("Can't find " + attrib + " in " + tag);
        }
        p2 = tag.indexOf ("=", p1);
        p3 = tag.indexOf("\"", p2);
        p4 = tag.indexOf("\"", p3+1);
        if (p3 < 0 || p4 < 0) {
            throw new MalformedURLException("Invalid " + attrib + " in " + tag);
        }
        String href = tag.substring(p3+1, p4);
        return href;
    }
}
```

Downloading an Entire Web Site

It would also be useful to have a program that reads the entire contents of a web site and saves it on your local hard disk. Sounds wasteful, but disk space is quite inexpensive nowadays, and this would allow you to peruse a web site when not connected to the Internet. Of course you couldn't run most of the CGI scripts that you downloaded, but at least you could navigate around the text and view the images. The LinkChecker program contains all the seeds of such a program: you need only to download the contents of each non-dynamic URL (see the test for HTML and directories near the end of routine checkOut() and the code in Recipe 17.6), create the requisite directories (Recipe 10.9), and create and write to a file on disk (see Chapter 9). This final step is left as an exercise for the reader.

18

Web Server Java: Servlets and JSP

18.0. Introduction

This chapter covers Web Server Java, but you won't find anything about writing CGI programs in Java here. Although it would be entirely possible to do so, it would not be efficient. The whole notion of CGI programs is pretty much passe. Every time a CGI program is invoked, the web server has to create a new heavyweight process in which to run it; this is inefficient. If it's interpreted in Java, the program has to be translated into machine code each time; this is even more inefficient.

Today's trend is toward building functionality into the web server: Microsoft ASP, PHP3, Java servlets, and JavaServer Pages™ (JSP*) are examples of this. None of these normally requires a separate process to be created for each request; the Java-based solutions run in a thread (see Chapter 24) inside the web server, and the Java bytecode need only be translated into machine code once in a long while, assuming a just-in-time (JIT) runtime system. Naturally, this book concentrates on the Java solutions.

We'll use two examples in this chapter. Consider the task of displaying a web page with five randomly chosen integer numbers (lottery players love this sort of thing). The Java code you need is simple:

```
// Part of file netweb/servlets_jsp/FiveInts.java
Random r = new Random();
for (int i=0; i<5; i++)
    System.out.println(r.nextInt());
```

---

* It has been said of Sun that when they copy something, they both improve upon it and give credit where credit's due in the name. Consider Microsoft ODBC and Java JDBC; Microsoft ASP and Java JSP. The same cannot be said of most large companies.

But of course you can't just run that and save its output into an HTML file because you want each person seeing the page to get a different set of numbers. If you wanted to mix that into a web page, you'd have to write code to `println()` a bit of HTML. This would be a Java servlet.

The servlet code could get messy, however, since you'd have to escape double quotes inside strings. Worse, if the webmaster wanted to change the HTML, he'd have to approach the programmer's sanctified source code and plead to have it changed. Imagine if you could give the webmaster a page containing a bit of HTML and the Java code you need, and have it magically compiled into Java whenever the HTML was changed. Imagine no longer, says the marketer, for that capability is here now, with JavaServer Pages.

The second example is a dictionary (list of terms); I'll present this both as a servlet and as a JSP.

I won't talk about how you get your servlet engine installed, nor exactly how you install your servlet. If you don't already have a servlet engine, though, I'd recommend downloading Tomcat from *http://jakarta.apache.org*. Tomcat is the official reference implementation—so designated by Sun—for the servlet and JSP standard. It is also (as you can infer from the URL) the official servlet engine for the ever-popular Apache web server.

18.1. First Servlet: Generating an HTML Page

Problem

You want a servlet to present some information to the user.

Solution

Override the `HttpServlet` method `service()`, or `doGet()`/`doPost()`.

Discussion

The abstract class `javax.servlet.Servlet` is designed for those who wish to structure an entire web server around the servlet notion. For example, in Sun's Java Web Server, there is a servlet subclass for handling plain HTML pages, another for processing CGI programs, and so on. Unless you are writing your own web server, you will probably not extend from this class, but rather its subclass `HttpServlet`, in the package `javax.servlet.http`. This class has a method:

```
public void service(HttpServletRequest req, HttpServletResponse resp)
throws ServletException, IOException;
```

The service method is passed two arguments, request and response. The request contains all the information about the request from the browser, including its input stream should you need to read data. The response argument contains information to get the response back to the browser, including the output stream to write your response back to the user.

But the web has several HTTP methods for passing data into a web page. Unimportant for plain HTML pages, this distinction becomes of interest when processing forms, i.e., web pages with fill-in-the-blank or choice items. Briefly, the GET method of HTTP is used to pass all the form data appended to the URL. GET URLs look like this, for example:

```
http://www.acmewidgets.com/cgi-bin/ordercgi?productId=123456
```

They have the advantage that the user can bookmark them, avoiding having to fill in the form multiple times. But there is a limit of about 1KB on the overall length of the URL. Since this must be a single string, there is an encoding that allows spaces, tabs, colons, and other characters to be presented as two hexadecimal digits: %20 is the character hexadecimal 20, or the ASCII space character. The POST method, by contrast, passes any parameters as input on the socket connection, after the HTTP headers.

The default implementation of the service() method in the HttpServlet class figures out which method was used to invoke the servlet. It dispatches to the correct method: doGet() if a GET request, doPost() if a POST request, etc., passing along the request and response arguments. So while you can, in theory, override the service() method, it's more common (and officially recommended) to override either doGet(), doPost(), or both.

The simplest HttpServlet is something like Example 18-1.

Example 18-1. HelloServlet.java

```java
import java.io.*;
import java.util.*;
import javax.servlet.*;
import javax.servlet.http.*;

/** Simple Hello World Servlet
 */
public class HelloServlet extends HttpServlet{
    public void doGet(HttpServletRequest request, HttpServletResponse response) throws
IOException {
        PrintWriter out = response.getWriter();
        response.setContentType("text/html");
        out.println("<H1>Hello from a Servlet</H1>");
        out.println("<P>This servlet ran at ");
```

Example 18-1. HelloServlet.java (continued)

```
        out.println(new Date().toString());
        out.println("<P>Courtesy of HelloServlet.java 1.2 ");
    }
}
```

The program will give output resembling Figure 18-1.

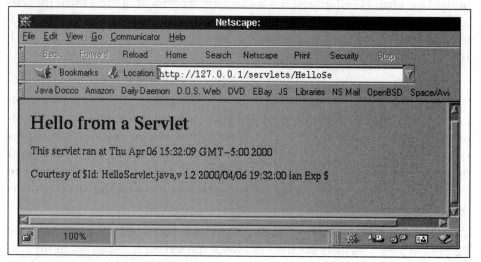

Figure 18-1. Hello from a servlet

You can do much more with servlets. Suppose you wanted to print a dictionary—a list of terms and their meanings—from within a servlet. The code would be pretty much as it was in Figure 18-1, except that you'd need a doGet() method instead of a doPost() method. Example 18-2 is the code for **TermsServlet**.

Example 18-2. TermsServlet.java

```
/** A Servlet to list the dictionary terms.
 */
public class TermsServlet extends HttpServlet {
    public void doGet(HttpServletRequest req, HttpServletResponse resp) throws
IOException {
        PrintWriter out = resp.getWriter();
        out.println("<HTML>");
        out.println("<TITLE>Ian Darwin's Computer Terms and Acronyms</TITLE>");
        out.println("<BODY>");
        out.println("<H1>Ian Darwin's Computer Terms and Acronyms</H1>");
        out.println("<TABLE BORDER=2>");
        out.println("<TR><TH>Term<TH>Meaning</TR>");
```

Example 18-2. TermsServlet.java (continued)

```
        // This part of the Servlet generates a list of lines like
        //   <TR> <TD>JSP <TD>Java Server Pages, a neat tool for ...
        TermsAccessor tax = new TermsAccessor("terms.txt");
        Iterator e = tax.iterator();
        while (e.hasNext()) {
            Term t = (Term)e.next();
            out.print("<TR><TD>");
            out.print(t.term);
            out.print("<TD>");
            out.print(t.definition);
            out.println("</TR>");
        }
        out.println("</TABLE>");
        out.println("<HR></HR>");
        out.println("<A HREF=\"servlet/TermsServletPDF
            \">Printer-friendly (Acrobat PDF) version</A>");
        out.println("<HR></HR>");
        out.println("<A HREF=\"mailto:compquest@darwinsys.com/subject=Question
            \">Ask about another term</A>");
        out.println("<HR></HR>");
        out.println("<A HREF=\"index.html\">Back to HS</A> <A HREF=\"../
            \">Back to DarwinSys</A>");
        out.println("<HR></HR>");
        out.println("<H6>Produced by $Id: TermsServlet.java,v 1.1 2000/04/06
            ian Exp $");
        out.print(" using ");
        out.print(tax.ident);
        out.println("</H6>");
    }
}
```

Debugging Tip for Servlets

Several servlet engines (e.g., Allaire JRun) generate a lot of very small log files spread over many different directories. It is worth investing the time to learn where your particular servlet engine records stack traces, standard error and output, and other messages.

See also Recipe 16.5, which shows how a servlet or other server component can communicate with a network-based logging tool.

18.2. Servlets: Processing Form Parameters

Problem

You want to process the data from an HTML form in a servlet.

Solution

Use the request object's getParameter() method.

Discussion

Each uniquely named INPUT element in the FORM on the HTML page makes an entry in the request object's list of parameters. These can be obtained as an enumeration, but more commonly you request just one. Figure 18-2 shows a simple form that asks you how many random numbers you want generated, and makes up that many for you.

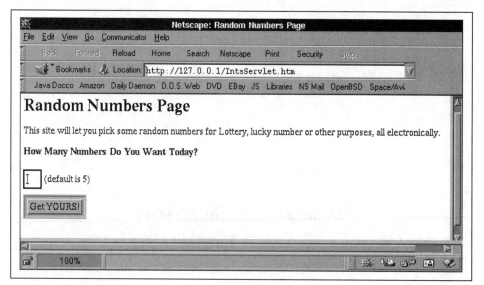

Figure 18-2. Random numbers HTML page

When I type the number 8 into the field and press the "Get Yours" button, I see the screen shot in Figure 18-3.

How does it work? The program obviously consists of both an HTML page and a Java servlet. The HTML page appears in Example 18-3; notice the FORM entry and the INPUT field.

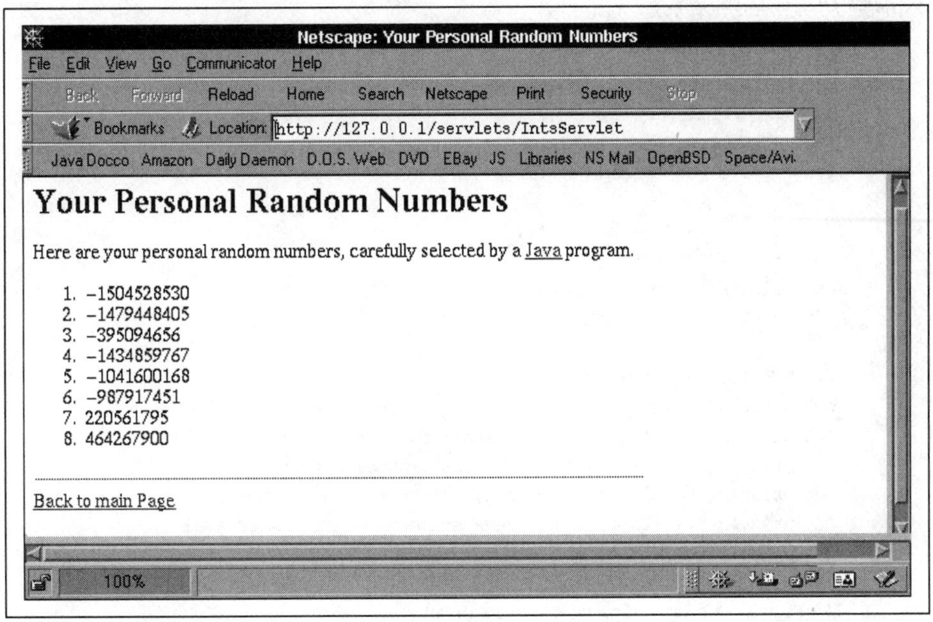

Figure 18-3. Random numbers servlet output

Example 18-3. IntsServlet.htm

```
<HTML>
<HEAD><TITLE>Random Numbers Page</TITLE></HEAD>
<BODY BGCOLOR="white">
<H1>Random Numbers Page</H1>
<P>This site will let you pick some random numbers for Lottery, lucky number
or other purposes, all electronically.</P>
<FORM METHOD=POST ACTION="/servlets/IntsServlet">
<H4>How Many Numbers Do You Want Today?</H4>
<INPUT NAME=howmany SIZE=2> (default is 5)
<BR>
<INPUT TYPE="SUBMIT" VALUE="Get YOURS!">
</FORM>
</BODY></HTML>
```

Example 18-4 shows the Java for the servlet. Watch for the use of getParameter().

Example 18-4. IntsServlet.java

```
import java.io.*;
import java.util.Random;
import javax.servlet.*;
import javax.servlet.http.*;

public class IntsServlet extends HttpServlet {
    protected final int DEFAULT_NUMBER = 5;
```

Example 18-4. IntsServlet.java (continued)

```
/** Called when the form is filled in by the user. */
public void doPost(HttpServletRequest req, HttpServletResponse resp)
throws IOException {
    resp.setContentType("text/html");
    PrintWriter out = resp.getWriter();

    // The usual HTML setup stuff.
    out.println("<HTML>");
    out.println("<HEAD>");
    out.println("<BODY BGCOLOR=\"white\">");

    // HTML for this page
    out.println("<TITLE>Your Personal Random Numbers</TITLE>");
    out.println("<H1>Your Personal Random Numbers</H1>");
    out.println("<P>Here are your personal random numbers,");
    out.println("carefully selected by a");
    out.println("<A HREF=\"http://java.sun.com\">Java</A> program.");
    out.println("<OL>");

    // Figure out how many numbers to print.
    int n = DEFAULT_NUMBER;
    String num=req.getParameter("howmany");
    if (num != null && num.length() != 0) {
        try {
            n = Integer.parseInt(num);
        } catch (NumberFormatException e) {
            out.println("<P>I didn't think much of ");
            out.println(num);
            out.println(" as a number.</P>");
        }
    }

    // Now actually generate some random numbers.
    Random r = new Random();
    for (int i=0; i<n; i++) {
        out.print("<LI>");
        out.println(r.nextInt(49));// for Lotto 6/49
    }
    out.println("</OL>");

    // Print a break and a back link.
    out.println("<HR></HR>");
    out.println("<A HREF=\"index.html\">Back to main Page</A>");
    out.println("</HTML>");
}
}
```

See Also

The online source includes OrderServlet, a slightly longer example.

18.3. Cookies

Problem

You want the client (the browser) to remember some bit of information for you.

Solution

Bake a cookie, and serve it to the client along with your response.

Discussion

Cookies were invented by Netscape as a debugging technique, but have since become ubiquitous: all modern browsers, including MSIE, and text browsers such as Lynx accept and store them. A cookie is, at heart, a small piece of text—a name and value pair—that the server side generates and sends to the client. The browser remembers them (nontransient cookies are stored to your hard disk; Netscape creates a file called *cookies* or *cookies.txt*, for example). The browser then sends them back to the server on any subsequent visit to a page from the same site. The Cookie class is part of the `javax.servlet.http` package, so any servlet implementation will include it. The constructor is passed a name and value, but there are other parameters you can set. Most important is the expiry time, which is in seconds from the time you first send it. The default is –1; if the value is negative, the cookie is not saved to disk; it becomes a "transient cookie" that exists only until the browser exits and is then forgotten. For cookies that are stored to disk, the expiry time is converted to a base of January 1, 1970, the beginning of Unix time and of the modern computing era.

When the browser visits a site that has sent it a cookie or cookies, it returns all of them as part of the HTTP headers. You retrieve them all (as an array) using the getCookies() method, and iterate through them looking for the one you want.

```
for (int i=0; i<mySiteCookies.length; i++) {
    Cookie c = mySiteCookies[i];
    if (c.getName().equals(name-you're-looking-for)) {
            someString = c.getValue();
            break;
    }
}
```

Suppose you want the user to pick a favorite color for the servlet to use as the background color for pages from that point on. Let's use a name of `prefs.bgcolor` for the color-coding cookie. The main servlet is `CookieServlet`, which checks for the cookie. If it was not set previously, it jumps off to an HTML page, which will eventually return here via another servlet. On the other hand, if the color cookie was previously set, `CookieServlet` (shown in Example 18-5) displays the welcome page with the user's color set.

Example 18-5. CookieServlet.java

```java
import java.io.*;
import java.util.*;
import javax.servlet.*;
import javax.servlet.http.*;

/** Simple Cookie-based Page Color Display servlet demo.
 */
public class CookieServlet extends HttpServlet {
    /** The preferences cookie name */
    protected final static String PREFS_BGCOLOR = "prefs.bgcolor";
    /** Where to go if we have not yet been customized. */
    protected final static String CUSTOMIZER = "/ColorCustomize.html";
    /** The user's chosen color, if any */
    protected String faveColor = null;

    public void doGet(HttpServletRequest request, HttpServletResponse response)
    throws ServletException, IOException {

        // Go through all the cookies we have, looking for a faveColor.
        Cookie[] mySiteCookies = request.getCookies();
        for (int i=0; i<mySiteCookies.length; i++) {
            Cookie c = mySiteCookies[i];
            if (c.getName().equals(PREFS_BGCOLOR)) {
                faveColor = c.getValue();
                break;
            }
        }

        // if we did not find a faveColor in a cookie,
        // punt to customization servlet to bake one up for us.
        if (faveColor == null) {
            ServletContext sc = getServletContext();

            // Requires Servlet API 2.1 or later!
            // RequestDispatcher rd =
            //   sc.getRequestDispatcher(CUSTOMIZER");
            //rd.forward(request, response);
```

Example 18-5. CookieServlet.java (continued)

```
            // Do it the old way
            response.sendRedirect(CUSTOMIZER);
        }

        // OK, we have a color, so we can do the page.
        PrintWriter out = response.getWriter();
        response.setContentType("text/html");

        out.println("<html><title>A Custom-Colored Page</title>");
        out.print("<body bgcolor=\"");
        out.print(faveColor);
        out.println("\">");
        out.println("<P>Welcome! We hope you like your colored page!</P>");
        out.println("</body></html>");
        out.flush();
    }
}
```

If the user has not yet set a color customization cookie, the `CookieServlet` passes
control (by sending an HTTP redirect in the old API, or by use of a
`ServletDispatcher` under the Servlet API 1.2 or later) to this HTML page.

```
<BODY BGCOLOR="pink">
<H1>Please choose a color</H1>
<FORM ACTION="/servlet/ColorCustServlet" METHOD=GET>
<SELECT NAME="color_name">
    <OPTION VALUE="green">Green</>
    <OPTION VALUE="white" SELECTED>White</>
    <OPTION VALUE="gray">Grey</>
</SELECT>
<INPUT TYPE="submit" VALUE="OK">
</FORM>
```

Finally, the HTML page will jump to the customization servlet (Example 18-6),
which contains the code shown here to save the user's preference as a cookie, and
then return to the `CookieServlet` by sending an HTTP "redirect," causing the
browser to load the specified replacement page.

Example 18-6. ColorCustServlet.java

```
import java.io.*;
import javax.servlet.*;
import javax.servlet.http.*;

/** Color customization servlet */
public class ColorCustServlet extends HttpServlet {
```

Example 18-6. ColorCustServlet.java (continued)

```
    protected final static String DEFAULT_COLOR = "white";
    protected String faveColor = DEFAULT_COLOR;

    public void doGet(HttpServletRequest request, HttpServletResponse response)
    throws IOException {
        response.setContentType("text/html");
        PrintWriter out = response.getWriter();

        String cand=request.getParameter("color_name");
        if (cand != null) {
            faveColor = cand;
            Cookie c = new Cookie(CookieServlet.PREFS_BGCOLOR, faveColor);
            c.setMaxAge(60*60*24*365);
            response.addCookie(c);
        }
        response.sendRedirect("/servlet/CookieServlet");
    }
}
```

Of course, there are issues to consider when using cookies. Some users disable cookies out of justifiable fear that web sites will use them for gathering more information than a person might want to have known. In this case, our servlet would keep coming back to the customization page. It should probably have a warning to the effect that "cookies must be enabled to view this site." Or you could use other techniques, such as session tracking (see Recipe 18.4).

And realistically, you probably want to keep more than one preference item for a user. If you let them set the screen background, you also need to set the text color, for example. It's probably better to keep the preferences in a database on the server side, and just set a token that identifies the user (possibly the database primary key). Even then, remember that cookies can be altered! See Recipe 18.11 for a program to allow modification of the cookies stored on your hard drive.

18.4. Session Tracking

Problem

You want to keep track of one user across several servlet invocations within the same browser session.

Solution

Use an `HttpSession` object.

Discussion

HTTP was designed to be a stateless protocol: you would connect to a server, download a laboratory report, and that would be the end of it. Then people started getting clever, and began using it for interactive applications. For such purposes as a shopping cart in an online mall, and tracking answers during an online quiz or moves in an online game, the notion of an HTTP session has evolved to keep track of a particular browser. Sessions can be identified either by use of a cookie (see Recipe 18.3) or by a Session Identifier that is added to the URL. In either case the session ends when the user's browser program exits, but will otherwise stick around for a long time (there is probably a major denial-of-service attack hidden in here, so beware).

Using a session is fairly simple within the Servlet API. You request the HttpSession object from the HttpRequest that is passed into your service() or doGet()/doPost() method. The session object behaves rather like a Hashtable (see Recipe 7.6) except that the method names are putValue() and getValue(). This allows you to store an arbitrary number of objects in the session and retrieve them later.

This program uses an HttpSession to keep track of a user's responses during a quiz about Java. There are some 20 categories; once you pick a category, you can answer all the multiple-choice questions in that topic. The first question looks like Figure 18-4.

After you've answered a few questions, it may look like Figure 18-5.

At the end of the quiz, you'll see the total number of questions that you answered correctly.

The Exam object (an object containing all the questions and answers, along with the number of correct answers) is loaded using an XamDataAccessor (the code for these two classes is not shown) and stored in a Progress object. Progress, an inner class inside the servlet, is a tiny data structure used to monitor your progress through one quiz. When you change topics, the Progress object is discarded and a new one created. The bulk of the code in Example 18-7 is taken up in checking and tracking your answers and in generating the HTML to show the results of your previous question (if any), as well as the question and possible answers for the current question.

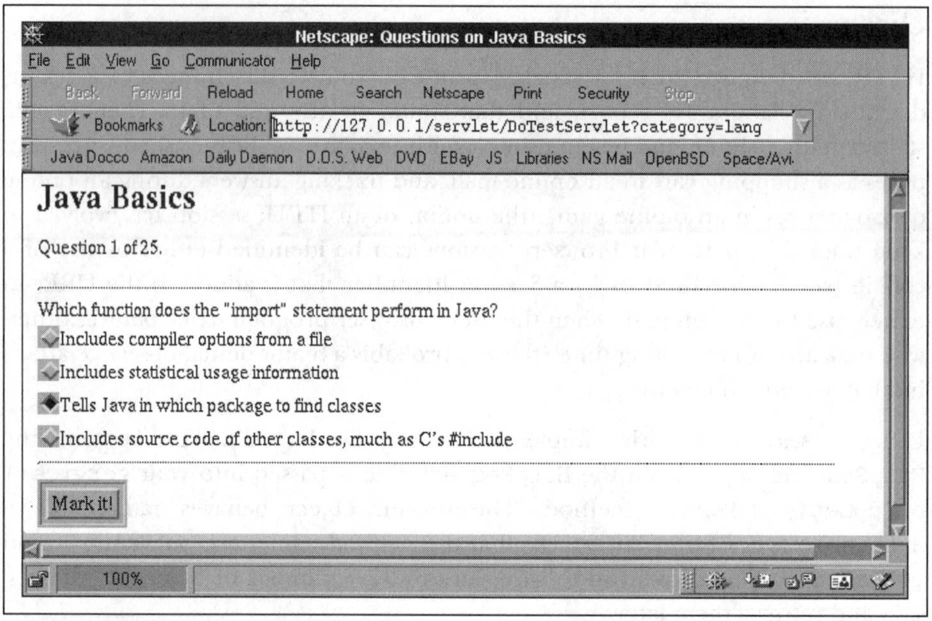

Figure 18-4. Quiz servlet starting

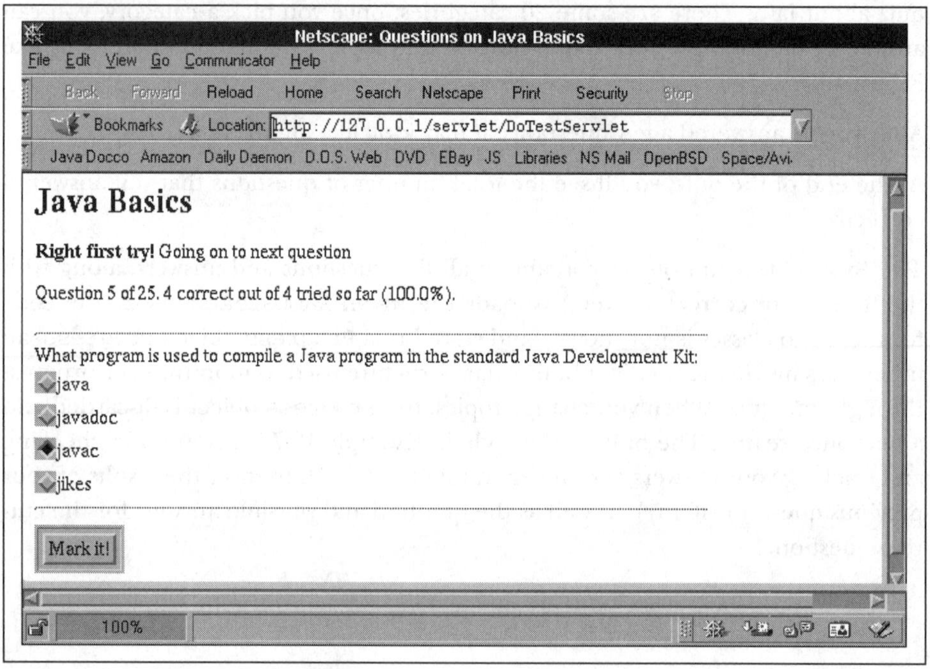

Figure 18-5. Quiz servlet several questions later

Example 18-7. DoTestServlet.java

```java
/** A Java Servlet to administer the tests over the Web.
 *  Saves exam and status session object to avoid having to reload it,
 *  but also to keep the exam constant during a session!
 */
public class DoTestServlet extends HttpServlet {

    /** Where to find the exams du jour */
    protected final static String DIRECTORY =
        "/home/ian/webs/daroadweb/quizzes-";
    /** The body color */
    protected final static String BGCOLOR = "white";

    /** An Inner Class to track the student's progress */
    class Progress {
        Exam exam;    // exam being taken
        boolean done;// exam is finished.
        String category;// name of exam, in effect
        int  curQuest;// Question number working on, 0-origin
        int  correct;// number gotten right on first try
    }

    /** Service is used to service each request. */
    public void service(HttpServletRequest request,
        HttpServletResponse response) throws IOException, ServletException {

        PrintWriter out = response.getWriter();
        HttpSession session;
        Progress progress;
        String reqCategory;

        // Set response type to HTML. Print the HTML header.
        response.setContentType("text/html");
        out.println("<HTML>");

        // Find the requested category
        reqCategory = request.getParameter("category");
        reqSubject  = request.getParameter("subject");// unix or java

        // Request the user's session, creating it if new.
        session = request.getSession(true);
        if (session.isNew()) {
            // out.println("<B>NEW SESSION</B>");
            progress = new Progress();
            progress.category = reqCategory;
            session.putValue("progress", progress);
        } else {
            progress = (Progress) session.getValue("progress");
        }
```

Example 18-7. DoTestServlet.java (continued)

```java
        if (reqCategory != null && progress.category != null &&
            !reqCategory.equals(progress.category)) {

            // CHANGE OF CATEGORIES
            // out.println("<B>NEW PROGRESS CUZ " +
            //   reqCategory + " != " +progress.category + "</B>");
            progress = new Progress();
            progress.category = reqCategory;
            session.putValue("progress", progress);
        }
        if (progress.exam == null) {
            XamDataAccessor ls = new XamDataAccessor();
            try {
                progress.exam = ls.load(DIRECTORY + subject + "/" +
                    progress.category + ".xam");
            } catch (IOException ex) {
                eHandler(out, ex, "We had some problems loading that exam!");
            } catch (NullPointerException ex) {
                eHandler(out, ex, "Hmmm, that exam file seems to be corrupt!");
            }
        }

        // Now that we have "exam", use it to get Title.
        out.print("<TITLE>Questions on ");
        out.print(progress.exam.getCourseTitle()); out.println("</TITLE>");
        out.print("<BODY BGCOLOR=\""); out.print(BGCOLOR); out.println("\">");
        out.print("<H1>");
        out.print(progress.exam.getCourseTitle());
        out.println("</H1>");

        // Guard against reloading last page
        if (progress.done) {
            out.println("<HR><a href=\"/quizzes/\">Another Quiz?</a>");
            out.flush();
            return;
        }

        // Are we asking a question, or marking it?
        out.println("<P>");
        String answer =request.getParameter("answer");
        int theirAnswer = -1;
        if (answer != null) {
            // MARK IT.
            Q q = progress.exam.getQuestion(progress.curQuest);
            theirAnswer = Integer.parseInt(answer);
            if (theirAnswer == q.getAns()) {
```

Example 18-7. DoTestServlet.java (continued)

```
                    // WE HAVE A RIGHT ANSWER -- HURRAH!
                    if (!q.tried) {
                        out.println("<P><B>Right first try!</B>");
                        progress.correct++;
                    } else
                        out.println("<P><B>Right. Knew you'd get it.</B>");
                    q.tried = true;// "Tried and true..."

                    if (++progress.curQuest >= progress.exam.getNumQuestions()) {
                        out.print("<P>END OF EXAM.");
                        if (progress.correct == progress.curQuest) {
                            out.println("<P><B>Awesome!</B> You got 100% right.");
                        } else {
                            out.print("You got ");
                            out.print(progress.correct);
                            out.print(" correct out of ");
                            out.print(progress.curQuest);
                            out.println(".");
                        }
                        out.println("<HR><a href=\"/quizzes/\">Another Quiz?</a>");

                        // todo invalidate "progress" in case user retries
                        progress.done = true;

                        // Return, so we don't try to print the next question!
                        return;

                    } else {
                        out.print("Going on to next question");
                        theirAnswer = -1;
                    }
                } else {
                    out.print("<B>Wrong answer</B>. Please try again.");
                    q.tried = true;
                }
            }

            // Progress?
            out.print("<P>Question ");
            out.print(progress.curQuest+1);
            out.print(" of ");
            out.print(progress.exam.getNumQuestions());
            out.print(". ");
            if (progress.curQuest >= 2) {
                out.print(progress.correct);
                out.print(" correct out of ");
```

Example 18-7. DoTestServlet.java (continued)

```java
                out.print(progress.curQuest);
                out.print(" tried so far (");
                double pct = 100.0 * progress.correct  / progress.curQuest;
                out.print((int) pct);
                out.println("%).");
        }


        // Now generate a form for the next (or same) question
        out.print("<FORM ACTION=/servlet/DoTestServlet METHOD=POST>");
        out.print("<INPUT TYPE=hidden NAME=category VALUE=");
                out.print(progress.category); out.println(">");
        out.println("<HR>");

        Q q = progress.exam.getQuestion(progress.curQuest);
        out.println(q.getQText());

        for (int j=0; j<q.getNumAnswers(); j++) {
                out.print("<BR><INPUT TYPE=radio NAME=answer VALUE=\"");
                out.print(j);
                out.print("\"");
                if (j==theirAnswer)
                    out.print(" CHECKED");
                out.print(">");
                out.print(q.getAnsText(j));
                out.println("</INPUT>");
            }
        out.println("<HR>");

        out.println("<INPUT TYPE=SUBMIT VALUE=\"Mark it!\"");
        out.println("</FORM>");
        out.println("</HTML>");
        out.close();
    }


    void eHandler(PrintWriter out, Exception ex, String msg) {
        out.println("<H1>Error!</H1>");
        out.print("<B>");
        out.print(msg);
        out.println("</B>");
        out.println("<pre>");
        ex.printStackTrace(out);
        out.flush();
        out.close();
    }
}
```

Debugging Tip for Servlets Using an HttpSession

Objects (such as `Exam` and `Progress` in the last example) are stored in the server for as long as your session lasts. If you change any such class so as to make it incompatible with the previous version, you will get mysterious "class cast errors" with the name of the class you changed. In these cases, you can simply close the browser (use File->Exit if using Netscape), and a new session object will be created. See also Recipe 9.17 for another way to avoid these `ClassCastException` errors.

18.5. Generating PDF from a Servlet

Problem

You want to make a printer-friendly document using a format like Adobe PDF.

Solution

Use `response.setContentType("application/pdf")` and a third-party Java API that can generate PDF.

Discussion

Portable Document Format (PDF) is a file format created by Adobe Systems Inc. PDF gives you full control over how your document looks, much more so than HTML, XML, or even Java's printing routines (see Chapter 12). Adobe Acrobat is a set of programs for reading and writing PDF. Adobe itself does not publish a Java API for generating PDF from scratch, but it does publish the file format specification (*Adobe Portable File Format Specification*) and explicitly gives everyone permission to write software to generate and/or process PDF files. PDF is a good fit for processing by an object-oriented language like Java, as it's an object-based text format. As a result, there are several PDF APIs available for Java, both free and commercial:

- Sitraka/KL Group (*http://www.klg.com*) has a PDF API as well as charting and other widgets, and JProbe, a leading tuning tool.

- StyleWriterEE (see *http://www.InetSoftCorp.com*).

- PDFLib GmbH (*http://www.pdflib.com/pdflib/*) produces PDFLib. PDFLib is mostly in C, with a Java wrapper; it also has bindings for several other popular languages.The source code is distributed, making it very cross-platform. It's free for noncommercial use; for commercial use, a small licensing fee is required.

- ReportLab (*http://www.reportlab.org*) is not for Java yet; it's entirely written in Python. You could probably use it within JPython (see Recipe 26.3). Watch for the possibility of future versions, though.

- Finally, since I couldn't decide which of these alternatives to use, I just went ahead and wrote my own, SPDF.

Go to *http://www.pdfzone.com* and look in the Toolbox section for others.

Like Perl, SPDF has several names. Perl on a good day is the Practical Extraction and Report Language, but on a bad day it's the Purely Eclectic Rubbish Lister. A true geek has to admire that kind of whimsy. SPDF can be the Simple PDF API, but it can also be the Stupid PDF API. Mostly the latter, I fear. Example 18-8 is a simple servlet that takes the user's name from the HTML form in Figure 18-6 and generates a custom-made shopping coupon with the customer's info imprinted into it, and a unique serial number (for which a `Date` object provides a cheap stand-in here) to prevent multiple uses of the coupon. I suspect there is a real window of opportunity for such coupons in conjunction with online web sites and large discount retail stores. Unfortunately, I'm too busy writing this book to exploit this marvelous opportunity, so I'll just release the source code to SPDF. If you get rich from it, send me some of the money, OK?

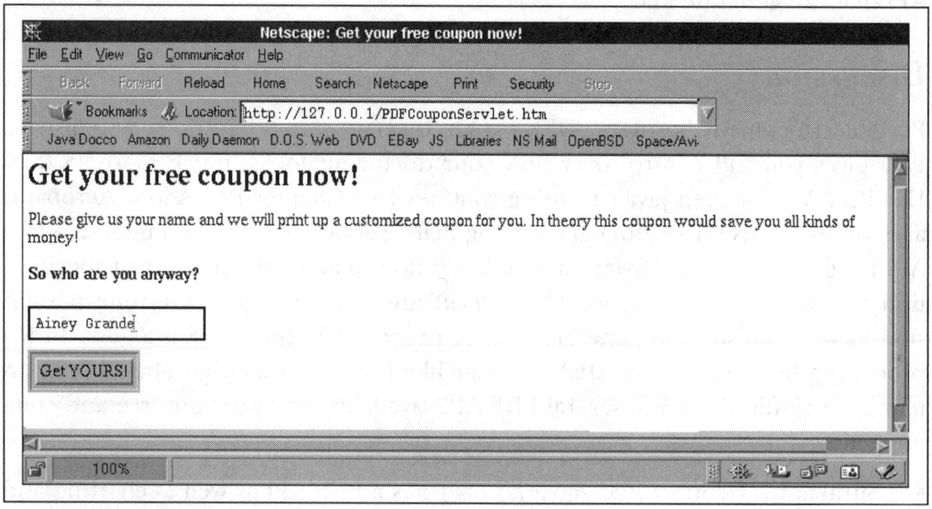

Figure 18-6. PDF coupon servlet

I'm not showing the source code for SPDF in this book, as the present version is pretty crude. No font support. No graphics. Single-page documents. It may be released, however; check out *http://www.darwinsys.com/freeware/spdf.html* if you're interested. Think of SPDF as the Standby PDF API, which you can use while you decide which of the other PDF APIs you really want to use.

When you click on the "Get Yours" button, the servlet is run, generating a PDF file and sending it back to the browser. My Unix version of Netscape tries to save it to disk since I don't have Acrobat loaded; the filename *MyCoupon.pdf* is provided by the `Content-disposition` header that I added to the response object. See Figure 18-7.

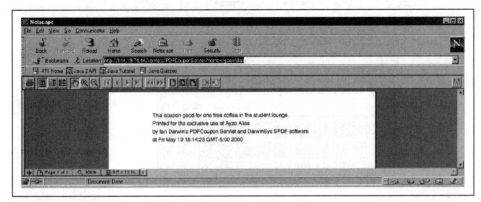

Figure 18-7. PDF coupon servlet save dialog

My test MS-Windows system's copy of Netscape has Acrobat installed, and will run Acrobat as a Netscape Plug-in to display it; see Figure 18-8.

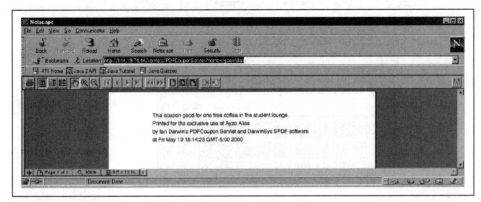

Figure 18-8. PDF coupon in Acrobat Reader

The basic SPDF API uses a PDF object to represent one PDF file. The PDF object has methods to set various things, to add pages to the object (and Page has methods to add text strings, moveTo operations, and others), and finally to write the file. Example 18-8 is the servlet that responds to the coupon request shown in Figure 18-6.

Example 18-8. PDFCouponServlet.java

```java
import java.io.*;
import java.util.*;
import javax.servlet.*;
import javax.servlet.http.*;
import com.darwinsys.spdf.*;

/** Simple PDF-based Coupon Printer Servlet
 */
public class PDFCouponServlet extends HttpServlet {
    public void doGet(HttpServletRequest request,
        HttpServletResponse response) throws IOException {

        PrintWriter out = response.getWriter();
        response.setContentType("application/pdf");

        // Tell browser to try to display inline, but if not,
        // to save under the given filename.
        response.setHeader("Content-disposition",
            "inline; filename=\"MyCoupon.pdf\"");

        PDF p = new PDF(out);
        Page p1 = new Page(p);
        p1.add(new MoveTo(p, 100, 600));
        p1.add(new Text(p,
            "This coupon good for one free coffee in the student lounge."));
        String name = request.getParameter("name");
        if (name == null)
            name = "unknown user";
        p1.add(new Text(p,
            "Printed for the exclusive use of " + name));
        p1.add(new Text(p,
            "by Ian Darwin's PDFCoupon Servlet and DarwinSys SPDF software"));
        p1.add(new Text(p, "at " + new Date().toString()));
        p.add(p1);
        p.setAuthor("Ian F. Darwin");

        // Write the PDF file page
        p.writePDF();
    }
}
```

Most of the Java PDF APIs are roughly similar. Example 18-9 is the `Terms` servlet
rewritten using PDFLib to generate a fancier PDF document with the same information as the HTML version.

Example 18-9. TermsServletPDF.java

```java
import javax.servlet.*;
import javax.servlet.http.*;
import java.io.*;
import java.util.*;
import com.pdflib.*;

/** Output the dictionary in fancy(?) PDF.
 * This version uses "PDFlib", from PDFLib.GmbH (www.pdflib.com).
 */
public class TermsServletPDF extends HttpServlet {
    /** A printwriter for getting the response. */
    PrintWriter out;

    /** Handle the get request. */
    public void doGet(HttpServletRequest request,
        HttpServletResponse response) throws ServletException {

        try {

            out = new PrintWriter(response.getOutputStream());

            int font;
            pdflib p = new pdflib();

            if (p.open_file("") == -1) {
                warning(response, "Couldn't create in-memory PDF file", null);
                return;
            }

            p.set_info("Title", "Dictionary Project");
            p.set_info("Author", "Ian F. Darwin, ian@darwinsys.com");
            p.set_info("Creator", "www.darwinsys.com/dictionary");

            p.begin_page(595, 842);

            font = p.findfont("Helvetica", "host", 0);

            p.setfont(font, 14);

            // for now just use one term from the Iterator
            Iterator e = new TermsAccessor("terms.txt").iterator();
            Term t = (Term)e.next();
            p.set_text_pos(50, 700);
```

Example 18-9. TermsServletPDF.java (continued)

```
            p.show("Term: ");
            p.continueText(t.term);
            p.set_text_pos(70, 666);
            p.show("Definition: ");
            p.continueText(t.definition);
            p.end_page();

            p.close();

            byte[] data = p.get_buffer();

            response.setContentType("application/pdf");
            response.getOutputStream().write(data);
        } catch (IOException e) {
            warning(response, "pdflib IO error:", e);
            return;
        } catch (Exception e) {
            warning(response, "pdflib error:", e);
            return;
        }
    }
```

The end of the servlet in Example 18-10 demonstrates a way to provide a user-friendly wrapper around the occasional exception traceback. Method `warning()` can also be used to print a generic error message without a traceback by passing `null` as the exception argument.

Example 18-10. TermsServletPDF error handling

```
    /** Generic error handler. Must call before any use of "out" */
    protected void warning(HttpServletResponse response,
        String error, Exception e) {
        response.setContentType("text/html");
        try {
            PrintWriter out = response.getWriter();
        } catch (IOException exc) {
            // egad - we can't tell the user a thing!
            System.err.println("EGAD! IO error " + exc +
                " trying to tell user about " + error + " " + e);
            return;
        }
        out.println("<H1>Error</H1>");
        out.print("<P>Oh dear. You seem to have run across an error in ");
        out.print("our dictionary formatter. We apologize for the inconvenience");
        out.print("<P>Error message is ");
        out.println(error);

        if (e != null) {
```

Example 18-10. TermsServletPDF error handling (continued)

```
                out.print("<P>Exception is: ");
                out.println(e.toString());
                out.print("Traceback is: ");
                out.print("<PRE>");
                e.printStackTrace(out);
                out.print("</PRE>");
        }
        System.out.print("DictionaryServletPDF: ");
        System.out.println(error);
        if (e != null) {
                System.out.println(e.toString());
        }
    }
}
```

18.6. HTML Meets Java: JSP

Problem

You have a web page that could use a jolt of Java.

Solution

Use the JavaServer Pages method of mixing HTML and Java.

Discussion

JavaServer Pages (JSP) shares some general syntax with Microsoft's ASP (Application Server Pages) and the free-software PHP (Programmable Hypertext Processor). They allow a mix of HTML and code; the code is executed on the server side, and the HTML plus the code results are printed as HTML. Because of Java's portability and JSP's full access to the entire Java API, JSP may be the most exciting web technology to come along since the online pizza demonstration. Example 18-11, for example, is the "five integers" code as a JSP.

Example 18-11. fiveints.jsp

```
<HTML>
<HEAD>
<TITLE>Your Personal Random Numbers</TITLE>
<H1>Your Personal Random Numbers</H1>
<P>Here are your personal random numbers,
carefully selected by a
<A HREF=\"http://java.sun.com\">Java</A> program.
<OL>
```

Example 18-11. fiveints.jsp (continued)

```
    <%
    java.util.Random r = new java.util.Random();
    for (int i=0; i<5; i++) {
        out.print("<LI>");
        out.println(r.nextInt());
    }
    %>
</OL>
<HR></HR>
<A HREF=\"index.html\">Back to main Page</A>
```

Notice how much more compact this is than the servlet version in Recipe 18.1. It should not surprise you to learn that JSPs are actually compiled into servlets, so most of what you know about servlets also applies to JSP. Let's look at another example that generates an HTML form and calls itself back when you activate the form, and also contains an HTML table to display the current month. Figure 18-9 and Example 18-12 show a JSP version of the `CalendarPage` program from Recipe 6.11.

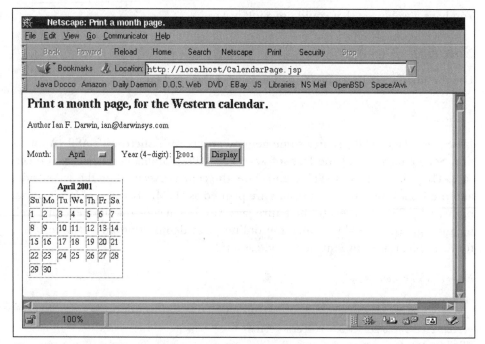

Figure 18-9. CalendarPage.jsp in action

Example 18-12. CalendarPage.jsp

```
<%@page import="java.util.*,java.text.*" %>

<head>
    <title>Print a month page.</title>
    <meta name="version"
</head>
<body bgcolor="white">
<h1>Print a month page, for the Western calendar.</h1>
<P>Author Ian F. Darwin, ian@darwinsys.com

<%  // First get the month and year from the form.
    boolean yyok = false;// -1 is a valid year, use boolean
    int yy = 0, mm = 0;
    String yyString = request.getParameter("year");
    if (yyString != null && yyString.length() > 0) {
        try {
            yy = Integer.parseInt(yyString);
            yyok = true;
        } catch (NumberFormatException e) {
            out.println("Year " + yyString + " invalid");
        }
    }
    Calendar c = Calendar.getInstance();
    if (!yyok)
        yy = c.get(Calendar.YEAR);

    String mmString = request.getParameter("month");
    if (mmString == null) {
        mm = c.get(Calendar.MONTH);
    } else {
        for (int i=0; i<months.length; i++)
            if (months[i].equals(mmString)) {
                mm = i;
                break;
            }
    }
%>


<form method=post action="CalendarPage.jsp">
    Month: <select name=month>
    <% for (int i=0; i<months.length; i++) {
        if (i==mm)
            out.print("<option selected>");
        else
            out.print("<option>");
        out.print(months[i]);
        out.println("</option>");
    }
    %>
```

Example 18-12. CalendarPage.jsp (continued)

```
    </select>
    Year (4-digit):
        <input type="text" size="5" name="year"
            value="<%= yy %>"></input>
    <input type=submit value="Display">
</form>
<%!
    /** The names of the months */
    String[] months = {
        "January", "February", "March", "April",
        "May", "June", "July", "August",
        "September", "October", "November", "December"
    };

    /** The days in each month. */
    int dom[] = {
            31, 28, 31, 30,/* jan feb mar apr */
            31, 30, 31, 31, /* may jun jul aug */
            30, 31, 30, 31/* sep oct nov dec */
    };
%>

<%
    /** The number of days to leave blank at the start of this month */
    int leadGap = 0;
%>
<table border=1>
<tr><th colspan=7><%= months[mm] %>   <%= yy %></tr>

<%      GregorianCalendar calendar = new GregorianCalendar(yy, mm, 1); %>

<tr><td>Su<td>Mo<td>Tu<td>We<td>Th<td>Fr<td>Sa</tr>

<%
        // Compute how much to leave before the first.
        // getDay() returns 0 for Sunday, which is just right.
        leadGap = calendar.get(Calendar.DAY_OF_WEEK)-1;

        int daysInMonth = dom[mm];
        if (calendar.isLeapYear(calendar.get(Calendar.YEAR)) && mm == 1)
            ++daysInMonth;

        out.print("<tr>");

        // Blank out the labels before 1st day of month
        for (int i = 0; i < leadGap; i++) {
            out.print("<td> ");
        }
```

Example 18-12. CalendarPage.jsp (continued)

```
        // Fill in numbers for the day of month.
        for (int i = 1; i <= daysInMonth; i++) {

            out.print("<td>");
            out.print(i);
            out.print("</td>");

            if ((leadGap + i) % 7 == 0) {// wrap if end of line.
                out.println("</tr>");
                out.print("<tr>");
            }
        }
    }
%>
</tr>
</table>
```

For another example, Example 18-13 shows the list of terms and definitions from Recipe 18.1 done as a JSP.

Example 18-13. terms.jsp

```
<HTML>
<HEAD>
    <TITLE>Ian Darwin's Computer Terms and Acronyms</TITLE>
    <%@ page import="java.io.*" %>
</HEAD>
<BODY BGCOLOR=white>
<H1>Ian Darwin's Computer Terms and Acronyms</H1>
<TABLE BORDER=2>
<TR><TH>Term<TH>Meaning</TR>
    <%
    // This part of the Servlet generates a list of lines like
    //   <TR> <TD>JSP <TD>Java Server Pages, a neat tool for ...

    // Filenames like this must NOT be read as parameters, since that
    // would allow any script kiddie to read any file on your system!!
    // In production code they would be read from a Properties file.
    String TERMSFILE = "/var/www/htdocs/hs/terms.txt";

    TermsAccessor tax = new TermsAccessor(TERMSFILE);
    Iterator it = tax.iterator();
    while (it.hasNext()) {
        Term t = it.next();
        out.print("<TR><TD>");
        out.print(t.term);
        out.print("</TD><TD>");
        out.print(t.definition);
        out.println("</TD></TR>");
    }
```

Example 18-13. terms.jsp (continued)

```
    %>
</TABLE>
<HR></HR>
<A HREF="/servlet/TermsServletPDF">Printer-friendly (Acrobat PDF) version</A>
<HR></HR>
<A HREF="mailto:compquest@darwinsys.com?subject=Question">Ask about another term</A>
<HR></HR>
<A HREF="index.html">Back to HS</A> <A HREF="../">Back to DarwinSys</A>
<HR></HR>
```

18.7. JSP Include/Forward

Problem

You want to write a "page-composite" JSP that includes other pages or passes control to another page.

Solution

Use `<jsp:include>` or `<jsp:forward>`.

Discussion

Suppose you have some common HTML code that you want to appear on every page, such as a navigator or header. You could copy it into each HTML and JSP file, but if it changed, you'd have to find all the files that used it and update each of them. It would be much easier to have one copy and include it everywhere you need it. Most webs servers feature such a mechanism already (e.g., server-side includes). However, using JSP's mechanism has some advantages, such as the ability to attach objects to a request, a topic I'll explore in Recipe 18.8.

The basic mechanism is simply to have `<jsp:include>` with a PAGE attribute naming the page to be included, and end with `</jsp:include>`. For convenience, you can put the / at the end of the opening tag and omit the closing tag. Much of this syntax is taken from XML namespaces (see Chapter 21). The FLUSH attribute is also required, and it must have the value TRUE; this is to remind you that, once you do an include, the contents of the output are actually written. Therefore, you can no longer do anything that involves sending HTTP headers, such as changing content type or transferring control using an HTTP redirect request. So a full JSP include might look like this:

```
<H2>News of the day</H2>
<jsp:include page="./news.jsp" flush="true" />
```

The `jsp:forward` request is similar to a `jsp:include`, but you don't get control back afterwards. The attribute `flush="true"` is required on some JSP engines (including the release of Tomcat at the time this book went to press) to remind you that once you do this include, you have committed your output (prior to the include, the output might be all in a buffer). Therefore, as I just stated, you can no longer do anything that might generate headers, including `setContentType()`, `sendRedirect()`, and so on.

An alternate include mechanism is `<%@include file="filename"%>`. This mechanism is a bit more efficient (the inclusion is done at the time the JSP is being compiled), but is limited to including text files (the file is read, rather than being processed as an HTTP URL; so if you include, say, a CGI script, the contents of your CGI script are revealed in the JSP output: not useful!). The `<jsp:include>` can include a URL of any type (HTML, servlet, JSP, CGI, even PHP or ASP).

18.8. JavaServer Pages Using a Servlet

Problem

It may seem that servlets and JSPs are mutually exclusive, but in fact they work well together. You can reduce the amount of Java coding in your JSP by passing control from a servlet to a JSP.

Solution

Use the Model-View-Controller paradigm, and implement it using `ServletDispatcher().forward()`.

Discussion

Model-View-Controller is a paradigm for building programs that interact well with the user. The *Model* is an object or collection that represents your data; the *View* is what the user sees; and the *Controller* responds to user request. Think of a slide-show (presentation) program: you probably have a text view, a slide view, and a sorter view. Yet when you change the data in any view, all the other views are updated immediately. This is because MVC allows a single model to have multiple views attached to it. MVC provides the basis for most well-designed GUI applications.

Using the Model-View-Controller paradigm, a servlet can be the controller and the JSP can be the view. A servlet, for example, could receive the initial request from the form, interrogate a database based upon the query, construct a collection of objects matching the user's query, and forward it to a JSP to be displayed (the servlet can attach data it found to the request). A good example of this is a search page, which might have only a few (or even one) form parameters, so using a JSP with a bean to receive the results would be overkill. A better design is to have a servlet retrieve the form parameter and contact the search API or database. From there, it would retrieve a list of pages matching the query. It could package these into a `Vector` or `ArrayList`, attach this to the request, and forward it to a JSP for formatting.

The basic syntax of this is:

```
ArrayList searchResultsList = // get from the query
RequestDispatcher disp;
disp = getServletContext().getRequestDispatcher("searchresults.jsp");
request.setAttribute("my.search.results", searchResultsList);
disp.forward(request, response);
```

This causes the servlet to pass the search results to the JSP. The JSP can retrieve the result set using this code:

```
ArrayList myList = (ArrayList) request.getAttribute("my.search.results");
```

You can then use a `for` loop to print the contents of the search request. Note that the URL in the `getRequestDispatcher()` call must be a call to the same web server, not to a server on a different port or machine.

18.9. Simplifying Your JSP with a JavaBean

Problem

You want to reduce the amount of Java coding in your JSP using a JavaBean component.

Solution

Use `<jsp:useBean>` with the name of your bean.

Discussion

JavaBeans is Java's component technology, analogous to COM components on MS-Windows. Recipes 23.7 and 23.8 contain a formula for packaging certain Java classes as JavaBeans. While JavaBeans were originally introduced as client-side, GUI-builder-friendly components, there is nothing in the JavaBeans specification that limits their use to the client-side or GUI. In fact, it's fairly common to use Java-Bean components with a JSP. It's also easy and useful, so let's see how to do it.

At the bare minimum, a JavaBean is an object that has a public no-argument constructor and follows the set/get paradigm. This means that there is regularity in the get and set methods. Consider a class, each instance of which represents one user account on a login-based web site. For the name, for example, the methods:

```
public void setName(String name);
public String getName();
```

allow other classes full control over the "name" field in the class but with some degree of encapsulation; that is, the program doesn't have to know the actual name of the field (which might be name, or myName, or anything else suitable). Other programs can even get a list of your get/set methods using introspection (see Recipe 25.2). Example 18-14 is the full class file; as you can see, it is mostly concerned with these set and get methods.

Example 18-14. User.java, a class usable as a bean

```
/** Represents one logged in user
 */
public class User {

    protected String name;
    protected String passwd;
    protected String fullName;
    protected String email;
    protected String city;
    protected String prov;
    protected String country;

    protected boolean editPrivs = false;
    protected boolean adminPrivs = false;

    /** Construct a user with no data -- must be a no-argument
     * constructor for use in jsp:useBean.
     */
    public User() {
    }

    /** Construct a user with just the name */
    public User(String n) {
        name = n;
    }

    /** Return the nickname. */
    public String getName() {
        return name;
    }

    public void setName(String nick) {
        name = nick;
    }
```

Example 18-14. User.java, a class usable as a bean (continued)

```java
    // The password is not public - no getPassword.

    /** Validate a given password against the user's. */
    public boolean checkPassword(String userInput) {
        return passwd.equals(userInput);
    }

    /** Set password */
    public void setPassword(String passwd) {
        this.passwd = passwd;
    }

    /** Get email */
    public String getEmail() {
        return email;
    }

    /** Set email */
    public void setEmail(String email) {
        this.email = email;
    }

    // MANY SIMILAR STRING-BASED SET/GET METHODS OMITTED

    /** Get adminPrivs */
    public boolean isAdminPrivileged() {
        return adminPrivs;
    }

    /** Set adminPrivs */
    public void setAdminPrivileged(boolean adminPrivs) {
        this.adminPrivs = adminPrivs;
    }

    /** Return a String representation. */
    public String toString() {
        return new StringBuffer("User[").append(name)
            .append(',').append(fullName).append(']').toString();
    }

    /** Check if all required fields have been set */
    public boolean isComplete() {
        if (name == null || name.length()==0 ||
            email == null || email.length()==0 ||
            fullName == null || fullName.length()==0 )
```

Example 18-14. User.java, a class usable as a bean (continued)

```
                return false;
        return true;
    }
}
```

The only methods that do anything other than set/get are the normal `toString()` and `isComplete()` (the latter returns true if all required fields have been set in the bean). If you guessed that this has something to do with validating required fields in an HTML form, give yourself a gold star.

We can use this bean in a JSP-based web page just by saying:

```
<jsp:useBean id="myUserBean" scope="request" class="User">
```

This creates an instance of the class called `myUserBean`. However, at present it is blank; no fields have been set. To fill in the fields, we can either refer to the bean directly within scriptlets, or, more conveniently, we can use `<jsp:setProperty>` to pass a value from the HTML form directly into the bean! This can save us a great deal of coding.

Further, if all the names match up, such as an HTML parameter "name" in the form and a `setName(String)` method in the bean, the entire contents of the HTML form can be passed into a bean using `property="*"`!

```
<jsp:setProperty name="myUserBean" property="*"/>
</jsp:useBean>
```

Now that the bean has been populated, we can check that it is complete by calling its `isComplete()` method. If it's complete, we print a response, but if not, we direct the user to go back and fill out all the required fields:

```
<% // Now see if they already filled in the form or not...
    if (!myUserBean.isComplete()) {
%>
            <TITLE>Welcome New User - Please fill in this form.</TITLE>
            <BODY BGCOLOR=White>
            <H1>Welcome New User - Please fill in this form.</H1>
                <FORM ACTION="name_of_this_page.jsp" METHOD=post>
                // Here we would output the form again, for them to try again.
                </FORM>
            <%
            } else {
            String nick = newUserBean.getName();
            String fullname = newUserBean.getFullName();
// etc...
            // Give the user a welcome
            out.println("Welcome " + fullname);
```

You'll see the full version of this JSP in Recipe 18.12.

See Also

You can extract even more Java out of the JSP, making it look almost like pure HTML, by using Java custom tags. *Custom tags* (also called custom actions) are a new mechanism for reducing the amount of Java code that must be maintained in a JSP. They have the further advantage of looking syntactically just like elements brought in from an XML namespace (see Recipe 21.0), making them more palatable both to HTML editor software and to HTML editor personware. Their disadvantage is that to write them requires a greater investment of time than, say, servlets or JSP. However, you don't have to write them to use them; there are several good libraries of custom tags available, one from Tomcat (*http://jakarta.apache.org*) and another from JRun (*http://jrun.allaire.com*). Sun is also working on a standard for a generic tag library. JSP tags are compiled classes, like applets or servlets, so any tag library from any vendor can be used with any conforming JSP engine. There are a couple of JSP custom tags in the source directory for the JabaDot program in Recipe 18.12.

18.10. JSP Syntax Summary

Problem

You can't remember all this post-HTML syntax.

Solution

Use the Table.

Discussion

Table 18-1 summarizes the syntax of JavaServer Pages. As the title implies, it contains only the basics; a more complete syntax can be downloaded from *http://java.sun.com/products/jsp/*.

Table 18-1. Basic JSP Syntax

Item	Syntax	Example
Scriptlet	`<% code;%>`	`<% mountain.setHeight(1000); %>`
Expression (to print)	`<%= expr %>`	`<%= mountain.getHeight() %>`
Declaration	`<%! decls; %>`	`<%! int height = 0; %>`
Include	`<jsp:include page="URL" flush=true />`	`<jsp:include page="./mountain-list.html" flush=true />`
Forward	`<jsp:forward page="url"/>`	`<jsp:forward page="./last-resort.html"/>`
Use bean	`<jsp:useBean .../>`	`<jsp:useBean class="x.ClimbBean" id="myClimbBean" scope="page"/>`

Table 18-1. Basic JSP Syntax (continued)

Item	Syntax	Example
Set property	`<jsp:setProperty ... />`	`<jsp:setProperty name="myClimbBean"` `property="*" />`
Page directive	`<%@ page ... %>`	`<%@ page import="java.io.*"` `errorPage="catcher.jsp" %>`
Comment	`<!-- comment -->`	`<%!-- This comment appears in HTML -->`
Hidden comment	`<%-- comment --%>`	`<%-- This comment is local to JSP --%>`

18.11. *Program: CookieCutter*

CookieCutter is a little program I wrote that allows you to display, modify, and even delete cookies. Since the banner-ad-tracking firm DoubleClick probably keeps a lot of information on your browsing habits, you want to befuddle them. After all, they are using a tiny bit of storage on your hard disk to rack up per-click profits, giving you nothing in return (directly, at least; obviously, ad sponsorship keeps some web sites on the air). In Figure 18-10, I am editing the cookie to, umm, "update" the personal identity cookie to an invalid number (a lot of 9's, and too many digits). A few lines above that, you can see the prefs.bgcolor cookie that I set to "green."

URL	Path	Name	Value	Expiry	Clie
www.computer...	/home/pri...	agent_it	9750405488095	1076313600	false
secure.webcon...	/cgi-bin	6772	000112172107...	1234099454	false
www.teknosurf...	/cgi-bin	teknoacc	306 32 50613	1109631679	false
boating.deneba...	/cgi-bin	lastLogin	2451660.1455	988224813	false
boating.deneba...	/cgi-bin	LastLogin...	04-25-2000%20...	988224813	false
.itworld.com	/agentIT	agent_it	5808302452981	1076331600	true
127.0.0.1	/servlet	prefs.bgco...	green	992022836	false
shaw.home.com	/flash	hitCount	1	962064687	false
www.QuickTak...	/qto	ShopperM...	SHOPPERMA...	1262303867	false
.doubleclick.net	/	id	abc999999	1920499140	true
.zdnet.com	/	cgversion	4	1041292706	true
.zdnet.com	/	browser	CC5C4C32382...	1041292706	true
.imgis.com	/	JEB2	16BC6907DF0...	1093136353	true
.netscape.com	/	NS_REG	SHA1=j%D6%9...	1293839982	true
.netscape.com	/	NS_REG	SHA1=+o%28+...	1293839982	true
.nscp-partners....	/	NS_REG	SHA1=%cf%dc...	978307192	true
.mediaplex.com	/	svid	937919745244...	1262285947	true

Figure 18-10. The CookieCutter display

I won't show the CookieCutter source code here as it doesn't really relate to web techniques (it's a client-side application), but it's included in the source archive for the book. CookieCutter also assumes your cookies are stored in the Netscape format; for the Microsoft Explorer format, you'll have to change the file-reading and file-writing code.

18.12. Program: JabaDot Web News Portal

Here is perhaps the most ambitious program developed in this book. It's the beginnings of a complete "news portal" web site, similar to *http://www.slashdot.org*, *http://www.deadly.org*, or *http://daily.daemonnews.org*. However (and as you should expect!), the entire site is written in Java. Or perhaps should I say "written in or by Java," since the JSP mechanism—which is written entirely in Java—turns the JSP pages into Java servlets that get run on this site. The web site is shown in Figure 18-11.

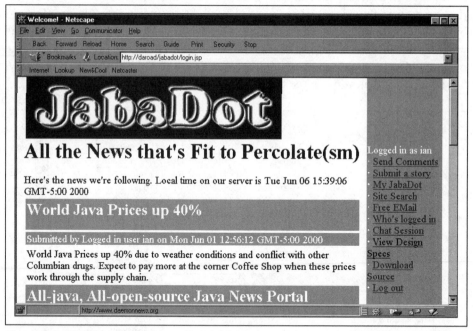

Figure 18-11. JabaDot welcome page

Like most portal sites, JabaDot allows some services (such as the current news items and of course the ubiquitous banner ads) without logging in, but requires a login for others. In this figure I am logged in as myself, so I have a list of all available services. The page that supports this view is *index.jsp* (Example 18-15), which contains a hodgepodge of HTML and Java code.

Example 18-15. index.jsp

```
<%@page errorPage="oops.jsp"%>
<HTML>
<TITLE>JabaDot - Java News For Ever(yone)</TITLE>
<P ALIGN=CENTER><jsp:include page="/servlet/AdRotator" flush="true"/></P>
<BODY BGCOLOR="#f0f0f0">
<%  HttpSession sess = request.getSession(true);
    User user = (User)sess.getValue("jabadot.login");
 %>
<TABLE>
<TD WIDTH=75% ALIGN="TOP">
    <!-- Most of page, at left -->
    <IMG SRC="logo.gif" ALIGN="LEFT"></IMG>
    <BR CLEAR="ALL">
    <jsp:include page="./news.jsp" flush="true"/>
</TD>
<TD WIDTH=25% BGCOLOR="#00cc00" ALIGN="TOP">
    <!-- Rest of page, at right -->
    <FONT COLOR=WHITE NAME="Helvetica,Arial">
    <% if (user == null) { %>
    <FORM ACTION=login.jsp METHOD=POST>
        Name: <INPUT TYPE=TEXT SIZE=8 NAME=nick>
        <br>
        Password: <INPUT TYPE=PASSWORD SIZE=8 NAME=pass>
        <br>
        <INPUT TYPE=SUBMIT VALUE="Login" ALIGN=CENTER>
    </FORM>
    <jsp:include page="public_services.html" flush="true"/>
    <% } else { %>
    Logged in as <%= user.getName() %>
    <jsp:include page="./logged_in_services.html" flush="true"/>
    <li><a href="logout.jsp">Log out</a>
    <% } %>
    </FONT>
</TD>
</TABLE>
</BODY>
</HTML>
```

As you can see, this code actually starts with a "page" tag (`%@page`) to specify an error handling page (the error page just prints the stack trace neatly, along with an apology). Then the output of the AdRotator servlet is included; the program just randomly selects a banner advertisement and outputs it as an HTML anchor around an IMG tag. Then I get the HttpSession object and, from that, the current User object, which is null if there is not a currently logged-in user. The User class was discussed when we talked about JavaBeans in JSPs (see Recipe 18.9); it's used as an ordinary object in most of these JSPs, but as a bean in the *newuser.jsp* page, when the user has entered all the fields on the "Create an Account" page.

Then there's an HTML table, which basically divides the rest of the page into two large columns. The left side of the page is fairly wide and contains the news stories, their headlines, the submitter's name, the time, optionally a URL, and the text of the news article. A future version will allow the user to send comments on the stories; as Slashdot has demonstrated, this is an important part of "community building," part of the art of keeping people coming back to your web site so you can show them more banner ads. :-)

The navigator part is displayed differently depending on whether you are logged in or not. If you're not, it begins with a login form, then lists the few services that are publicly available as HTML anchors, with the unavailable services in italic text. If you are logged in, there is a full list of links and a logout page at the end.

Before you log in, you must create an account. The trick here is that we require the user to give a valid email address, which we'll use for various authentication purposes and, just possibly, to send them a monthly newsletter by email. To ensure that the user gives a valid email address, we email to them the URL from which they must download the password. Figure 18-12 shows the entry page for this. This form is processed by *newuser.jsp*.

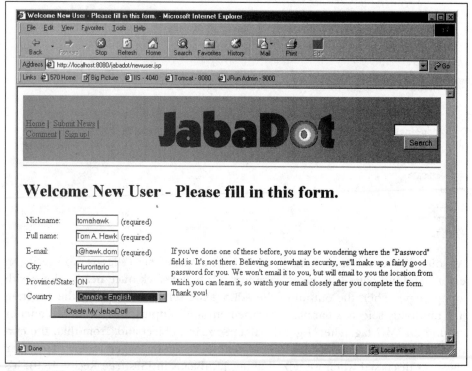

Figure 18-12. newuser.jsp in action

Example 18-16 is the source for *newuser.jsp*. As mentioned previously, this gets a
User object as a JavaBean (see Recipe 18.9).

Example 18-16. newuser.jsp

```
<%@page errorPage="oops.jsp" import="jabadot.*, java.io.*" %>
<%! java.util.Random r = new java.util.Random(); %>
<jsp:useBean id="newUserBean" scope="request" class="jabadot.User">
    <jsp:setProperty name="newUserBean" property="*"/>
</jsp:useBean>
<jsp:useBean id="mailBean" scope="request" class="jabadot.Mailer"/>
<html>
<%@include file="header.html" %>
<%
    User user = (User)session.getAttribute("jabadot.login");
    if (user != null) {
%>
<TITLE>You're already logged on!</TITLE>
<H1>You are logged on!</H1>
<P>Please <A href="logout.jsp">log out</A> before
trying to create a new account.  Thank you!
<%  return;
    }
%>
<% // Now see if they already filled in the form or not...
    if (!newUserBean.isComplete()) {
        // out.println("<!-- in new -->");
%>
        <TITLE>Welcome New User - Please fill in this form.</TITLE>
        <BODY BGCOLOR=White>
        <H1>Welcome New User - Please fill in this form.</H1>
        <TABLE>
        <TD>
        <FORM ACTION="newuser.jsp" METHOD=post>
            <table><!-- inner table so fields line up -->
            <tr><td>Nickname:</td>
                <td><INPUT TYPE=TEXT SIZE=10 NAME="name"> (required)</td></tr>
            <tr><td>Full name:</td>
                <td><INPUT TYPE=TEXT SIZE=10 NAME="fullName"> (required)</td></tr>
            <tr><td>E-mail:</td>
                <td><INPUT TYPE=TEXT SIZE=10 NAME="email"> (required)</td></tr>
            <tr><td>City:</td>
                <td><INPUT TYPE=TEXT SIZE=10 NAME="city"></td></tr>
            <tr><td>Province/State:</td>
                <td><INPUT TYPE=TEXT SIZE=10 NAME="prov"></td></tr>
            <tr><td>Country</td>
                <td><select name="location">
                <jsp:include page="country_select.html" flush="true"/>
                </select>
                </td></tr>
```

Example 18-16. newuser.jsp (continued)

```
            <tr><td colspan=2 align="center">
                <INPUT TYPE=SUBMIT VALUE="Create My JabaDot!"></tr>
            </table>
        </FORM>
        <TD>
        <P>If you've done one of these before, you may be wondering where
        the "Password" field is. It's not there. Believing somewhat in
        security, we'll make up a fairly good password for you.
        We won't email it to you, but will email to you the location
        from which you can learn it, so watch your email closely
        after you complete the form. Thank you!
        </TABLE>
<%      return;
        }

        // out.println("<!-- in get -->");
        String nick = newUserBean.getName();
        if (UserDB.getInstance().getUser(nick) != null) {
%>
            <P>It seems that that user name is already in use!
            Please go back and pick another name.
            <% return;
            } %>
<%
        String fullname = newUserBean.getFullName();
        String email = newUserBean.getEmail();
%>
        <!-- Give the user a welcome -->
        Welcome <%= fullname %>.
        We will mail you (at <%= email %>) with a URL
        from which you can download your initial password.

        <jsp:setProperty name="newUserBean"
            property="editPrivileged" value="false"/>
        <jsp:setProperty name="newUserBean"
            property="adminPrivileged" value="false"/>
<%
        // Generate initial random password and store it in the User
        String newPass = Password.getNext().toString();
        newUserBean.setPassword(newPass);

        // NOW add the user to the persistent database.
        UserDB.getInstance().addUser(newUserBean);

        // Create a temporary HTML file containing the full name
        // and the new password, and mail the URL for it to the user.
        // This will confirm that the user gave us a working email.
        // NEVER show the nickname and the password together!
```

Example 18-16. newuser.jsp (continued)

```
        String tempDir = JDConstants.getProperty("jabadot.tmp_links_dir");
        File tempLink = File.createTempFile(
            r.nextInt()+"$PW", ".html", new File(tempDir));
        PrintWriter pw = new PrintWriter(new FileWriter(tempLink));
        pw.print("<HTML><BODY>");
        pw.print("Greetings ");
        pw.print(newUserBean.getFullName());
        pw.print(". Your new password for accessing JabaDot is <B>");
        pw.print(newPass);
        pw.print("</B>. Please remember this, or better yet, ");
        pw.print("<a href=\"/jabadot/index.jsp\">");
        pw.print("login</a> now!");
        pw.print("You may want to visit \"My Jabadot\"");
        pw.print("and change this password after you log in.");
        pw.println("</HTML>");
        pw.close();

        // Now we have to mail the URL to the user.
        mailBean.setFrom(JDConstants.getProperty("jabadot.mail_from"));
        mailBean.setSubject("Welcome to JabaDot!");
        mailBean.addTo(email);
        mailBean.setServer(JDConstants.getProperty("jabadot.mail.server.smtp"));

        // Get our URL, strip off "newuser.jsp", append "/tmp/"+tmpname
        StringBuffer getPW_URL = HttpUtils.getRequestURL(request);
        int end = getPW_URL.length();
        int start = end - "newuser.jsp".length();
        getPW_URL.delete(start,end).append("tmp/").append(tempLink.getName());
        mailBean.setBody("To receive your JabaDot password,\n" +
            "please visit the URL " + getPW_URL);

        // Now send the mail.
        mailBean.doSend();

        // AVOID the temptation to sess.setAttribute() here, since
        // the user has not yet verified their password!
    %>
```

Once you create an account and read the email containing the link for the password, you can return to the site and log in normally. The login form is handled by *login.jsp*, shown in Example 18-17.

Example 18-17. login.jsp

```
<%@page errorPage="oops.jsp" import="jabadot.*" %>
<HTML>
<%
    User user = (User)session.getAttribute("jabadot.login");
```

Example 18-17. login.jsp (continued)

```
    if (user != null) {
        session.setAttribute("jabadot.message",
            "<H1>You're already logged on!</H1>"+
            "(as user " + user.getName() + "). Please" +
            "<a href=\"logout.jsp\">" +
            "logout</a> if you wish to log in as a different user.");
        response.sendRedirect("/jabadot/");
    }
    String nick = request.getParameter("nick");
    String pass = request.getParameter("pass");
    if (nick == null || nick.length() == 0 ||
        pass == null || pass.length() == 0) {
%>
        <!-- Must use jsp include not @ include here since
          ** tomcat complains if it sees the @ include twice.
          ** Can't just include it once at beginning, since we
          ** do a redirect at the end of this jsp if successful.
          -->
        <jsp:include page="./header.html" flush="true" />
        <TITLE>Missing name/password!</TITLE>
        <BODY BGCOLOR=WHITE>
        <H1>Missing name/password!</H1>
        <P>Please enter both a name and a password in the form.
<%      return;
    }


    User u = UserDB.getInstance().getUser(nick);
    if (u == null || !u.checkPassword(pass)) {
%>
        <jsp:include page="./header.html" flush="true" />
        <TITLE>Invalid name/password</TITLE>
        <BODY BGCOLOR=WHITE>
        <H1>Invalid name/password</H1>
        <P>We could not find that name and password combination.
        Please try again if you have an account, else go create one.
<%      return;
    }


    // Hallelujeah! WE FINALLY GOT THIS ONE LOGGED IN.

    session.setAttribute("jabadot.login", u); // login flag
    //session.setAttribute("jabadot.ads", new AdServlet());
    session.setAttribute("jabadot.message",
        "<H1>Welcome back, " + u.getFullName() + "</H1>");

    // For non-admin logins, provide a 3-hour timeout
    if (!u.isAdminPrivileged()) {
        session.setMaxInactiveInterval(3600*3);
```

Example 18-17. login.jsp (continued)

```
    }

    // Send Redirect back to top, so user sees just this in URL textfield.
    response.sendRedirect("/jabadot/");
%>
```

After ensuring that you're not already logged in, this page gets the username and password from the HTML form, checks that both are present, looks up the name in the password database and, if found, validates the password. If either the name or the password is wrong, I report a generic error (this is deliberate security policy to avoid giving malicious users any more information than they already have*). If you log in, I put the User object representing you into the HttpSession, set a little greeting, and pass control to the main page via a redirect.

Whether logged in or not, you can send a general comment to the system's administrators via the *submit.jsp* page. This simply generates the HTML form shown in Figure 18-13.

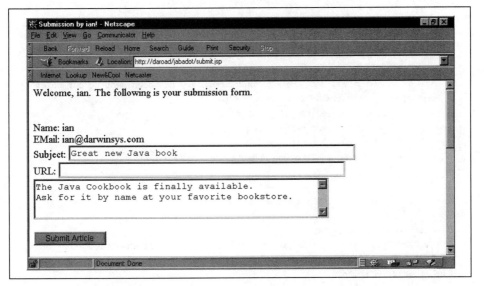

Figure 18-13. Input form for comments.jsp

This form is processed by *comments.jsp*, shown in Example 18-18, when you press the "Submit Article" button.

---

* This ancient advice comes from the early days of Unix; you'd be surprised how many sites still don't get it.

Example 18-18. comments.jsp

```
<%@page errorPage="oops.jsp" %>
<%@page import="jabadot.*, javax.mail.*" %>
<jsp:useBean id="mailBean" scope="request" class="jabadot.Mailer">
    <jsp:setProperty name="mailBean" property="*"/>
</jsp:useBean>
<%
    User user = (User)session.getAttribute("jabadot.login");

    mailBean.setFrom(JDConstants.getProperty("jabadot.mail_from"));
    mailBean.setSubject("Comment from jabadot site");
    mailBean.addTo(JDConstants.getProperty("jabadot.mail_comments_to"));
    mailBean.setServer(JDConstants.getProperty("jabadot.mail.server.smtp"));

    String message = request.getParameter("message");
    if (message != null)
        mailBean.setBody(message);

    // See if they already filled in the form or not...
    if (mailBean.isComplete()) {
        try {
            mailBean.doSend();

            // Now attach a thank you note and send them to the index page
            session.setAttribute("jabadot.message",
                "<H1>Mail sent</H1><p>Your commentary has been sent to our chief" +
                " pickle.<b>Thank you.</b></p>");
            response.sendRedirect("/jabadot/");
            // No return from sendRedirect
        } catch (MessagingException ex) {
            throw new IllegalArgumentException(ex.toString());
        }
    }
    // ELSE - mailbean is NOT complete, put up form.
%>
    <%@include file="header.html" %>
    <P ALIGN=CENTER><jsp:include page="/servlet/AdServlet" flush="true"/></P>
    <TITLE>Send Comments</TITLE>
    <BODY BGCOLOR="white">

    <DIV ALIGN="CENTER">
    <BLOCKQUOTE>

    <FORM METHOD="POST" ACTION="comments.jsp">

    <P>Please send us your feedback on this site.
<%  if (user != null) { %>
        <P>Since you are logged in, you can use
        <A href="mailto:<%=JDConstants.getProperty(
            // This subject= without quotes WORKS but doesn't feel good :-)
```

Example 18-18. comments.jsp (continued)

```
                "jabadot.mail_comments_to")%>?subject=Comments about JabaDot">
        this <I>mailto</I> link</A>.</P>
<%  } %>
    <P>Name: <INPUT TYPE="TEXT" NAME="name" SIZE="15"
    VALUE="<%= user==null?"":user.getFullName()%>"> 
        Email:<INPUT TYPE="TEXT" NAME="from" SIZE="15"
        VALUE="<%= user==null?"":user.getEmail()%>"></P>
    <P>City:     <INPUT TYPE="TEXT" NAME="City" SIZE="15"
    VALUE="<%= user==null?"":user.getCity() %>"> 
        State: <INPUT TYPE="text" NAME="State" SIZE="15"
        VALUE="<%= user==null?"":user.getProv() %>"></P>
    <P>Country: <INPUT TYPE="text" NAME="country" size="15"
    VALUE="<%= user==null?"": user.getCountry() %>"></P>
    <TEXTAREA NAME="message" ROWS="8" COLS="50" WRAP="physical">
<%= message %>
    </TEXTAREA>
    <P><INPUT TYPE="submit" VALUE="Send Comments"></P>
    </FORM>

    </BLOCKQUOTE>
    </DIV>
    </BODY>
```

This page starts off like the first one. I particularly like the code that displays a mailto: URL only if the user is logged in. SPAM perpetrators (see Chapter 19) are notorious for automatically loading entire web sites just to look for mailto: URLs. This is a good way to fence these rodents out, since they normally won't go to the trouble of signing up for a service and providing a real (working) email address just to get one mailto: URL from your site. There are easier ways to find mailto:'s on other sites; hopefully the SPAM perps will go there. For extra fun, make up a unique email address for each user to send mail to, so if you do get spammed, you have an idea who might have done it.

See Also

There is more to servlets and JSPs than I've got room to tell you about. These technologies offer an interesting partitioning of code and functionality. The JSP can be concerned primarily with getting the input and displaying the results. A JSP can forward to a servlet, or can include or jump to any other local web resource, like an audio file. Servlets and JSP are primary parts of the Java Enterprise Edition, and are becoming very important web server technologies.

For an opposing view (that JSPs are the wrong solution to the wrong problem), surf on over to *http://www.servlets.com*. For more information on servlets and JSPs, refer to the O'Reilly books *Java Servlet Programming* and *JavaServer Pages*.

19

Java and Electronic Mail

19.0. Introduction

Sending and receiving email from a program is easy with Java. If you are writing an applet, you can simply trick the browser into composing and sending it for you. Otherwise, you can use the JavaMail Extension (package `javax.mail`) to both send and read mail. JavaMail provides three general categories of classes, known as `Messages`, `Transports`, and `Stores`. A `Message`, of course, represents one email message. A `Transport` is a way of sending a `Message` from your application into the network or Internet. A `Store` represents stored email messages, and can be used to retrieve them as `Message` objects. That is, a `Store` is the inverse of a `Transport`, or, looked at another way, a `Transport` is for sending email and a `Store` is for reading it. One other class, `Session`, is used to obtain references to the appropriate `Store` and/or `Transport` objects that you need to use.

Being an extension, the JavaMail package must be downloaded separately from Sun's web site and is not part of the core API. It's worth it, though. For the cost of a few minutes' downloading time, you get the ability to send and receive electronic mail over a variety of network protocols. JavaMail is also included in the Java 2 Enterprise Edition (J2EE), so if you have J2EE you do not need to download JavaMail.

Finally, as you might have guessed from Chapter 15, it's not that big a stretch to write code that contacts an SMTP server yourself and pretends to be a mail program. Hey, why pretend? You really have a mail program at that point!

19.1. Sending Email: Browser Version

Problem

You want an applet to permit the user to compose and send email.

Solution

Use a mailto: URL, but hide it in some Java code.

Discussion

Since most web browsers are now configured with either built-in or linked-in email clients, you can use the mailto: URL as a poor-person's email composer to have users contact you. Many people prefer this to a fill-in-the-blank "mail" form connected to a CGI script or servlet (see Chapter 18), since they can use a specialized tool and save their own copy of the mail either in their log file or by CC'ing their own account. While you could use a mailto: URL directly in HTML, experience suggests that a species of parasite called a SPAM perpetrator will attach itself permanently to your mailbox if you do. Permanently, but not symbiotically, since this alleged life-form offers nothing in return to its host.

```
<H1>Test</H1> <P>Here is how to <A HREF="mailto:spam-
magnet@darwinsys.com?subject=Testing Mailto URL&cc=dilbert@office.comics">contact
us</A>
```

My approach is to hide the mailto: URL inside a Java applet, where SPAM perps are less likely to notice it. The applet uses showDocument() to activate the mailto: URL.

```
String theURL = "mailto:" + username;
URL targetURL = new URL(theURL);
getAppletContext.showDocument(targetURL);
```

Further, I break the email address into two parts and provide the @ directly, so it won't be seen even if the SPAM-spider is clever enough to look into the PARAM parts of the APPLET tag. Since I know you won't actually deploy this code without changing TARGET1 and TARGET2—the PARAM tags for the mail receiver's email name and host domain—you're fairly safe from SPAM with this. Example 19-1 is the Java applet class.

Example 19-1. MailtoButton.java

```
import java.applet.*;
import java.awt.*;
import java.awt.event.*;
import java.net.*;
```

Example 19-1. MailtoButton.java (continued)

```java
import java.util.*;

/**
 * MailtoButton -- look like a mailto, but not visible to spiders.
 */
public class MailtoButton extends Applet {
    /** The label that is to appear in the button */
    protected String label = null;
    /** The width and height */
    protected int width, height;
    /** The string form of the URL to jump to */
    protected String targetName, targetHost;
    /** The URL to jump to when the button is pushed. */
    protected URL targetURL;
    /** The name of the font */
    protected String fontName;
    protected String DEFAULTFONTNAME = "helvetica";
    /** The font */
    protected Font theFont;
    /** The size of the font */
    protected int fontSize = 18;
    /** The HTML PARAM for the user account -- keep it short */
    private String TARGET1 = "U";// for User
    /** The HTML PARAM for the hostname -- keep it short */
    private String TARGET2 = "H";// for Host
    // Dummy
    private String BOGON1 = "username";// happy strings-ing, SPAM perps
    private String BOGON2 = "hostname";// ditto.
    /** The string for the Subject line, if any */
    private String subject;

    /** Called from the browser to set up. We want to throw various
     * kinds of exceptions but the API predefines that we don't, so we
     * limit ourselves to the ubiquitous IllegalArgumentException.
     */
    public void init() {
        // System.out.println("In LinkButton::init");
        try {
            if ((targetName = getParameter(TARGET1)) == null)
                throw new IllegalArgumentException(
                    "TARGET parameter REQUIRED");
            if ((targetHost = getParameter(TARGET2)) == null)
                throw new IllegalArgumentException(
                    "TARGET parameter REQUIRED");

            String theURL = "mailto:" + targetName + "@" + targetHost;

            subject = getParameter("subject");
            if (subject != null)
```

Example 19-1. MailtoButton.java (continued)

```java
                theURL += "?subject=" + subject;

            targetURL = new URL(theURL);

        } catch (MalformedURLException rsi) {
            throw new IllegalArgumentException("MalformedURLException " +
                rsi.getMessage());
        }


        label = getParameter("label");// i.e., "Send feedback"
        if (label == null)
                throw new IllegalArgumentException("LABEL is REQUIRED");

        // Now handle font stuff.
        fontName = getParameter("font");
        if (fontName == null)
            fontName = DEFAULTFONTNAME;
        String s;
        if ((s = getParameter("fontsize")) != null)
            fontSize = Integer.parseInt(s);
        if (fontName != null || fontSize != 0) {
            System.out.println("Name " + fontName + ", size " + fontSize);
            theFont = new Font(fontName, Font.BOLD, fontSize);
        }

        Button b = new Button(label);
        b.addActionListener(new ActionListener() {
            public void actionPerformed(ActionEvent e) {
                if (targetURL != null) {
                    // showStatus("Going to " + target);
                    getAppletContext().showDocument(targetURL);
                }
            }
        });
        if (theFont != null)
            b.setFont(theFont);
        add(b);
    }

    /** Give Parameter info to the AppletViewer, just for those
     * writing HTML without hardcopy documentation :-)
     */
    public String[][] getParameterInfo() {
        String info[][] = {
            { "label","string","Text to display" },
            { "fontname","name","Font to display it in" },
            { "fontsize","10-30?","Size to display it at" },
```

Example 19-1. MailtoButton.java (continued)

```
                // WARNING - these intentionally lie, to mislead spammers who
                // are incautious enough to download and run (or strings) the
                // .class file for this Applet.

                { "username","email-account",
                    "Where do you want your mail to go today? Part 1" },
                { "hostname","host.domain",
                    "Where do you want your mail to go today? Part 2" },
                { "subject","subject line",
                    "What your Subject: field will be." },
            };
            return info;
        }
    }
```

Example 19-2 shows the program in a simple HTML page, to show you the syntax
of using it.

Example 19-2. MailtoButton.htm

```
<HTML><HEAD>
<TITLE>Darwin Open Systems: Feedback Page</TITLE></HEAD>
<BODY BGCOLOR="White">
<H1>Darwin Open Systems: Feedback Page</H1>
<P>So, please, send us your feedback!</P>
<APPLET CODE=MailtoButton WIDTH=200 HEIGHT=40>
    <PARAM NAME="H" VALUE="www.darwinsys.com">
    <PARAM NAME="U" VALUE="wile_e_coyote">
    <PARAM NAME="subject" VALUE="Acme Widgets Feedback">
    <PARAM NAME="label" VALUE="Send Feedback by Mail">
    <PARAM NAME="font" VALUE="Helvetica">
    <PARAM NAME="fontsize" VALUE="16">
    <P>Your browser doesn't recognize Java Applets.
    Please use the non-Java CGI-based feedback form.</P>
</APPLET>
<P>You should get an acknowledgement by email shortly. Thank you
for your comments!</P>
<HR>
<P>Here is a traditional "CGI"-style form to let you to send feedback
if you aren't running Java or if your browser doesn't support
email composition.</P>
<FORM METHOD=POST ACTION="http://www.darwinsys.com/bin/feedback.cgi">
    <TEXTAREA NAME=message ROWS=5 COLS=60></TEXTAREA>
    <BR>
    <INPUT TYPE=SUBMIT VALUE="Send Feedback"></INPUT>
</FORM>
<P>Thank you for your comments.</P>
```

Of course, not everybody uses a full-featured browser, and the light version doesn't include the email composer. The page therefore features a traditional CGI-based form for the benefit of those poor souls in need of a Java-based browser. Figure 19-1 is a screenshot in Netscape 4, showing the Compose window resulting from pressing the Feedback button.

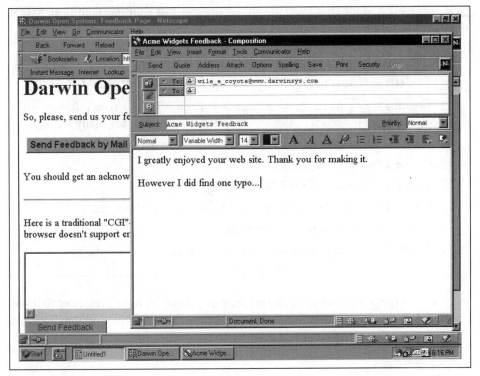

Figure 19-1. MailToButton

The CGI form is a workaround, though. Better yet is to provide a full-blown mail composer.

19.2. *Sending Email: For Real*

Problem

You need to send email, and the browser trick in Recipe 19.1 won't cut it.

Solution

Provide a real email client.

Discussion

A real email client allows the user considerably more control. Of course, it also requires more work. In this recipe I'll build a simple version of a mail sender, relying upon the JavaMail standard extension in package `javax.mail` and `javax.mail.internet` (the latter contains classes that are specific to Internet email protocols). This first example shows the steps of sending mail over SMTP, the standard Internet mail protocol. The steps are listed in the sidebar.

Ian's Basic Steps: Sending Email over SMTP

1. Create a `java.util.Properties` (see Recipe 7.3) to pass information about the mail server, as the JavaMail API allows room for many settings.

2. Load the `Properties` with at least the hostname of the SMTP mail server.

3. Create a `Session` object.

4. Create a `Message` from the `Session` object.

5. Set the From, To, CC addresses, and Subject in the `Message`.

6. Set the message text into the message body.

7. Finally, use the static method `Transport.send()` to send the message!

As is usual in Java, you must catch certain exceptions. This API requires that you catch the `MessagingException`, which indicates some failure of the transmission. Class `Sender` is shown in Example 19-3.

Example 19-3. Sender.java

```java
import java.io.*;
import java.util.*;
import javax.mail.*;
import javax.mail.internet.*;

/** sender -- send an email message.
 */
public class Sender {

    /** The message recipient. */
    protected String message_recip = "spam-magnet@darwinsys.com";
    /* What's it all about, Alfie? */
    protected String message_subject = "Re: your mail";
    /** The message CC recipient. */
    protected String message_cc = "nobody@erewhon.com";
    /** The message body */
    protected String message_body =
```

Example 19-3. Sender.java (continued)

```
        "I am unable to attend to your message, as I am busy sunning " +
        "myself on the beach in Maui, where it is warm and peaceful. " +
        "Perhaps when I return I'll get around to reading your mail. " +
        "Or perhaps not.";

    /** The JavaMail session object */
    protected Session session;
    /** The JavaMail message object */
    protected Message mesg;

    /** Do the work: send the mail to the SMTP server.   */
    public void doSend() {

        // We need to pass info to the mail server as a Properties, since
        // JavaMail (wisely) allows room for LOTS of properties...
        Properties props = new Properties();

        // Your LAN must define the local SMTP server as "mailhost"
        // for this simple-minded version to be able to send mail...
        props.put("mail.smtp.host", "mailhost");

        // Create the Session object
        session = Session.getDefaultInstance(props, null);
        session.setDebug(true);// Verbose!

        try {
            // create a message
            mesg = new MimeMessage(session);

            // From Address - this should come from a Properties...
            mesg.setFrom(new InternetAddress("nobody@host.domain"));

            // TO Address
            InternetAddress toAddress = new InternetAddress(message_recip);
            mesg.addRecipient(Message.RecipientType.TO, toAddress);

            // CC Address
            InternetAddress ccAddress = new InternetAddress(message_cc);
            mesg.addRecipient(Message.RecipientType.CC, ccAddress);

            // The Subject
            mesg.setSubject(message_subject);

            // Now the message body.
            mesg.setText(message_body);
            // XXX I18N: use setText(msgText.getText(), charset)
```

Example 19-3. Sender.java (continued)

```
                // Finally, send the message!
                Transport.send(mesg);

        } catch (MessagingException ex) {
            while ((ex = (MessagingException)ex.getNextException()) != null) {
                ex.printStackTrace();
            }
        }
    }


    /** Simple test case driver */
    public static void main(String[] av) {
        Sender sm = new Sender();
        sm.doSend();
    }
}
```

Of course, a program that can only send one message to one address is not useful in the long run. The second version (not shown here, but in the source tree accompanying this book) allows the To, From, Mailhost, and Subject to come from the command line, and reads the mail text either from a file or from the standard input.

19.3. Mail-Enabling a Server Program

Problem

You want to send mail notification from within a program.

Solution

Use the `javax.mail` API directly, or this `Mailer` wrapper.

Discussion

It is not uncommon to want to send email from deep within a non-GUI program such as a server. Here, I package all the standard code into a class called `Mailer`, which has a series of "set" methods to set the sender, recipient, mail server, etc. You simply call the `Mailer` method `doSend()` after setting the recipient, sender, subject, and the message text, and `Mailer` does the rest. Very convenient! So convenient, in fact, that `Mailer` is part of the `com.darwinsys.util` package.

For extra generality, the lists of To, CC, and BCC recipients can be set in one of three ways:

- By passing a string containing one or more recipients, such as "ian, robin"

- By passing an `ArrayList` containing all the recipients as strings

- By adding each recipient as a string

A "full" version will allow the user to type the recipients, the subject, the text, and so on into a GUI, and have some control over the header fields. The `MailComposeBean` (which we'll meet in Recipe 19.9) does all of these, using a Swing-based GUI. `MailComposeBean` uses this `Mailer` class to interface with the JavaMail API. Example 19-4 contains the code for the `Mailer` class.

Example 19-4. Mailer.java

```
package com.darwinsys.util;

import java.io.*;
import java.util.*;
import javax.mail.*;
import javax.mail.internet.*;

/** Mailer. No relation to Norman. Sends an email message.
 */
public class Mailer {
    /** The javamail session object. */
    protected Session session;
    /** The sender's email address */
    protected String from;
    /** The subject of the message. */
    protected String subject;
    /** The recipient ("To:"), as Strings. */
    protected ArrayList toList = new ArrayList();
    /** The CC list, as Strings. */
    protected ArrayList ccList = new ArrayList();
    /** The BCC list, as Strings. */
    protected ArrayList bccList = new ArrayList();
    /** The text of the message. */
    protected String body;
    /** The SMTP relay host */
    protected String mailHost;
    /** The verbosity setting */
    protected boolean verbose;

    /** Get from */
    public String getFrom() {
        return from;
    }

    /** Set from */
    public void setFrom(String fm) {
```

Example 19-4. Mailer.java (continued)

```java
        from = fm;
    }

    /** Get subject */
    public String getSubject() {
        return subject;
    }

    /** Set subject */
    public void setSubject(String subj) {
        subject = subj;
    }

    // SETTERS/GETTERS FOR TO: LIST

    /** Get tolist, as an array of Strings */
    public ArrayList getToList() {
        return toList;
    }

    /** Set to list to an ArrayList of Strings */
    public void setToList(ArrayList to) {
        toList = to;
    }

    /** Set to as a string like "tom, mary, robin@host". Loses any
     * previously-set values. */
    public void setToList(String s) {
        toList = tokenize(s);
    }

    /** Add one "to" recipient */
    public void addTo(String to) {
        toList.add(to);
    }

    // SETTERS/GETTERS FOR CC: LIST

    /** Get cclist, as an array of Strings */
    public ArrayList getCcList() {
        return ccList;
    }

    /** Set cc list to an ArrayList of Strings */
    public void setCcList(ArrayList cc) {
        ccList = cc;
    }
```

Example 19-4. Mailer.java (continued)

```java
/** Set cc as a string like "tom, mary, robin@host". Loses any
 * previously-set values. */
public void setCcList(String s) {
    ccList = tokenize(s);
}

/** Add one "cc" recipient */
public void addCc(String cc) {
    ccList.add(cc);
}

// SETTERS/GETTERS FOR BCC: LIST

/** Get bcclist, as an array of Strings */
public ArrayList getBccList() {
    return bccList;
}

/** Set bcc list to an ArrayList of Strings */
public void setBccList(ArrayList bcc) {
    bccList = bcc;
}

/** Set bcc as a string like "tom, mary, robin@host". Loses any
 * previously-set values. */
public void setBccList(String s) {
    bccList = tokenize(s);
}

/** Add one "bcc" recipient */
public void addBcc(String bcc) {
    bccList.add(bcc);
}

// SETTER/GETTER FOR MESSAGE BODY

/** Get message */
public String getBody() {
    return body;
}

/** Set message */
public void setBody(String text) {
    body = text;
}

// SETTER/GETTER FOR VERBOSITY
```

Example 19-4. Mailer.java (continued)

```java
/** Get verbose */
public boolean isVerbose() {
    return verbose;
}

/** Set verbose */
public void setVerbose(boolean v) {
    verbose = v;
}

/** Check if all required fields have been set before sending.
 * Normally called e.g., by a JSP before calling doSend.
 * Is also called by doSend for verification.
 */
public boolean isComplete() {
    if (from == null    || from.length()==0) {
        System.err.println("doSend: no FROM");
        return false;
    }
    if (subject == null || subject.length()==0) {
        System.err.println("doSend: no SUBJECT");
        return false;
    }
    if (toList.size()==0) {
        System.err.println("doSend: no recipients");
        return false;
    }
    if (body == null || body.length()==0) {
        System.err.println("doSend: no body");
        return false;
    }
    if (mailHost == null || mailHost.length()==0) {
        System.err.println("doSend: no server host");
        return false;
    }
    return true;
}

public void setServer(String s) {
    mailHost = s;
}

/** Send the message.
 */
public synchronized void doSend() throws MessagingException {

    if (!isComplete())
        throw new IllegalArgumentException(
```

Example 19-4. Mailer.java (continued)

```
                "doSend called before message was complete");

/** Properties object used to pass props into the MAIL API */
Properties props = new Properties();
props.put("mail.smtp.host", mailHost);

// Create the Session object
if (session == null) {
    session = Session.getDefaultInstance(props, null);
    if (verbose)
        session.setDebug(true);// Verbose!
}

// create a message
final Message mesg = new MimeMessage(session);

InternetAddress[] addresses;

// TO Address list
addresses = new InternetAddress[toList.size()];
for (int i=0; i<addresses.length; i++)
    addresses[i] = new InternetAddress((String)toList.get(i));
mesg.setRecipients(Message.RecipientType.TO, addresses);

// From Address
mesg.setFrom(new InternetAddress(from));

// CC Address list
addresses = new InternetAddress[ccList.size()];
for (int i=0; i<addresses.length; i++)
    addresses[i] = new InternetAddress((String)ccList.get(i));
mesg.setRecipients(Message.RecipientType.CC, addresses);

// BCC Address list
addresses = new InternetAddress[bccList.size()];
for (int i=0; i<addresses.length; i++)
    addresses[i] = new InternetAddress((String)bccList.get(i));
mesg.setRecipients(Message.RecipientType.BCC, addresses);

// The Subject
mesg.setSubject(subject);

// Now the message body.
mesg.setText(body);

// Finally, send the message! (use static Transport method)
// Do this in a Thread as it sometimes is too slow for JServ
new Thread() {
    public void run() {
```

Example 19-4. Mailer.java (continued)

```java
            try {
                Transport.send(mesg);
            } catch (MessagingException e) {
                throw new IllegalArgumentException(
                "Transport.send() threw: " + e.toString());
            }
        }
    }.start();
}

/** Convenience method that does it all with one call. */
public static void send(String mailhost,
    String recipient, String sender, String subject, String message)
throws MessagingException {
    Mailer m = new Mailer();
    m.setServer(mailhost);
    m.addTo(recipient);
    m.setFrom(sender);
    m.setSubject(subject);
    m.setBody(message);
    m.doSend();
}

/** Convert a list of addresses to an ArrayList. This will work
 * for simple names like "tom, mary@foo.com, 123.45@c$.com"
 * but will fail on certain complex (but RFC-valid) names like
 * "(Darwin, Ian) <ian@darwinsys.com>".
 * Or even "Ian Darwin <ian@darwinsys.com>".
 */
protected ArrayList tokenize(String s) {
    ArrayList al = new ArrayList();
    StringTokenizer tf = new StringTokenizer(s, ",");
    // For each word found in the line
    while (tf.hasMoreTokens()) {
        // trim blanks, and add to list.
        al.add(tf.nextToken().trim());
    }
    return al;
}
}
```

19.4. Sending MIME Mail

Problem

You need to send a multipart, MIME-encoded message.

Solution

Use the Part, man.

Discussion

Way back in the old days when the Internet was being invented, most email was composed using the seven-bit ASCII character set. You couldn't send messages containing characters from international character sets. Then some enterprising soul got the idea to convert non-ASCII files into ASCII using a form of encoding known as UUENCODE (the UU is a reference to UUCP, one of the main transport protocols used for email and file transfer at a time when Internet access was prohibitively expensive for the masses). But this was pretty cumbersome, so eventually the Multimedia Internet Mail Exchange format, or MIME, was born. MIME has grown over the years to support, as its name implies, a variety of multimedia types in addition to supporting odd characters. MIME typing has become very pervasive due to its use on the Web. As you probably know, every file that your web browser downloads—and a typical web page may contain from 1 to 20, 40, or more files depending on how hog-wild the graphics are—is classified by the web server; this "MIME type" tells the browser how to display the contents of the file. Normal HTML pages are given a type of text/html. Plain text is, as you might guess, text/plain. Images have types such as image/gif, image/jpeg, image/png, and so on. Other types include application/ms-word, application/pdf, audio/au, etc.

Mail *attachments* are files attached to a mail message. MIME is used to classify attachments, so they can be deciphered by a mail reader the same way that a browser decodes files it downloads. Plain text and HTML text are the two most popular, but something called Visual Basic Script, or VBS, was popularized (along with major weaknesses in the design of a certain desktop operating system) by several famous viruses including the so-called "love bug" virus.

The point of all this? The JavaMail extension is designed to make it easy for you to send and receive all normal types of mail, including mail containing MIME-typed data. For example, if you wish to encode a stream containing audio data, you can do so. And, as importantly for Java, if you wish to encode a Reader containing characters in an 8- or 16-bit character encoding, you can do that too.

The API makes you specify each separate MIME-encoded portion of your message as a Part. A Part represents a chunk of data that may need special handling by MIME encoders when being sent, and MIME decoders (in your email client) when being read. Example 19-5 is an example of sending a text/html attachment along with plain text.

Example 19-5. SendMime.java (partial listing)

```
/** The text/plain message body */
protected String message_body =
    "I am unable to attend to your message, as I am busy sunning " +
    "myself on the beach in Maui, where it is warm and peaceful. " +
    "Perhaps when I return I'll get around to reading your mail. " +
    "Or perhaps not.";
/* The text/html data. */
protected String html_data =
    "<HTML><HEAD><TITLE>My Goodness</TITLE></HEAD>" +
    "<BODY><P>You <EM>do</EM> look a little " +
    "<font color=green>GREEN </FONT>" +
    "around the edges..." +
    "</BODY></HTML>";

/** Do the work: send the mail to the SMTP server.  */
public void doSend() throws IOException, MessagingException {

        // create a session and message as before

        // Addresses, Subject set as before

        // Now the message body.
        Multipart mp = new MimeMultipart();

        BodyPart textPart = new MimeBodyPart();
        textPart.setText(message_body);// sets type to "text/plain"

        BodyPart pixPart = new MimeBodyPart();
        pixPart.setContent(html_data, "text/html");

        // Collect the Parts into the MultiPart
        mp.addBodyPart(textPart);
        mp.addBodyPart(pixPart);

        // Put the MultiPart into the Message
        mesg.setContent(mp);

        // Finally, send the message as before
        Transport.send(mesg);
```

N.B. This example requires JavaMail API Version 1.2 or later, due to a bug/limitation in earlier versions.

19.5. Providing Mail Settings

Problem

You want a way to automatically provide server host, protocol, user, and password.

Solution

Use a `Properties` object.

Discussion

You may remember from Recipe 7.7 that `java.util.Properties` is a list of name/value pairs, and that my `FileProperties` extends `Properties` to provide loading and saving. In several places in this chapter, I use a `FileProperties` object to preload a large variety of settings, instead of hardcoding them or having to type them all on the command line. When dealing with JavaMail, you must specify the mail hostname, username and password, protocol to use (IMAP, POP, or mailbox for reading), and so on. I store this information in a properties file, and most of the programs in this chapter will use it. Here is my default file, *MailClient.properties*:

```
# This file contains my default Mail properties.
#
# Values for sending
Mail.address=ian@darwinsys.com
Mail.send.proto=smtp
Mail.send.host=localhost
Mail.send.debug=true
#
# Values for receiving
Mail.receive.host=localhost
Mail.receive.protocol=mbox
Mail.receive.user=*
Mail.receive.pass=*
Mail.receive.root=/var/mail/ian
```

The last two, `pass` and `root`, can have certain predefined values. Since nobody concerned with security would store unencrypted passwords in a file on disk, I allow you to set `pass=ASK` (in uppercase), which causes some of my programs to prompt for a password. The JavaMail API allows use of `root=INBOX` to mean the default storage location for your mail.

The keys in this list of properties intentionally begin with a capital letter, since the property names used by the JavaMail API begin with a lowercase letter. The names are rather long, so they, too, are coded. But it would be circular to encode them in a `Properties` object; instead, they are embedded in a Java interface called MailConstants, shown in Example 19-6.

Example 19-6. MailConstants.java

```
/** Simply a list of names for the Mail System to use.
 * If you "implement" this interface, you don't have to prefix
 * all the names with MailProps in your code.
 */
public interface MailConstants {
    public static final String PROPS_FILE_NAME = "MailClient.properties";

    public static final String SEND_PROTO = "Mail.send.protocol";
    public static final String SEND_USER  = "Mail.send.user";
    public static final String SEND_PASS  = "Mail.send.password";
    public static final String SEND_ROOT  = "Mail.send.root";
    public static final String SEND_HOST  = "Mail.send.host";
    public static final String SEND_DEBUG = "Mail.send.debug";

    public static final String RECV_PROTO = "Mail.receive.protocol";
    public static final String RECV_PORT  = "Mail.receive.port";
    public static final String RECV_USER  = "Mail.receive.user";
    public static final String RECV_PASS  = "Mail.receive.password";
    public static final String RECV_ROOT  = "Mail.receive.root";
    public static final String RECV_HOST  = "Mail.receive.host";
    public static final String RECV_DEBUG = "Mail.receive.debug";
}
```

The fields in this interface can be referred to by their full names, e.g., MailConstants.RECV_PROTO. However, that is almost as much typing as the original long string (Mail.receive.protocol).* As a shortcut, programs that use more than a few of the fields will claim to implement the interface, and then can refer to the fields as part of their class, e.g., RECV_PROTO. This is a bit of a trick on the compiler: the interface has no methods so anybody can implement it, but in so doing "inherit" all the fields (remember that fields in an interface can only be final, not non-final).

19.6. Sending Mail Without Using JavaMail

Problem

You want to send mail, but don't want to require `javax.mail`.

---

* A bit like typing BorderLayout.NORTH instead of just "North".

Solution

This is a Really Bad Idea. You *can* implement the SMTP protocol yourself, but you shouldn't.

Discussion

Implementing an Internet protocol from the ground up is not for the faint of heart. To get it right, you need to read and study the requisite Internet RFC* pseudo-standards. I make no pretense that this mail sender fully conforms to the relevant RFCs; in fact, it almost certainly does not. The toy implementation here uses a simpler send-expect sequencing to keep in sync with the SMTP server at the other end. Indeed, this program has little to recommend it for serious use; I can only say that I had it around, and it's a good illustration of how simple a mail sender can be. Reading it may help you to appreciate the JavaMail API, which handles not just SMTP but also POP, IMAP, and many other protocols. Do *not* use this code in production; use the JavaMail API instead!

The basic idea of SMTP is that you send requests like MAIL, FROM, RCPT, and DATA in ASCII over an Internet socket (see Recipe 15.1). Even if your mail contains 8- or 16-bit characters, the control information must contain only "pure ASCII" characters. This suggests either using the byte-based stream classes from `java.io` (see Recipe 9.1) or using `Readers/Writers` with ASCII encoding. Further, if the data contains 8- or 16-bit characters, it should be encoded using MIME (see Recipe 19.4). This trivial example uses only the ASCII character set to send a plain text message.

When I run this program, it traces the SMTP transaction in the same way sendmail does with the –v option under Unix (this resemblance is intentional). The <<< and >>> are not part of the protocol; they are printed by the program to show the direction of communication (>>> means outgoing, from client to server, and <<< means the opposite). Lines starting with these symbols are the actual lines that an SMTP client and server exchange. You may notice that the server sends lines with both a three-digit numeric code and a text message, while the client sends four-letter words, commands like HELO and MAIL to tell the server what do to. The data sent in response to the line beginning with code 354 (the actual mail message) is not shown.

```
daroad.darwinsys.com$ jr SmtpTalk localhost ian
+ jikes +E SmtpTalk.java
+ java SmtpTalk localhost ian
```

---

* RFC stands for "Request For Comments," a reflection on the community-based standards process that was the norm when the Internet was young.

```
    SMTP Talker ready
    <<< 220 darwinsys.com ESMTP Sendmail 8.9.3/8.9.3; Thu, 23 Dec 1999 16:02:00
    >>> HELO darwinsys.com
    <<< 250 darwinsys.com Hello ian@localhost [127.0.0.1], pleased to meet you
    >>> MAIL From:<MAILER-DAEMON@daroad.darwinsys.com>
    <<< 250 <MAILER-DAEMON@daroad.darwinsys.com>... Sender ok
    >>> RCPT To:<ian>
    <<< 250 <ian>... Recipient ok
    >>> DATA
    <<< 354 Enter mail, end with "." on a line by itself
    >>> .
    <<< 250 QAA00250 Message accepted for delivery
    >>> QUIT
    <<< 221 darwinsys.com closing connection daroad.darwinsys.com$
```

The program, shown in Example 19-7, is straightforward, if not very elegant.

Example 19-7. SmtpTalk.java

```java
import java.io.*;
import java.net.*;
import java.util.*;

/**
 * SMTP talker class, usable standalone (as a SendMail(8) backend)
 * or inside applications such as JabaDex that need to send mail..
 *
 * OBSOLETE!! Use javax.mail instead, now that it's available!
 *
 */
public class SmtpTalk implements SysExits {
    // SysExits is a simple interface that just defines the
    // System.exit() codes to make this compatible with Sendmail.

    BufferedReader is;
    PrintStream os;
    private boolean debug = true;
    private String host;

    /** A simple main program showing the class in action.
     *
     * TODO generalize to accept From arg, read msg on stdin
     */
    public static void main(String[] argv) {
        if (argv.length != 2) {
            System.err.println("Usage: java SmtpTalk host user");
            System.exit(EX_USAGE);
        }

        try {
            SmtpTalk st = new SmtpTalk(argv[0]);
```

Example 19-7. SmtpTalk.java (continued)

```java
            System.out.println("SMTP Talker ready");

            st.converse("MAILER-DAEMON@daroad.darwinsys.com",
                argv[1], "Test message", "Hello there");
        } catch (SMTPException ig) {
            System.err.println(ig.getMessage());
            System.exit(ig.getCode());
        }
    }

    /** Constructor taking a server hostname as argument.
     */
    SmtpTalk(String server) throws SMTPException {
        host = server;
        try {
            Socket s = new Socket(host, 25);
            is = new BufferedReader(
                new InputStreamReader(s.getInputStream()));
            os = new PrintStream(s.getOutputStream());
        } catch (NoRouteToHostException e) {
            die(EX_TEMPFAIL, "No route to host " + host);
        } catch (ConnectException e) {
            die(EX_TEMPFAIL, "Connection Refused by " + host);
        } catch (UnknownHostException e) {
            die(EX_NOHOST, "Unknown host " + host);
        } catch (IOException e) {
            die(EX_IOERR, "I/O error setting up socket streams\n" + e);
        }
    }

    /** Send a command with an operand */
    protected void send_cmd(String cmd, String oprnd) {
        send_cmd(cmd + " " + oprnd);
    }

    /* Send a command with no operand */
    protected void send_cmd(String cmd) {
        if (debug)
            System.out.println(">>> " + cmd);
        os.print(cmd + "\r\n");
    }

    /** Send_text sends the body of the message. */
    public void send_text(String text) {
        os.print(text + "\r\n");
    }

    /** Expect (read and check for) a given reply */
    protected boolean expect_reply(String rspNum) throws SMTPException {
```

Example 19-7. SmtpTalk.java (continued)

```
        String s = null;
        try {
            s = is.readLine();
        } catch(IOException e) {
            die(EX_IOERR,"I/O error reading from host " + host + " " + e);
        }
        if (debug) System.out.println("<<< " + s);
        return s.startsWith(rspNum + " ");
    }

    /** Convenience routine to print message & exit, like
     * K&P error(), perl die(1,), ...
     * @param ret Numeric value to pass back
     * @param msg Error message to be printed on stdout.
     */
    protected void die(int ret, String msg) throws SMTPException {
        throw new SMTPException(ret, msg);
    }

    /** send one Mail message to one or more recipients via smtp
     * to server "host".
     */
    public void converse(String sender, String recipients,
            String subject, String body) throws SMTPException {

        if (!expect_reply("220")) die(EX_PROTOCOL,
            "did not get SMTP greeting");

        send_cmd("HELO", "darwinsys.com");
        if (!expect_reply("250")) die(EX_PROTOCOL,
            "did not ack our HELO");

        send_cmd("MAIL", "From:<"+sender+">");// no spaces!
        if (!expect_reply("250")) die(EX_PROTOCOL,
            "did not ack our MAIL command");

        StringTokenizer st = new StringTokenizer(recipients);
        while (st.hasMoreTokens()) {
            String r = st.nextToken();
            send_cmd("RCPT", "To:<" + r + ">");
            if (!expect_reply("250")) die(EX_PROTOCOL,
                "didn't ack RCPT " + r);
        }
        send_cmd("DATA");
        if (!expect_reply("354")) die(EX_PROTOCOL,"did not want our DATA!");

        send_text("From: " + sender);
        send_text("To: " + recipients);
```

Example 19-7. SmtpTalk.java (continued)

```
        send_text("Subject: " + subject);
        send_text("");
        send_text(body + "\r");

        send_cmd(".");
        if (!expect_reply("250")) die(EX_PROTOCOL,"Mail not accepted");

        send_cmd("QUIT");
        if (!expect_reply("221")) die(EX_PROTOCOL,"Other end not closing down");
    }
}
```

19.7. Reading Email

Problem

You need to read mail.

Solution

Use a JavaMail `Store`.

Discussion

The JavaMail API is designed to be easy to use. `Store` encapsulates the information and access methods for a particular type of mail storage; the steps for using it are listed in the sidebar.

Ian's Basic Steps: Reading Email Using Store

1. Get a `Session` object using `Session.getDefaultInstance()`. You can pass `System.getProperties()` as the `Properties` argument.

2. Get a `Store` from the `Session` object.

3. Get the root `Folder`.

4. If the root `Folder` can contain subfolders, list them.

5. For each `Folder` that can contain messages, call `getMessages()`, which returns an array of `Message` objects.

6. Do what you will with the messages (usually, display the headers and let the user select which message to view).

Sun provides a `Store` class for the IMAP transport mechanism, and optionally for POP3.* In these examples I use the Unix mbox protocol† (when I started with Unix there was no POP3 protocol; it was traditional to access your mail spool file directly on a server). However, you could use all these programs with the POP or IMAP stores just by passing the appropriate protocol name where "mbox" appears in the following examples. I've tested several of the programs using Sun's POP store and several POP servers (CUCIpop and PMDF).

I delete most of the email I get on one of my systems, so there were only two messages to be read when I ran my first "mailbox lister" program:

```
daroad.darwinsys.com$ java MailLister mbox localhost - - /var/mail/ian
Getting folder /var/mail/ian.
Name: ian(/var/mail/ian)
No New Messages
irate_client@nosuchd  Contract in Hawaii
mailer-daemon@kingcr  Returned mail: Data format error
daroad.darwinsys.com$
```

The main program shown in Example 19-8 takes all five arguments from its command line.

Example 19-8. MailLister.java

```java
import com.darwinsys.util.*;
import java.util.Properties;
import javax.mail.*;
import javax.mail.internet.*;

/**
 * List all available folders.
 */
public class MailLister {
    static StringFormat fromFmt =
        new StringFormat(20, StringFormat.JUST_LEFT);
    static StringFormat subjFmt =
        new StringFormat(40, StringFormat.JUST_LEFT);

    public static void main(String[] argv) throws Exception {
        String fileName = MailConstants.PROPS_FILE_NAME;
        String protocol = null;
        String host = null;
        String user = null;
        String password = null;
```

---

* The POP3 `Store` classes must be downloaded and manually installed from *http://java.sun.com/products/javamail/*.

† This is free (GPL) software, which can be downloaded from the Giant Java Tree, *http://www.gjt.org*.

Example 19-8. MailLister.java (continued)

```java
        String root = null;

        // If argc == 1, assume it's a Properties file.
        if (argv.length == 1) {
            fileName = argv[0];
            FileProperties fp = new FileProperties(fileName);
            fp.load();
            protocol = fp.getProperty(MailConstants.RECV_PROTO);
            host = fp.getProperty(MailConstants.RECV_HOST);
            user = fp.getProperty(MailConstants.RECV_USER);
            password = fp.getProperty(MailConstants.RECV_PASS);
            root = fp.getProperty(MailConstants.RECV_ROOT);
        }
        // If not, assume listing all args in long form.
        else if (argv.length == 5) {
            protocol = argv[0];
            host = argv[1];
            user = argv[2];
            password = argv[3];
            root = argv[4];
        }
        // Otherwise give up.
        else {
            System.err.println(
                "Usage: MailLister protocol host user pw root");
            System.exit(0);
        }

        boolean recursive = false;

        // Start with a Session object, as usual
        Session session = Session.getDefaultInstance(
            System.getProperties(), null);
        session.setDebug(false);

        // Get a Store object for the given protocol
        Store store = session.getStore(protocol);
        store.connect(host, user, password);

        // Get Folder object for root, and list it
        // If root name = "", getDefaultFolder(), else getFolder(root)
        Folder rf;
        if (root.length() != 0) {
            System.out.println("Getting folder " + root + ".");
            rf = store.getFolder(root);
        } else {
            System.out.println("Getting default folder.");
            rf = store.getDefaultFolder();
        }
```

Example 19-8. MailLister.java (continued)

```java
        rf.open(Folder.READ_WRITE);

        if (rf.getType() == Folder.HOLDS_FOLDERS) {
            Folder[] f = rf.list();
            for (int i = 0; i < f.length; i++)
                listFolder(f[i], "", recursive);
        } else
                listFolder(rf, "", false);
    }

    static void listFolder(Folder folder, String tab, boolean recurse)
    throws Exception {
        folder.open(Folder.READ_WRITE);
        System.out.println(tab + "Name: " + folder.getName() + '(' +
            folder.getFullName() + ')');
        if (!folder.isSubscribed())
            System.out.println(tab + "Not Subscribed");
        if ((folder.getType() & Folder.HOLDS_MESSAGES) != 0) {
            if (folder.hasNewMessages())
                System.out.println(tab + "Has New Messages");
            else
                System.out.println(tab + "No New Messages");
            Message[] msgs = folder.getMessages();
            for (int i=0; i<msgs.length; i++) {
                Message m = msgs[i];
                Address from = m.getFrom()[0];
                String fromAddress;
                if (from instanceof InternetAddress)
                    fromAddress = ((InternetAddress)from).getAddress();
                else
                    fromAddress = from.toString();
                StringBuffer sb = new StringBuffer();
                fromFmt.format(fromAddress, sb, null);
                sb. append(" ");
                subjFmt.format(m.getSubject(), sb, null);
                System.out.println(sb.toString());
            }
        }
        if ((folder.getType() & Folder.HOLDS_FOLDERS) != 0) {
            System.out.println(tab + "Is Directory");
        if (recurse) {
            Folder[] f = folder.list();
            for (int i=0; i < f.length; i++)
                listFolder(f[i], tab + "", recurse);
            }
        }
    }
}
```

This program has the core of a full mail reader but doesn't actually fetch the articles. To display a message, you have to get it (by number) from the folder, then call methods like getSubject(), getFrom(), and others. The listFolder() method does this to obtain identifying information on each message, and formats them using the StringFormat class from Recipe 3.5.

If we add a GUI and a bit of code to get all the relevant header fields, we can have a working mail reader. We'll show the messages in a tree view, since some protocols let you have more than one folder containing messages. For this we'll use a JTree widget, the Swing GUI component for displaying text or icons in a tree-like view. The objects stored in a JTree must be Node objects, but we also want them to be Folders and Messages. I handled this by subclassing DefaultMutableNode and adding a field for the folder or message, though you could also subclass Folder and implement the Node interface. Arguably, the way I did it is less "pure OO," but also less work. Example 19-9 is my MessageNode; FolderNode is similar, but simpler in that its toString() only calls the Folder's getName() method.

Example 19-9. MessageNode.java

```java
import javax.mail.*;
import javax.mail.internet.*;
import javax.swing.tree.*;

/** A Mutable Tree Node that is also a Message. */
public class MessageNode extends DefaultMutableTreeNode {
    Message m;

    StringFormat fromFmt = new StringFormat(20, StringFormat.JUST_LEFT);
    StringFormat subjFmt = new StringFormat(30, StringFormat.JUST_LEFT);

    MessageNode(Message m) {
        this.m = m;
    }

    public String toString() {
        try {
            Address from = m.getFrom()[0];

            String fromAddress;
            if (from instanceof InternetAddress)
                fromAddress = ((InternetAddress)from).getAddress();
            else
                fromAddress = from.toString();

            StringBuffer sb = new StringBuffer();
            fromFmt.format(fromAddress, sb, null);
            sb. append("  ");
```

Example 19-9. MessageNode.java (continued)

```
            subjFmt.format(m.getSubject(), sb, null);
            return sb.toString();
        } catch (Exception e) {
            return e.toString();
        }
    }
}
```

These are all put together into a mail reader in Recipe 19.8.

19.8. Program: MailReaderBean

Example 19-10 shows the complete `MailReaderBean` program. As the name implies, it can be used as a bean in larger programs, but also has a `main` method for standalone use. Clicking on a message displays it in the message view part of the window; this is handled by the `TreeSelectionListener` called `tsl`.

Example 19-10. MailReaderBean.java

```
import java.awt.*;
import java.awt.event.*;
import javax.swing.*;
import javax.swing.tree.*;
import javax.swing.event.*;
import javax.mail.*;
import javax.mail.internet.*;

/**
 * Display a mailbox or mailboxes.
 * This is the generic version in javasrc/email, split off from
 * JabaDex because of the latter's domain-specific "implements module" stuff.

 */
public class MailReaderBean extends JSplitPane {

    private JTextArea bodyText;

    /* Construct a mail reader bean with all defaults.
     */
    public MailReaderBean() throws Exception {
        this("smtp", "mailhost", "user", "nopasswd", "/");
    }

    /* Construct a mail reader bean with all values. */
    public MailReaderBean(
        String protocol,
        String host,
        String user,
```

Example 19-10. MailReaderBean.java (continued)

```
        String password,
        String rootName)
    throws Exception {

        super(VERTICAL_SPLIT);

        boolean recursive = false;

        // Start with a Mail Session object
        Session session = Session.getDefaultInstance(
            System.getProperties(), null);
        session.setDebug(false);

        // Get a Store object for the given protocol
        Store store = session.getStore(protocol);
        store.connect(host, user, password);

        // Get Folder object for root, and list it
        // If root name = "", getDefaultFolder(), else getFolder(root)
        FolderNode top;
        if (rootName.length() != 0) {
            // System.out.println("Getting folder " + rootName + ".");
            top = new FolderNode(store.getFolder(rootName));
        } else {
            // System.out.println("Getting default folder.");
            top = new FolderNode(store.getDefaultFolder());
        }
        if (top == null || !top.f.exists()) {
            System.out.println("Invalid folder " + rootName);
            return;
        }

        if (top.f.getType() == Folder.HOLDS_FOLDERS) {
            Folder[] f = top.f.list();
            for (int i = 0; i < f.length; i++)
                listFolder(top, new FolderNode(f[i]), recursive);
        } else
                listFolder(top, top, false);

        // Now that (all) the foldernodes and treenodes are in,
        // construct a JTree object from the top of the list down,
        // make the JTree scrollable (put in JScrollPane),
        // and add it as the MailComposeBean's Northern child.
        JTree tree = new JTree(top);
        JScrollPane treeScroller = new JScrollPane(tree);
        treeScroller.setBackground(tree.getBackground());
        this.setTopComponent(treeScroller);

        // The Southern (Bottom) child is a textarea to display the msg.
```

Example 19-10. MailReaderBean.java (continued)

```java
    bodyText = new JTextArea(15, 80);
    this.setBottomComponent(new JScrollPane(bodyText));

    // Add a notification listener for the tree; this will
    // display the clicked-upon message
    TreeSelectionListener tsl = new TreeSelectionListener() {
        public void valueChanged(TreeSelectionEvent evt) {
            Object[] po = evt.getPath().getPath();// yes, repeat it.
            Object o = po[po.length - 1];// last node in path
            if (o instanceof FolderNode) {
                // System.out.println("Select folder " + o.toString());
                return;
            }
            if (o instanceof MessageNode) {
                bodyText.setText("");
                try {
                    Message m = ((MessageNode)o).m;

                    bodyText.append("To: ");
                    Object[] tos = m.getAllRecipients();
                    for (int i=0; i<tos.length; i++) {
                        bodyText.append(tos[i].toString());
                        bodyText.append(" ");
                    }
                    bodyText.append("\n");

                    bodyText.append("Subject: " + m.getSubject() + "\n");
                    bodyText.append("From: ");
                    Object[] froms = m.getFrom();
                    for (int i=0; i<froms.length; i++) {
                        bodyText.append(froms[i].toString());
                        bodyText.append(" ");
                    }
                    bodyText.append("\n");

                    bodyText.append("Date: " + m.getSentDate() + "\n");
                    bodyText.append("\n");

                    bodyText.append(m.getContent().toString());

                    // Start reading at top of message(!)
                    bodyText.setCaretPosition(0);
                } catch (Exception e) {
                    bodyText.append(e.toString());
                }
            } else
                System.err.println("UNEXPECTED SELECTION: " + o.getClass());
        }
    };
```

Example 19-10. MailReaderBean.java (continued)

```
        tree.addTreeSelectionListener(tsl);
    }

    static void listFolder(FolderNode top, FolderNode folder, boolean recurse)
    throws Exception {
        // System.out.println(folder.f.getName() + folder.f.getFullName());
        if ((folder.f.getType() & Folder.HOLDS_MESSAGES) != 0) {
            Message[] msgs = folder.f.getMessages();
            for (int i=0; i<msgs.length; i++) {
                MessageNode m = new MessageNode(msgs[i]);
                Address from = m.m.getFrom()[0];
                String fromAddress;
                if (from instanceof InternetAddress)
                    fromAddress = ((InternetAddress)from).getAddress();
                else
                    fromAddress = from.toString();
                top.add(new MessageNode(msgs[i]));
            }
        }
        if ((folder.f.getType() & Folder.HOLDS_FOLDERS) != 0) {
            if (recurse) {
                Folder[] f = folder.f.list();
                for (int i=0; i < f.length; i++)
                    listFolder(new FolderNode(f[i]), top, recurse);
            }
        }
    }

    /* Test unit - main program */
    public static void main(String[] args) throws Exception {
        final JFrame jf = new JFrame("MailReaderBean");
        String mbox = "/var/mail/ian";
        if (args.length > 0)
            mbox = args[0];
        MailReaderBean mb = new MailReaderBean("mbox", "localhost",
            "", "", mbox);
        jf.getContentPane().add(mb);
        jf.setSize(640,480);
        jf.setVisible(true);
        jf.addWindowListener(new WindowAdapter() {
            public void windowClosing(WindowEvent e) {
            jf.setVisible(false);
            jf.dispose();
            System.exit(0);
            }
        });
    }
}
```

It's a minimal, but working, mail reader. I'll merge it with a mail sender in Recipe 19.9 to make a complete mail client program.

19.9. Program: MailClient

This program is a simplistic GUI-based mail client. It uses the Swing GUI components (see Chapter 13) along with JavaMail. The program loads a `Properties` file (see Recipe 7.7) to decide what mail server to use for outgoing mail (see Recipe 19.2), as well as the name of a mail server for incoming mail and a `Store` class (see this chapter's Introduction and Recipe 19.5). The main class, `MailClient`, is simply a `JComponent` with a `JTabbedPane` to let you switch between reading mail and sending mail.

When first started, the program behaves as a mail reader, as shown in Figure 19-2.

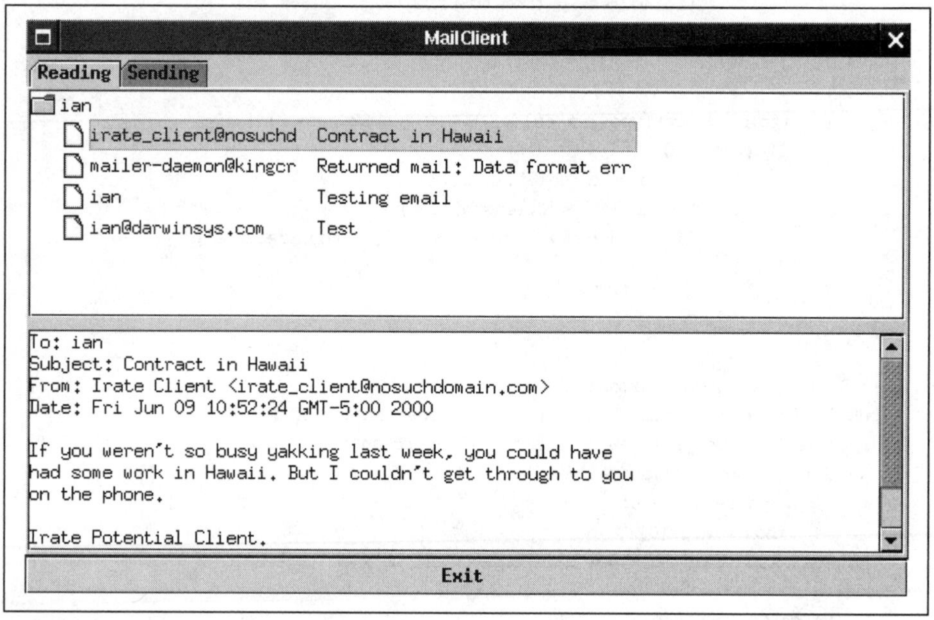

Figure 19-2. Mail Client in reading mode

You can click on the Sending tab to make it show the Mail Compose window, shown in Figure 19-3. I am typing a message to an ISP about some SPAM I received.

The code is pretty simple; it uses the `MailReaderBean` presented earlier and a similar `MailComposeBean` for sending mail. Example 19-11 is the main program.

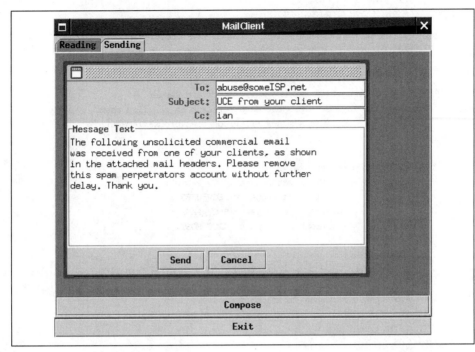

Figure 19-3. Mail Client in compose mode

Example 19-11. MailClient.java

```java
import com.darwinsys.util.FileProperties;
import java.awt.*;
import java.awt.event.*;
import javax.swing.*;
import java.io.*;
import java.util.*;

/** Standalone MailClient GUI application.
 */
public class MailClient extends JComponent implements MailConstants {
    /** The quit button */
    JButton quitButton;
    /** The read mode */
    MailReaderBean mrb;
    /** The send mode */
    MailComposeFrame mcb;

    /** Construct the MailClient JComponent a default Properties filename */
    public MailClient() throws Exception {
        this(PROPS_FILE_NAME);
    }
```

Example 19-11. MailClient.java (continued)

```java
/** Construct the MailClient JComponent with no Properties filename */
public MailClient(String propsFileName) throws Exception {
    super();

    // Get the Properties for the mail reader and sender.
    // Save them in System.properties so other code can find them.
    FileProperties mailProps = new FileProperties(propsFileName);
    mailProps.load();

    // Gather some key values
    String proto = mailProps.getProperty(RECV_PROTO);
    String user  = mailProps.getProperty(RECV_USER);
    String pass  = mailProps.getProperty(RECV_PASS);
    String host  = mailProps.getProperty(RECV_HOST);

    if (proto==null)
        throw new IllegalArgumentException(RECV_PROTO + "==null");

    // Protocols other than "mbox" need a password.
    if (!proto.equals("mbox") && (pass == null || pass.equals("ASK"))) {
        String np;
        do {
            // VERY INSECURE -- should use JDialog + JPasswordField!
            np = JOptionPane.showInputDialog(null,
            "Please enter password for " + proto + " user   " +
                user + " on " + host + "\n" +
                "(warning: password WILL echo)",
            "Password request", JOptionPane.QUESTION_MESSAGE);
        } while (np == null || (np != null && np.length() == 0));
        mailProps.setProperty(RECV_PASS, np);
    }

    // Dump them all into System.properties so other code can find.
    System.getProperties().putAll(mailProps);

    // Construct the GUI
    // System.out.println("Constructing GUI");
    setLayout(new BorderLayout());
    JTabbedPane tbp = new JTabbedPane();
    add(BorderLayout.CENTER, tbp);
    tbp.addTab("Reading", mrb = new MailReaderBean());
    tbp.addTab("Sending", mcb = new MailComposeFrame());
    add(BorderLayout.SOUTH, quitButton = new JButton("Exit"));
    // System.out.println("Leaving Constructor");
}

/** "main program" method - run the program */
public static void main(String[] av) throws Exception {
```

Example 19-11. MailClient.java (continued)

```
        final JFrame f = new JFrame("MailClient");

        // Start by checking that the javax.mail package is installed!
        try {
            Class.forName("javax.mail.Session");
        } catch (ClassNotFoundException cnfe) {
            JOptionPane.showMessageDialog(f,
                "Sorry, the javax.mail package was not found\n(" + cnfe + ")",
                "Error", JOptionPane.ERROR_MESSAGE);
            return;
        }

        // create a MailClient object
        MailClient comp;
        if (av.length == 0)
            comp = new MailClient();
        else
            comp = new MailClient(av[0]);
        f.getContentPane().add(comp);

        // Set up action handling for GUI
        comp.quitButton.addActionListener(new ActionListener() {
            public void actionPerformed(ActionEvent e) {
                f.setVisible(false);
                f.dispose();
                System.exit(0);
            }
        });
        f.addWindowListener(new WindowAdapter() {
            public void windowClosing(WindowEvent e) {
                f.setVisible(false);
                f.dispose();
                System.exit(0);
            }
        });

        // Set bounds. Best at 800,600, but works at 640x480
        // f.setLocation(140, 80);
        // f.setSize     (500,400);
        f.pack();

        f.setVisible(true);
    }
}
```

The `MailReaderBean` used in the Reading tab is exactly the same as the one shown in Recipe 19.7.

The `MailComposeBean` used for the Sending tab is a GUI component for composing a mail message. It uses the `Mailer` class from Recipe 19.2 to do the actual sending. Example 19-12 shows the `MailComposeBean` program.

Example 19-12. MailComposeBean.java

```java
import com.darwinsys.util.*;
import java.awt.*;
import java.awt.event.*;
import javax.swing.*;
import java.util.*;
import java.io.*;
import javax.activation.*;
import javax.mail.*;
import javax.mail.internet.*;

/** MailComposeBean - Mail gather and send Component Bean.
 *
 * Can be used as a Visible bean or as a Non-Visible bean.
 * If setVisible(true), puts up a mail compose window with a Send button.
 * If user clicks on it, tries to send the mail to a Mail Server
 * for delivery on the Internet.
 *
 * If not visible, use addXXX(), setXXX(), and doSend() methods.
 *
 */
public class MailComposeBean extends JPanel {

    /** The parent frame to be hidden/disposed; may be JFrame, JInternalFrame
     * or JPanel, as necessary */
    private Container parent;

    private JButton sendButton, cancelButton;
    private JTextArea msgText;// The message!

    // The To, Subject, and CC lines are treated a bit specially,
    // any user-defined headers are just put in the tfs array.
    private JTextField tfs[], toTF, ccTF, subjectTF;
    // tfsMax MUST == how many are current, for focus handling to work
    private int tfsMax = 3;
    private final int TO = 0, SUBJ = 1, CC = 2, BCC = 3, MAXTF = 8;

    /** The JavaMail session object */
    private Session session = null;
    /** The JavaMail message object */
    private Message mesg = null;

    private int mywidth;
    private int myheight;
```

Example 19-12. MailComposeBean.java (continued)

```java
    /** Construct a MailComposeBean with no default recipient */
    MailComposeBean(Container parent, String title, int height, int width) {
        this(parent, title, null, height, width);
    }

    /** Construct a MailComposeBean with no arguments (needed for Beans) */
    MailComposeBean() {
        this(null, "Compose", null, 300, 200);
    }

    /** Constructor for MailComposeBean object.
     *
     * @param parentContainer parent. If JFrame or JInternalFrame,
     * will setvisible(false) and dispose() when
     * message has been sent. Not done if "null" or JPanel.
     * @param titleTitle to display in the titlebar
     * @param recipientEmail address of recipient
     * @param heightHeight of mail compose window
     * @param widthWidth of mail compose window
     */
    MailComposeBean(Container parent, String title, String recipient,
            int width, int height) {
        super();

        this.parent = parent;

        mywidth = width;
        myheight = height;

        // THE GUI
        Container cp = this;
        cp.setLayout(new BorderLayout());


        // Top is a JPanel for name, address, etc.
        // Centre is the TextArea.
        // Bottom is a panel with Send and Cancel buttons.
        JPanel tp = new JPanel();
        tp.setLayout(new GridLayout(3,2));
        cp.add(BorderLayout.NORTH, tp);

        tfs = new JTextField[MAXTF];

        tp.add(new JLabel("To: ", JLabel.RIGHT));
        tp.add(tfs[TO] = toTF = new JTextField(35));
        if (recipient != null)
            toTF.setText(recipient);
        toTF.requestFocus();
```

Example 19-12. MailComposeBean.java (continued)

```java
        tp.add(new JLabel("Subject: ", JLabel.RIGHT));
        tp.add(tfs[SUBJ] = subjectTF = new JTextField(35));
        subjectTF.requestFocus();

        tp.add(new JLabel("Cc: ", JLabel.RIGHT));
        tp.add(tfs[CC] = ccTF = new JTextField(35));

        // Centre is the TextArea
        cp.add(BorderLayout.CENTER, msgText = new JTextArea(70, 10));
        msgText.setBorder(BorderFactory.createTitledBorder("Message Text"));

        // Bottom is the apply/cancel button
        JPanel bp = new JPanel();
        bp.setLayout(new FlowLayout());
        bp.add(sendButton = new JButton("Send"));
        sendButton.addActionListener(new ActionListener() {
            public void actionPerformed(ActionEvent e) {
                try {
                    doSend();
                } catch(Exception err) {
                    System.err.println("Error: " + err);
                    JOptionPane.showMessageDialog(null,
                        "Sending error:\n" + err.toString(),
                        "Send failed", JOptionPane.ERROR_MESSAGE);
                }
            }
        });
        bp.add(cancelButton = new JButton("Cancel"));
        cancelButton.addActionListener(new ActionListener() {
            public void actionPerformed(ActionEvent e) {
                maybeKillParent();
            }
        });
        cp.add(BorderLayout.SOUTH, bp);
    }

    public Dimension getPreferredSize() {
        return new Dimension(mywidth, myheight);
    }
    public Dimension getMinimumSize() {
        return getPreferredSize();
    }

    /** Do the work: send the mail to the SMTP server.
     *
     * ASSERT: must have set at least one recipient.
     */
    public void doSend() {
```

Example 19-12. MailComposeBean.java (continued)

```java
try {
    Mailer m = new Mailer();

    FileProperties props =
        new FileProperties(MailConstants.PROPS_FILE_NAME);
    String serverHost = props.getProperty(MailConstants.SEND_HOST);
    if (serverHost == null) {
        JOptionPane.showMessageDialog(parent,
            "\"" + MailConstants.SEND_HOST +
                "\" must be set in properties"
            "No server!",
            JOptionPane.ERROR_MESSAGE);
        return;
    }
    m.setServer(serverHost);

    String tmp = props.getProperty(MailConstants.SEND_DEBUG);
    m.setVerbose(tmp != null && tmp.equals("true"));

    String myAddress = props.getProperty("Mail.address");
    if (myAddress == null) {
        JOptionPane.showMessageDialog(parent,
            "\"Mail.address\" must be set in properties",
            "No From: address!",
            JOptionPane.ERROR_MESSAGE);
        return;
    }
    m.setFrom(myAddress);

    m.setToList(toTF.getText());
    m.setCcList(ccTF.getText());
    // m.setBccList(bccTF.getText());

    if (subjectTF.getText().length() != 0) {
        m.setSubject(subjectTF.getText());
    }

    // Now copy the text from the Compose TextArea.
    m.setBody(msgText.getText());
    // XXX I18N: use setBody(msgText.getText(), charset)

    // Finally, send the sucker!
    m.doSend();

    // Now hide the main window
    maybeKillParent();
```

Example 19-12. MailComposeBean.java (continued)

```java
        } catch (MessagingException me) {
            me.printStackTrace();
            while ((me = (MessagingException)me.getNextException()) != null) {
                me.printStackTrace();
            }
            JOptionPane.showMessageDialog(null,
                "Mail Sending Error:\n" + me.toString(),
                "Error", JOptionPane.ERROR_MESSAGE);
        } catch (Exception e) {
            JOptionPane.showMessageDialog(null,
                "Mail Sending Error:\n" + e.toString(),
                "Error", JOptionPane.ERROR_MESSAGE);
        }
    }


    private void maybeKillParent() {
        if (parent == null)
            return;
        if (parent instanceof Frame) {
            ((Frame)parent).setVisible(true);
            ((Frame)parent).dispose();
        }
        if (parent instanceof JInternalFrame) {
            ((JInternalFrame)parent).setVisible(true);
            ((JInternalFrame)parent).dispose();
        }
    }


    /** Simple test case driver */
    public static void main(String[] av) {
        final JFrame jf = new JFrame("DarwinSys Compose Mail Tester");
        System.getProperties().setProperty("Mail.server", "mailhost");
        System.getProperties().setProperty("Mail.address", "nobody@home");
        MailComposeBean sm =
            new MailComposeBean(jf,
            "Test Mailer", "spam-magnet@darwinsys.com", 500, 400);
        sm.setSize(500, 400);
        jf.getContentPane().add(sm);
        jf.setLocation(100, 100);
        jf.setVisible(true);
        jf.addWindowListener(new WindowAdapter() {
            public void windowClosing(WindowEvent e) {
            jf.setVisible(false);
            jf.dispose();
            System.exit(0);
            }
```

Example 19-12. MailComposeBean.java (continued)

```
        });
        jf.pack();
    }
}
```

Further, the `MailComposeBean` program is a JavaBean, so it can be used in GUI builders and even have its fields set within a JSP (see Recipe 18.8). It has a main method, which allows it to be used standalone (primarily for testing).

To let you compose one or more email messages concurrently, messages being composed are placed in a `JDesktopPane`, Java's implementation of Multiple-Document Interface (MDI). Example 19-13 shows how to construct a multi-window email implementation. Each `MailComposeBean` must be wrapped in a `JInternalFrame`, which is what you need to place components in the `JDesktopPane`. This wrapping is handled inside `MailReaderFrame`, one instance of which is created in the `MailClient` constructor. The `MailReaderFrame` method `newSend()` creates an instance of `MailComposeBean` and shows it in the `JDesktopFrame`, returning a reference to the `MailComposeBean` so that the caller can use methods such as `addRecipient()` and `send()`. It also creates a Compose button and places it below the desktop pane, so you can create a new composition window by clicking the button.

Example 19-13. MailComposeFrame.java

```
import java.awt.*;
import java.awt.event.*;
import javax.swing.*;

/** A frame for (possibly) multiple MailComposeBean windows.
 */
public class MailComposeFrame extends JPanel {
    JDesktopPane dtPane;
    JButton newButton;
    protected int nx, ny;

    /** To be useful here, a MailComposeBean has to be inside
     * its own little JInternalFrame.
     */
    public MailComposeBean newSend() {

        // Make the JInternalFrame wrapper
        JInternalFrame jf = new JInternalFrame();

        // Bake the actual Bean
        MailComposeBean newBean =
            new MailComposeBean(this, "Compose", 400, 250);
```

Example 19-13. MailComposeFrame.java (continued)

```
        // Arrange them on the diagonal.
        jf.setLocation(nx+=10, ny+=10);

        // Make the new Bean be the contents of the JInternalFrame
        jf.setContentPane(newBean);
        jf.pack();
        jf.toFront();

        // Add the JInternalFrame to the JDesktopPane
        dtPane.add(jf);
        return newBean;
    }

    /* Construct a MailComposeFrame, with a Compose button. */
    public MailComposeFrame() {

        setLayout(new BorderLayout());

        dtPane = new JDesktopPane();
        add(dtPane, BorderLayout.CENTER);

        newButton = new JButton("Compose");
        newButton.addActionListener(new ActionListener() {
            public void actionPerformed(ActionEvent e) {
                newSend();
            }
        });
        add(newButton, BorderLayout.SOUTH);
    }
}
```

The file *TODO.txt* in the email source directory lists a number of improvements that would have to be added to the `MailClient` program to make it functional enough for daily use (delete and reply functionality, menus, templates, aliases, and much more). But it is a start, and provides a structure to build on.

See Also

Sun maintains a mailing list specifically for the JavaMail API. Read about the `javamail-interest` list near the bottom of the main API page, at *http://java.sun.com/products/javamail/*. This is also a good place to find other provider classes; Sun has a POP3 provider, and there is a list of third-party products. You can also download the complete source code for the JavaMail API from Sun's community source project; there is a link to this on the main API page.

There are now several books that discuss Internet mail. David Wood's *Programming Internet Email* (O'Reilly) discusses all aspects of Internet email, with an emphasis on Perl but with a chapter and examples on JavaMail. Similarly, Kevin Johnson's *Internet Email Protocols: A Developer's Guide* (Addison-Wesley) covers the protocols and has appendixes on various programming languages, including Java. *The Programmer's Guide to Internet Mail: Smtp, Pop, Imap, and Ldap,* by John Rhoton (Digital Press) and *Essential E-Mail Standards: RFCs and Protocols Made Practical* by Pete Loshin (John Wiley) cover the protocols without much detail on Java implementation. *Internet E-Mail: Protocols, Standards, and Implementation* by Lawrence E. Hughes (Artech House Telecommunications) covers a great deal of general material, but emphasizes Microsoft technologies and doesn't say much about JavaMail. Finally, the books *Stopping Spam: Stamping Out Unwanted Email and News Postings* by Alan Schwartz and Simson Garfinkel (O'Reilly) and *Removing the Spam: Email Processing and Filtering* (Addison-Wesley) by Geoff Mulligan aren't about JavaMail, but discuss what is now perhaps the biggest problem facing Internet mail users.

20

Database Access

20.0. Introduction

Java can be used to access many kinds of databases. A *database* can be something as simple as a text file or a fast key/value pairing on disk (DBM format), as sophisticated as a relational database management system (DBMS), or as exotic as an object database.

Regardless of how your data is actually stored, in a reasonable application you'll want to write a class called an *accessor* to mediate between the database and the rest of the application. For example, if you are using JDBC, the answers to your query will come back packaged in an object called a ResultSet, but it would not make sense to structure the rest of your application around the ResultSet because it's JDBC-specific. In a Personal Information Manager application, for example, the primary classes might be Person, Address, and Meeting. You would probably write a PersonAccessor class to request the names and addresses from the database (probably using JDBC), and generate Person and Address objects from them. The DataAccessor objects would also take updates from the main program and store them into the database.*

Java DataBase Connectivity (JDBC) consists of classes in package java.sql and some JDBC Level 2 extensions in package javax.sql. (SQL is the Standard Query Language, used by relational database software to provide a standard command language for creating, modifying, updating, and querying relational databases.)

---

* If this reminds you of Enterprise4 JavaBeans, you're right. If you're familiar with EJB, you can think of simple entity beans as a specialized kind of data accessor.

Why was JDBC invented? Java is highly portable, but many databases previously lacked a portable interface and were tied to one particular language or platform. JDBC is designed to fill that gap.

JDBC is patterned very loosely on Microsoft's Open DataBase Connectivity (ODBC). Sun's Java group borrowed several general ideas from Microsoft, who in turn borrowed some of it from prior art in relational databases. While ODBC is C- and pointer-based (`void *` at that), JDBC is based on Java and is therefore portable, as well as being network-aware and having better type checking.

JDBC comes in two parts: the portable JDBC API provided with Java, and the database-specific driver usually provided by the DBMS vendor or a third party. These drivers have to conform to a particular interface (called `Driver`, unsurprisingly) and map from the generic calls into something the existing database code can understand.

JDBC deals with *relational databases* only. No flat files (although several drivers have been written that map from flat files to the JDBC API) and no DBM files (though you could write a driver that used one DBM file for each table in a database). Through this clever division of labor, JDBC can provide access to any relational database, be it local or remote (remote databases are accessed using client sockets, as discussed in Chapter 15). In addition to the drivers from database vendors, there is also a JDBC-ODBC bridge in the standard JDK and JRE; this allows you to use JDBC with an existing MS-Windows database. Its performance is weaker because it adds an extra layer, but it does work.

One fairly common form of database that I do not cover is the so-called Xbase format, which is a series of commercial databases (dBase, FoxBase, etc.) common in the MS-DOS and MS-Windows world. If you wanted to decode such a database in Java, you'd probably start with the Xbase file format, documented at *http:// www.e-bachmann.dk/docs/xbase.htm*. Alternately, you might find a useful driver in the Microsoft ODBC-32 software, and use the JDBC-to-ODBC bridge to convert your data to a newer format such as a relational database.

This chapter is an overview of several database techniques, emphasizing JDBC, so that you know what this technology looks and feels like.

20.1. Text-File Databases

Problem

You wish to treat a text file as a database.

Solution

Write an `Accessor` class that returns objects of the correct type.

Discussion

On the JabaDot web site (see Recipe 18.12) there is a list of users. Each user has a login name, full name, password, email address, privilege level, and so forth, and is represented by a `User` object. These are stored in the `User` database.

There are several versions of this database, so I have an abstract class to represent all the user data accessors, called `UserDB`. One of its main functions is to read the database; this can be done in the constructor or in the `getUsers()` method.

Of course, for efficiency, we want to do this reading only once, even though we may have many users visiting the site. So the design pattern (see the Introduction to Chapter 8) known as *singleton* (ensure one single instance exists) is used; anybody wanting a `UserDB` object does not construct one (the constructor is private), but must call `getInstance()`. Unsurprisingly, `getInstance()` returns the same value to anyone who calls it. The only implication of this is that some of the methods must be `synchronized` (see Chapter 24) to prevent complications when more than one user accesses the (single) `UserDB` object concurrently.

The code in Example 20-1 uses a class called `JDConstants` (JabaDot constants), which is a wrapper around a `Properties` object (see Recipe 7.3) to get values such as the location of the database.

Example 20-1. UserDB.java

```
package jabadot;

import java.io.*;
import java.util.*;
import java.sql.SQLException;// Only used by JDBC version
import java.lang.reflect.*;// For loading our subclass class.

/** A base for several "database" accessors for User objects.
 * We use a Singleton access method for efficiency and to enforce
 * single access on the database, which means we can keep an in-memory
 * copy (in an ArrayList) perfectly in synch with the database.
 *
 * We provide field numbers, which are 1-based (for SQL), not 0 as per Java.
 */
public abstract class UserDB {

    public static final int NAME= 1;
    public static final int PASSWORD= 2;
```

Example 20-1. UserDB.java (continued)

```
public static final int FULLNAME = 3;
public static final int EMAIL= 4;
public static final int CITY= 5;
public static final int PROVINCE= 6;
public static final int COUNTRY= 7;
public static final int PRIVS= 8;

protected ArrayList users;

protected static UserDB singleton;

/** Static code block to intialize the Singleton. */
static {
    String dbClass = null;
    try {
        dbClass = JDConstants.getProperty("jabadot.userdb.class");
        singleton = (UserDB)Class.forName(dbClass).newInstance();
    } catch (ClassNotFoundException ex) {
        System.err.println("Unable to instantiate UserDB singleton " +
            dbClass + " (" + ex.toString() + ")");
        throw new IllegalArgumentException(ex.toString());
    } catch (Exception ex) {
        System.err.println(
        "Unexpected exception: Unable to initialize UserDB singleton");
        ex.printStackTrace(System.err);
        throw new IllegalArgumentException(ex.toString());
    }
}

/** In some subclasses the constructor will probably load the database,
 *  while in others it may defer this until getUserList().
 */
protected UserDB() throws IOException, SQLException {
    users = new ArrayList();
}

/** "factory" method to get an instance, which will always be
 * the Singleton.
 */
public static UserDB getInstance() {
    if (singleton == null)
        throw new IllegalStateException("UserDB initialization failed");
    return singleton;
}

/** Get the list of users. */
public ArrayList getUserList() {
    return users;
}
```

Example 20-1. UserDB.java (continued)

```
    /** Get the User object for a given nickname */
    public User getUser(String nick) {
        Iterator it = users.iterator();
        while (it.hasNext()) {
            User u = (User)it.next();
            if (u.getName().equals(nick))
                return u;
        }
        return null;
    }

    public synchronized void addUser(User nu) throws IOException, SQLException {
        // Add it to the in-memory list
        users.add(nu);

        // Add it to the on-disk version
        // N.B. - must be done in subclass.
    }

    public abstract void setPassword(String nick, String newPass)
    throws SQLException;

    public abstract void deleteUser(String nick)
    throws SQLException;
}
```

In the initial design, this information was stored in a text file. The UserDB class reads this text file and returns a collection of User objects, one per user. There are also various "get" methods, such as the one that finds a user by login name. The basic approach is to open a BufferedReader (see Chapter 9), read each line, and (for non-blank, non-comment lines) construct a StringTokenizer (see Recipe 3.2) to retrieve all the fields. If the line is well-formed (has all its fields), construct a User object and add it to the collection.

The file format is simple; one user per line:

```
#name:passwd:fullname:email:City:Prov:Country:privs
admin:secret1:JabaDot Administrator:ian@darwinsys.com:Toronto:ON:CA:A
ian:secret2:Ian Darwin:ian@darwinsys.com:Toronto:ON:Canada:E
```

So the UserDBText class is a UserDB implementation that reads this file and creates a User object for each non-comment line in the file. Example 20-2 shows how it works.

Example 20-2. UserDBText.java

```java
package jabadot;

import java.io.*;
import java.util.*;
import java.sql.SQLException;

/** A trivial "database" for User objects, stored in a flat file.
 * <P>
 * Since this is expected to be used heavily, and to avoid the overhead
 * of re-reading the file, the "Singleton" Design Pattern is used
 * to ensure that there is only ever one instance of this class.
 */
public class UserDBText extends UserDB {
    protected final static String DEF_NAME =
        "/home/ian/src/jabadot/userdb.txt";

    protected String fileName;

    protected UserDBText() throws IOException,SQLException {
        this(DEF_NAME);
    }

    /** Constructor */
    protected UserDBText(String fn) throws IOException,SQLException {
        super();
        fileName = fn;
        BufferedReader is = new BufferedReader(new FileReader(fn));
        String line;
        while ((line = is.readLine()) != null) {
            //name:password:fullname:City:Prov:Country:privs

            if (line.startsWith("#")) {// comment
                continue;
            }

            StringTokenizer st =
                new StringTokenizer(line, ":");
            String nick = st.nextToken();
            String pass = st.nextToken();
            String full = st.nextToken();
            String email = st.nextToken();
            String city = st.nextToken();
            String prov = st.nextToken();
            String ctry = st.nextToken();
            User u = new User(nick, pass, full, email,
                city, prov, ctry);
```

Example 20-2. UserDBText.java (continued)

```
            String privs = st.nextToken();
            if (privs.indexOf("A") != -1) {
                u.setAdminPrivileged(true);
            }
            users.add(u);
        }
    }


protected PrintWriter pw;

public synchronized void addUser(User nu) throws IOException,SQLException {
    // Add it to the in-memory list
    super.addUser(nu);

    // Add it to the on-disk version
    if (pw == null) {
        pw = new PrintWriter(new FileWriter(fileName, true));
    }
    pw.println(toDB(nu));
    // toDB returns: name:password:fullname:City:Prov:Country:privs
    pw.flush();
}


protected String toDB(User u) {
    // #name:password:fullName:email:City:Prov:Country:privs
    char privs = '-';
    if (adminPrivs)
        privs = 'A';
    else if (editPrivs)
        privs = 'E';

    return new StringBuffer()
        .append(u.name).append(':')
        .append(u.password).append(':')
        .append(u.fullName).append(':')
        .append(u.email).append(':')
        .append(u.city).append(':')
        .append(u.prov).append(':')
        .append(u.country).append(':')
        .append(u.privs)
        .toString();
    }
}
```

This version does not have any "set" methods, which would be needed to allow a user to change his/her password, for example. Those will come later.

See Also

If your text-format data file is in a format similar to the one used here, you may be able to massage it into a form where the `SimpleText` driver (see online source *contrib/JDBCDriver-Moss*) can be used to access the data using JDBC (see Recipe 20.3).

20.2. DBM Databases

Problem

You need to access a DBM file.

Solution

Use my code, or SleepyCat's code, to interface DBM from Java.

Discussion

Unix systems are commonly supplied with some form of DBM or DB* data file, often called a *database*. These are not relational databases, but are key/value pairs, rather like a `java.util.Hashtable` that is automatically persisted to disk whenever you called its `put()` method. This format is also used on MS-Windows by a few programs; for example, the Win32 version of Netscape keeps its history in a *history.db* or *netscape.hst* file, which is in this format. Not convinced?

```
daroad.darwinsys.com$ pwd
/c/program files/netscape/users/ian
daroad.darwinsys.com$ file *.hst
netscape.hst: Berkeley DB Hash file (Version 2, Little Endian, Bucket Size 4096,
Bucket Shift 12, Directory Size 256, Segment Size 256, Segment Shift 8, Overflow
Point 8, Last Freed 36, Max Bucket 184, High Mask 0xff, Low Mask 0x7f, Fill Factor
54, Number of Keys 733)
daroad.darwinsys.com$
```

The Unix *file* command† decodes file types; it's what Unix people rely on instead of (or in addition to) filename extensions.

So the DBM format is a nice, general mapping from keys to values. But how can we use it in Java? There is no publicly defined mapping for Java, so I wrote my own. It uses a fair bit of native code, that is, C code called from Java that in turn calls the

---

* DBM is the original format; DB is a newer, more general format. DBM is actually now a front-end to DB, but because it's a bit simpler, I've used it for this example. GDBM is the FSF's implementation.

† The version of `file(1)` in Linux and BSD systems was originally written by your humble scribe.

DBM library. I'll discuss native code in Recipe 26.4. For now it suffices to know that we can initialize a DBM file by calling the relevant constructor, passing the name of our DB file. We can iterate over all the key/value pairs by calling firstkey() once and then nextkey() repeatedly until it returns null. Both byte arrays and objects can be stored and retrieved; it is up to the programmer to know which is which (hint: use one or the other within a given DBM file). Objects are serialized using normal Java object serialization (see Recipe 9.16). Here is the API for the DBM class:

```
public DBM(String fileName) throws IOException;
public Object nextkey(Object) throws IOException;
public byte[] nextkey(byte[]) throws IOException;
public Object firstkeyObject() throws IOException;
public byte[] firstkey() throws IOException;
public void store(Object,Object) throws IOException;
public void store(byte[],byte[]) throws IOException;
public Object fetch(Object) throws IOException;
public byte[] fetch(byte[]) throws IOException;
public void close();
```

A simple program to print out the sites we have visited as listed in our Netscape history is shown in Example 20-3.

Example 20-3. ReadHistNS.java

```
import java.io.IOException;

/** Demonstration of reading the MS-Windows Netscape History
 * under UNIX using DBM.java.
 */
public class ReadHistNS {
    public static void main(String[] unused) throws IOException {
        DBM d = new DBM("netscape.hst");
        byte[] ba;
        for (ba = d.firstkey(); ba != null; ba = d.nextkey(ba)) {
            System.out.println("Key=\"" + new String(ba) + '"');
            byte[] val = d.fetch(ba);
            for (int i=0; i<16&&i<val.length; i++) {
                System.out.print((short)val[i]);
                System.out.print(' ');
            }
        }
    }
}
```

The DBM format is an emulation of an older format, built on top of the DB library. Because of this, the filename must end in *.pag*, so I copied the history file to the name shown in the DBM constructor call.

A longer program, which includes both storing and retrieving in a DBM file, is the DBM version of the `UserDB` class, `UserDBDBM`. This is shown in Example 20-4.

Example 20-4. UserDBDBM.java

```java
package jabadot;

import java.io.*;
import java.util.*;
import java.sql.SQLException;

/** A trivial "database" for User objects, stored in a flat file.
 * <P>
 * Since this is expected to be used heavily, and to avoid the overhead
 * of re-reading the file, the "Singleton" Design Pattern is used
 * to ensure that there is only ever one instance of this class.
 */
public class UserDBDBM extends UserDB {
    protected final static String DEF_NAME =
        "/home/ian/src/jabadot/userdb";    // It appends .pag

    protected DBM db;

    /** Default Constructor */
    protected UserDBDBM() throws IOException,SQLException {
        this(DEF_NAME);
    }

    /** Constructor */
    protected UserDBDBM(String fn) throws IOException,SQLException {
        super();

        db = new DBM(fn);
        String k;
        Object o;

        // Iterate through contents of DBM, adding into list.
        for (o=db.firstkeyObject(); o!=null; o=db.nextkey(o)) {
            // firstkey/nextkey give Key as Object, cast to String.
            k = (String)o;
            o = db.fetch(k);       // Get corresponding Value (a User)
            users.add((User)o);     // Add to list.
        }
    }

    /** Add one user to the list, both in-memory and on disk. */
    public synchronized void addUser(User nu) throws IOException, SQLException {
        // Add it to the in-memory list
        super.addUser(nu);
```

Example 20-4. UserDBDBM.java (continued)

```
        // Add it to the on-disk version: store in DB with
        // key = nickname, value = object.
        db.store(nu.getName(), nu);
    }
}
```

See Also

SleepyCat software (*http://www.sleepycat.com*) provides an improved version of Berkeley DBM and includes a Java driver for it. The Free Software Foundation provides GDBM, another DBM-like mechanism.

20.3. JDBC Setup and Connection

Problem

You want to access a database via JDBC.

Solution

Use `Class.forName()` and `DriverManager.getConnection()`.

Discussion

While DB and friends have their place, most of the modern database action is on relational databases, and accordingly Java Database action is on JDBC. So the bulk of this chapter is devoted to JDBC.

This is not the place for a tutorial on relational databases. I'll assume that you know a little bit about the Structured Query Language (SQL), the universal language used to control relational databases. SQL has *queries* like "SELECT * from userdb", which means to select all columns (the *) from all rows (entries) in a database table named userdb (all rows are selected because there is no "where" clause on the SELECT statement). SQL also has *updates* like INSERT, DELETE, CREATE, and DROP. If you need more information on SQL or relational databases, there are many good books that will introduce you to the topic in more detail.

JDBC has two Levels, JDBC 1 and JDBC 2. Level 1 is included in all JDBC implementation and drivers; Level 2 is optional, and requires a Level 2 driver. This chapter concentrates on common features, primarily Level 1.

The first step in using JDBC 1 is to load your database's driver. This is performed using some Java JVM magic. The class `java.lang.Class` has a method called `forName()` that takes a string containing the full Java name for a class and loads

---

Ian's Basic Steps: Using a JDBC Query

1. Load the appropriate `Driver` class, which has the side effect of registering with the `DriverManager`.

2. Get a `Connection` object, using `DriverManager.getConnection()`:

   ```
   Connection con = DriverManager.getConnection (dbURL, name, pass);
   ```

3. Get a `Statement` object, using the `Connection` object's `createStatement()`:

   ```
   Statement stmt = con.createStatement();
   ```

4. Get a `ResultSet` object, using the `Statement` object's `executeQuery()`:

   ```
   ResultSet rs = stmt.executeQuery("select * from MyTable");
   ```

5. Iterate over the `ResultSet`:

   ```
   while (rs.next()) {
       int x = rs.getInt("CustNO");
   ```

6. Close the `ResultSet`.

7. Close the `Statement`.

8. Close the `Connection`.

---

the class, returning a `Class` object describing it. This is typically used in introspection (see Chapter 25), but can be used anytime to ensure that a class has been correctly configured into your CLASSPATH. This is the use that we'll see here. And, in fact, part of the challenge of installing JDBC drivers is ensuring that they are in your CLASSPATH, both at compile time and at deployment time. But wait, there's more! In addition to checking your CLASSPATH, this method also registers the driver with another class called the `DriverManager`. How does it work? Each valid JDBC driver has a bit of method-like code called a *static initializer*. This is used whenever the class is loaded—just what the doctor ordered! So the static block registers the class with the `DriverManager` when you call `Class.forName()` on the driver class.

For the curious, the static code block in a `Driver` called `BarFileDriver` looks something like this:

```
/** Static code block, to initialize with the DriverManager. */
static {
    try {
        DriverManager.registerDriver(new BarFileDriver());
    } catch (SQLException e) {
        DriverManager.println("Can't load driver" +
                              "darwinsys.sql.BarFileDriver");
    }
}
```

Example 20-5 shows a bit of code that tries to load two drivers. The first is the
JDBC-to-ODBC bridge described in the Introduction. The second is one of the
commercial drivers from Oracle.

Example 20-5. LoadDriver.java

```
import java.awt.*;
import java.sql.*;

/** Load some drivers.  */
public class LoadDriver {

    public static void main(String[] av) {
        try {

            // Try to load the jdbc-odbc bridge driver
            // Should be present on Sun JDK implementations.
            Class c = Class.forName("sun.jdbc.odbc.JdbcOdbcDriver");
            System.out.println("Loaded " + c);

            // Try to load an Oracle driver.
            Class d = Class.forName("oracle.jdbc.driver.OracleDriver");
            System.out.println("Loaded " + d);
        } catch (ClassNotFoundException ex) {
            System.err.println(ex);
        }
    }
}
```

As expected, the first load succeeds and the second fails, since I don't have Oracle
installed on my notebook:

```
daroad.darwinsys.com$ java LoadDriver
Loaded class sun.jdbc.odbc.JdbcOdbcDriver
java.lang.ClassNotFoundException: oracle/jdbc/driver/OracleDriver
daroad.darwinsys.com$
```

It is also possible to preregister a driver using the –D option to load it into the System Properties; in this case, you can skip the `Class.forName()` step:

```
java -Djdbc.drivers=com.acmewidgets.AcmeDriver:foo.bar.OhMyDriver MyClass
```

Once you have registered the driver, you are ready to connect to the database.

20.4. Connecting to a JDBC Database

Problem

You need to connect to the database.

Solution

Use `DriverManager.getConnection()`.

Discussion

The static method `DriverManager.getConnection()` lets you connect to the database using a URL-like syntax for the database name (for example, *jdbc: dbmsnetproto://server:4567/mydatabase*) and a login name and password. The "dbURL" that you give must begin with `jdbc:`. The rest of it can be in whatever form the driver vendor's documentation requires, and is checked by the driver. The `DriverManager` asks each driver you have loaded (if you've loaded one) to see if it can handle a URL of the form you provided. The first one that responds in the affirmative gets to handle the connection, and its `connect()` method is called for you (by `DriverManager.getConnection()`).

There are four types of drivers defined by Sun (not in the JDBC specification, but in their less formal documentation); these are shown in Table 20-1.

Table 20-1. JDBC driver types

Type	Name	Notes
1	JDBC-ODBC Bridge	Provides JDBC API access.
2	Java and Native Driver	Java code calls Native DB driver.
3	Java and Middleware	Java contacts middleware server.
4	Pure Java	Java contacts (possibly remote) DB directly.

Table 20-2 shows some interesting drivers. I'll use the ODBC bridge driver and IDB in examples for this chapter. Some drivers work only locally (like the JDBC-ODBC bridge), while others work across a network. For details on different types of drivers, please refer to the books listed at the end of this chapter. Most of these drivers are commercial products. *Instant Database* is a clever freeware product (from *http://www.enhydra.org*); the driver and the entire database management system reside inside the same Java Virtual Machine as the client (the database is stored on disk like any other, of course). This eliminates the interprocess communication overhead of some databases. However, you can't have multiple JVM processes updating the same database at the same time.

Table 20-2. Some JDBC drivers

Driver class	Start of dbURL	Database
`sun.jdbc.odbc.JdbcOdbcDriver`	`jdbc:odbc:`	Bridge to Microsoft ODBC (included with JDK)
`jdbc.idbDriver`	`jdbc:idb:`	Instant Database

Table 20-2. Some JDBC drivers (continued)

Driver class	Start of dbURL	Database
oracle.jdbc.Driver.OracleDriver	jdbc:oracle:thin: @server:port#:dbname	Oracle
postgresql.Driver	jdbc:postgres:// host/database	PostGreSQL (freeware database; see *http://www.postgresql.org*)
org.gjt.mm.mysql.Driver	jdbc:mysql://host/ database	MySql (freeware database; see *http://www.mysql.org*)

Example 20-6 is a sample application that connects to a database. Note that we now have to catch the checked exception SQLException, as we're using the JDBC API. (The Class.forName() method is in java.lang, and so is part of the standard Java API, not part of JDBC.)

Example 20-6. Connect.java

```
import java.awt.*;
import java.sql.*;

/** Load a driver and connect to a database.
 */
public class Connect {

    public static void main(String[] av) {
        String dbURL = "jdbc:odbc:Companies";
        try {
            // Load the jdbc-odbc bridge driver
            Class.forName("sun.jdbc.odbc.JdbcOdbcDriver");

            // Enable logging
            DriverManager.setLogStream(System.err);

            System.out.println("Getting Connection");
            Connection conn =
                DriverManager.getConnection(dbURL, "ian", "");// user, passwd

            // If a SQLWarning object is available, print its
            // warning(s).  There may be multiple warnings chained.

            SQLWarning warn = conn.getWarnings();
            while (warn != null) {
                System.out.println("SQLState: " + warn.getSQLState());
                System.out.println("Message:  " + warn.getMessage());
                System.out.println("Vendor:   " + warn.getErrorCode());
                System.out.println("");
                warn = warn.getNextWarning();
            }
        }
```

Example 20-6. Connect.java (continued)

```
        // Process the connection here...

        conn.close();// All done with that DB connection

    } catch (ClassNotFoundException e) {
        System.out.println("Can't load driver " + e);
    } catch (SQLException e) {
        System.out.println("Database access failed " + e);
    }
  }
}
```

I've enabled two verbosity options in this example. The use of `DriverManager.setLogStream()` causes any logging to be done to the standard error, and the `Connection` object's `getWarnings()` prints any additional warnings that come up.

When I run it on a system that doesn't have ODBC installed, I get the following outputs. They are all from the `setLogStream()` except for the last one, which is a fatal error:

```
Getting Connection
JDBC to ODBC Bridge: Checking security
*Driver.connect (jdbc:odbc:Companies)
JDBC to ODBC Bridge: Checking security
JDBC to ODBC Bridge 1.2001
Current Date/Time: Fri Jun 16 16:18:45 GMT-5:00 2000
Loading JdbcOdbc library
Unable to load JdbcOdbc library
Unable to load JdbcOdbc library
Unable to allocate environment
Database access failed java.sql.SQLException: driver not found: jdbc:odbc:
Companies
```

On a system with JDBC installed, the connection goes further and verifies that the named database exists and can be opened.

20.5. Sending a JDBC Query and Getting Results

Problem

You're getting tired of all this setup and want to see results.

Solution

Get a `Statement` and use it to execute a query. You'll get a set of results, a `ResultSet` object.

Discussion

The `Connection` object can generate various kinds of statements; the simplest is a `Statement` created by `createStatement()` and used to send your SQL query as an arbitrary string:

```
Statement stmt = conn.createStatement();
stmt.executeUpdate("select * from myTable");
```

The result of the query is returned as a `ResultSet` object. The `ResultSet` works like an iterator in that it lets you access all the rows of the result that match the query. This process is shown in Figure 20-1.

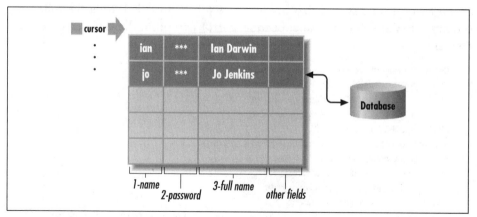

Figure 20-1. ResultSet illustrated

Typically, you use it like this:

```
while (rs.next()) {
    int i = rs.getInt(1);    // or getInt("UserID");
```

As the comment suggests, you can retrieve elements from the `ResultSet` either by their column index (which starts at one, unlike most Java things, which typically start at zero) or column name. In JDBC 1, you must retrieve the values in increasing order by the order of the SELECT (or by their column order in the database if the query is SELECT *). In JDBC 2, you can retrieve them in any order (and in fact, many JDBC 1 drivers don't enforce the retrieving of values in certain orders). If you want to learn the column names (a sort of introspection), you can use a `ResultSet`'s `getResultSetMetaData()` method, described in Recipe 20.10.

There are many types of data in SQL, and there are methods to get them from a ResultSet; the common ones are shown in Table 20-3.

Table 20-3. Data type mappings between SQL and JDBC

JDBC method	SQL type	Java type
getBit()	BIT	boolean
getByte()	TINYINT	byte
getShort()	SMALLINT	short
getInt()	INTEGER	int
getLong()	BIGINT	long
getReal()	REAL	float
getDouble()	DOUBLE	double
getString()	CHAR	String
getString()	VARCHAR	String
getString()	LONGVARCHAR	String
getDate()	DATE	java.sql.Date
getTimeStamp()	TIME	java.sql.Date
getObject()	BLOB	Object

Assuming that we have a relational database containing the User data, we can retrieve it as demonstrated in Example 20-7. This program retrieves any or all entries that have a username of ian and prints the ResultSets in a loop. It prints lines like:

```
User ian is named Ian Darwin
```

The source code is shown in Example 20-7.

Example 20-7. UserQuery.java

```java
import jabadot.*;

import java.sql.*;
import java.io.*;
import java.util.*;

/** Look up one use from the relational database using JDBC.
 */
public class UserQuery {

    public static void main(String[] fn)
        throws ClassNotFoundException, SQLException, IOException {

        // Load the database driver
```

Example 20-7. UserQuery.java (continued)

```java
        Class.forName(JDConstants.getProperty("jabadot.userdb.driver"));

        System.out.println("Getting Connection");
        Connection conn = DriverManager.getConnection(
            JDConstants.getProperty("jabadot.dburl"));

        Statement stmt = conn.createStatement();

        ResultSet rs = stmt.executeQuery(
            "SELECT * from userdb where name='ian'");

        // Now retrieve (all) the rows that matched the query
        while (rs.next()) {

            // Field 1 is login name
            String name = rs.getString(1);

            // Password is field 2 - do not display.

            // Column 3 is fullname
            String fullName = rs.getString(3);

            System.out.println("User " + name + " is named " + fullName);
        }

        rs.close();   // All done with that resultset
        stmt.close();// All done with that statement
        conn.close();// All done with that DB connection
        System.exit(0);// All done with this program.
    }
}
```

Note that a `ResultSet` is tied to its `Connection` object; if the `Connection` is closed, the `ResultSet` becomes invalid. You should either extract the data from the `ResultSet` before closing it, or cache it in a `CachingRowSet`, an experimental RowSet subclass currently available from Sun's Java web site (`RowSet` is a JDBC 2 subclass of `ResultSet`).

20.6. *Using JDBC Parameterized Statements*

Problem

You want to save the overhead of parsing, compiling, and otherwise setting up a statement that will be called multiple times.

Solution

Use a PreparedStatement.

Discussion

An SQL query consists of textual characters. The database must first parse a query and then compile it into something that can be run in the database. This can add up to a lot of overhead if you are sending a lot of queries. In some types of applications, you'll use a number of queries that are the same syntactically but have different values:

```
select * from payroll where personnelNo = 12345;
select * from payroll where personnelNo = 23740;
select * from payroll where personnelNo = 97120;
```

In this case, the statement only needs to be parsed and compiled once. But if you keep making up select statements and sending them, the database will mindlessly keep parsing and compiling them. Better to use a *prepared statement* in which the variable part is replaced by a special marker (a question mark in JDBC). Then the statement need only be parsed (or organized, optimized, compiled, or whatever) once.

```
PreparedStatement ps = conn.prepareStatement(
    "select * from payroll where personnelNo = ?;")
```

Before you can use this prepared statement, you must fill in the blanks with the appropriate set methods. These take a parameter number (starting at one, not zero like most things in Java) and the value to be plugged in. Then use executeQuery() with no arguments, since the query is already stored in the statement:

```
ps.setInt(1, 12345);
rs = ps.executeQuery();
```

If there is more than one parameter, you address them by number; for example, if there were a second parameter of type double, its value would be set by:

```
ps.setDouble(2, 12345);
```

Example 20-8 is the JDBC version of the User accessor, UserDBJDBC. It uses prepared statements for inserting new users, changing passwords, and setting the last login date.

Example 20-8. UserDBJDBC.java

```
package jabadot;

import java.sql.*;
import java.io.*;
import java.util.*;
```

Example 20-8. UserDBJDBC.java (continued)

```java
/** A UserDB using JDBC and a relational DBMS.
 * We use the inherited getUser ("Find the User object for a given nickname")
 * since we keep everything in memory in this version.
 */
public class UserDBJDBC extends UserDB {

    protected final static String DB_URL =
        JDConstants.getProperty("jabadot.userdb.url");
    protected PreparedStatement setPasswordStatement;
    protected PreparedStatement addUserStmt;
    protected PreparedStatement setLastLoginStmt;
    protected PreparedStatement deleteUserStmt;

    /** Default constructor */
    protected UserDBJDBC()
    throws ClassNotFoundException, SQLException, IOException {
        this(DB_URL);
    }

    /** Constructor */
    public UserDBJDBC(String fn)
    throws ClassNotFoundException, SQLException, IOException {
        super();

        // Load the database driver
        Class.forName("jdbc.idbDriver");

        Connection conn = DriverManager.getConnection(fn,
            "www", "");// user, password

        Statement stmt = conn.createStatement();

        ResultSet rs = stmt.executeQuery("select * from userdb");

        while (rs.next()) {
            //name:password:fullname:City:Prov:Country:privs

            // Get the fields from the query.
            String nick = rs.getString(1);
            String pass = rs.getString(2);
            String full = rs.getString(3);
            String email = rs.getString(4);
            String city = rs.getString(5);
            String prov = rs.getString(6);
            String ctry = rs.getString(7);
            int iprivs = rs.getInt(8);

            // Construct a user object from the fields
```

Example 20-8. UserDBJDBC.java (continued)

```java
        User u = new User(nick, pass, full, email,
            city, prov, ctry, iprivs);

        // Add it to the in-memory copy.
        users.add(u);
    }
    stmt.close();
    rs.close();// All done with that resultset

    // Set up the PreparedStatements now so we don't have to
    // re-create them each time needed.
    addUserStmt = conn.prepareStatement(
        "insert into userdb values (?,?,?,?,?,?,?,?)");
    setPasswordStatement = conn.prepareStatement(
        "update userdb SET password = ? where name = ?");
    setLastLoginStmt = conn.prepareStatement(
        "update userdb SET lastLogin = ? where name = ?");
    deleteUserStmt = conn.prepareStatement(
        "delete from userdb where name = ?");
}

/** Add one user to the list, both in-memory and on disk. */
public synchronized void addUser(User nu)
throws IOException, SQLException {
    // Add it to the in-memory list
    super.addUser(nu);

    // Copy fields from user to DB
    addUserStmt.setString(1, nu.name);
    addUserStmt.setString(2, nu.password);
    addUserStmt.setString(3, nu.fullName);
    addUserStmt.setString(4, nu.email);
    addUserStmt.setString(5, nu.city);
    addUserStmt.setString(6, nu.prov);
    addUserStmt.setString(7, nu.country);
    addUserStmt.setInt   (8, nu.getPrivs());

    // Store in persistent DB
    addUserStmt.executeUpdate();
}

public void deleteUser(String nick) throws SQLException {
    // Find the user object
    User u = getUser(nick);
    if (u == null) {
        throw new SQLException("User " + nick + " not in in-memory DB");
    }
    deleteUserStmt.setString(1, nick);
```

Example 20-8. UserDBJDBC.java (continued)

```
        int n = deleteUserStmt.executeUpdate();
        if (n != 1) {// not just one row??
            /*CANTHAPPEN */
            throw new SQLException("ERROR: deleted " + n + " rows!!");
        }

        // IFF we deleted it from the DB, also remove from the in-memory list
        users.remove(u);
    }

    public synchronized void setPassword(String nick, String newPass)
    throws SQLException {

        // Find the user object
        User u = getUser(nick);

        // Change it in DB first; if this fails, the info in
        // the in-memory copy won't be changed either.
        setPasswordStatement.setString(1, newPass);
        setPasswordStatement.setString(2, nick);
        setPasswordStatement.executeUpdate();

        // Change it in-memory
        u.setPassword(newPass);
    }

    /** Update the Last Login Date field. */
    public synchronized void setLoginDate(String nick, java.util.Date date)
    throws SQLException {

        // Find the user object
        User u = getUser(nick);

        // Change it in DB first; if this fails, the date in
        // the in-memory copy won't be changed either.
        // Have to convert from java.util.Date to java.sql.Date here.
        // Would be more efficient to use java.sql.Date everywhere.
        setLastLoginStmt.setDate(1, new java.sql.Date(date.getTime()));
        setLastLoginStmt.setString(2, nick);
        setLastLoginStmt.executeUpdate();

        // Change it in-memory
        u.setLastLoginDate(date);
    }
}
```

Another example of prepared statements is given in Recipe 20.8.

20.7. Using Stored Procedures with JDBC

Problem

You want to use a procedure stored in the database (a stored procedure).

Solution

Use a `CallableStatement`.

Discussion

A *stored procedure* is a series of SQL statements[*] stored as part of the database for use by any SQL user or programmer, including JDBC developers. Stored procedures are used for the same reasons as prepared statements: efficiency and convenience. Typically, the database administrator (DBA) at a large database shop will set up stored procedures and tell you what they are called, what parameters they require, and what they return. Putting the stored procedure itself into the database is totally database-dependent and not discussed here.

Suppose that I wish to see a list of user accounts that had not been used for a certain length of time. Instead of coding this logic into a JDBC program, I might define it using database-specific statements to write and store a procedure in the database, and then use the following code. Centralizing this logic in the database has some advantages for maintenance and also, in most databases, for speed.

```
CallableStatment cs = conn.prepareCall("{ call ListDefunctUsers }");
ResultSet rs = cs.executeQuery();
```

I then process the `ResultSet` in the normal way.

20.8. Changing Data Using a ResultSet

Problem

You want to change the data using a `ResultSet`.

Solution

If you have JDBC 2 and a conforming driver, you can request an updatable `ResultSet` when you create the statement object. Then, when you're on the row you want to change, use the `update()` methods, and end with `updateRow()`.

---

[*] And possibly some database-dependent utility statements.

Discussion

You need to create the statement with the attribute `ResultSet.CONCUR_UPDATABLE` as shown in Example 20-9. Do an SQL SELECT with this statement. When you are on the row (there is only one row that matches this particular query because it is selecting on the primary key), use the appropriate update method for the type of data in the column you want to change, passing in the column name or number and the new value. You can change more than one column in the current row this way. When you're done, call `updateRow()` on the `ResultSet`. Assuming that you didn't change the autocommit state, the data will be committed to the database.

Example 20-9. ResultSetUpdate.java (partial listing)

```
try {
    con = DriverManager.getConnection(url, user, pass);
    stmt = con.createStatement(
        ResultSet.TYPE_SCROLL_SENSITIVE, ResultSet.CONCUR_UPDATABLE);
    rs = stmt.executeQuery("SELECT * FROM Users where nick=\"ian\"");

    // Get the resultset ready, update the passwd field, commit
    rs.first();
    rs.updateString("password", "unguessable");
    rs.updateRow();

    rs.close();
    stmt.close();
    con.close();
} catch(SQLException ex) {
    System.err.println("SQLException: " + ex.getMessage());
}
```

20.9. Changing Data Using SQL

Problem

You wish to insert or update data, create a new table, delete a table, or otherwise change the database.

Solution

Instead of `executeQuery()`, use `executeUpdate()` and SQL commands to make the change.

Discussion

The `executeUpdate()` method is used when you want to make a change to the database, as opposed to getting a list of rows with a query. You can implement either data changes like `insert` or `update`, data structure changes like `create table`, or almost anything that you can do by sending SQL directly to the database through its own update command interface or GUI.

The program listed in Example 20-10 converts the `User` database from the text file format of Recipe 20.1 into a relational database. Note that I destroy the table before creating it, just in case there was an older version in place. If there was not, `executeUpdate()` simply indicates this in its return code; it doesn't throw an exception. Then the program creates the table and its index. Finally, it goes into a loop reading the lines from the text file; for each, a prepared statement is used to insert the user's information into the database.

Example 20-10. TextToJDBC.java

```java
package jabadot;

import java.sql.*;
import java.io.*;
import java.util.*;

/** Convert the database from text form to JDBC form.
 */
public class TextToJDBC {

    protected final static String TEXT_NAME = "userdb.txt";
    protected final static String DB_URL = "jdbc:idb:userdb.prp";

    public static void main(String[] fn)
    throws ClassNotFoundException, SQLException, IOException {

        BufferedReader is = new BufferedReader(new FileReader(TEXT_NAME));

        // Load the database driver
        Class.forName("jdbc.idbDriver");

        System.out.println("Getting Connection");
        Connection conn = DriverManager.getConnection(
            DB_URL, "ian", "");// user, password

        System.out.println("Creating Statement");
        Statement stmt = conn.createStatement();

        System.out.println("Creating table and index");
        stmt.executeUpdate("DROP TABLE userdb");
```

Example 20-10. TextToJDBC.java (continued)

```java
        stmt.executeUpdate("CREATE TABLE userdb (\n" +
            "name     char(12) PRIMARY KEY,\n" +
            "password char(20),\n" +
            "fullName char(30),\n" +
            "email    char(60),\n" +
            "city     char(20),\n" +
            "prov     char(20),\n" +
            "country  char(20),\n" +
            "privs    int\n" +
            ")");
        stmt.executeUpdate("CREATE INDEX nickIndex ON userdb (name)");
        stmt.close();

        // put the data in the table
        PreparedStatement ps = conn.prepareStatement(
            "INSERT INTO userdb VALUES (?,?,?,?,?,?,?,?)");

        String line;
        while ((line = is.readLine()) != null) {
            //name:password:fullname:City:Prov:Country:privs

            if (line.startsWith("#")) {// comment
                continue;
            }

            StringTokenizer st =
                new StringTokenizer(line, ":");
            String nick = st.nextToken();
            String pass = st.nextToken();
            String full = st.nextToken();
            String email = st.nextToken();
            String city = st.nextToken();
            String prov = st.nextToken();
            String ctry = st.nextToken();
            // User u = new User(nick, pass, full, email,
            //   city, prov, ctry);
            String privs = st.nextToken();
            int iprivs = 0;
            if (privs.indexOf("A") != -1) {
                iprivs |= User.P_ADMIN;
            }
            if (privs.indexOf("E") != -1) {
                iprivs |= User.P_EDIT;
            }
            ps.setString(1, nick);
            ps.setString(2, pass);
            ps.setString(3, full);
            ps.setString(4, email);
```

Example 20-10. TextToJDBC.java (continued)

```
            ps.setString(5, city);
            ps.setString(6, prov);
            ps.setString(7, ctry);
            ps.setInt(8, iprivs);
            ps.executeUpdate();
        }
        ps.close();    // All done with that statement
        conn.close();  // All done with that DB connection
        return;        // All done with this program.
    }
}
```

Once the program has run, the database is populated and ready for use by the UserDBJDBC data accessor shown in Recipe 20.5.

20.10. *Finding JDBC Metadata*

Problem

You want to learn about a database or table.

Solution

Read the documentation provided by your vendor or database administrator. Or ask the software for a MetaData object.

Discussion

There are two classes of *metadata* (data about data) that you can ask for: DatabaseMetaData and ResultSetMetaData. Each of these has methods that let you interrogate particular aspects. The former class is obtained from a get method in a Connection object; the latter from a get method in the given ResultSet. First, let's look at RawSQLServlet, a "generic query" formatter. The user enters a query (which must begin with SELECT) into an HTML form, and a servlet (see Recipe 18.1) passes the query on to a database using JDBC. The response is interrogated and formatted into a neat little HTML table, using the column names from the ResultSetMetaData as the headings for the HTML table. Figure 20-2 shows the form for inputting the query and the resulting response from the servlet. The code for the RawSQLServlet class is in Example 20-11. The nice part about this program is that it responds to whatever columns are in the ResultSet, which need not be in the same order as they are in the database. Consider the two queries:

```
    select name, address from userdb
    select address, name from userdb
```

Any code that depends upon knowing the order in the database would look very strange indeed if the user query requested fields in a different order than they were stored in the database.

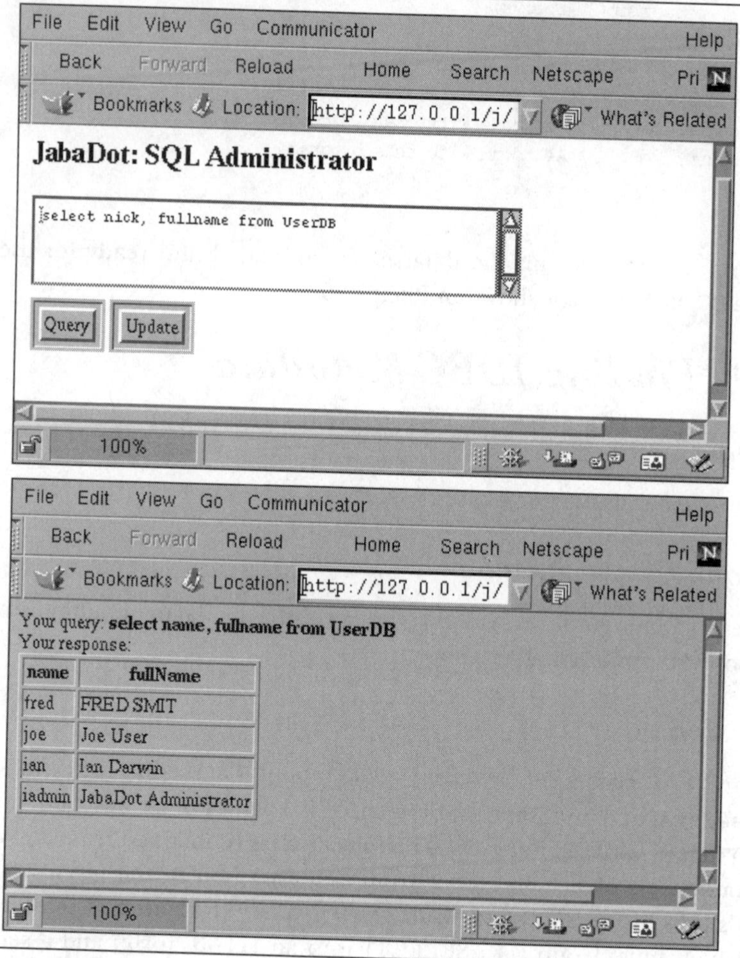

Figure 20-2. RawSQLServlet in action

Example 20-11. RawSQLServlet.java

```
import com.darwinsys.util.FileProperties;

import javax.servlet.*;
import javax.servlet.http.*;
import java.sql.*;
import java.io.*;
import java.util.*;
```

Example 20-11. RawSQLServlet.java (continued)

```java
/** Process a raw SQL query; use ResultSetMetaData to format it.
 */
public class RawSQLServlet extends HttpServlet {
    public final static String PROPS_FILE = "JDBCMeta.properties";

    /** The name of the JDBC Driver */
    protected String DRIVER;

    /** The DB connection object */
    protected Connection conn;

    /** The JDBC statement object */
    protected Statement stmt;

    /** Initialize the servlet. */
    public void init() throws ServletException {
        try {
            // Get a Properties to load from
            FileProperties fp = new FileProperties(PROPS_FILE);

            // Load the database driver
            DRIVER = fp.getProperty("driver");
            Class.forName(DRIVER);

            // Get the connection
            log(getClass() + ": Getting Connection");
            Connection conn = DriverManager.getConnection (
                fp.getProperty("dburl"),
                fp.getProperty("user"),
                fp.getProperty("password"));


            log(getClass() + ": Creating Statement");
            stmt = conn.createStatement();
        } catch (IOException ex) {
            log(getClass() + ": init: could not load props file " + PROPS_FILE);
        } catch (ClassNotFoundException ex) {
            log(getClass() + ": init: Could not load SQL driver " + DRIVER);
        } catch (SQLException ex) {
            log(getClass() + ": init: SQL Error: " + ex);
        }
    }

    /** Do the SQL query */
    public void doPost(HttpServletRequest request,
        HttpServletResponse response) throws ServletException, IOException {

        String query = request.getParameter("sql");
```

Example 20-11. RawSQLServlet.java (continued)

```java
        response.setContentType("text/html");
        PrintWriter out = response.getWriter();

        if (query == null) {
            out.println("<b>Error: malformed query, contact administrator</b>");
            return;
        }

        // NB MUST also check for admin privs before proceding!
        if (!query.toLowerCase().startsWith("select")) {
            throw new SecurityException("You can only select data");
        }

        try {// SQL
            out.println("<br>Your query: <b>" + query + "</b>");
            ResultSet rs = stmt.executeQuery(query);

            out.println("<br>Your response:");

            ResultSetMetaData md = rs.getMetaData();
            int count = md.getColumnCount();
            out.println("<table border=1>");
            out.print("<tr>");
            for (int i=1; i<=count; i++) {
                out.print("<th>");
                out.print(md.getColumnName(i));
            }
            out.println("</tr>");
            while (rs.next()) {
                out.print("<tr>");
                for (int i=1; i<=count; i++) {
                    out.print("<td>");
                    out.print(rs.getString(i));
                }
                out.println("</tr>");
            }
            out.println("</table>");
            // rs.close();
        } catch (SQLException ex) {
            out.print("<B>" + getClass() + ": SQL Error:</B>\n" + ex);
            out.print("<pre>");
            ex.printStackTrace(out);
            out.print("</pre>");
        }
    }

    public void destroy() {
        try {
```

Example 20-11. RawSQLServlet.java (continued)

```
            conn.close();// All done with that DB connection
        } catch (SQLException ex) {
            log(getClass() + ": destroy: " + ex);
        }
    }
}
```

The servlet as shown is not thread safe (see Recipe 24.5) because you can't really assume that the `Connection` object is thread safe. However, this servlet is used only by the administrator. A servlet connecting to a database should probably save only the driver class name and URL in its `init()` method, and get the `Connection` in its `service()`/`doGet()`/`doPost()` method. However, this will likely be very slow. One solution is to use a *connection pool*: you preallocate a certain number of `Connection` objects, hand them out on demand, and the servlet returns its connection to the pool when done. Writing a simple connection pool is easy, but writing a connection pool reliable enough to be used in production is very hard. For this reason, JDBC 2 introduced the notion of having the driver provide connection pooling. However, this is an optional feature—check your driver's documentation. Also, Enterprise JavaBeans (EJB) running in an application server usually provide connection pooling; if the servlet engine runs in the same process, this can be a very efficient solution.

Database metadata

The second example (see Example 20-12) uses a `DatabaseMetaData` to print out the name and version number of the database product and its default *transaction isolation* (basically, the extent to which users of a database can interfere with each other; see any good book on databases for information on transactions and why it's often really important to know your database's default transaction isolation).

Example 20-12. JDBCMeta.java

```
import com.darwinsys.util.FileProperties;

import java.awt.*;
import java.sql.*;

/** A database MetaData query
 */
public class JDBCMeta {

    public static void main(String[] av) {
        int i;
        try {
            FileProperties fp = new FileProperties("JDBCMeta.properties");
```

Example 20-12. JDBCMeta.java (continued)

```
            // Load the driver
            Class.forName(fp.getProperty("driver"));

            // Get the connection
            Connection conn = DriverManager.getConnection (
                fp.getProperty("dburl"),
                fp.getProperty("user"),
                fp.getProperty("password"));

            // Get a Database MetaData as a way of interrogating
            // the names of the tables in this database.
            DatabaseMetaData meta = conn.getMetaData();

            System.out.println("We are using " + meta.getDatabaseProductName());
            System.out.println("Version is " + meta.getDatabaseProductVersion() );

            int txisolation = meta.getDefaultTransactionIsolation();
            System.out.println("Database default transaction isolation is " +
                txisolation + " (" +
                transactionIsolationToString(txisolation) + ").");

            conn.close();

            System.out.println("All done!");

        } catch (java.io.IOException e) {
            System.out.println("Can't load PROPERTIES " + e);
        } catch (ClassNotFoundException e) {
            System.out.println("Can't load driver " + e);
        } catch (SQLException ex) {
            System.out.println("Database access failed:");
            System.out.println(ex);
        }
    }

    /** Convert a TransactionIsolation int (defined in java.sql.Connection)
     * to the corresponding printable string.
     */
    public static String transactionIsolationToString(int txisolation) {
        switch(txisolation) {
            case Connection.TRANSACTION_NONE:
                // transactions not supported.
                return "TRANSACTION_NONE";
            case Connection.TRANSACTION_READ_UNCOMMITTED:
                // All three phenomena can occur
                return "TRANSACTION_NONE";
            case Connection.TRANSACTION_READ_COMMITTED:
                // Dirty reads are prevented; non-repeatable reads and
```

Example 20-12. JDBCMeta.java (continued)

```
              // phantom reads can occur.
                  return "TRANSACTION_READ_COMMITTED";
              case Connection.TRANSACTION_REPEATABLE_READ:
                  // Dirty reads and non-repeatable reads are prevented;
                  // phantom reads can occur.
                  return "TRANSACTION_REPEATABLE_READ";
              case Connection.TRANSACTION_SERIALIZABLE:
                  // All three phenomena prvented; slowest!
                  return "TRANSACTION_SERIALIZABLE";
              default:
                  throw new IllegalArgumentException(
                          txisolation + " not a valid TX_ISOLATION");
          }
      }
}
```

When you run it, in addition to some debugging information, you'll see something like this. The details, of course, depend on your database:

```
> java JDBCMeta
Enhydra InstantDB - Version 3.13
The Initial Developer of the Original Code is Lutris Technologies Inc.
Portions created by Lutris are Copyright (C) 1997-2000 Lutris Technologies,
Inc.All Rights Reserved.
We are using InstantDB
Version is Version 3.13
Database default transaction isolation is 0 (TRANSACTION_NONE).
All done!
>
```

20.11. Program: JDAdmin

The JDAdmin program lets a privileged user view and administer the user database for the JabaDot web site shown in Recipe 18.12. It doesn't use the accessors that we so carefully built up in this chapter, as it needs to be able to make any change at all to the database, including recovering from corrupted data introduced by potential bugs in future versions of the accessor. Instead, it makes extensive use of the PreparedStatement class (see Recipe 20.6).

The user interface (shown in Figure 20-3) is a simple JTable controlled by the MyTableModel class defined at the end of the source. This controls the display of the fields and allows and handles the editing of the password field.

The Schema class used here simply defines public constants for the fields within the database. These field numbers begin at one; I subtract one from the field number when I need Java-origin numbers.

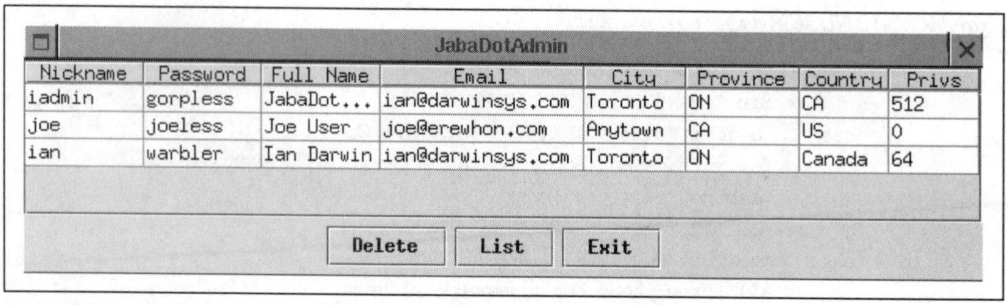

Figure 20-3. JDAdmin user interface

Example 20-13 shows the first working version of the program. It allows you to reset the password of a forgetful user and to delete a defunct account. One plausible extension is to add a text field and a button to allow you to execute an arbitrary SQL statement, as in Recipe 20.10.

Example 20-13. JDAdmin.java

```java
package jabadot;

import java.util.*;
import java.sql.*;
import java.awt.*;
import java.awt.event.*;
import javax.swing.*;
import javax.swing.table.*;

/** A User Database Administrator program
 * This does NOT use the UserDB interface as it needs
 * to be able to do ANYTHING to the database,
 * to go beyond, and to repair any errors introduced
 * by bugs in the UserDB code and/or queries. :-)
 *
 * If using InstantDB, therefore, you MUST NOT RUN THIS PROGRAM
 * while users have access to the system, or the database will
 * get worse instead of better!
 */
public class JDAdmin extends JFrame {

    /** the list of users */
    protected ArrayList userList = new ArrayList();
    /** The database connection */
    protected Connection conn;
    /** A Statement for listing users */
    protected PreparedStatement listUsersStatement;
    /** A Statement for deleting users */
    protected PreparedStatement deleteUserStatement;
    /** A Statement for resetting passwords for forgetful users */
    protected PreparedStatement setPasswordStatement;
```

Example 20-13. JDAdmin.java (continued)

```
/** The main table */
protected JTable theTable;

/** Main program -- driver */
public static void main(String av[]) throws Exception {
    JDAdmin aFrame = new JDAdmin();
    aFrame.populate();
    // aFrame.pack();
    aFrame.setSize(600,450);
    aFrame.setVisible(true);
}

/** Constructor */
public JDAdmin() throws SQLException {
    super("JabaDotAdmin");

    // INIT THE DB
    // Do this before the GUI, since JDBC does more-delayed
    // type checking than Swing...

    String dbDriver = JDConstants.getProperty("jabadot.userdb.driver");
    try {
        Class.forName(dbDriver);
    } catch (ClassNotFoundException ex) {
        JOptionPane.showMessageDialog(this,
            "JDBC Driver Failure:\n" + ex, "Error",
            JOptionPane.ERROR_MESSAGE);
    }
    conn = DriverManager.getConnection(
        JDConstants.getProperty("jabadot.userdb.url"));
    listUsersStatement = conn.prepareStatement("select * from userdb");
    deleteUserStatement =
        conn.prepareStatement("delete from userdb where name = ?");
    setPasswordStatement = conn.prepareStatement(
        "update userdb SET password = ? where name = ?");

    // INIT THE GUI
    Container cp = getContentPane();
    cp.setLayout(new BorderLayout());
    cp.add(new JScrollPane(theTable = new JTable(new MyTableModel())),
        BorderLayout.CENTER);
    JPanel bp = new JPanel();
    JButton x;
    bp.add(x = new JButton("Delete"));
    x.addActionListener(new ActionListener() {
        public void actionPerformed(ActionEvent ex) {
            int r = theTable.getSelectedRow();
            if (r == -1) {
```

Example 20-13. JDAdmin.java (continued)

```java
                    JOptionPane.showMessageDialog(JDAdmin.this,
                        "Please select a user to delete", "Error",
                        JOptionPane.ERROR_MESSAGE);
                    return;
                }
                int i = JOptionPane.showConfirmDialog(JDAdmin.this,
                        "Really delete user?", "Confirm",
                        JOptionPane.YES_NO_OPTION);
                switch(i) {
                    case 0:
                        try {
                            delete(r);
                        } catch (SQLException e) {
                            JOptionPane.showMessageDialog(JDAdmin.this,
                            "SQL Error:\n" + e, "Error",
                            JOptionPane.ERROR_MESSAGE);
                        }
                        break;
                    case 1:
                        // nothing to do.
                        break;
                    default:
                        System.err.println("showConfirm: unex ret " + i);
                }
            }
        });
        bp.add(x = new JButton("List"));
        x.addActionListener(new ActionListener() {
            public void actionPerformed(ActionEvent ex) {
                try {
                    populate();
                } catch (SQLException e) {
                    JOptionPane.showMessageDialog(JDAdmin.this,
                    "SQL Error:\n" + e, "Error",
                    JOptionPane.ERROR_MESSAGE);
                }
            }
        });
        bp.add(x = new JButton("Exit"));
        x.addActionListener(new ActionListener() {
            public void actionPerformed(ActionEvent ex) {
                System.exit(0);
            }
        });

        cp.add(bp, BorderLayout.SOUTH);

    }
```

Example 20-13. JDAdmin.java (continued)

```java
/** Get the current list of users from the database
 * into the ArrayList, so the display will be up-to-date
 * after any major change.
 */
public void populate() throws SQLException {
    ResultSet rs = listUsersStatement.executeQuery();
    userList.clear();
    while (rs.next()) {
        String nick = rs.getString(1);
        // System.out.println("Adding " + nick);
        User u = new User(nick, rs.getString(UserDB.PASSWORD),
            rs.getString(UserDB.FULLNAME),
            rs.getString(UserDB.EMAIL),
            rs.getString(UserDB.CITY),
            rs.getString(UserDB.PROVINCE),
            rs.getString(UserDB.COUNTRY),
            rs.getInt(UserDB.PRIVS));
        userList.add(u);
    }
    rs.close();
    theTable.repaint();
}


/** Delete the given user, by row number
 * (row number in the display == index into the ArrayList).
 * Use a JDBC PreparedStatement; if it succeeds, then also
 * remove the user object from the ArrayList.
 */
public void delete(int x) throws SQLException {
    User u = (User)userList.get(x);
    String nick = u.getName();
    deleteUserStatement.setString(1, nick);
    int n;
    switch (n = deleteUserStatement.executeUpdate()) {
        case 0:
            // no match!
            JOptionPane.showMessageDialog(this,
                "No match for user " + nick, "Error",
                JOptionPane.ERROR_MESSAGE);
            break;
        case 1:
            // OK
            JOptionPane.showMessageDialog(this,
                "User " + nick + " deleted.", "Done",
                JOptionPane.INFORMATION_MESSAGE);
            userList.remove(x);
            break;
        default:
```

Example 20-13. JDAdmin.java (continued)

```java
                    // Ulp! Deleted too many! -- n
                    JOptionPane.showMessageDialog(this,
                        "Oops, we deleted " + n + " users!!", "Error",
                        JOptionPane.ERROR_MESSAGE);
            }
            theTable.repaint();
    }


// class extends TableModel...
class MyTableModel extends AbstractTableModel {

    /** Returns the number of items in the list. */
    public int getRowCount() {
        return userList.size();
    }


    /** Return the width of the table */
    public int getColumnCount() {
        return 8;
    }


    /** Get the name of a given column */
    public String getColumnName(int i) {
        switch(i) {
        case UserDB.NAME-1:return "Nickname";
        case UserDB.PASSWORD-1:return "Password";
        case UserDB.FULLNAME-1:return "Full Name";
        case UserDB.EMAIL-1:return "Email";
        case UserDB.CITY-1:return "City";
        case UserDB.PROVINCE-1:return "Province";
        case UserDB.COUNTRY-1:return "Country";
        case UserDB.PRIVS-1:return "Privs";
        default: return "??";
        }
    }


    /** Returns a data value for the cell at columnIndex and rowIndex.
     * MUST BE IN SAME ORDER as setValueAt();
     */
    public Object getValueAt(int row, int col) {
        User u = (User) userList.get(row);
        switch (col) {
        case UserDB.NAME-1: return u.getName();
        case UserDB.PASSWORD-1: return u.getPassword();
        case UserDB.FULLNAME-1: return u.getFullName();
        case UserDB.EMAIL-1: return u.getEmail();
        case UserDB.CITY-1: return u.getCity();
        case UserDB.PROVINCE-1:return u.getProv();
```

Example 20-13. JDAdmin.java (continued)

```
            case UserDB.COUNTRY-1:return u.getCountry();
            case UserDB.PRIVS-1:return new Integer(u.getPrivs());
            default: return null;
            }
    }

    /** Set a value in a cell. MUSE BE IN SAME ORDER AS getValueAt. */
    public void setValueAt(Object val, int row, int col)  {
            User u = (User) userList.get(row);
            switch (col) {
            // DB Schemas start at one, Java columns at zero.
            case UserDB.PASSWORD-1:
                String newPass = (String)val;// Get new value
                try {
                    setPasswordStatement.setString(1, newPass);// ready,
                    setPasswordStatement.setString(2, u.getName());// steady,
                    setPasswordStatement.executeUpdate();// and update!
                } catch (SQLException ex) {
                    JOptionPane.showMessageDialog(null,
                        "SQL Error:\n" + ex.toString(), "SQL Error",
                        JOptionPane.ERROR_MESSAGE);
                    break;
                }
                u.setPassword(newPass);// bypassed if DB update failed
                break;

            // Only password cells are editable.
            default:
                JOptionPane.showMessageDialog(null,
                    "setValueAt" + val.getClass() + "," + val, "Logic error",
                    JOptionPane.ERROR_MESSAGE);
                break;
            }
    }

    /** Only password cells are editable. */
    public boolean isCellEditable(int rowIndex, int columnIndex) {
            return columnIndex == UserDB.PASSWORD-1;
    }
    }
}
```

This version is a standalone Java application. Given that we have an administrator level of privilege in the database, it might make sense to reimplement this as a web application under the administration functions. But then again, keeping it as a standalone application ensures that it will be run only on the server (my database does not listen for or accept network connections, folks, so don't bother trying).

See Also

The file *jdk1.x/docs/guide/jdbc/getstart/introTOC.doc.html* is provided with the JDK and gives some guidance on JDBC. JDBC is given extensive coverage in O'Reilly's *Database Programming with JDBC and Java,* and Addison Wesley's *JDBC Database Access from Java: A Tutorial and Annotated Reference* is also recommended. For general information on databases, you might want to consult *Joe Celko's Data and Databases* (Morgan Kaufman) or any of many other good general books.

21

XML

21.0. Introduction

The Extensible Markup Language, or XML, is a portable, human-readable format for exchanging text or data between programs. XML derives from its parent standard SGML, as does the HTML language used on web pages worldwide. XML, then, is HTML's younger but more capable sibling. And since most developers know at least a bit of HTML, parts of this discussion will be couched in terms of comparisons with HTML. XML's lesser-known grandparent is IBM's GML (General Markup Language), and one of its cousins is Adobe FrameMaker's Maker Interchange Format (MIF). Example 21-1 depicts the family tree.

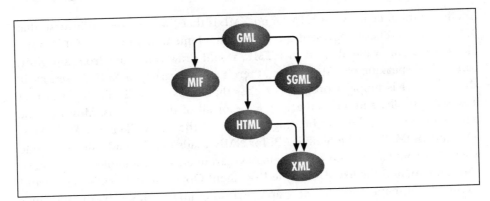

Figure 21-1. XML's ancestry

One way of thinking about XML is that it's HTML cleaned up, consolidated, and with the ability to define your own tags. It's HTML with tags that can and should identify the informational content as opposed to the formatting. Another way of perceiving XML is as a general interchange format for such things as business-to-business communications over the Internet, or as a human-editable* description of things as diverse as word-processing files and Java documents. XML is all these things, depending on where you're coming from as a developer and where you want to go today—and tomorrow.

Because of the wide acceptance of XML, it is used as the basis for many other formats, including the Open Office (*http://www.openoffice.org*) save file format, the SVG graphics file format, and many more.

From SGML, both HTML and XML inherit the syntax of using angle brackets (< and >) around *tags*, each pair of which delimits one part of an XML document, called an *element*. An element may contain content (like a <P> tag in HTML) or may not (like an <HR> in HTML). While HTML documents can begin with either an <HTML> tag or a <DOCTYPE...> tag (or, informally, with neither), an XML file must always begin with an XML prolog, which is at least the following:

```
<?xml version="1.0"?>
```

The question mark is a special character used to identify the XML prolog (it's syntactically similar to the % used in ASP and JSP).

HTML has a number of elements that accept attributes, such as:

```
<BODY BGCOLOR=white> ... </body>
```

XML attribute values (such as the 1.0 for the version in the prolog, or the white in BGCOLOR) must be quoted. In other words, quoting is optional in HTML, but required in XML.

Another difference between HTML and XML is that XML is case-sensitive, so that BODY, Body, and body represent three different element names. The BODY example shown here, while allowed in HTML, would draw complaint from any XML parser. And speaking of XML parsing, there's a great variety of XML parsers available. A parser is simply a program or class that reads an XML file, looks at it at least syntactically, and lets you access some or all of the elements. Most of these parsers conform to the Java bindings for one of the two well-known XML APIs, SAX and DOM. SAX, the Simple API for XML, reads the file and calls your code when it encounters certain events, such as start-of-element, end-of-element, start-of-document, and the like. DOM, the Document Object Model, reads the file and constructs an in-memory tree or graph corresponding to the elements and their

---

* Although you can edit XML using *vi*, Emacs, notepad, or simpletext, it is considered preferable to use an XML-aware editor. XML's structure is more complex, and parsing programs far less tolerant of pic-ayune error, than was ever the case in the HTML world. XML files are kept as plain text for debugging purposes, for ease of transmission across wildly incompatible operating systems, and (as a last resort) for manual editing to repair software disasters.

attributes and contents in the file. This tree can be traversed, searched, modified (even constructed from scratch, using DOM), or written to a file.

An alternative API called JDOM has also been released into the open source field. JDOM, by Brett McLaughlin and Jason Hunter, has the advantage of being aimed primarily at Java (DOM itself is designed to work with many different programming languages). JDOM is available at *http://www.jdom.org*, and has been accepted as a JSR (Java Standards Request) for the Sun Community Standards Process.

But how does the parser know if an XML file contains the correct elements? Well, the simpler, "non-validating" parsers don't; they simply check that the XML is syntactically correct, or *well-formed*. Validating parsers check that the XML file conforms to a given Document Type Definition (DTD) or an XML *Schema*. DTDs are inherited from SGML; their syntax is discussed in Recipe 21.4. Schemas are newer than DTDs and, while more complex, provide such object-based features as inheritance. DTDs are written in a special meta-language derived from SGML, while XML Schemas are written in "pure" XML.

In addition to parsing XML, you can use an XML processor to transform it into some other format, such as HTML. This is a natural for use in a servlet (see Chapter 18): if a given web browser client can support XML, just write the data as-is, but if not, transform the data into HTML. There are two transformation languages, XML-T and XML-FO, which we'll look at first; for more complex operations on XML, there are two parsing APIs that we'll cover later.

If you need to control how an XML document is displayed, you can use XSL-FO (Extensible Style Language: Formatted Objects). XSL-FO is an extended version of the HTML stylesheet concept that allows you to specify formatting for particular elements. However, the XSL-FO standard isn't complete yet. And XML-FO can be complex; you are basically specifying a batch formatting language to describe how your textual data is formatted for the printed page. A comprehensive reference implementation is FOP, which produces Acrobat PDF output and is available from *http://xml.apache.org*.

21.1. Transforming XML with XSLT

Problem

You need to make significant changes to the output format.

Solution

Use XSLT; it is fairly easy to use and does not require writing much Java.

Discussion

XSLT, or Extensible Style Language for Transformations, allows you a great deal of control over the output format. It can be used to change an XML file from one DTD into another, as might be needed in a business-to-business (B2B) application where information is passed from one industry-standard DTD to a site that uses another. It can also be used to render XML into another format such as HTML. Think of XSLT as a scripting language for transforming XML.

You need a set of classes called an *XSLT processor*. One freely available XSLT processor is the Apache project's Xalan (formerly available from Lotus/IBM as the Lotus XSL processor). To use this, you create an XSL processor by calling the factory method `getProcessor()`, then call its parse method passing in two `XSLTInputSources` (one for the XML document and one for the XSL stylesheet) and one `XSLTResultTarget` for the output file.

Assume you have a file of people's names, addresses, and so on, stored in an XML document such as the file *people.xml*, shown in Example 21-1.

Example 21-1. people.xml

```
<?xml version="1.0"?>
<people>
<person>
    <name>Ian Darwin</name>
    <email>ian@darwinsys.com</email>
    <country>Canada</country>
</person>
<person>
    <name>Another Darwin</name>
    <email type="intranet">ad</email>
    <country>Canada</country>
</person>
</people>
```

You can transform the *people.xml* file into HTML by using the following command:

```
$ java XSLTransform people.xml people.xsl people.html
```

Figure 21-2 shows the resulting HTML file opened in a browser.

Let's look at the file *people.xsl* (shown in Example 21-2). Since an XSL file is an XML file, it must be well-formed according to the syntax of XML. As you can see, it contains some XML elements but is mostly (well-formed) HTML.

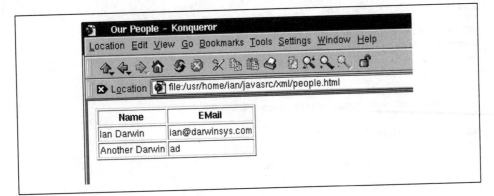

Figure 21-2. XML to HTML final result

Example 21-2. people.xsl

```
<?xml version="1.0"?>
<xsl:stylesheet xmlns:xsl="http://www.w3.org/1999/XSL/Transform" version="1.0">
<xsl:template match="/">

<html>
<head><title>Our People</title></head>
<body>

    <table border="1">
    <tr>
        <th>Name</th>
        <th>EMail</th>
    </tr>

    <xsl:for-each select="people/person">
        <tr>
            <td><xsl:value-of select="name"/></td>
            <td><xsl:value-of select="email"/></td>
        </tr>
    </xsl:for-each>

    </table>

</body></html>
</xsl:template>
</xsl:stylesheet>
```

The program **XSLTransform** appears in Example 21-3.

Example 21-3. XSLTransform.java

```java
import org.apache.xalan.xslt.*;
import java.net.*;
import java.io.*;

/**
 * Demonstrate transforming a file using XSLT.
 */
public class XSLTransform {

    public static void main(String[] args) {

        try {
            // Require three input args
            if (args.length != 3) {
                System.out.println("Usage: java XSLTransform "
                    + "<input XML file> <input XSL file> <output file>");
                System.exit(1);
            }

            XSLTProcessor myProcessor = XSLTProcessorFactory.getProcessor();
            XSLTInputSource xmlSource = new XSLTInputSource(args[0]);
            XSLTInputSource xslStylesheet = new XSLTInputSource(args[1]);
            XSLTResultTarget xmlOutput = new XSLTResultTarget(args[2]);
            myProcessor.process(xmlSource, xslStylesheet, xmlOutput);
        }
        catch (org.xml.sax.SAXException exc) {
            System.err.println("Found invalid XML during processing:");
            exc.printStackTrace();
        }
    }
}
```

See Also

A new development in progress is the use of *translets*. Sun is developing a program that will read a stylesheet and generate a `Translet` class, which is a compiled Java program that transforms XML according to the stylesheet. This will eliminate the overhead of reading the stylesheet each time a document is translated. See *http:// www.sun.com/xml/developers/xsltc/*.

21.2. Parsing XML with SAX

Problem

You want to make one quick pass over an XML file, extracting certain tags or other information as you go.

Solution

Simply use SAX to create a document handler and pass it to the SAX parser.

Discussion

The XML `DocumentHandler` interface specifies a number of "callbacks" that your code must provide. In one sense this is similar to the `Listener` interfaces in AWT and Swing, as covered briefly in Recipe 13.4. The most commonly used methods are `startElement()`, `endElement()`, and `text()`. The first two, obviously, are called at the start and end of an element, and `text()` is called when there is character data. The characters are stored in a large array, and you are passed the base of the array and the offset and length of the characters that make up your text. Conveniently, there is a string constructor that takes exactly these arguments. Hmmm, I wonder if they thought of that . . .

To demonstrate this, I wrote a simple program using SAX to extract names and email addresses from an XML file. The program itself is reasonably simple, and is shown in Example 21-4.

Example 21-4. SaxLister.java

```
import java.io.*;
import org.xml.sax.*;
import org.xml.sax.helpers.*;
import org.apache.xerces.parsers.SAXParser;

/** Simple lister - extract name and email tags from a user file.
 * Updated for SAX 2.0
 */
public class SaxLister {

    class PeopleHandler extends DefaultHandler {

        boolean name = false;
        boolean mail = false;

        public void startElement(String nsURI, String strippedName,
```

Example 21-4. SaxLister.java (continued)

```
            String tagName, Attributes attributes)
        throws SAXException {
            if (tagName.equalsIgnoreCase("name"))
                name = true;
            if (tagName.equalsIgnoreCase("email"))
                mail = true;
        }


        public void characters(char[] ch, int start, int length) {
            if (name) {
                System.out.println("Name:   " + new String(ch, start, length));
                name = false;
            } else if (mail) {
                System.out.println("Email: " + new String(ch, start, length));
                mail = false;
            }
        }
    }


    public void list() throws Exception {
        XMLReader parser = XMLReaderFactory.createXMLReader(
            "org.apache.xerces.parsers.SAXParser");// should load properties
        parser.setContentHandler(new PeopleHandler());
        parser.parse("people.xml");
    }


    public static void main(String[] args) throws Exception {
        new SaxLister().list();
    }
}
```

When run, it prints the listing:

```
$ java SaxLister users.xml
Name:  Ian Darwin
Email: ian@darwinsys.com
$
```

One problem with SAX is that it is, well, simple, and therefore doesn't scale well, as you can see by thinking about this program. Imagine trying to handle 12 different tags and doing something different with each one. For more involved analysis of an XML file, the Document Object Model (DOM) may be better suited. (On the other hand, DOM requires keeping the entire tree in memory, so there are some scalability issues with extremely large XML documents.) And with SAX, you can't really "navigate" a document, since you have only a stream of events, not a real structure. For that, you want DOM or JDOM.

21.3. Parsing XML with DOM

Problem

You want to examine an XML file in detail.

Solution

Use DOM to parse the document, and process the resulting in-memory tree.

Discussion

The Document Object Model (DOM) is a tree-structured representation of the information in an XML document. It consists of several interfaces, the most important of which is the *node*. All are in the package *org.w3c.dom*, reflecting the influence of the World Wide Web Consortium (*http://www.w3.org*) in creating and promulgating the DOM. The DOM interfaces are shown in Table 21-1.

Table 21-1. DOM interfaces

Interface	Function
Document	Top-level representation of an XML document
Node	Representation of any node in the XML tree
Element	An XML element
Text	A textual string

You don't have to implement these interfaces; the parser generates them. When you get to creating or modifying XML documents in Recipe 21.5, then you can create nodes. But even then there are implementing classes. Parsing an XML document with DOM is syntactically similar to processing a file with XSL, that is, you get a reference to a parser and call its methods with objects representing the input files. The difference is that the parser returns an XML DOM, a tree of objects in memory. Example 21-5 is code that simply parses an XML document.

Example 21-5. XParse.java

```
import java.io.*;
import org.w3c.dom.*;
import com.sun.xml.tree.*;
import org.xml.sax.SAXException;
import org.xml.sax.SAXParseException;

/** Parse an XML file using DOM.
 */
public class XParse {
```

Example 21-5. XParse.java (continued)

```java
    /** Convert the file */
    public static void parse(String fileName) {
        try {
            System.err.println("Parsing " + fileName + "...");

            // Make the document a URL so relative DTD works.
            String uri = "file:" + new File(fileName).getAbsolutePath();

            XmlDocument doc = XmlDocument.createXmlDocument(uri);
            System.out.println("Parsed OK");

        } catch (SAXParseException ex) {
            System.err.println("+================================+");
            System.err.println("|          *Parse Error*         |");
            System.err.println("+================================+");
            System.err.println("+ Line " + ex.getLineNumber ()
                               + ", uri " + ex.getSystemId ());
            System.err.println(ex.getClass());
            System.err.println(ex.getMessage());
            System.err.println("+================================+");
        } catch(SAXException ex) {
            System.err.println("+================================+");
            System.err.println("|         *SAX XML Error*        |");
            System.err.println("+================================+");
            System.err.println(ex.toString());
        } catch (IOException ex) {
            System.err.println("+================================+");
            System.err.println("|     *Input/Output Error*       |");
            System.err.println("+================================+");
            System.err.println(ex.toString());
        }
    }

    public static void main(String[] av) {
        if (av.length == 0) {
            System.err.println("Usage: XParse file");
            return;
        }
        for (int i=0; i<av.length; i++) {
            parse(av[i]);
        }
    }
}
```

You then traverse the document. You can use the defined **TreeWalker** interface, or you can just use the algorithm shown in Example 21-6.

Example 21-6. XTW.java (partial listing)

```
/* Process all the nodes, recursively. */
protected void doRecursive(Node p) {
    if (p == null) {
        return;
    }
    NodeList nodes = p.getChildNodes();
    int numElem = nodes.getLength();
    Debug.println("xml-tree", "Element has " + numElem + " children");
    for (int i=0; i<numElem; i++) {
        Node n = nodes.item(i);
        if (n == null) {
            continue;
        }

        doNode(n);

    }
}
```

A full code example using this approach is given in Recipe 21.6.

21.4. Verifying Structure with a DTD

Problem

Up to now, I have simply provided XML and asserted that it is valid. Now you want to verify the structure using a Document Type Definition (DTD).

Solution

Write the DTD and refer to it in one or more XML documents.

Discussion

This is not the place for a full dissertation on creating a Document Type Definition. Briefly, a DTD consists of a header and a list of the elements and any attributes. The DTD is written in a special language that allows you to specify the elements and attributes. Example 21-7 is *people.dtd*, a DTD for the *people.xml* file used earlier in this chapter.

Example 21-7. people.dtd

```
<!ELEMENT people (person)*>
<!ELEMENT person (name, email, country)>

<!ELEMENT name (#PCDATA)>
<!ATTLIST email type CDATA #IMPLIED>
<!ELEMENT email (#PCDATA)>
<!ELEMENT country (#PCDATA)>
```

To verify that a file conforms to a DTD, you do two things:

1. Refer to the DTD from within the XML file, as is sometimes seen in HTML documents. The <!DOCTYPE> line should follow the <?xml> line but precede any actual data.

   ```
   <?xml version="1.0"?>
   <!DOCTYPE people SYSTEM "people.dtd">

   <people>
   <person>
           <name>Ian Darwin</name>
           <email>ian@darwinsys.com</email>
           <country>Canada</country>
   </person>
   ```

2. Pass true as a second argument to the createXMLDocument() method; true means "enforce document validity."

   ```
   XmlDocument doc = XmlDocument.createXmlDocument(uri);
   ```

Now any elements found in the document that are not valid according to the DTD will result in an exception being thrown.

21.5. Generating Your Own XML with DOM

Problem

You want to generate your own XML files or modify existing documents.

Solution

Use DOM or JDOM; parse or create the document, and call its write method.

Discussion

Sun's XmlDocument class has a write() method that can be called with either an OutputStream or a Writer. To use it, create an XML document object using the XmlDocument constructor. Create nodes, and append them into the tree. Then call the document's `write()` method. For example, suppose you want to generate a poem in XML. Running the program and letting the XML appear on the standard output might look something like this:

```
$ jikes +E -d . DocWrite.java
$ java DocWrite
<?xml version="1.0" encoding="UTF-8"?>

<Poem>
  <Stanza>
    <Line>Once, upon a midnight dreary</Line>
    <Line>While I pondered, weak and weary</Line>
  </Stanza>
</Poem>
$
```

The code for this is fairly short; see Example 21-8.

Example 21-8. DocWrite.java

```java
import java.io.*;
import org.w3c.dom.*;
import com.sun.xml.tree.*;

/** Make up and write an XML document
 */
public class DocWrite {

    public static void main(String[] av) throws IOException {
        DocWrite dw = new DocWrite();
        XmlDocument doc = dw.makeDoc();
        doc.write(System.out);
    }

    /** Generate the XML document */
    protected XmlDocument makeDoc() {
        try {
            XmlDocument doc = new XmlDocument();

            Node root = doc.createElement("Poem");
            doc.appendChild(root);

            Node stanza = doc.createElement("Stanza");
            root.appendChild(stanza);

            Node line = doc.createElement("Line");
            stanza.appendChild(line);
            line.appendChild(doc.createTextNode("Once, upon a midnight dreary"));
            line = doc.createElement("Line");
```

Example 21-8. DocWrite.java (continued)

```
            stanza.appendChild(line);
            line.appendChild(doc.createTextNode("While I pondered, weak and weary"));

            return doc;

        } catch (Exception ex) {
            System.err.println("+=============================+");
            System.err.println("|          XML Error          |");
            System.err.println("+=============================+");
            System.err.println(ex.getClass());
            System.err.println(ex.getMessage());
            System.err.println("+=============================+");
            return null;
        }
    }
}
```

A more complete program, of course, would create an output file and have better error reporting. It would also have more lines of the poem than I can remember.

Sun's XmlDocument class is not a committed part of the standard, which is why the code imports com.sun.xml.tree.*. However, other vendors' APIs will likely have similar functionality. In Version 2 of the XML DOM API, you can use the new XMLReaderFactory.createXMLReader(), which takes the name of the parser as a string argument, which can in turn be loaded from a properties file (see Recipe 7.7). This avoids having the parser class name compiled into your application.

21.6. Program: xml2mif

Adobe FrameMaker* uses an interchange language called MIF (Maker Interchange Format), which is vaguely related to XML but is not well-formed. Let's look at a program that uses DOM to read an entire document and generate code in MIF for each node. This program was used to create some earlier chapters of the book you are now reading.

The main program, shown in Example 21-9, is called XmlForm; it parses the XML and calls one of several output generator classes. This could be used as a basis for generating other formats.

---

* Previously from Frame Technologies, a company that Adobe ingested.

Example 21-9. XmlForm.java

```java
import java.io.*;
import org.w3c.dom.*;
import com.sun.xml.tree.*;

/** Convert a simple XML file to text.
 */
public class XmlForm {
    protected Reader is;
    protected String fileName;

    protected static PrintStream msg = System.out;

    /** Construct a converter given an input filename */
    public XmlForm(String fn) {
        fileName = fn;
    }

    /** Convert the file */
    public void convert(boolean verbose) {
        try {
            if (verbose)
                System.err.println(">>>Parsing " + fileName + "...");
            // Make the document a URL so relative DTD works.
            String uri = "file:" + new File(fileName).getAbsolutePath();
            XmlDocument doc = XmlDocument.createXmlDocument(uri);
            if (verbose)
                System.err.println(">>>Walking " + fileName + "...");
            XmlFormWalker c = new GenMIF(doc, msg);
            c.convertAll();

        } catch (Exception ex) {
            System.err.println("+================================+");
            System.err.println("|          *Parse Error*         |");
            System.err.println("+================================+");
            System.err.println(ex.getClass());
            System.err.println(ex.getMessage());
            System.err.println("+================================+");
        }
        if (verbose)
            System.err.println(">>>Done " + fileName + "...");
    }

    public static void main(String[] av) {
        if (av.length == 0) {
            System.err.println("Usage: XmlForm file");
            return;
        }
```

Example 21-9. XmlForm.java (continued)

```
        for (int i=0; i<av.length; i++) {
            String name = av[i];
            new XmlForm(name).convert(true);
        }
        msg.close();
    }
}
```

The actual MIF generator is not shown here—it's not really XML-related—but is included in the online source code for the book.

See Also

XML is an area of rapid change. Schemas are becoming "real." New APIs (and acronyms!) continue to appear. XML-RPC and SOAP let you build distributed applications using XML and HTTP as the program interchange. The W3C has many new XML standards coming out. Several web sites track the changing XML landscape, including the official W3C site (*http://www.w3.org/xml/*) and O'Reilly's XML site (*http://www.xml.com*).

Sun's Java API for XML Parsing (JAXP), included with the Java 2 SDK 1.4 and later, provides convenience routines for accessing a variety of different parsers. This also includes SAX, DOM, and XSLT in the standard set of Java APIs for the first time.

And many books compete to cover XML. These range from the simple *XML: A Primer* by Simon St. Laurent to the comprehensive *XML Bible* by the prolific Elliotte Rusty Harold. In between is *Learning XML* by Erik T. Ray (O'Reilly). O'Reilly's *Java and XML* by Brett McLaughlin covers these topics in more detail, and also covers XML publishing frameworks such as Apache's *Cocoon* and XML information channels using RSS.

22

Distributed Java: RMI

22.0. Introduction

A *distributed system* is a program or set of programs that runs using more than one computing resource. Distributed computing covers a wide spectrum, from intra-process distributed applications (which Java calls threaded applications, discussed in Chapter 24), through intra-system applications (such as a network client and server on the same machine), to applications where a client program and a server program run on machines far apart (such as a web application).

Distributed computing was around for a long time before Java. Some traditional distributed mechanisms include RPC (remote procedure call) and CORBA. Java adds RMI (Remote Method Invocation), its own CORBA support, and EJB (Enterprise JavaBeans) to the mix. This chapter covers only RMI in detail, but these other technologies are discussed briefly.

At its simplest level, *remote procedure call* is the ability to run code on another machine and have it behave as much as possible like a local method call. Most versions of Unix use remote procedure calls extensively: Sun's NFS, YP/NIS, and NIS+ are all built on top of Sun's RPC. Windows NT implements large parts of the Unix DCE Remote Procedure Call and can interoperate with it. Each of these defines its own slightly ad hoc method of specifying the interface to the remote call. Sun's RPC uses a program called rpcgen, which reads a protocol specification and writes both the client and server network code. These are both Unix-specific; they have their place, but aren't as portable as Java.

Java Remote Methods Invocation (RMI) is a type of remote procedure call* that is network-independent, lightweight, and totally portable, as it's written in pure Java. I discuss RMI in this chapter in enough detail to get you started.

CORBA is the Object Management Group's (OMG) Common Object Request Broker Architecture, a sort of remote procedure call for programs written in C, C++, Java, Ada, Smalltalk, and others to call methods in objects written in any of those languages. It provides a transport service called the Internet Inter-Orb Protocol (IIOP) that allows object implementations from different vendors to interoperate. There is now a version of RMI over IIOP, making it possible to claim that RMI is CORBA-compliant.

Enterprise JavaBeans (EJB) is a distributed object mechanism used primarily for building reusable distributed objects that provide both business logic and database storage. There are several types of EJBs, including *session beans*, which do something (a shopping cart bean is a good example) and *entity beans*, which represent something (usually the things stored in a database; in our shopping cart example, the entity beans would be the objects available for purchase).

CORBA and EJB are of interest primarily to enterprise developers; they are covered briefly in O'Reilly's *Java Enterprise in a Nutshell*. A more detailed presentation will have to wait until O'Reilly decides to develop an *Enterprise Java Cookbook*. You can read about EJB in the O'Reilly book *Enterprise JavaBeans*.

Ian's Basic Steps: RMI

1. Define (or locate) the remote interface in agreement with the server.

2. Write your server.

3. Run *rmic* (Java RMI stub compiler) to generate the network glue.

4. Write the client.

5. Ensure that the RMI registry is running.

6. Start the server.

7. Run one or more clients.

---

* Both RMI and CORBA should really be called "remote method calls," as they both emphasize remote *objects*.

22.1. Defining the RMI Contract

Problem

You want to define the communications exchange between client and server.

Solution

Define a Java interface.

Discussion

RMI procedures are defined using an existing Java mechanism: interfaces. An interface is similar to an abstract class, but a class can implement more than one interface. RMI remote interfaces must be subclassed from `java.rmi.Remote`,[*] and both the client and server must be in the same Java package. All parameters and return values must be either primitives (`int`, `double`, etc.), or implement `Serializable` (as do most of the standard types like `String`). Or, as we'll see in Recipe 22.5, they can also be `Remote`.

Figure 22-1 shows the relationships between the important classes involved in an RMI implementation. The developer need only write the interface and two classes, the client application and the server object implementation. The RMI stub or proxy and the RMI skeleton or adapter are generated for you by the *rmic* program (see Recipe 22.3), while the RMI Registry and other RMI classes at the bottom of the figure are provided as part of RMI itself.

Example 22-1 is a simple `RemoteDate` getter interface, which lets us find out the date and time on a remote machine.

Example 22-1. RemoteDate.java

```
package darwinsys.distdate;

import java.rmi.*;
import java.util.Date;

/** A statement of what the client & server must agree upon. */
public interface RemoteDate extends java.rmi.Remote {
```

---

[*] You might not have known that interfaces can *extend* other interfaces, just as classes extend classes. It's worth knowing this, however. Indeed, there are a few examples of this in the standard API: `LayoutManager2` extends `LayoutManager`, and both are interfaces.

Example 22-1. RemoteDate.java (continued)

```
    /** The method used to get the current date on the remote */
    public Date getRemoteDate() throws java.rmi.RemoteException;

    /** The name used in the RMI registry service. */
    public final static String LOOKUPNAME = "RemoteDate";
}
```

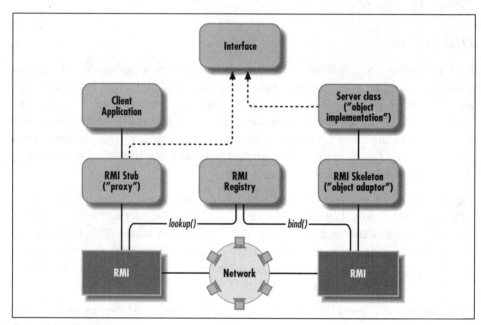

Figure 22-1. RMI overview

It's necessary for this file to list all the methods that will be callable from the server by the client. The lookup name is an arbitrary name that is registered by the server and looked up by the client to establish communications between the two processes. While most authors just hardcode this string in both programs, I find this error-prone, so I usually include the lookup name in the interface.

"So interfaces can contain variables?" you say. No variables indeed, but interfaces may contain non-variable (`final`) fields, as here. Putting the lookup name here ensures that both server and client really agree, and that is what this interface is all about, after all. I've seen other developers waste a considerable amount of time tracking down spelling mistakes in the lookup names of various remote services, so I prefer doing it this way.

22.2. RMI Client

Problem

You want to write a client to use an RMI service.

Solution

Locate the object and call its methods.

Discussion

Assume for now that the server object is running remotely. To locate it, you use `Naming.lookup()`, passing in the lookup name. This gives you a reference to a *proxy object*, an object that, like the real server object, implements the remote interface but runs in the same Java Virtual Machine as your client application. Here we see the beauty of interfaces: the proxy object implements the interface, so your code can use it just as it would use a local object providing the given service. And the remote object also implements the interface, so the proxy object's remote counterpart can use it exactly as the proxy is used. Example 22-2 shows the client for the `RemoteDate` service.

Example 22-2. DateClient.java

```
package darwinsys.distdate;

import java.rmi.*;
import java.util.*;

/* A very simple client for the RemoteDate service. */
public class DateClient {

    /** The local proxy for the service. */
    protected static RemoteDate netConn = null;

    public static void main(String[] args) {
        try {
            netConn = (RemoteDate)Naming.lookup(RemoteDate.LOOKUPNAME);
            Date today = netConn.getRemoteDate();
            System.out.println(today.toString()); // XX use a DateFormat...
        } catch (Exception e) {
            System.err.println("RemoteDate exception: " + e.getMessage());
            e.printStackTrace();
        }
    }
}
```

Also in the online source/RMI directory are *DateApplet.htm* and *DateApplet.java*, which together provide an example of using the server. In DateApplet, the connection is set up in the applet's init() method. The actual RMI call is done at the start of paint(), so it is updated any time the screen is painted.

22.3. RMI Server

Problem

The client looks good on paper, but will be lonely without a server to talk to.

Solution

You need to write two parts for the server, an implementation class and a main method. These can be in the same class or separated for clarity.

Discussion

The server-side code has to do a bit more work; see the sidebar.

Ian's Basic Steps: RMI Server

1. Define (or locate) the remote interface in agreement with the client.

2. Specify the remote interface being implemented.

3. Define the constructor for the remote object.

4. Provide implementations for the methods that can be invoked remotely.

5. Create and install a security manager.

6. Create one or more instances of a remote object.

7. Register at least one of the remote objects with the RMI remote object registry.

This implementation divides the server into the traditional two parts, a main program and an implementation class. It is just as feasible to combine these in a single class. The main program shown in Example 22-3 simply constructs an instance of the implementation and registers it with the lookup service.

Example 22-3. DateServer.java

```
package darwinsys.distdate;

import java.rmi.*;

public class DateServer {
    public static void main(String[] args) {

        // You may want a SecurityManager for downloading of classes:
        // System.setSecurityManager(new RMISecurityManager());

        try {
            // Create an instance of the server object
            RemoteDateImpl im = new RemoteDateImpl();

            System.out.println("DateServer starting...");
            // Locate it in the RMI registry.
            Naming.rebind(RemoteDate.LOOKUPNAME, im);

            System.out.println("DateServer ready.");
        } catch (Exception e) {
            System.err.println(e);
            System.exit(1);
        }
    }
}
```

The `Naming.bind()` method creates an association between the lookup name and the instance of the server object. This method will fail if the server already has an instance of the given name, requiring you to call `rebind()` to overwrite it. But since that's exactly where you'll find yourself if the server crashes (or you kill it while debugging) and you restart it, many people just use `rebind()` all the time.

The implementation class must implement the given remote interface. See Example 22-4.

Example 22-4. RemoteDateImpl.java

```
package darwinsys.distdate;

import java.rmi.*;
import java.rmi.server.*;
import java.util.*;

public class RemoteDateImpl extends UnicastRemoteObject implements RemoteDate
{
    /** Construct the object that implements the remote server.
     * Called from main, after it has the SecurityManager in place.
```

Example 22-4. RemoteDateImpl.java (continued)

```
     */
    public RemoteDateImpl() throws RemoteException {
        super();// sets up networking
    }

    /** The remote method that "does all the work". This won't get
     * called until the client starts up.
     */
    public Date getRemoteDate() throws RemoteException {
        return new Date();
    }
}
```

Using the server

Once you've compiled the implementation class, you can run *rmic* (RMI compiler) to build some glue files and install them in the client's CLASSPATH:

```
$ jikes -d . RemoteDateImpl.java
$ ls darwinsys/distdate
DateApplet$1.class        DateClient.class          RemoteDate.class
DateApplet.class          DateServer.class          RemoteDateImpl.class
$ rmic -d . darwinsys.distdate.RemoteDateImpl
$ ls darwinsys/distdate
DateApplet$1.class        DateServer.class          RemoteDateImpl_Skel.class
DateApplet.class          RemoteDate.class          RemoteDateImpl_Stub.class
DateClient.class          RemoteDateImpl.class
$
```

You must also ensure that TCP/IP networking is running, and then start the RMI registry program. If you're doing this by hand, just type the command *rmiregistry* in a separate window, or start or background it on systems that support this.

See Also

See the documentation in *jdk1.x/docs/guide/rmi/getstart.doc.html*.

22.4. Deploying RMI Across a Network

Problem

As shown so far, the server and the client must be on the same machine—some distributed system!

Solution

Get the RMI registry to dish out the client stubs on demand.

Discussion

RMI does not provide true *location transparency*, which means that you must at some point know the network name of the machine the server is running on. The server machine must be running the RMI registry program as well, though there's no need for the RMI registry to be running on the client side.

Now the RMI registry needs to send the client stubs to the client. The best way to do this is to provide an HTTP URL and ensure that the stub files can be loaded from your web server. This can be done by passing the HTTP URL into the RMI server's startup by defining it in the system properties:

```
java -Djava.rmi.server.codebase=http://serverhost/stubsdir/ ServerMain
```

In this example, `serverhost` is the TCP/IP network name of the host where the RMI server and registry are running, and `stubsdir` is some directory relative to the web server from which the stub files can be downloaded.

Be careful to start the RMI registry in its own directory, away from where you are storing (or building!) the RMI stubs. If RMI can find the stubs in its own CLASSPATH, it will assume they are universally available and won't download them!

The only other thing to do is to change the client's view of the RMI lookup name to something like *rmi://serverhost/foo_bar_name*. And for security reasons, the installation of the RMI Security Manager, which was optional before, is now a requirement.

22.5. Program: RMI Callbacks

One major benefit of RMI is that almost any kind of object can be passed as a parameter or return value of a remote method. The recipient of the object will not know ahead of time the class of the actual object it will receive. If the object is of a class that implements `Remote` (`java.rmi.Remote`), then in fact the returned object will be a proxy object that implements at least the declared interface. If the object is not remote, it must be serializable, and then a copy of it will be transmitted across the Net. The prime example of this is a `String`. It makes no sense to write an RMI proxy object for `String`. Why? Remember from Chapter 3 that `String` objects are immutable! Once you have a `String`, you can copy it locally but never change it. So `String`s, like most other core classes, can be copied across the RMI connection just as easily as they are copied locally. But `Remote` objects will cause an RMI proxy to be delivered. So what is stopping the caller from passing an

RMI object that is also itself a proxy? Nothing at all, and this is the basis of the powerful RMI callback mechanism.

An RMI callback occurs when the client of one service passes an object that is the proxy for another service. The recipient can then call methods in the object it received, and be calling back (hence the name) to where it came from. Think about a stock ticker service. You write a server that runs on your desktop and notifies you when your stock moves up or down. This server is also a remote object. You then pass this server object to the stock ticker service, which remembers it and calls its methods when the stock price changes. See Figure 22-2 for the big picture.

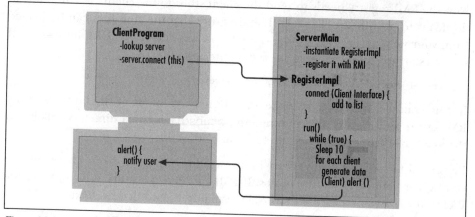

Figure 22-2. RMI callback service

The code for the callback service comes in several parts. Because there are two servers, there are also two interfaces. The first is the interface for the `TickerServer` service. There is only one method, `connect()`, which takes one argument, a `Client`:

```
package com.darwinsys.callback;

import com.darwinsys.client.*;

import java.rmi.*;

public interface TickerServer extends java.rmi.Remote {
    public static final String LOOKUP_NAME = "Ticker Service";
    public void connect(Client d) throws java.rmi.RemoteException;
}
```

`Client` is the interface that displays a stock price change message on your desktop. It also has only one method, `alert()`, which takes a `String` argument:

```
package com.darwinsys.client;

import java.rmi.*;

/** Client -- the interface for the client callback */
public interface Client extends Remote {
    public void alert(String mesg) throws RemoteException;
}
```

Now that you've seen both interfaces, let's look at the `TickerServer` implementation (Example 22-5). Its constructor starts a background thread to "track" stock prices; in fact, this implementation just calls a random number generator. A real implementation might use a third RMI service to track actual stock data. The `connect()` method is trivial; it just adds the given client (which is really an RMI proxy for the client server running on your desktop). The run method runs forever; and on each iteration, after sleeping for a while, it picks a random stock movement and reports it to any and all clients that are registered. If there's an error on a given client, the client is removed from the list.

Example 22-5. TickerServerImpl.java

```
package com.darwinsys.callback;

import com.darwinsys.client.*;

import java.rmi.*;
import java.rmi.server.*;
import java.util.*;

/** This is the main class of the server */
public class TickerServerImpl
    extends UnicastRemoteObject
    implements TickerServer, Runnable
{
    ArrayList list = new ArrayList();

    /** Construct the object that implements the remote server.
     * Called from main, after it has the SecurityManager in place.
     */
    public TickerServerImpl() throws RemoteException {
        super();// sets up networking
    }

    /** Start background thread to track stocks :-) and alert users. */
    public void start() {
        new Thread(this).start();
    }
```

Example 22-5. TickerServerImpl.java (continued)

```java
/** The remote method that "does all the work". This won't get
 * called until the client starts up.
 */
public void connect(Client da) throws RemoteException {
    System.out.println("Adding client " + da);
    list.add(da);
}

boolean done = false;
Random rand = new Random();

public void run() {
    while (!done) {
        try {
            Thread.sleep(10 * 1000);
            System.out.println("Tick");
        } catch (InterruptedException unexpected) {
            System.out.println("WAHHH!");
            done = true;
        }
        Iterator it = list.iterator();
        while (it.hasNext()){
            String mesg = ("Your stock price went " +
                (rand.nextFloat() > 0.5 ? "up" : "down") + "!");
            // Send the alert to the given user.
            // If this fails, remove them from the list
            try {
                ((Client)it.next()).alert(mesg);
            } catch (RemoteException re) {
                System.out.println(
                    "Exception alerting client, removing it.");
                System.out.println(re);
                it.remove();
            }
        }
    }
}
```

As written, this code is not thread safe; things might go bad if one client connects while we are running through the list of clients. I'll show how to fix this in Recipe 24.5.

This program's "server main" is trivial, so I don't include it here; it just creates an instance of the class we just saw, and registers it. More interesting is the client application shown in Example 22-6, which is both the RMI client to the connect() method and the RMI server to the alert() method in the server in Example 22-5.

Example 22-6. Callback ClientProgram.java

```java
package com.darwinsys.client;

import com.darwinsys.callback.*;

import java.io.*;
import java.rmi.*;
import java.rmi.server.*;

/** This class tries to be all things to all people:
 *   - main program for client to run.
 *   - "server" program for remote to use Client of
 */
public class ClientProgram extends UnicastRemoteObject implements Client
{
    protected final static String host = "localhost";

    /** No-argument constructor required as we are a Remote Object */
    public ClientProgram() throws RemoteException {
    }

    /** This is the main program, just to get things started. */
    public static void main(String[] argv) throws IOException, NotBoundException {
        new ClientProgram().do_the_work();
    }

    /** This is the server program part */
    private void do_the_work() throws IOException, NotBoundException {

        System.out.println("Client starting");

        // First, register us with the RMI registry
        // Naming.rebind("Client", this);

        // Now, find the server, and register with it
        System.out.println("Finding server");
        TickerServer server =
            (TickerServer)Naming.lookup("rmi://" + host + "/" +
            TickerServer.LOOKUP_NAME);

        // This should cause the server to call us back.
        System.out.println("Connecting to server");
        server.connect(this);

        System.out.println("Client program ready.");
    }
```

Example 22-6. Callback ClientProgram.java (continued)

```
    /** This is the client callback */
    public void alert(String message) throws RemoteException {
        System.out.println(message);
    }
}
```

In this version, the client server `alert()` method simply prints the message in its console window. A more realistic version would receive an object containing the stock symbol, a timestamp, and the current price and relative price change; it could then consult a GUI control to decide whether the given price movement is considered noticeable, and pop up a `JOptionPane` (see Recipe 13.7) if so.

22.6. Program: RMIWatch

Here's a program I put together while teaching Java courses for Learning Tree (*http://www/learningtree.com*). In one exercise, each student starts the RMI registry on his or her machine and uses `Naming.rebind()` (as in Recipe 22.3) to register with it. Some students come up with interesting variations on the theme of registering. So this program contacts the RMI registry on each of a batch of machines, and shows the instructor graphically which machines have RMI running and what is registered. A red flag shows machines that don't even have the registry program running: a black flag shows machines that are dead to the (networked) world.

This program also uses many ideas from elsewhere in the book. A Swing GUI (Chapter 13) is used. The layout is a `GridLayout` (discussed briefly in Recipe 13.2). A default list of machines to watch is loaded from a `Properties` object. (Recipe 7.7). For each host, an `RMIPanel` is constructed. This class is both a `JComponent` (Recipe 13.1) and a thread (Chapter 24). As a `JComponent`, it can be run in a panel, and as a thread, it can run independently and then sleep for 30 seconds (by default; settable in the properties file) so it isn't continually hammering away at the RMI registry on all the machines (the network traffic could be awesome). This program combines all these elements, and comes out looking like the display in Figure 22-3 (alas, we don't have color pages in this book).

Example 22-7 is the main class, `NetWatch`, which creates the `JFrame` and all the `RMIPanels` and puts them together.

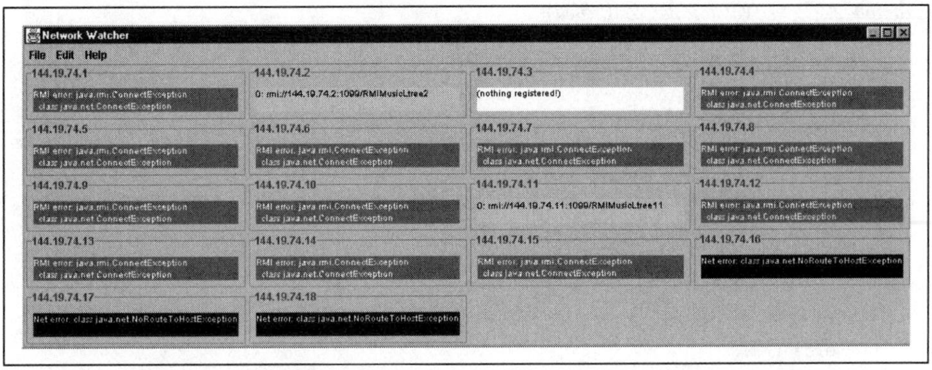

Figure 22-3. NetWatch watching the class

Example 22-7. NetWatch.java

```java
public class NetWatch {
    public static void main(String[] argv) {

        Properties p = null;

        NetFrame f = new NetFrame("Network Watcher", p);

        try {
            FileInputStream is = new FileInputStream("NetWatch.properties");
            p = new Properties();
            p.load(is);
            is.close();
        } catch (IOException e) {
            JOptionPane.showMessageDialog(f,
                e.toString(), "Properties error",
                JOptionPane.ERROR_MESSAGE);
        }

        // NOW CONSTRUCT PANELS, ONE FOR EACH HOST.

        // If arguments, use them as hostnames.
        if (argv.length!=0) {
            for (int i=0; i<argv.length; i++) {
                f.addHost(argv[i], p);
            }
        // No arguments. Can we use properties?
        } else if (p != null && p.size() > 0) {
            String net = p.getProperty("netwatch.net");
            int start = Integer.parseInt(p.getProperty("netwatch.start"));
            int end = Integer.parseInt(p.getProperty("netwatch.end"));
            for (int i=start; i<=end; i++) {
```

Example 22-7. NetWatch.java (continued)

```
                    f.addHost(net + "." + i, p);
                }
                for (int i=0; ; i++) {
                    String nextHost = p.getProperty("nethost" + i);
                    if (nextHost == null)
                        break;
                    f.addHost(nextHost, p);
                }
            }
            // None of the above. Fall back to localhost
            else {
                f.addHost("localhost", p);
            }

            // All done. Pack the Frame and show it.
            f.pack();
            // UtilGUI.centre(f);
            f.setVisible(true);
            f.addWindowListener(new WindowAdapter() {
                public void windowClosing(WindowEvent e) {
                    System.exit(0);
                }
            });
    }
}
```

The per-machine class, RMIPanel (shown in Example 22-8), is both a JComponent and a Runnable (for use with a thread). This class is instantiated once for each machine being monitored. Its run method loops, getting the list of registered objects from the given machine's RMI registry, and checks the contents to see if the expected string is present, setting the state to one of several integer values defined in the parent class NetPanel (EMPTY, DUBIOUS, FINE, etc.) based on what it finds. This state value is used to decide what color to paint this particular RMIPanel in the setState() method of the parent class NetPanel, which we have no reason to override.

Example 22-8. RMIPanel.java

```
/** Displays one machine's status, for RMI.
 */
public class RMIPanel extends NetPanel implements Runnable {

    public RMIPanel(String host, Properties p) {
        super(host, p);
    }
```

Example 22-8. RMIPanel.java (continued)

```
    /** Keep the screen updated forever, unless stop()ped. */
    public void run() {
        String thePort = props.getProperty("rmiwatch.port", "");
        String theURL = "rmi://" + hostName + ":" + thePort;
        while (!done) {
            try {
                String[] names = Naming.list(theURL);
                ta.setText("");
                for (int i=0; i<names.length; i++) {
                    ta.append(i + ": " + names[i] + "\n");
                }
                // If we didn't get an exception, host is up.
                String expect = props.getProperty("rmiwatch.expect");
                String fullText = ta.getText();
                if (fullText.length() == 0) {
                    ta.setText("(nothing registered!)");
                    setState(EMPTY);
                } else if (expect != null && fullText.indexOf(expect)==-1) {
                    setState(DUBIOUS);
                } else setState(FINE);
            } catch (java.rmi.ConnectIOException e) {
                setState(DOWN);
                ta.setText("Net error: " + e.detail.getClass());
            } catch (java.rmi.ConnectException e) {
                setState(NOREG);
                ta.setText("RMI error: " + e.getClass().getName() + "\n" +
                    "   " + e.detail.getClass());
                // System.err.println(hostName + ":" + e);
            } catch (RemoteException e) {
                setState(NOREG);
                ta.setText("RMI error: " + e.getClass().getName() + "\n" +
                    "   " + e.detail.getClass());
            } catch (MalformedURLException e) {
                setState(DOWN);
                ta.setText("Invalid host: " + e.toString());
            } finally {
                // sleep() in "finally" so common "down" states don't bypass.
                // Randomize time so we don't make net load bursty.
                try {
                    Thread.sleep((int)(sleepTime * MSEC * 2 * Math.random()));
                } catch (InterruptedException e) {
                    /*CANTHAPPEN*/
                }
            }
        }
    }
}
```

The last part is `NetPanel`, shown in Example 22-9. Notice the state variable definitions, and the `setState()` method that calls `setBackground()` to set the correct color given the state.

Example 22-9. NetPanel.java

```
/** Displays one machine's status.
 * Part of the NetWatch program: watch the network
 * on a bunch of machines (i.e., in a classroom or lab).
 * <P>Each non-abstract subclass just needs to implement run(),
 * which must, in a while (!done) loop:
 * <UL><LI>Try to contact the host
 * <LI>call setState(); (argument below)
 * <LI>call ta.setText();
 * <LI>Thread.sleep(sleepTime * MSEC);
 * </UL>
 */
public abstract class NetPanel extends JPanel implements Runnable {
    /** The name of this host */
    protected String hostName;
    /** The text area to display a list of stuff */
    protected JTextArea ta;
    /** Properties, passed in to constructor */
    protected Properties props;
    /** Default sleep time, in seconds. */
    protected static int DEFAULT_SLEEP = 30;
    /** Sleep time, in seconds. */
    protected int sleepTime = DEFAULT_SLEEP;
    /** Conversion */
    protected int MSEC = 1000;
    /** The constant-width font, shared by all instances. */
    protected static Font cwFont;
    /** The states */
    /** The state for: has "expect"ed name registered. */
    protected final static int FINE = 1;
    /** The state for: does not have expected name registered. */
    protected final static int DUBIOUS = 2;
    /** The state for: Server has nothing registered. */
    protected final static int EMPTY = 3;
    /** The state for: host is up but not running RMI */
    protected final static int NOREG = 4;
    /** The state for: host unreachable, not responding, ECONN, etc. */
    protected final static int DOWN = 5;
    /** The color for when a machine is FINE */
    protected static final Color COLOR_FINE = Color.green;
    /** The color for when a machine is DUBIOUS */
    protected static final Color COLOR_DUBIOUS = Color.yellow;
    /** The color for when a machine is EMPTY */
    protected static final Color COLOR_EMPTY = Color.white;
```

Example 22-9. NetPanel.java (continued)

```java
    /** The color for when a machine has NOREG */
    protected static final Color COLOR_NOREG = Color.red;
    /** The color for when a machine is NOREG */
    protected static final Color COLOR_DOWN = Color.black;

    /** State of the monitored host's RMI registry, up or down.
     * Initially set 0, which isn't one of the named states, to
     * force the background color to be set on the first transition.
     */
    protected int state = 0;

    public NetPanel(String host, Properties p) {
        hostName = host;
        props = p;
        String s = props.getProperty("rmiwatch.sleep");
        if (s != null)
            sleepTime = Integer.parseInt(s);
        // System.out.println("Sleep time now " + sleepTime);

        // Maybe get font name and size from props?
        if (cwFont == null)
            cwFont = new Font("lucidasansTypewriter", Font.PLAIN, 10);

        // Gooey gooey stuff.
        ta = new JTextArea(2, 26);
        ta.setEditable(false);
        ta.setFont(cwFont);
        add(BorderLayout.CENTER, ta);
        setBorder(BorderFactory.createTitledBorder(hostName));

        // Sparks. Ignition!
        new Thread(this).start();
    }

    boolean done = false;
    /** Stop this Thread */
    public void stop() {
        done = true;
    }

    /** True if the given host is believed to be up. */
    protected int getState() {
        return state;
    }

    /** Record the new state of the current machine.
     * If this machine has changed state, set its color
     * @param newState - one of the five valid states in the introduction.
```

Example 22-9. NetPanel.java (continued)

```
        */
    protected void setState(int newState) {
        if (state /*already*/ == newState)
            return;  // nothing to do.
        switch(newState) {
            case FINE:// Server has "expect"ed name registered.
                ta.setBackground(COLOR_FINE);
                ta.setForeground(Color.black);
                break;
            case DUBIOUS:// Server does not have expected name registered.
                ta.setBackground(COLOR_DUBIOUS);
                ta.setForeground(Color.black);
                break;
            case EMPTY:// Server has nothing registered.
                ta.setBackground(COLOR_EMPTY);
                ta.setForeground(Color.black);
                break;
            case NOREG:// host is up but not running RMI
                ta.setBackground(COLOR_NOREG);
                ta.setForeground(Color.white);
                break;
            case DOWN:// host unreachable, not responding, ECONN, etc.
                ta.setBackground(COLOR_DOWN);
                ta.setForeground(Color.white);
                break;
            default:
                throw new IllegalStateException("setState("+state+") invalid");
            }
        state = newState;
    }
}
```

See Also

The term *distributed computing* covers a lot of terrain. Here I've shown only the basics of RMI. For more on RMI, see the O'Reilly book *Java Distributed Computing* by Jim Farley. Jim's book also offers some information on CORBA. It's now possible to use RMI to access CORBA objects, or vice versa, using a new (late 2000) mechanism called RMI-IIOP. See *http://java.sun.com/products/rmi-iiop/*.

The newest and potentially most important distributed mechanism for large-scale computing projects is Enterprise JavaBeans, part of the Java 2 Enterprise Edition (J2EE). See the O'Reilly book *Enterprise JavaBeans*, by Richard Monson-Haefel.

You can also think of servlets and JSP as a kind of distributed computing, used primarily as the gateway into these other distributed object mechanisms. See Chapter 18 for details.

23

Packages and Packaging

23.0. Introduction

One of the better aspects of the Java language is that it has defined a very clear packaging mechanism for categorizing and managing the external API. Contrast this with a language like C, where external symbols may be found in the C library itself or in any of dozens of other libraries, with no clearly defined naming conventions.* APIs consist of one or more packages; packages consist of classes; classes consist of methods and fields. Anybody can create a package, with one important restriction: you or I cannot create a package whose name begins with the four letters java. Packages named java. or javax. are reserved for use by Sun Microsystems' Java developers. When Java was new, there were about a dozen packages in a structure that is very much still with us; some of these are shown in Table 23-1.

Table 23-1. Java packages basic structure

Name	Function
java.applet	Applets for browser use
java.awt	Graphical User Interface
java.lang	Intrinsic classes (strings, etc.)
java.net	Networking (sockets)
java.io	Reading and writing
java.util	Utilities (collections, date)

---

* This is not strictly true. On Unix, at least, there is a distinction between normal include files and those in the *sys* subdirectory, and many structures have names beginning with one or two letters and an underscore, like pw_name, pw_passwd, pw_home, and so on in the password structure. But this is nowhere near as consistent as Java's java.* naming conventions.

Many packages have since been added, but the initial structure has stood the test of time fairly well. In this chapter I show you how to create and document your own packages, and then discuss a number of issues related to deploying your package in various ways on various platforms.

23.1. Creating a Package

Problem

You want to create your own package.

Solution

Put a package statement at the front of each file, and recompile with −d.

Discussion

The package statement must be the very first non-comment statement in your Java source file, preceding even import statements, and must give the full name of the package. Package names are expected to start with your domain name backward: for example, my Internet domain is *darwinsys.com*, so most of my packages begin with com.darwinsys and a project name. The utility classes used in this book are in the package com.darwinsys.util, and each source file begins with:

```
package com.darwinsys.util;
```

Once you have package statements in place, be aware that the Java runtime and even the compiler will expect the class files to be found in their rightful place, that is, in the subdirectory corresponding to the full name somewhere in your CLASS-PATH settings. For example, the class file for com.darwinsys.util.FileIO must *not* be in the file *FileIO.class* in my class path, but must be in *com/darwinsys/util/FileIO.class* relative to one of the directories or archives in my CLASSPATH. Accordingly, it is customary to use the −d command-line argument when compiling. This argument must be followed by a directory name (often . is used to signify the current directory), to specify where to build the directory tree. For example, I often say:

```
javac -d . *.java
```

which creates the path (e.g., *com/darwinsys/util/*) relative to the current directory, and puts the class files into that subdirectory. This makes life easy for subsequent compilations, and also for creating archives, which I will do in Recipe 23.3.

23.2. *Documenting Classes with Javadoc*

Problem

You have heard about this thing called "code reuse," and would like to promote it by allowing other developers to use your classes.

Solution

Use Javadoc.

Discussion

Javadoc is one of the great inventions of the early Java years. Like so many good things, it was not wholly invented by the Java folk; earlier projects such as Knuth's Literate Programming had combined source code and documentation in a single source file. But the Java folk did a good job on it and came along at the right time. Javadoc is to Java classes what manpages are to Unix or Windows Help is to MS-Windows applications: it is a standard format that everybody expects to find and knows how to use. Learn it. Use it. Write it. Live long and prosper (well, perhaps not). But all that HTML documentation that you refer to when writing Java code, the complete reference for the JDK—did you think they hired dozens of tech writers to produce it? Nay, that's not the Java way. Java's developers wrote the documentation comments as they went along, and when the release was made, they ran Javadoc on all the zillions of public classes, and generated the documentation bundle at the same time as the JDK. You can, should, and really must do the same when you are preparing classes for other developers to use.

All you have to do to use Javadoc is to put special "doc comments" into your Java source files. These begin with a slash and two stars (/**), and must appear immediately before the definition of the class, method, or field that they document. Doc comments placed elsewhere are ignored.

There is a series of keywords, prefixed by the at sign (@), that can appear inside doc comments in certain contexts. These are listed in Table 23-2.

Table 23-2. Javadoc keywords

Keyword	Use
@author	Author name(s)
@version	Version identifier
@parameter	Argument name and meaning (methods only)
@since	JDK version in which introduced (primarily for Sun use)

Table 23-2. Javadoc keywords (continued)

Keyword	Use
@return	Return value
@throws	Exception class and conditions under which thrown
@deprecated	Causes deprecation warning
@see	Cross-reference

Example 23-1 is a somewhat contrived example that shows almost every usage of a javadoc keyword. The output of running this through Javadoc is shown in a browser in Figure 23-1.

Example 23-1. JavadocDemo.java

```
import java.applet.*;
import java.awt.*;
import java.awt.event.*;

/**
 * JavadocDemo - a simple applet to show JavaDoc comments.
 * <P>Note: this is just a commented version of HelloApplet.
 * @see java.applet.Applet
 * @see javax.swing.JApplet
 */
public class JavadocDemo extends Applet {

    /** init() is an Applet method called by the browser to initialize.
     * Init normally sets up the GUI, and this version is no exception.
     * @return None.
     */
    public void init() {
        // We create and add a pushbutton here,
        // but it doesn't do anything yet.
        Button b;
        b = new Button("Hello");
        add(b);                     // connect Button into Applet
    }

    /** paint() is an AWT Component method, called when the
     *  component needs to be painted. This one just draws colored
     * boxes in the Applet's window.
     *
     * @param g A java.awt.Graphics that we use for all our
     * drawing methods.
     */
    public void paint(Graphics g) {
        int w = getSize().width, h=getSize().height;
```

Example 23-1. JavadocDemo.java (continued)

```
        g.setColor(Color.yellow);
        g.fillRect(0, 0, w/2, h);
        g.setColor(Color.green);
        g.fillRect(w/2, 0, w, h);
        g.setColor(Color.black);
        g.drawString("Welcome to Java", 50, 50);
    }


    /** Show makes a component visible; this method became deprecated
     * in the Great Renaming of JDK1.1.
     * @since 1.0
     * @deprecated Use setvisible(true) instead.
     */
    public void show() {
        setVisible(true);
    }


    /** An Applet must have a public no-argument constructor.
     * @throws java.lang.IllegalArgumentException on Sundays.
     */
    public JavadocDemo() {
        if (new java.util.Date().getDay() == 0) {
            throw new IllegalArgumentException("Never On A Sunday");
        }
    }
}
```

The Javadoc tool works fine for one class, but really comes into its own when dealing with a package or collection of packages. It generates thoroughly interlinked and cross-linked documentation, just like that which accompanies the standard JDK. There are several command-line options; I normally use -author and -version to get it to include these items, and often -link to tell it where to find the standard JDK to link to. Run *javadoc –help* for a complete list of options. Figure 23-1 shows one view of the documentation that the previous class generates when run as:

```
$ javadoc -author -version JavadocDemo.java
```

Be aware that one of the (many) generated files will have the same name as the class, with the extension *.html.* If you write an applet and a sample HTML file to invoke it, the *.html* file will be silently overwritten with the Javadoc output. For this reason, I recommend using a different filename or the filename extension *.htm* for the HTML page that invokes the applet. Alternately, use the *–d directory* option to tell it where to put the generated files if you don't want them in the same directory.

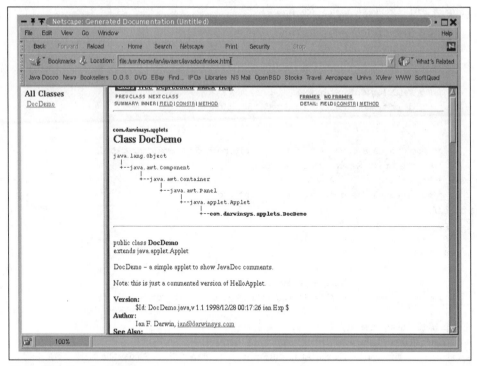

Figure 23-1. Javadoc in action

See Also

The output that Javadoc generates is fine for most purposes. It is possible to write your own `Doclet` class to make the Javadoc program into a class documentation verifier, a Java-to-MIF or Java-to-RTF documentation generator, or whatever you like. Those are actual examples; see the Javadoc tools documentation that comes with the JDK for documents and examples, or go to *http://java.sun.com/j2se/javadoc/*. A tool for testing Java files to ensure that they have adequate Javadoc comments can be downloaded from *http://www.znerd.demon.nl/doclint/*. This tool is a Javadoc `Doclet`!

Javadoc is for programmers using your classes; for a GUI application, users will probably appreciate standard online help. This is the role of the Java Help API, which is not covered in this book but is fully explained in the O'Reilly book *Creating Effective JavaHelp*, which every GUI application developer should read.

23.3. *Archiving with jar*

Problem

You want to create a Java archive (JAR) file.

Solution

Use *jar*.

Discussion

The *jar* archiver is Java's standard tool for building archives. Archives serve the same purpose as the program libraries that some other programming languages use. Java normally loads its standard classes from archives, a fact you can verify by running a simple Hello World program with the −verbose option:

```
java -verbose HelloWorld
```

To create an archive is a simple process. The *jar* tool takes several command-line arguments: the most common are c for create, t for table of contents, and x for extract. The archive name is specified with −f and a filename. The options are followed by the files and directories to be archived. For example:

```
jar cvf /tmp/MyClasses.jar .
```

The dot at the end is important; it means "the current directory." This command creates an archive of all files in the current directory and its subdirectories into the file */tmp/MyClasses.jar*.

Some applications of JAR files require an extra file in the JAR called a *manifest*. This file lists the contents of the JAR and their attributes. The attributes are in the form name: value, as used in email headers, properties files (see Recipe 7.7), and elsewhere. Some attributes are required by the application, while others are optional. For example, Recipe 23.6 discusses running a main program directly from a JAR; this requires a Main-Program header. You can even invent your own headers, such as:

```
MySillyAttribute: true
MySillynessLevel: high (5'11")
```

You store this in a file called, say, *manifest.stub*, and pass it to *jar* with the −m switch. *jar* includes your attributes in the manifest file it creates:

```
jar -cv -m manifest.stub -f /tmp/com.darwinsys.util.jar .
```

The *jar* program and related tools add additional information to the manifest, including a listing of all the other files included in the archive.

23.4. Running an Applet from a JAR

Problem

You want to optimize downloading time for an applet by putting all the class files into one JAR file.

Solution

jar the applet and supporting files. Deploy the JAR file in place of the class file on the web server. Use `<APPLET CODE="MyClass" ARCHIVE="MyAppletJar.jar" ...>`.

Discussion

Once you've deployed the JAR file on the web server in place of the class file, you only need to refer to it in the APPLET tag in the HTML. The syntax for doing this is to use an `ARCHIVE="name of jar file"` attribute on the APPLET tag.

See Also

You can also store other resources such as GIF images for use by the applet. You then need to use `getResource()` instead of trying to open the file directly; see Step 5 in the sidebar in Recipe 23.11.

23.5. Running an Applet with a JDK

Problem

You want to use an applet on an intranet or the Internet, but it needs a modern JDK to run.

Solution

Use the Java Plug-in.

Discussion

Sun's Java Plug-in allows your applet to run with a modern JDK even if the user has an ancient browser (Netscape 2, 3, or 4), or an anti-standard-Java browser (Microsoft Explorer might come to mind). For Netscape, the plug-in runs as a

Netscape Plug-in. For Microsoft, the plugin runs as an ActiveX control. The Java Plug-in was previously a separate download, but is included in the Java Runtime Environment (JRE) in all modern JDK versions.

The HTML code needed to make a single applet runnable in either of those two modes rather boggles the mind. However, there is a convenient tool (which Sun provides for free) that converts a plain applet tag into a hairy mess of HTML that is "bilingual": both of the major browsers will interpret it correctly and do the right thing. Note that since browser plug-ins are platform-dependent, the Plug-in is platform-dependent. Sun provides versions for Solaris and MS-Windows; other vendors provide it ported to various platforms. Learn more at Java's Plug-in page, *http://java.sun.com/products/plugin/*.

To try it out, I started with a simple JApplet subclass, the HelloApplet program from Recipe 25.8. Since this is a JApplet, it requires Swing support, which is not available in older Netscape versions or newer MSIE versions. Here are some screen-shots, and the "before and after" versions of a simple HTML page with an applet tag run through the converter. Example 23-2 shows a simple applet HTML page.

Example 23-2. HelloApplet.html

```
<html>
<title>Hello Applet</title>
<body bgcolor="white">
<h1>Hello Applet</h1>
<hr>
<applet code=HelloApplet width=300 height=200>
    <param name="buttonlabel" value="Toggle Drawing">
</applet>
<hr>
</html>
```

When I run this under Netscape, it dies because Netscape 4 doesn't fully support Swing. So I need to convert it to use the Java Plugin. Editing the HTML by hand is possible (there is a spec on the Java web site, *http://java.sun.com*), but messy. I decide to use the HTMLConverter instead. It pops up a simple dialog window (shown at the top of Figure 23-2), in which I browse to the directory containing the HTML page. Note that the program will convert *all* the HTML files in a direc-tory, so approach with caution if you have a lot of files.

When I click on the Convert button, it chugs for a while, and then pops up the window shown at the bottom of Figure 23-2 to show what it did.

By the time the HTMLConverter is finished with it, the once-simple HTML file is simple no more. See Example 23-3 for the finished version.

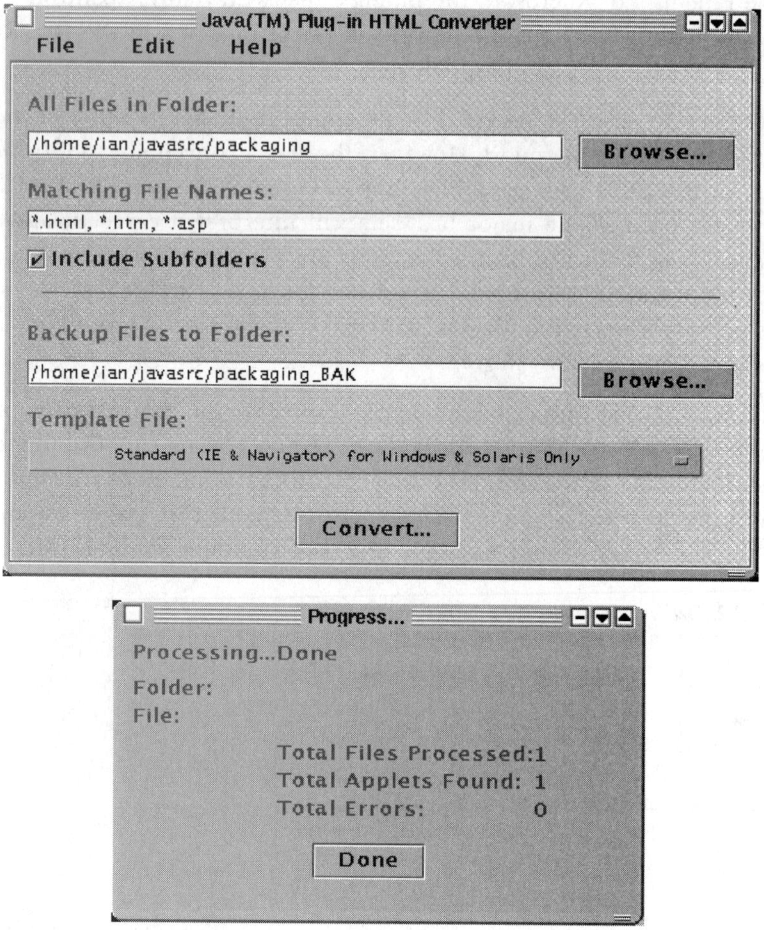

Figure 23-2. HTML converter

Example 23-3. HTML converter output

```
<html>
<title>Hello Applet</title>
<body bgcolor="white">
<h1>Hello Applet</h1>
<hr>
<!--"CONVERTED_APPLET"-->
<!-- CONVERTER VERSION 1.3 -->
<OBJECT classid="clsid:8AD9C840-044E-11D1-B3E9-00805F499D93"
WIDTH = 300 HEIGHT = 200  codebase="http://java.sun.com/products/plugin/1.3/jinstall-
13-win32.cab#Version=1,3,0,0">
<PARAM NAME = CODE VALUE = HelloApplet >
```

Example 23-3. HTML converter output (continued)

```
<PARAM NAME="type" VALUE="application/x-java-applet;version=1.3">
<PARAM NAME="scriptable" VALUE="false">
<PARAM NAME = "buttonlabel" VALUE ="Toggle Drawing">
<COMMENT>
<EMBED type="application/x-java-applet;version=1.3"  CODE = HelloApplet WIDTH = 300
HEIGHT = 200 buttonlabel = "Toggle Drawing"  scriptable=false pluginspage="http://
java.sun.com/products/plugin/1.3/plugin-install.html"><NOEMBED></COMMENT>

</NOEMBED></EMBED>
</OBJECT>

<!--
<APPLET CODE = HelloApplet WIDTH = 300 HEIGHT = 200>
<PARAM NAME = "buttonlabel" VALUE ="Toggle Drawing">


</APPLET>
-->
<!--"END_CONVERTED_APPLET"-->

<hr>
</html>
```

Sun's documentation makes the amusing claim that "this may look complicated, but it's not really." Your mileage may vary; mine did. The key point is that, since I used the default template, it built a version of the file that can be used with either MSIE (the OBJECT version) or Netscape (the EMBED version); both are cleverly interwoven to appear as ignorable comments to the other. Figure 23-3 shows this page running under Netscape, and Figure 23-4 shows it under MSIE.

23.6. Running a Program from a JAR

Problem

You want to distribute a single large file containing all the classes of your application, and run the main program from within the JAR.

Solution

Create a JAR file with a `Main-Class:` line in the manifest; run the program with the *java –jar* option.

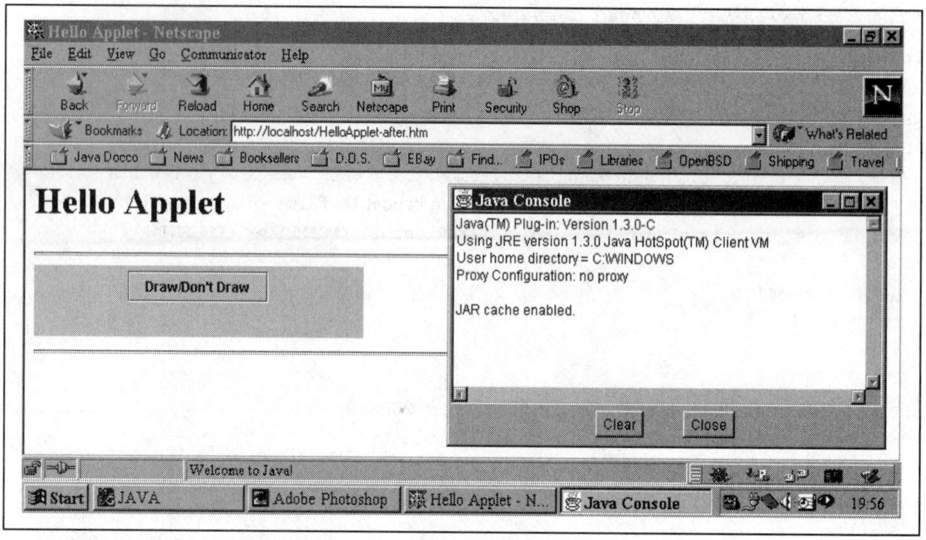

Figure 23-3. Applet working in Netscape using Java Plug-in

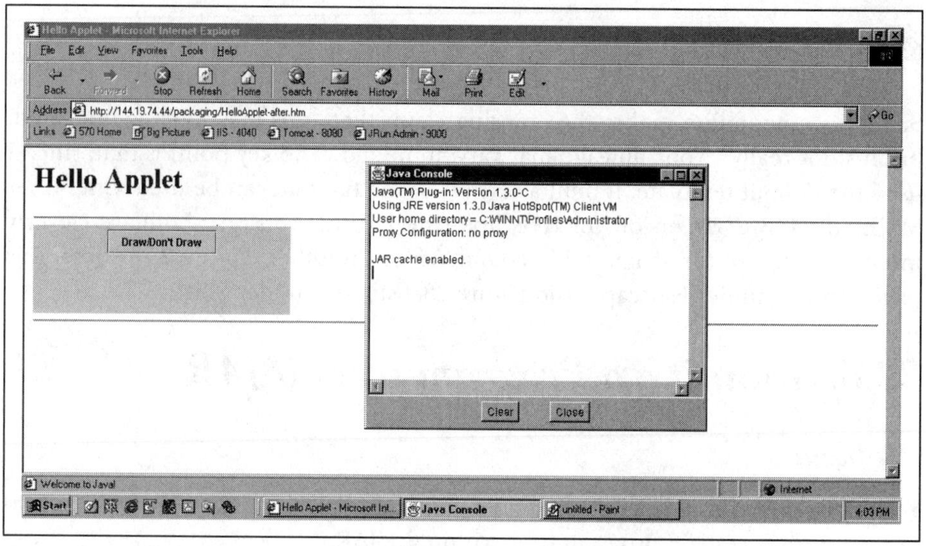

Figure 23-4. Applet working in Microsoft Internet Explorer using Java Plug-in

Discussion

The *java* command has a -jar option that tells it to run the main program found within a JAR file. In this case, it will also find classes it needs to load from within the same JAR file. How does it know which class to run? You must tell it. Create a one-line entry like this:

```
Main-class: HelloWorld
```

in a file called, say, *manifest.stub*, and assuming that you want to run the program HelloWorld. Then give the following commands:

```
C:> jikes HelloWorld.java
C:> jar cvmf manifest.stub hello.jar HelloWorld.class
C:> java -jar hello.jar
Hello, World of Java
C:>
```

You can now copy the JAR file anywhere and run it the same way. You do not need to add it to your CLASSPATH or list the name of the main class.

23.7. *Preparing a Class as a JavaBean*

Problem

You have a class that you would like to install as a JavaBean.

Solution

Make sure the class meets the JavaBeans requirements; create a JAR file containing the class, a manifest, and any ancillary entries.

Discussion

There are three kinds of Java components that are called JavaBeans:

- Visual components for use in GUI builders, as discussed in this chapter.

- Components that are used in JavaServer Pages (JSP). Examples of these are given in Chapter 18.

- Enterprise JavaBeans (EJB) has features for building enterprise-scale applications. Creating and using EJB is more involved than regular JavaBeans and would take us very far afield, so EJB is not covered in this book. When you need to learn about EJB functionality, turn to the O'Reilly book *Enterprise Java-Beans*.

What all three kinds of beans have in common are certain naming paradigms. All public properties should be accessible by get/set accessory methods. For a given property Prop of type Type, the following two methods should exist (note the capitalization):

```
public Type getProp();
public void setProp(Type)
```

For example, the various AWT and Swing components that have textual labels all have the following pair of methods:

```
public String getText();
public void setText(String newText);
```

You should use this set/get design pattern (set/get methods) for methods that control a bean. Indeed, this is useful even in non-bean classes for regularity. The "bean containers"—the Bean Builders, the JSP mechanism, and the EJB mechanism—all use Java introspection (see Chapter 25) to find the set/get method pairs, and some use these to construct properties editors for your bean. Bean-aware IDEs, for example, provide editors for all standard types (colors, fonts, labels, etc.). You can supplement this with a `BeanInfo` class to provide or override information.

The bare minimum a class requires to be usable as a JavaBean in a GUI Builder is the following:

- The class must implement `java.io.Serializable`.

- The class must have a no-argument constructor.

- The class should use the set/get paradigm.

- The class file should be packaged into a JAR file with the *jar* archiver program (see Recipe 23.8).

Here is a sample bean that may be a useful addition to your Java GUI toolbox, the `LabelText` widget. It combines a label and a one-line text field into a single unit, making it easier to compose GUI applications. There is a test program in the source directory that sets up three `LabelText` widgets, and is shown in Figure 23-5.

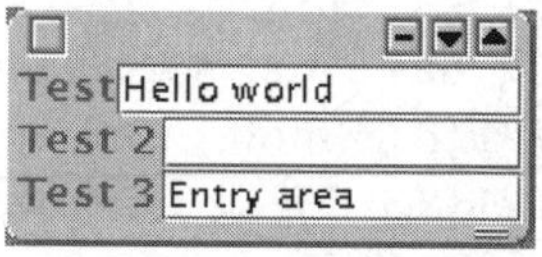

Figure 23-5. LabelText bean

The code for `LabelText` is shown in Example 23-4. Notice that it is serializable and uses the set/get paradigm for most of its public methods. Most of the public set/get methods simply delegate to the corresponding methods in the label or the text field. There isn't really a lot to this bean, but it's a good example of aggregation, as well as being a good example of a bean.

Example 23-4. LabelText.java

```java
import java.awt.*;
import java.awt.event.*;
import javax.swing.*;

/** A label and text combination, inspired by
 * the LabelText control in Guy Eddon's ActiveX Components book
 * (2nd Edition, p. 203). But done more, simply.
 *
 */
public class LabelText extends JPanel implements java.io.Serializable {
    /** The label component */
    protected JLabel theLabel;
    /** The label component */
    protected JTextField theTextField;

    /** Construct the object with no initial values.
     * To be usable as a JavaBean there MUST be a no-argument constructor.
     */
    public LabelText() {
        this("(LabelText)", 12);
    }

    /** Construct the object with the label and a default textfield size */
    public LabelText(String label) {
        this(label, 12);
    }

    /** Construct the object with given label and textfield size */
    public LabelText(String label, int numChars) {
        super();
        setLayout(new BoxLayout(this, BoxLayout.X_AXIS));
        theLabel = new JLabel(label);
        add(theLabel);
        theTextField = new JTextField(numChars);
        add(theTextField);
    }

    /** Get the label's horizontal alignment */
    public int getLabelAlignment() {
        return theLabel.getHorizontalAlignment();
    }

    /** Set the label's horizontal alignment */
    public void setLabelAlignment(int align) {
        switch (align) {
        case JLabel.LEFT:
        case JLabel.CENTER:
        case JLabel.RIGHT:
```

Example 23-4. LabelText.java (continued)

```
            theLabel.setHorizontalAlignment(align);
            break;
        default:
            throw new IllegalArgumentException(
                "setLabelAlignment argument must be one of JLabel aligners");
        }
    }

    /** Get the text displayed in the text field */
    public String getText() {
        return theTextField.getText();
    }

    /** Set the text displayed in the text field */
    public void setText(String text) {
        theTextField.setText(text);
    }

    /** Get the text displayed in the label */
    public String getLabel() {
        return theLabel.getText();
    }

    /** Set the text displayed in the label */
    public void setLabel(String text) {
        theLabel.setText(text);
    }

    /** Set the font used in both subcomponents. */
    public void setFont(Font f) {
        theLabel.setFont(f);
        theTextField.setFont(f);
    }

    /** Adds the ActionListener to receive action events from the textfield */
    public void addActionListener(ActionListener l) {
        theTextField.addActionListener(l);
    }

    /** Remove an ActionListener from the textfield. */
    public void removeActionListener(ActionListener l) {
        theTextField.removeActionListener(l);
    }
}
```

Once it's compiled, it's ready to be pickled into a JAR. JavaBeans people really talk like that!

23.8. Pickling Your Bean into a JAR

Problem

You need to package your bean for deployment.

Solution

"Pickle your bean into a JAR," that is, create a JAR archive containing it and a manifest file.

Discussion

In addition to the compiled file, you need a manifest prototype, which needs only the following entries:

```
Name: LabelText.class
Java-Bean: true
```

If these lines are stored in a file called *LabelText.stub*, we can prepare the whole mess for use as a bean by running the *jar* command (see Recipe 23.3):

```
jar cvfm labeltext.jar LabelText.stub LabelText.class
```

Now we're ready to install *labeltext.jar* as a JavaBean. However, the curious may wish to examine the JAR file in detail. The **x** option to *jar* asks it to extract files:

```
$ jar xvf *.jar
      0 Sat Nov 18 20:03:40 EST 2000 META-INF/
    106 Sat Nov 18 20:03:42 EST 2000 META-INF/MANIFEST.MF
   1829 Wed Jan 17 20:03:30 EST 2001 LabelText.class
```

The *MANIFEST.MF* file is based upon the manifest file (*LabelText.stub*); let's examine it:

```
$ more  META-INF/MANIFEST.MF
Manifest-Version: 1.0
Name: LabelText.class
Java-Bean: true
Created-By: 1.2 (Sun Microsystems Inc.)
```

Not much exciting has happened besides the addition of a few lines. But the class is now ready for use as a JavaBean. For a GUI builder, either copy it into the *beans* directory or use the bean installation wizard as appropriate.

See Also

There are many good books available on JavaBeans technology. O'Reilly's entry is *Developing JavaBeans*, by Robert Englander. You can also find information on Java-Beans at Sun's web site, *http://java.sun.com/products/javabeans/*.

23.9. Packaging a Servlet into a WAR File

Problem

You have a servlet and other web resources, and want to package them into a single file for deploying to the server.

Solution

Use *jar* to make a web archive (WAR) file.

Discussion

Servlets are server-side components for use in web servers, and are discussed in Chapter 18. They can be packaged for easy installation into a web server. A *web application* in the Servlet API specification is a collection of HTML and/or JSP pages, servlets, and other resources. A typical directory structure might include the following:

index.html, foo.jsp
> Web pages

WEB-INF
> Server directory

WEB-INF/web.xml
> Descriptor

WEB-INF/classes
> Directory for servlets and any classes used by them or by JSP

WEB-INF/lib
> Directory for any JAR files of classes needed by classes in the *WEB-INF/classes* directory

Once you have prepared the files in this way, you just package them up with *jar*:

```
jar cvf MyWebApp.war .
```

You then deploy the resulting WAR file into your web server. For details on this, consult the web server documentation.

23.10. "Write Once, Install Anywhere"

Problem

You want your application program to be installable by users who have not yet earned a Ph.D. in software installation, and on a variety of platforms.

Solution

Use an installer.

Discussion

The process of installing software is non-trivial. Unix command-line geeks will be quite happy to extract a gzipped tar file and set their PATH manually; but if you want your software to be used by the larger masses, you need something simpler. As in, point and click. There are several tools that try to automate this process. The better ones will create startup icons on MacOS, MS-Windows, and even some of the UNIX desktops (CDE, KDE, GNOME).

I've had good results with ZeroG Software's commercial InstallAnywhere. It ensures that there is a JVM installed and has both web-based and application installation modes: that is, you can install the application from a web page or you can run the installer explicitly. See *http://www.zerog.com.*

Sitraka (formerly KL Group) DeployDirector is a newer entry that promises to automate deployment of client-side applications on hundreds or thousands of desktops. It works with Java Web Start (see Recipe 23.11). I haven't tried it. See *http://www.sitraka.com/deploy/.*

InstallShield has long been the leader in the MS-Windows installation world, but they have had more competition in the Java world. They can be reached at *http:// www.installshield.com.*

Recipe 23.11 discusses Java Web Start, Sun's new web-based application installer.

23.11. Java Web Start

Problem

You have an application (not an applet) and need to distribute it electronically.

Solution

Sun's Java Web Start combines browser-based ease of use with applet-like "sandbox" security (which can be overridden on a per-application basis) and "instant update" downloading, but also lets you run a full-blown application on the user's desktop.

Discussion

Java Web Start (JWS*) is a new technology for providing application downloads over the Web. It is distinct from applets (see Chapter 17), which require special methods and run in a browser framework. JWS lets you run ordinary GUI-based applications. It is aimed at people who want the convenience of browser access combined with full application capabilities. The user experience is as follows. You see a link to an application you'd like to launch. If you've previously installed JWS (explained toward the end of this recipe), you can just click on its Launch link and be running the application in minutes. Figure 23-6 shows the startup screen that appears after clicking a Launch link for my JabaDex application.

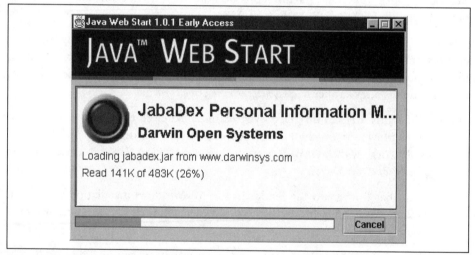

Figure 23-6. Starting JabaDex as a JWS application

After the application is downloaded successfully, it will start running. This is shown in slightly compressed form in Figure 23-7.

For your convenience, JWS caches the JAR files and other pieces needed to run the application. You can later restart the application (even when not connected to the Web) using the JWS application launcher. In Figure 23-8 I have JabaDex in my

---

* JWS used to stand for Java Web Server, which was discontinued, so the acronym has been recycled. Things recycle quickly on the Web.

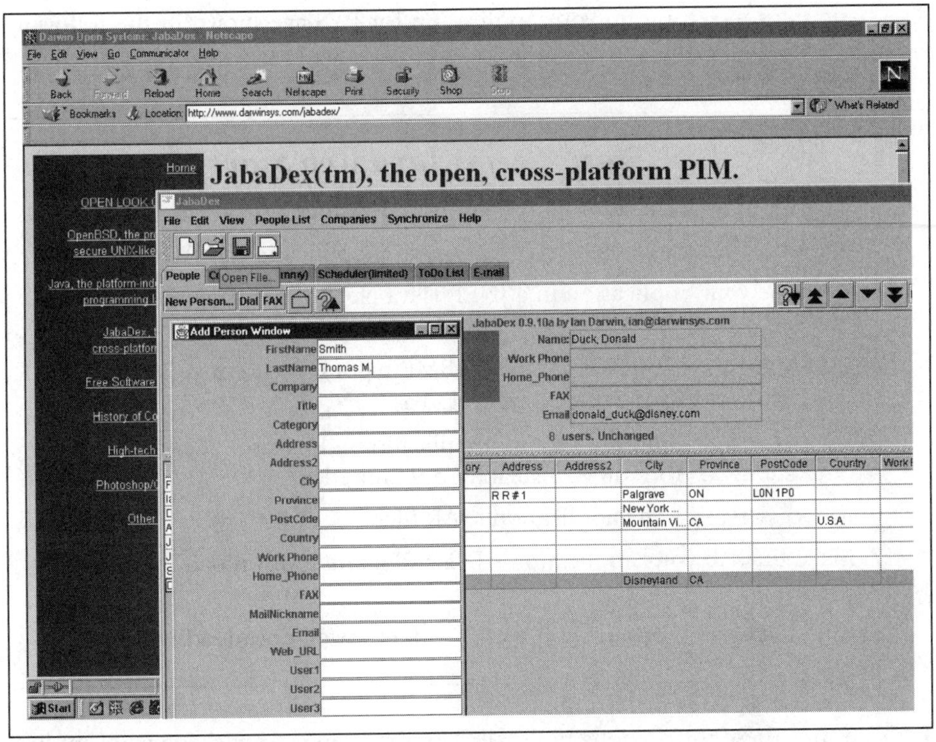

Figure 23-7. JabaDex up and running

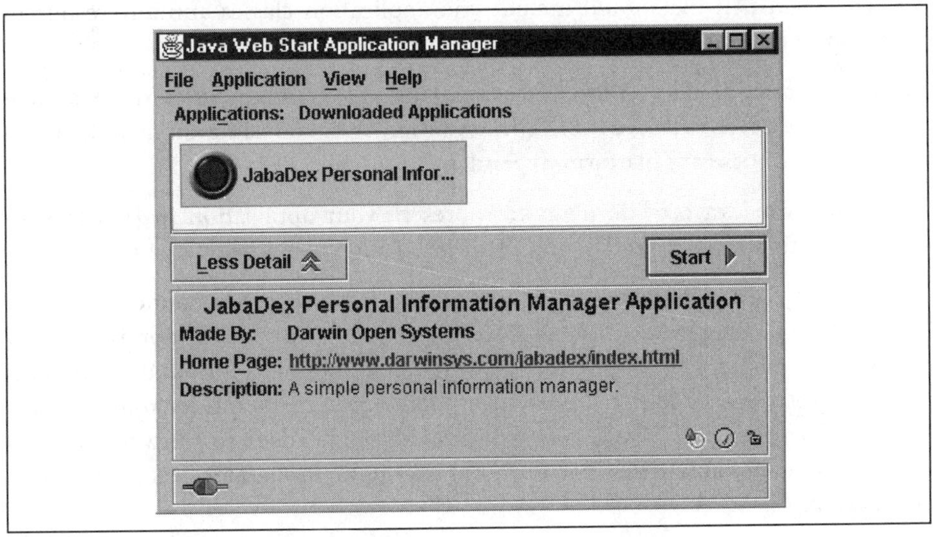

Figure 23-8. JWS application control screen

JWS launcher. JWS also allows you to create desktop shortcuts and start menu
entries on systems that support these.

The basic steps in setting up your application for JWS are shown in the following sidebar.

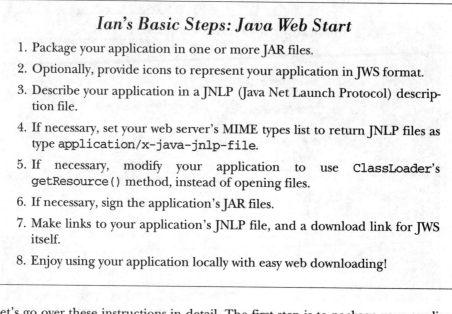

Ian's Basic Steps: Java Web Start

1. Package your application in one or more JAR files.

2. Optionally, provide icons to represent your application in JWS format.

3. Describe your application in a JNLP (Java Net Launch Protocol) description file.

4. If necessary, set your web server's MIME types list to return JNLP files as type `application/x-java-jnlp-file`.

5. If necessary, modify your application to use `ClassLoader`'s `getResource()` method, instead of opening files.

6. If necessary, sign the application's JAR files.

7. Make links to your application's JNLP file, and a download link for JWS itself.

8. Enjoy using your application locally with easy web downloading!

Let's go over these instructions in detail. The first step is to package your application in one or more JAR files. The *jar* program was described earlier in this chapter. The main JAR file should include the application classes and any resources such as properties files, images, and the like.

You should also include on the web site any JAR files containing extra APIs, such as JavaMail, `com.darwinsys.util`, or any other APIs. You can even include native code files, but these are platform-dependent.

Optionally, you can provide icons to represent your application in JWS format. The application icons should be in GIF or JPEG and should be 64×64 bits.

The next step is to describe your application in a JNLP (Java Net Launch Protocol) description file. The JNLP file is an XML file. The official specification is at *http://java.sun.com/products/javawebstart/download-spec.html* and a less formal description is in the Developer's Guide at the web site *http://java.sun.com/products/javawebstart/docs/developersguide.html.* The file I used for enabling JabaDex to run with JWS is a subset of the allowable XML elements, but should be moderately self-explanatory. See Example 23-5.

Example 23-5. JabaDex.jnlp

```
<?xml version="1.0" encoding="utf-8"?>
<!-- JNLP File for JabaDex Application -->
<jnlp spec="1.0+"
      codebase="http://www.darwinsys.com/"
      href="/jabadex/">
      <information>
         <title>JabaDex Personal Information Manager Application</title>
         <vendor>Darwin Open Systems</vendor>
         <homepage href="/"/>
         <description>JabaDex Personal Information Manager Application</description>
         <description kind="short">A simple personal information manager.</description>
         <icon href="images/jabadex.jpg"/>
         <offline-allowed/>
      </information>
      <security>
            <all-permissions/>
      </security>
      <resources>
         <j2se version="1.3"/>
         <j2se version="1.2"/>
         <jar href="jabadex.jar"/>
         <jar href="com-darwinsys-util.jar"/>
      </resources>
      <application-desc main-class="JDMain"/>
   </jnlp>
```

If necessary, set your web server's MIME types list to return JNLP files as of type
`application/x-java-jnlp-file`. How you do this depends entirely on what
web server you are running; it should be just a matter of adding an entry for the
filename extension *.jnlp* to map to this type.

Also if necessary, modify your application to get its `ClassLoader` and use one of
its `getResource()` methods, instead of opening files. Any images or other
resources that you need should be opened this way. For example, to explicitly load
a properties file, you could use `getClassLoader()` and `getResource()`, as
shown in Example 23-6.

Example 23-6. GetResourceDemo (partial listing)

```
// Find the ClassLoader that loaded us.
// Regard it as the One True Classloader for this app.
ClassLoader loader = this.getClass().getClassLoader();

// Use the loader's getResource() method to open the file.
InputStream is = loader.getResourceAsStream("widgets.properties");
if (is == null) {
    System.err.println("Can't load properties file");
```

Example 23-6. GetResourceDemo (partial listing) (continued)

```
    return;
}

// Create a Properties object
Properties p = new Properties();

// Load the properties file into the Properties object
try {
    p.load(is);
} catch (IOException ex) {
    System.err.println("Load failed: " + ex);
    return;
}
```

Notice that `getResource()` returns a `java.net.URL` object here, while `getResourceAsStream()` returns an `InputStream`.

If you want the application to have "non-sandbox" (i.e., full application) permissions, you must sign the application's JAR files. The procedure to sign a JAR file digitally is described in Recipe 23.12. If you request full permissions and don't sign all your application JAR files, the sad note shown in Figure 23-9 will display.

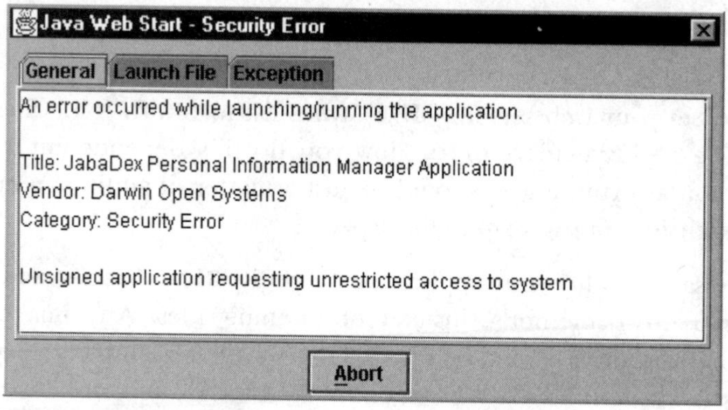

Figure 23-9. Unsigned application failure

If you self-sign (i.e., use a test certificate), the user will see a warning dialog like the one in Figure 23-10.

Finally, make links to your application's JNLP file in the web page, and optionally a download link for JWS itself. JWS is a compiled program that must be loaded before the user can download any JWS-enabled applications; it runs as a "helper application" for the browsers. As such, there is a binary program that you can

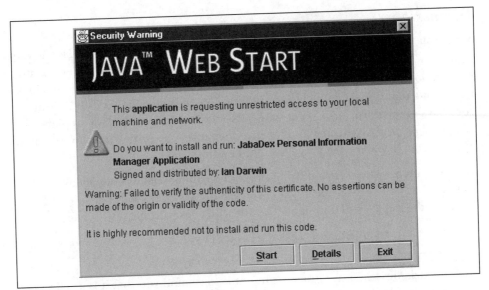

Figure 23-10. Unverifiable certificate warning

download from the JWS home page. In theory, you could write your own implementation of this helper from the *JNLP Specification*, if you needed to.

Actually, if the user has JWS installed, you don't need the download link; if they
don't, the Launch link will not function correctly. The *Developer's Guide* shows how
you can use client-side HTML scripting (JavaScript or VBScript) to make only one
of these links appear. The Launch link must refer to the JNLP file:

```
If you have JWS installed, you can <a href="jabadex.jnlp">lauchh JabaDex<</a>
If not, you should <a href="http://java.sun.com/products/javawebstart/">
read about Java Web Start</a>.
```

You should now be ready to use your application in a downloadable fashion!

See Also

The JWS home page at *http://java.sun.com/products/javawebstart/*.

23.12. Signing Your JAR File

Problem

You want to digitally sign your JAR file.

Solution

Get or forge a digital certificate, and use the `jarsigner` program.

Discussion

A JAR file can be digitally signed to verify the identity of its creator. This is very similar to digital signing of web sites: consumers are trained not to enter sensitive information such as credit card numbers into a web form unless the "padlock" icon shows that it is digitally signed. Signing JAR files uses the security API in the core Java 2 platform. You can sign JAR files for use with Java applets (see Chapter 17) or JWS (Recipe 23.11). In either case, the `jarsigner` tool is used. This program is part of the Java 2 standard edition.

You can purchase a certificate from one of the commercial signing agencies when you are ready to go live. Meanwhile, for testing, you can "self-sign" a certificate. Here are the steps needed to sign a JAR file with a test certificate:

1. Create a new key in a new "keystore" as follows:

   ```
   keytool -genkey -keystore myKeystore -alias myself
   ```

   The alias "myself" is arbitrary; its intent is to remind you that it is a self-signed key so you don't put it into production by accident.

2. The program will prompt you in the terminal window for information about the new key. It will ask for a password for protecting the keystore. Then it will ask for your name, department, organization, city, state, country, and so on. This information will go into the new keystore file on disk.

3. Create a self-signed test certificate:

   ```
   keytool -selfcert -alias myself -keystore myKeystore
   ```

   You will have to give the keystore password, and then `keytool` will generate the certificate.

4. You may want to verify that the steps up to here worked correctly. You can list the contents of the keystore:

   ```
   keytool -list -keystore myKeystore
   ```

   The output should look something like the following:

   ```
   Keystore type: jks
   Keystore provider: SUN
   Your keystore contains 1 entry:

   myself, Mon Dec 18 11:05:27 EST 2000, keyEntry,
   Certificate fingerprint (MD5): 56:9E:31:81:42:07:BF:FF:42:01:CB:42:51:42:96:
   B6
   ```

5. You can now sign the JAR file with your test certificate:

   ```
   jarsigner -keystore myKeystore test.jar myself
   ```

The `jarsigner` tool will update the META-INF directory of your JAR file to contain certificate information and digital signatures for each entry in the archive.

This can take a while, depending on the speed of your CPU, the number of entries in the archive, and so on. The end result is a signed JAR file that will be acceptable to applet-enabled browsers, Java Web Start, and any other mechanisms that require a signed JAR file.

See Also

For more information on signing and permissions, see the O'Reilly book *Java Security*. For more information on the other JDK tools mentioned here, see the documentation that accompanies the release of the JDK you are using.

24

Threaded Java

24.0. Introduction

We live in a world of multiple activities. A person may be talking on the phone while doodling or reading a memo. A FAX machine may scan one FAX while receiving another and printing a third. We expect the GUI programs we use to be able to respond to a menu while updating the screen. But ordinary computer programs can do only one thing at a time. The conventional computer programming model—that of writing one statement after another, punctuated by repetitive loops and binary decision-making—is sequential at heart.

Sequential processing is straightforward, but not as efficient as it could be. To enhance performance, Java offers threading, the capability to handle multiple flows of control within a single application or process. Java provides thread support and, in fact, requires threads: the Java runtime itself is inherently multithreaded. For example, Windows system action handling and Java's garbage collection—that miracle that lets us avoid having to free everything we allocate, as we must do when working in languages at or below C level—run in separate threads.

While most modern operating systems—POSIX P1003, Sun Solaris, the Distributed Computing Environment (OSF/DCE) for Unix, Windows NT/95, and MacOS—provide threads, Java is the first mainstream programming language to have intrinsic support for threaded operations built right into the language. The semantics of `java.lang.Object`, of which all objects are instances, includes the notion of "monitor locking" of objects, and some methods (`notify`, `notifyall`, `wait`) that are only meaningful in the context of a multithreaded application. Java also has language keywords such as `synchronized` to control the behavior of threaded applications.

So what, precisely, do we mean by threaded Java? Threads can be defined in several ways, but the easiest to understand is this: threads are multiple flows of control within a single program or process. Just as multitasking allows a single operating system to give the appearance of running more than one program at the same time on a single-processor computer, so multithreading can allow a single program or process to give the appearance of working on more than one thing at the same time. With multithreading, applications can handle more than one activity at the same time, leading to more interactive graphics and more responsive GUI applications (the program can draw in a window while responding to a menu, with both activities occurring more or less independently), more reliable network servers (if one client does something wrong, the server continues communicating with the others), and so on.

Note that I did not say "multiprocessing" in the previous paragraph. The term multi-tasking is sometimes erroneously called multiprocessing, but that term in fact refers to the less-common case of two or more CPUs running under a single operating system. Actually, multiprocessing is nothing new: IBM mainframes did it in the 1970s, Sun SPARCstations did it in the late 1980s, and Intel PCs did it in the 1990s. True multiprocessing* allows you to have more than one process running concurrently on more than one CPU. Java's support for threading will support multiprocessing under certain circumstances, if the operating system and the JVM support it as well. Consult your system documentation for details.

24.1. *Running Code in a Different Thread*

Problem

You need to write a threaded application.

Solution

Write code that implements `Runnable`; instantiate and start it.

---

*   By which I mean SMP, *symmetric multiprocessing*, in which either the operating system or the application programs can be run on any of the available CPUs. At some point, the OS may be running on three of the four processors on a given system, while at some later time all four processors may be running user processes. On systems such as Solaris 2.x, it is even possible for one (threaded) process to be running on several CPUs concurrently. The implications for server responsiveness are exciting, and this is part of Sun's commercial success in the Internet server marketplace.

Discussion

There are two ways to implement threading, and both require you to implement the Runnable interface. Runnable has only one method, whose signature is:

```
public void run();
```

You must provide an implementation of the run() method. When this method returns, the thread is used up and can never be restarted or reused. Note that there is nothing special in the compiled class file about this method; it's an ordinary method and you could call it yourself. But then what? There wouldn't be the special magic that launches it as an independent flow of control, so it wouldn't run concurrently with your main program or flow of control. For this, you need to invoke the magic of thread creation.

One way to do this is simply to subclass from java.lang.Thread (which also implements this interface; you do not need to declare redundantly that you implement it). This approach is shown in Example 24-1. Class ThreadsDemo simply prints a series of Xs and Ys; the order in which they appear is indeterminate, since there is nothing in either Java or the program to determine the order of things.

Example 24-1. ThreadsDemo1.java

```
/**
 * Threaded demo application, as a Threads subclass.
 */
public class ThreadsDemo1 extends Thread {
    String mesg;
    int count;

    /** Run does the work: print a message, "count" number of times */
    public void run() {
        while (count-- > 0) {
            println(mesg);
            try {
                Thread.sleep(100);// 100 msec
            } catch (InterruptedException e) {
                return;
            }
        }
        println(mesg + " all done.");
    }

    void println(String s) {
        System.out.println(s);
    }

    /**
     * Construct a ThreadsDemo1 object.
```

Example 24-1. ThreadsDemo1.java (continued)

```
    * @paramString mMessage to display
    * @paramint nHow many times to display it
    */
   public ThreadsDemo1(String m, int n) {
       count = n;
       mesg  = m;
       setName(m + " runner Thread");
   }


   /**
    * Main program, test driver for ThreadsDemo1 class.
    */
   public static void main(String[] argv) {
       // could say: new ThreadsDemo1("Hello from X", 10).run();
       // could say: new ThreadsDemo1("Hello from Y", 15).run();
       // But then it wouldn't be multi-threaded!
       new ThreadsDemo1("Hello from X", 10).start();
       new ThreadsDemo1("Hello from Y", 15).start();
   }
}
```

What if you can't subclass **Thread** because you're already subclassing another class, such as **JApplet**? There are two other ways to do it: have a class implement the **Runnable** interface, or use an inner class to provide the **Runnable** implementation. Example 24-2 is code that implements **Runnable**.

Example 24-2. ThreadsDemo2.java

```
public class ThreadsDemo2 implements Runnable {
    String mesg;
    Thread t;
    int count;

    /**
     * Construct a ThreadDemo object
     *
     * @paramString mMessage to display
     * @paramint nHow many times to display it
     */
    public ThreadsDemo2(String m, int n) {
        count = n;
        mesg  = m;
        t = new Thread(this);
        t.setName(m + " printer thread");
    }
```

The run method itself does not change, so I've omitted it from this listing. To complete the discussion, Example 24-3 is a version of this class that uses an inner class to provide the run method.

Example 24-3. ThreadsDemo3.java

```java
public class ThreadsDemo3 {
    String mesg;
    Thread t;
    int count;

    /**
     * Main program, test driver for ThreadsDemo3 class.
     */
    public static void main(String argv[]) {
        new ThreadsDemo3("Hello from X", 10);
        new ThreadsDemo3("Hello from Y", 15);
    }

    /**
     * Construct a ThreadDemo object
     *
     * @paramString mMessage to display
     * @paramint nHow many times to display it
     */
    public ThreadsDemo3(String m, int n) {
        count = n;
        mesg  = m;
        t = new Thread(new Runnable() {
            public void run() {
                while (count-- > 0) {
                    System.out.println(mesg);
                    try {
                        Thread.sleep(100);// 100 msec
                    } catch (InterruptedException e) {
                        return;
                    }
                }
                System.out.println(mesg + " thread all done.");
            }
        });
        t.start();
    }
}
```

Here, the run method is part of the anonymous inner class declared in the statement beginning `t = new Thread(...)`. This runs with no interaction with other classes, so it's a good use of an inner class.

To summarize, there are three ways of having a Runnable:

- Extend Thread as ThreadsDemo1 did. This works best for standalone applications that don't need to extend another class.

- Implement the Runnable interface. This works for applets that extend JApplet and cannot extend Thread, due to single inheritance.

- Construct a Thread passing an inner class that is a Runnable. This is best for tiny run methods with little outside interaction.

Thread life cycle methods

There are other methods that I should mention briefly, starting with the Thread constructors: Thread(), Thread("Thread Name"), Thread(Runnable), etc. The no-argument and name-argument constructors are used only when subclassing. But what's in a name? Well, by default, a thread's name is composed of the class name and a number such as a sequence number or the object's hashcode; on JDK 1.3 it uses sequence numbers, such as Thread-0, Thread-1, and so on. These are not very interesting when you need to look at them in a debugger, so assigning names like "Clock Ticker Thread" or "Background Save Thread" will make your life easier when (not if) you wind up having to debug your threaded application. Because of this, there are also getName()/setName(String) methods, which return or change the thread's name, respectively.

We've seen already that the start() method begins the process of assigning CPU time to a thread, resulting in its run() method being called. The corresponding stop() method is deprecated; see Recipe 24.3, where I also discuss interrupt(), which interrupts whatever the thread is doing. The method boolean isAlive() returns true if the thread has neither finished nor been terminated by a call to its stop() method. Also deprecated are suspend()/resume(), which pause and continue a thread; they are prone to corruption and deadlocking, so they should not be used. If you've created multiple threads, you can join() a thread to wait for it to finish; see Recipe 24.4.

The methods int getPriority()/void setPriority(int) show and set the priority of a thread; higher-priority threads get first chance at the CPU. Finally, wait()/notify()/notifyAll() allow you to implement classical semaphore handling, for such paradigms as producer/consumer relationships. There are a few other methods: see the Javadoc page for the Thread class.

24.2. Displaying a Moving Image with Animation

Problem

You need to update a graphical display while other parts of the program are running.

Solution

Use a background thread to drive the animation.

Discussion

One common use of threads is an *animator*, a class that displays a moving image. This program, Animator, does just that. To simplify, it uses a small drawn rectangle instead of a graphical image (see Recipe 12.6). This version is an applet, so we see it here in the AppletViewer (Figure 24-1).

Figure 24-1. Animator

Example 24-4 is the code for the Animator program.

Example 24-4. Animator.java (applet)

```
// graphics/Sprite.java
import java.applet.*;
import java.awt.*;
import java.awt.event.*;
import java.util.*;
```

Example 24-4. Animator.java (applet) (continued)

```java
/** A Sprite is one Image that moves around the screen on its own */
class Sprite extends Component implements Runnable {
    protected static int spriteNumber = 0;
    protected Thread t;
    protected int x, y;
    protected Bounce parent;
    protected Image img;
    protected boolean done = false;

    /** Construct a Sprite with a Bounce parent: construct
     * and start a Thread to drive this Sprite.
     */
    Sprite(Bounce parent, Image img) {
        super();
        this.parent = parent;
        this.img = img;
        setSize(img.getWidth(this), img.getHeight(this));
        t = new Thread(this);
        t.setName("Sprite #" + ++spriteNumber);
        t.start();
    }

    /** Stop this Sprite's thread. */
    void stop() {
        System.out.println("Stopping " + t.getName());
        done = true;
    }

    /**
     * Run one Sprite around the screen.
     * This version is very stupid, and just moves them around
     * at some 45-degree angle.
     */
    public void run() {
        int width = parent.getSize().width;
        int height = parent.getSize().height;
        // Random location
        x = (int)(Math.random() * width);
        y = (int)(Math.random() * height);
        // Flip coin for x & y directions
        int xincr = Math.random()>0.5?1:-1;
        int yincr = Math.random()>0.5?1:-1;
        while (!done) {
            width = parent.getSize().width;
            height = parent.getSize().height;
            if ((x+=xincr) >= width)
                x=0;
            if ((y+=yincr) >= height)
```

Example 24-4. Animator.java (applet) (continued)

```
                y=0;
        if (x<0)
            x = width;
        if (y<0)
            y = height;
        // System.out.println("Move " + t.getName() + " from " +
        //   getLocation() + " to " + x + "," + y);
        setLocation(x, y);
        repaint();
        try {
            Thread.sleep(250);
        } catch (InterruptedException e) {
            return;
        }
        }
    }
    }

    /** paint -- just draw our image at its current location */
    public void paint(Graphics g) {
        g.drawImage(img, 0, 0, this);
    }
}


// graphics/Bounce.java
/** This is the main class; create and start Sprites. */
public class Bounce extends Applet implements ActionListener {
    Panel p;
    Image img;
    Vector v;

    public void init() {
        Button b = new Button("Start");
        b.addActionListener(this);
        setLayout(new BorderLayout());
        add("North", b);
        add("Center", p = new Panel());
        p.setLayout(null);
        String imgName = getParameter("imagefile");
        if (imgName == null) imgName = "duke.gif";
        img = getImage(getCodeBase(), imgName);
        MediaTracker mt = new MediaTracker(this);
        mt.addImage(img, 0);
        try {
            mt.waitForID(0);
        } catch(InterruptedException e) {
            throw new IllegalArgumentException(
                "InterruptedException while loading image " + imgName);
        }
```

Example 24-4. Animator.java (applet) (continued)

```
        if (mt.isErrorID(0)) {
            throw new IllegalArgumentException(
                "Couldn't load image " + imgName);
        }
        v = new Vector();
    }

    public void actionPerformed(ActionEvent e) {
        System.out.println("Creat-ing another one!");
        Sprite s = new Sprite(this, img);
        p.add(s);
        v.addElement(s);
    }

    public void stop() {
        for (int i=0; i<v.size(); i++) {
            ((Sprite)(v.get(i))).stop();
        }
        v.clear();
    }
}
```

24.3. Stopping a Thread

Problem

You need to stop a thread.

Solution

Don't use the `Thread.stop()` method; instead, use a `boolean` tested at the top of the main loop in the `run()` method.

Discussion

While you can use the thread's `stop()` method, Sun recommends against it. That's because the method is so drastic that it can never be made to behave reliably in a program with multiple active threads. That is why, when you try to use it, the compiler will generate deprecation warnings. The recommended method is to use a `boolean` variable in the main loop of the `run()` method. The program in Example 24-5 prints a message endlessly until its `shutDown()` method is called; it then sets the controlling variable `done` to false, which terminates the loop. This causes the `run()` method to return, ending the thread. The `ThreadStoppers` program in the source directory for this chapter has a main program that instantiates and starts this class, and then calls the `shutDown()` method.

Example 24-5. StopBoolean.java

```java
public class StopBoolean extends Thread {
    protected boolean done = false;
    public void run() {
        while (!done) {
            System.out.println("StopBoolean running");
            try {
                sleep(720);
            } catch (InterruptedException ex) {
                // nothing to do
            }
        }
        System.out.println("StopBoolean finished.");
    }
    public void shutDown() {
        done = true;
    }
}
```

Running it looks like this:

```
StopBoolean running
StopBoolean running
StopBoolean running
StopBoolean running
StopBoolean running
StopBoolean running
StopBoolean running
StopBoolean finished.
```

But what if your thread is blocked reading from a network connection? You then cannot check a boolean, as the thread that is reading is asleep. This is what the stop method was designed for, but as we've seen, it is now deprecated. Instead, you can simply close the socket. The program shown in Example 24-6 intentionally deadlocks itself by reading from a socket that you are supposed to write to, simply to demonstrate that closing the socket does in fact terminate the loop.

Example 24-6. StopClose.java

```java
import java.io.*;
import java.net.*;

public class StopClose extends Thread {
    protected Socket io;

    public void run() {
        try {
            io = new Socket("localhost", 80);// HTTP
            BufferedReader is = new BufferedReader(
```

Example 24-6. StopClose.java (continued)

```
                    new InputStreamReader(io.getInputStream()));
                System.out.println("StopClose reading");

                // The following line will deadlock (intentionally), since HTTP
                // enjoins the client to send a request (like "GET / HTTP/1.0")
                // and a null line, before reading the response.

                String line = is.readLine();// DEADLOCK

                // Should only get out of the readLine if an interrupt
                // is thrown, as a result of closing the socket.

                // So we shouldn't get here, ever:
                System.out.println("StopClose FINISHED!?");
            } catch (IOException ex) {
                System.err.println("StopClose terminating: " + ex);
            }
        }

    public void shutDown() throws IOException {
        if (io != null) {
            // This is supposed to interrupt the waiting read.
            io.close();
        }
    }
}
```

When run, it prints a message that the close is happening:

```
StopClose reading
StopClose terminating: java.net.SocketException: Resource temporarily unavailable:
Resource temporarily unavailable
```

"But wait," you say. "What if I want to break the wait, but not really terminate the socket?" A good question, indeed, and there is no perfect answer. You can, however, *interrupt* the thread that is reading; the read will be interrupted by a `java.io.InterruptedIOException`, and you can retry the read. The file *Intr.java* in this chapter's source code shows this.

24.4. *Rendezvous and Timeouts*

Problem

You need to know whether something finished, or whether it finished in a certain length of time.

Solution

Start that "something" in its own thread and call its `join()` method with or without a timeout value.

Discussion

The `join()` method of the target thread is used to suspend the current thread until the target thread is finished (returns from its run method). This method is overloaded; a version with no arguments will wait forever for the thread to terminate, while a version with arguments will wait up to the specified time. For a simple example, I'll create (and start!) a simple thread that just reads from the console terminal, and the main thread will simply wait for it. When I run the program, it looks like this:

```
darwinsys.com$ java Join
Starting
Joining
Reading
hello from standard input # waits indefinitely for me to type this line
Thread Finished.
Main Finished.
darwinsys.com$
```

Example 24-7 is the code for the `join()` demo.

Example 24-7. Join.java

```java
public class Join {
    public static void main(String[] args) {
        Thread t = new Thread() {
            public void run() {
                System.out.println("Reading");
                try {
                    System.in.read();
                } catch (java.io.IOException ex) {
                    System.err.println(ex);
                }
                System.out.println("Thread Finished.");
            }
        };
        System.out.println("Starting");
        t.start();
        System.out.println("Joining");
        try {
            t.join();
        } catch (InterruptedException ex) {
            // should not happen:
            System.out.println("Who dares interrupt my sleep?");
```

Example 24-7. Join.java (continued)

```
        }
        System.out.println("Main Finished.");
    }
}
```

As you can see, it uses an inner class `Runnable` (see Recipe 24.1) in `Thread t` to be runnable.

24.5. Thread Communication: Synchronized Code

Problem

You need to protect certain data from access by multiple threads.

Solution

Use the `synchronized` keyword on the method or code you wish to protect.

Discussion

I discussed the `synchronized` keyword briefly in Recipe 16.4. This keyword specifies that only one thread at a time is allowed to run the given code. You can synchronize methods or smaller blocks of code. It is easier and safer to synchronize entire methods, but this can be more costly in terms of blocking threads that could run. Simply add the `synchronized` keyword on the method. For example, many of the methods of `Vector` (see Recipe 7.3) are synchronized.* This ensures that the vector does not become corrupted or give incorrect results when two threads update or retrieve from it at the same time.

Bear in mind that threads can be interrupted at almost any time and control given to another thread. Consider the case of two threads appending to a data structure at the same time. Let's suppose we have the same methods as `Vector`, but we're operating on a simple array. The `add()` method simply uses the current number of objects as an array index, then increments it:

```
1 public void add(Object obj) {
2    data[max] = obj;
3    max = max + 1;
4 }
```

---

* The corresponding methods of `ArrayList` are not synchronized; this makes nonthreaded use of an `ArrayList` about 20 to 30 percent faster (see Recipe 7.17).

Threads A and B both wish to call this method. Now suppose that Thread A gets interrupted after line 2 but before line 3, and then Thread B gets to run. Thread B does line 2, overwriting the contents of data[max]; we've now lost all reference to the object that Thread A passed in! Thread B then increments max in line 3, and returns. Later, Thread A gets to run again; it resumes at line 3 and increments max past the last valid object. So not only have we lost an object, but we have an un-initialized reference in the array. This state of affairs is shown in Figure 24-2.

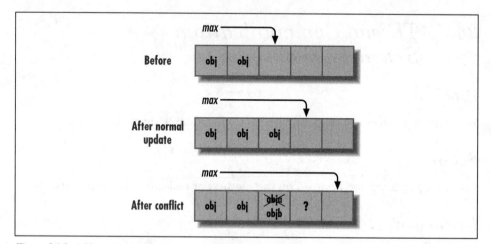

Figure 24-2. Add method in operation: normal and failed updates

Now you might think, "No problem, I'll just combine lines 2 and 3":

```
data[max++] = obj;
```

As the talk show host sometimes says, "Bzzzzt! Thanks for playing!" This change makes the code a bit shorter, but has absolutely no effect on reliability. Interrupts don't happen conveniently on Java statement boundaries; they can happen between any of the many JVM machine instructions that correspond to your program. The code can still be interrupted after the store and before the increment. The only good solution is to use Java synchronization.

Making the method synchronized means that any invocations of it will wait if one thread has already started running the method:

```
public synchronized void add(Object obj) {
    ...
}
```

Anytime you wish to synchronize some code, but not an entire method, use the synchronized keyword on an un-named code block within a method, as in:

```
synchronized (someObject) {
    // this code will execute in one thread at a time
}
```

The choice of object is up to you. Sometimes it makes sense to synchronize on the object containing the code, as in Example 24-8. For synchronizing access to an `ArrayList`, it would make sense to use the `ArrayList` instance, as in:

```
synchronized(myArrayList) {
    if (myArrayList.indexof(someObject) != -1) {
        // do something with it.
    }
    // else create an object and add it... }
```

Example 24-8 is a servlet (see Recipe 18.1) that I wrote for use in the classroom, following a suggestion from Scott Weingust (*scottw@sysoft.ca*). It lets you play a quiz show game of the style where the host asks a question and the first person to press their buzzer (buzz in) gets to try to answer the question correctly. To ensure against having two people buzz in simultaneously, the code uses a synchronized block around the code that updates the boolean buzzed variable. And for reliability, any code that accesses this boolean is also synchronized.

Example 24-8. BuzzInServlet.java

```
import javax.servlet.*;
import javax.servlet.http.*;
import java.io.*;

/** A quiz-show "buzzer" servlet: the first respondent wins the chance
 * to answer the skill-testing question. Correct operation depends on
 * running in a Servlet container that CORRECTLY implements the Servlet
 * spec, that is, a SINGLE INSTANCE of this servlet class exists, and it
 * is run in a thread pool. This class does not implement "SingleThreadModel"
 * so a correct Servlet implementation will use a single instance.
 * <p>
 * If you needed to work differently, you could synchronize on an object
 * stored in the Servlet Application Context, at a slight increased cost
 * in terms of system overhead.
 */
public class BuzzInServlet extends HttpServlet {

    /** This controls the access */
    protected static boolean buzzed = false;
    /** who got the buzz? */
    protected static String winner;

    /** doGet is called from the contestants web page.
     * Uses a synchronized code block to ensure that
     * only one contestant can change the state of "buzzed".
     */
    public void doGet(HttpServletRequest request, HttpServletResponse response)
    throws ServletException, IOException
    {
        boolean igotit = false;
```

Example 24-8. BuzzInServlet.java (continued)

```java
        // Do the synchronized stuff first, and all in one place.
        synchronized(this) {
            if (!buzzed) {
                igotit = buzzed = true;
                winner = request.getRemoteHost() + '/' + request.getRemoteAddr();
            }
        }


        response.setContentType("text/html");
        PrintWriter out = response.getWriter();

        out.println("<html><head><title>Thanks for playing</title></head>");
        out.println("<body bgcolor=\"white\">");

        if (igotit) {
            out.println("<b>YOU GOT IT</b>");
            getServletContext().log("BuzzInServlet: WINNER " +
                request.getRemoteUser());
            // TODO - output HTML to play a sound file :-)
        } else {
            out.println("Thanks for playing, " + request.getRemoteAddr());
            out.println(", but " + winner + " buzzed in first");
        }
        out.println("</body></html>");
    }

    /** The Post method is used from an Administrator page (which should
     * only be installed in the instructor/host's localweb directory).
     * Post is used for administrative functions:
     * 1) to display the winner;
     * 2) to reset the buzzer for the next question.
     * <p>
     * In real life the password would come from a Servlet Parameter
     * or a configuration file, instead of being hardcoded in an "if".
     */
    public void doPost(HttpServletRequest request, HttpServletResponse response)
    throws ServletException, IOException
    {
        response.setContentType("text/html");
        PrintWriter out = response.getWriter();

        if (request.getParameter("password").equals("syzzy")) {
            out.println("<html><head><title>Welcome back, host</title><head>");
            out.println("<body bgcolor=\"white\">");
            String command = request.getParameter("command");
            if (command.equals("reset")) {
                // Synchronize what you need, no more, no less.
                synchronized(this) {
                    buzzed = false;
```

Example 24-8. BuzzInServlet.java (continued)

```
                winner = null;
            }
            out.println("RESET");
        } else if (command.equals("show")) {
            synchronized(this) {
                out.println("<b>Winner is: </b>" + winner);
            }
        }
        else {
            out.println("<html><head><title>ERROR</title><head>");
            out.println("<body bgcolor=\"white\">");
            out.println("ERROR: Command " + command + " invalid.");
        }
    } else {
        out.println("<html><head><title>Nice try, but... </title><head>");
        out.println("<body bgcolor=\"white\">");
        out.println(
            "Your paltry attempts to breach security are rebuffed!");
    }
    out.println("</body></html>");
    }
}
```

There are two HTML pages that lead to the servlet. The contestant's page simply has a large link (`<a href=/servlet/BuzzInServlet>`). Anchor links generate an HTML GET, so the servlet engine calls `doGet()`.

```
<html><head><title>Buzz In!</title></head>
<body>
<h1>Buzz In!</h1>
<p>
<font size=+6>
<a href="servlet/BuzzInServlet">
Press here to buzz in!
</a>
</font>
```

The HTML is pretty plain, but it does the job. Figure 24-3 shows the look and feel.

The game show host has access to an HTML form with a POST method, which calls the `doPost()` method. This displays the winner to the game show host, and also resets the "buzzer" for the next question. A password is provided; it's hardcoded here, but in reality the password would come from a properties file (Recipe 7.7) or a servlet initialization parameter (see the *Java Servlet Programming* book).

```
<html><head><title>Reset Buzzer</title></head>
<body>
<h1>Display Winner</h1>
```

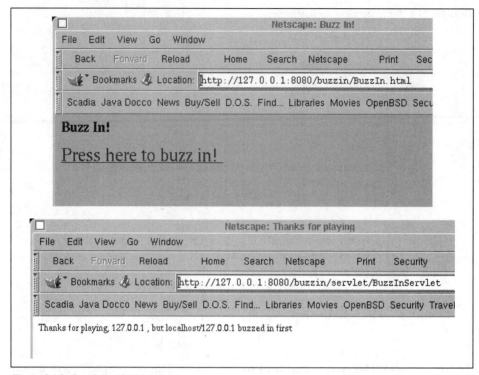

Figure 24-3. BuzzInServlet in action

```
<p>
<b>The winner is:
<form method="post" action="servlet/BuzzInServlet">
    <input type="hidden" name="command" value="show">
    <input type="hidden" name="password" value="syzzy">
    <input type="submit" name="Show" value="Show">
</form>
<h1>Reset Buzzer</h1>
<p>
<b>Remember to RESET before you ask the contestants each question!</b>
<form method="post" action="servlet/BuzzInServlet">
    <input type="hidden" name="command" value="reset">
    <input type="hidden" name="password" value="syzzy">
    <input type="submit" name="Reset" value="RESET!">
</form>
```

The game show host functionality is shown in Figure 24-4.

For a more complete game, of course, the servlet would keep a `Stack` (Recipe 7.15) of people in the order they buzzed in, in case the first person doesn't answer the question correctly. Access to this would have to be synchronized too, of course.

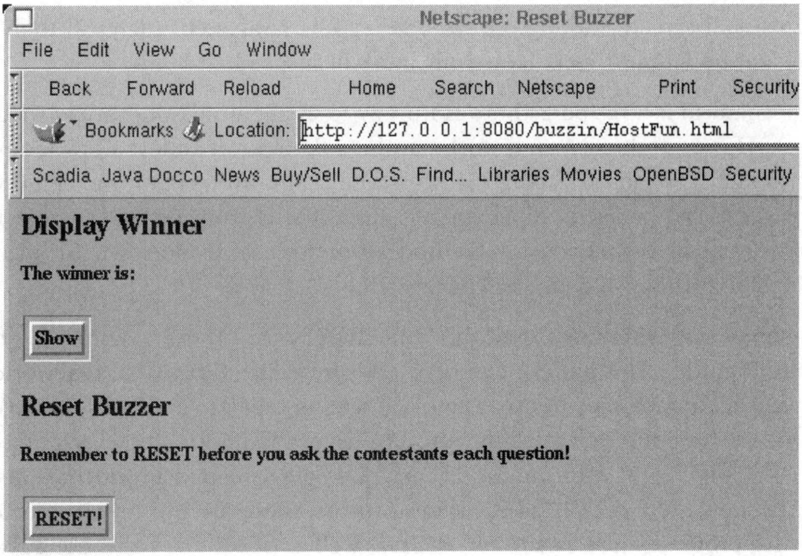

Figure 24-4. BuzzInServlet game show host function

24.6. Thread Communication: wait() and notifyAll()

Problem

The `synchronized` keyword lets you lock out multiple threads, but doesn't give you much communication between them.

Solution

Use `wait()` and `notifyAll()`. Very carefully.

Discussion

Three methods appear in `java.lang.Object` that allow you to use any object as a synchronization target: `wait()`, `notify()`, and `notifyAll()`.

`wait()`

> Causes the current thread to block in the given object until awakened by a `notify()` or `notifyAll()`.

`notify()`

> Causes a randomly selected thread waiting on this object to be awakened. It must then try to regain the monitor lock. If the "wrong" thread is awakened, your program can deadlock.

`notifyAll()`

Causes all threads waiting on the object to be awakened; each will then try to regain the monitor lock. Hopefully one will succeed.

The mechanism is a bit odd: there is no way to awaken only the thread that owns the lock. However, that's how it works, and it's the reason almost all programs use `notifyAll()` instead of `notify()`. Also note that both `wait()` and the notification methods can be used only if you are already synchronized on the object; that is, you must be in a synchronized method within, or a code block synchronized on, the object that you wish your current thread to `wait()` or `notify()` upon.

For a simple introduction to `wait()` and `notify()`, I'll use a simple Producer-Consumer model. This pattern can be used to simulate a variety of real-world situations in which one object is creating or allocating objects (producing them), usually with a random delay, while another is grabbing the objects and doing something with them (consuming them). A single-threaded Producer-Consumer model is shown in Example 24-9. As you can see, there are no threads created, so the entire program—the `read()` in main as well as `produce()` and `consume()`— runs in the same thread. You control the production and consumption by entering a line consisting of letters. Each p causes one unit to be produced, while each c causes one unit to be consumed. So if I run it and type pcpcpcpc, the program will alternate between producing and consuming. If I type pppccc, the program will produce three units and then consume them. See Example 24-9.

Example 24-9. ProdCons1.java

```java
public class ProdCons1 {

    /** Throughout the code, this is the object we synchronize on so this
     * is also the object we wait() and notifyAll() on.
     */
    protected LinkedList list = new LinkedList();

    protected void produce() {
        int len = 0;
        synchronized(list) {
            Object justProduced = new Object();
            list.addFirst(justProduced);
            len = list.size();
            list.notifyAll();
        }
        System.out.println("List size now " + len);
    }

    protected void consume() {
        Object obj = null;
        int len = 0;
        synchronized(list) {
```

Example 24-9. ProdCons1.java (continued)

```
            while (list.size() == 0) {
                try {
                    list.wait();
                } catch (InterruptedException ex) {
                    return;
                }
            }
            obj = list.removeLast();
            len = list.size();
        }
        System.out.println("Consuming object " + obj);
        System.out.println("List size now " + len);
    }

    public static void main(String[] args) throws IOException {
        ProdCons1 pc = new ProdCons1();
        int i;
        while ((i = System.in.read()) != -1) {
            char ch = (char)i;
            switch(ch) {
                case 'p':pc.produce(); break;
                case 'c':pc.consume(); break;
            }
        }
    }
}
```

The part that may seem strange is using `list` instead of the main class as the synchronization target. Each object has its own wait queue, so it does matter which object you use. In theory, any object can be used as long as your `synchronized` target and the object in which you run `wait()` and `notify()` are one and the same object. Of course, it is good to refer to the object that you are protecting from concurrent updates, so I used `list` here.

Hopefully, you're now wondering what this has to do with thread synchronization. There is only one thread, but the program *seems* to work:

```
> jikes +E -d . ProdCons1.java
> java ProdCons1
pppccc
List size now 1
List size now 2
List size now 3
Consuming object java.lang.Object@d9e6a356
List size now 2
Consuming object java.lang.Object@d9bea356
List size now 1
Consuming object java.lang.Object@d882a356
List size now 0
```

But this program is not quite right. If I enter even one more c's than p's, think about what happens. The `consume()` method does a `wait()`, but it is no longer possible for the `read()` to proceed. The program, we say, is *deadlocked*: it is waiting on something that can never happen. Fortunately, this simple case is detected by the Java runtime:

```
ppccc
List size now 1
List size now 2
Consuming object java.lang.Object@18faf0
List size now 1
Consuming object java.lang.Object@15bc20
List size now 0
Dumping live threads:
 'gc' tid 0x1a0010, status SUSPENDED flags DONTSTOP
  blocked@0x19c510 (0x1a0010->|)
 'finaliser' tid 0x1ab010, status SUSPENDED flags DONTSTOP
  blocked@0x10e480 (0x1ab010->|)
 'main' tid 0xe4050, status SUSPENDED flags NOSTACKALLOC
  blocked@0x13ba20 (0xe4050->|)
Deadlock: all threads blocked on internal events
Abort (core dumped)
```

Indeed, the `read()` is never executed, because there's no way for `produce()` to get called and so the `notify()` can't happen. To fix this, I want to run the producer and the consumer in separate threads. There are several ways to accomplish this. I'll just make `consume()` and `produce()` into inner classes `Consume` and `Produce` that extend `Thread`, and their `run()` method will do the work of the previous methods. In the process, I'll replace the code that reads from the console with code that causes both threads to loop for a certain number of seconds, and change it to be a bit more of a simulation of a distributed Producer-Consumer mechanism. The result of all this is the second version, `ProdCons2`, shown in Example 24-10.

Example 24-10. ProdCons2.java

```java
import java.util.*;
import java.io.*;

public class ProdCons2 {

    /** Throughout the code, this is the object we synchronize on so this
     * is also the object we wait() and notifyAll() on.
     */
    protected LinkedList list = new LinkedList();
    protected int MAX = 10;
    protected boolean done = false; // Also protected by lock on list.
```

Example 24-10. ProdCons2.java (continued)

```
/** Inner class representing the Producer side */
class Producer extends Thread {

    public void run() {
        while (true) {
            Object justProduced = getRequestFromNetwork();
            // Get request from the network - outside the synch section.
            // We're simulating this actually reading from a client, and it
            // might have to wait for hours if the client is having coffee.
            synchronized(list) {
                    while (list.size() == MAX) // queue "full"
                    try {
                        System.out.println("Producer WAITING");
                        list.wait(); // Limit the size
                    } catch (InterruptedException ex) {
                        System.out.println("Producer INTERRUPTED");
                    }
                list.addFirst(justProduced);
                if (done)
                    break;
                list.notifyAll();// must own the lock
                System.out.println("Produced 1; List size now " + list.size());
                // yield();
            }
        }
    }

    Object getRequestFromNetwork() {// Simulation of reading from client
        // try {
        //   Thread.sleep(10); // simulate time passing during read
        // } catch (InterruptedException ex) {
        //   System.out.println("Producer Read INTERRUPTED");
        // }
        return(new Object());
    }
}

/** Inner class representing the Consumer side */
class Consumer extends Thread {
    public void run() {
        while (true) {
            Object obj = null;
            int len = 0;
            synchronized(list) {
                while (list.size() == 0) {
                    try {
                        System.out.println("CONSUMER WAITING");
                        list.wait();// must own the lock
```

Example 24-10. ProdCons2.java (continued)

```java
                            } catch (InterruptedException ex) {
                                System.out.println("CONSUMER INTERRUPTED");
                            }
                        }
                        if (done)
                            break;
                        obj = list.removeLast();
                        list.notifyAll();
                        len = list.size();
                        System.out.println("List size now " + len);
                    }
                    process(obj);// Outside synch section (could take time)
                    //yield();
                }
            }

            void process(Object obj) {
                // Thread.sleep(xxx) // Simulate time passing
                System.out.println("Consuming object " + obj);
            }
        }

        ProdCons2(int nP, int nC) {
            for (int i=0; i<nP; i++)
                new Producer().start();
            for (int i=0; i<nC; i++)
                new Consumer().start();
        }

        public static void main(String[] args)
        throws IOException, InterruptedException {

            // Start producers and consumers
            int numProducers = 2;
            int numConsumers = 2;
            ProdCons2 pc = new ProdCons2(numProducers, numConsumers);

            // Let it run for, say, 30 seconds
            Thread.sleep(30*1000);

            // End of simulation - shut down gracefully
            synchronized(pc.list) {
                pc.done = true;
                pc.list.notifyAll(); // Wake up any waiters!
            }
        }
    }
```

I'm happy to report that all is well with this. It will happily run for long periods of time, neither crashing nor deadlocking. After running for some time, I captured this tiny bit of the log:

```
Produced 1; List size now 118
Consuming object java.lang.Object@2119d0
List size now 117
Consuming object java.lang.Object@2119e0
List size now 116
```

By varying the number of producers and consumers started in the constructor method, you can observe different queue sizes that all seem to work correctly.

24.7. Background Saving in an Editor

Problem

You need to save the user's work periodically in an interactive program.

Solution

Use a background thread.

Discussion

This code fragment creates a new thread to handle background saves, as in most word processors:

```java
public class AutoSave extends Thread {
    FileSaver model;

    public AutoSave(FileSaver m) {
        super("AutoSave Thread");
        // setDaemon(true);// so we don't keep the main app alive
        model = m;
    }

    public void run() {
        while (true) {// entire run method runs forever.
            try {
                sleep(300*1000);
            } catch (InterruptedException e) {
                // do nothing with it
            }
            if (model.wantAutoSave() && model.hasUnsavedChanges())
                model.saveFile(null);
        }
    }
```

As you can see in the `run()` method, this code sleeps for five minutes (300 seconds), then checks if it should do anything. If the user has turned autosave off or hasn't made any changes since the last save, there is nothing to do. Otherwise, we call the `saveFile()` method in the main program, which saves the data to the current file. Better would be to save it to a recovery file of some name, as the better word processors do.

What's not shown is that now the `saveFile()` method must be synchronized, and what's more, whatever method shuts down the main program must also be synchronized on the same object. It's easy to see why if you think about how the save method would work if the user clicked on the Save button at the same time that the autosave method called it, or if the user clicked on Exit while the file save method had just opened the file for writing. The "save to recovery file" strategy gets around some of this, but it still needs a great deal of care.

24.8. Threaded Network Server

Problem

You want a network server to be multithreaded.

Solution

Either create a thread when you accept a connection, or pre-create a pool of threads and have each wait on the `accept()` call.

Discussion

Networking (see Chapters 15 through 17) and threads are two very powerful APIs that are a standard part of the Java platform. Used alone, each can increase the reach of your Java programming skills. A common paradigm is a threaded network server, which can either preallocate a certain number of threads, or can start a new thread each time a client connects. The big advantage is that each thread can block on read, without causing other client threads to delay.

One example of a threaded socket server was discussed in Recipe 16.4; another is shown here. It seems to be some kind of rite (or wrong) of passage for Java folk to write a web server entirely in Java. This one is fairly small and simple; if you want a full-bodied flavor, check out the Apache Foundation's Apache (written in C) and Tomcat (pure Java) servers, or the World Wide Web Consortium's `jigsaw` server. The main program of mine constructs one instance of class `Httpd`. This creates a socket and waits for incoming clients in the `accept()` method. Each time there is a return from `accept()`, we have another client, so we create a new thread to process that client. This happens in the `main()` and `runserver()` methods, which are near the beginning of Example 24-11.

Example 24-11. Httpd.java

```java
/**
 * A very very simple Web server.
 *
 * NO SECURITY. ALMOST NO CONFIGURATION. NO CGI. NO SERVLETS.
 *
 * This version is threaded. I/O is done in Handler.
 */
public class Httpd {
    /** The default port number */
    public static final int HTTP = 80;
    /** The server socket used to connect from clients */
    protected ServerSocket sock;
    /** A Properties, for loading configuration info */
    protected Properties wsp;
    /** A Properties, for loading mime types into */
    protected Properties mimeTypes;
    /** The root directory */
    protected String rootDir;

    public static void main(String argv[]) {
        System.out.println("DarwinSys JavaWeb Server 0.1 starting...");
        Httpd w = new Httpd();
        if (argv.length == 2 && argv[0].equals("-p")) {
            w.startServer(Integer.parseInt(argv[1]));
        } else {
            w.startServer(HTTP);
        }

        w.runServer();
        // NOTREACHED
    }

    /** Run the main loop of the Server. Each time a client connects,
     * the ServerSocket accept() returns a new Socket for I/O, and
     * we pass that to the Handler constructor, which creates a Thread,
     * which we start.
     */
    void runServer() {
        while (true) {
            try {
                Socket clntSock = sock.accept();
                new Handler(this, clntSock).start();
            } catch(IOException e) {
                System.err.println(e);
```

Example 24-11. Httpd.java (continued)

```java
                    }
            }
    }


    /** Construct a server object for a given port number */
    Httpd() {
        super();
        // A ResourceBundle can't load from the same basename as your class,
        // but a simple Properties can.
        wsp=loadProps("httpd.properties");
        rootDir = wsp.getProperty("rootDir", ".");
        mimeTypes = loadProps(wsp.getProperty("mimeProperties", "mime.properties"));
    }


    public void startServer(int portNum) {
        String portNumString = null;
        if (portNum == HTTP) {
            portNumString = wsp.getProperty("portNum");
            if (portNumString != null) {
                portNum = Integer.parseInt(portNumString);
            }
        }
        try {
            sock = new ServerSocket(portNum);
        } catch(NumberFormatException e) {
            System.err.println("Httpd: \"" + portNumString +
                "\" not a valid number, unable to start server");
            System.exit(1);
        } catch(IOException e) {
            System.err.println("Network error " + e);
            System.err.println("Unable to start server");
            System.exit(1);
        }
    }


    /** Load the Properties. */
    protected Properties loadProps(String fname) {
        Properties sp = new Properties();

        try {
            // Create input file to load from.
            FileInputStream ifile = new FileInputStream(fname);

            sp.load(ifile);
        } catch (FileNotFoundException notFound) {
            System.err.println(notFound);
            System.exit(1);
        } catch (IOException badLoad) {
```

Example 24-11. Httpd.java (continued)

```
            System.err.println(badLoad);
            System.exit(1);
        }
        return sp;
    }


}
```

The `Handler` class—shown in its current form in Example 24-12—is the part that knows the HTTP protocol, or at least a small subset of it. You may notice near the middle that it parses the incoming HTTP headers into a `Hashmap`, but does nothing with them. Here is a log of one connection:

```
Connection accepted from localhost/127.0.0.1
Request: Command GET, file /, version HTTP/1.0
hdr(Connection,Keep-Alive)
hdr(User-Agent,Mozilla/4.6 [en] (X11; U; OpenBSD 2.8 i386; Nav))
hdr(Pragma,no-cache)
hdr(Host,127.0.0.1)
hdr(Accept,image/gif, image/jpeg, image/pjpeg, image/png, */*)
hdr(Accept-Encoding,gzip)
hdr(Accept-Language,en)
hdr(Accept-Charset,iso-8859-1,*,utf-8)
Loading file //index.html
END OF REQUEST
```

At this stage of evolution, the server is getting ready to create an `HttpServletRequest` object (described in Recipe 18.1's discussion of servlets), but it is not sufficiently evolved to do so. This file is a snapshot of work in progress. More interesting is the `Hashtable` used as a cache; once a file has been read from disk, the program will not reread it, to save disk I/O overhead. This means you have to restart the server if you change files; comparing the timestamps (see Recipe 10.1) and reloading files if they have changed is left as an exercise for the reader.

Example 24-12. Handler.java

```java
import java.io.*;
import java.net.*;
import java.text.*;
import java.util.*;

/** Called from Httpd to handle one connection.
 * We are created with just a Socket, and read the
 * HTTP request, extract a name, read it (saving it
 * in Hashtable h for next time), and write it back.
 */
```

Example 24-12. Handler.java (continued)

```java
public class Handler extends Thread {
    /** The Socket that we read from and write to. */
    Socket clntSock;
    /** inputStream, from Viewer */
    BufferedReader is;
    /** outputStream, to Viewer */
    PrintStream os;
    /** Main program */
    Httpd parent;
    /** The default filename in a directory. */
    final static String DEF_NAME = "/index.html";

    /** The Hashtable used to cache all URLs we've read.
     * Static, shared by all instances of Handler (one per request).
     */
    static Hashtable h = new Hashtable();

    /** Construct a Handler */
    Handler(Httpd prnt, Socket sock) {
        super("client thread");
        parent = prnt;
        clntSock = sock;
        // First time, put in null handler.
        if (h.size() == 0) {
            h.put("", "<HTML><BODY><B>Unknown server error");
        }
    }

    protected static final int RQ_INVALID = 0, RQ_GET = 1, RQ_HEAD = 2,
        RQ_POST = 3;

    public void run() {
        String request;// what Viewer sends us.
        int methodType = RQ_INVALID;
        try {
            System.out.println("Connection accepted from " +
                clntSock.getInetAddress());
            is = new BufferedReader(new InputStreamReader(
                clntSock.getInputStream()));
            // Must do before any chance of errorResponse being called!
            os = new PrintStream(clntSock.getOutputStream());

            request = is.readLine();
            if (request == null || request.length() == 0) {
                // No point nattering: the sock died, nobody will hear
                // us if we scream into cyberspace... Could log it though.
                return;
            }
```

Example 24-12. Handler.java (continued)

```java
        // Use a StringTokenizer to break the request into its three parts:
        // HTTP method, resource name, and HTTP version
        StringTokenizer st = new StringTokenizer(request);
        if (st.countTokens() != 3) {
            errorResponse(444, "Unparseable input " + request);
            return;
        }
        String rqCode = st.nextToken();
        String rqName = st.nextToken();
        String rqHttpVer = st.nextToken();
        System.out.println("Request: Command " + rqCode +
                ", file " + rqName + ", version " + rqHttpVer);


        // Read headers, up to the null line before the body,
        // so the body can be read directly if it's a POST.
        HashMap map = new HashMap();
        String hdrLine;
        while ((hdrLine = is.readLine()) != null &&
                hdrLine.length() != 0) {
            int ix;
            if ((ix=hdrLine.indexOf(':')) != -1) {
                String hdrName = hdrLine.substring(0, ix);
                String hdrValue = hdrLine.substring(ix+1).trim();
                System.out.println("hdr("+hdrName+","+hdrValue+")");
                map.put(hdrName, hdrValue);
            } else {
                System.err.println("INVALID HEADER: " + hdrLine);
            }
        }

        // check that rqCode is either GET or HEAD or ...
        if ("get".equalsIgnoreCase(rqCode))
            methodType = RQ_GET;
        else if ("head".equalsIgnoreCase(rqCode))
            methodType = RQ_HEAD;
        else if ("post".equalsIgnoreCase(rqCode))
            methodType = RQ_POST;
        else {
            errorResponse(400, "invalid method: " + rqCode);
            return;
        }

        // A bit of paranoia may be a good thing...
        if (rqName.indexOf("..") != -1) {
            errorResponse(404, "can't seem to find: " + rqName);
            return;
        }
```

Example 24-12. Handler.java (continued)

```
                // Someday: new MyRequest(clntSock, rqName, methodType);
                // new MyResponse(clntSock, os);

                // if (isServlet(rqName)) [
                //      doServlet(rqName, methodType, map);
                // else
                    doFile(rqName, methodType == RQ_HEAD, os /*, map */);
                os.flush();
                clntSock.close();
        } catch (IOException e) {
            System.out.println("IOException " + e);
        }
        System.out.println("END OF REQUEST");
    }


    /** Processes one file request */
    void doFile(String rqName, boolean headerOnly, PrintStream os)
    throws IOException {
        File f;
        byte[] content = null;
        Object o = h.get(rqName);
        if (o != null && o instanceof byte[]) {
            content = (byte[])o;
            System.out.println("Using cached file " + rqName);
            sendFile(rqName, headerOnly, content, os);
        } else if ((f = new File(parent.rootDir + rqName)).isDirectory()) {
            // Directory with index.html? Process it.
            File index = new File(f, DEF_NAME);
            if (index.isFile()) {
                doFile(rqName + DEF_NAME, index, headerOnly, os);
                return;
            }
            else {
                // Directory? Do not cache; always make up dir list.
                System.out.println("DIRECTORY FOUND");
                doDirList(rqName, f, headerOnly, os);
                sendEnd();
            }
        } else if (f.canRead()) {
            // REGULAR FILE
            doFile(rqName, f, headerOnly, os);
        }
        else {
            errorResponse(404, "File not found");
        }
    }

    void doDirList(String rqName, File dir, boolean justAHead, PrintStream os) {
```

Example 24-12. Handler.java (continued)

```
        os.println("HTTP/1.0 200 directory found");
        os.println("Content-type: text/html");
        os.println("Date: " + new Date().toString());
        os.println("");
        if (justAHead)
            return;
        os.println("<HTML>");
        os.println("<TITLE>Contents of directory " + rqName + "</TITLE>");
        os.println("<H1>Contents of directory " + rqName + "</H1>");
        String fl[] = dir.list();
        Arrays.sort(fl);
        for (int i=0; i<fl.length; i++)
            os.println("<BR><A HREF=\"" + fl[i] + "\">" +
            "<IMG ALIGN=absbottom BORDER=0 SRC=\"internal-gopher-unknown\">" +
            ' ' + fl[i] + "</A>");
    }


    /** Send one file, given a File object. */
    void doFile(String rqName, File f, boolean headerOnly, PrintStream os)
    throws IOException {
        System.out.println("Loading file " + rqName);
        InputStream in = new FileInputStream(f);
        byte c_content[] = new byte[(int)f.length()];
        // Single large read, should be fast.
        int n = in.read(c_content);
        h.put(rqName, c_content);
        sendFile(rqName, headerOnly, c_content, os);
        in.close();
    }


    /** Send one file, given the filename and contents.
     * boolean justHead - if true, send heading and return.
     */
    void sendFile(String fname, boolean justHead,
        byte[] content, PrintStream os) throws IOException {
        os.println("HTTP/1.0 200 Here's your file");
        os.println("Content-type: " + guessMime(fname));
        os.println("Content-length: " + content.length);
        os.println("");
        if (justHead)
            return;
        os.write(content);
    }


    /** The type for unguessable files */
    final static String UNKNOWN = "unknown/unknown";
    String guessMime(String fn) {
        String lcname = fn.toLowerCase();
```

Example 24-12. Handler.java (continued)

```
        int extenStartsAt = lcname.lastIndexOf('.');
        if (extenStartsAt<0) {
            if (fn.equalsIgnoreCase("makefile"))
                return "text/plain";
            return UNKNOWN;
        }
        String exten = lcname.substring(extenStartsAt);
        String guess = parent.mimeTypes.getProperty(exten, UNKNOWN);

        // System.out.println("guessMime: input " + fn +
        //   ", extention " + exten + ", result " + guess);

        return guess;
    }

    /** Sends an error response, by number, hopefully localized. */
    protected void errorResponse(int errNum, String errMsg) {

        // Check for localized messages
        ResourceBundle messages = ResourceBundle.getBundle("errors");

        String response;
        try { response = messages.getString(Integer.toString(errNum)); }
        catch (MissingResourceException e) { response=errMsg; }

        // Generate and send the response
        os.println("HTTP/1.0 " + errNum + " " + response);
        os.println("Content-type: text/html");
        os.println("");
        os.println("<HTML>");
        os.println("<HEAD><TITLE>Error " + errNum + "--" + response +
            "</TITLE></HEAD>");
        os.println("<H1>" + errNum + " " + response + "</H1>");
        sendEnd();
    }

    /** Send the tail end of any page we make up. */
    protected void sendEnd() {
        os.println("<HR>");
        os.println("<ADDRESS>Java Web Server,");
        String myAddr = "http://www.darwinsys.com/freeware/";
        os.println("<A HREF=\"" + myAddr + "\">" +
            myAddr + "</A>");
        os.println("</ADDRESS>");
        os.println("</HTML>");
        os.println("");
    }
}
```

From a performance point of view, it may be better to pre-create a pool of threads and cause each one to run the handler when a connection comes along. This is how servlet engines drive ordinary servlets to high levels of performance; it avoids the overhead of creating a Thread object for each request.

This may never replace the Apache web server, but there it is: small, simple, and threaded.

See Also

There are several issues I have not discussed. Scheduling of threads is not necessarily preemptive; it may be cooperative. This means that, on some platforms, the threads mechanism does not interrupt the running thread periodically to give other threads a "fair" chance to get CPU time. Therefore, in order to be portable to all Java platforms, your code *must* use yield() or wait() periodically (or some other method that causes the thread to be suspended, such as reading or writing). I also didn't get into priorities. The priority model is more limited than some other thread models, such as POSIX threads.

All in all, it's important to understand that *threaded classes require careful design.* For this reason, you should refer to a good book on threaded Java before unleashing anything threaded upon the world. Recommendations include *Concurrent Programming in Java* by Doug Lea (Addison Wesley), *Multithreaded Programming with Java Technology* by Lewis et al (Prentice Hall), and *Java Threads* by Scott Oaks and Henry Wong (O'Reilly).

25

Introspection, or *"A Class Named Class"*

25.0. Introduction

The class `java.lang.Class` and the reflection package `java.lang.reflect` provide a number of mechanisms for gathering information from the Java Virtual Machine. Known collectively as *introspection* or *reflection*, these facilities allow you to load classes on the fly, to find methods and fields in classes, to generate listings of them, and to invoke methods on dynamically loaded classes. There is even a mechanism to let you construct a class from scratch (well, actually, from an array of bytes) while your program is running. This is about as close as Java lets you get to the magic, secret internals of the Java machine.

The JVM Interpreter is a large program, normally written in C and/or C++, that implements the Java Virtual Machine abstraction. You can get the source for Sun's and other JVMs via the Internet, and could study the JVM for months. Here we concentrate on just a few aspects, and only from the point of view of a programmer using the JVM's facilities, not how it works internally; that is an implementation detail that varies from one vendor's JVM to another.

I'll start with loading an existing class dynamically, move on to listing the fields and methods of a class and invoking methods, and end by creating a class on the fly using a `ClassLoader`. One of the more interesting aspects of Java, and one that accounts for both its flexibility (applets, servlets) and part of its perceived speed problem, is the notion of *dynamic loading*. For example, even the simplest "Hello Java" program has to load the class file for your `Hello` class, the class file for its parent (usually `java.lang.Object`), the class for `PrintStream` (since you used `System.out`), the class for `PrintStream`'s parent, and so on. To see this in action, try something like this:

```
java -verbose HelloJava | more
```

To take another example, a browser can download an applet's bytecode file over the Internet and run it on your desktop. How does it load the class file into the running JVM? We discuss this little bit of Java magic in Recipe 25.3. The chapter ends with replacement versions of the JDK tools *javap* and AppletViewer—the latter doing what a browser does, loading applets at runtime—and a cross-reference tool that you can use to become a famous Java author by publishing your very own reference to the complete Java API.

25.1. Getting a Class Descriptor

Problem

You want to get a `Class` object from a class name or instance.

Solution

If the class name is known at compile time, you can get the class instance using the compiler keyword `.class`, which works on any object. However, the `Object` class does not have `class` as a field, so this strikes some observers as a bit of a hack. Nonetheless, it works. Use it.

Otherwise, if you have an object (an instance of a class), you can call the `java.lang.Object` method `getClass()`, which returns the `Class` object for the object's class (now that was a mouthful!):

```
import java.util.*;
/**
 * Show the Class keyword and getClass() method in action.
 */
public class ClassKeyword {
    public static void main(String[] argv) {
        System.out.println("Trying the ClassName.class keyword:");
        System.out.println("Object class: " + Object.class);
        System.out.println("String class: " + String.class);
        System.out.println("Calendar class: " + Calendar.class);
        System.out.println("Current class: " + ClassKeyword.class);
        System.out.println();

        System.out.println("Trying the instance.getClass() method:");
        System.out.println("Robin the Fearless".getClass());
        System.out.println(Calendar.getInstance().getClass());
    }
}
```

When we run it, we see:

```
C:\javasrc\reflect>java  ClassKeyword
Trying the ClassName.class keyword:
```

```
Object class: class java.lang.Object
String class: class java.lang.String
Calendar class: class java.util.Calendar
Current class: class ClassKeyword
Trying the instance.getClass() method:
class java.lang.String
class java.util.GregorianCalendar
C:\javasrc\reflect>
```

Nothing fancy, but as you can see, you can get the Class object for any class known at compile time, whether part of a package or not.

25.2. Finding and Using Methods and Fields

Problem

You need more to find arbitrary method or field names in arbitrary classes.

Solution

Use the reflection package `java.lang.reflect`.

Discussion

If you just wanted to find fields and methods in one particular class, you wouldn't need this; you could simply create an instance of the class using new and refer to its fields and methods directly. This allows you to find methods and fields in any class, even classes that have not yet been written! Given a class object created as in Recipe 25.1, you can obtain a list of constructors, a list of methods, or a list of fields. The method getMethods() lists the methods available for a given class as an array of Method objects. Since constructor methods are treated specially by Java, there is also a getConstructors() method, which returns an array of Constructor objects. Even though "class" is in the package java.lang, the Constructor, Method, and Field objects it returns are in java.lang.reflect, so you need an import of this package. The ListMethods class (Example 25-1) shows how to do this.

Example 25-1. ListMethods.java

```
import java.lang.reflect.*;

/**
 * List the Constructors and methods
 */
```

Example 25-1. ListMethods.java (continued)

```
public class ListMethods {
    public static void main(String[] argv) throws ClassNotFoundException {
        if (argv.length == 0) {
            System.err.println("Usage: ListMethods className");
            return;
        }
        Class c = Class.forName(argv[0]);
        Constructor[] cons = c.getConstructors();
        printList("Constructors", cons);
        Method[] meths = c.getMethods();
        printList("Methods", meths);
    }
    static void printList(String s, Object[] o) {
        System.out.println("*** " + s + " ***");
        for (int i=0; i<o.length; i++)
            System.out.println(o[i].toString());
    }
}
```

For example, you could run Example 25-1 on a class like `java.lang.String` and get a fairly lengthy list of methods; I'll only show part of the output so you can see what it looks like:

```
> java ListMethods java.lang.String
*** Constructors ***
public java.lang.String()
public java.lang.String(java.lang.String)
public java.lang.String(java.lang.StringBuffer)
public java.lang.String(byte[])
// and many more...
*** Methods ***
public static java.lang.String java.lang.String.copyValueOf(char[])
public static java.lang.String java.lang.String.copyValueOf(char[],int,int)
public static java.lang.String java.lang.String.valueOf(char)
// and more valueOf() forms...
public boolean java.lang.String.equals(java.lang.Object)
public final native java.lang.Class java.lang.Object.getClass()
// and more java.lang.Object methods...
public char java.lang.String.charAt(int)
public int java.lang.String.compareTo(java.lang.Object)
public int java.lang.String.compareTo(java.lang.String)
```

You can see that this could be extended (almost literally) to write a `BeanMethods` class that would list only the set/get methods defined in a JavaBean (see Recipe 23.7).

Alternately, you can find a particular method and invoke it, or find a particular field and refer to its value. Let's start by finding a given field, since that's the easiest.

Example 25-2 is code that, given an `Object` and the name of a field, finds the field (gets a `Field` object), then retrieves and prints the value of that `Field` as an `int`.

Example 25-2. FindField.java

```
import java.lang.reflect.*;
import java.util.*;

/** This class shows using Reflection to get a field from another class. */
public class FindField {

    public static void main(String[] unused)
    throws NoSuchFieldException, IllegalAccessException {

        // Create instance of FindField
        FindField gf = new FindField();

        // Create instance of target class (YearHolder defined below).
        Object o = new YearHolder();

        // Use gf to extract a field from o.
        System.out.println("The value of 'currentYear' is: " +
            gf.intFieldValue(o, "currentYear"));
    }

    int intFieldValue(Object o, String name)
    throws NoSuchFieldException, IllegalAccessException {
        Class c = o.getClass();
        Field fld = c.getField(name);
        int value = fld.getInt(o);
        return value;
    }
}

/** This is just a class that we want to get a field from */
class YearHolder {
    /** Just a field that is used to show getting a field's value. */
    public int currentYear = Calendar.getInstance().get(Calendar.YEAR);
}
```

What if we need to find a method? The simplest way is to use the methods `getMethod()` and `invoke()` to do the deed. But this is not altogether trivial. Suppose that somebody gives us a reference to an object. We don't know its class, but have been told that it should have this method:

```
public void work(String s) { }
```

We wish to invoke `work()`. To find the method, we must make an array of `Class` objects, one per item in the calling list. So in this case, we make an array containing only a reference to the class object for `String`. Since we know the name of the class at compile time, we'll use the shorter invocation `String.class` instead of `Class.forName()`. This, plus the name of the method as a string, gets us entry into the `getMethod()` method of the `Class` object. If this succeeds, we have a `Method` object. But guess what? In order to invoke the method, we have to construct yet another array, this time an array of `Object` references, actually containing the data to be passed to the invocation. We also, of course, need an instance of the class in whose context the method is to be run. For this demonstration class, we need to pass only a single string, as our array consists only of the string. Example 25-3 is the code that finds the method and invokes it.

Example 25-3. GetMethod.java

```java
import java.lang.reflect.*;

/** This class is just here to give us something to work on,
 * with a println() call that will prove we got here. */
class X {
    public void work(String s) {
        System.out.println("Working on \"" + s + "\"");
    }
}

/**
 * Get a given method, and invoke it.
 */
public class GetMethod {

    public static void main(String[] argv) {
        try {
            Class clX = X.class; // or Class.forName("X");
            // To find a method we need the array of matching Class types.
            Class[] argTypes = {
                String.class
            };

            // Now find a Method object for the given method.
            Method worker = clX.getMethod("work", argTypes);

            // To INVOKE the method, we need its actual arguments, as an array.
            Object[] theData = {
                "Chocolate Chips"
            };

            // The obvious last step: invoke the method.
            worker.invoke(new X(), theData);
        } catch (Exception e) {
```

Example 25-3. GetMethod.java (continued)

```
            System.err.println("Invoke() failed: " + e);
        }
    }
}
```

Not tiny, but still not bad. In most programming languages, you couldn't do that in the 40 lines it took us here.

A word of caution: when the arguments to a method are of a primitive type such as `int`, you do not pass `Integer.class` into `getMethod()`. Instead, you must use the class object representing the primitive type `int`. The easiest way to find this class is in the `Integer` class, as a public constant named `TYPE`, so you'd pass `Integer.TYPE`. The same is true for all the primitive types; for each, the corresponding wrapper class has the primitive class referred to as `TYPE`.

25.3. Loading and Instantiating a Class Dynamically

Problem

You want to load classes dynamically, just like browsers load your applets and web servers load your servlets.

Solution

Use `java.lang.class.forName("ClassName");` and the class's `newInstance()` method.

Discussion

Suppose you are using Java as an extension language in a larger application and want customer developers to be able to write Java classes that can run in the context of your application. You would probably want to define a small set of methods that these extension programs would have, and that you could call for such purposes as initialization, operation, and termination. The best way to do this is, of course, to publish a given possibly abstract class that provides those methods, and get the developers to subclass from it. Sound familiar? It should. This is just how web browsers such as Netscape allow the deployment of applets.

We'll leave the thornier issues of security and of loading a class file over a network socket for now, and assume that the user can install the classes into the application directory or into a directory that appears in CLASSPATH at the time the program is run. First, let's define our class. We'll call it Cooklet (see Example 25-4), to avoid infringing on the overused word *applet*. And we'll initially take the easiest path from ingredients to cookies before we complicate it.

Example 25-4. Cooklet.java

```java
/** A simple class, just to provide the list of methods that
 * users need to provide to be usable in our application.
 * Note that the class is abstract so you must subclass it,
 * but the methods are non-abstract so you don't have to provide
 * dummy versions if you don't need a particular functionality.
 */
public abstract class Cooklet {

    /** The initialization method. The Cookie application will
     * call you here (AFTER calling your no-argument constructor)
     * to allow you to initialize your code
     */
    public void initialize() {
    }

    /** The work method. The cookie application will call you
     * here when it is time for you to start cooking.
     */
    public void work() {
    }

    /** The termination method. The cookie application will call you
     * here when it is time for you to stop cooking and shut down
     * in an orderly fashion.
     */
    public void terminate() {
    }
}
```

Now, since we'll be baking, err, making this available to other people, we'll probably want to cook up a demonstration version available too; see Example 25-5.

Example 25-5. DemoCooklet.java

```java
public class DemoCooklet extends Cooklet {
    public void work() {
        System.out.println("I am busy baking cookies.");
    }
    public void terminate() {
        System.out.println("I am shutting down my ovens now.");
    }
}
```

But how does our application use it? Once we have the name of the user's class, we need to create a `Class` object for that class. This can be done easily using the static method `Class.forName()`. Then we can create an instance of it using the `Class` object's `newInstance()` method; this will call the class's no-argument constructor. Then we simply cast the newly constructed object to our `Cooklet` class, and we can call its methods! It actually takes longer to describe this code than to look at the code, so let's do that now; see Example 25-6.

Example 25-6. Cookies.java

```
/**
 * This is the part of the Cookies application that loads
 * the user-defined subclass.
 */
public class Cookies {
    public static void main(String[] argv) {
        System.out.println("Cookies Application Version 0.0");
        Cooklet cooklet = null;
        String cookletClassName = argv[0];
        try {
            Class cookletClass = Class.forName(cookletClassName);
            Object cookletObject = cookletClass.newInstance();
            cooklet = (Cooklet)cookletObject;
        } catch (Exception e) {
            System.err.println("Error " + cookletClassName + e);
        }
        cooklet.initialize();
        cooklet.work();
        cooklet.terminate();
    }
}
```

And if we run it?

```
$ javac Cookies DemoCooklet
Cookies Application Version 0.0
I am busy baking cookies.
I am shutting down my ovens now.
$
```

Of course, this version has rather limited error handling. But you already know how to fix that. Your `ClassLoader` can also place classes into a package by constructing a `Package` object; you should do this if loading any reasonable-sized set of application classes.

25.4. Constructing a Class from Scratch

Problem

You need to load a class and run its methods.

Solution

Write and use your own `ClassLoader`.

Discussion

A `ClassLoader`, of course, is a program that loads classes. There is one class loader built into the Java Virtual Machine, but your application can create additional ones as needed. Learning to write and run a working class loader and use it to load a class and run its methods is a nontrivial exercise. In fact, you rarely need to write a class loader, but knowing how is helpful in understanding how the JVM finds classes, creates objects, and calls methods.

`ClassLoader` itself is abstract; you must subclass it to provide a `loadClass()` method that loads classes as you wish. It can load the bytes from a network connection, a local disk, RAM, a serial port, or anywhere else. Or you can construct the class file in memory yourself if you have access to a compiler.

You must call this class loader's `loadClass()` method for any classes you wish to load from it. Note that it will be called to load all classes required for classes you load (parent classes that aren't already loaded, for example). However, the JVM will still load classes that you instantiate with the new operator "normally" via CLASSPATH.

To write a class loader, you need to subclass `ClassLoader` and implement at least `findClass()` and `loadClass()`. The `loadClass()` method needs to get the class file into a byte array (typically by reading it), convert the array into a `Class` object, and return the result.

What? That sounds a bit like "And Then a Miracle Occurs . . . " And it is. The miracle of class creation, however, happens down inside the JVM, where you don't have access to it. Instead, your `ClassLoader` has to call the final `defineClass()` method in your superclass (which is `java.lang.ClassLoader`). This is illustrated in Figure 25-1, where a stream of bytes containing a hypothetical Chicken class is converted into a ready-to-run Chicken class in the JVM by calling the `defineClass()` method.

Figure 25-1. ClassLoader in action

What next?

To use your `ClassLoader` subclass, you need to instantiate it and call its `loadClass()` method with the name of the class you want to load. This gives you a `Class` object for the named class; the `Class` object in turn lets you construct instances, find and call methods, etc. Refer back to Recipe 25.2.

25.5. Performance Timing

Problem

You need to know how long a Java program takes to run.

Solution

Call `System.currentTimeMillis()` before and after invoking the target class dynamically.

Discussion

The simplest technique is to save the JVM's accumulated time before and after dynamically loading a main program, and calculating the difference between those times. Code to do just this is presented in Example 25-7; for now, just remember that we have a way of timing a given Java class.

One way of measuring the efficiency of a particular operation is to run it many times in isolation. The overall time the program takes to run thus approximates the total time of many invocations of the same operation. Gross numbers like this can be compared if you want to know which of two ways of doing something is more efficient. Consider the case of string concatenation versus `println()`. The code:

```
println("Time is " + n.toString() + " seconds");
```

creates a `StringBuffer`, appends the string `"Time is "`, the value of n as a string, and `" seconds"`, and finally converts the finished `StringBuffer` to a `String` and passes that to `println()`. Suppose you have a program that does a lot of this, such as a Java servlet (see Chapter 18) that creates a lot of HTML this way, and you expect (or at least hope) that your web site will be sufficiently busy that doing this efficiently will make a difference. There are two ways of thinking about this:

- Theory A: This string concatenation is inefficient.

- Theory B: String concatenation doesn't matter; `println()` is inefficient too.

A proponent of Theory A might answer that since `println()` just puts stuff into a buffer, it really doesn't matter, and that the string concatenation is the expensive part.

How to decide between Theory A and Theory B? Assume you are willing to write a simple test program that tests both theories. One way of proceeding might be to disassemble the resulting bytecodes and count the CPU cycles each uses. This is an interesting theoretical exercise, and a good subject for a computer science dissertation. But we need the results quickly, so we will just write a simple program both ways and time it. `StringPrintA` is the timing program for Theory A:

```
public class StringPrintA {
    public static void main(String[] argv) {
        Object o = "Hello World";
        for (int i=0; i<100000; i++) {
            System.out.println("<p><b>" + o.toString() + "</b></p>");
        }
    }
}
```

`StringPrintAA` is the same, but explicitly uses a `StringBuffer` for the string concatenation. `StringPrintB` is the tester for Theory B:

```
public class StringPrintB {
    public static void main(String[] argv) {
        Object o = "Hello World";
        for (int i=0; i<100000; i++) {
            System.out.print("<p><b>");
            System.out.print(o.toString());
            System.out.print("</b></p>");
            System.out.println();
        }
    }
}
```

Timing results

I ran `StringPrintA`, `StringPrintAA`, and `StringPrintB` twice each on a single 400 MHz Intel Celeron. Here are the results:

StringPrintA	17.23, 17.20 seconds
StringPrintAA	17.23, 17.23 seconds
StringPrintB	27.59, 27.60 seconds

Moral: Don't guess. If it matters, time it.

Another moral: Multiple calls to `System.out.print()` cost more than the same number of calls to a `StringBuffer`'s `append()` method, by a factor of 1.5 (or 150%). Theory B wins; the extra `println` calls appear to save a string concatenation, but make the program take substantially longer.

A shell script to run these timing tests appears in file *stringprinttimer.sh* in the online source.

Timing program

It's pretty easy to build a simplified time command in Java, given that you have `System.currentTimeMillis()` to start with. Call `Time.java`, shown in Example 25-7, before and after running a program, and you'll know how long it took. But remember that `System.currentTimeMillis()` returns clock time, not necessarily CPU time. So you must run it on a machine that isn't running a lot of background processes. And note also that I use dynamic loading (see Recipe 25.3) to let you put the Java class name on the command line.

Example 25-7. Time.java

```java
import com.darwinsys.util.QuickTimeFormat;
import java.lang.reflect.*;

/**
 * Time the main method of another class, for performance tuning.
 */
public class Time {
    public static void main(String[] argv) throws Exception {
        // Instantiate target class, from argv[0]
        Class c = Class.forName(argv[0]);

        // Find its static main method (use our own argv as the signature).
        Class[] classes = { argv.getClass() };
        Method main = c.getMethod("main", classes);

        // Make new argv array, dropping class name from front.
        String nargv[] = new String[argv.length - 1];
```

Example 25-7. Time.java (continued)

```
        System.arraycopy(argv, 1, nargv, 0, nargv.length);

        Object[] nargs = { nargv };

        System.err.println("Starting class " + c);

        // About to start timing run. Important to not do anything
        // (even a println) that would be attributed to the program
        // being timed, from here until we've gotten ending time.

        // Get current (i.e., starting) time
        long t0 = System.currentTimeMillis();

        // Run the main program
        main.invoke(null, nargs);

        // Get ending time, and compute usage
        long t1 = System.currentTimeMillis();

        long runTime = t1 - t0;

        System.err.println(
            "runTime="  + QuickTimeFormat.msToSecs(runTime));
    }
}
```

Of course, you can't directly compare the results from the operating system time command with results from running this program. There is a rather large, but fairly constant, initialization overhead—the JVM startup and the initialization of Object and System.out, for example—that is included in the former and excluded from the latter. One could even argue that my Time program is more accurate, as it excludes this constant overhead. But as noted, it must be run on a single-user, non-server machine to give repeatable results. And no fair running an editor in another window while waiting for your timed program to complete!

25.6. *Printing Class Information*

Problem

You want to print all the information about a class, similar to the way *javap* does.

Solution

Get a Class object, call its getFields() and getMethods(), and print the results.

Discussion

The JDK includes a program called *javap*, the Java Printer. Sun's JDK version normally prints the outline of a class file—a list of its methods and fields—but can also print out the Java bytecodes or machine instructions. The Kaffe package did not include a version of *javap*, so I wrote one and contributed it (see Example 25-8). The Kaffe folk have expanded it somewhat, but it still works basically the same. My version doesn't print the bytecodes; it behaves rather like Sun's behaves when you don't give theirs any command-line options.

The `getFields()` and `getMethods()` methods return array of `Field` and `Method` respectively; these are both in package `java.lang.reflect`. I use a `Modifiers` object to get details on the permissions and storage attributes of the fields and methods. In many implementations you can bypass this, and simply call `toString()` in each `Field` and `Method` object. Doing it this way gives me a bit more control over the formatting.

Example 25-8. MyJavaP.java

```
import java.io.*;
import java.util.*;
import java.lang.reflect.*;

/**
 * JavaP prints structural information about classes.
 * For each class, all public fields and methods are listed.
 * "Reflectance" is used to look up the information.
 */
public class MyJavaP {

    /** A "Modifier" object, to decode modifiers of fields/methods */
    Modifier m = new Modifier();

    /** Simple main program, construct self, process each class name
     * found in argv.
     */
    public static void main(String[] argv) {
        MyJavaP pp = new MyJavaP();

        if (argv.length == 0) {
            System.err.println("Usage: javap className [...]");
            System.exit(1);
        } else for (int i=0; i<argv.length; i++)
            pp.doClass(argv[i]);
    }

    /** Format the fields and methods of one class, given its name.
     */
```

Example 25-8. MyJavaP.java (continued)

```
    protected void doClass(String className) {

        try {
            Class c = Class.forName(className);
            System.out.println(m.toString(c.getModifiers()) + ' ' + c + " {");
            int i, mods;
            Field fields[] = c.getFields();
            for (i = 0; i < fields.length; i++) {
                if (!m.isPrivate(fields[i].getModifiers())
                  && !m.isProtected(fields[i].getModifiers()))
                    System.out.println("\t" + fields[i]);
            }

            Method methods[] = c.getMethods();
            for (i = 0; i < methods.length; i++) {
                if (!m.isPrivate(methods[i].getModifiers())
                  && !m.isProtected(methods[i].getModifiers()))
                    System.out.println("\t" + methods[i]);
            }
        } catch (ClassNotFoundException e) {
            System.err.println("Error: Class " +
                className + " not found!");
        } catch (Exception e) {
            System.err.println(e);
        } finally {
            System.out.println("}");
        }
    }
}
```

25.7. *Program: CrossRef*

We've all seen those books that consist entirely of listings of the Java API for version thus-and-such of the JDK. I don't suppose you thought the authors of these works sat down and typed the entire contents from scratch. As a programmer, you would have realized, I hope, that there must be a way to obtain that information from Java. But you might not have realized how easy it is! If you've read this chapter faithfully, you now know that there is one true way: make the computer do the walking. Example 25-9 is a program that puts most of the techniques together. This version generates a cross-reference listing, but by overriding the last few methods you could easily convert it to print the information in any format you like, including an API Reference book. You'd need to deal with the details of this or that publishing software—FrameMaker, troff, T$_{E}$X, or whatever—but that's the easy part.

This program makes fuller use of the reflection API than did `JavaP` in Recipe 25.6. It also uses the `java.util.zip` classes (see Recipe 9.18) to crack the JAR archive containing the class files of the API. Each class file found in the archive is loaded and listed; the listing part is similar to `JavaP`.

Example 25-9. CrossRef.java

```java
import java.io.*;
import java.util.*;
import java.util.zip.*;
import java.lang.reflect.*;

/**
 * CrossRef prints a cross-reference about all classes named in argv.
 * For each class, all public fields and methods are listed.
 * "Reflectance" is used to look up the information.
 *
 * It is expected that the output will be post-processed e.g.,
 * with sort and awk/perl. Try:
 *    java CrossRef |
 *         uniq | # squeeze out polymorphic forms early
 *         sort | awk '$2=="method" { ... }' > crossref-methods.txt
 * The part in "{ ... }" is left as an exercise for the reader. :-(
 *
 */
public class CrossRef {
    /** Counter of fields/methods printed. */
    protected static int n = 0;

    /** A "Modifier" object, to decode modifiers of fields/methods */
    protected Modifier m = new Modifier();

    /** True if we are doing classpath, so only do java. and javax. */
    protected static boolean doingStandardClasses = true;

    /** Simple main program, construct self, process each .ZIP file
     * found in CLASSPATH or in argv.
     */
    public static void main(String[] argv) {
        CrossRef xref = new CrossRef();

        xref.doArgs(argv);
    }

    protected void doArgs(String[] argv) {

        if (argv.length == 0) {
            // No arguments, look in CLASSPATH
            String s = System.getProperties().getProperty("java.class.path");
```

Example 25-9. CrossRef.java (continued)

```java
            //  break apart with path sep.
            String pathSep = System.getProperties().
                getProperty("path.separator");
            StringTokenizer st = new StringTokenizer(s, pathSep);
            // Process each classpath
            while (st.hasMoreTokens()) {
                String cand = st.nextToken();
                System.err.println("Trying path " + cand);
                if (cand.endsWith(".zip") || cand.endsWith(".jar"))
                    processOneZip(cand);
            }
        } else {
            // We have arguments, process them as zip files
            doingStandardClasses = false;
            for (int i=0; i<argv.length; i++)
                processOneZip(argv[i]);
        }

        System.err.println("All done! Found " + n + " entries.");
        System.exit(0);
    }


    /** For each Zip file, for each entry, xref it */
    public void processOneZip(String classes) {
        ArrayList entries = new ArrayList();

        try {
            ZipFile zippy =
                new ZipFile(new File(classes));
            Enumeration all = zippy.entries();
            // For each entry, get its name and put it into "entries"
            while (all.hasMoreElements()) {
                entries.add(((ZipEntry)(all.nextElement())).getName());
            }
        } catch (IOException err) {
            System.err.println("IO Error: " + err);
            return;
        }

        // Sort the entries (by class name)
        Collections.sort(entries);

        // Process the entries
        for (int i=0; i< entries.size(); i++) {
            doClass((String)entries.get(i));
        }
    }
```

Example 25-9. CrossRef.java (continued)

```java
/** Format the fields and methods of one class, given its name.
 */
protected void doClass(String zipName) {
    if (System.getProperties().getProperty("debug.names") != null)
        System.out.println("doClass(" + zipName + ");");

    // Ignore package/directory, other odd-ball stuff.
    if (zipName.endsWith("/")) {
        System.err.println("Starting directory " + zipName);
        return;
    }
    // Ignore META-INF stuff
    if (zipName.startsWith("META-INF/")) {
        return;
    }
    // Ignore images, HTML, whatever else we find.
    if (!zipName.endsWith(".class")) {
        System.err.println("Ignoring " + zipName);
        return;
    }
    // If doing CLASSPATH, Ignore com.sun.* which are "internal API".
    if (doingStandardClasses && zipName.startsWith("com.sun")){
        return;
    }

    // Convert the zip file entry name, like
    //    java/lang/Math.class
    // to a class name like
    //    java.lang.Math
    String className = zipName.replace('/', '.').
        substring(0, zipName.length() - 6);// 6 for ".class"
    if (System.getProperties().getProperty("debug.names") != null)
        System.err.println("ZipName " + zipName +
            "; className " + className);
    try {
        Class c = Class.forName(className);
        printClass(c);
    } catch (ClassNotFoundException e) {
        System.err.println("Error: Class " +
            className + " not found!");
    } catch (Exception e) {
        System.err.println(e);
    }
    // System.err.println("in gc...");
    System.gc();
    // System.err.println("done gc");
}
```

Example 25-9. CrossRef.java (continued)

```java
    /**
     * Print the fields and methods of one class.
     */
    protected void printClass(Class c) {
        int i, mods;
        startClass(c);
        try {
            Object[] fields = c.getFields();
            Arrays.sort(fields);
            for (i = 0; i < fields.length; i++) {
                Field field = (Field)fields[i];
                if (!m.isPrivate(field.getModifiers())
                 && !m.isProtected(field.getModifiers()))
                    putField(field, c);
                else System.err.println("private field ignored: " + field);
            }

            Method methods[] = c.getDeclaredMethods();
            // Arrays.sort(methods);
            for (i = 0; i < methods.length; i++) {
                if (!m.isPrivate(methods[i].getModifiers())
                  && !m.isProtected(methods[i].getModifiers()))
                    putMethod(methods[i], c);
                else System.err.println("pvt: " + methods[i]);
            }
        } catch (Exception e) {
            System.err.println(e);
        }
        endClass();
    }


    /** put a Field's information to the standard output.
     * Marked protected so you can override it (hint, hint).
     */
    protected void putField(Field fld, Class c) {
        println(fld.getName() + " field " + c.getName() + " ");
        ++n;
    }
    /** put a Method's information to the standard output.
     * Marked protected so you can override it (hint, hint).
     */
    protected void putMethod(Method method, Class c) {
        String methName = method.getName();
        println(methName + " method " + c.getName() + " ");
        ++n;
    }
    /** Print the start of a class. Unused in this version,
     * designed to be overridden */
```

Example 25-9. CrossRef.java (continued)

```
    protected void startClass(Class c) {
    }


    /** Print the end of a class. Unused in this version,
     * designed to be overridden */
    protected void endClass() {
    }


    /** Convenience routine, short for System.out.println */
    protected final void println(String s) {
        System.out.println(s);
    }
}
```

You probably noticed the methods `startClass()` and `endClass()`, which are null. These are placeholders designed to make it easy for subclassing when you need to write something at the start and end of each class. One example might be a fancy text formatting application in which you need to output a bold header at the beginning of each class. Another would be XML (see Chapter 21), where you'd want to write a tag like `<class>` at the front of each class, and `</class>` at the end. Example 25-10 is, in fact, a working XML-specific subclass that generates (limited) XML for each field and method.

Example 25-10. CrossRefXML.java

```
import java.io.*;
import java.lang.reflect.*;

/** This class subclasses CrossRef to output the information in XML.
 */
public class CrossRefXML extends CrossRef {

    public static void main(String[] argv) {
        CrossRef xref = new CrossRefXML();
        xref.doArgs(argv);
    }


    /** Print the start of a class.
     */
    protected void startClass(Class c) {
        println("<class><classname>" + c.getName() + "</classname>");
    }


    protected void putField(Field fld, Class c) {
        println("<field>" + fld + "</field>");
        ++n;
    }
```

Example 25-10. CrossRefXML.java (continued)

```
    /** put a Method's information to the standard output.
     * Marked protected so you can override it (hint, hint).
     */
    protected void putMethod(Method method, Class c) {
        println("<method>" + method + "</method>");
        ++n;
    }


    /** Print the end of a class.
     */
    protected void endClass() {
        println("</class>");
    }
}
```

By the way, if you publish a book using either of these and get rich, "Remember, remember me!"

25.8. *Program: AppletViewer*

Another JDK tool that can be replicated is the AppletViewer. This uses the reflection package to load a class that is subclassed from `Applet`, instantiate an instance of it, and `add()` this to a frame at a given size. This is a good example of reflection in action: you can use these techniques to dynamically load any subclass of a given class. Suppose we have a simple applet like the `HelloApplet` in Example 25-11.

Example 25-11. HelloApplet.java

```
import java.applet.*;
import java.awt.*;
import javax.swing.*;
import java.awt.event.*;


/**
 * HelloApplet is a simple applet that toggles a message
 * when you click on a Draw button.
 */
public class HelloApplet extends JApplet {

    /** The flag which controls drawing the message. */
    protected boolean requested;

    /** init() is an Applet method called by the browser to initialize */
    public void init() {
        JButton b;
        requested = false;
        Container cp = (Container)getContentPane();
```

Example 25-11. HelloApplet.java (continued)

```
        cp.setLayout(new FlowLayout());
        cp.add(b = new JButton("Draw/Don't Draw"));
        b.addActionListener(new ActionListener() {
            /*  Button - toggle the state of the "requested" flag, to draw or
             *  not to draw.
             */
            public void actionPerformed(ActionEvent e) {
                String arg = e.getActionCommand();
                // Invert the state of the draw request.
                requested = !requested;
                do_the_work();
            }
        });
    }


    /** paint() is an AWT Component method, called when the
     *  component needs to be painted.
     */
    public void do_the_work() {
        /* If the Draw button is selected, draw something */
        if (requested) {
            showStatus("Welcome to Java!");
        } else {
            showStatus("");// retract welcome? :-)
        }
    }
}
```

If we run it in my AppletViewer,* it shows up as a window with just the Draw button showing; if you press the button an odd number of times, the screen shows the welcome label (Figure 25-2).

Figure 25-2. My AppletViewer showing simple applet

---

* My AppletViewer doesn't parse the HTML as the real one does, so you invoke it with just the name of the Applet subclass on its command line. The size is therefore hardcoded, at least until somebody gets around to writing code to extract the CLASS, WIDTH, and HEIGHT attributes from the APPLET tag in the HTML page like the real McCoy does.

Example 25-12 is the code for the main part of the AppletViewer, which creates a
JFrame, and then loads the Applet class dynamically and adds it to the JFrame.

Example 25-12. AppletViewer.java main program

```java
import java.awt.*;
import java.awt.event.*;
import javax.swing.*;
import java.applet.*;
import java.lang.reflect.*;
import java.net.*;
import java.util.*;


/*
 * AppletViewer - a simple Applet Viewer program.
 */
public class AppletViewer {
    /** The main Frame of this program */
    JFrame f;
    /** The AppletAdapter (gives AppletStub, AppletContext, showStatus) */
    static AppletAdapter aa = null;
    /** The name of the Applet subclass */
    String appName = null;
    /** The Class for the actual applet type */
    Class ac = null;
    /** The Applet instance we are running, or null. Can not be a JApplet
     * until all the entire world is converted to JApplet. */
    Applet ai = null;
    /** The width of the Applet */
    final int WIDTH = 250;
    /** The height of the Applet */
    final int HEIGHT = 200;

    /** Main is where it all starts.
     * Construct the GUI. Load the Applet. Start it running.
     */
    public static void main(String[] av) {
        new AppletViewer(av.length==0?"HelloApplet":av[0]);
    }


    /** Construct the GUI for an Applet Viewer */
    AppletViewer(String appName) {
        super();

        this.appName = appName;

        f = new JFrame("AppletViewer");
        f.addWindowListener(new WindowAdapter() {
            public void windowClosing(WindowEvent e) {
                f.setVisible(false);
```

Example 25-12. AppletViewer.java main program (continued)

```
                f.dispose();
                System.exit(0);
            }
    });
    Container cp = f.getContentPane();
    cp.setLayout(new BorderLayout());

    // Instantiate the AppletAdapter which gives us
    // AppletStub and AppletContext.
    if (aa == null)
        aa = new AppletAdapter();

    // The AppletAdapter also gives us showStatus.
    // Therefore, must add() it very early on, since the Applet's
    // Constructor or its init() may use showStatus()
    cp.add(BorderLayout.SOUTH, aa);

    showStatus("Loading Applet " + appName);

    loadApplet(appName , WIDTH, HEIGHT);// sets ac and ai
    if (ai == null)
        return;

    // Now right away, tell the Applet how to find showStatus et al.
    ai.setStub(aa);

    // Connect the Applet to the Frame.
    cp.add(BorderLayout.CENTER, ai);

    Dimension d = ai.getSize();
    d.height += aa.getSize().height;
    f.setSize(d);
    f.setVisible(true);// make the Frame and all in it appear

    showStatus("Applet " + appName + " loaded");

    // Here we pretend to be a browser!
    ai.init();
    ai.start();
}

/*
 * Load the Applet into memory. Should do caching.
 */
void loadApplet(String appletName, int w, int h) {
    // appletName = ... extract from the HTML CODE= somehow ...;
    // width = ditto
    // height = ditto
```

Example 25-12. AppletViewer.java main program (continued)

```
        try {
            // get a Class object for the Applet subclass
            ac = Class.forName(appletName);
            // Construct an instance (as if using no-argument constructor)
            ai = (Applet) ac.newInstance();
        } catch(ClassNotFoundException e) {
            showStatus("Applet subclass " + appletName + " did not load");
            return;
        } catch (Exception e ){
            showStatus("Applet " + appletName + " did not instantiate");
            return;
        }
        ai.setSize(w, h);
    }

    public void showStatus(String s) {
        aa.getAppletContext().showStatus(s);
    }
}
```

For `Applet` methods to work, two additional classes must be defined: `AppletStub` and `AppletContext`. The `AppletStub` is the tie-in between the applet and the browser, and the `AppletContext` is a set of methods used by the applet. Although in a real browser they are probably implemented separately, I have combined them into one class (see Example 25-13). Note that the scope of applets that will work without throwing exceptions is rather limited, since so many of the methods here are at present dummied out. This AppletViewer is not a full replacement for Sun's AppletViewer; it has only been tested with a basic Hello World applet, and is simply provided as a starting point for those who want to fill in the gaps and make a full-blown applet viewer program.

Example 25-13. AppletAdapter.java, partial AppletStub and AppletContext

```
import java.awt.*;
import java.awt.event.*;
import java.applet.*;
import java.net.*;
import java.util.*;

/*
 * AppletAdaptor: partial implementation of AppletStub and AppletContext.
 *
 * This code is far from finished, as you will see.
 *
 */
public class AppletAdapter extends Panel implements AppletStub, AppletContext {
    /** The status window at the bottom */
```

Example 25-13. AppletAdapter.java, partial AppletStub and AppletContext (continued)

```java
Label status = null;

/** Construct the GUI for an Applet Status window */
AppletAdapter() {
    super();

    // Must do this very early on, since the Applet's
    // Constructor or its init() may use showStatus()
    add(status = new Label());

    // Give "status" the full width
    status.setSize(getSize().width, status.getSize().height);

    showStatus("AppletAdapter constructed");// now it can be said
}


/****************** AppletStub **********************/
/** Called when the applet wants to be resized.  */
public void appletResize(int w, int h) {
    // applet.setSize(w, h);
}

/** Gets a reference to the applet's context.  */
public AppletContext getAppletContext() {
    return this;
}

/** Gets the base URL.  */
public URL getCodeBase() {
    return getClass().getResource(".");
}

/** Gets the document URL.  */
public URL getDocumentBase() {
    return getClass().getResource(".");
}

/** Returns the value of the named parameter in the HTML tag.  */
public String getParameter(String name) {
    String value = null;
    return value;
}
/** Determines if the applet is active.  */
public boolean isActive() {
    return true;
}
```

Example 25-13. AppletAdapter.java, partial AppletStub and AppletContext (continued)

```java
/*********************** AppletContext ***********************/

/** Finds and returns the applet with the given name. */
public Applet getApplet(String an) {
    return null;
}

/** Finds all the applets in the document */
public Enumeration getApplets() {
    class AppletLister implements Enumeration {
        public boolean hasMoreElements() {
            return false;
        }
        public Object nextElement() {
            return null;
        }
    }
    return new AppletLister();
}

/** Create an audio clip for the given URL of a .au file */
public AudioClip getAudioClip(URL u) {
    return null;
}

/** Look up and create an Image object that can be paint()ed */
public Image getImage(URL u)  {
    return null;
}

/** Request to overlay the current page with a new one - ignored */
public void showDocument(URL u) {
}

/** as above but with a Frame target */
public void showDocument(URL u, String frame)  {
}

/** Called by the Applet to display a message in the bottom line */
public void showStatus(String msg) {
    if (msg == null)
        msg = "";
    status.setText(msg);
}
}
```

It is left as an exercise for the reader to implement getImage() and other methods in terms of other recipes used in this book.

See Also

We have not investigated all the ins and outs of reflection or the `ClassLoader` mechanism, but I hope I've given you a basic idea of how it works.

Perhaps the most important omissions are `SecurityManager` and `ProtectionDomain`. Only one `SecurityManager` can be installed in a given instance of JVM (e.g., to prevent a malicious applet from providing its own!). A browser, for example, provides a `SecurityManager` that is far more restrictive than the standard one. Writing such a `SecurityManager` is left as an exercise for the reader, but an important exercise for anyone planning to load classes over the Internet! (For more information about security managers and the Java Security APIs, see O'Reilly's *Java Security*, by Scott Oaks.) A `ProtectionDomain` can be provided with a `ClassLoader` to specify all the permissions needed for the class to run.

I've also left unexplored some other topics in the JVM; see the O'Reilly books *The Java Virtual Machine* and *The Java Language,* or Sun's JVM Specification document *(http://java.sun.com/docs/books/vmspec/)* for a lifetime of reading enjoyment and edification!

The Byte Code Engineering Library (BCEL) is a third-party toolkit for building and manipulating class files. BCEL was written by Markus Dahm and is available for free from *http://bcel.sourceforge.net.* Source code is included.

26

Using Java with
Other Languages

26.0. Introduction

Java has several methods of running programs written in other languages. You can invoke a compiled program or executable script using `Runtime.exec()`, as I'll describe in Recipe 26.1. Or you can drop down to C level with Java's "native code" mechanism, and call compiled functions written in C/C++. From there, you can call to functions written in just about any language. Not to mention that you can contact programs written in any language over a socket (see Chapter 15), with HTTP services (see Chapter 17), or with Java clients in RMI or CORBA clients in a variety of languages (see Chapter 22).

There is an element of system dependency here, of course. You can only run MS-Windows applications under MS-Windows, and Unix applications under Unix. So some of the recipes in this chapter aren't portable, though in a few cases I try to make them at least run on MS-Windows *or* Unix.

26.1. Running a Program

Problem

You want to run a program.

Solution

Use one of the `exec()` methods in the `java.lang.Runtime` class.

Discussion

The `exec()` method in the `Runtime` class lets you run an external program. The command line you give will be broken into strings by a simple `StringTokenizer` (Recipe 3.2) and passed on to the operating system's "execute a program" system call. As a simple example, here is a simple program that uses `exec()` to run kwrite, a windowed text editor program.* On MS-Windows, you'd have to change the name to notepad or wordpad, possibly including the full pathname, e.g., *c:\\ WINDOWS\\NOTEPAD.EXE* (double backslashes because the backslash is special in Java strings).

```
// file ExecDemoSimple.java
public class ExecDemoSimple {
    public static void main(String av[]) throws java.io.IOException {

        // Run the "notepad" program or a similar editor
        Process p = Runtime.getRuntime().exec("kwrite");

    }
}
```

When you compile and run it, the appropriate editor window appears:

```
$ jr ExecDemoSimple
+ jikes +E -d . ExecDemoSimple.java
+ java ExecDemoSimple # causes a KWrite window to appear.
$
```

Example 26-1 runs the MS-Windows or Unix version of Netscape, assuming Netscape was installed in the default directory. It passes as an argument the name of a help file, offering a kind of primitive "help" mechanism, as displayed in Figure 26-1.

Example 26-1. ExecDemoNS.java

```
import com.darwinsys.util.*;

import java.awt.event.*;
import javax.swing.*;

import java.io.*;
import java.net.*;
import java.awt.*;

/**
 * ExecDemoNS shows how to execute a 32-bit Windows program from within Java.
 */
```

---

* `kwrite` is Unix-specific; it's a part of the K Desktop Environment (KDE). See *http://www.kde.org*.

Example 26-1. ExecDemoNS.java (continued)

```java
public class ExecDemoNS extends JFrame {
    /** The name of the help file. */
    protected final static String HELPFILE = "./help/index.html";

    /** The path to the Netscape binary  */
    protected static String netscape;

    /** A process object tracks one external running process */
    Process p;

    /** main - instantiate and run */
    public static void main(String av[]) throws Exception {
        new ExecDemoNS().setVisible(true);
    }

    /** Constructor - set up strings and things. */
    public ExecDemoNS() {
        super("ExecDemo: Netscape");
        String osname = System.getProperty("os.name");
        if (osname == null)
            throw new IllegalArgumentException("no os.name");
        netscape = // Windows or Unix only for now, sorry Mac fans
            (osname.toLowerCase().indexOf("windows")!=-1) ?
            "c:/program files/netscape/communicator/program/netscape.exe" :
            "/usr/local/netscape/netscape";

        Container cp = getContentPane();
        cp.setLayout(new FlowLayout());
        JButton b;
        cp.add(b=new JButton("Exec"));
        b.addActionListener(new ActionListener() {
            public void actionPerformed(ActionEvent evt) {
                doHelp();
            }
        });
        cp.add(b=new JButton("Wait"));
        b.addActionListener(new ActionListener() {
            public void actionPerformed(ActionEvent evt) {
                doWait();
            }
        });
        cp.add(b=new JButton("Exit"));
        b.addActionListener(new ActionListener() {
            public void actionPerformed(ActionEvent evt) {
                System.exit(0);
            }
        });
```

Example 26-1. ExecDemoNS.java (continued)

```java
        pack();
    }

    /** Start the help, in its own Thread. */
    public void doHelp() {

        new Thread() {
            public void run() {

                try {
                    // Get the URL for the Help File
                    URL helpURL = this.getClass().getClassLoader().
                        getResource(HELPFILE);

                    // Start Netscape from the Java Application. A Java
                    // Applet would not be allowed to, nor need to :-)

                    p = Runtime.getRuntime().exec(netscape + " " + helpURL);

                    Debug.println("trace", "In main after exec");

                } catch (Exception ex) {
                    JOptionPane.showMessageDialog(ExecDemoNS.this,
                        "Error" + ex, "Error",
                        JOptionPane.ERROR_MESSAGE);
                }
            }
        }.start();

    }


    public void doWait() {
        try {
            p.waitFor();// wait for process to complete
            Debug.println("trace", "Process is done");
        } catch (Exception ex) {
            JOptionPane.showMessageDialog(this,
                "Error" + ex, "Error",
                JOptionPane.ERROR_MESSAGE);
        }
    }

}
```

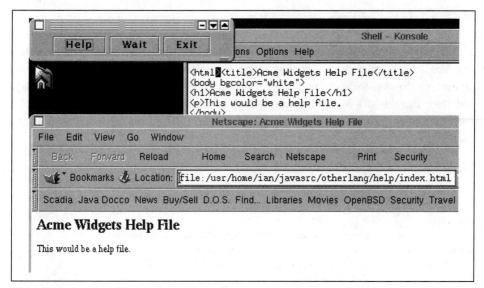

Figure 26-1. ExecDemoNS in action

26.2. Running a Program and Capturing Its Output

Problem

You want to run a program but also capture its output.

Solution

Use the `Process` object's `getInputStream();` read and copy the contents to `System.out` or wherever you want them.

Discussion

A program's standard and error output does not automatically appear anywhere. Arguably, there should be an automatic way to make this happen. But for now, you need to add a few lines of code to grab the program's output and print it:

```
// part of ExecDemoLs.java
p = Runtime.getRuntime().exec(PROGRAM);

// getInputStream gives an Input stream connected to
// the process p's standard output (and vice versa). We use
// that to construct a BufferedReader so we can readLine() it.
BufferedReader is =
    new BufferedReader(new InputStreamReader(p.getInputStream()));
```

```
    while ((line = is.readLine()) != null)
        System.out.println(line);
```

This is such a common occurrence that I've packaged it up into a class called ExecAndPrint, part of my package com.darwinsys.util. ExecAndPrint has several overloaded forms of its run() method (see the documentation for details), but they all take at least a command, and optionally an output file to which the command's output is written. Example 26-2 shows the code for some of these methods.

Example 26-2. ExecAndPrint.java (partial listing)

```
/** Need a Runtime object for any of these methods */
protected static Runtime r = Runtime.getRuntime();


/** Run the command given as a String, printing its output to System.out */
public static int run(String cmd) throws IOException {
    return run(cmd, new OutputStreamWriter(System.out));
}


/** Run the command given as a String, print its output to "out" */
public static int run(String cmd, Writer out) throws IOException {

    String line;

    Process p = r.exec(cmd);

    FileIO.copyFile(new InputStreamReader(p.getInputStream()), out, true);
    try {
        p.waitFor();// wait for process to complete
    } catch (InterruptedException e) {
        return -1;
    }
    return p.exitValue();
}
```

As a simple example of using exec() directly along with ExecAndPrint, I'll create three temporary files, list them (directory listing), and then delete them. When I run the ExecDemoFiles program, it lists the three files it has created:

```
-rw-------  1 ian  wheel  0 Jan 29 14:29 file1
-rw-------  1 ian  wheel  0 Jan 29 14:29 file2
-rw-------  1 ian  wheel  0 Jan 29 14:29 file3
```

Its source code is in Example 26-3.

Example 26-3. ExecDemoFiles.java

```
// Get and save the Runtime object.
Runtime rt = Runtime.getRuntime();

// Create three temporary files
rt.exec("mktemp file1");
rt.exec("mktemp file2");
rt.exec("mktemp file3");

// Run the "ls" (directory lister) program
// with its output printed back to us.
String[] args = { "ls", "-l", "file1", "file2", "file3" };
ExecAndPrint.run(args);

rt.exec("rm file1 file2 file3");
```

A process isn't necessarily destroyed when the Java program that created it exits or
bombs out. Simple text-based programs will be, but window-based programs like
kwrite, Netscape, or even a Java-based JFrame application will not. For example,
our ExecDemoNS program started Netscape, and when the Exit button is pressed,
ExecDemoNS exits but Netscape stays running. What if you want to be sure a process has completed? The Process object has a waitFor() method that lets you
do so, and an exitValue() that tells you the "return code" from the process.
Finally, should you wish to forcibly terminate the other process, you can do so with
the Process object's destroy() method, which takes no argument and returns
no value. Example 26-4 is ExecDemoWait, a program that runs whatever program
you name on the command line (along with arguments), captures the program's
standard output, and waits for the program to terminate.

Example 26-4. ExecDemoWait.java

```
// A Runtime object has methods for dealing with the OS
Runtime r = Runtime.getRuntime();
Process p;              // Process tracks one external native process
BufferedReader is;      // reader for output of process
String line;

// Our argv[0] contains the program to run; remaining elements
// of argv contain args for the target program. This is just
// what is needed for the String[] form of exec.
p = r.exec(argv);

System.out.println("In Main after exec");

// getInputStream gives an Input stream connected to
// the process p's standard output. Just use it to make
// a BufferedReader to readLine() what the program writes out.
```

Example 26-4. ExecDemoWait.java (continued)

```
is = new BufferedReader(new InputStreamReader(p.getInputStream()));

while ((line = is.readLine()) != null)
    System.out.println(line);

System.out.println("In Main after EOF");
try {
    p.waitFor();     // wait for process to complete
} catch (InterruptedException e) {
    return;
}
System.err.println("Process done, exit status was " + p.exitValue());
return;
```

See Also

You wouldn't normally use any form of `exec()` to run one Java program from another in this way; instead, you'd probably create it as a thread within the same process, as this is generally quite a bit faster (the Java interpreter is already up and running, so why wait for another copy of it to start up?). See Chapter 24.

There isn't anything special to say about running Perl scripts, per se. However, two free packages—perljvm and PerlCaffeine—allow you to compile Perl source into Java bytecode. This code can then be interpreted at full speed by any JVM interpreter or Java runtime. If you are a Perl user, you can probably find these modules on CPAN, the Comprehensive Perl Archive Network.

26.3. *Mixing Java and Scripts with BSF*

Problem

You want to interface Java components to an existing scripting language.

Solution

Use the Bean Scripting Framework (BSF).

Discussion

Many scripting languages are used in the computing field today: VB, Perl, Python, JavaScript, Tcl/TK, REXX, and others. A project that originated at IBM, the Bean Scripting Framework (BSF) aims to provide a way to allow all of them to interoperate with Java.

The BSF consists of a management API, an engine API for driving different scripting languages, and a series of plug-ins for different scripting languages. The management API lets you either evaluate an expression in the given scripting language, such as "2+2" (which is so simple as to be valid in most supported languages), or run a script stored in a script file. In this example I'll use JPython, a pure-Java (certified) implementation of the scripting language Python (see *http:// www.python.org* or the O'Reilly book *Learning Python*).

While it is convenient (and efficient) to run JPython in the same JVM as the calling program, this is not by any means a requirement; for example, it is possible to use BSF with scripting languages written in some native language. BSF and the scripting plug-in are responsible for dealing with whatever "plumbing"—external connections or processes—this requires. In fact, BSF currently supports the languages listed in Table 26-1.

Table 26-1. Languages supported by BSF

Language	Description
JPython	Java implementation of Python
Jacl	Java implementation/interface for Tcl
Bean Markup Language (BML)	Related language, from IBM
LotusXSL	XML stylesheets (see Recipe 21.1)
NetRexx	REXX variant
Netscape Rhino	JavaScript implementation
Pnuts	Scripting language for accessing Java APIs
Microsoft Active Scripting Format (MASF)	Microsoft analog of BSF

BSF could also support MacOS Apple Scripting or almost any other language, though I don't know of an implementation at present.

Example 26-5 uses JPython to evaluate and print the value of 22/7, a crude approximation of `Math.PI`, using the management API's `eval()` function.

Example 26-5. BSFSample.java

```
import com.ibm.cs.util.*;
import com.ibm.bsf.*;
import java.io.*;

/** Sample of using Bean Scripting Framework with JPython */
public class BSFSample {
    public static void main(String[] args) {
        BSFManager manager = new BSFManager();

        // register scripting language
```

Example 26-5. BSFSample.java (continued)

```
        String[] fntypes = { ".py" };
        manager.registerScriptingEngine("jpython",
            "com.ibm.bsf.engines.jpython.JPythonEngine", fntypes);

        try {
            BSFEngine jpythonengine = manager.loadScriptingEngine("jpython");

            // try an expression
            Object r = manager.eval("jpython", "testString", 0, 0, "22.0/7");
            System.out.println("Result type is " + r.getClass().getName());
            System.out.println("Result value is " + r);
        } catch (Exception ex) {
            System.err.println(ex.toString());
        }
        System.out.println("Scripting demo done.");
        return;
    }
}
```

This program prints the following output:

```
$ java BSFSample
'import exceptions' failed; using string-based exceptions
Result type is org.python.core.PyFloat
Result value is 3.142857142857143
Scripting demo done.
$
```

The exceptions failure is probably due to my having installed JPython in a non-standard location and not setting the environment variable(s) needed to find it. Further, the first time you run it, JPython spits out a bunch of nattering about your CLASSPATH, one line for each JAR file that it finds. These can be a bit surprising when they pop up from a script, but JPython doesn't seem to know or care whether it's being run interactively or dynamically.

```
packageManager: processing new jar, "/usr/local/java/swingall.jar"
```

The following longer example uses the `LabelText` bean from Recipe 23.7 and a push button to run a Python script that collects the text from the `LabelText` instance and displays it on the standard output. Here is the little script, *buttonhandler.py*:

```
print "Hello";
print bean.getText();
```

When I ran this, I typed the famous words that Alexander Graham Bell apparently sent to his assistant Watson, and had the Java program send them to the Python script.

Sure enough, when I clicked on the button, I got this on the standard output (as shown in Figure 26-2):

```
Script output: -->
Hello
Mr. Watson, come here
<-- End of Script output.
```

Figure 26-2. BSFSample in action

Nothing you couldn't do in Java, of course, but in this example the `LabelText` bean is registered with the BSF as a bean, and the `JButton`'s action handler runs a script that gets that text and displays it. Example 26-6 shows the source code for the script-using program.

Example 26-6. BSFAction.java

```java
import com.ibm.cs.util.*;
import com.ibm.bsf.*;
import javax.swing.*;
import java.awt.*;
import java.awt.event.*;
import java.io.*;

/** Longer sample of using Bean Scripting Framework with JPython */
public class BSFAction {
    protected String FILENAME = "buttonhandler.py";
    protected BSFManager manager;
    protected BSFEngine jpythonengine;
    protected String language;
    protected String script;

    public static void main(String[] args) {
        new BSFAction();
    }

    BSFAction() {

        // Construct the Bean instance
        LabelText bean = new LabelText("Message to Python script");

        try {
```

Example 26-6. BSFAction.java (continued)

```
            manager = new BSFManager();

            // register scripting language
            String[] fntypes = { ".py" };
            manager.registerScriptingEngine("jpython",
                "com.ibm.bsf.engines.jpython.JPythonEngine", fntypes);
            jpythonengine = manager.loadScriptingEngine("jpython");

            // Tell BSF about the bean.
            manager.declareBean("bean", bean, LabelText.class);

            // Read the script file into BSF
            language = manager.getLangFromFilename(FILENAME);
            script = IOUtils.getStringFromReader(
                new FileReader(FILENAME));

        } catch (Exception ex) {
            System.err.println(ex.toString());
            System.exit(0);
        }

        System.out.println("Scripting setup done, building GUI.");

        final JFrame jf = new JFrame(getClass().getName());

        Container cp = jf.getContentPane();
        cp.setLayout(new FlowLayout());

        cp.add(bean);// add the LabelText

        JButton b = new JButton("Click me!");
        cp.add(b);           // and the button under it.
        b.addActionListener(new ActionListener() {
            public void actionPerformed(ActionEvent evt) {
                try {

                    // When the button is pressed, run the script.
                    System.out.println("Script output: -->");
                    manager.exec(language, FILENAME, 0, 0, script);
                    System.out.println("<-- End of Script output.");
                } catch (BSFException bse) {
                    JOptionPane.showMessageDialog(jf,
                        "ERROR: " + bse, "Script Error",
                        JOptionPane.ERROR_MESSAGE);
                }
            }
        });
```

Example 26-6. BSFAction.java (continued)

```
        // A Quit button at the bottom
        JButton qb = new JButton("Quit");
        cp.add(qb);
        qb.addActionListener(new ActionListener() {
            public void actionPerformed(ActionEvent evt) {
                System.exit(0);
            }
        });

        // Routine JFrame setup
        jf.pack();
        jf.setVisible(true);
    }
}
```

See Also

Information on the Bean Scripting Framework is currently located on IBM's alphaWorks web site, under *http://oss.software.ibm.com/developerworks/projects/bsf/*.

JPython has been taken under a new umbrella and renamed Jython; see *http://www.jython.org*.

There are many other projects that aim to blend Java with other languages. As a single example, check out the OmegaHat project's interface at *http://www.omegahat.org/RSJava/*. R, itself a clone of S (*http://cm.bell-labs.com/cm/ms/departments/sia/S/*) is the statistical package used to produce the charts back in Figure 5-1. This interface lets you use Java inside R or S, and also to call R or S from Java code.

26.4. Blending in Native Code (C/C++)

Problem

You wish to call native C/C++ functions from Java, either for efficiency or to access hardware- or system-specific features.

Solution

Use JNI, the Java Native Interface.

Discussion

Java lets you load *native* or compiled code into your Java program. Why would you want to do such a thing? One reason might be to access OS-dependent functionality. Another is speed: native code will likely run faster than Java, at least at present. Like everything else in Java, this mechanism is subject to security restrictions; for example, applets are not allowed to access native code.

The native code language bindings are defined for code that has been written in the C or C++ language. If you need to access a language other than C/C++, write a bit of C/C++ and have it pass control to other functions or applications, using any mechanism defined by your operating system.

Due to such system-dependent features as the interpretation of header files and the allocation of the processor's general-purpose registers, your native code may need to be compiled by the same C compiler used to compile the Java runtime for your platform. For example, on Solaris you can use SunPro C, or maybe gcc. On Win32 platforms, use Microsoft Visual C++ Version 4.x or higher (32 bit). For other platforms, see your Java vendor's documentation.

Also note that the details in this section are for Java 1.1's Java Native Interface (JNI) that differs in some details from 1.0 and from Microsoft's native interface.

The steps to call native code are summarized in the following sidebar and detailed below.

Ian's Basic Steps: Java Calling Native Code

1. Write Java code that calls a native method.
2. Compile this Java code.
3. Create an *.h* file using *javah*.
4. Write a C function that does the work.
5. Compile the C code into a loadable object.
6. Try it!

The first step is to write Java code that calls a native method. To do this, use the keyword `native` to indicate that the method is native, and provide a static code block that loads your native method using `System.loadLibrary()`. (The dynamically loadable module is created in Step 5.) Static blocks are executed when the class containing them is loaded; loading the native code here ensures it is in memory when needed!

Object variables that your native code may modify should carry the `volatile` modifier. The file *HelloWorld.java*, shown in Example 26-7, is a good starting point.

Example 26-7. HelloWorld.java

```
/**
 * A trivial class to show Java Native Interface 1.1 usage from Java.
 */
public class HelloWorld {
    int myNumber = 42;        // used to show argument passing

    // declare native class
    public native void displayHelloWorld();

    // Application main, call its display method
    public static void main(String[] args) {
        System.out.println("HelloWorld starting; args.length="+
            args.length+"...");
        for (int i=0; i<args.length; i++)
            System.out.println("args["+i+"]="+args[i]);
        HelloWorld hw = new HelloWorld();
        hw.displayHelloWorld();// call the native function
        System.out.println("Back in Java, \"myNumber\" now " + hw.myNumber);
    }

    // Static code blocks are executed once, when class file is loaded
    static {
        System.load("libhello.so");
    }
}
```

The second step is simple; just use *javac HelloWorld* as you normally would. You probably won't get any compilation errors on a simple program like this; if you do, correct them and try the compilation again.

Next, you need to create an *.h* file. Use *javah* to produce files:

```
javah -jni HelloWorld          // produces HelloWorld.h
```

The `-jni` is required; without it, you get incompatible 1.0 output.

The *.h* file produced is a "glue" file, not really meant for human consumption and particularly not for editing. But by inspecting the resulting *.h* file, you'll see that the C method's name is composed of the name `Java`, the package name (if any), the class name, and the method name:

```
void Java_HelloWorld_displayHelloWorld(JNIEnv *env, jobject this);
```

Then, create a C function that does the work. You must use the same function signature as is used in the *.h* file:

```
void Java_HelloWorld_displayHelloWorld(JNIEnv *env, jobject this) {
```

This function can do whatever it wishes. Note that it is passed two arguments: a JVM environment, and a handle for the this object. Table 26-2 shows the correspondence between Java types and the C types (JNI types) used in the C code.

Table 26-2. Java and JNI types

Java type	JNI	Java array type	JNI
byte	jbyte	byte[]	jbyteArray
short	jshort	short[]	jshortArray
int	jint	int[]	jintArray
long	jlong	long[]	jlongArray
float	jfloat	float[]	jfloatArray
double	jdouble	double[]	jdoubleArray
char	jchar	char[]	jcharArray
boolean	jboolean	boolean[]	jbooleanArray
void	jvoid		
Object	jobject	Object[]	jobjectArray
Class	jclass		
String	jstring		
array	jarray		
Throwable	jthrowable		

Example 26-8 is a complete C native implementation. Passed an object of type HelloWorld, it increments the integer myNumber contained in the object.

Example 26-8. HelloWorld.c

```
#include <jni.h>
#include "HelloWorld.h"
#include <stdio.h>

/*
 * This is the 1.1 implentation of displayHelloWorld.
 */
void Java_HelloWorld_displayHelloWorld(JNIEnv *env, jobject this)
{
    jfieldID fldid;
    jint n, nn;

    (void)printf("Hello from a Native Method\n");

    if (this == NULL) {
        fprintf(stderr, "Input pointer is null!\n");
        return;
```

Example 26-8. HelloWorld.c (continued)

```
    }
    if ((fldid = (*env)->GetFieldID(env,
        (*env)->GetObjectClass(env, this), "myNumber", "I")) == NULL) {
        fprintf(stderr, "GetFieldID failed");
        return;
    }

    n = (*env)->GetIntField(env, this, fldid);/* retrieve myNumber */
    printf("\"myNumber\" value is %d\n", n);

    (*env)->SetIntField(env, this, fldid, ++n);/* increment it! */
    nn = (*env)->GetIntField(env, this, fldid);

    printf("\"myNumber\" value now %d\n", nn); /* make sure */
    return;
}
```

Finally, you compile the C code into a loadable object. Naturally, the details depend on platform, compiler, etc. For example, on Windows 95:

```
> set JAVAHOME=C:\java            # or wherever
> set INCLUDE=%JAVAHOME%\include;%INCLUDE%
> set LIB=%JAVAHOME%\lib;%LIB%
> cl HelloWorld.c -Fehello.dll -MD -LD javai.lib
```

And on Unix:

```
$ export JAVAHOME=/local/java    # or wherever
$ cc -I$JAVAHOME/include -I$JAVAHOME/include/solaris \
-G HelloWorld.c -o libhello.so
```

Example 26-9 is a makefile for Unix.

Example 26-9. Unix makefile

```
# Makefile for the 1.1 Java Native Methods examples for
# Learning Tree International Course 471/478.
# Has been tested on Solaris both with "gcc" and with SunSoft "cc".
# On other platforms it will certainly need some tweaking; please
# let me know how much! :-)

# Configuration Section

CSRCS   = HelloWorld.c
JAVAHOME= /local/jdk1.1.2
INCLUDES= -I$(JAVAHOME)/include -I$(JAVAHOME)/include/solaris
LIBDIR   = $(JAVAHOME)/lib/sparc/green_threads
CLASSPATH= $(JAVAHOME)/lib/classes.zip:.
```

Example 26-9. Unix makefile (continued)

```
all:     testhello testjavafromc

# This part of the Makefile is for C called from Java, in HelloWorld
testhello:hello.all
        @echo
        @echo "Here we test the Java code \"HelloWorld\" that calls C code."
        @echo
        LD_LIBRARY_PATH=`pwd`:. java HelloWorld

hello.all:HelloWorld.class libhello.so

HelloWorld.class: HelloWorld.java
        javac HelloWorld.java

HelloWorld.h:HelloWorld.class
        javah -jni HelloWorld

HelloWorld.o::HelloWorld.h

libhello.so:$(CSRCS) HelloWorld.h
    $(CC) $(INCLUDES) -G $(CSRCS) -o libhello.so

# This part of the Makefile is for Java called from C, in javafromc
testjavafromc:javafromc.all hello.all
    @echo
    @echo "Now we test HelloWorld using javafromc instead of java"
    @echo
    LD_LIBRARY_PATH="$(LIBDIR):." CLASSPATH="$(CLASSPATH)" ./javafromc HelloWorld
    @echo
    @echo "That was, in case you didn't notice, C->Java->C. And,"
    @echo "incidentally, a replacement for JDK program \"java\" itself!"
    @echo


javafromc.all:javafromc

javafromc:javafromc.o
    $(CC) -L$(LIBDIR) javafromc.o -ljava -o $@

javafromc.o:javafromc.c
    $(CC) -c $(INCLUDES) javafromc.c

clean:
    rm -f core *.class *.o *.so HelloWorld.h
clobber: clean
    rm -f javafromc
```

And you're done! Just run the Java interpreter on the class file containing the main program. Assuming that you've set whatever system-dependent settings are necessary (possibly including both CLASSPATH and LD_LIBRARY_PATH or its equivalent), the program should run as follows:

```
C> java HelloWorld
Hello from a Native Method// from C
"myNumber" value is 42// from C
"myNumber" value now 43// from C
Value of myNumber now 43// from Java
```

Congratulations! You've called a native method. However, you've given up portability; the Java class file now requires you to build a loadable object for each operating system and hardware platform. Multiply {MS-Windows 95/98, MS-Windows CE, Me, and NT, MacOS, Sun Solaris, HP/UX, Linux, OpenBSD, NetBSD, FreeBSD} times {Intel, SPARC, PowerPC, HP-PA, Sun3} and you begin to see the portability issues. Your native code can be used in server code and desktop applications, but is normally not permitted in web browsers.

Beware that problems with your native code can and will crash the runtime process right out from underneath the Java Virtual Machine. The JVM can do nothing to protect itself from poorly written C/C++ code. Memory must be managed by the programmer; there is no automatic garbage collection of memory obtained by the system runtime allocator. You're dealing directly with the operating system and sometimes even the hardware, so, "Be careful. Be very careful."

See Also

If you need more information on Java Native Methods, you might be interested in the comprehensive treatment found in *Essential JNI: Java Native Interface* by Rob Gordon (Prentice Hall).

26.5. Calling Java from Native Code

Problem

You need to go the other way, calling Java from C/C++ code.

Solution

Use JNI again.

Discussion

In 1.1, JNI provides an interface for calling Java from C, with calls to:

1. Create a JVM

2. Load a class

3. Find and call a method from that class (i.e., main)

This lets you add Java to legacy code. That can be useful for a variety of purposes, but entails treating Java code as an extension language (just define or find an interface like `Applet` or `Servlet`, and let your customers subclass from it).

This is not discussed in detail here, but there's a full code example in the code archive in directory *src/native1.1*.

26.6. Program: DBM

This program lets you use the original Unix DBM (database access method) routines from Java. DBM is actually emulated using the newer Berkeley Database (DB) routines, but the DBM interface is more traditional, and simpler. DBM was used in Recipe 20.2 to provide a name-to-login database, which is similar to how many modern Unixes actually store name and password information. That recipe also showed how to use it to display your Netscape history, even under MS-Windows.

I'll now show the Java version of the DBM library, *DBM.java* (see Example 26-10).

Example 26-10. DBM.java

```
import java.io.*;

/** This class provides a dbm-compatible interface to the Unix-style
 * database access methods described in dbm(3) (which is on some Unixes
 * a front-end to db(3).
 * <P>Each unique record in the database is a unique key/value pair,
 * similar to a java.util.Hashtable but stored on persistent medium, not
 * kept in memory. Dbm was originally optimized for Unix for fast
 * access to individual key/value pairs.
 */
public class DBM {
    /** Since you can only have one DBM database in use at a time due
     * to implementation restrictions, we enforce this rule with a
     * class-wide boolean.
     */
    protected static boolean inuse = false;

    /** Save the filename for messages, etc. */
    protected String fileName;
```

Example 26-10. DBM.java (continued)

```java
/** Construct a DBM given its filename */
public DBM(String file) {
    synchronized(this) {
        if (inuse)
            throw new IllegalArgumentException(
                "Only one DBM object at a time per Java Machine");
        inuse = true;
    }
    fileName = file;
    int retCode = dbminit(fileName);
    if (retCode < 0)
        throw new IllegalArgumentException(
            "dbminit failed, code = " + retCode);
}

// Static code blocks are executed once, when class file is loaded.
// This is here to ensure that the shared library gets loaded.
static {
    System.loadLibrary("jdbm");
}

protected ByteArrayOutputStream bo;

/** serialize an Object to byte array. */
protected byte[] toByteArray(Object o) throws IOException {
    if (bo == null)
        bo = new ByteArrayOutputStream(1024);
    bo.reset();
    ObjectOutputStream os = new ObjectOutputStream(bo);
    os.writeObject(o);
    os.close();
    return bo.toByteArray();
}

/** un-serialize an Object from a byte array. */
protected Object toObject(byte[] b) throws IOException {
    Object o;

    ByteArrayInputStream bi = new ByteArrayInputStream(b);
    ObjectInputStream os = new ObjectInputStream(bi);
    try {
        o = os.readObject();
    } catch (ClassNotFoundException ex) {
        // Convert ClassNotFoundException to I/O error
        throw new IOException(ex.getMessage());
    }
    os.close();
```

Example 26-10. DBM.java (continued)

```java
        return o;
    }

    protected native int dbminit(String file);

    protected native int dbmclose();

    /** Public wrapper for close method. */
    public void close() {
        this.dbmclose();
        inuse = false;
    }

    protected void checkInUse() {
        if (!inuse)
            throw new IllegalStateException("Method called when DBM not open");
    }

    protected native byte[] dbmfetch(byte[] key);

    /** Fetch using byte arrays */
    public byte[] fetch(byte[] key) throws IOException {
        checkInUse();
        return dbmfetch(key);
    }

    /** Fetch using Objects */
    public Object fetch(Object key) throws IOException {
        checkInUse();
        byte[] datum = dbmfetch(toByteArray(key));
        return toObject(datum);
    }

    protected native int dbmstore(byte[] key, byte[] content);

    /** Store using byte arrays */
    public void store(byte[] key, byte[] value) throws IOException {
        checkInUse();
        dbmstore(key, value);
    }

    /** Store using Objects */
    public void store(Object key, Object value) throws IOException {
        checkInUse();
        dbmstore(toByteArray(key), toByteArray(value));
    }
```

Example 26-10. DBM.java (continued)

```
    protected native int delete(Object key);

    public native byte[] firstkey() throws IOException;

    public Object firstkeyObject() throws IOException {
        return toObject(firstkey());
    }

    public native byte[] nextkey(byte[] key) throws IOException;

    public Object nextkey(Object key) throws IOException {
        byte[] ba = nextkey(toByteArray(key));
        if (ba == null)
            return null;
        return toObject(ba);
    }

    public String toString() {
        return "DBM@" + hashCode() + "[" + fileName + "]";
    }
}
```

Notice how the methods `toByteArray()` and `toObject()`, the inverses of each
other, convert between an object and an array of bytes using `ByteArrayStreams`.
These provide the functionality of reading from or writing to a buffer that is in
memory, instead of the usual buffer that has been read from or written to a disk
file or socket.

See Also

A more complete and widely used implementation of DBM for Java is available
from SleepyCat Software, the heirs-apparent to the Berkeley DBM software. Their
SleepyCat DBM can be downloaded for free, in source form, under the Berkeley
(University of California at Berkeley) software license. Check out *http://
www.sleepycat.com*.

Afterword

Writing this book has been a humbling experience. It has taken far longer than I had predicted, or than I would like to admit. And, of course, it's not finished yet. Despite my best efforts and those of the technical reviewers, editors, and many other talented folks, a book this size is bound to contain errors, omissions, and passages that are less clear than they might be. Please, let us know by email if you happen across any of these things. There will be subsequent editions that incorporate changes sent in by readers just like you!

It has been said that you don't really know something until you've taught it. I have found this true of lecturing, and find it equally true of writing.

I tell my students that when Java was very young, it was possible for one person to study hard and know almost everything about Java. When Java 1.1 came out, this was no longer true. With Java 2, anybody who tells you they "know all about Java" should cause your "bogozity" detector to go off at full volume. And the amount you need to know keeps growing. How can you keep up? Java books? Java magazines? Java courses? Conferences? There is no single answer; all of these are useful to some people. Sun's Java software division has several programs that you should be aware of:

- JavaOne, their annual conference (*http://java.sun.com/javaone/*)
- The Java Developer Connection, a free web-based service for getting the latest APIs, news, and views (*http://developer.java.sun.com*)
- The Java Community Process (*http://java.sun.com/aboutJava/communityprocess/*), the home of open Java standardization and enhancement
- Java Developer Essentials, a fee-based CD-ROM subscription to all the Java APIS, tools, and other material (*http://www.sun.com/developers/tools/*)

As you know, the Java API is divided into packages. A package is normally considered "core" if its package name begins with `java`, and an optional extension if its package name begins with `javax`. But there is already one exception to this rule: `javax.swing.*` which is core.

I maintain a comprehensive listing of the major Java APIs produced and promulgated by the Java division of Sun Microsystems on my web site, at *http://www.darwinsys.com/java/java-api.html.*

As you can see, there is no end of Java APIs to learn about. And there are still more books to be written . . . and read.

Index

We'd like to hear your suggestions for improving our indexes. Send email to *index@oreilly.com.*

About the Author

Ian F. Darwin divides his non-family time between writing (books, courses, and magazine articles), teaching Java and Unix courses, and consulting for Java and Unix projects. He is the original author of two four-day Java programming courses taught by Learning Tree International. He's also the author of *Checking C Programs with Lint*, published by O'Reilly in 1988. Of his second O'Reilly book, *X Window System User's Guide: Volume 3, OPEN LOOK*, little can be said except that he placed the final manuscript in Tim O'Reilly's hands the same week that Sun announced they were discontinuing OPEN LOOK in favor of the Common Desktop Environment; the ill-fated "Vol3OL" was published only in a CD-ROM compilation available from *http://www.darwinsys.com*. (Sun has recently announced its move from CDE to GNOME, which makes Ian glad he did not write a *Volume 3, CDE Edition*.) Ian's open source freeware contributions include the *file(1)* command used on Linux and BSD, a couple of Photoshop image-file-format plug-ins, and *JabaDex*, a personal information manager written in Java, plus some ongoing maintenance of OpenBSD, the proactively secure Unix-like system. He used to fly small airplanes and teach scuba diving, but he's been too busy lately as a computerist and family man to enjoy such ups and downs.

Ian's wife and three children raise Plymouth Barred Rock chickens. They believe that it complements Ian's book writing, since the Plymouth Barred Rock breed was "cooked up" by blending the Dominique and Black Java breeds.

Colophon

Our look is the result of reader comments, our own experimentation, and feedback from distribution channels. Distinctive covers complement our distinctive approach to technical topics, breathing personality and life into potentially dry subjects.

The animal on the cover of *Java Cookbook* is a domestic chicken. Domestic chickens (*Gallus gallus*) are descended from the wild red jungle fowl of India. Domesticated over 8,000 years ago in the area that is now Vietnam and Thailand, chickens are raised for meat and eggs, and the males for sport as well (though cockfighting is currently against the law in many places).

With their big, heavy bodies and small wings, these birds are well suited to living on the ground, and they can fly at most only short distances. Their four-toed feet are designed for scratching in the dirt, where they find the elements of their usual diet: worms, bugs, seeds, and various plant matter.

A male chicken is called a rooster or cock, and a female is known as a hen. The incubation period for a chicken egg is about three weeks; newly hatched chickens are precocial, meaning they have downy feathers and can walk around on their own right after emerging from the egg. They're also not dependent on their mothers for food; not only can they procure their own, but they also can live for up to a week post-hatch on egg yolk that remains in their abdomen after birth.

The topic of chickens comes up frequently in ancient writings. Chinese documents date their introduction to China to 1400 B.C., Babylonian carvings mention them in 600 B.C., and Aristophanes wrote about them in 400 B.C. The rooster has long symbolized courage: the Romans thought chickens were sacred to Mars, god of war, and the first French Republic chose the rooster as its emblem.

Emily Quill was the production editor and copyeditor for *Java Cookbook*. Claire Cloutier, Colleen Gorman, and Jane Ellin conducted quality control reviews, and Edith Shapiro, Sada Preisch, Lucy Muellner, Linley Dolby, and Matt Hutchinson provided production assistance. Ellen Troutman-Zaig wrote the index.

Hanna Dyer designed the cover of this book, based on a series design by Edie Freedman. The cover image is a 19th-century engraving from the Dover Pictoral Archive. Emma Colby produced the cover layout with QuarkXPress 4.1 using Adobe's ITC Garamond font.

Melanie Wang and David Futato designed the interior layout, based on a series design by Nancy Priest. Mike Sierra implemented the design in FrameMaker 5.5.6. The heading font is Bitstream Bodoni, the text font is ITC New Baskerville, and the code font is Constant Willison. The illustrations that appear in the book were produced by Robert Romano and Jessamyn Read using Macromedia FreeHand 9 and Adobe Photoshop 6. This colophon was written by Leanne Soylemez.

Whenever possible, our books use a durable and flexible lay-flat binding. If the page count exceeds this binding's limit, perfect binding is used.